RESEARCH METHODS IN PSYCHOLOGY

RESEARCH METHODS IN PSYCHOLOGY

Investigating Human Behavior

PAUL G. NESTOR
RUSSELL K. SCHUTT
University of Massachusetts Boston

Los Angeles | London | New Delhi
Singapore | Washington DC

Los Angeles | London | New Delhi
Singapore | Washington DC

FOR INFORMATION:

SAGE Publications, Inc.
2455 Teller Road
Thousand Oaks, California 91320
E-mail: order@sagepub.com

SAGE Publications Ltd.
1 Oliver's Yard
55 City Road
London EC1Y 1SP
United Kingdom

SAGE Publications India Pvt. Ltd.
B 1/I 1 Mohan Cooperative Industrial Area
Mathura Road, New Delhi 110 044
India

SAGE Publications Asia-Pacific Pte. Ltd.
33 Pekin Street #02-01
Far East Square
Singapore 048763

Executive Editor: Jerry Westby
Assistant Editor: Eve Oettinger
Editorial Assistant: Erim Sarbuland
Production Editor: Brittany Bauhaus
Permissions Editor: Karen Ehrmann
Copy Editor: Kim Husband
Typesetter: C&M Digitals (P) Ltd.
Proofreader: Jennifer Gritt
Indexer: Diggs Publication Services, Inc.
Cover Designer: Bryan Fishman
Marketing Manager: Erica DeLuca

Printed in the United States of America

Library of Congress Cataloging-in-Publication Data

Nestor, Paul G.

Research methods in psychology : investigating human behavior / Paul G. Nestor, Russell K. Schutt.

p. cm.
Includes bibliographical references and index.

ISBN 978-1-4129-6049-6 (pbk.)

1. Human behavior. 2. Human behavior—Research. 3. Psychology—Research. I. Schutt, Russell K. II. Title.

BF199.N37 2012 150.72—dc22 2010046456

This book is printed on acid-free paper.

11 12 13 14 15 10 9 8 7 6 5 4 3 2 1

Brief Contents

Detailed Contents

Preface

"Forget What You Know About Good Study Habits" headlines an article appearing in *The New York Times* on September 6, 2010. In this well-researched article, science journalist Benedict Carey describes scientific findings that, he asserts, debunk conventional wisdom about what constitutes good study habits. Among these is the popular notion that studying in the same location improves retention. It does not: Carey notes that several laboratory studies point to better learning for research participants who study in alternating rooms. So too, he asserts, is there a lack of any research evidence to support the fashionable idea of teaching to learning styles, such as using different approaches for students who are "left-brained" versus those who are "right-brained." As a recent review by Pashler and colleagues (2009) published in the journal *Psychological Science in the Public Interest* concluded, "The contrast between the enormous popularity of the learning-styles approach within education and the lack of evidence for its utility, is, in our opinion, striking and disturbing" (p. 117).

Now let us use the foregoing to explain why we wrote this book. First, we hope it is abundantly clear from our example that *research matters*. As the engine of discovery, research tells us how things work, what works, and what doesn't. Research involves a way of thinking that is embodied in the scientific method and is vital to how we know and learn. It is the scientific method that is the heart and soul of our book. However, let us hasten to add that the scientific method is not a proverbial ball and chain, shackling creativity, but a set of tools to broaden and build thinking about research. And as you can see in our example of when the learning-styles approach encountered the scientific method, it withered and evaporated.

But how would you have known? After all, wouldn't common sense tell you that matching teaching with learning styles would enhance student learning? These questions bring us to another pivotal reason that drove and inspired us to write this book. We want our book to teach you to recognize, understand, and appreciate scientific research. We aim to do so by placing research within a broad and rich cultural context of the "public square." To this end, our approach is unique in casting the scientific method widely, in aligning it not only with rigorous testing of ideas but also with the generation of new ideas, spawned by imagination and curiosity. Thus, our aspiration for writing this book is to imbue in you a sense of excitement about psychological research. Far from drudgery, research, as we frame it throughout the text, provides the best method for investigating questions that matter to all of us. So in this text, you will learn both to design and to critique research as you explore a diverse array of case examples of how to investigate such lively, timeless topics as happiness and altruism, facial expression of emotion, 9/11 memories, and brain plasticity training.

TEACHING AND LEARNING GOALS

Our purpose in writing this book is to make teaching and learning about research methods in psychology both fun and rewarding. We bring you into the world of psychological research. Here you will find a culture in its own right that is governed by a way of thinking. At center stage is a set of rules and procedures that is collectively known as the scientific method. To engage you, we take you inside various research studies and we ask you to wear alternating hats. With one of these hats, you play the role of the researcher: How does one come up with research ideas? Why must ideas be subjected to the scientific method? How might you design a study to test your ideas? With another hat, you become a research consumer learning how to appraise and critique theory and design. Our aim is for you to develop a mindset of skepticism without cynicism and more rigorous and disciplined thinking while still remaining flexible, open minded, imaginative, innovative, and inventive. With yet another hat, you will experience research as a participant: How do you imagine yourself as a participant? Do you understand the tasks, measures, and procedures required of the participants? Do you think these methods capture what the research intended to study? By playing these alternating roles, we hope to spark your curiosity and creativity and to share with you our passion so that you too learn the joy of conducting sound research. To accomplish our goals, we employed an approach that is novel and unique in that it melds two distinct yet complementary themes. First is our commitment to make the case for the scientific method and for the role of research in the world today. We do so by building an evidence-based argument derived from psychological research in cognitive science. From this research emerges a model of the human mind that has been sculpted by evolution to favor subjective impression, anecdotes, and personal testimony over cold, hard objective statistics of science. These biases of the mind have been likened to "cognitive illusions," and cognitive studies have shown that such endemic and systemic misperceptions and distortions lead to errors of logical reasoning that we all share and for which the scientific method is the best antidote. We hope that our book will convince you, as a member of our jury, of the indispensability of the scientific method.

Second, we use the findings of cognitive science to guide our text in a way that is most conducive to learning, understanding, and appreciation. We contextualize informational content. For example, statistical reasoning is woven into the text and tied to specific research examples that are chosen to illuminate how results of any scientific study are probabilistic in nature, a matter of calculating odds via mathematical formulae, which are presented in Chapter 10. Similarly, we emphasize a narrative approach that likens psychological theory to storytelling that can be used in study design and data interpretation. In a nutshell, then, we have used the science of psychology as a guide for writing the text and for accomplishing our teaching and learning goals.

ORGANIZATION OF THE BOOK

The way the book is organized reflects our commitment to making research methods interesting. Each chapter is structured around at least one particular published, peer-reviewed study that we selected for innovativeness and inventiveness as well as for impact on our understanding of exciting, cutting-edge topics at the forefront of psychology. Through the lens of these studies, we aim to provide you with a context to stimulate and facilitate learning of various research methods—bringing them to life and infusing them with meaning and practical application. In this sense, our book is anchored in a case-study approach to learning. Using particular published investigations as a storyline, we have tried to provide you with a narrative for learning.

The first three chapters introduce you to the why and how of research in general. In Chapter 1, we take you inside the study by Iyengar, Wells, and Schwartz (2006), "Doing Better but Feeling Worse. Looking for the 'Best' Job Undermines Satisfaction." To whet your appetite, Chapter 1 includes Iyengar and colleagues' maximization-satisficer scale. We encourage you to take the maximization-satisficer scale to help you understand what participants in their research experienced. Also in Chapter 1 we compare and contrast science and pseudoscience. In addition, you learn about limits of common-sense reasoning and why, because of our natural propensities for cognitive illusions, we need the scientific method. Chapter 2 continues with our hands-on, roll-up-the-sleeves approach, highlighted by a very simple but ingenious experiment by Strack, Martin, and Stepper (1988), "Inhibiting and Facilitating Conditions of the Human Smile: A Nonobtrusive Test of the Facial Feedback Hypothesis." Here you too can easily reenact Strack and company's experimental task by simply holding a pen between your teeth to facilitate smiling or between your lips to inhibit smiling. Chapter 3 highlights issues of research ethics by taking you inside Stanley Milgram's research on obedience to authority. It also introduces you to different research philosophies.

Chapters 4 and 5 cover essential research techniques of measurement and sampling. In Chapter 4, you learn about the ins and outs of developing a measurement tool, taking the case of a recently developed instrument for assessing *mental health*. This provides an interesting contrast to the *Diagnostic and Statistical Manual of Mental Disorders Fourth Edition Text Revision* (DSM-IV-TR), which is widely used for assessing mental illness. Chapter 4 also covers the school of psychology dedicated to standardized measurement, known as psychometrics. Here we use IQ testing as the case example. In Chapter 5, we use research on happiness to illustrate the process of sampling and the method of survey research based on samples. In Chapters 6, 7, and 8, you learn about different experimental approaches. Chapter 6 presents as an example of a single-factor experiment a groundbreaking study—a randomized clinical trial examining the effects of computerized cognitive training on memory decline in aging. Chapter 7 presents complex factorial designs and takes you behind the scenes to learn how eye-gaze and emotional expression of faces interact to influence observers' judgments. Chapter 8 delves into quasiexperiments. This, as you will learn, is a critical research approach in that it offers a much-needed experimental methodology for studying those countless topics in human psychology for which key variables cannot be truly controlled and manipulated. Our chapter describes a brain imaging study examining memories of the 9/11 terrorist attacks.

We devote Chapter 9 to small-N design, an important research approach for clinical, behavioral, and counselling psychology. Chapter 10 brings together many of the statistical and data analytic issues introduced in the prior chapters. Consistent with the earlier chapters, we organize and contextualize statistics and data analysis with reference to a fascinating study published in the prestigious interdisciplinary journal *Science,* "Spending Money on Others Promotes Happiness" by Dunn, Aknin, and Norton (2008). Chapter 11 is dedicated to qualitative methods. These techniques are intended to go beyond numbers. They are used to study and understand phenomena in terms of the meanings people attach to them, thereby preserving and capturing the complexities and diversities of human behavior. Finally, in Chapter 12 you will learn about report writing in APA style. We emphasize the general structure of an APA-formatted paper along with the APA rules for citations and referencing. We encourage you to think of APA style not as an obstacle but as a means to help structure your writing. We come full circle in Chapter 12, using as a sample paper of APA report writing the Iyengar and colleagues study that we first introduced in Chapter 1.

DISTINCTIVE FEATURES

Case study approach provides a narrative for learning. Each chapter is organized around a study selected from the psychological literature that we carefully deconstruct to illustrate the procedures, logic, and design of research. Studies we selected as cases range from classic investigations to cutting-edge experiments in positive psychology, cognitive neuroscience, developmental psychology, social psychology, and clinical psychology.

Experiential, hands-on, roll-up-the-sleeves approach to learning. Elegant but simple experiments are presented that can be customized for both in-class exercises and course projects. Studies are presented from multiple perspectives and can be easily adapted for role-playing exercises with students acting as researchers, participants, or consumers of science. The text is illustrated with examples of study stimuli, such as faces and eyes, in order to bring to life the actual experimental tasks. In addition, we also include questionnaires and measurement scales that you can take in order to provide a fuller understanding of the research experience.

Research in the News is a special section in each chapter. Each of these sections summarizes a science story that attests to the relevance of research methods. Each piece describes an important study. You can evaluate the extent to which the journalistic account is true to the actual research study. You will learn the difference between peer-reviewed scientific articles and journalistic pieces.

Ethics in Action sections highlight the APA Ethics Code as applied to research and scholarship. These are questions presented at the end of the chapter to help stimulate your thinking about this important aspect of research practice. In addition, a chapter on research ethics (Chapter 3) includes up-to-date information on institutional review boards and HIPAA (health information) rules. You will learn about issues in ethical practice in part through the rich literature on Stanley Milgram's laboratory-based investigations of obedience to authority.

Cultural and developmental perspectives are emphasized. You will learn about research that illuminates how culture shapes our thinking and how our thinking shapes culture. In our coverage of measurement of intelligence (Chapter 4), you will learn the nuts and bolts of experiments on stereotype threat that have provided compelling evidence of the deleterious effects of racial bias on IQ in African American students. You will learn in Chapter 8 of experimental studies of constructivist theories of culture as we highlight the work of Ying-yi Hong, Michael W. Morris, Chi-yue Chiu, and Veronica Benet-Martinez in the *America Psychologist* (2000), "Multicultural Minds: A Dynamic Constructivist Approach to Culture and Cognition." Also in Chapter 8, you learn of different experimental designs used in developmental psychology through the lens of a longitudinal design examining brain maturation in children diagnosed with attention deficit hyperactivity disorder.

Integrated statistical reasoning elements introduced in each chapter, culminating in Chapter 10, which is exclusively devoted to data analyses. We present the rationale and logic of statistical reasoning first as a countervailing force to what cognitive scientists often refer to as our "probability-blind" minds. We continue in subsequent chapters to build a conceptual understanding of the nature of statistical reasoning, emphasizing, for example, in Chapter 4 the statistical properties of scales of measurement and in Chapter 7 the depiction of correlations via scatter diagrams. Chapter 10 presents descriptive and inferential statistics in the context of real-life studies.

Reporting writing is presented according to the recently updated *Publication Manual of the American Psychological Association* (Sixth Edition, 2009). You will learn about APA-style report writing in Chapter 12. Both paper and poster presentation are covered. You will also read the actual prepublication manuscript kindly provided by Sheena Iyengar (Iyengar, Wells, & Schwartz, 2006), "Doing Better But Feeling Worse. Looking for the 'Best' Job Undermines Satisfaction." This sample of APA report writing describes the study that we used as a case illustration in Chapter 1.

Extensive resources are presented on a Student Study Site on the web:

- To reinforce learning, methodological topics are reviewed with answers presented in the form of the popular television program *Jeopardy* for which students must come up with the correct answers.

- Interactive exercises describe actual research studies and pose questions about them corresponding to topics throughout the book.

- Journal articles from *Psychological Science, Psychological Science in the Public Interest,* and other related periodicals that are used in the interactive exercises and as examples in text chapters are available in PDF form for easy downloading.

- Web-based exercises facilitate explorations of topics introduced throughout the text.

- Practice exercises in SPSS and STATA with which to extend students' ability to use statistics.

Acknowledgments

Our thanks first to Jerry Westby, publisher and senior editor for SAGE Publications. Jerry's consistent support and exceptional vision have made it possible for this project to flourish, while his good cheer and collegiality have even made it all rather fun. Editor extraordinaire Leah Mori also contributed vitally, while production was managed with great expertise and good cheer by Brittany Bauhaus, assisted by publishing's most conscientious and effective copyeditor, Kim Husband. And we continue to be grateful to work with what has become the world's best publisher in social science, SAGE Publications, and their exceptional marketing manager, Erica DeLuca.

We also are indebted to the first-rate psychologists recruited by Jerry Westby to critique our book. Their thoughtful suggestions and cogent insights have helped improve every chapter. They are:

Elizabeth Arnott-Hill, *Chicago State University*

Deborah Baldwin, *University of Tennessee*

Vicki Black Bishop, *Northern Arizona University*

Cynthia Bostick, *California State University–Dominguez Hills*

Mary Jo Carnot, *Chadron State College*

Lawrence Cohen, *University of Delaware*

Chris Goode, *Georgia State University*

Nicholas Herrera, *DePaul University*

Brian Hock, *Austin Peay State University*

Karen Holmes, *Norfolk State University*

Katherine Hooper, *University of North Florida*

Steven Hoover, *St. Cloud State University*

Joel Hughes, *Kent State University*

Amy Hyman, *Florida International University*

Keith Jones, *Texas Tech University*

Sarah Kulkofsky, *Texas Tech University*

James Kuterbach, *Pennsylvania State University*

Sean Laraway, *San Jose State University*

Christopher Leupold, *Elon University*

Susan Lima, *University of Wisconsin*

Donald Loffredo, *University of Houston*

Connie Meinholdt, *Ferris State University*

Padraig O'Seaghdha, *Lehigh University*

Elizabeth Sheehan, *Georgia State University*

L. James Smart, *Miami University*

Carrie Smith, *University of Delaware*

Emily Stark, *Minnesota State University–Mankato*

Seth Surgan, *Worcester State College*

John Wallace, *Ball State University*

Sandra Waters, *North Carolina Central University*

Michael Young, *Southern Illinois University*

The quality of *Research Methods in Psychology*: *Investigating Human Behavior* benefits increasingly from the wisdom and creativity of our growing SAGE author group. Our profound gratitude to SAGE authors: Ronet Bachman (University of Delaware), Dan Chambliss (Hamilton College), Joe Check (University of Massachusetts, Boston), and Ray Engel (University of Pittsburgh). We also thank Sheena Iyengar (Columbia University) for allowing us to use as a stellar example of report writing her pre-publication manuscript (Iyengar, Wells, & Schwartz, 2006) "Doing Better But Feeling Worse. Looking for the 'Best' Job Undermines Satisfaction."

The interactive exercises on the website began with a series of exercises developed in a project at the University of Massachusetts, Boston. We had the great fortune to recruit Christian Chan, doctoral candidate in clinical psychology, and Lane Standige and Kathryn Stoeckert, who wrote interactive exercises, checked websites, and exercises. We are extremely grateful for their talented assistance. We also thank Chris Goldy for his excellent photographs.

No scholarly book project can succeed without good library resources, and for these we continue to incur a profound debt to the Harvard University library staff and their extraordinary collection. We also have benefited from the resources maintained by the excellent librarians at the University of Massachusetts Boston.

Most important, we thank our families for their love and support. Patti Nestor and Beth Schutt deserve canonization for their loving patience, humor, perspective, and wisdom, for which we are eternally indebted and forever grateful. And to our daughters, Molly Ann Nestor, Bridget Aileen Nestor, and Julia Ellen Schutt, we are blessed by your lives.

—Paul G. Nestor
—Russell K. Schutt
Boston, Massachusetts

CHAPTER 1

Uncommon Sense

Scientific Method and Human Reasoning

DOING BETTER BUT FEELING WORSE

Psychology—broadly defined as the scientific study of people, the mind, and behavior—focuses attention on virtually endless questions about how we feel, think, behave, believe, and interact. We begin this chapter by focusing on questions about feelings of well-being—feelings that motivate much of our activity, influence how we view the world, what we remember, and how we behave with others. Ask yourself the following question: Do you always shoot for the best, or are you okay with settling for "good enough"? When you are looking for professional work after receiving your college degree (congratulations!), will you shoot for the best possible outcome in terms of job satisfaction and salary or will you be happy with hitting a certain target—a certain income that's good enough?

Barry Schwartz (2004) and colleagues set out to look at how happy recent college graduates are with the job choices they made. They found an interesting and surprising result, but before delving into the details of the study, let's imagine that you are a participant in the Schwartz study. What we want to know first is how much you would agree or disagree with the following set of 13 statements. We will explain the ideas more fully, but first just please indicate the degree to which you agree with each statement by recording a number between 1 (disagree completely) and 7 (agree completely).

1. Whenever I'm faced with a choice, I try to imagine what all the other possibilities are, even ones that aren't present at the moment. ___

2. No matter how satisfied I am with my job, it's only right for me to be on the lookout for better opportunities. ___

3. When I am in the car listening to radio, I often check other stations to see if something better is playing, even if I am relatively satisfied with what I'm listening to. ___

4. When I watch TV, I channel surf, often scanning through the available options even while attempting to watch one program. ___

5. I treat relationships like clothing: I expect to try a lot on before finding the perfect fit. ___

6. I often find it difficult to shop for a gift for a friend. ___

7. Renting videos is really difficult. I'm always struggling to pick the best one. ___

8. When shopping, I have a hard time finding clothing that I really love. ___

9. I'm a big fan of lists that attempt to rank things (the best movies, the best singers, the best athletes, the best novels, etc.). ___

10. I find that writing is very difficult, even if it's just writing a letter to a friend, because it's so hard to word things just right. I often do several drafts of even simple things. ___

11. No matter what I do, I have the highest standards for myself. ___

12. I never settle for second best. ___

13. I often fantasize about living in ways that are quite different from my actual life. ___

Schwartz and colleagues gave the "Maximization Scale"—this set of 13 statements—to thousands of people and found the highest score was 75. While the researchers did not use a sharp cutoff to distinguish maximizers from satisficers, they considered people whose average ratings are higher than 4 (the scale's midpoint) to be maximizers and those whose average ratings are lower than the midpoint as satisficers (Schwartz, 2004). So if you scored above 52 (i.e., scale's midpoint of 4 multiplied by the13 items), you are thought to be a person who always has to perform an exhaustive check of all the available choices to make sure you pick the best. From finding a TV channel or picking a restaurant to searching for the "best" job, you generally try to exhaust all possibilities before making your final choice. On the other hand, if you have a score of 52 or less, you are a satisficer—you set standards for yourself and you will choose the first option that meets that standard.

Now let's switch hats from research participant to research investigator *a la* Sheena Iyengar, Rachael Wells, and Barry Schwartz (2006). Who do you predict is more likely to be satisfied with their choices and who do you believe will make the "best" choice? Iyengar and company investigated this question by categorizing 548 graduating students in the fall of their senior year and then followed them during the next year as they searched for jobs. When interviewed again the following summer, maximizers had found jobs that paid 20% more on average than the satisficers' jobs, but maximizers were less satisfied with the outcome of their job search and were more pessimistic, stressed, tired, worried, overwhelmed, and depressed. Maximizers felt worse even though they had done better than satisficers, the researcher reasoned, because considering so many choices led to unrealistic expectations that increased the likelihood of feelings of regret, disappointment, dissatisfaction, and sadness. In fact, the researchers reported that maximizers were more likely to fantasize about jobs they hadn't applied for and to wish they had pursued even more jobs than they did.

The findings are somewhat surprising. On one hand, the maximizers' careful search for the best job paid off. They found jobs that paid 20% more on average than the satisficers' jobs. You might have expected this finding; after all, most advisors encourage recent college graduates searching for jobs to perform an extensive search of all opportunities and to carefully weigh all options before arriving at a final choice. This did pay off for the maximizers in higher salaries. The unexpected finding was that the maximizers derived less satisfaction from their choices than did the satisficers. They were "doing better but feeling worse" (i.e., the title of the article by Iyengar, Wells, & Schwartz, 2006). They were satisfied with their final job selection, perhaps in part because their extensive job searches made them more aware of other options and caused them to second-guess, leading them to feelings of regret and to ask themselves, "What if . . . ?" So as one headline summarizing the study (Jarrett, 2006) aptly put it: "Are you a grumpy maximizer or a happy satisficer?" (*The British Psychological Society Research Digest*, March 3, 2006).

THE SCIENTIFIC METHOD

Let us use the study by Schwartz and colleagues to learn how psychology acquires knowledge through the use of the scientific method. As you will learn throughout the book, the scientific method is the cornerstone of research. We will flesh out various key features of the scientific method throughout the book. But as a starting point, let's think of the scientific method as the veritable rules of the game of research. These rules reflect procedures and techniques for conducting and evaluating psychological research. Together, these rules, procedures, and techniques form a unified conceptual framework—a formal way of thinking about a problem, idea, or question. Just as any game will have a set of rules, procedures, and techniques to govern play, so too does the scientific method lay out a foundation for how information is collected, measured, examined, and evaluated. In this sense, then, the scientific method serves as a playbook or toolbox for psychological research.

The origins of the scientific method, most scholars agree, may be traced to the school of philosophy known as empiricism, which holds that knowledge is gained through experience, observation, and experiment. In science, the term *empirical* is used to denote information gained objectively from observation or experimentation. This information, commonly referred to as data, is described as empirical because it can be measured and evaluated statistically. These data constitute empirical evidence against which all scientific knowledge is tested.

Empirical evidence differs from anecdotal evidence, which refers to impressions—opinions of just one person, usually, that are not translated into a quantifiable form. Investigative journalism may use such anecdotal evidence. Likewise, a very different methodology is used in legal reasoning and jurisprudence, one that emphasizes customs, precedence, and morality using techniques of cross-examination, persuasion, and rhetoric. A legal framework is thus very different, in both substance and procedures, from the scientific method.

The scientific method is crucial to research because it minimizes bias by providing the rules by which observations are collected and results are evaluated. *Bias* is a familiar term that often indicates unfair practices that wrongly discriminate against others. Within the framework of the scientific method, bias reflects a subtle process that comes in many different forms, all of which can be fatal to a research study. In fact, if you were marooned on an island and in order to be rescued you had to come up with the most important reason for the scientific method, its *raison d'etre,* or reason for being, you could do a lot worse than the following: The scientific method exists largely as a countervailing force to biases that operate at virtually all steps in the research process and that can distort and negate a study.

What Is a Scientific Question?

Many questions that might interest us may not, however, be researchable. That is, some questions may deal with topics for which the scientific method is moot.

These include questions of religion and faith that fall well beyond the realm of science and for which empiricism would be considered an anathema and maybe even an apostasy. Philosophers often distinguish two types of questions: those that they call "is" questions from those that they call "ought" questions. This philosophical distinction (known as **is-ought**) may help us understand what is meant by a scientific or "researchable" question. "Is" questions can be answered by facts or empirical data, and these answers are independent of social, cultural, political, and religious preference. These so-called "is" questions, many would argue, are the exclusive domain of scientific research. These are questions that can be best addressed through scientific research.

On the other hand are the "ought" questions, that call upon cultural values and ethical considerations, but cannot be answered solely on the basis of scientific evidence. Does God exist? Should capital punishment be overturned? Should same-sex marriage be legalized? Ought questions address the values inherent in laws and customs and are influenced by beliefs that can reflect ideology, politics and interpretation of rights. "These "ought" questions are influenced by beliefs that reflect ideology, politics, and, at least for same-sex marriage and capital punishment, constitutional law. Here science may help to contribute to the debate, but science in itself certainly cannot provide any direct, definitive answers to these questions. These questions we will leave to philosophers, theologians, and constitutional scholars.

The scientific method thus aims to answer scientific questions. Scientific questions and their answers are commonly framed in reference to a particular theory. In psychology, **theory** is defined as a coherent set of propositions that are used as principles to describe, understand, and explain psychological or behavioral phenomena. Theories often address questions of "how," as in the case of Schwartz and colleagues, who studied how maximizing relates to feelings of well-being. Ideas for a study often spring from psychological theories. We in turn use the scientific method to assess the quality of any psychological theory.

In psychology, theory often influences all aspects of a study. Not only does it serve as the source of inspiration for the seminal idea of a study, its influence will continue through the final interpretation of the results (Kuhn, 1962). Indeed, we can see the influence of the Schwartz and colleagues theory of the paradoxical effect of choice on satisfaction and happiness on how they interpreted their findings.

From Theory to Testable Hypothesis

A theory generates testable hypotheses, which are evaluated empirically with the scientific method. A **testable hypothesis** is framed as a statement, often in the form of a prediction that is made prior to the actual collection of data. A testable hypothesis is therefore described as **a priori**, meaning that it exists before experimentation or observation. A priori hypotheses constitute a key feature of the scientific method. By formulating hypotheses before data collection and analysis, a scientist is less likely to be prone to error and bias by bending the theory to fit the numbers.

In direct contradistinction are hypotheses that are formulated after the data are collected and analyzed. These hypotheses, described as **post hoc** (in Latin, "after this"), pose serious problems for the scientific method. Post hoc hypotheses increase the likelihood of error and bias. The notion is the more you look the more likely it is you will find something—the more hypotheses you test post hoc, the more likely it is that one of these will by chance be wrongly accepted as true. Post hoc hypotheses are therefore held in disfavor and require statistical adjustments that essentially raise the ante, increasing the threshold for what would be accepted as a genuine or significant finding.

Variables and Measurement

A researcher will identify, often based on theory, key variables to investigate scientifically. A **variable** is simply defined as any characteristic that can take on different values or can vary across research participants. Variables can include age, gender, weight, height, education, attitude, income, and virtually any other attribute that can assume multiple values or can vary in people. For example, Schwartz and colleagues focus on three key variables—maximizer/satisficer, satisfaction, and salary. Each of these variables had a range of values that was recorded using objective measurements. The scientific method requires objective measurement of identifiable and specifiable variables. Schwartz and colleagues used an objective measurement to categorize subjects as either satisficers or maximizers. If something in psychology cannot be measured, then it cannot be investigated scientifically.

Systematic Observation and Data Collection

Science often begins with simple observation, which can serve as a source of both evidence and ideas. Charles Darwin, for example, generated the theory of evolution by natural selection exclusively on the basis of simple observation. In his later 1872 book *The Expression of the Emotions in Man and Animals*, and again relying exclusively on observation, Darwin would make the case that all mammals regularly display emotion in their faces. Often in research, our observations are collected systematically and quantified by sampling a population. A **population** is defined as any entire collection of people, animals, plants, or things, all of which can be referred to as units, from which we may collect information. Because a population is too large to study in its entirety, a sample is generally selected for study. A **sample** is defined as a group of units selected from a larger group that is known as the *population*. Schwartz and colleagues selected a sample of 548 graduating students for their study. Thus, they had a sample size (notation for sample size is n) of 548 college graduating seniors who are referred to as *research participants* ($n = 548$).

How a researcher selects a sample from a larger population is critically important for the scientific method. A researcher tries to maximize what is referred to as **generalizability**—the extent to which findings that are derived from a sample can be applied to a wider population. Remember, a major reason for the scientific method is to combat bias, and a key source of potential bias can originate from how a sample is selected. For example, case studies can be seriously if not fatally flawed by selecting only those cases that fit preconceived ideas. This sort of "cherry picking"—that is, deliberately picking only cases that support your view while ignoring those opposing your view—is an anathema to the scientific method. This can lead to a particular form of bias, **sample bias**, which means that some members of the population are less likely than others to be included in the study (Trochim, 2006). Such exclusion of certain members or subgroups of a population

Exhibit 1.1   Sample and Cross-Population Generalizability

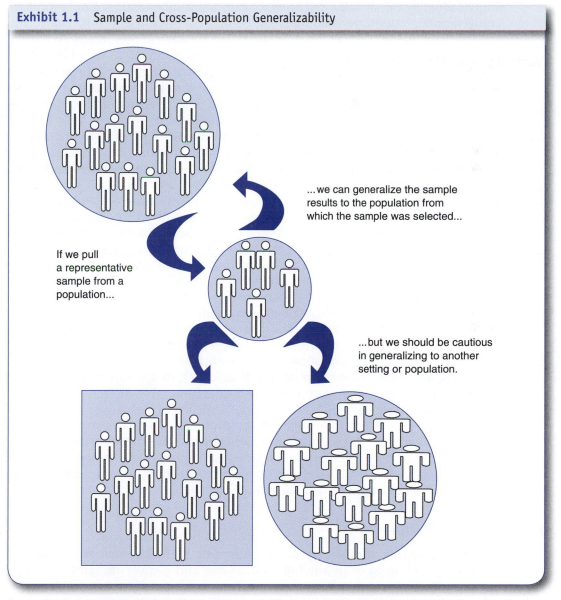

...we can generalize the sample results to the population from which the sample was selected...

If we pull a representative sample from a population...

...but we should be cautious in generalizing to another setting or population.

Source: Schutt, R. K. (2009). *Investigating the social world: The process and practice of research* (6th ed., p. 53). Thousand Oaks, CA: Pine Forge Press.

under study can produce misleading results (see Exhibit 1.1). We will discuss sampling at greater length in Chapter 5.

Evaluating Evidence and Theory

The scientific method thus requires the collection of observations, such as responses to questions, test scores, or ratings; these observations are categorized or quantified systematically, and numeric values are either assigned or computed. These number values are what constitute empirical evidence. In this regard, you can see that Schwartz and colleagues computed for each of their research participants a maximization score that could range from a low of 13 to a high of 91. Higher scores meant higher maximization. They later interviewed these research participants, used an objective rating scale to assess job satisfaction, and also recorded their yearly salary. They therefore had objective, quantitative measures of maximization, job satisfaction, and yearly salary.

The scientific method uses statistics to test relationships between and among objective, quantifiable measures that are derived from either experimentation or observation. Schwartz and colleagues tested statistically the relationship among their three measures. We will not at this point delve into the details of statistical testing. For now, two basic points are important to emphasize. Statistics are computed on the sample, which in this case consisted of 548 graduating college seniors. The sample statistics are assumed to provide estimates of the population, in this case graduating college seniors. All statistics are based on the logic of **probability**, and they all use the same criterion for evaluation. The question asked and answered by statistical tests may be stated as follows: In light of the data, what is the probability that the obtained results are due to chance? If the statistical analyses of the data show that the obtained results are highly unlikely due to chance, then the predicted relationship between, for example, high maximization and high salary but low job satisfaction is considered to be highly likely. If, on the other hand, the statistical analyses of the data show that the obtained results are likely due to chance, then there is no empirical evidence in support of the expected relationship of high maximization and high salary but low satisfaction.

The statistical evidence therefore provides a means to evaluate or test a theory. Schwartz and colleagues interpreted their empirical findings as support for the theory that maximizers may end up unhappy because they become debilitated by unrealistically high expectations when faced with an array of choices. From their findings, they reasoned that choice had a paradoxical effect on satisfaction—more choices, less satisfaction (see Exhibit 1.2).

Reliability and Validity

All sound research studies rely on the scientific method. However, as we will learn, different areas of psychology often pose and answer research scientific questions differently. Psychologists investigate these questions from a hypothetical research "toolbox" consisting of a variety of methods and techniques, each with its own advantages and disadvantages. Two important standards are used to judge the scientific quality of these methods and techniques as well as the results that they produce. First is reliability, which simply means *consistency.* Not all data are created as equal, as wise psychologists have often noted. A reliable study is one that produces data that can be replicated, that is, repeated with the same results. Whenever you read about a result of a study, always find out if it has been replicated, and if it has, then you can have greater confidence in its reliability.

Even more important in evaluating research is validity, which is defined as the extent to which a study provides a true measure of what it is *meant* to investigate. A reliable study may not necessarily be valid. For example, studies may consistently classify a certain percentage of college graduates as maximizers, but these results might be explained by other personality traits that may be related to but presumably conceptually distinct from the maximizer/satisficer classification. Could we reasonably argue that maximizers are really just perfectionists? Likewise, other factors might be related to maximization/satisficer categorization, and these could seriously detract from the validity of the conclusions of the Schwartz study. As an example, let's say you discover that the distinction varies with college major, financial need, or graduate school plans. How then can we conclude that the differences in salary and happiness can be solely attributable to differences in scores on the maximization/satisficer scale? Other aspects of how a study is designed and carried out can also influence the extent to which its conclusions are judged as unbiased, meaningful, and valid. How a study sample is selected from a population and how representative it is can influence validity.

We will learn that there are different types of validity, all of which, however, address the same question: "How true are our conclusions?" In evaluating validity, you will learn to look for what are known as confounds or confounding variables, which are unwanted sources of influence that can be viewed, much to the dismay of the researcher, as viable alternative explanations for the result of a study. "Those darn confounds" is a damning phrase that can make researchers cringe, as it cuts to the heart or validity of a study. In many studies, researchers use what is referred to as a control variable in order to measure an unwanted source of influence that could invalidate the conclusions of a study. The aim is to be able to rule out the effect of a control variable on the results of a study. So for the Schwartz study, a personality test to measure perfectionism could have served as a control variable. This could have allowed the researchers to show that perfectionism had no bearing on their findings. This, then, would rule out perfectionism as an explanation, thereby strengthening the validity of their conclusion that maximizers may end up unhappy because they become debilitated by unrealistically high expectations when faced with an array of choices.

Exhibit 1.2 Simplified Version of the Scientific Method

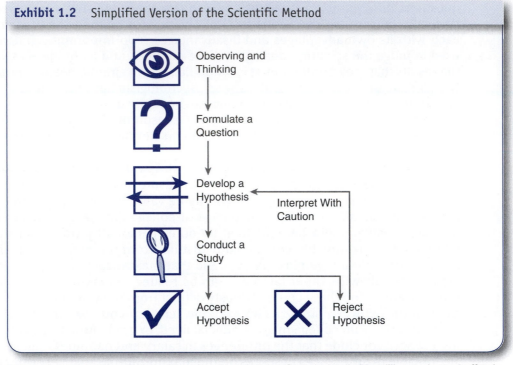

Source: Adapted from *Scientific Method Steps*, from "How the Scientific Method Works," by William Harris. HowStuffWorks.

METHODS AND TOOLS OF PSYCHOLOGICAL RESEARCH

In this book we will learn about of variety of research tools that psychologists use to investigate scientific questions. Each of these tools has its own advantages and disadvantages, and each will be judged by the extent to which it can reliably and validly address the research question posed by a study. Below, we will introduce some of the different types of methods commonly used in psychological research, as well as some of the different types of study design. Oftentimes, a research study will incorporate different techniques, combining, for example, survey measures with interviews and observational rating scales.

True Experiments

An **experiment** is a controlled investigation in which one or more variables are manipulated. Variables will differ in the degree to which they can be controlled or manipulated. We will learn that in a "true experiment," the researcher controls who conducts the study, what is studied, and how the study is conducted. That is, a researcher designs an experiment in which a particular aspect of the study is systematically altered or manipulated. This is defined as the **independent variable**, an element of the study that you as a researcher systematically manipulate, change,

Exhibit 1.3   Table 1 Research Toolbox

True experiments	Random assignment of participants to groups and manipulation of one or more independent variables.
Quasiexperiments	Experiments in which random assignment is not possible to groups.
Descriptive research	Studies that focus on the distribution of variables, the quantitative association of variables; causation cannot be established.
Survey design	Research in which information is obtained from a sample of individuals through their responses to specific questions.
Performance-based measures	Studies of data collected from standardized tests.
Single-subject designs	Systematic investigation of one or a few cases.
Qualitative research	Qualitative methods, such as participant observation, intensive interviewing, and focus groups used to study and understand phenomena in terms of the meanings people attach to them.

or select. The effects of the manipulation of the independent variable are examined and measured by the dependent variable. That is, the dependent variable is the observed effect, result, or outcome that is measured in response to a systematic change in the independent variable. Why the term *true experiment*? As we will learn in Chapter 6, the term *true experiment* is restricted to those independent variables, such as a placebo and an experimental drug, that can be randomly assigned. Random assignment helps to ensure that research participants are similar prior to the manipulation of the independent variable. Thus, the thinking is that any subsequent differences in the dependent variable can be attributed to manipulation of the independent variable rather than to confounding factors (Exhibit 1.4).

Exhibit 1.4   Three Key Variables

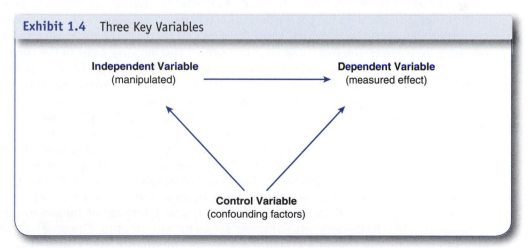

Source: From *Designing and Conducting Health Systems Research Projects: Volume 1. Proposal Development and Fieldwork*, by Corlien M. Varkevisser, Inda Pathmanathan and Ann Brownlee. Published by Canada's International Development Research Centre.

Quasiexperiments

In real life, random assignment is not possible, so a true experiment is neither practical nor plausible for many scientific questions studied by psychologists. Enter **quasi-experimental** studies (*quasi* means "as if" in Latin) for investigations that aim to examine the effects of an independent variable that cannot be directly manipulated or randomly assigned on a dependent variable. Gender, race, age, ethnicity, socio-economic status (SES), locale, diagnosis, personality traits, and personal history are just some examples of independent variables that cannot be directly manipulated by an experimenter. Rather, for these kinds of variables, an experimenter either selects participants who have a particular characteristic or studies participants who have been exposed to specified events, such as war or trauma, or might live in certain settings or situations, such as a neighborhood or a geographic region. Ideally, you will try to control for as many variables as possible so that the interpretation of the relationship between the independent and dependent variables is not unduly confounded by unwanted influences. However, in reality, this is seldom possible, so special statistical techniques may be used to remove the effects of potential confounds.

Descriptive Research

Researchers often aim to examine the relationship between two or more variables. For example, following Schwartz and colleagues, let's imagine that you sought to investigate the relationship in a sample of recent college graduates among three variables: maximization/satisficer score, levels of happiness, and current salary. To do so, you would compute what is referred to as a **correlation** between a pair of variables. A correlation is a statistic that is computed by a specific formula; this statistic provides an index of how closely related two variables are. This statistic, known as the correlation coefficient (symbolized as r), can range from .00 to +1.00 and .00 to −1.00. If there is no relationship between two variables, that is, variation in one variable has nothing to do with variation in the other variable, then the correlation value will be .00 or close to .00. The closer a correlation between two variables is to 1.00, either +1.00 or −1.00, the stronger is the relationship between the two variables. The positive and negative signs of the correlation coefficient tell the direction of the relationship between the two variables. A positive correlation coefficient (a "plus" sign) means that there is a positive linear relationship—as scores on one variable increase, so do scores on the other variable. For example, as scores on IQ increase, so do grades. This correlation helps psychologists establish the validity of IQ. A negative correlation coefficient (indicated by a "minus" sign) means that there is a negative linear relationship: As scores on one variable increase, scores on the other variable decrease. For example, as IQ increases, accident rates decrease. This negative relationship might also be used as evidence of validity of IQ, suggesting that higher IQ is associated with healthy functioning, as indicated by fewer accidents.

Descriptive research thus entails looking at the way one set of measurements goes up or down in tandem with another set of measurements. The chief advantage of correlational research is that it allows for the quantitative comparison of variables that cannot be manipulated directly. However, correlation can only look at relations among variables at one point in time. And also as we will learn, the most important limitation is that a correlation can only indicate whether two sets of measurements tend to vary together; it cannot determine causality, that is, whether one variable causes the other.

Naturalistic Observation

Naturalistic observation is a type of descriptive research used to collect behavioral data in natural environments as opposed to laboratory or other controlled settings. For example, naturalistic observation provides a means to study animal behavior in its natural habitat. Developmental psychologists also use naturalistic observation to investigate children interacting with caregivers. This research approach is not simply a collection of subjective impressions but rather the systematic study of well-defined, measurable observations that can be repeated by others. An important disadvantage of naturalistic observation is the lack of control of the countless variables that could influence behavior in the natural environment. However, careful observation is often important in the process of research, as it can help the researcher to pose a scientific question and to formulate a hypothesis.

Survey Design

A survey is typically comprised of a set of questions asking respondents about their activities, opinions, attitudes, or preferences. Using self-report measures, such as the maximization-satisficer scale, a survey provides a relatively inexpensive way to collect a lot of data quickly and to formulate and test a hypothesis. A survey is, however, limited by what people are capable of reporting accurately.

Performance-Based Measures

Standardized tests, such as the college-board examination, are perhaps the best example of performance-based measures. In psychology, performance-based measures constitute a well-known psychometric approach for investigating variables such as intelligence, personality traits, and aptitude (the psychometric approach is covered in detail in Chapter 4). With this approach, test performance is scored and compared to a statistical average derived from a normative or standardization sample taken from a wider population. For example, a well-known psychometric test of intelligence is the Wechsler Adult Intelligence Scale–Fourth Edition (WAIS-IV; Wechsler, 2008). This test provides a measure of a variety of cognitive abilities, such as vocabulary, mental arithmetic, spatial reasoning, and using blocks to construct designs, performance on all of which is summarized in the form of an intelligence quotient (IQ). IQ is computed by comparing a person's test score to that of a normative group of peers of similar ages. The advantage of the psychometric approach rests largely on the extensive reliability and validity studies that are performed in the development and construction of an instrument, such as the WAIS-IV. An important disadvantage, however, is that psychometric measures are often criticized for being culturally biased in their construction and selection of test items and tasks. An additional important consideration is the extent to which the normative or standardization sample for a psychometric test is truly representative of the diversity of the general population or an appropriate bench-mark for an individual test taker of an ethnic or racial minority.

Small-N and Single-Subject Designs

Single-Subject Designs are used to test the effectiveness of a particular intervention on one person or a small set of very similar cases and to monitor client progress. In this design (also known as a single-case or **small-N design**), between one and nine research participants are the target of an intervention. The structure of this design makes it useful for research on interventions in behavior analysis and clinical practice (Saville, 2003; Yarnold, 1992). Specifically, clinicians in their practice must make assessments, establish goals and outcomes for an intervention, deliver the intervention, and then evaluate client progress in terms of the desired outcome(s). In parallel fashion, researchers (or clinician/researchers) using a single-subject design assess a client (or a few clients) using a systematic measurement procedure, they monitor client progress by making repeated measurements in terms of the desired outcomes, and they then evaluate the efficacy of the intervention. In this way, clinicians can improve their ability to monitor their effectiveness and also contribute to a body of research on a treatment. A major disadvantage of this research design is uncertainty about whether the findings from one case or a few cases are applicable to others.

Qualitative Research

In many instances, researchers may seek to study questions for which numerical or empirical answers may not provide the most complete answers, such as questions of values and meanings people attach to human behavior and beliefs. For example, how and why is it that people from Western cultures tend to value independence and individualism in contrast to the high value people of Eastern cultures give to interdependence and collectivism? An even deeper question might be to address the fundamental nature of such categories as individualism and collectivism. For these questions of how and why, researchers often use what are referred to as qualitative methods, such as participant observation, intensive interviewing, and focus groups. These techniques are intended *to go beyond numbers* in order to study and understand phenomena in terms of the meanings people attach to them, thereby preserving and capturing the complexities and diversities of human behavior. While often complemented by quantitative approaches summarized in Table 1, qualitative methods are especially well suited for exploring research questions as well as for helping to define preliminary questions that can then be studquantitatively. We will learn more about qualitative methods or research in Chapter 2. Chapter 11 will also present qualitative research in much more detail.

CULTURE AND PSYCHOLOGICAL SCIENCE

The science of psychology does not occur in a vacuum. How we think about psychological problems, ask questions, design studies, and interpret results occur within a larger societal context, which is referred to as **culture**. Culture may be best defined as the rich and intricate melding of shared meanings, communal practices and rituals, and collective discourses and beliefs about human life that prevails in a given group or society (Shweder & Sullivan, 1993). These common patterns of beliefs, symbols, feelings, and customs are acquired and transmitted socially, although how the mechanisms through which this occurs have yet to be established. Some researchers, for example, have introduced the term *memes* as the genetic DNA of culture, and like genes, memes are postulated to act as units through which group ways of life spread from one mind to another (e.g., Dawkins, 1976/1989; Pinker, 1997) According to this school of thought, culture is generated by information-processing mechanisms situated in human minds and sculpted by evolution (Barkow, Cosmides, & Tooby, 1992).

Cultural Research

Why is understanding and appreciating culture vital to research in psychology? Because culture generates profound psychological differences among people, and such diversity enriches human life (Wilson, Van Vugt, & O'Gorman, 2008). To understand human psychology more fully and to study it more deeply therefore requires research that takes into account cultural influences. How can this be done? In the preceding section, you learned about the different kinds of research designs, all of which involved collecting data from a sample of people. In many instances, studies using these designs will sample people from a single culture. As you have learned earlier in this chapter, this poses a significant limitation for a study, which we refer to as the problem of generalizability. When a researcher uses a culturally homogeneous sample, results cannot be generalized to a wider population of people. This is not necessarily fatal, but it certainly is something a researcher should think about in designing a study and interpreting results.

On the other hand, certain fields within psychology are devoted to the study of culture. For example, a researcher in the field of **cultural psychology** studies how culture shapes our thinking and how our thinking shapes culture (e.g., Nisbett, Peng, Choi, & Norenzayan, 2001). A related but distinct field of study is **cross-cultural psychology**. Here the primary object is to investigate the universality of psychological processes across different cultures rather than to study how local cultural practices might shape psychological processes. So whereas a cross-cultural researcher might examine whether certain personality traits such as extraversion and introversion are universal across a variety of cultures, a cultural psychologist might be interested how particular cultures shape how personality traits are expressed and displayed (McAdams & Pals, 2006).

SCIENCE VERSUS PSEUDOSCIENCE

In philosophical terms, the scientific method represents an **epistemology**, that is, a way of knowing that is exclusively reliant upon objective, empirical investigation. Its techniques must be **transparent** so that the methods, procedures, and data analyses of any study can be easily reproduced. This transparency allows for other researchers to see if the same study can be repeated with the same finding. As we have learned in this chapter, when a result is replicated, we have greater confidence that the finding is reliable.

Science builds knowledge through the replication of studies and findings. The maximizing study clearly meets the requirements of transparency in methods and procedures so that other researchers can see if they can independently replicate these findings. Their methods and procedures are open to public scrutiny, as you can easily see by the availability of the 13-item test that Schwartz and colleagues used to categorize their research participants as either satisficers or maximizers. Transparency also allows for **peer review**, the process by which other independent reviewers (meaning no relationship with the researchers whose work is under review) evaluate the scientific merit of the work. These peer reviews essentially determine whether the work will be accepted for publication. Schwartz and his colleagues submitted their study to the peer-reviewed journal *Psychological Science* and, following careful scientific scrutiny from peer reviewers, the journal editor accepted the study for publication.

Reliable and valid knowledge is thus knowledge that has a high probability of being true because it has been systematically acquired and empirically tested; that is, it has been produced and evaluated by the scientific method. Now let us consider knowledge gained not through the scientific method but through other means, such as intuition, impression, gut reactions, or experience. We may be convinced that this knowledge is also true and valid. However, it is not based on empirical evidence generated by the scientific method. Instead, it might be based on authoritarian or expert evidence of what a person tells you to believe or it might be based on testimonial or anecdotal evidence offered by a person who believes the knowledge to be true because of personal subjective experience.

The crux of the problem arises when the methods of establishing evidence and the body of knowledge generated from these techniques are claimed to represent a legitimate scientific field of study. Consider the well-known case of astrology that uses horoscopes to predict personality and behavior; many people may swear by astrology and believe it to be scientific. However, astrology, along with extrasensory perception, alien-abduction reports, out-of-body experiences, the lunar lunacy effect, rebirthing therapy, and handwriting analysis are just some of examples of what is referred to as **pseudoscience**. In popular psychology, pseudoscientific beliefs are dubious but fascinating claims that are touted as "scientifically proven" and bolstered by fervent, public testimonials of believers who have experienced first hand or who have claimed to have witnessed the phenomenon.

Recognizing Pseudoscience

History tells us that with advancements over time, some fields of study come to be seen as pseudoscientific: Today's pseudoscience could be yesterday's science. Take for example, **phrenology**, a now defunct field of study that was once considered a science in the 19th century. The major, unified belief of phrenology held that bumps and fissures of the skull determined the character and personality of a person. Phrenologists believed that various psychological attributes, including personality traits, intellectual faculties, and moral character, could all be assessed by running their fingertips and palms over the skulls of a patient to feel for enlargements or indentations (see **Exhibit 1.5**). Advances in neurology would

Exhibit 1.5   This porcelain head for sale in a New Orleans antique store shows the sections of the brain, as detailed by 19th-century phrenologists. They believed that each section was responsible for a particular human personality trait. If a section were enlarged or shrunken, the personality would be likewise abnormal. Doctors, particularly those doing entry examinations at American prisons, would examine the new inmate's head for bumps or cavities to develop a criminal profile. For example, if the section of brain responsible for "acquisitiveness" was enlarged, the offender probably was a thief. Lombroso and his school combined phrenology with other models that included external physical appearance traits that could single out criminals from the general population.

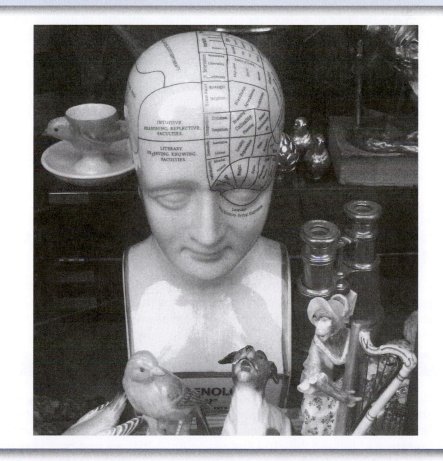

Source: Photo taken by Cecil Greek.

relegate phrenology to the dustbin of pseudoscience. However, some of its assumptions have come to influence modern neuroscience and neuropsychology. Among these are the centrality of the brain as the organ of the mind and the localization of certain mental functions across particular brain regions.

Psychology professor Scott Lilienfeld of Emory University has identified "The 10 Commandments of Helping Students Distinguish Science from Pseudoscience in Psychology," and he proposes these rules as a way for us to understand better what science is and what science isn't. According to Lilienfeld (2005), just as we cannot grasp fully the concept of cold without understanding hot, we cannot grasp fully the concept of scientific thinking without an understanding of pseudoscientific beliefs—specifically those beliefs that at first blush appear scientific but are not. Among the warning signs of pseudoscience laid out by Lilienfeld (2005) are:

- A tendency to invoke ad hoc hypotheses, which can be thought of as "escape hatches" or loopholes, as a means of immunizing claims from falsification.
- An absence of self-correction and an accompanying intellectual stagnation.
- An emphasis on confirmation rather than refutation.
- A tendency to place the burden of proof on skeptics, not proponents, of claims.
- Excessive reliance on anecdotal and testimonial evidence to substantiate claims.
- Evasion of the scrutiny afforded by peer review.
- Absence of "connectivity" (Stanovich, 1997), that is, a failure to build on existing scientific knowledge.
- Use of impressive-sounding jargon whose primary purpose is to lend claims a facade of scientific respectability.
- An absence of boundary conditions (Hines, 2003), that is, a failure to specify the settings under which claims do not hold.

Now none of these warning signs alone is sufficient to render a discipline as pseudoscientific. But the more warning signs that are present, the more reason to suspect pseudoscientific machinations are at work.

WHY PSEUDOSCIENCE?

Why are we so susceptible to pseudoscience? Recall that theories help us to understand how a particular phenomenon works. In this case, we want to understand how, in theory, pseudoscience might work. To do so, we examine the scientific literature of human thinking and reasoning. What we find may very well surprise you, as this research shows that humans commonly reason with unseen and persistent biases. As you will see, pseudoscience preys on these biases, which can only be combated by (you guessed it!), the scientific method. As Lilienfeld (2005) noted, the scientific method provides a "tool box" to prevent researchers from confirming their own biases

Cognitive Illusions

Cognitive psychologists study how we think and make decisions. One of the most striking contributions cognitive psychologists have made over the past decades is the finding that laypersons and experts alike tend to make consistent, systematic, deeply ingrained, and often insidious mistakes of reasoning that reflect our poor grasp of logic and probability theory. So important is this discovery that its principal pioneer, originator, and founding figure, psychology professor Daniel Kahneman, won the 2002 Nobel Prize in Economic Sciences. The body of empirical evidence underlying this program of research comes from a rather simple but elegant study design in which cognitive psychologists devised a vast array of confusing questions that most people answer incorrectly because of their poor grasp of logic and probability theory. The correct answers are so counterintuitive that they elicit strong emotions of disbelief comparable to those produced by familiar optical illusions. For example, in the optical illusion in **Exhibit 1.6**, your visual system deceives you so that the figure in the background seems larger, although they are exactly the same size. In the same way, **cognitive illusions** occur when our thinking deceives us, and these occur

Exhibit 1.6   Cool Brain Trick: In Depth

Which monster is larger?

Note: To most people, the one in the background seems larger, though in fact they are exactly the same size. But the depth cues in the picture (the receding tunnel) give the 2D image a 3D feel. Although both monsters create the same size image in our eyes, our brains take the depth cues into account, which results in a perception of the upper monster as farther away—making it seem larger.

Source: From *Mind Sights* by Roger Shepard. Copyright © 1990 Roger Shepard. Published by W. H. Freeman & Company. Reprinted by permission of the author.

because of curious blind spots, or mental tunnels in our minds (e.g., Piatelli-Palmarini, 1994).

The human mind, these studies tell us, is "probability blind," meaning that it is naturally endowed to favor subjective impressions and personal anecdotes over cold, hard statistics. These **heuristic biases** for the subjective over the objective act as mental shortcuts that can distort logical reasoning. We all, expert and novice alike, use these heuristic biases regularly, naturally, and automatically in making a variety of decisions, such as marrying a partner, picking a stock, or diagnosing a disease (not even medical doctors are immune to heuristic biases). When faced with making decisions for which available information is incomplete or overly complex, we rely on simplifying heuristics, or efficient rules of thumb (e.g., Piatelli-Palmarini, 1994). Michael Shermer, prolific journalist and scholar, who specializes in the study of pseudoscience, perhaps says it best and with panache in his August 2008 *Scientific American* column "Skeptic," explaining why subjective anecdotes often trump cold hard data, when he writes, " . . . we have evolved brains that pay attention to anecdotes because false positives (believing there is a connection between A and B when there is not) are usually harmless, whereas false negatives (believing there is no connection between A and B when there is) may take you out of the gene pool" (p. 42).

Confirmatory Bias

Confirmatory bias has been described as a ubiquitous phenomenon that comes in many guises (Nickerson, 1988). It is considered a primary source of errors in human reasoning, and researchers have argued that our natural and universal tendency for confirmatory bias is major reason why pseudoscience has persisted and flourished over time (Sternberg, 2007). As Sternberg wrote, " . . . people want to believe, and so they find ways to believe" (p. 292). **Confirmatory bias** is defined as a natural tendency of the human mind to actively seek out and assign more weight to any kind of evidence that favors existing beliefs, expectations, or a hypothesis in hand (Nickerson, 1998). Nickerson identified several scenarios in which confirmatory bias may contaminate scientific research. One common scenario occurs when a researcher restricts attention to a favored hypothesis, which is defined as either explanation of a phenomenon or a prediction of a theoretical relationship (e.g., income predicts happiness) that requires empirical testing. (We will elaborate more on the meaning of hypothesis in Chapter 2.) Others include preferential treatment of that which supports existing beliefs, looking only or primarily for positive cases, a form of "cherry-picking" we discussed earlier in relation to sample bias, and overweighting positive confirmatory instances (Nickerson, 1998). Thus, a common mistake, confirmatory bias reflects a kind of selective thinking and observation—choosing to look only at things that are in line with our preferences or beliefs. **Exhibit 1.7** depicts the difference between selective observation and a related error in reasoning, overgeneralization.

Philosophers of science have long viewed confirmatory bias as a major threat or danger to research. Enter the work of Sir Karl Popper (1959), whose central idea,

Exhibit 1.7 The Difference Between Selective Observation and Overgeneralization

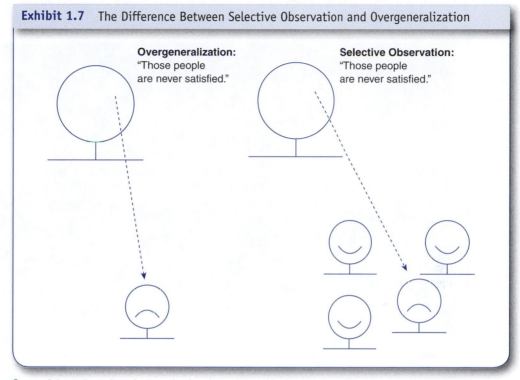

Overgeneralization:
"Those people
are never satisfied."

Selective Observation:
"Those people
are never satisfied."

Source: Schutt, R. K. (2009). *Investigating the social world: The process and practice of research* (6th ed., p. 6). Thousand Oaks, CA: Pine Forge Press.

referred to as the **doctrine of falsification**, was that scientists should aim to falsify their theories rather than confirm them. In the Popper approach, a scientist ought to investigate a theory by producing tests that disconfirm it rather than confirm it. As Nobel Prize Winner Eric R. Kandel writes in his autobiography, *In Search of Memory* (2006), " . . . Being on the wrong side of an interpretation was unimportant, Popper argued. The greatest strength of the scientific method is its ability to disprove a hypothesis" (p. 96). This is because, as Popper argued, confirming evidence could be consistent with several different theoretical explanations. In fact, theories entail many assumptions, some of which are undoubtedly wrong. If, however, there is no way to disconfirm, then there is no way to eliminate false theories and their assumptions.

Thus, for Popper, disconfirmation is an all-or-nothing affair: A single result can either disconfirm the hypothesis or else it does not (Koslowski, 1996). Consider the famous Popper example of "black swans" in which he observed that only a single black swan is required to falsify the theory that all "swans are white" even though there are thousands of white swans in evidence. Thus, if hypotheses or theories can stand the test of disproof, then they earn scientific acceptance. Theories should therefore be open to disproof. Falsification fits with the **self-correcting** nature of science in which information accumulates with new advances and discoveries. In stark contrast, pseudosciences are neither

Exhibit 1.8   Disconfirmation of "All Swans Are White"

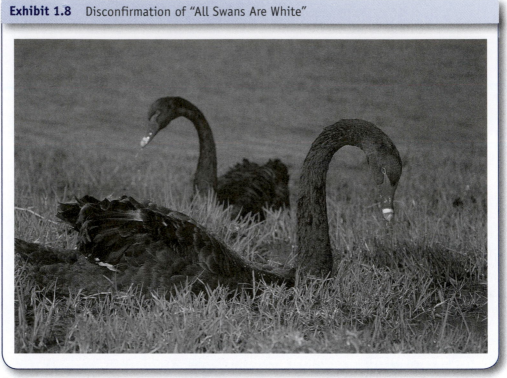

Source: Stockbyte/Thinkstock.

self-correcting nor cumulative but instead are stagnant and show little or no progress in accumulating knowledge (**Exhibit 1.8**).

Uncommon Sense

We can see that our minds might very well be naturally endowed to confirm our existing beliefs. Our inclination for what we consider to be "common sense"—for what seems intuitively obvious—can run counter to understanding the physical world and the social world. As developmental psychologists have noted, even before the development of language, 1-year-old babies possess a rich understanding of the physical world and the social world, with the former referred to as a "naïve physics" and the latter as a "naïve psychology" (Bloom & Weisberg, 2007). This evolved adaptation gives children a head start for understanding and learning about objects and people. By the same token, however, it inevitably conflicts with scientific discoveries, sowing the seeds of resistance in children to learning and accepting certain scientific facts. Indeed, as Carey (2000) noted, the challenge in teaching science to children is "not what the student lacks, but what the student *has,* namely alternative conceptual frameworks for the phenomena covered by the theories we are trying to teach" (p. 14).

Bloom and Weisberg (2007) proposed that people come to "resist certain scientific findings because many of these findings are unnatural and unintuitive"

(p. 997). Even commonsense psychology poses a major obstacle for understanding science. As an example, Bloom and Weisberg point to the philosophy of **dualism**, which holds that the mind is a nonphysical substance that is fundamentally different from the physical brain. They noted that children naturally believe that certain aspects of psychology, such as morality, love, and play, are solely dependent upon the immaterial nature of the interior life of the soul. And these intuitions are often further solidified and transmitted by cultural authorities. On the other hand, as we have learned earlier in this chapter, dualism touches upon questions of meaning spirituality that are not necessarily suited to science and empiricism. And for many, including scientists, for these domains of human experience, only religion can provide deep insights. In fact, the prestigious scientific organization National Academy of Sciences (NAS) endorses the value of dualism and has made clear that science and religion are not at all at odds with each other. In a 2008 publication titled *Science, Evolution and Creationism*, the Committee on Revising Science and Creationism (2008) stated, "Many scientists have written eloquently about how their scientific studies have increased their awe and understanding of a creator. The study of science need not lessen or compromise faith" (p. 54). Thus, we can see that pseudoscience can be appealing on many fronts. It often preys on our heuristic biases, capitalizing on our evolved and developed resistance to the uncommon sense of science.

CONCLUSIONS

In this chapter, we likened the scientific method to a toolbox of procedures and techniques that allows a researcher to ask, study, and answer particular questions about psychology. In philosophical terms, these questions are referred to as "is" questions and defined as those that can be answered by facts or empirical data, with these answers independent of social, cultural, political, and religious context. On the other hand are "ought' questions that fall outside the domain of the scientific method, meaning that their ultimate answers and final directives hinge upon a collective, usually democratic, understanding of decency, justice, and fairness.

Scientific questions are commonly framed in reference to a particular theory that in turn leads to a testable hypothesis that specifies key variables to be investigated. Objective measurement of these variables is critical, because if something in psychology cannot be measured, then it cannot be investigated scientifically. Observations can then be collected systematically and quantified by sampling a population. These observations, translated into number values, are what constitute empirical evidence. Statistics are computed to test hypothesized relationships between and among objective, quantifiable measures. Statistics allow the researcher to assess the likelihood that the obtained results are due to chance; a finding that is unlikely due to chance is typically interpreted as supportive of the hypothesis of the study. Reliability and validity are two important standards that are used to judge the scientific quality of any research study.

Within the toolbox are several different kinds of research methods and designs. These, we learned, include experimental design, quasiexperimental design, descriptive research, surveys, performance-based measures, small-N studies, and qualitative methods. Each approach has its advantages and disadvantages, which will be discussed throughout the book. The degree to which variables can be manipulated is an important feature in deciding on a research approach. In a true experimental design, the independent variable is under complete control or manipulation by the researcher, and its effects on the dependent variable can thus be directly tested. By contrast, a quasiexperimental design is used for independent variables that cannot be directly manipulated or randomly assigned. Descriptive research also allows for comparison of variables that cannot be manipulated directly. We also learned that how we think about psychological problems, ask questions, design studies, and interpret results occur within a larger societal context, which is referred to as culture.

Finally, we learned that the scientific method represents an epistemology, that is, a way of knowing that is exclusively reliant upon objective, empirical investigation. Its techniques must be transparent so that the methods, procedures, and data analyses of any study can be easily reproduced. Pseudoscience, on the other hand, relies not on empirical evidence but on anecdotal testimonial accounts. Pseudoscientific beliefs are dubious but fascinating claims that are touted as "scientifically proven" and bolstered by fervent, public testimonials of believers who have experienced first hand or who have claimed to have witnessed the phenomenon. We theorized that pseudoscience preys on our naturally evolved and universal tendency for confirmatory bias.

END OF CHAPTER

Chapter Highlights

- The scientific method is the conceptual framework we use to design, conduct, and evaluate theories and to test hypotheses.

- The scientific method is empirical, meaning that information is gained objectively from observation or experiment and represented as variables.

- A variable is defined as any characteristic or attribute that can take on more than one value or can vary across participants in a research study.

- The scientific method uses statistics to test relationships between and among objective, quantifiable measures of specified variables.

- All statistics are based on the logic of probability and they all use the same criterion for evaluation. The question asked and answered by statistical tests may be stated as follows: In light of the data, what is the probability that the obtained results are due to chance?

- There are a variety of research tools and research designs. These include experimental design, quasiexperimental design, descriptive research, surveys, performance-based measures, small-N studies, and qualitative methods. Reliability and validity are the main standards that psychologists use in evaluating each of these research techniques and procedures.

- Understanding and appreciating culture is vital to research in psychology. How we think about psychological problems, ask questions, design studies, and interpret results occur within a larger societal context, which is referred to as culture.

- The scientific method exists largely as a countervailing force to biases that operate at virtually all steps in the research process and that can distort and negate a study.

- The human mind is "probability blind," meaning that it is naturally endowed to favor subjective impressions over cold, hard statistics. These heuristic biases for the subjective over the objective act as mental shortcuts that distort logical reasoning.

- Pseudoscience preys on heuristic biases, which can only be combated by the scientific method.

- Pseudoscience remains a powerful force that seems to satisfy a deep-rooted need etched into our collective consciousness to understand how the world works and how we fit into the grand cosmos.

Key Terms

A priori   5

Bias   4

Cognitive illusions   20

Confirmatory bias   20

Confounding variables   9

Confounds   9

Control variable   9

Correlation   12

Correlational research   12

Cross-cultural psychology   15

Cultural psychology   15

Culture   14

Data   4

Dependent variable   11

Doctrine of falsification   21

Dualism   23

Empiricism   4

Epistemology   15

Experiment   10

Experimental design   10

Generalizability   6

Heuristic biases   20

Hypothesis   5

Independent variable   10

Is-ought   5

Naturalistic observation   13

Research in the News

Examples abound of new pseudoscientific disciplines. Perhaps there is no better example than the best-selling tome *The Secret* by television producer Rhonda Byrne. It became a blockbuster, No. 1 on *The New York Times* best-seller list when it was featured not once but twice by television personality Oprah Winfrey's popular show. What is so evidently alluring about *The Secret* is its central idea, known as the Law of Attraction, which states that wishing can make things come true, something very young children could resonate to in their beliefs about the Tooth Fairy and Santa Claus. Whether you want money, a new home, or even a regular parking space, just ask, believe you will get it, and you will get it, guaranteed! *The Secret*'s mantra is a simple and ancient idea: Ask. Believe. Receive. This is positive thinking with a guarantee, and of course, there are no guarantees in psychology. Explain how *The Secret* meets the seven warning signs of pseudoscience.

Activity Questions

1. As a cross-cultural psychologist, you have been hired to help researchers design studies that have greater generalizability. What would you recommend in terms of sampling? What kinds of measures might be most helpful? What kind of study design would you recommend?

2. The question of whether creation should be taught as a science has long been debated in the public arena and in the courts across the land. In *McLean v. Arkansas* (*McLean v. Arkansas Board of Education*, Decision January 5, 1982), Judge William Overton ruled that "creation science" was not scientific and should not be taught

in Arkansas public schools. Judge Overton cited the lack of falsifiability as one of the reasons he determined "creation science" to be not scientific and why it should not be taught in Arkansas public schools. In his conclusion, Judge Overton explained his reasoning as to why he used falsifiability as a criterion to determine the creation science was not a science. He wrote that a methodology cannot be described as scientific if to begins with a conculsion and does not change regardless of evidence to the contrary. Explain how and why you think Judge Overton came to use lack of falsfiability as a criterion for deciding against "creation science." Explain how psychological research of heuristic biases might influence other legal rulings on "creation science."

3. In a May 9, 2010, article in the *Chronicle of Higher Education,* titled "The New War Between Science and Religion," Mano Singham writes about "the new war that pits those who argue that science and 'moderate' forms of religion are compatible worldviews against those who think they are not" [paragraph 1]. As you also learned in Chapter 1, the prestigious National Academy of Sciences endorses the position for the compatibility of science and religion. Weigh both the pros and cons of this debate. How might the philisophical distinction between questions of *ought* versus *is* be used to shed light on this debate?

4. Suppose you have been hired as a developmental psychologist to help design a curriculum to teach science and the scientific method to elementary school children. As a research psychologist, you know before the development of language, 1-year-old babies possess a rich understanding of the physical world and the social world, with the former referred to as a "naïve physics" and the latter as a "naïve psychology" (Bloom & Weisberg, 2007). Moreover, you also know that as psychologist Susan Carey (2000) noted, the challenge in teaching science to children is "not what the student lacks, but what the student *has,* namely alternative conceptual frameworks for the phenomena covered by the theories we are trying to teach" (p. 14). Organize a formal discussion, first addressing people's commonsense intuitive understanding of psychology ("naïve psychology") and why it comes so naturally to us. Address how it could contribute to scientific resistance for understanding the workings of the brain and mind.

5. Heuristic biases come in many forms. Consider the following example from "Where Mistakes of Reason Rule Our Minds" (Piatelli-Palmarini, 1994):

Steve is very shy and withdrawn, invariably helpful, but with little interest in people or the world of reality. A meek and tidy soul, he has a need for order and structure, and a passion for detail.

Which is more likely, that Steve is a librarian or farmer? Now, if you are like most people you will pick librarian. You will do so even though you have been provided background statistics that indicated that there are far more farmers than librarians. Your blind spots or cognitive illusions let the librarian stereotype override the fact that there are far more farmers than librarians. You neglect or ignore hard, cold statistical evidence about the higher base rate or incidence of farmers over librarians in favor of impressionistic, subjective, intuitive, stereotypical information. Try with a group of naïve students and see how they respond.

Review Questions

1. What is a scientific question? Compare and contrast scientific questions and legal questions.

2. In the maximization study, how would you state the major hypothesis of the study? How did theory influence the formation of the hypothesis?

3. State the independent and dependent variables of the maximization study. How were they selected and measured?

4. What was the sample size of the maximization study? What implication does sample size have on statistical analysis? Would you consider this a random sample? Why or why not?

5. All statistics are based on the logic of probability. Explain how this works. How do statistics address question as to whether a study's results are to be believed?

6. Describe the different kinds of studies that are part of the research toolbox.

7. What are confounds and how might they be controlled?

8. How can you tell the difference between pseudoscience and real science?

9. Why do you think pseudoscience is often so appealing? According to cognitive psychologists, how do our minds that make us susceptible to pseudoscience?

10. Explain how the scientific method tries to stamp out confirmatory bias.

CHAPTER 2

The Foundations of Psychological Research

FACIAL EXPRESSIONS OF EMOTION

The headline of the Jan 16, 2009, article in *Time* magazine by John Cloud exclaimed, "How to lift your mood? Try smiling." You might respond, Wow! Why didn't I think of that? Or you might dismiss at first blush (no pun intended) as preposterous the claim made in the headline that smiling can actually lead to improved mood. You might think to yourself, everyone knows our emotions don't

29

work this way—we smile as a result of being happy, smiling doesn't cause us to be happy. However, as we will learn in this chapter, the scientific method can be applied to this chicken-and-egg question as to what comes first, the simple act of smiling or the positive emotional feeling. And what you will learn in this chapter might surprise you, and the claim in this headline could seem less preposterous than you might have originally thought.

As you recall from Chapter 1, there are several techniques available in the research toolbox from which you can choose. The research methods and design you choose depend greatly on the questions asked and the answers you hope to discover. There are two very broad research approaches used by researchers: **experimental** and **nonexperimental** designs. For example, studies that use naturalistic observation methodology are nonexperimental in that actions and events are carefully measured and catalogued but independent variables cannot be directly manipulated and extraneous factors that can confound results are difficult to control. Nonexperimental designs encompass several types of studies, including studies referred to as quasiexperimental, correlational, survey, and single-subject or small-N research. Thus, if you wanted to examine the relationship of smiling and positive mood using a nonexperimental design, you might have participants watch a comedy film, record the number of times each participant smiled, and then have participants complete a questionnaire on their mood. Suppose you found a relationship between increases in smiles and positive mood. Could you conclude that there is a causal relationship between smiling and positive mood? As you know, the answer to this important question is "no."

On the other hand, an experimental study can be used when the researcher wants to test cause and effect, such as investigating whether smiling causes positive changes in emotional feelings. In an experimental design, a researcher is able to exercise control over the variable or variables that are assumed to be the causal agent(s) producing the predicted effect. In this chapter, we will learn about the nature of these variables, and we will also learn that causality in human psychological research even with an experimental design is surprisingly complex. But for now, the important message is that only an experimental design allows for testing of cause-and-effect relationships.

THE GOALS OF SCIENCE

Paul Ekman is a world-renowned psychologist who has devoted his career to studying facial expressions of emotions. In the 1960s as a young psychology professor at the University of California at San Francisco (UCSF), Ekman found that most social scientists understood emotional expression in the face to be *culturally determined* by a set of learned social conventions. He had a very different idea, one that could be traced to Charles Darwin's 1872 book *The Expression of the Emotions in Man and Animals,* in which Darwin argues that all mammals communicate their emotions through facial expression. Malcolm Gladwell, in a delightful 2002 *New Yorker* piece, described how an undaunted and inspired Ekman set out to discover the rules governing how we express emotions in our faces. Ekman began, Gladwell writes, by challenging the idea that such rules are learned social or cultural conventions.

Ekman first traveled to places like Japan, Brazil, and Argentina, carrying photographs of men and women posing various distinctive faces. Everywhere he went in the developed world, people agreed on what those expressions meant. But because these people all lived in developed countries, they, Ekman knew, could still have picked up the same cultural rules watching the same movies and televisions shows. The indefatigable Ekman, armed with his trusty photographs, next traveled to the most remote villages in the jungles of Papua New Guinea, and there he found, lo and behold, that these tribe folk also had no problem interpreting various facial expressions of emotions. In this very important sense, then, as you recall from Chapter 1, Ekman began his work as a true *cultural psychologist*.

Over the next half century, Paul Ekman would build a program of psychological research around his breakthrough discovery that facial expressions of emotions were not socially learned but rather are the universal products of evolution. His nonexperimental studies of facial expression across cultures would be extended to elegant experimental studies by him and other researchers (see also, e.g., Leppanen, & Nelson, 2009; Mandal & Ambady, 2004). Together, this research established the human face as an exquisite and efficient organ of emotional communication.

Exhibit 2.1   Universal Expressions of Seven Major Categories of Facial Emotions

Eve Ekman, the daughter of psychologist Paul Ekman, demonstrates the seven major categories of facial expressions. Top row, from left to right: Fear, anger, happiness, contempt. Bottom row: surprise, disgust, and sadness.

Source: Paul Ekman, PhD/Paul Ekman Group, LLC.

Description

The principal objective of research is to provide a scientific understanding of the topic of investigation. Scientific understanding entails two distinct but related processes: description and explanation. We first describe the phenomenon that we intend to study. This may seem obvious, but careful and precise definitions of key concepts and the measures we develop for those concepts are critical for scientific understanding.

Generally, researchers describe and define terms both conceptually and operationally. A **conceptual definition** provides the meaning, often rather broad in scope, of an abstract term, such as *intelligence*, *anxiety*, or *emotion*. Very similar to what you would find in a dictionary, a conceptual definition demarcates a semantic or linguistic meaning of a psychological term, that is, its usage in words, texts, and language. For example, intelligence as a concept may be defined as the general ability that enables an individual to comprehend the world and to deal effectively with its challenges (Wechsler, 1997). For Ekman, the term *emotions* represents another key concept that he defines broadly as a rapid and coordinated response system that evolved to enable humans to react quickly and effectively to events that affect their welfare (Ekman, 2003). In this conceptual definition of emotions as a response system, facial expressions are a critical medium of communication.

Operational definitions follow from conceptual definitions. An **operational definition** indicates how a concept is coded, measured, or quantified. It may be as simple

Table 2.1 Operational Definitions for Producing Seven Major Categories of Facial Expressions of Emotions

Seven Major Categories of Facial Expessions of Emotions

(adapted from Duenwald, 2005)

SADNESS: The eyelids droop as the inner corners of the brows rise and, in extreme sadness, draw together. The corners of the lips pull down, and the lower lip may push up in a pout.

SURPRISE: The upper eyelids and brows rise, and the jaw drops open.

ANGER: Both the lower and upper eyelids tighten as the brows lower and draw together. Intense anger raises the upper eyelids as well. The jaw thrusts forward, the lips press together, and the lower lip may push up a little.

CONTEMPT: This is the only expression that appears on just one side of the face: One half of the upper lip tightens upward.

DISGUST: The nose wrinkles and the upper lip rises while the lower lip protrudes.

FEAR: The eyes widen and the upper lids rise, as in surprise, but the brows draw together. The lips stretch horizontally.

HAPPINESS: The corners of the mouth lift in a smile. As the eyelids tighten, the cheeks rise and the outside corners of the brows pull down.

Source: From "The physiology of . . . facial expressions: A self-conscious look of fear, anger, or happiness can reveal more than a lie detector" by Mary Duenwald. January 2005, *Discover* magazine.

as an operational definition of gender in which female is coded as 1 and male as 2 (or vice versa). No single operational definition can capture fully the concept it is intended to measure. An operational definition is among several possible objective and measurable indicators of a concept. We will learn more about the relationships of variables and concepts in Chapter 4 when we discuss psychological constructs.

In the Ekman work, the Facial Action Coding System provides the operational definition of various facial expressions of emotions. The coding system defines specific combinations of facial muscle movements that are universally and discretely generated when certain emotions are elicited (see **Table 2.1** and **Exhibit 2.2**). In essence, specific sequences of facial muscle contractions are predictive of particular emotional expressions. Thus, we see that an important aspect of a scientific description and explanation is establishing *predictive relationships* between two events or occurrences.

Exhibit 2.2 The Facial Affect Coding System breaks down the muscles associated with facial expressions of various emotions. For example, the orbicularis oculi and zygomaticus are activated to produce a smile, the corrugator is activated during frowning in anger, and the levator is used to produce the grimace of disgust (from Niedenthal, 2007).

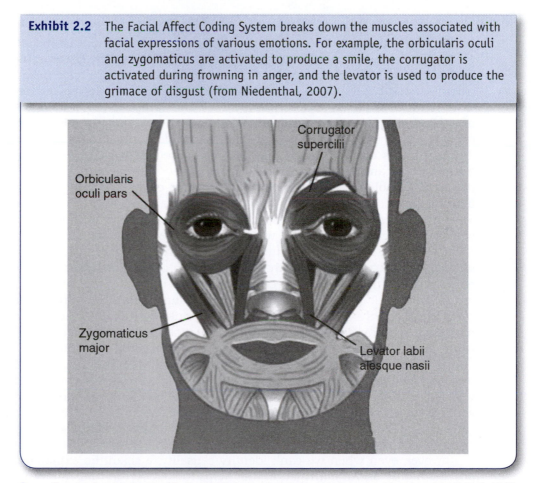

Source: From "Embodying Emotion" by Paul M. Niedenthal in *Science, 316,* January 1, 2010. Copyright © 2010, AAAS. Reprinted with permission.

Note also that the coding system is transparent so that a researcher can learn these patterns of facial muscle movements and design studies to replicate as well to extend findings about human emotional expression across different cultures. In 1967, Ekman traveled to the highlands of Papua New Guinea to conduct research with the Fore people, who had never been exposed to movies, television, magazines, or many foreigners, but who nevertheless recognized facial expressions of emotions exactly as Westerners did. Through the use of the Facial Action Coding System, Ekman identified seven discrete emotional expressions that humans in different cultures develop a similar capacity to recognize: happiness, sadness, fear, anger, surprise, disgust, and contempt. The generalizability of such findings was especially impressive. You can try your luck at identifying facial expressions of these seven emotions as portrayed by the actor in **Exhibit 2.1**. You will find descriptions of the particular combinations of facial action units for each expression in **Table 2.1**.

Explanation

Description and explanation are the goals of science. Explanation can include both prediction as well as establishing cause and effect. Causality, however, is not a simple matter. In fact, philosophers since the time of Aristotle have debated the true essence of causality. For our purposes, let's think of causality as requiring three kinds of evidence, as described by Cook and Campbell (1979). The first kind of evidence is that of **temporal precedence**. This evidence establishes that the cause *precedes* the effect. Thus, one step toward demonstrating smoking causes lung cancer is data demonstrating temporal precedence: Smoking cigarettes occurred first, and lung cancer, tragically, followed. The second type of evidence needed to establish causality is **covariation of the cause and effect**. This means that when the cause is present, the effect occurs, and when the cause is absent, the effect does not occur. Thus, we need to know that people who smoke cigarettes contract lung cancer, and those who do not smoke do not contract lung cancer. Third, causality requires the elimination of **alternative explanations**. In other words, a researcher must show that nothing other than a causal variable could be responsible for the observed effect; that is, there is no other plausible explanation for the relationship. In our smoking example, suppose a third variable, such as social class, could explain the relationship of smoking and lung cancer. This alternative explanation could come into play if cancer victims were found to come from socio-economic strata different from those of healthy individuals.

As you can see, these three prongs of causality are difficult standards to meet in human psychological research. This holds even with a true experimental design, which ostensibly allows the researcher to test whether changes in an independent variable causes changes in the dependent variable. The problem is that it is impossible in human studies to control for all extraneous, **confounding** (see Chapter 1), or so-called **third variables** that could account for the observed effect.

However, even when we can't identify causality, a scientific explanation can provide highly useful information that helps to specify the rules under which a certain phenomenon occurs. As an example of a scientific explanation governing facial expression of emotions, consider the Ekman Facial Action Coding System.

In this coding scheme, each of the seven universal facial expressions presented in **Exhibit 2.1** can be decomposed into a specific sequence of microaction units as outlined in **Table 2.1**. For example, the facial expression of disgust can be broken down into microaction units of wrinkling the nose and raising the upper lip while protruding the lower lip (try it yourself).

Practical Knowledge

Scientific understanding through the process of description and explanation often leads to interesting practical application. Studies are often categorized as either **basic research** or **applied research**. Basic research addresses fundamental questions about the nature of abstract psychological processes and ideas, such as emotion, intelligence, reasoning, and social behavior. Applied research addresses important questions that are thought to be of immediate relevance in solving practical problems. What television advertisements are most effective in reducing illicit drug use in children? What is the most effective teaching method for learning math? Do early-intervention programs, such as Head Start, lead to better outcomes? Such questions are investigated and studied in applied research. In fact, a major area of interest and study in applied research is called **program evaluation**. Program evaluation studies the effects on behavior of large-scale policy changes and as well social reforms and innovations occurring in government, schools, courts, prisons, businesses, health care, housing, and so forth.

In reality, these distinctions often blur and the basic and applied research designation is probably most accurately viewed as falling along a continuum. Both are essential and of equal importance, with scientific progress depending on the combined efforts and fruits of basic and applied research. Moreover, basic research often has exceptionally important applications that are impossible to predict. For example, the principles and findings from Ekman's basic research on facial expression of emotion are now applied in a variety of settings. The most high-profile of these settings is public safety, including the CIA, the FBI, and the Department of Defense. But other areas of clinical application are also prominent, as in modulating facial expression of emotions as an important psychotherapy technique in treatment of debilitating mental problems (Linehan, Heard, & Armstrong, 1993). In addition, the June 2008 issue of the *Journal of the American Academy of Dermatology* features an article by Alam and colleagues reviewing evidence that botulinum toxin injections ("botox") may have an antidepressant effect by reducing frowning and other negative facial expressions. "Can looking better make you feel happier?" is the engaging question that is included in the title and is the focus of the Alam and colleagues review.

SOURCES OF RESEARCH IDEAS

Generating ideas may very well be one of the most exciting aspects of the research process. In this the first step of the research process, our mindset may become more expansive, curious, and creative, as we would like to generate novel ideas or new ways to think about old problems. While the scientific method provides us with a prescriptive, disciplined, and objective format to test the veracity of our ideas, the question for us to consider now is how we actually come up with the ideas in the first place.

Starting With Observation

Suppose you have no formal experience in research but you have always been curious about the human face. In many ways, you have chosen a wonderful topic for research that can be studied by the power of simple *observation*. Science often begins with simple observation, which can serve as a source of both evidence and ideas. Charles Darwin, for example, generated the theory of evolution by natural selection exclusively on the basis of simple observation. In his later 1872 book *The Expression of the Emotions in Man and Animals,* and again relying exclusively on observation, Darwin would make the case that all mammals regularly display emotion in their faces. For us mere mortals, we might look for the "agony of defeat and the thrill of victory" etched on the faces of the athletes when watching our favorite sport. See for example **Exhibit 2.4** from Sandy Nicholson's (2008) book *2nd: The Face of Defeat,* which in many ways captures the power of observing facial expression of emotions.

Often in research, our observations will need to be broken down into simpler units that allow for more precise quantification and measurement. Indeed, as we have learned about the research of Paul Ekman, the complexity of human emotion is much easier to study by making it simpler. At the risk of hyperbole, how elegantly simple and brilliant is the Ekman system of decoding various facial expressions into distinct sets of specific muscle movements? In a similar vein, as we will see later in this chapter, Strack and colleagues showed how two simple positions of holding a pen either gently between the teeth or tightly between the lips induced facial expressions of smiling and frowning, respectively (Strack, Martin, & Stepper, 1988).

Observations often act to restrict our attention, but sometimes we might stumble upon an important discovery that may not have been of primary interest to us. This is why we want to emphasize that during the earlier phases of research when we are trying to generate ideas, narrowing the focus of observation may be counterproductive, stifling perhaps our imagination and creativity. Here you might be better served by a frame of mind in which your attention and observation act not so much as a narrow spotlight of illumination of a particular area of interest but as a lantern casting a diffuse radiance over the panoply of experience (Lehrer, 2009). Such a prepared yet open mind increases the chances of accidentally discovering something fortunate. This is known as the **serendipity** effect. Lore also has it that the seeds of Isaac Newton's law of universal gravitation can be traced to his observations of the famed apple falling out of a tree. The point is that serendipity teaches us the value of keeping our minds and hearts open for the unexpected, unlikely, and counterintuitive.

Starting With Theory

In many instances, your research question will flow directly from a theory. For example, as we have learned, Charles Darwin was the among the first to raise the question of whether physiological changes may lead to, if not very well be the cause of, an emotion as opposed to being just the consequence of that emotion. Echoing the sentiments of Darwin, the 19th-century psychologist William James in 1884 and Danish physiologist Carl Lange in 1887, each working independently, developed remarkably similar ideas as to the nature of human emotions. They each theorized that emotions are feelings that come about as a *result* of physiological changes, such as perspiration, rapid heartbeat, muscular tension, and dryness of mouth, created by the **autonomic nervous system** that regulates bodily reactions to stress (Lang, 1994). Known as the **James–Lange theory,** it addresses the chicken-and-egg question by stating that the physiological changes come first, followed by the experience of emotional feelings (Ellsworth, 1994). So, for example, according to this theory, you see a bear, your muscles tense, your heart races, you feel afraid. In the 1920s, Walter Cannon and Philip Bard would argue that the James-Lange theory got it backward, and in what became known as the **Cannon–Bard theory** of emotional experiences, these researchers proposed that emotions come first, followed by bodily changes.

As a rapprochement of these two theories, consider recent research by Niedenthal (2007) on the ways in which various emotional states can be encoded in particular bodily movements and postures. To illustrate her point, Niedenthal offers the following amusing "thought experiment":

> A man goes into a bar to tell a new joke. Two people are already in the bar. One is smiling and one is frowning. Who is more likely to "get" the punch line and appreciate his joke? Here is another: Two women walking over a bridge. One is afraid of heights, so her heart pounds and her hands tremble. The other is not afraid at all. On the other side of a bridge, they encounter a man. Which of the two women is more likely to believe that she has just met the man of her dreams? (p. 1002)

As Niedenthal wrote, in both these scenarios, the first person, as you would guess, is the correct answer. How is this so intuitively obvious to us? Each vignette involves processing of emotions—the smiling approachable patron or the woman's fear of heights. When we perceive and think about their emotions, we experience or more precisely re-experience in ourselves those subtle physical and mental changes of the relevant emotions. This re-experiencing is referred to as the "embodiment" of emotion. It involves perceptual, somatovisceral (body), and motoric re-experiencing of the relevant emotion. The **embodiment theory of emotion** thus proposes a dynamic interplay of specific bodily states and their associated emotions. A schematic of the theory taken from Niedenthal is presented in **Exhibit 2.3**. On the left side, you see that the picture of a snarling bear triggers a cascade of events across the brain and somatovisceral systems. On the right side, simply thinking about the snarling bear is enough to re-engage parts of the original visual system, which in turn reactivate parts of the brain and somatovisceral organs originally triggered. As experimental support for this theory, Niedenthal cited studies that have shown that (a) when people adopt emotion-specific bodily postures, they report experiencing the associated emotions; (b) when people make facial expressions or emotional gestures, their

Exhibit 2.3   Schematic of the Embodiment Theory of Emotion

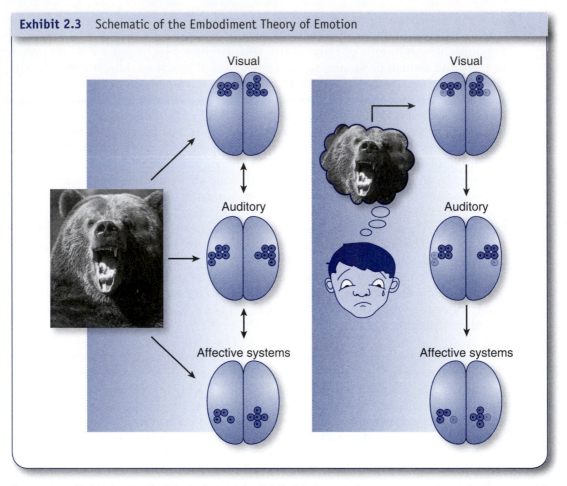

Source: From "Embodying Emotion" by Paul M. Niedenthal in *Science, 316,* January 1, 2010. Copyright © 2010, AAAS. Reprinted with permission. Bear photo: © Getty Images/Ablestock.com/Thinkstock.

perceptions and impressions are affected; and (c) inhibiting people's motor movements can interfere with their experience of emotion.

Thus, we see the genesis of a research question. We can trace the research questions of Paul Ekman to competing views of the James–Lange and Cannon–Bard theories of emotion, which gave way to the modern-day embodiment theory of emotion. We see how Ekman posed his questions in such a way that could be directly answered using the scientific method.

Literature

Scientific literature can also serve as a fountain for new ideas. These ideas may come to us when we consider empirical findings of various peer-reviewed studies that are published in scientific **journals**. These journals constitute the scientific literature. **Table 2.2** presents a partial list of major peer-reviewed publications in

Table 2.2   Some Important Peer-Reviewed Journals for Psychological Research

Empirical Articles	Review Articles
Behavior Therapy	*American Psychologist*
Child Development	*Annual Review of Psychology*
Cognitive Psychology	*Psychological Bulletin*
Developmental Psychology	*Psychological Review*
Journal of Abnormal Psychology Science	
Journal of Applied Psychology	
Journal of Educational Psychology	
Journal of Experimental Child Psychology	
Journal of Experimental Psychology: General	
Journal of Experimental Psychology: Learning, Memory, and Cognition	
Journal of Experimental Psychology: Human Perception and Performance	
Journal of Personality and Social Psychology	
Proceedings of the National Academy of Sciences	
Psychological Assessment	
Psychological Science	
Neuropsychology	
Science	

psychology. In looking at this list, you see that the peer-reviewed publications fall into one of two categories: **empirical articles** and **review articles**. An empirical article reports on a particular study and is written in a certain format divided into sections with an *Abstract, Introduction* (which will contain a review of the relevant literature that is the focus of the study), *Method, Results,* and *Discussion.* A review article examines several studies of a particular phenomenon, such as facial expressions of emotion. It evaluates the methodology used across different studies, examines the degree to which findings are robust across various conditions, settings and procedures, and comments on the extent to which the empirical findings allow for general theoretical conclusions.

An additional potential wealth of inspiration for new ideas may be found in the **popular science** literature, often written by eminent scientists who aim to explain science for a general audience. An example of an outstanding work of popular science is the book by renowned evolutionist Professor David Sloan Wilson of Binghamton University, *Evolution for Everyone: How Darwin's Theory Can Change the Way We Think About Our Lives* (2007). Closely related to popular science is **science journalism** that often focuses on recent developments in science that are judged newsworthy. Malcolm Gladwell's (2002) piece in the *New Yorker* on Paul Ekman is a classic example of science journalism. Both popular science and science journalism fulfill an important public service of bringing peer-reviewed publications borne of the scientific method into popular political and cultural discourse.

Pieces in both popular science and science journalism are often exceptionally well-written works of literary distinction: lively, clear, and engaging and free of technical jargon. The downside is that this popular literature lacks the critical sense of proportionality, cautiousness, and tentativeness that is fundamental to the scientific method. Scientific findings can be oversold, if not downright sensationalized. Michael Shermer, prolific science journalist and scholar, warns of such overselling in the area of brain scan studies, citing as an example of sensationalizing findings a November 11, 2007, *New York Times* opinion piece titled "This Is Your Brain on Politics." by Marco Iacoboni and colleagues. Likewise, in a November 7, 2009, *New York Times Book Review,* eminent psychologist Steven Pinker criticized science journalist Malcolm Gladwell, opining " . . . when a writer's education on a topic consists in interviewing an expert, he is apt to offer generalizations that are banal, obtuse or flat wrong."

How then might you view this popular literature? We emphasize these works of journalism only as a source of ideas that might inspire and motivate you to pursue a formal line of investigation using the scientific method. These journalistic pieces represent important **secondary sources**, that is, second-hand media accounts of scientific work. They are best used as clues to lead you to the **primary source**, the first-hand empirical report published in a peer-reviewed journal.

Consider an interesting newspaper article by journalist Javier Zarracina that appeared in the April 4, 2010, *Boston Globe* titled, "A Life Lesson From the Majors. Smile, You'll Live Longer." The newspaper account describes an empirical study published in the peer-reviewed journal *Psychological Science* by researchers Ernest L. Abel and Michael Kruger (2010) titled "Smile Intensity in Photographs Predicts Longevity." With a sample of 230 photos of baseball players culled from the Baseball Register for 1952, Abel and Kruger coded the intensity of players' expressions as either *no smile, partial smile* (only movement of muscles around the mouth, that is, only contractions of the zygomatic major muscles), or *full smile* (movement of muscles around the mouth and corners of the eyes, that is, contraction of both zygomatic and obicularis oculi muscles). They also compiled life data for the baseball players and controlled for other longevity factors, such as education, marital status, and body mass index. Their results showed that players with full smiles lived the longest, to 79.9 years, which is nearly 2 years more than the typical life expectancy for an American. Even a partial smile added to longevity, with these players living for 74.9 years, on average, 2 full years more than those who exhibited no smile. Their findings demonstrated an overall gain of 7 years of life for smiling players. In addition, by including ratings of each of the player's headshot on a three-point attractiveness scale, the researchers effectively ruled out perceived attractiveness as an *alternative explanation* for their findings: Unlike a player's smile, a player's perceived attractiveness did not influence his longevity.

One of the *Research in the News* exercises at the end of this chapter features the Abel and Kruger (2010) study along with its media account. It provides a sound example of how you can go from a secondary source from a newspaper to a primary source of an empirical study published in a peer-reviewed journal. And lest you smirk and think after reading the newspaper account that the Abel and Kruger study is a fluke, you would soon learn otherwise. Indeed, you would learn from the primary source that their findings add to those of numerous other studies that have shown the face to be an intriguing barometer of emotions. These include studies that have linked marriage stability and satisfaction with smile intensity of childhood photos and college yearbook photos (Harker & Keltner, 2001; Hertenstein et al., 2009). Likewise, Todorov and colleagues (2005) showed that their research participants who made split-second judgments of competence from faces of political candidates predicted the outcomes of U.S. congressional elections better than chance (e.g., 68% of the Senate race in 2004).

Searching the Literature

The Internet has been described as a godsend for researchers and scholars, especially for those who like to work in their pajamas (Tuhus-Dubrow, 2008)! Tracking down a published peer-reviewed article on the Internet can often be done in a matter of seconds, all from the comfort of your home. In addition, many researchers have very accessible and highly informative websites that include articles that can be identified by typing their name into a search engine such as Google and then easily downloaded free of charge. Internet traveling, so to speak, from hyperlink to hyperlink may also lead to an *online serendipity* of stumbling onto an unexpected article that could add a new dimension to your thinking or perhaps lead you down a very different path from your original idea.

A branch of Google called Google Scholar (http://scholar.google.com) specializes in searches of the scholarly and scientific literature: Just type a researcher's name, such as "Paul Ekman," and within seconds you will have access to a corpus of scholarly and scientific work on facial expression of emotion. Two excellent websites for major psychological organizations are American Psychological Association (www.apa.org) and Association for Psychological Science (www.psychologicalscience.org). **PsycINFO** and **PsycLIT** are specialized, noncommercial search engines sponsored by the American Psychological Association (APA) to serve as databases for citations and abstracts of the world's literature in psychology and related fields. So too is the **Social Sciences Citation Index** (SSCI), which includes articles from not only psychology but also related fields, such as sociology and criminology. With SSCI, you can identify a "key article" on your topic. SSCI will then provide you with a list of articles that have cited your key article. This list will give you a start in developing a bibliography of articles relevant to your topic.

These websites are not free and are **proprietary**, open only to subscribers. For example, websites of scientific journals are generally proprietary, meaning that only paid subscribers can access their contents of peer-reviewed articles. Most college and university libraries have subscriptions to a number of proprietary websites that can be accessed through the library system. Consulting with the library staff of your college or university will help you learn how to access proprietary websites of scholarly information.

Let the Searcher Beware!

Elizabeth Kirk (2002) offers some excellent guidelines for evaluating information from the Internet that are available on the Johns Hopkins University web page: www.library. jhu.edu/researchhelp/general/evaluating. Kirk's main take-home point is that you should never use information that cannot be verified by other independent sources. To make her point about the dangers of accepting Internet information as gospel, she cites the famous Latin phrase *caveat lector*: Let the reader beware. She lists several criteria against which all information should be evaluated. Among these are authority (e.g., Who wrote it?), publishing body (e.g., Who is the sponsor of the site?), point of view or bias (e.g. Does the website advocate a point of view or sell media products, such as books, pamphlets, videos, etc.?), connection to the scientific literature (e.g., Does it cite references to peer-reviewed articles?), verifiability and transparency (e.g., Is the methodology open to public scrutiny and able to be reproduced?), and timelines (e.g., What is the date, and does the information get updated?). Kirk concludes by citing Yeats: "Cast a cold eye . . . on everything you read. . . . Look for other sources that can authenticate or corroborate what you find. . . . Learn to be skeptical and then learn to trust your instincts. . . ." Last, keep in mind that general search engines such as the family of Google search tools can be very useful, but they are commercially based and derive a portion of their revenues through advertisement.

Researchers have now begun to study how the Internet may shape scholarship. In a 2008 article in the prestigious peer-reviewed journal *Science,* University of Chicago sociologist James Evans argues that the Internet may paradoxically have a narrowing effect on thinking and research, suggesting that good ideas may be ignored and lost. Other scholars, such as anthropologist Alex Bentley of Durham University in England, quoted in the *Boston Sunday Globe* of November 23, 2008 by journalist Rebecca Tuhus-Dubrow, have warned that the Internet "makes academic research a popularity contest" dominated by search engines that order or prioritize information in ways that may have little to do with scientific merit or impact. Further complicating matters is that some commercial search engines may sell spaces to advertisers; in turn, this may affect how these search engines browse for information, how they list information, and how they update information.

The common lesson is that the tremendous benefits of the Internet, especially in the early phases of generating ideas, may also come with some potential costs. As we know from Chapter 1, we are all prone to confirmatory bias, which may lead us to only search for information on the Internet that supports our positions and ideas. We should always remain cognizant that the Internet and the search tools used to navigate the electronic world have limitations that may affect how we search and gather information in ways we may not fully appreciate.

RESEARCH STRATEGIES

In conducting research, we are attempting to connect theory with empirical data, that is, evidence we obtained through scientific studies. As we have learned, researchers may make this connection by starting with a psychological theory and testing some of its implications with data. This is the process of **deductive research**; it is most often the strategy used in experimental studies. Alternatively, researchers may develop a connection between psychological theory by first systematically collecting observations, measurements, or data and then developing a theory that explains the patterns in the data. This **inductive research** approach is most often used in nonexperimental studies, such as those that use naturalistic observation methods. As you'll see, a research study can draw on both inductive and deductive strategies.

Thus, two of the most important elements of all scientific research strategies are (a) data and (b) theory. Data are the empirical observations that allow for evaluating a theory. A theory is a set of propositions that explains a variety of occurrences. A theory performs three major functions: organization, explanation, and prediction. A good theory is one that is parsimonious and precise as well as powerful in its breadth and depth of explanation. It can explain a variety of occurrences with the fewest theoretical assertions. **Exhibit 2.4** depicts the link between theory and data. As you can see, a deductive research strategy will begin with a theory from which particular statements are drawn and then tested by collecting data. By contrast, an inductive strategy first examines the data and then derives a theory to explain the patterns shown in the data.

Inductive Research

Inductive research entails reasoning from particular data or empirical observations to a general theory. In Chapter 1, we were introduced to different research methods and designs. Among those that are probably best suited for an inductive research approach is the naturalistic observation method. Often used in **qualitative research** (which will be discussed in Chapter 11), a

Exhibit 2.4 The Links Between Theory and Data

Ideas: What we think

Theory

Inductive reasoning

Deductive reasoning

Data

Reality: What we observe

Source: Schutt, R. K. (2009). *Investigating the social world: The process and practice of research* (6th ed., p. 41). Thousand Oaks, CA: Pine Forge Press.

naturalistic observation design studies people in their natural settings so that their behaviors and words can be put into their proper context. Such descriptive study of people is also sometimes referred to as **ethnography**. Here observation, it is important to emphasize, does not mean the casual "seeing" of everyday life that leads to haphazard impressions. To the contrary, for this research methodology to be effective, observation must be *systematic,* which means that it must be conducted carefully, with precise description that allows for consistent or reliable cataloging of data and the orderly classification and analysis of that information (Adler & Adler, 1994). While qualitative researchers use naturalistic observation methods that tend to avoid predetermining categories of action that can be precisely measured, they, like their quantitative counterparts, make sure their studies yield reliable and valid data. In short, the aim of qualitative research is to understand context—the what, how, when, and where of an event or an action. It yields data regarding meanings, concepts, definitions, characteristics, metaphors, symbols, and descriptions of events or actions (Berg, 2004). As such, it is ideally suited for an inductive research approach.

Inductive research also fits well with quantitative studies that use naturalistic observation. Consider a study by David Sloane Wilson and his then graduate student Kevin Kniffin (Kniffin & Wilson, 2004) published in the peer-reviewed journal *Evolution and Human Behavior.* Here you find a highly user-friendly, naturalistic observation methodology to investigate to what extent attractiveness of faces is influenced by physical traits or nonphysical features such as knowing, liking, and respecting the person. Kniffin and Wilson (2004) had a college student sample rate photographs of classmates they knew taken from their high school yearbooks for familiarity, liking, respect, and physical attractiveness. Then the researchers had the same photographs rated for physical attractiveness by another person of the same age and sex as the yearbook owner who did not know the people in the photographs. Kniffin and Wilson reasoned that if the ratings of physical attractiveness were based solely on physical traits observable in the photographs, then the two raters should be in agreement, regardless of what one knew of their nonphysical qualities of knowing, liking, or respecting the person in the photograph.

Their simple study showed that it was not the physical qualities but rather the nonphysical qualities that had a pronounced influence on the assessment of physical attractiveness of these yearbook photographs. As Wilson (2007) wrote in *Evolution for Everyone,* "As the theory predicts, it is not how well you *know* a person (familiarity per se) but how well you regarded him or her (liking and respect) that makes the biggest difference" (p. 121). Wilson induced an evolutionary interpretation of the data from the yearbook study, theorizing that attractiveness is largely determined by nonphysical features, such as trustworthiness and respect, as knowing these qualities of a person is vital for adaptation, fitness, and reproduction. To underscore his point, Wilson (2007) presented in *Evolution for Everyone* the amusing anecdote of the iconic photograph of Abraham Lincoln as an example of a "person made beautiful by his nonphysical qualities" (p. 123). Wilson tells the story that people regarded Lincoln in his lifetime as hideously ugly. Lincoln, himself, Wilson recounted, even poked fun at his appearance, as when accused of being two-faced, Lincoln quipped, "If I had two faces, think I'd be wearing this one?" Yet his non-physical qualities embodied in his personal history, character, and accomplishments have made the pictorial image of Lincoln among the most admired, revered, and, yes, beautiful.

Deductive Research

In deductive research, reasoning proceeds from a general theory to particular data. Theories, however, are not directly testable. Thus, hypotheses must be derived from a theory. These hypotheses are then tested and the ensuing results are used to evaluate how well the theory works—that is, how well it describes, explains, and predicts the nature of the phenomenon under study. A hypothesis is defined as a specific testable statement that can be evaluated by empirical observations or data. It is different from generalizations that are embedded in a theory. A **generalization** is a broad statement

Exhibit 2.5   Nonphysical Beauty of Abraham Lincoln

Source: © Steven Synn/iStockphoto.com.

that cannot be directly tested but rather needs to be translated into one or more hypotheses. That is, a theory will consist of a host of generalizations, and each generalization can lead to one or more hypotheses. Only hypotheses are directly testable. This is so because a hypothesis proposes a specific relationship between two or more variables that must be measurable. And as we know, one of these variables will be the independent variable that is hypothesized to predict, influence, or cause variation in the dependent variable. In deductive research, then, the investigators formulate one or more hypotheses and develop particular methods and procedures of measurement and/or experimentation. This yields data that serve as a direct test of a given hypothesis.

Hypotheses can be worded in several different ways, and identifying the independent and dependent variables is sometimes difficult. When in doubt, try to rephrase the hypothesis as an "if-then" statement: "If the independent variable increases (or decreases), then the dependent variable increases (or decreases). **Exhibit 2.6** (Examples of Hypotheses) presents several hypotheses with their independent and dependent variables and their "if-then" equivalents. **Exhibit 2.6** demonstrates another feature of hypotheses: **direction of association**. When researchers hypothesize that one variable increases as the other variable increases, the direction of the association is positive (Hypotheses 1 and 2). When one variable decreases as the other variable decreases, the direction of association is also positive. But when one variable increases as the other decreases, or vice versa, the direction of the association is negative or inverse. Hypothesis 2 states a negative or inverse association between increased age and reduced motor speed. Hypothesis 4 is a special case in which the independent variable is categorical (which we will discuss Chapter 4), as in this example, where students study for an exam, either in the library or in their dorms. This qualitative variable cannot be said to increase or decrease. In this case, the concept of direction of association does not apply, and the hypothesis simply states one category or level of the independent variable is associated with higher values of the dependent variable.

As we know from Chapter 1, both the strength and direction of the association or relationship between two variables can be measured statistically by the correlation coefficient (symbolized as r), which can range from .00 to +1.00 and .00 to −1.00. If there is no relationship between two variables—that is, variation in one variable has nothing to do with variation in the other variable—then the correlation value will be .00 or close to .00. The closer a correlation between two variables is to 1.00, either +1.00 or −1.00, the stronger is the relationship between the two variables. The positive and negative signs of the correlation coefficient tell the direction of the association between the two variables. A positive correlation coefficient (a "plus" sign) means that there is a positive linear relationship: As scores on one variable increase, so do scores on the other variable. A negative correlation coefficient indicated by a "minus" sign means that there is a negative linear relationship: As scores on one variable increase, scores on the other variable decrease.

Exhibit 2.6   Examples of Hypotheses

Original Hypothesis	Independent Variable	Dependent Variable	IF-THEN Hypothesis	Direction of Association
1. Deeper encoding of words, better memory	Levels of encoding	Recall of words	IF encoding level increases, THEN memory increases	+
2. Older age, reduced motor speed	Age	Motor speed	IF age increases, THEN, motor speed decreases	−
3. Higher SAT scores, better GPAs	SAT	GPA	IF SATs are higher, THEN GPAs are higher	+
4. Exam grades are higher for students who study in the library vs. dorm	Place of study	Exam grade	IF place of study is the library THEN exam grades are higher compared to those who study in dorm	NA

Source: Schutt, R. K. (2009). *Investigating the social world: The process and practice of research* (6th ed., p. 43). Thousand Oaks, CA: Pine Forge Press.

The Research Circle

In reality, the process of conducting research designed to test explanations for psychological phenomena involves a dynamic interplay of moving from theory to data and then back to theory. This process can be characterized as a **research circle**. As **Exhibit 2.7** shows, deductive and inductive research processes can be closely intertwined. With deductive research, theory gives birth to hypotheses, which are then tested by data. With inductive research, data give birth to an **empirical generalization**—a statement that describes patterns found in the data, from which a theory is formulated. The goals of inductive and deductive research approaches are identical: to develop and formulate theories, a set of general propositions that serve to organize and interpret data or to generate predictions for events and actions for which no data have yet to be obtained.

SUBSTANCE OF PSYCHOLOGICAL RESEARCH

In this next section, we examine the substance of psychological research, the nuts and bolts of formulating a hypothesis drawn from theory, creating variables, devising an experimental task, and analyzing data. To learn about the substance of psychological research, we use a simple experiment by Strack and colleagues (Strack, Martin, & Stepper, 1998), published in the peer-reviewed periodical *Journal of Personality and Social Psychology* (*JPSP*), titled "Inhibiting and Facilitating Conditions of the Human Smile: A Nonobtrusive Test of the Facial Feedback Hypothesis."

Exhibit 2.7   The Research Circle

Source: Schutt, R. K. (2009). *Investigating the social world: The process and practice of research* (6th ed., p. 42). Thousand Oaks, CA: Pine Forge Press.

We chose this study mainly because it is a rather straightforward experiment that we think would be fun for you to replicate. It also, of course, had direct bearing on the research question on smiling and emotion that began this chapter.

Facial Expression and Emotion

We know that a good theory generates testable hypotheses that can be evaluated empirically with the scientific method. Recall also that a testable hypothesis is framed as a statement often in the form of a prediction that is made prior to the actual collection of data. Strack and colleagues devised their experiment as a test of the **facial feedback hypothesis**. The facial feedback hypothesis originates from the James–Lange theory of emotion. In contemporary research, the facial feed-back hypothesis falls under the embodiment theory of emotion (Niedenthal, 2007), which we discussed earlier. The idea is that facial movements by themselves can re-enact particular emotional feelings and that these emotional feelings can be created by simply "tricking" a person into making specific facial contractions. Thus, in the Strack and company study, some participants held a pencil between their teeth while performing a laboratory task that involved rating the funniness of different cartoons. Holding the pencil in the mouth this way covertly induced the individuals to smile—and the corresponding emotion state of happiness. Other participants were instructed to hold a pencil between their lips without touching the pencil with their teeth, and this covertly induced the individuals to frown. (see **Exhibit 2.8**). Strack and colleagues specifically hypothesized that participants who

Exhibit 2.8 Participants in the Strack et al. (1988) study either held a pen between the lips to inhibit smiling, as in the left panel, or else held the pen between the teeth to facilitate smiling

Source: © Chris Goldy.

were led to smile would judge the cartoons as funnier than participants who were led to frown. You can see that this is an excellent example of hypothesis: It is (a) derived from the embodiment theory of emotion, (b) presented as an a priori prediction, and (c) eminently testable.

Creating Independent and Dependent Variables

You can also see this is a very simple but ingenious method to create an independent variable: One group of participants rated funny cartoons while holding a pen between their teeth (inducing a smile) whereas another group of participants rated the same cartons while holding a pen between their lips without it touching their lips (inducing a frown). No fancy technology, just a familiar pen held in the mouth in different positions to create the independent variable. The independent variable had three conditions or **levels**, two of which were whether participants held a pen between either their teeth or lips. Every independent variable must have two or more levels. Why? Because you want to compare levels of an independent variable on a dependent variable, and thus you need at least two levels for comparison. Strack and company wanted to see whether perceived funniness of cartoons changed as a function of whether participants held a pen between either their teeth (inducing a smile) or their lips (inducing a frown).

In addition, they had a third condition or level in which a third group of participants rated the funniness of cartoons while holding a pen in their nondominant hand that they would not normally use for writing. Participants assigned to this nondominant hand condition formed the **control group** for the study, meaning that they did not make facial muscle contractions intended to induce either a smile or a frown. Thus, we can see that the Strack and company study created an independent variable with three levels of conditions: participants with the pen either held with their teeth (teeth condition) or lips (lip condition) or with their nondominant hand (nondominant condition). In addition, they used *random assignment* (see Chapter 1) in allotting participants to one of these three conditions. By using random assignment, as you recall from Chapter 1, these researchers ensured that each participant had an equal chance of being assigned to ether the teeth, lips, or nondominant hand conditions.

All participants completed the same task: That is, they rated the funniness of different cartoons while holding a pen either held tightly between their lips (lips condition), gently between their teeth (teeth condition), or with their nondominant condition). Note that the researchers labeled their independent variable as "condition" with three levels, but they could have easily called it something else such as "pen hold" with three levels—teeth, lips, and nondominant hand. A researcher has leeway in naming an independent variable, although simple and sensible labels are of course preferable. As you also know, the dependent variable is the observed effect, result, or outcome that is measured in response to a change in the independent variable. In the Strack and company study, the dependent variable was the humor ratings their research participants completed. The researcher also has leeway in labeling a dependent variable, but it makes little or no sense to use arbitrary names. For example, there is no better name for the dependent variable in the Strack and company study than humor "ratings" of cartoons that they had their participants complete.

We learned earlier in the chapter about the difference between conceptual and operational definitions. Using this distinction here, we can think of both independent and dependent variables as falling under the category of operational definitions. The independent variable specifies the operations that will be used as a manipulation— for example, what participants will do or how they might be grouped. The dependent variable specifies the operations that will be used to measure the effects of the independent variable on performance, which can be assessed, for example, by ratings scores, observational recordings, physiological response, test scores, and the like. A control variable is a potential source of influence on the dependent variable that you as a researcher desire to hold constant. You are not interested in studying the effects of a control variable, but it often can be an unwanted source of influence that you need to assess. Recall from Chapter 1 that this unwanted source of influence can also be referred to as *confounds*, which can include so-called third variables. Thus, you aim to rule out any effect a control variable may have on the dependent and independent variables.

To recap, a researcher examines the effects of changes of an independent variable on a dependent variable while using control variables to rule out extraneous sources of influence (e.g., confounds, third variables). The independent variable is what you change, the dependent variable is what you observe, and the control variable is what you keep constant or quantify, if it can't be held constant. Strack and colleagues, for example, held a variety of factors constant. These included a cover story, testing setting, and the testing stimuli (cartoons), meaning that all participants heard the same cover story, were tested in the same laboratory setting, and rated the same cartoons. These would be examples of control variables that Strack and colleagues held constant, as they did not want the setting or cartoons to affect the relationship of the independent variable of facial contractions on the dependent variable of humor ratings.

Unfortunately, though, there are countless other variables in addition to the independent variable that could have easily influenced the dependent variable. Indeed, it is impossible to have enough control variables to rule out all the possible extraneous, potentially confounding factors that could influence the relationship between the independent and dependent variables. These other factors could vary with or contaminate the relation of the independent and dependent variables. This, as we recall from Chapter 1, is a major problem of confounding variables, which occurs when one or more variables that are thought to be extraneous based on the theory under investigation are in fact related to both the independent and dependent variables. When this happens, you might want to scream "Damn!" as these confounding variables can pose alternative explanations for findings of a study.

For example, Strack and colleagues did not want the cognitive interpretation that people might make about their facial actions to influence their ratings of humor or to confound their results. That is why the researchers presented the cover story, which they hoped would ensure that their participants enacted the desired facial movements (i.e., smile vs. frown) without being aware of or recognizing the corresponding emotion (i.e., happy vs. sad) or the real purpose of the study. Strack and colleagues also addressed the potential confounding problem of differences in difficulty among the three conditions. They did so by having their participants, while holding the pen in their mouth (lips vs. teeth), rate the degree of difficulty they experienced as they used the pen to complete their ratings. These ratings of difficulty served as a control variable, as the researchers did not want the degree of difficulty of the pen position to influence the humor ratings of cartoons. This allowed them to rule out different degrees of difficulty for the three experimental conditions as an alternative explanation for their findings.

Evaluating With Statistics

As we learned in Chapter 1, a testable hypothesis is evaluated statistically. If the statistical analyses of the data show that the obtained results are highly unlikely due to chance, then the hypothesis is accepted—the predicted relationship between, for example, two variables is considered to be highly likely. If, on the other hand, the statistical analyses of the data show that the obtained results are likely due to chance, then the hypothesis is rejected. Statistical probabilities are set at levels of significance in the form of *probability (p)-values*. Traditionally, *p*-values of .05 or less indicate that an obtained finding is statistically significant, meaning that there is a 5% chance or less that the obtained results are due to chance. Thus, *statistical significance* simply means that a finding is unlikely due to chance at a certain level of probability, usually .05 or less.

Now let us look at the results of the Strack and company study of 92 male and female undergraduate students at the University of Illinois (Study 1). Their hypothesis predicted that participants who were led to smile would rate the cartoons as funnier than participants who were led to frown. **Table 2.3** compares average or mean (*M*) funniness ratings as well as difficulty ratings for the participants who held the pen gently between the teeth, or tightly between the lips, or in the non-dominant hand. Ratings were made on a range of 0 to 9, with a lower value indicating lower funniness and difficulty, and higher value indicating higher funniness and difficulty. As predicted by the facial feedback hypothesis, participants induced to smile by holding the pen gently between their teeth gave the cartoons the highest funniness ratings (*M* = 5.14), followed by those who held the pen in their non-dominant hand (*M* = 4.77), and participants led to frown by holding the pen with their lips gave the cartoons the lowest funniest ratings (*M* = 4.32).

The million-dollar statistical question pertains to the different mean ratings among the three groups of participants. The question, put simply, is whether these differences are statistically significant or are simply a matter of chance. The good news for Strack and colleagues is that their statistical analyses indicated that the differences among the means were unlikely due to chance at a probability level of less than .05 ($p < .05$). This meant that the likelihood is less than 5 out of 100 that these differences were due to chance. Strack and company also needed to demonstrate that their humor rating results were not confounded by any differences in difficulty that their participants may have experienced in using a pen that they held either between their teeth, between their lips, or in their dominant hands.

Here, too, the news was good. As you can see in **Table 2.3**, even though participants led to smile evaluated the cartoons as the funniest, they also found writing with the pen held gently between their teeth to be the most difficult in relation to the other two groups. Thus, the researchers could correctly conclude that the differing degree of difficulty of holding the pen in either the teeth or lips did not confound how research participants rated the funniness of the cartoons.

HOW TO READ SCIENTIFIC LITERATURE

The scientific method entails a skeptical mindset, meaning that all knowledge is constantly questioned and all empirical evidence is subjected to rigorous scrutiny with respect to both reliability and validity (Gernsbacher, 2006). A reliable study, as we learned in Chapter 1, is one that can be replicated; the findings can be consistently demonstrated across independent research studies. For a useful reminder, think of the headline borrowed from Kosslyn and Rosenberg (2001), "Reliability: You can count on it!" A valid study is one that provides a true test of what is meant to be measured or investigated. A useful headline might read, "Validity: What does it really mean?" (Kosslyn & Rosenberger, 2001). In general, such **skepticism** fits with the self-correcting and ever-changing nature of science. As we also learned in Chapter 1, it clearly resonates with the importance that all claims stand the test of falsification: Scientific understanding advances only when new empirical evidence refutes or falsifies prior knowledge, rendering it obsolete or wrong.

A large portion of the research process requires evaluating prior studies with a thoughtful skepticism that is informed by the scientific method. The aim of

Table 2.3   Rating of Funniness and Difficulty (Ratings ranged on a scale from 0 to 9, with lower ratings indicating lower funniness and difficulty and higher ratings indicating higher funniness and difficulty)

Cartoon	Position of Pen		
	Lip	Hand	Teeth
First	3.90	5.13	5.09
Second	4.00	4.10	4.19
Third	4.47	4.67	5.78
Fourth	4.90	5.17	5.50
Mean funniness	4.32	4.77	5.14
Mean difficulty	4.47	2.72	4.91

Source: From "Inhibiting and facilitating conditions of the human smile: A nonobtrusive test of the facial feedback hypothesis" by F. Strack, L. L. Martin and S. Stepper in *Journal of Personality and Social Psychology, 54,* 768–777. Copyright © 1988 American Psychological Association.

research is to improve on previous studies, to assess, for example, the extent to which the findings are reproducible, replicable, or **robust** given different conditions, settings, and samples. How does one learn to evaluate research and to become a critical consumer of the science of psychology? In this section, we approach this problem from two related perspectives. We first present how to evaluate research from a general or macro perspective of an educated consumer. Moving from our lofty philosophical armchair, we then focus on specific and more technical aspects of a particular study or research report. Steeped in our burgeoning knowledge of the toolbox of methods and designs of psychological research, we present a step-by-step process for the professional reviewer.

What Does It All Mean?

Oftentimes, we will learn about interesting research second-hand through science journalism, such as a newspaper account or a television story. As we know, science journalism can be an excellent source for generating ideas. However, it is not subject to the peer-review process of a scientific journal. The great concern is that science journalism may not provide an accurate account of a study. If learning about a study from a secondary source, such as a newspaper article or a television show, keep in mind the goals of popular media are to attract attention, sell issues, and increase ratings; these outlets are not subject to the rigors of scientific peer review of professional journals, such as the *JPSP*, which published the Strack and company study. Thus, in order to critique a study, you must go to the primary source. In our example, you would read the Strack and colleagues study published in *JPSP*. You will find that the *JPSP* is a top-tier peer-reviewed periodical that caries the prestigious imprimatur of the American Psychological Association (APA). As we know, for a study to be published in an APA journal, it must past the muster of reliability and validity as evaluated through the rigors of peer review. So your first general criterion for evaluating a study is to *consider the source*: where an empirical report such as the Strack and company study is published. A credible source requires peer review.

Next, look to see if the goals of the study are clearly defined and articulated. Then consider whether the methods and design of the study are sufficient to achieve its goals. Ask yourself, "If I had to design this study to test this hypothesized relationship, what would I do?" In other words, you want to evaluate whether the study provides the best method for achieving the goals of the research. Here a mental template might be helpful: Begin with the broad distinction of whether you would classify a study as either experimental or nonexperimental. For example, Strack and colleagues aimed to examine whether facial muscle contractions could cause changes in emotional responses to cartoons. To test a causal relationship such as this requires an experiment of the kind carried out by Strack and colleagues. On the other hand, a correlational study, an important nonexperimental design in our proverbial research toolbox, does not allow you to infer causality. Indeed, a correlational study might demonstrate an important empirical relationship between two or more variables. However, a *correlation does not imply causation,* meaning that a relationship between two variables does not mean that changes in one cause changes in another.

Also, in developing an eye of a critical consumer of research, keep in mind our discussion of pseudoscience in Chapter 1. We know that sound research has a clear *connection to previous studies.* How does the study fit with previous research? If it is a truly novel discovery, what made it so? Did it correct a flaw that prevented other studies from demonstrating these results? Also, always keep in mind the difference between anecdotal and empirical evidence. Personal testimonial accounts can be very moving and convincing, but we know such anecdotes do not constitute evidence for the scientific method.

Last, look at *who funded the research.* Major federal funding agencies and private foundations fund only research proposals that have been evaluated carefully and ranked high by a panel of experts, or peer reviewers. The funding agencies also often monitor the progress of the research. This does not guarantee that every such project is good, but it goes a long way toward ensuring some worthwhile products. On the other hand, research that is funded by organizations that have a preference for a particular outcome should be given particularly close scrutiny (Locke, Silverman, & Spirduso, 1998).

Professional Review

Now let's go back in time and imagine being asked by the editor of the *Journal of Personality and Psychology* to serve as a peer reviewer of the Strack and company study. Your task as a peer reviewer is to provide an opinion as to the scientific merit of the study. The manuscript in front of you will be organized into a specific format with specific sections: Abstract, Introduction, Method, Results, and Discussion. You carefully read the manuscript, and for each of these sections, there are particular questions to consider that will help you to critique the study and to offer an opinion as to its scientific merit.

Abstract

The **abstract** summarizes the major points of the study. As a reviewer, you want to learn from the abstract the problem under investigation, the procedures used to study the problem, the results, the conclusions, and the implications of the research findings. The Strack and company abstract provided a concise description of their study, including its rationale, methodology, results, and theoretical conclusions. From reading the abstract, you should understand the main finding or contribution of the study.

Introduction

The **introduction** identifies the problem to be investigated and why it is important. In reviewing the introduction, look to see if the problem and rationale have been cast in a psychological theory, which should serve as a framework for the study, defining its key concepts and terms. Two general questions are helpful guides for reading an introduction: What is the study about and why does it matter? More formal questions are: What is the theory and hypothesis and how are they related?

For both these sets of questions, clear answers can be easily inferred from reading the introduction of the Strack and company study.

That is, Strack and colleagues devised their experiment as a test of what is referred to in the literature as the facial feedback hypothesis. The facial feedback hypothesis, which originates from the James–Lange theory of emotion, states that facial movements by themselves can induce particular emotional feelings and that these emotional feelings can be created by simply "tricking" a person into making specific facial contractions. Strack and colleagues specifically hypothesized that participants who held a pen gently between their teeth would induce smiling, which in turn would lead to significantly higher ratings of the funniness of cartoons than would participants who held a pen tightly between their lips that presumably induced frowning. Thus, you can see that this is an excellent example of a hypothesis as it is derived from theory, presented as an a priori prediction, and eminently testable.

Method

The **method** section details the operations and procedures that the researcher used in the study. Two helpful hints in reading the method: First, the method section should provide sufficient detail so that another researcher could reproduce the study. Second, you as a reader should be able to put yourself in the shoes of a participant and understand exactly what the participant actually was instructed to do in the study. How participants were recruited and how the study sample was formed should be clearly stated in the method. In reading the method, look for any signs of sample bias that occur when participants are not randomly selected. Also, consider how representative is the sample, as this will affect the generalizability of the study results.

The method section should also make clear operational definitions for both the independent and dependent variables. What was the experimental task? Were participants randomly assigned to different levels of the independent variable? Now let's see how the Stark and company method fared. We know that they recruited their participants from the student body at the University of Illinois. This would not be considered a random sample. Also keep in mind that a sample of college students has limited generalizability. So on these two criteria, the Strack and colleagues study came up a bit short. On the other hand, the experimental task was ingenious, especially well designed to test the hypothesis. The cover story was elaborate and convincing and very likely eliminated methodological problems of earlier studies by preventing participants from being aware of the emotional feeling associated with the particular facial muscle activity of smile versus frown. In addition, the cover story provided a means to minimize the problem of **demand characteristics**. Demand characteristics are cues available that tip off participants to the scientific hypothesis of the researcher and influence how participants respond to study stimuli. The researchers also collected difficulty ratings as a control variable in order to assess whether their results would be influenced by these extraneous factors. Finally, the method should include a clear statement on **informed consent** procedures, which we discuss in Chapter 3. No research should be done without informed consent of the participants.

Results

The **results** section presents the major statistical findings of the study. The results include both **descriptive statistics** and **inferential statistics**. Descriptive statistics summarize the data, usually in the form of averages and standard deviations (a statistical measure of variability). Inferential statistics in the form of tests of significance tell the probability of whether the observed differences found in the study were produced by random, or chance, factors. Also important for inferential statistics is an estimate of what is known as **effect size**. The effect size refers to the strength of the predicted or hypothesized relationship between the independent variable and dependent variable. For the Strack and company study, the effect size can be evaluated by looking at the difference in funniness ratings for the teeth condition ($M = 5.14$) versus the lip condition ($M = 4.32$). While these differences reached statistical significance, the effect size appeared rather modest, reflecting a difference of less than one funniness rating point.

Overall, Strack and colleagues provided clear descriptive data in the form of mean funniness ratings as well as mean difficulty ratings for each of their three conditions. They also used inferential statistics to determine that the differences in the funniness ratings were unlikely due to chance. With the exception of failing to provide any statistical estimate of effect size, the results section provided the reader with the necessary descriptive and inferential statistics that are critical to test the facial feedback hypothesis.

Discussion

In the **discussion** section, the major findings of the study are often restated but typically only in narrative form, and the theoretical meaning of the results is discussed. Important questions to consider in reading the discussion are: Do the empirical findings support the inferences and explanations? Does the discussion section duly express tentativeness and exercise cautiousness, which are essential to the scientific method? Are alternative interpretations carefully considered?

Perhaps the most important question for the discussion section is whether the limitations of the study are thoughtfully and explicitly discussed. These limitations may be related to the extent to which the operations and procedures adequately capture the intended phenomena. Is the experiment too unrealistic, too contrived—clever but lacking any real application to life? The extent to which a study or experiment approximates the actual real-life phenomenon under investigation refers to **ecological validity**. Related to but different from questions of ecological validity are those that pertain to the generalizability of the study and how representative or culturally diverse is the sample. These considerations fall under the general or broader category of **external validity** (ecological validity is one particular aspect of external validity). Strack and company used a college sample. They devised a simple yet ingenious experimental task. But a fair question to ask is whether the experimental task was too contrived. Probably not, but this potential limitation was not considered in the discussion. They also did not discuss the limitations of generalizability of their college student sample. On the other hand,

Strack and colleagues provided theoretical interpretations that were well supported by their empirical findings. Also on a positive note, their discussion raised the possibility of additional follow-up studies. Overall, the discussion could be improved by addressing more fully the limitations of the study. However, to be fair, the Strack and company study was written for experts in their particular area and published in a top-tier psychology journal that assumes a level of knowledge and experience in research well beyond what we have assumed in writing this textbook.

Literature Review

All psychological research presented in peer-reviewed journals generally begins with a literature review. Some psychology journals are exclusively devoted to publishing literature reviews of particular topics of interest. Consider, for example, what the prestigious *Psychological Bulletin* seeks to publish, as described on their web page:

> Integrative reviews or research syntheses focus on empirical studies and seek to summarize past research by drawing overall conclusions from many separate investigations that address related or identical hypotheses. A research synthesis typically presents the authors' assessments of the (a) state of knowledge concerning the relations of interest; (b) critical assessments of the strengths and weaknesses in past research; and (c) important issues that research has left unresolved, thereby directing future research so it can yield a maximum amount of new information. (http://www.apa.org/pubs/journals/bul/)

As you can see from this description, literature reviews serve an extremely important function in developing a scientific understanding of a topic. A sound literature review creates and evaluates a body of knowledge that is drawn from a synthesis of empirical findings across independent studies.

A critical reading of any literature review, however, should pay close attention to several factors. First, how were the empirical studies selected for review? A major limitation is that authors of reviews are relatively free to select studies and can choose on their own those empirical findings viewed as relevant. Two independent reviewers of the very same topic could reach very different conclusions! We know from Chapter 1 the problems of confirmatory bias. It is not hard to imagine how confirmatory bias may influence a reviewer to seek only empirical findings that fit with a certain school of thought. Second, most traditional reviews lack an objective benchmark to evaluate the strength of different empirical findings gleaned across various studies. How does one weigh the importance of one empirical finding over the other? Third, literature reviews are limited by **publication bias**. That is, reviews are based on studies that have been published. Studies often are unpublished because of negative findings, such as failing to replicate a certain phenomenon or effect. A review generally does not take into consideration unpublished studies, instead focusing exclusively on empirical findings that have been reported in peer-reviewed journals. Publication bias can be a particular problem for studies examining the effectiveness of a particular drug. In fact, all drug studies, often referred as "trials," must now be filed with the Federal Drug Administration (FDA), including negative trials in which the drug failed to show the predicted effect. The FDA requires this in order to limit the effects of publication bias in its reviews of drug studies.

Because of these difficulties reviews now often incorporate meta-analysis as a method to provide a more unbiased evaluation of the literature. Meta-analysis is a statistical tool that provides an objective metric to weigh the strength of results from individual studies. The metric used provides an estimate of effect size (strength or magnitude of the demonstrated findings) for the results of each study included in the review. The effect size statistic allows for studies to be directly and objectively compared with each other. The average effect size across studies can be computed to provide an objective indicator of the overall strength of the empirical findings. This, in turn, might also provide an index of the degree generalizability of the empirical findings, as the review includes many studies varying in settings, samples, procedures, and time periods. Meta-analysis provides a statistical means to combat the biases of any reviewer.

CONCLUSIONS

Researchers aim to describe and explain thoughts, actions, and events in terms of a theory. However, a theory cannot be tested directly. Thus, researchers perform experimental and nonexperimental studies to test hypotheses that are derived from a theory. A dynamic interplay ensues, with data obtained through hypothesis testing acting as the lifeline for both building and evaluating a theory. A good theory, then, will be one that can account for a wide variety of data with the fewest explanatory concepts. A theory gains power when it can organize ideas and facts into a coherent pattern and predict the results of future research. Causality, though, will be difficult to establish for any theory in psychology, as even highly controlled experiments cannot rule out all potential confounding factors. Evidence for causality should establish (a) temporal precedence, (b) covariation of cause and effect, and (c) elimination of alternative explanations. The best benchmark remains the degree to which a theory can account for findings that are robust across various conditions, settings, and procedures.

Both inductive and deductive reasoning can figure prominently in theory formation and explanatory research. We have likened this process to a research circle in which deductive reasoning goes from theory to hypotheses to data, whereas inductive reasoning goes from data to empirical generalizations to theory. Ideas, as the so-called grist for the mill for research aimed toward building scientific theory, can come from many sources. The most important of these is the psychological literature, which consists of studies that have met the rigors of peer review. Scientific journalism and popular science literature can be two other potential sources for ideas, but articles and reports appearing in these two venues are not subject to peer review. As such, these secondary sources can best serve as clues to lead you to the primary source, the first-hand empirical report published in a peer-reviewed journal.

Finally, evaluating the scientific merit of research is a key skill. We hope you become an educated consumer of psychological research! Always consider the source, and in order to critique a study, go to the primary source. Keep in mind that correlation cannot prove causation and anecdotes are not evidence for the scientific method. When reading a primary source of an empirical article, evaluate whether the abstract summarizes the study, the introduction defines key concepts, the method specifies operations and procedures, the results present descriptive and inferential statistics, and the discussion covers interpretation of the findings as well as limitations of the research.

END OF CHAPTER

Chapter Highlights

- Researchers describe and define terms both conceptually and operationally, with the former providing the meaning, often rather broad in scope, of an abstract term, such as *intelligence*, *anxiety*, or *emotion*, and the latter specifying how a concept is coded, measured, or quantified.

- Researchers aim to develop theories that will provide parsimonious and precise explanation of the nature of the phenomenon under investigation.

- Because a theory cannot be tested directly, researchers perform experimental and nonexperimental studies to test hypotheses that are derived from a theory.

- Data obtained through hypothesis testing act as the lifeline for both building and evaluating a theory.

- A good theory is one that can account for a wide variety of data with the fewest explanatory concepts. A theory gains power when it can organize ideas and facts into a coherent pattern and predict the results of future research.

- Deductive and inductive reasoning can figure prominently in theory formation and explanatory research, which we have likened to a research circle in which deductive reasoning goes from theory to hypotheses to data, whereas inductive reasoning goes from data to empirical generalizations to theory.

- Ideas are generated from a variety of sources: observation, theory, and searching the literature, most notably peer-reviewed journals but also written works in science journalism and popular science.

- Empirical articles contain the following sections: Abstract, Introduction, Method, Results, Discussion, and References. The abstract summarizes the study, the introduction defines key concepts, the method specifies operations and procedures, the results present descriptive and inferential statistics, and the discussion covers interpretation of the findings as well as limitations of the research.

- A traditional literature review article evaluates the methodology used across different studies, examines the degree to which findings are robust across various conditions, settings, and procedures, and comments on the extent to which the empirical findings allow for general theoretical conclusions.

- Meta-analysis provides a more unbiased review of the literature than traditional literature reviews.

Key Terms

Abstract   54

Alternative explanation   34

Applied research   35

Autonomic nervous system   37

Basic research   35

Cannon–Bard theory of emotion   37

Conceptual definition   32

Confounding   34

Control group   49

Control variable   50

Covariation of the cause
and effect   34

Deductive research   43

Demand characteristics   55

Descriptive statistics   56

Direction of association   45

Discussion   56

Ecological validity   56

Effect size   56

Embodiment theory of emotion   37

Empirical articles   38

Empirical generalization   47

Ethnography   44

Experimental   30

External validity   56

Facial feedback hypothesis   48

Generalization   45

Inductive research   43

Inferential statistics   56

Informed consent   55

Introduction   54

James–Lange theory   37

Journals   38

Levels   49

Meta-analysis   58

Method   55

Nonexperimental   30

Operational definition   33

Popular science   39

Primary source   40

Program evaluation   35

Proprietary   42

PsycINFO   41

PsycLIT   41

Publication bias   57

Qualitative research   43

Research circle   47

Results   56

Review articles   39

Robust   53

Science journalism   40

Secondary sources   40

Serendipity   36

Skepticism   52

Social Sciences Citation Index (SSCI)   41

Temporal precedence   34

Third variable   34

Research in the News

1. Consider an interesting newspaper article by journalist Javier Zarracina that appeared in the April 4, 2010, *Boston Globe* titled "A Life Lesson From the Majors. Smile, You'll Live Longer." The newspaper account describes an empirical study published in the peer-reviewed journal *Psychological Science* by researchers Ernest L. Abel and Michael Kruger (2010) titled "Smile Intensity in Photographs Predicts Longevity." Read the Abel and Kruger (2010) paper and provide a critique as both an educated consumer of psychological research and a professional reviewer of the study.

2. In the *Time* January 16, 2009, article "How to Lift Your Mood? Try Smiling," John Cloud tells the story how of being coaxed during his workouts by his personal trainer: "Relax your face." Cloud writes that he remained skeptical about his trainer's advice until he read a January 2009 *Journal of Personality and Social Psychology* study by Matsumoto and Willingham (2009) that compared facial expressions in two groups of judo athletes—blind and sighted competitors from the 2004 Olympics in Athens. This study prompted Cloud to discover one of the oldest questions in the study of emotion as to whether we all learn facial expression through our culture or are they genetically coded for everyone. By the end of his enjoyable piece, Cloud concludes, " . . . the emotional train does run in two directions between your brain, which may be screaming from the pain that your trainer is causing, and your face, which can—if you draw it into a relaxed expression—inform your brain that it shouldn't be protesting so much. So next time you're working out and grimacing push your facial muscles into submission. Look blank. You will find it's easier to get through one more rep."

What makes this piece an example of science journalism? How would you describe the reporting methods used in this article? How do the style, organization, and content of science journalism compare with the scientific method of peer-reviewed studies? Do you think Cloud's conclusions are supported by the scientific literature?

Activity Questions

1. Researchers in psychology "play" with ideas that require conceptual and operational definitions, such topics as maximization, happiness, intelligence, anxiety, impulsivity, attention, and emotion. For each of these, provide conceptual and operational definitions.

2. Independent, dependent, and control variables also fall under the "must know" category. To understand them requires practice. Here are some study situations. For each of these, name the three kinds of variables.

   a. You want to see if different instructional sets influence performance on a cognitive test. One instructional set presents the cognitive test as an ability-diagnostic measure of intelligence and the other instructional set presents the cognitive test as an ability-nondiagnostic laboratory measure of problem solving unrelated to intelligence.

      Independent (what you change/manipulate) variable: instructional set

      Dependent (what you observe/measure) variable: scores on cognitive test

      Control (what you hold constant) variable: cognitive test, same test given under the two instructional sets

   b. You want to see if facial expressions can influence perception. You decide to have subjects look at cartoons and rate them on a funniness scale either while holding a pen between their lips, which makes it impossible to contract either of the two smiling muscles, or while holding a pen clenched between their teeth, which has the opposite effect of making them smile.

      Independent (what you change/manipulate) variable: facial expression induced by either holding a pen between lips or clenched between teeth

      Dependent (what you observe/measure) variable: funniness scores/ratings

      Control (what you hold constant) variable: cartoons, same whether viewed while holding a pen between lips or clenched between teeth; funniness scale

   c. You been hired to evaluate the effectiveness of two diets: South Beach vs. Atkins. You want to make sure both dieting groups weigh about the same before starting either the South Beach or Atkins diet. So you weigh everyone before the diet and at the completion of the diet 6 weeks later.

      Independent (what you change/manipulate) variable: diet (South Beach vs. Atkins)

      Dependent (what you observe/measure) variable: difference in weight before and after

      Control (what you hold constant) variable: prediet weight; length of time (6 weeks) on respective diets

   d. You want to study the influence of Alzheimer's disease on memory while controlling for age. What this means is that you will have two groups of people of about the same age; one group will be diagnosed with Alzheimer's disease and the other group will be your control group of healthy persons.

      Independent (what you change/manipulate) variable: group (Alzheimer's disease vs. control)

      Dependent (what you observe/measure) variable: scores on memory test

      Control (what you hold constant) variable: age, memory test, same given to both groups

3. Transform each of the following statements or problems into at least two testable hypotheses.

   a. Talking on cell phones while driving should be against the law.

   b. Listening to Mozart will make people smarter.

   c. Steroids increase home runs in baseball.

   d. Eating a vegetarian diet increases your grade-point average.

   e. Money can buy you happiness.

4. In virtually all experiments, there is a degree of deception as researchers need to avoid creating bias by providing too much information before subjects have completed a study. What do you think about the ethics of deception in psychological research?

5. High school yearbooks can be used to study faces. Recall the Kniffin and Wilson (2004) study in which participants rated photographs of people they knew taken from their high school yearbooks. Then these same photographs were rated by another person of the same age and sex as the yearbook owner who did not know the people in the photographs. This would be a rather straightforward exercise to do in class, provided students have their high school yearbooks! Students rate the attractiveness of photographs of graduates they knew from their own yearbook, and then these same photographs are rated by another student of the same age and sex as the yearbook owner who does not know the people in the photographs. You can collect data and then combine them with ratings from other students who participated in the exercise. What are your independent and dependent variables? What is your hypothesis and why? What are your expected results and why?

6. Consider the following "thought experiment" taken from psychologist Paula M. Niedenthal's (2007) review published in *Science*, "Embodying Emotion":

   A man goes into a bar to tell a new joke. Two people are already in the bar. One is smiling and one is frowning. Who is more likely to "get" the punch line and appreciate his joke? (p. 1002)

   You probably could easily guess correctly that the smiling person would get the joke. But describe how the experimental study of Strack and colleagues could be used as evidence for your answer.

Review Questions

1. Why is a naturalistic observational methodology considered to be a nonexperimental study? What are the strengths and limitations of nonexperimental studies?

2. Describe how Paul Ekman's studies of facial expression of emotions addressed cross-cultural differences.

3. Compare and contrast deductive and inductive research strategies.

4. Identify and explain the three criteria for establishing cause and effect.

5. Describe how a researcher develops and uses conceptual and operational definitions.

6. Describe how there are the three kinds of evidence that are needed to establish causality. Why should a psychological researcher always be skeptical about interpreting evidence of causality?

7. How might a third variable serve to confound the interpretation of results? What should a researcher do when concerned about third variables?

8. Explain how it is that a theory cannot be directly tested. If this is so, how does a researcher go about evaluating a theory?

9. When obtained results achieve statistical significance, what does that mean precisely?

10. External validity and ecological validity are two important considerations in evaluating research. What do they mean? How are they related? How are they different?

11. What considerations should you keep in mind when using popular search engines such as Google Scholar?

12. Science journalism and popular science represent two interesting sources for developing thoughts and ideas about research. How would you use these sources as leads in pursuing a research question?

13. How might confirmatory bias on the part of the researcher contaminate a literature review? What can be done to reduce confirmatory bias in literature reviews?

14. What is peer review and why it important?

15. How would you review each of the sections of an empirical article?

16. What is the purpose of a control group?

17. Explain how an obtained result could achieve statistical significance but be of a small effect size.

18. Explain the fundamental truism that you cannot infer causality on the basis of correlation.

19. Explain how a correlation coefficient contains two critical pieces of information about the relationship of two variables: (a) the strength of the relationship and (b) the direction of the relationship.

20. How does publication bias influence a literature review?

CHAPTER 3

Ethics in Behavioral Research

Let's begin with a thought experiment (or a trip down memory lane, depending on your prior exposure to this example). One spring morning as you are drinking coffee and reading the newspaper, you notice a small ad for a psychology experiment at the local university. "Earn money and learn about yourself," it says. Feeling a bit bored with your job as a high school teacher, you call and schedule an evening visit to the lab.

WE WILL PAY YOU $45 FOR ONE HOUR OF YOUR TIME

Persons Needed for a Study of Memory

You arrive at the assigned room at the university, ready for an interesting hour or so, and are impressed immediately by the elegance of the building and the professional appearance of the personnel. In the waiting room, you see a man dressed in a lab technician's coat talking to another visitor—a middle-aged fellow dressed in casual attire. The man in the lab coat turns and introduces himself and

65

explains that, as a psychologist, he is interested in the question of whether people learn things better when they are punished for making a mistake. He quickly convinces you that this is a very important question for which there has been no adequate answer; he then explains that his experiment on punishment and learning will help to answer this question. Then he announces,

"I'm going to ask one of you to be the teacher here tonight and the other one to be the learner."

"The experimenter" [as we'll refer to him from now on] says he will write either "teacher" or "learner" on small identical slips of paper and then asks both of you to draw one. Yours says "teacher."

The experimenter now says, in a matter-of-fact way,

"All right. Now the first thing we'll have to do is to set the Learner up so that he can get some type of punishment."

He leads you both behind a curtain, sits the Learner down, attaches a wire to his left wrist and straps both of his arms to the chair so that he cannot remove the wire (**Exhibit 3.1**). The wire is connected to a console with 30 switches and a large dial on the other side of the room. When you ask what the wire is for, the experimenter says he will demonstrate. He then asks you to hold the end of the wire, walks back to the control console, flips several switches and focuses his attention on the dial. You hear a clicking noise, see the dial move, and then feel an electric shock in your hand. The shock increases and the dial registers more current when the experimenter flips the next switch on the console.

"Oh, I see," you say. "This is the punishment. Couldn't it cause injury?" The experimenter explains that the machine is calibrated so that it will not cause permanent injury, but acknowledges that when it is turned up all the way it is very, very

Exhibit 3.1   Learner Strapped in Chair With Electrodes

Source: From the film *OBEDIENCE* © 1968 by Stanley Milgram, © Renewed 1993 by Alexandra Milgram, and distributed by Penn State, Media Sales.

painful and can result in severe, although momentary, discomfort.

Now you walk back to the other side of the room (so that the Learner is behind the curtain) and sit before the console (**Exhibit 3.2**). The experimental procedure has four simple steps: (1) You read aloud a series of word pairs, like "blue box," "nice day," "wild duck," and so forth. (2) Next, you read one of the first words from those pairs and a set of four words, one of which contains the original paired word. For example, you might say, "blue: sky ink box lamp." (3) The Learner states the word that he thinks was paired with the first word you read ("blue"). If he gives a correct response, you compliment him and move on to the next word. If he makes a mistake, you flip a switch on the console. This causes the Learner to feel a shock on his wrist. (4) After each mistake, you are to flip the next switch on the console, progressing from left to right. You note that there is a label corresponding to every 5th mark on the dial, with the 1st mark labeled "slight shock," the 5th mark labeled "moderate shock," the 10th "strong shock," and so on through "very strong shock," "intense shock," "extreme intensity shock," and "danger: severe shock."

You begin. The Learner at first gives some correct answers, but then he makes a few errors. Soon you are beyond the 5th mark ("slight shock") and are moving in the direction of more and more severe shocks. You recall having heard about this experiment and so you know that as you turn the dial, the Learner's responses increase in intensity from a grunt at the 15th mark ("strong shock") to painful groans at higher levels, anguished cries to "get me out of here" at the "extreme intensity shock" levels, to a deathly silence at the highest level. You also know that as you proceed and indicate your discomfort at administering the stronger shocks, the experimenter will inform you that "The experiment requires that you continue," and occasionally, "It is absolutely essential that you continue." Please mark on the console below the most severe shock that you would agree to give the Learner (**Exhibit 3.3**).

You may very well recognize that this thought experiment is a slightly simplified version of the famous **"obedience" experiments by Stanley Milgram** begun at Yale University in 1960. Did you know that Milgram also surveyed Yale undergraduates and asked them to indicate at what level they would terminate their "shocks"? The average (mean) maximum shock level predicted by the Yale undergraduates was 9.35, corresponding to a "strong" shock. Only one student predicted that he would provide a stimulus above that level, but only barely so, for he said he would stop at

Exhibit 3.2   Milgram's "Shock Generator"

Source: From the film *OBEDIENCE* © 1968 by Stanley Milgram, © Renewed 1993 by Alexandra Milgram, and distributed by Penn State, Media Sales.

Exhibit 3.3 Shock Meter

Source: Schutt, R. K. (2009). *Investigating the social world: The process and practice of research* (6th ed., p. 70). Thousand Oaks, CA: Pine Forge Press.

the "very strong" level. Responses were similar from nonstudent groups who were asked the same question.

What was the actual average level of shock administered by the 40 New Haven adults who volunteered for the experiment? It was 24.53, or a level higher than "extreme intensity shock" and just short of the "danger: severe shock" level. Twenty-five (62.5%) of Milgram's original 40 subjects complied with the experimenter's demands all the way to the top of the scale (originally labeled simply as "XXX"). And lest you pass this result off as simply the result of the subjects having thought that the experiment wasn't real, we hasten to point out that there is abundant evidence from the subjects' own observed high stress and their subsequent reports that they really believed that the Learner was receiving actual, hurtful shocks.

Are you surprised by the subjects' responses? By the Yale undergraduates' predictions of so many compassionate responses? By your own response? (We leave it to you to assess how accurately you predicted the response you would have given if you had been an actual subject.)

Of course, our purpose in introducing this little "experiment" is not to focus attention on the prediction of obedience to authority; instead, we want to introduce the topic of research ethics by encouraging you to think about research from the standpoint of the people who are the subjects of behavioral research. We refer to Stanley Milgram's research on obedience throughout this chapter, since it is fair to say that this research ultimately had as profound an influence on the way that psychologists think about research ethics as it had on the way that psychologists understand obedience to authority.

Every psychologist needs to consider how to practice the discipline ethically, whether that practice involves clinical care about personal problems, research to learn about human behavior, or a mixture of both. Although the 15 ethical standards in the "research and publication" category are but a fraction of the 83 standards in the American Psychological Association's entire 2002 **Code of Conduct**, it is not possible to draw a clear dividing line between ethics applicable to clinical and research practice: Whenever we interact with other people as psychologists, we must give paramount importance to the rational concerns and emotional needs that will shape their responses to our actions. It is here that ethical research practice begins, with the recognition that our research procedures involve people who deserve as much respect for their well-being as we do.

HISTORICAL BACKGROUND

Formal procedures for the protection of participants in research grew out of some widely publicized abuses. A defining event occurred in 1946, when the **Nuremberg War Crime Trials** exposed horrific medical experiments conducted by Nazi doctors and others in the name of "science". In the 1970s, Americans were shocked to learn that researchers funded by the U.S. Public Health Service had followed 399 low-income African American men in the **Tuskegee syphilis study** in the 1930s, collecting data to learn about the "natural" course of the illness (**Exhibit 3.4**). Many participants were not informed of their illness and were denied treatment until 1972, even though a cure (penicillin) was developed in the 1950s.

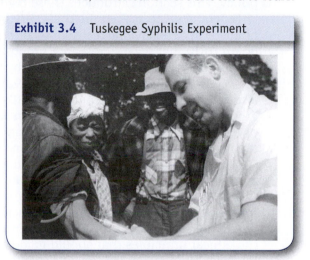

Exhibit 3.4   Tuskegee Syphilis Experiment

Egregious violations of human rights like these resulted, in the United States, in the creation of a National Commission for the Protection of Human Subjects of Biomedical and Behavioral Research. The Commission's 1979 **Belmont Report** (U.S. Department of Health, Education, and Welfare, 1979) established three basic ethical principles for the protection of human subjects (**Exhibit 3.5**):

Exhibit 3.5   Belmont Report Principles

Respect for Persons

Beneficence   Justice

- *Respect for persons:* Treating persons as autonomous agents and protecting those with diminished autonomy

- *Beneficence:* Minimizing possible harms and maximizing benefits

- *Justice:* Distributing benefits and risks of research fairly

The Department of Health and Human Services and the Food and Drug Administration then translated these principles into specific regulations that were adopted in 1991 as the **Federal Policy for the Protection of Human Subjects**.

This policy has shaped the course of social science research ever since, and you will have to take it into account as you design your own research investigations. Professional associations like the American Psychological Association, university review boards, and ethics committees in other organizations also set standards for the treatment of human subjects by their members, employees, and students, although these standards are all designed to comply with the federal policy. This section introduces these regulations.

Federal regulations require that every institution that seeks federal funding for biomedical or behavioral research on human subjects have an **institutional review board (IRB)** that reviews research proposals. IRBs at universities and other agencies apply ethical standards that are set by federal regulations but can be expanded or specified by the IRB itself (Sieber, 1992). To promote adequate review of ethical issues, the regulations require that IRBs include members with diverse backgrounds. The **Office for Protection from Research Risks** in the National Institutes of Health monitors IRBs, with the exception of research involving drugs (which is the responsibility of the Federal Food and Drug Administration).

The American Psychological Association (APA) started the process of developing an ethics code in 1938, when it formed a committee to consider the issue (Korn, 1997). Work on a formal APA ethics code then began in 1947 (Fisher, 2003). A committee reviewed more than 1,000 descriptions of "critical incidents" in which practicing psychologists had been confronted by ethical issues, deliberated about the ethical principles that should guide decisions in such incidents, and sought feedback from APA members. The resulting ethics code was published in 1953 and has subsequently been revised nine times (Fisher, 2003).

ETHICAL PRINCIPLES

The 2002 APA Ethics Code, the most recent version, contains 151 enforceable Ethical Standards as well as five General Principles. The General Principles are meant to be general "aspirational" values that capture the discipline's "moral vision" and are consistent with the Belmont Report's three ethical principles, while the Ethical Standards are meant to apply to all APA members and to be enforced by the APA Ethics Committee. In addition, more than half of the state boards that license psychologists as well as numerous other bodies stipulate that psychologists must comply with the APA Ethics Code. Violations of the Code can be investigated by the APA Ethics Committee and lead to sanctions ranging from a reprimand to expulsion. (Detailed procedures are available at http://www.apa.org/ethics/code/index.aspx.) Of course, legal actions by aggrieved parties are also a possibility, but violations of the Code are not in and of themselves legal violations (Fisher, 2003).

Fifteen of the Code's 151 Enforceable Standards pertain specifically to research and publication, but many others—on competence, human relations, privacy and confidentiality, and assessment—have direct implications for research practice. The APA's General Principles for ethical practice reflect this view of research ethics as part of a commitment to overarching ethical principles across all areas of psychological practice. We present these principles first as a foundation for our own discussion of specific ethical standards (APA, 2010).

Principle A: Beneficence and Nonmaleficence

Psychologists strive to benefit those with whom they work and take care to do no harm. In their professional actions, psychologists seek to safeguard the welfare and rights of those with whom they interact professionally and other affected persons, and the welfare of animal subjects of research. When conflicts occur among psychologists' obligations or concerns, they attempt to resolve these conflicts in a responsible fashion that avoids or minimizes harm. Because psychologists' scientific and professional judgments and actions may affect the lives of others, they are alert to and guard against personal, financial, social, organizational, or political factors that might lead to misuse of their influence. Psychologists strive to be aware of the possible effect of their own physical and mental health on their ability to help those with whom they work.

Principle B: Fidelity and Responsibility

Psychologists establish relationships of trust with those with whom they work. They are aware of their professional and scientific responsibilities to society and to the scientific communities in which they work. Psychologists uphold professional standards of conduct, clarify their professional roles and obligations, accept appropriate responsibility for their behavior, and seek to manage conflicts of interest that could lead to exploitation or harm. Psychologists consult with, refer to, or cooperate with other professionals and institutions to the extent needed to serve the best interests of those with whom they work. They are concerned about the ethical compliance of their colleagues' scientific and professional conduct. Psychologists strive to contribute a portion of their professional time for little or no compensation or personal advantage.

Principle C: Integrity

Psychologists seek to promote accuracy, honesty, and truthfulness in the science, teaching, and practice of psychology. In these activities, psychologists do not steal, cheat, or engage in fraud, subterfuge, or intentional misrepresentation of fact. Psychologists strive to keep their promises and to avoid unwise or unclear commitments. In situations in which deception may be ethically justifiable to maximize benefits and minimize harm, psychologists have a serious obligation to consider the need for, the possible consequences of, and their responsibility to correct any resulting mistrust or other harmful effects that arise from the use of such techniques.

Principle D: Justice

Psychologists recognize that fairness and justice entitle all persons to access to and benefit from the contributions of psychology and to equal quality in the processes, procedures, and services being conducted by psychologists.

Psychologists exercise reasonable judgment and take precautions to ensure that their potential biases, the boundaries of their competence, and the limitations of their expertise do not lead to or condone unjust practices.

Principle E: Respect for People's Rights and Dignity

Psychologists respect the dignity and worth of all people and the rights of individuals to privacy, confidentiality, and self-determination. Psychologists are aware that special safeguards may be necessary to protect the rights and welfare of persons or communities whose vulnerabilities impair autonomous decision making. Psychologists are aware of and respect cultural, individual, and role differences, including those based on age, gender, gender identity, race, ethnicity, culture, national origin, religion, sexual orientation, disability, language, and socioeconomic status and consider these factors when working with members of such groups. Psychologists try to eliminate the effect on their work of biases based on those factors, and they do not knowingly participate in or condone activities of others based upon such prejudices.

Did Stanley Milgram respect these principles in the obedience experiments? It is unfair to judge his research in light of principles adopted 40 years later, but it is still instructive to ask the question. No doubt you already want to know more of the details in order to evaluate whether Milgram took "care to do no harm" and established "relationships of trust" with his subjects. We will report many of these details in this chapter. But do you also see that we have to convert these abstract principles into concrete standards before we can hope to evaluate the degree of harm, trust, and other features of a research project, no matter how current that project is or what details we have learned about it?

We have organized our discussion of ethical standards for research under four headings that reflect the five APA principles:

- to achieve valid results;
- to maintain professional integrity;
- to protect research subjects;
- to encourage appropriate application.

Each of these principles became a focus of debate about Milgram's experiments, so we will return frequently to that debate in order to keep our discussion realistic. We will also refer frequently to the 2002 APA Code in order to keep our treatment current. You will soon realize that there is no simple answer to the question of what is (or isn't) ethical research practice or, more generally, which practices are consistent with the APA's general principles. The issues are just too complicated and the relevant principles too subject to different interpretations. But we do promise that by the time you finish this chapter, you will be aware of the major issues in research ethics and be able to make informed, defensible decisions about the ethical conduct of psychological research.

Bear in mind that no specific ethical standard can implement fully the intent of an abstract principle. In addition, you will soon realize that most of the specific standards help to implement more than one of the five principles. So as you read about the standards in each of the following sections, ask yourself two questions: (1) Do these standards capture the intent of the general principle? (2) Do these standards help to implement any other general principles?

Achieving Valid Results (Principle B: Fidelity and Responsibility)

Commitment to achieving valid results is the necessary starting point for ethical research practice. Simply put, we have no business asking people to answer questions, submit to observations, or participate in experimental procedures if we are simply seeking to verify our existing prejudices or convince others to take action on behalf of our personal interests. It is the pursuit of objective knowledge about human behavior—the goal of validity—that motivates and justifies our investigations and gives us some claim to the right to influence others to participate in our research. Knowledge is the foundation of human progress as well as the basis for our expectation that we, as behavioral scientists, can help people to achieve a brighter future. If we approach our research projects objectively, setting aside our personal predilections in the service of learning a bit more about human behavior, we can honestly represent our actions as potentially contributing to the advancement of knowledge.

The details in Milgram's 1963 article and 1974 book on the obedience experiments make a compelling case for his commitment to achieving valid results—to learning how and why obedience influences behavior. In Milgram's (1963) own words,

> It has been reliably established that from 1933–45 millions of innocent persons were systematically slaughtered on command. . . . Obedience is the psychological mechanism that links individual action to political purpose. It is the dispositional cement that binds men to systems of authority . . . for many persons obedience may be a deeply ingrained behavior tendency. . . . Obedience may [also] be ennobling and educative and refer to acts of charity and kindness, as well as to destruction. (p. 371)

Milgram (1963) then explains how he devised experiments to study the process of obedience in a way that would seem realistic to the subjects and still allow "important variables to be manipulated at several points in the experiment" (p. 372). Every step in the experiment was carefully designed—and documented—to ensure that subjects received identical stimuli and that their responses were measured carefully.

Milgram's (1963) attention to validity is also apparent in his reflections on "the particular conditions" of his experiment, for, he notes, "understanding of the phenomenon of obedience must rest on an analysis of [these conditions]" (p. 377). These particular conditions included the setting for the experiment at

Yale University, its purported "worthy purpose" to advance knowledge about learning and memory, and the voluntary participation of the subject as well as of the Learner—as far as the subject knew. The importance of some of these "particular conditions" (such as the location at Yale) was then tested in subsequent replications of the basic experiment (Milgram, 1965).

However, not all psychologists agreed that Milgram's approach could achieve valid results. The "Behavioral Study of Obedience" was published in 1963 in the *Journal of Abnormal and Social Psychology.* In the next year, the *American Psychologist* published a critique of the experiment's ethics by psychologist Diana Baumrind (1964). Her critique begins with a rejection of the external validity—the generalizability—of the experiment. Because

> [T]he laboratory is unfamiliar as a setting and the rules of behavior ambiguous. . . . Therefore, the laboratory is not the place to study degree of obedience or suggestibility, as a function of a particular experimental condition.

> [And so,] the parallel between authority-subordinate relationships in Hitler's Germany and in Milgram's laboratory is unclear. (Baumrind, 1964, p. 423)

Stanley Milgram (1964) quickly published a rejoinder in which he disagreed with (among other things) the notion that it is inappropriate to study obedience in a laboratory setting: "A subject's obedience is no less problematical because it occurs within a social institution called the psychological experiment" (p. 850).

Milgram (1974) also pointed out that his experiment had been replicated in other places and settings with the same results, that there was considerable evidence that subjects had believed that they actually were administering shocks, and that the "essence" of his experimental manipulation—the request that subjects comply with a legitimate authority—was shared with the dilemma faced by people in Nazi Germany, soldiers at the My Lai massacre in Vietnam, and even cultists who drank poison in Jonestown, Guyana, at the command of their leader, Jim Jones (Miller, 1986).

Diana Baumrind (1985) was still not convinced. In a follow-up article in the *American Psychologist*, she argued that "Far from illuminating real life, as he claimed, Milgram in fact appeared to have constructed a set of conditions so internally inconsistent that they could not occur in real life" (p. 171).

Do you agree with Milgram's assumption that obedience could fruitfully be studied in the laboratory? Do you find merit in Baumrind's criticism? Will your evaluation of the ethics of Milgram's experiments be influenced by your answers to these questions? Should our standards differ when we judge the results of a study to provide valid information about important social psychological processes?

We can't answer these questions for you, but before you dismiss them as inappropriate when we are dealing with ethical standards for the treatment of human subjects, bear in mind that both Dr. Milgram and his strongest critic, Dr. Baumrind, buttressed their ethical arguments with assertions about the external validity (or invalidity) of the experimental results. It is hard to justify *any* risk for human subjects, or even *any* expenditure of time and resources, if our findings tell us nothing about human behavior.

Maintaining Professional Integrity (Principle C)

How can you assess the validity of an experiment or other research method? The scientific concern with validity requires in turn that scientists be open in disclosing their methods and honest in presenting their findings (APA Ethics Code). By contrast, research distorted by political or personal pressures to find particular outcomes or to achieve the most marketable results is unlikely to be carried out in an honest and open fashion. In order to assess the validity of a researcher's conclusions and the ethics of their procedures, you need to know exactly how the research was conducted. This means that articles or other reports must include a detailed methodology section, perhaps supplemented by appendices containing the research instruments or websites or other contact information where more information can be obtained.

Stanley Milgram's research exemplifies adherence to the goal of honesty and openness. His initial 1963 article included a detailed description of study procedures, including the text of the general introduction, the procedures involved in the learning task, "shock generator," administration of the "sample shock," the shock instructions and the preliminary practice run, the standardized feedback from the "victim" and from the experimenter, and the measures used. Many more details, including pictures, were provided in Milgram's (1974) subsequent book (**Exhibit 3.6**).

The act of publication itself is a vital element in maintaining openness and honesty. Others can review and question study procedures and so generate an open dialogue with the researcher. Although Milgram disagreed sharply with Diana Baumrind's criticisms of his experiments, their mutual commitment to

Exhibit 3.6   Diagram of Milgram Experiment

Student

Experimenter

Teacher

Source: Schutt, R. K. (2009). *Investigating the social world: The process and practice of research* (6th ed., p. 75). Thousand Oaks, CA: Pine Forge Press.

public discourse in journals widely available to psychologists resulted in more comprehensive presentation of study procedures and more thoughtful discourse about research ethics. Almost 50 years later, this commentary continues to inform debates about research ethics.

Openness about research procedures and results goes hand in hand with honesty in research design. Openness is also essential if researchers are to learn from the work of others. In spite of this need for openness, some researchers may hesitate to disclose their procedures or results to prevent others from building on their ideas and taking some of the credit. You may have heard of the long legal battle between a U.S. researcher, Dr. Robert Gallo, and a French researcher, Dr. Luc Montagnier, about how credit for discovering the AIDS virus should be allocated. Although a public dispute such as this one is unusual—even more unusual is its resolution through an agreement announced by then-President Ronald Reagan and then-Prime Minister Jacques Chirac (Altman, 1987)—concerns with priority of discovery are common. Scientists are like other people in their desire to be first. Enforcing standards of honesty and encouraging openness about research are the best solutions to these problems (as exemplified by the chronology of discovery that Gallo and Montagnier jointly developed as part of the agreement).

Protecting Research Participants (Principle A: Beneficence and Nonmaleficence)

Protection of research participants is the most important ethical principle, so you will probably not be surprised to learn that several specific ethical standards in the APA Code pertain to it. We will again focus attention on the obedience experiments, since the most serious charge leveled against the ethics of Milgram's study was that he had harmed his subjects. We will organize our discussion of the APA Standards in this area in four subcategories:

- Avoid harming research participants (Standard 3.04).
- Obtain informed consent (Standards 3.10, 8.02–8.06).
- Avoid deception in research, except in limited circumstances (Standards 8.07, 8.08).
- Maintain privacy and confidentiality (Standards 4.01–4.07).

Avoid Harming Research Participants

Although this standard may seem straightforward, it can be difficult to interpret in specific cases and harder yet to define in a way agreeable to all behavioral scientists. Does it mean that subjects should not be at all harmed psychologically as well as physically? That they should feel no anxiety or distress whatever during the study or only after their involvement ends? Should the possibility of any harm, no matter how remote, deter research?

Before we address these questions with respect to Milgram's experiments, a verbatim transcript of one session will give you an idea of what participants experienced (Milgram, 1965):

150 volts delivered. You want me to keep going?

165 volts delivered. That guy is hollering in there. There's a lot of them here. He's liable to have a heart condition. You want me to go on?

180 volts delivered. He can't stand it! I'm not going to kill that man in there! You hear him hollering? He's hollering. He can't stand it. . . . I mean who is going to take responsibility if anything happens to that gentleman?

[The experimenter accepts responsibility.] All right.

195 volts delivered. You see he's hollering. Hear that. Gee, I don't know. *[The experimenter says: "The experiment requires that you go on."]* I know it does, sir, but I mean—hugh—he don't know what he's in for. He's up to 195 volts.

210 volts delivered.

225 volts delivered.

240 volts delivered. (p. 67)

This experimental manipulation generated "extraordinary tension" (Milgram, 1963):

Subjects were observed to sweat, tremble, stutter, bite their lips, groan and dig their fingernails into their flesh. . . . . Full-blown, uncontrollable seizures were observed for 3 subjects. [O]ne . . . seizure so violently convulsive that it was necessary to call a halt to the experiment [for that individual]. (p. 375)

An observer (behind a one-way mirror) reported (Milgram, 1963), "I observed a mature and initially poised businessman enter the laboratory smiling and confident. Within 20 minutes he was reduced to a twitching, stuttering wreck, who was rapidly approaching a point of nervous collapse" (p. 377).

From critic Diana Baumrind's (1964) perspective, this emotional disturbance in subjects was "potentially harmful because it could easily effect an alteration in the subject's self-image or ability to trust adult authorities in the future" (p. 422). Stanley Milgram (1964) quickly countered that

[M]omentary excitement is not the same as harm. As the experiment progressed there was no indication of injurious effects in the subjects; and as the subjects themselves strongly endorsed the experiment, the judgment I made was to continue the experiment. (p. 849)

When Milgram (1964) surveyed subjects in a follow-up, 83.7% endorsed the statement that they were "very glad" or "glad" "to have been in the experiment," 15.1% were "neither sorry nor glad," and just 1.3% were "sorry" or "very sorry" to have participated. Interviews by a psychiatrist a year later found no evidence "of any traumatic reactions" (p. 197). Subsequently, Milgram (1977) argued that "the central moral justification for allowing my experiment is that it was judged acceptable by those who took part in it" (p. 21).

Milgram (1963) also attempted to minimize harm to subjects with postexperiment procedures "to assure that the subject would leave the laboratory in a state of well being" (p. 374). "A friendly reconciliation was arranged between the subject and the victim, and an effort was made to reduce any tensions that arose as a result of the experiment" (p. 374).

In some cases, the "dehoaxing" (or "**debriefing**") discussion was extensive, and all subjects were promised (and later received) a comprehensive report (Milgram, 1964). Professor Baumrind (1964) was unconvinced, writing, "It would be interesting to know what sort of procedures could dissipate the type of emotional disturbance just described" (p. 422; quoting Milgram, 1964).

In a later article, Baumrind (1985) dismissed the value of the self-reported "lack of harm" of subjects who had been willing to participate in the experiment—although noting that still 16% did *not* endorse the statement that they were "glad" they had participated in the experiment. Baumrind (1985) also argued that research indicates that most introductory psychology students who have participated in a deception experiment report a decreased trust in authorities as a result—a tangible harm in itself.

Many social scientists, ethicists, and others concluded that Milgram's procedures had not harmed subjects and so were justified for the knowledge they produced, but others sided with Baumrind's criticisms (Miller, 1986). What is your opinion at this point? Does Milgram's debriefing process relieve your concerns? Are you as persuaded by the subjects' own endorsement of the procedures as was Milgram?

What about possible harm to the subjects of **Zimbardo's prison simulation study** at Stanford University (Haney, Banks, & Zimbardo, 1973)? The study was designed to investigate the impact of social position on behavior—specifically, the impact of being either a guard or a prisoner in a prison, a "total institution." The researchers selected apparently stable and mature young male volunteers and asked them to sign a contract to work for 2 weeks as a guard or a prisoner in a simulated prison. Within the first 2 days after the prisoners were incarcerated by the guards in a makeshift basement prison, the prisoners began to be passive and disorganized, while the guards became sadistic—verbally and physically aggressive (Exhibit 3.7). Five prisoners were soon released for depression, uncontrollable crying, fits of rage, and, in one case, a psychosomatic rash. Instead of letting things continue for 2 weeks as planned, Zimbardo and his colleagues terminated the experiment after 6 days in order to avoid harming subjects.

Through discussions in special postexperiment encounter sessions, feelings of stress among the participants who played the role of prisoner seemed to be

Exhibit 3.7 Chart of Guard and Prisoner Behavior

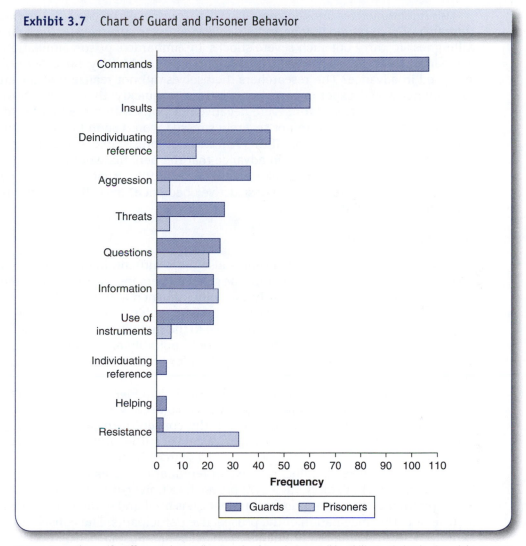

relieved; follow-up during the next year indicated no lasting negative effects on the participants and some benefits in the form of greater insight.

Would you ban such experiments because of the potential for harm to subjects? Does the fact that Zimbardo's and Milgram's experiments seemed to yield significant insights into the effect of a social situation on human behavior—insights that could be used to improve prisons or perhaps lessen the likelihood of another Holocaust—make any difference (Reynolds, 1979)? Do you believe that this benefit outweighs the foreseeable risks?

Well-intentioned researchers may also fail to foresee all the potential problems. Milgram (1974) reported that he and his colleagues were surprised by the subjects' willingness to carry out such severe shocks. In Zimbardo's prison simulation, all the participants signed consent forms, but how could they have been fully informed in advance? The researchers themselves did not realize that the study participants would experience so much stress so quickly, that some prisoners would have to be released for severe negative reactions within the first few days, or that even those who were not severely stressed would soon be begging to be released from the mock prison. If this risk was not foreseeable, was it acceptable for the researchers to presume in advance that the benefits would outweigh the risks? And are you concerned, like Arthur Miller (1986), that real harm "could result from *not doing* research on destructive obedience" (p. 138) and other troubling human behaviors?

Obtain Informed Consent

The requirement of informed consent is also more difficult to define than it first appears. To be informed, consent must be given by persons who are competent to consent, have consented voluntarily, are fully informed about the research, and have comprehended what they have been told (Reynolds, 1979). Yet you probably realize, like Diana Baumrind (1985), that due to the inability to communicate perfectly, "Full disclosure of everything that could possibly affect a given subject's decision to participate is not possible, and therefore cannot be ethically required" (p. 165).

Obtaining informed consent creates additional challenges for researchers. The researcher's actions and body language should help to convey his verbal assurance that consent is voluntary. The language of the consent form must be clear and understandable to the research participants and yet sufficiently long and detailed to explain what will actually happen in the research. Exhibits 3.8 and 3.9, from the authors' own research, illustrate two different approaches to these tradeoffs. The consent form in Exhibit 3.8 was approved by a university for a social psychology experiment with undergraduate students. It is brief and to the point but leaves quite a bit to the imagination of the prospective participants. The consent form in Exhibit 3.9 reflects the requirements of an academic hospital's IRB. Because the hospital is used to reviewing research proposals involving drugs and other treatment interventions with hospital patients, it requires a very detailed and lengthy explanation of procedures and related issues, even for a simple survey. You can probably imagine that the requirement that prospective participants sign such lengthy consent forms can reduce their willingness to participate in research and perhaps influence their responses if they do agree to participate (Larson, 1993).

As in Milgram's study, experimental researchers whose research design requires some type of subject deception try to get around this problem by withholding some information before the experiment begins but then debriefing subjects at the end. In the debriefing, the researcher explains to the subject what happened in the experiment and why and responds to questions. A carefully designed debriefing procedure can help research participants learn from the experimental research

Exhibit 3.8   UMB Consent Form

University of Massachusetts at Boston

Department of Psychology

100 Morrissey Boulevard

Boston, MA 02125-3393

Consent Form for the Project: "Examining Gaze Evoked Inhibition of Return and Its Implications for Social Communication"

Introduction and Contact Information

You have been asked to take part in a research project as described below. The researcher will explain the project to you in detail. You should feel free to ask questions. If you have further questions later, Paul Nestor, the person mainly responsible for this study, will discuss them with you. His telephone number is 617-287-6387.

Description of the Project

You have been asked to take part in a research study on eye gaze. This research seeks to improve our understanding of gaze processing as a key component underlying social communication, which will provide researchers with a better understanding of how problems associated with gaze processing are relevant for certain disorders, including schizophrenia and autism. The results of this study will be especially beneficial to the fields of psychology, medicine, and computer vision.

If you decide to take part in this research study, here is what will happen:

You will first fill out a few questionnaires that will ask you some background questions about yourself and also some questions about your thinking and beliefs. Then, you will sit in front of a computer screen, and the experimenter will mount the headset of an eye tracker device on your head. This device will determine your gaze position throughout the experiment. Prior to the experiment, a calibration procedure will be performed in order to maximize the system's precision of measurement. In this procedure, a dot will appear at nine different positions on the screen. You will be asked to track that dot, that is, to keep looking at it wherever it appears.

Afterwards, there will be a number of experimental trials. Before each trial, the experimenter will verbally explain to you the task that you have to complete. The tasks will require you to respond to a target either by pressing a button on a joystick or by shifting your eyes to the target. Your button press or eye movement will indicate your response. The first few trials will be practice trials that allow you to familiarize yourself with the interface. In the subsequent trials, you will be asked to perform as quickly and accurately as possible. The time from completing the questionnaires to the completion of the experiment will be approximately one hour and a half.

After the experiment, the experimenter will ask you some questions about your experience with the interface. She will ask you about the difficulty of each task and what you liked or disliked about it.

Risks or Discomforts

The equipment is not harmful to the eyes. It may happen that you feel discomfort after wearing the headset for some time. In that case, you should inform the experimenter, who will remove the headset immediately. After a break of a few minutes you can decide whether you want to continue your participation or quit the experiment.

(Continued)

Exhibit 3.8 (Continued)

By participating in this study, you will be part of the scientific effort to understand the importance of eye gaze processing in social communication. You will actively participate in the ongoing research by performing in the experimental tasks and delivering your feedback. Moreover, you will receive $10 for your participation.

Confidentiality

All information you provide throughout your assessment is confidential. None of the information will identify you by name. All information will be given a code number, and access to the data will be limited to the research team. The data will be stored in a locked file and destroyed after the research has been concluded.

Participation and Rights

The decision whether or not to take part in this research study is voluntary on your part. You do not have to participate. If you do decide to take part in this study, you may terminate your participation at any time. If you wish to terminate your participation in the research study, you simply inform Kristy Klein (617-319-7056) of your decision. Whatever you decide will in no way penalize you or affect your grade or status as a student.

You may also write or call a representative of the Institutional Review Board (IRB), at the University of Massachusetts at Boston, which oversees research involving human subjects. The Institutional Review Board may be reached at the following address: IRB, Office of Research and Sponsored Programs, Quinn Administration Building-2-015, University of Massachusetts at Boston, 100 Morrissey Boulevard, Boston, MA 02125-3393. You can contact the Board by telephone at (617) 287-5370 or at human.subjects@umb.edu.

I HAVE READ THE CONSENT FORM. MY QUESTIONS HAVE BEEN ANSWERED. MY SIGNATURE ON THIS FORM MEANS THAT I UNDERSTAND THE INFORMATION AND I CONSENT TO PARTICIPATE IN THIS STUDY. I ALSO CERTIFY THAT I AM 18 YEARS OF AGE OR OLDER.

_____   _____   _____

  Signature of Participant   Date   Signature of Researcher

_____   _____

  Printed Name of Participant   Printed Name of Researcher

Source: Schutt, R. K. (2009). *Investigating the social world: The process and practice of research* (6th ed., p. 81). Thousand Oaks, CA: Pine Forge Press.

and grapple constructively with feelings elicited by the realization that they were deceived (Sieber, 1992). However, even though debriefing can be viewed as a substitute, in some cases, for securing fully informed consent prior to the experiment, debriefed subjects who disclose the nature of the experiment to other participants can contaminate subsequent results (Adair, Dushenko, & Lindsay, 1985). Unfortunately, if the debriefing process is delayed, the ability to lessen any harm resulting from the deception is also reduced.

For a study of the social background of men who engage in homosexual behavior in public facilities, Laud Humphreys (1970) decided that truly informed consent would be impossible to obtain. Instead, he first served as a lookout—a

Exhibit 3.9 BIDMC Consent Form

**Research Consent Form for Social and
Behavioral Research**

Dana-Farber/Harvard Cancer Center

BIDMC/BWH/CH/DFCI/MGH/Partners Network Affiliates   OPRS 11-05

Protocol Title: <u>ASSESSING COMMUNITY HEALTH WORKERS' ATTITUDES AND KNOWLEDGE ABOUT
EDUCATING COMMUNITIES ABOUT CANCER CLINICAL TRIALS</u>

DF/HCC Principal Research Investigator / Institution: Dr. Russell Schutt, Ph.D. / Beth Israel
Deaconess Medical Center and Univ. of Massachusetts, Boston

DF/HCC Site-Responsible Research Investigator(s) / Institution(s):

Lidia Schapira, M.D. / Massachusetts General Hospital

Interview Consent Form

A. INTRODUCTION

We are inviting you to take part in a research study. Research is a way of gaining new knowledge.

A person who participates in a research study is called a "subject." This research study is evaluating whether community health workers might be willing and able to educate communities about the pros and cons of participating in research studies.

It is expected that about 10 people will take part in this research study.

An institution that is supporting a research study either by giving money or supplying something that is important for the research is called the "sponsor." The sponsor of this protocol is National Cancer Institute and is providing money for the research study.

This research consent form explains why this research study is being done, what is involved in participating in the research study, the possible risks and benefits of the research study, alternatives to participation, and your rights as a research subject. The decision to participate is yours. If you decide to participate, please sign and date at the end of the form. We will give you a copy so that you can refer to it while you are involved in this research study.

If you decide to participate in this research study, certain questions will be asked of you to see if you are eligible to be in the research study. The research study has certain requirements that must be met. If the questions show that you can be in the research study, you will be able to answer the interview questions.

If the questions show that you cannot be in the research study, you will not be able to participate in this research study.

Page 1 of 6

DFCI Protocol Number:	06-085	Date DFCI IRB Approved this Consent Form:	January 16, 2007
Date Posted for Use:	January 16, 2007	Date DFCI IRB Approval Expires:	August 13, 2007

(Continued)

Exhibit 3.9 (Continued)

**Research Consent Form for Social and
Behavioral Research**

Dana-Farber/Harvard Cancer Center

BIDMC/BWH/CH/DFCI/MGH/Partners Network Affiliates   OPRS 11-05

We encourage you to take some time to think this over and to discuss it with other people and to ask questions now and at any time in the future.

B. <u>WHY IS THIS RESEARCH STUDY BEING DONE?</u>

Deaths from cancer in general and for some specific cancers are higher for black people compared to white people, for poor persons compared to nonpoor persons, and for rural residents compared to non-rural residents. There are many reasons for higher death rates between different subpopulations. One important area for changing this is to have more persons from minority groups particpate in research about cancer. The process of enrolling minority populations into clinical trials is difficult and does not generally address the needs of their communities. One potential way to increase particpation in research is to use community health workers to help educate communities about research and about how to make sure that researchers are ethical. We want to know whether community health workers think this is a good strategy and how to best carry it out.

C. <u>WHAT OTHER OPTIONS ARE THERE?</u>

Taking part in this research study is voluntary. Instead of being in this research study, you have the following option:

- Decide not to participate in this research study.

D. <u>WHAT IS INVOLVED IN THE RESEARCH STUDY?</u>

<u>Before the research starts (screening):</u> After signing this consent form, you will be asked to answer some questions about where you work and the type of community health work you do to find out if you can be in the research study.

 If the answers show that you are eligible to participate in the research study, you will be eligible to participate in the research study. If you do not meet the eligibility criteria, you will not be able to participate in this research study.

<u>After the screening procedures confirm that you are eligible to participate in the research study:</u>
You will participate in an interview by answering questions from a questionnaire. The interview will take about 90 minutes. If there are questions you prefer not to answer we can skip those questions. The questions are about the type of work you do and your opinions about participating in research. If you agree, the interview will be taped and then transcribed. Your name and no other information about you will be associated

Page 2 of 6

DFCI Protocol Number:	06-085	Date DFCI IRB Approved this Consent Form:	January 16, 2007
Date Posted for Use:	January 16, 2007	Date DFCI IRB Approval Expires:	August 13, 2007

Research Consent Form for Social and Behavioral Research

Dana-Farber/Harvard Cancer Center

BIDMC/BWH/CH/DFCI/MGH/Partners Network Affiliates   OPRS 11-05

with the tape or the transcript. Only the research team will be able to listen to the tapes. Immediately following the interview, you will have the opportunity to have the tape erased if you wish to withdraw your consent to taping or participation in this study. You will receive $30.00 for completing this interview.

After the interview is completed: Once you finish the interview there are no additional interventions.

...

N. DOCUMENTATION OF CONSENT

My signature below indicates my willingness to participate in this research study and my understanding that I can withdraw at any time.

_____   _____
Signature of Subject   Date
or Legally Authorized Representative

_____   _____
Person obtaining consent   Date

To be completed by person obtaining consent:

The consent discussion was initiated on _____ (date) at _____ (time.)

☐ A copy of this signed consent form was given to the subject or legally authorized representative.

For Adult Subjects

☐ The subject is an adult and provided consent to participate.

☐ The subject is an adult who lacks capacity to provide consent and his/her legally authorized representative:

   ☐ gave permission for the adult subject to participate

   ☐ did not give permission for the adult subject to participate

Page 6 of 6

| DFCI Protocol Number: | 06-085 | Date DFCI IRB Approved this Consent Form: | January 16, 2007 |
| Date Posted for Use: | January 16, 2007 | Date DFCI IRB Approval Expires: | August 13, 2007 |

"watch queen"—for men who were entering a public bathroom in a city park with the intention of having sex. In a number of cases, he then left the bathroom and copied the license plate numbers of the cars driven by the men. One year later, he visited the homes of the men and interviewed them as part of a larger study of social issues. Humphreys changed his appearance so that the men did not recognize him. In *Tearoom Trade* (1970), his book on this research, Humphreys concluded that the men who engaged in what were viewed as deviant acts were, for the most part, married, suburban men whose families were unaware of their sexual practices. But debate has continued ever since about Humphreys' failure to tell the men what he was really doing in the bathroom or why he had come to their homes for the interview. He was criticized by many, including some faculty members at the University of Washington who urged that his doctoral degree be withheld. However, many other professors and some members of the gay community praised Humphreys for helping to normalize conceptions of homosexuality (Miller, 1986).

If you were to serve on your university's IRB, would you allow this research to be conducted? Can students who are asked to participate in research by their professor be considered to be able to give informed consent? Do you consider "informed consent" to be meaningful if the true purpose or nature of an experimental manipulation is not revealed?

The process and even possibility of obtaining informed consent must take into account the capacity of prospective participants to give informed consent. Children cannot legally give consent to participate in research; instead, they must in most circumstances be given the opportunity to give or withhold their *assent* to participate in research, usually by a verbal response to an explanation of the research. In addition, a child's legal guardian must give written informed consent to have the child participate in research (Sieber, 1992). There are also special protections for other populations that are likely to be vulnerable to coercion—prisoners, pregnant women, mentally disabled persons, and educationally or economically disadvantaged persons. Would you allow research on prisoners, whose ability to give informed consent can be questioned? What special protections do you think would be appropriate?

Avoid Deception in Research, Except in Limited Circumstances

Deception occurs when subjects are misled about research procedures to determine how they would react to the treatment if they were not research subjects. Deception is a critical component of many psychological experiments, in part because of the difficulty of simulating real world stresses and dilemmas in a laboratory setting. The goal is to get subjects "to accept as true what is false or to give a false impression" (Korn, 1997, p. 4). In Milgram's (1964) experiment, for example, deception seemed necessary because the subjects could not be permitted to administer real electric shocks to the "stooge," yet it would not have made sense to order the subjects to do something that they didn't find to be so troubling. Milgram (1992) insisted that the deception was absolutely essential. The results of many other psychological and social psychological experiments would be worthless if subjects understood what was really happening to them while the experiment was in progress. The real question: Is this sufficient justification to allow the use of deception?

Gary Marshall and Philip Zimbardo (1979) sought to determine the physiological basis of emotion by injecting student volunteers with adrenaline so that their heart rate and sweating would increase and then placing them in a room with a student "stooge" who acted silly. But the students were told that they were being injected with a vitamin supplement in order to test its effect on visual acuity (Korn, 1997). Piliavin and Piliavin (1972) staged fake seizures on subway trains in order to study helpfulness (Korn, 1997). Would you vote to allow such deceptive practices in research if you were a member of your university's IRB? What about less dramatic instances of deception in laboratory experiments with psychology students like yourself?

Do you believe that deception itself is the problem? Aronson and Mills's (1959) study of severity of initiation to groups is a good example of experimental research that does not pose greater-than-everyday risks to subjects but still uses deception. This study was conducted at an all-women's college in the 1950s. The student volunteers who were randomly assigned to the "severe initiation" experimental condition had to read a list of embarrassing words. We think it's fair to say that even in the 1950s, reading a list of potentially embarrassing words in a laboratory setting and listening to a taped discussion are unlikely to increase the risks to which students are exposed in their everyday lives. Moreover, the researchers informed subjects that they would be expected to talk about sex and could decline to participate in the experiment if this requirement would bother them. None dropped out.

To further ensure that no psychological harm was caused, Aronson and Mills (1959) explained the true nature of the experiment to subjects after the experiment. The subjects did not seem perturbed: "None of the Ss expressed any resentment or annoyance at having been misled. In fact, the majority were intrigued by the experiment, and several returned at the end of the academic quarter to ascertain the result" (p. 179).

Are you satisfied that this procedure caused no harm? Do you react differently to the **debriefing** by Aronson and Mills than you did to Milgram's debriefing? The minimal deception in the Aronson and Mills experiment, coupled with the lack of any ascertainable risk to subjects and a debriefing, satisfies the ethical standards for research of most psychologists and IRBs, even today.

What scientific or educational or applied value would make deception justifiable, even if there is some potential for harm? Who determines whether a non-deceptive intervention is "equally effective"? Diana Baumrind (Miller, 1986) suggested that personal "introspection" would have been sufficient to test Milgram's hypothesis and has argued subsequently that intentional deception in research violates the ethical principles of self-determination, protection of others, and maintenance of trust between people and so can never be justified (Baumrind, 1985). How much risk, discomfort, or unpleasantness might be seen as affecting willingness to participate? When should a postexperimental "attempt to correct any misconception" due to deception be deemed sufficient? Can you see why an institutional review board, representing a range of perspectives, is an important tool for making reasonable, ethical research decisions when confronted with such ambiguity?

Maintain Privacy and Confidentiality

Maintaining privacy and confidentiality is another key ethical standard for protecting research participants, and the researcher's commitment to that standard should be included in the informed consent agreement (Sieber, 1992). Procedures to protect each subject's privacy such as locking records and creating special identifying codes must be created to minimize the risk of access by unauthorized persons. However, statements about confidentiality should be realistic: Laws allow research records to be subpoenaed and may require reporting child abuse; a researcher may feel compelled to release information if a health- or life-threatening situation arises and participants need to be alerted. Also, the standard of confidentiality does not apply to observation in public places and information available in public records.

There is one exception to some of these constraints: the National Institutes of Health can issue a "Certificate of Confidentiality" to protect researchers from being legally required to disclose confidential information. Researchers who are focusing on high-risk populations or behaviors, such as crime, substance abuse, sexual activity, or genetic information, can request such a certificate. Suspicions of child abuse or neglect must still be reported, and in some states researchers may still be required to report such crimes as elder abuse (Arwood & Panicker, 2007).

The Health Insurance Portability and Accountability Act (HIPAA) passed by Congress in 1996 created much more stringent regulations for the protection of health care data. As implemented by the U.S. Department of Health and Human Services in 2000 (and revised in 2002), the HIPAA Final Privacy Rule applies to oral, written and electronic information that "relates to the past, present or future physical or mental health or condition of an individual" (Cava, Cushman, & Goodman, 2007, n.p.). The HIPAA Rule requires that researchers have valid authorization for any use or disclosure of "protected health information" (PHI) from a health care provider. Waivers of authorization can be granted in special circumstances (Cava, Cushman, & Goodman, 2007).

Encouraging Appropriate Application
(Principle D: Justice; Principle E: Respect for People's Rights)

Scientists must also consider the uses to which their research is put. Although many scientists believe that personal values should be left outside the laboratory, some feel that it is proper—even necessary—for scientists to concern themselves with the way their research is used.

Stanley Milgram made it clear that he was concerned about the phenomenon of obedience precisely because of its implications for people's welfare. As you have already learned, his first article (Milgram, 1963) highlighted the atrocities committed under the Nazis by citizens and soldiers who were "just following orders." In his more comprehensive book on the obedience experiments (Milgram, 1974), he also used his findings to shed light on the atrocities committed in the Vietnam War at My Lai, slavery, the destruction of the American Indian population, and the internment of Japanese Americans during World War II. Milgram makes no explicit attempt to "tell us what to do" about this problem. In fact, as a dispassionate psychological researcher, Milgram (1974) tells us, "What the present study [did was] to give the dilemma [of obedience to authority] contemporary form by treating it as subject matter for experimental inquiry, and with the aim of understanding rather than judging it from a moral standpoint" (p. xi).

Yet it is impossible to ignore the very practical implications of Milgram's investigations, which Milgram took pains to emphasize. His research highlighted the extent of obedience to authority and identified multiple factors that could be manipulated to lessen blind obedience (such as encouraging dissent by just one group member, removing the subject from direct contact with the authority figure, increasing the contact between the subject and the victim).

A widely publicized experiment on the police response to domestic violence provides an interesting cautionary tale about the uses of science. Lawrence Sherman and Richard Berk (1984) arranged with the Minneapolis police department for the random assignment of persons accused of domestic violence to be either arrested or simply given a warning. The results of this field experiment indicated that those who were arrested were less likely subsequently to commit violent acts against their partners. Sherman (1993) explicitly cautioned police departments not to adopt mandatory arrest policies based solely on the results of the Minneapolis experiment, but the results were publicized in the mass media and encouraged many jurisdictions to change their policies (Binder & Meeker, 1993; Lempert, 1989). Although we now know that the original finding of a deterrent effect of arrest did not hold up in many other cities where the experiment was repeated, Sherman (1992) later suggested that implementing mandatory arrest policies might have prevented some subsequent cases of spouse abuse (pp. 150–153). In particular, in a follow-up study in Omaha, arrest warrants reduced repeat offenses among spouse abusers who had already left the scene when police arrived. However, this Omaha finding was not publicized, so it could not be used to improve police policies. So how much publicity is warranted and at what point in the research should it occur?

Social scientists who conduct research on behalf of specific organizations may face additional difficulties when the organization, instead of the researcher, controls the final report and the publicity it receives. If organizational leaders decide that particular research results are unwelcome, the researcher's desire to have findings used appropriately and reported fully can conflict with contractual obligations. Researchers can often anticipate such dilemmas in advance and resolve them when the contract for research is negotiated—or simply decline a particular research opportunity altogether. But often, such problems come up only after a report has been drafted, or the problems are ignored by a researcher who needs to have a job or needs to maintain particular personal relationships. These possibilities cannot be avoided entirely, but because of them, it is always important to acknowledge the source of research funding in reports and to consider carefully the sources of funding for research reports written by others.

CONCLUSIONS

The extent to which ethical issues are a problem for researchers and their subjects varies dramatically with the type of research design. Much survey research, in particular, creates few ethical problems. In fact, researchers from Michigan's Institute for Survey Research interviewed a representative national sample of adults and found that 68% of those who had participated in a survey were somewhat or very interested in participating in another; the more times respondents had been interviewed, the more willing they were to participate again. Presumably they would have felt differently if they had been treated unethically (Reynolds, 1979). On the other hand, some experimental studies in the social sciences that have put people in uncomfortable or embarrassing situations have generated vociferous complaints and years of debate about ethics (Reynolds, 1979; Sjoberg, 1967), although you now know that most of the subjects of those experiments are not among those voicing concern (Milgram, 1974).

The evaluation of ethical issues in a research project should be based on a realistic assessment of the overall potential for harm and benefit to research subjects rather than just an apparent inconsistency between any particular aspect of a research plan and a specific ethical guideline. For example, full disclosure of "what is really going on" in an experimental study is unnecessary if subjects are unlikely to be harmed. The requirement that subjects give signed, informed consent to participate in research can be waived when their participation is anonymous and the research procedures do not involve any increase in risk beyond what they normally experience. In order to make such realistic and balanced assessments, researchers must make every effort to foresee all possible risks and to weigh the possible benefits of the research against these risks. They should consult with individuals having different perspectives to develop a realistic risk/benefit assessment, and they should try to maximize the benefits to, as well as minimize the risks for, potential research subjects (Sieber, 1992).

Ultimately, these decisions about ethical procedures are not just up to you, as a researcher, to make. Your university's IRB sets the human subjects protection standards for your institution and will require that researchers—even, in most cases, students—submit their research proposal to the IRB for review. So we leave you with the instruction to review the APA guidelines, consult your university's procedures for the conduct of research with human subjects, and then proceed accordingly.

END OF CHAPTER

Chapter Highlights

- Stanley Milgram's obedience experiments led to intensive debate about the extent to which deception could be tolerated in psychological research and how harm to subjects should be evaluated.

- Egregious violations of human rights by researchers, including scientists in Nazi Germany and researchers in the Tuskegee syphilis study, led to adoption of federal ethical standards for research on human subjects.

- The 1979 Belmont Report developed by a national commission established three basic ethical standards for the protection of human subjects: respect for persons, beneficence, and justice.

- The Department of Health and Human Services adopted in 1991 a Federal Policy for the Protection of Human Subjects. This policy requires that every institution seeking federal funding for biomedical or behavioral research on human subjects have an institutional review board to exercise oversight.

- The APA's most recent Ethics Code was adopted in 2002. It contains 151 enforceable Ethical Standards and five General Principles.

- The APA's standards for the protection of human subjects require avoiding harm, obtaining informed consent, avoiding deception except in limited circumstances, and maintaining privacy and confidentiality.

- Scientific research should maintain high standards for validity and be conducted and reported in an honest and open fashion.

- Effective debriefing of research participants after an experiment can help to reduce the risk of harm due to the use of deception in the experiment.

Key Terms

Belmont Report   69

Beneficence   69

Certificate of Confidentiality   88

Code of Conduct, American Psychological Association   68

Debriefing   78

Federal Policy for the Protection of Human Subjects   69

Health Insurance Portability and Accountability Act (HIPAA)   88

Institutional review board (IRB)   70

Justice   69

Nuremberg War Crime Trials   69

Obedience experiments by Stanley Milgram   67

Research in the News

"You need subjects and they're hard to get." Developmental psychologist Deborah Linebarger (Belluck, 2009, p. 1) made this statement in an article about scientists who use their own children in their research. Since Jonas Salk injected his children with polio vaccine, researcher/parents have studied their children's response to tickling, tested their children's cognition, scanned their brains, and recorded their children's every verbal utterance and visible behavior. But Robert M. Nelson (Belluck, 2009, p. 1) at Philadelphia's Children's Hospital Center for Research Integrity is troubled. "The role of the parent is to protect the child. Once that parent becomes an investigator, it sets up an immediate potential conflict of interest." Even Dr. Linebarger acknowledges that, "When you mix being a researcher with being a parent, it can put your kids in an unfair place" (Belluck, 2009, p. 1). What is your opinion? What are the advantages and disadvantages to researchers of using their own children as research participants? What are the advantages and disadvantages to their children? Do you think that this approach to research is good for science?

Activity Questions

1. Should psychologists be permitted to conduct replications of Milgram's obedience experiments? Zimbardo's prison simulation? Can you justify such research as permissible within the current APA ethical standards? If not, do you believe these standards should be altered so as to permit Milgram-type research?

2. How do you evaluate the current APA ethical code? Is it too strict or too lenient, or just about right? Are the enforcement provisions adequate? What provisions could be strengthened?

3. Does debriefing solve the problem of subject deception? How much must researchers reveal after the experiment is over as well as before it begins?

4. Investigate the standards and operations of your university's IRB. Interview one IRB member and one researcher whose research has been reviewed by the IRB (after receiving the appropriate permissions!). How well do typical IRB meetings work to identify the ethical issues in proposed research? Do researchers feel that their proposals are treated fairly? Why or why not?

5. The Collaborative Institutional Training Initiative (CITI) offers an extensive online training course in the basics of human subjects protections issues. Go the public access CITI site at https://www.citiprogram.org/rcrpage.asp?affiliation=100 and

complete the course in social and behavioral research. Write a short summary of what you have learned.

6. Read the entire APA Ethics Code at the website of the APA Ethics Office, http://www .apa.org/ethics/homepage.html. Discuss the difference between the aspirational standards and the enforceable standards.

Review Questions

1. Describe the history of egregious violations of human rights in the United States that prompted the creation of a National Commission for the Protection of Human Subjects of Biomedical and Behavioral Research.

2. Describe the three basic ethical principles for the protection of human subjects established in the 1979 Belmont Report (Department of Health, Education, and Welfare, 1979).

3. How did the Belmont Report set the stage for the 1991 Federal Policy for the Protection of Human Subjects and the creation of institutional review boards?

4. What were the major ethical issues raised by the *Tearoom Trade* study?

5. Why would an ethicist dismiss as irrelevant reports that research subjects were unharmed by partaking in the Milgram study?

6. What should a researcher do to insure that participants are truly informed?

7. Under what circumstances, if any, is deception in research ever justified?

8. Describe a thoughtful and comprehensive debriefing. What is the objective? What should you do if a participant becomes upset with the study? What are the pros and cons of debriefing subjects immediately following their participation or waiting until the completion of data collection?

9. Compare and contrast the ethical violations in the Milgram study with those of the Zimbardo prison simulation study.

10. What is a Certificate of Confidentiality? How and why might a researcher request it and who would issue it?

11. What are the safeguards a researcher must put in place to protect confidentiality and privacy of research participants?

Ethics in Action

Now that we have formally introduced the critical topic of ethics in research, we begin a new exercise that is intended to highlight fascinating yet all too common ethical dilemmas and challenges in science.

The April 21, 2010, *New York Times* article by Amy Harmon titled "Tribe Wins Fight to Limit Research of Its DNA" reverberates with ethical and cultural ramifications for all researchers to take to heart. The article states that beginning in 1990, researchers from Arizona State had enrolled members of the Havasupai Indians of the Grand Canyon as participants in studies that they hoped might reveal genetic clues to the tribe's devastating rate of diabetes.

> But they learned that their blood samples had been used to study many other things, including mental illness and theories of the tribe's geographical origins that contradict their traditional stories. The geneticist responsible for the research has said that she had obtained permission for wider-range genetic studies. Acknowledging a desire to "remedy the wrong that was done," the university's Board of Regents . . . agreed to pay $700,000 to the 41 of the tribe's members, return the blood samples and provide other forms of assistance to the impoverished Havasupai—a settlement that legal experts said was significant because it implied that *the rights of research subjects can be violated when they are not fully informed about how their DNA might be used.* (Italics added for emphasis; n.p.)

As you can see, this case raises substantial ethical issues. First and foremost is the question of informed consent. How would you improve the informed consent form for these studies? Dr. Markow, the geneticist and principal investigator of the studies, described in the article as defending her actions as ethical, is quoted as saying, "I was doing good science" (n.p.). Tribal council member Carletta Tilousi countered, "I'm not against scientific research. I just want it to be done right. They used our blood for all these studies, people got degrees and grants, and they never asked our permission" (n.p.).

What do you think about these two different positions and opinions? How might these issues of misuse of data apply to psychological research? The case also underscores the ethical obligation, emphasized in the APA Ethics Code, for psychological researchers to exercise cultural sensitivity in their work. For example, many members of the tribe expressed concern that they had unknowingly participated in research that could potentially damage the tribe, perhaps calling into question sacred cultural beliefs and even sovereign rights to tribal land. How might a researcher become culturally sensitive in working with ethnic and racial minorities?

C H A P T E R   4

Conceptualization and Measurement

MEASURING MENTAL HEALTH AND MENTAL ILLNESS

Have you ever thought about what it means to be mentally healthy? If you go to the research literature for some clues, you will most likely come away thinking that to be mentally healthy means you do not have a diagnosable mental disorder or mental disability. But you might think otherwise. Mental health, you may propose, is not simply the absence of mental illness but something much more positive. You might imagine a mentally healthy person as happy, thriving, and flourishing in life. You might think of mental health and mental illness as two separate categories, characteristics, or features to describe people. Curious, you play around with these ideas and you come up with an analogy that grabs you. You reason: Height and weight are two distinct physical features of people, and perhaps mental health and mental illness are two distinct psychological features of people. Your task, as you see it, is to understand the meaning of mental health. What are the characteristics of a mentally healthy person? Can a subset of people be identified who show optimal mental health and who might be classified as flourishing? What percent of U.S. adults might be classified as flourishing? Is complete mental health more than the absence of mental illness?

DEVELOPING AND DEFINING CONSTRUCTS

Excited by these questions, you start to think more formally about how to cast your ideas into a psychological theory. A psychological theory is important because it will provide a conceptual framework for your study. It specifies the conceptual meaning of key terms and it identifies how variables are to be measured or operationalized. It explains the rationale for the importance of particular concepts that are under study and why particular variables and their measurements are chosen. In short, a conceptual framework can be thought of as a network of interlocking relationships linking theoretical ideas to concrete variables and their measurements. Notice that this is a purely abstract process enacted in the workings of your mind as you transform your rather inchoate ideas into a clearly defined theory.

Theoretical Constructs

A theory unites concepts with their corresponding variables and their distinct forms of measurements. It does so by translating abstract concepts into particular calculable variables, each of which will include a form of objective measurement. In a scientific theory, abstract concepts are formally referred to as constructs. A **construct** is specified in a theory in order to describe, explain, and predict a wide range of related empirical findings. Constructs that are studied in psychology, such as intelligence, personality, memory, anxiety, or attention, are not directly observable material entities. Nor is a breadth and depth of a construct fully captured by any a single referent, indicator, or variable. Rather, a construct encompasses several referents or indicators, which are cast as variables that in turn can be measured by collecting data from multiple instruments, such as physiological recordings, objective pencil-and-paper tests, and behavior rating scales. As we will learn later in the chapter, the quality of a construct depends greatly on the extent to which data collected from its multiple indicators cohere into consistent and logical patterns of relationships.

Operational Definitions of Constructs

A construct needs to be translated into an *operational definition*. An operational definition, as you recall, provides a recipe for specifying variables that are to be used to measure a construct. For example, the construct of anxiety can be operationalized in the form of three distinct variables—measures of psychophysiology, observational ratings, and self-report. These represent three different *dependent variables* of the same construct, anxiety. An operational definition of a construct is, however, not limited to specifying how to measure it. Rather, in laboratory studies, an operational definition spells out the conditions under which the construct is expected to occur. That is, an operational definition identifies the *independent variables* that are expected to produce the construct.

Consider, for example, a laboratory study by Bushman and Baumeister (1998) aimed at investigating conditions that produce interpersonal violence. Here interpersonal violence represents the construct under investigation. The researchers first devised a laboratory task that is intended to simulate conditions under which interpersonal violence is theorized to occur. What can they *ethically* have research participants do that will make them respond violently to another person? What laboratory task would approximate conditions that lead to interpersonal violence in the real world? Likewise, what dependent variable could be used to measure the effect of a laboratory task on interpersonal violence? Recall from Chapter 2, researchers are always worried that their experiments might be too unrealistic, too contrived, or too clever so that their studies lack any application to real life. Recall that the extent to which a study or experiment approximates the actual real-life phenomenon under investigation refers to *ecological validity*. Experimenters aim to design ecologically valid studies.

The study began with an ordinary task in which research participants wrote brief essays expressing their opinions on abortion that they thought would be critically evaluated by another participant. The researchers in reality randomly marked the essays as good ("No suggestions. Great essay!") or bad ("This is one of the worst essays I have ever read!"). Next the participants competed in a reaction-time test against the person they believed had marked their essays. The researchers rigged the game so that all participants, regardless of whether they had been either insulted or praised, always won. When they won, the research participants were told that they could blast their opponent with a loud noise with the decibel level set by them. However, reminiscent of the Milgram study (see Chapter 3), there was no actual opponent and no one actually received the blast. Researchers recorded the exact decibel level the participants blasted their fictitious opponent as the dependent measure of interpersonal violence.

Bushman and Baumeister (1998) used what is referred to as a *staged manipulation* (see Chapter 6) that they hoped would mimic or approximate in the laboratory conditions that lead to interpersonal violence in the real world. As a staged manipulation, the essay writing exercise served as a ruse to insult and anger at least half of the research participants randomly assigned to that study condition. Continuing with the deception, the researchers had participants play a competitive reaction-time game rigged so that they always won. Completing the subterfuge, Bushman and Baumeister told the insulted participants as well as the praised participants that their game opponent had been the grader of their exam. For these researchers, the critical question hung in the balance: Could these contrived conditions actually produce differences between insulted versus praised groups? Would insulted participants differ from praised participants in delivering loud noises to their opponents who they believed had earlier graded their essays? The premise was straightforward: Insulted parties would respond aggressively in a competitive game against an opponent they believed had offended them earlier.

Notice how closely tied a theoretical construct is to its independent and dependent variables. Here the theoretical construct of interpersonal violence was put into its operational form when participants were randomly assigned to the study condition in which their essays received the worst grades. This staged manipulation served as the independent variable that the researchers manipulated for the purpose of trying to insult their study participants. And as already mentioned, the dependent variable measured the decibel level of noise that the participants delivered in the reaction-time game to their ostensible opponent, the person they believed had earlier either insulted or praised their essay. This led to the intriguing question of whether an insulted person would seek revenge.

Bushman and Baumeister were thus interested in the dynamics of interpersonal violence. Under what conditions would people act violently? To operationalize their construct of interpersonal violence, they used as a dependent variable the degree to which participants would choose to blast another person with a loud noise. Recall that the researchers randomly assigned participants to having their essays either praised or insulted. This staged manipulaserved as the independent variable, the effects of which the researchers measured on the dependent variable–decibel level of noise that the participants delivered in the reaction-time game to their ostensible opponent, the person they believed had earlier either insulted or praised their essay. This led to the intriguing question of whether an insulted person would seek revenge.

Bushman and Baumeister also had all their participants take a pencil-and-paper test of narcissism, a personality trait that is characterized by an inflated sense of importance and self-esteem. This represented another theoretical construct in their study. Based on prior works (e.g., Baumeister, Smart, & Boden, 1996), they theorized that people with high levels of narcissism would respond aggressively toward a person they believed to have insulted them. As Bushman and Baumeister (1998) reported (in "Study 2"), their findings indicated increased levels of aggressive responses as measured by decibel level of noise delivered by insulted participants who had scored high on narcissism against the person they believed had offended them by trashing their essays.

Exhibit 4.1 provides a simple depiction of one of the ways in which Bushman and Baumeister tested influences of the personality trait of narcissism on the construct of interpersonal violence. Perceived threat links the independent variable of narcissism to the dependent variable of level of aggressive response directed toward the perceived offender. As shown in Exhibit 4.1, perceived threat mediates the

Exhibit 4.1	Perceived threat as an intervening variable mediates the relationship between narcissism and aggressive response of "blasting" perceived insulter (Bushman & Baumeister, 1998)

Independent Variable →→→ **Intervening Variable** →→→ **Dependent Variable**

Narcissism →→→ Perceived Threat →→→ Decibel Level/Blasting Perceived Insulter

Source: From "Threatened egotism, narcissism, self-esteem, and direct and displaced aggression" by B. J. Bushman and R. F. Baumeister in *Journal of Personality and Social Psychology, 75,* 219–229. Copyright © 1998 American Psychological Association.

relationship of narcissism and aggressiveness directed toward a perceived offender in response to the staged manipulation of insulting or praising participants. In this formu perceived threat is an example of what is referred to as an intervening variable, which is defined as a hypothetical internal state that is used to explain relationbetween independent and dependent variables. Intervening variables often represent theoretical constructs that link inputs or conditions that researchers use as their independent variables with the outputs used to measure them (dependent variables).

To summarize, the structure of a scientific theory begins with abstract constructs, which in turn are translated or operationalized into measurable independent and dependent variables. A sound program of research depends greatly on the extent to which these operations capture the nature of the theoretical constructs under investigation. The scientific validity of a theory or a theoretical construct hinges on the extent to which it describes, predicts, and explains those empirical relationships that are uncovered between independent and dependent variables. In many instances, relationships between independent and dependent variables will be linked, connected, or mediated by intervening variables, hypothetical internal states that are critical components of the deductive structure of a theory.

Building Constructs

Now let's return to the more uplifting research question of *mental health* vs. *mental illness,* which social scientist Corey L. M. Keyes (2007) studied in a paper published in the *American Psychologist* titled "Promoting and Protecting Mental Health as Flourishing: A Complementary Strategy for Improving National Mental Health." In this paper, Keyes adopted a conceptual framework rooted in the school of psychology known as positive psychology. Defined as the scientific study of ordinary human strengths and virtues, **positive psychology** seeks to learn about human thriving, flourishing, optimism, resilience, joy, and capabilities (Seligman, 1991). Positive psychology researchers ask: "What is the nature of the effectively functioning human being who successfully applies evolved adaptations and learned skills?" (Sheldon & King, 2001). For Keyes, and indeed for a burgeoning number of other researchers (e.g., Seligman, 1991), positive psychology provides a theoretical framework to study attitudes, actions, and feelings.

Through the lens of positive psychology, Keyes aimed to flesh out the meanings of two theoretical constructs, mental health and mental illness. First, with regard to mental health, he theorized mental health as an enduring sense of well-being and happiness that a person regularly experiences in life. From his positive psychology perspective, mental health constituted well-being or happiness. As such, he cited the Surgeon General's definition of mental health as " . . . a state of successful performance of mental function, resulting in productive activities, fulfilling relationships with people, and the ability to adapt to change and cope with adversity" (U.S. Public Health Service, 1999, p. 4). For defining the construct of mental illness, Keyes turned to a familiar source, the American Psychiatric Association's *Diagnostic and Statistical Manual of Mental Disorders, Third Edition-Revised* (DSM-III-R). In general, the DSM defines two components that are both necessary in order to establish the presence of a diagnosable mental disorder. One component is the presence of particular symptoms of a specific disorder, and these lists of symptoms are presented in the DSM; the other component is evidence that the symptoms have interfered with aspects of everyday functioning in such areas as work, leisure, school, and interpersonal relationships.

For these dual constructs of mental health and mental illness, Keyes used several methods of measurement that served as operational definitions. For example, he had participants rate how frequently they felt six different positive states of mind: (a) cheerful, (b) in good spirits, (c) extremely happy, (d) calm and peaceful, (e) satisfied, and (f) full of life. Additional measures of emotional well-being tapped the degree to which participants experience helplessness, resilience, and intimacy, as well as the extent to which they express satisfaction in meeting their life goals. He complemented these self-reported ratings of feelings and emotions with questions about behavior related to activities of daily life. These variables were presented in the form of question items such as, What kind of activities of daily living does a person regularly do? Keyes identified several different variables related to daily functioning. Among these, he examined aspects of daily living that can be limited by health, such as lifting and carrying groceries, climbing several flights of stairs, walking more than one mile, performing vigorous activities like running and lifting heavy objects, and performing moderate activity, such as bowling and vacuuming. Keyes also targeted another aspect of functioning in relation to work by asking about missed days of work or shortened work days due to mental illness. All participants also underwent a diagnostic interview via telephone by researchers trained on the DSM. Keyes identified four different forms of mental illness: (1) major depressive episode, (2) generalized anxiety disorder; (3) panic disorder, and (4) alcohol dependence during the past 12 months. For each of these mental disorders, the DSM provides a list of symptoms that must be present in order for a particular diagnosis to be met.

Thus we can see that both mental health and mental illness represented hypothetical constructs that Keyes inferred from related sets of behaviors, emotions, attitudes, and experiences. Keyes investigated these two constructs using two different forms of measurements, self-report ratings of everyday feelings and activities as well as DSM diagnostic interviews via telephone. As we will learn later in this chapter, the validity of these constructs rests largely on two important findings. First is the extent to which these different measured variables of the same construct coalesce, converge, or correlate. Second is the extent to which these different variables distinguish or discriminate the construct of mental health from the construct of mental illness. Remember, the reason for this study was to investigate the idea that mental health is very different from mental illness, and that the mere absence of mental illness does not make a person mentally healthy.

MEASUREMENT OF PSYCHOLOGICAL CONSTRUCTS

In psychological research, we investigate whether our hypothetical constructs reflect objective reality. We do so through the process of **measurement**, which is defined simply as the assignment of numerals to objects or events according to some objective rule (see **Exhibit 4.2**).

These objects or events are variables, which we select as indicators to measure a given construct. A variable will in turn specify a form of measurement. Returning to the example of anxiety, let's imagine that we used three different variables. First, galvanic skin response (GSR) would be a psy-

Exhibit 4.2   Definition of Measurement

Measurement

"... assign numbers to a variable according to objective rules that reflect the features of the construct under investigation..."

chophysiological variable that could be used to measure the physical aspects of anxiety; GSR is a form of measure that essentially provides an objective recording of changes in electrical properties of the skin. A second variable could be scores on a self-report measure of psychological aspects of anxiety; here the form of measurement is an objective, multiple-choice-like test consisting of a set of questions or items that a participant answers. A third variable for the construct of anxiety could use as a form of measurement an observation rating scale that trained observers might complete on the basis of videotaped interviews. Thus, we have one hypothetical construct, anxiety, operationalized with three different variables, each using a different form of measurement: GSR, self-report, and observational.

Advantages of Multiple Methods

Overall, keep in mind that the variables and particular measurement operations chosen for a study should be consistent with the research question. As you can see, Keyes chose variables and particular measurement operations that were aimed toward investigating and addressing the question of whether mental health reflects more than simply the absence of mental illness. To address these questions, he used two kinds of methods of measurement, self-report and interview. These two methods of measurement provided him with data to classify participants into five distinct groups: (1) mental illness and languishing; (2) pure mental illness; (3) pure languishing; (4) moderately mentally healthy; and (5) completely mentally healthy and flourishing. Classifying people into these groups would provide a means for Keyes to test not only his idea that mental health means more than the absence of mental illness but also the idea that pure languishing, the least desirable of the mental health diagnoses, proved to be more dysfunctional than pure mental illness. As an example, adults with pure mental illness had higher levels of positive functioning than adults with pure languishing in regard to life goals, resilience, and friendships. On the basis of these findings, Keyes (2007) concluded that languishing could often be worse than the presence of a diagnosable mental illness.

Multiple methods of measurement are essential in order for us to develop a complete understanding of a phenomenon, such as the relationship between mental heath and mental illness. Just as we learned in Chapter 1 that we have at our disposal different types of study designs and approaches, such as experimental and nonexperimental, we see in this chapter that we have at our disposal different types of methods of measurement. In the next section of this chapter, we will learn to evaluate the reliability and validity of these different methods of measurement. For now, however, keep in mind the importance of using different forms of measurement of the same construct. By doing so, you can test whether these multiple methods of measurement are related, and the degree to which they are adds to our understanding of a given construct. We will discuss more on this later in the chapter.

Levels of Measurement

We defined measurement as the process by which numbers are used to designate objects or events according to some objective *rule*. By rule, we mean, the way numbers are used to represent a particular **scale** of measurement. A variable can have one of four scales of measurement. There are nominal, ordinal, interval, and ratio (see **Exhibit 4.3**).

Nominal Level of Measurement

The **nominal level of measurement** (also called the categorical or qualitative level) identifies variables whose values have no mathematical interpretation; they vary in kind or quality but not in amount. In fact, it is conventional to refer to the values of nominal variables as "attributes" instead of values. "State" (referring to the United

Exhibit 4.3 Four Levels of Measurement

Nominal	Categorical, including dichotomies, no ranking
Ordinal	Ranks on a scale, numerical degrees, distances unequal
Interval	Ranks with equal distance, but no true zero point
Ratio	Ranks with equal distance, true zero point means absence of the quantity

Source: Adapted from "Levels of Measurement," Research Assessment Adviser.

States) is one example. The variable has 50 attributes (or categories or qualities). We might indicate specific states with numbers, so California might be represented by the value 1 and Oregon with the value 2 and so on, but these numbers do not tell us anything about the difference between the states except that they are different. Oregon is not one unit more of "state" than California, nor is it twice as much "state." Nationality, occupation, religious affiliation, and region of the country are also measured at the nominal level. A nominal scale thus classifies data according to a category only.

Keyes made good use of nominal scales of measurement. For example, the DSM diagnoses he used for mental illness are categorical in nature. That is, diagnoses of major depression and alcohol abuse represent two separate categories. While any given participant may meet criteria for more than one diagnosis at any one time (often referred to as co-occurring or comorbid conditions), each diagnosis is defined by a distinct set of criteria in the form of specific symptoms that delineate each form of mental illness. A diagnosis of "major depression" does not represent more mental illness than a diagnosis of "alcohol abuse;" they are two different *kinds* of mental illness in the DSM scheme. Exhibit 4.4 presents an example of a nominal level of measurement with four groups or categories.

Exhibit 4.4 Nominal Level of Measurement With Four Groups

Source: From "Data Collection and Analysis" *Neuroscience for Kids* by Dr. Eric H. Chudler, Department of Bioengineering, University of Washington.

Although the attributes of categorical variables do not have a mathematical meaning, they must be assigned to cases with great care. The attributes we use to measure, or categorize, cases must be mutually exclusive and exhaustive:

- A variable's attributes or values are **mutually exclusive** if every case can have only one attribute.

- A variable's attributes or values are **exhaustive** when every case can be classified into one of the categories.

When a variable's attributes are mutually exclusive and exhaustive, every case corresponds to one, and only one, attribute. We know this sounds pretty straight-forward, and in many cases it is. However, what we think of as mutually exclusive and exhaustive categories may really be so only because of social convention; when these conventions change, or if they differ between the societies in a multi-country study, appropriate classification at the nominal level can become much more complicated.

The Special Case of Dichotomies

Dichotomies, variables having only two values, are a special case from the stand-point of levels of measurement. The values or attributes of a variable such as gender clearly vary in kind or quality, but not in amount. Thus, the variable is categorical—measured at the nominal level. Yet we can also think of the variable as indicating the presence of the attribute "female" (or "male") or not. Viewed in this way, there is an inherent order: A female has more of the "female" attribute (it is present) than a male (the attribute is not present). So what do you answer to the test question, "What is the level of measurement of 'gender'?" "Nominal," of course, but you'll find that when a statistical procedure requires that variables be quantitative, a dichotomy can be perfectly acceptable.

As we can see from the graphs (see **Exhibit 4.5**), changing the number assigned to "male" and "female" does not change the number of men and women partici-pants in a study. We still have the same number of men and women in the data set.

Exhibit 4.5   Dichotomous Data Use a Nominal Scale of Measurement

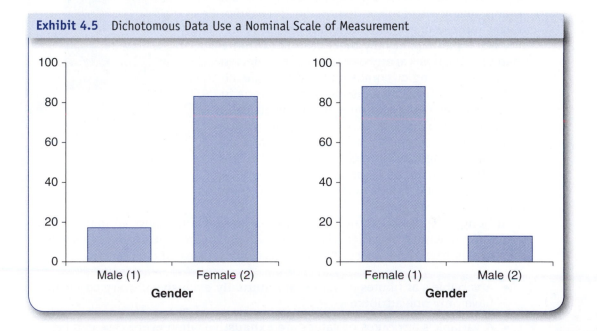

Ordinal Level of Measurement

The first of the three quantitative levels is the **ordinal level of measurement**. At this level, the numbers assigned to response choices allow for "greater than" and "less than" distinctions. And because this level of measurement allows for a ranking of responses, such as degree of agreement or frequency of occurrence, ordinal level of measurement is sometimes referred as a ranking scale. Oftentimes, research participants are asked to rank the frequency of occurrence of a particular emotion or behavior on a numerical scale. For example, Keyes asked participants to rate how frequently in the past 30 days they felt (a) cheerful, (b) in good spirits, (c) extremely happy, (d) calm and peaceful, (e) satisfied, and (f) full of life. For each of these positive emotions, participants rated how frequently they had experienced each on a scale by selecting only one of the five numbered responses (typically presented from left to right) with 1 = *none of the time,* 2 = *a little of the time,* 3 = *some of the time,* 4 = *most of the time,* or 5 = *all of the time.* Researchers commonly referred to this metric as a **Likert scale**, named after its originator, psychologist Rensis Likert (Likert, 1932). Keyes also used a Likert scale when he asked participants to "rate their life overall these days" on a scale ranging from 0 (worst possible life overall) to 10 (best possible life overall).

A simple depiction of an ordinal scale of measurement is presented in **Exhibit 4.6**. Here imagine that respondents participated in a driving test in which they rank-ordered four different cars on a one-to-four scale, with 1 for most favorite and 4 for least favorite. **Exhibit 4.6** simply shows that ranking always involves an ordinal scale, such as that used by Olympic judges. Other common examples of an ordinal level of measurement are grades, military rank, and socioeconomic status (see **Exhibit 4.7**).

As with nominal variables, the different values of a variable measured at the ordinal level must be mutually exclusive and exhaustive. They must cover the range of observed values and allow each case to be assigned no more than one value. Often instruments that use an ordinal level of measurement simply ask respondents to rate

Exhibit 4.6   Ordinal Level of Measurement for Car Preference

Mercedes Benz 1
Lincoln Continental 2
Volkswagen 3
Volvo 4

Volkswagen 1
Mercedes Benz 2
Volvo 3
Lincoln Continental 4

Volvo 1
Volkswagen 2
Mercedes Benz 3
Lincoln Continental 4

Exhibit 4.7 Always Ordinal, Ranking

Ranking

Whenever something, such as a performance or a set of objects, is rank ordered, an ordinal level of measurement is used.

their responses to some questions or statements along a continuum of, for example, strength of agreement, level of importance, or relative frequency. A key limitation of the ordinal level of measurement is that you cannot assume that respondents perceive the differences between response scale points as equidistant. You cannot assume, taking an example from Keyes's rating of positive emotions, that the distance or difference between "all of the time" and "most of the time" is equal to the distance or difference between "a little of the time" and "none of the time." While these points on the response scale are intended to reflect an order of frequency ("all of the time" to "none of the time"), the numbers that you would assign to each of the response scale points (e.g., *all of the time* = 5, *most of the time* = 4, *some of the time* = 3, *a little of the time* = 2, and *none of the time* = 1) do not indicate the magnitude of difference between any two points on this ordinal response scale. For instance, say you answered "all of the time," which is assigned and coded with a value of 5 for how frequently you felt cheerful in the past 30 days, and another participant responded with "none of the time," which we coded with a value of 1. You cannot say that the "all of the time" response is 5 times greater than the "none of the time" response just because you decided to code these responses as, respectively, 5 and 1.

Interval Level of Measurement

An **interval level of measurement** has all the characteristics of nominal and ordinal scales of measurement. That is, like a nominal scale, it gives a name or category for each observation, with the number serving as a code for a label (e.g., 1 = *females*, 2 = *males*). Like an ordinal scale, responses are numerically ordered or ranked from lowest to highest on some particular characteristic. But in addition, an interval level of measurement by definition uses a scale on which the distances between any two points are of known size. The numbers indicating the values of a variable at the interval level of measurement represent fixed measurement units but have no absolute, or fixed, zero point.

What this means is that a zero value on an interval scale does not indicate the complete absence of the measured variable. This is true even if the scaled values happen to carry the name "zero." The Fahrenheit scale illustrates the issue (see **Exhibit 4.8**). A temperature of 0° Fahrenheit does not represent the complete absence of temperature, defined as the absence of any molecular kinetic energy.

Rather, 0° Fahrenheit became a handy convention for temperature measurement for largely accidental reasons of history. The key point is that because an interval scale has no true zero point, ratio measurements make no sense. For example, we cannot state that the ratio of 40° to 20° Fahrenheit is the same as the ratio of 100° to 50°. After all, if the "zero" degree applied at the temperature that Fahrenheit happens to measure as 10°, the two ratios would instead be 30 to 10 and 90 to 40 and would no longer be equivalent. For this reason, that is, the absence of true zero point in an interval scale, we cannot say that 80° is "twice as hot" as 40°. Such a claim would assume a true zero point that an interval scale lacks. Remember, as with all interval scales, that decision about where to "start" the Fahrenheit temperature scale is arbitrary and is not tied to an underlying physical reality of atmospheric climate.

Exhibit 4.8   Fahrenheit temperature uses an interval level of measurement

Source: © Comstock/Thinkstock.

Thus, an interval-level measure is created by a scale that has fixed measurement units but no absolute or fixed zero point. The numbers can therefore be added and subtracted, but ratios are not meaningful. Again, the values must be mutually exclusive and exhaustive. In psychology, standardized measures of intelligence, personality, and aptitude typically use an interval level of measurement, just as do education tests such as the SATs and GREs. That is, these standardized measures use an arbitrary zero point, as there is, for example, no such thing as no intelligence, no personality, and the like. Likewise, as with our example of temperature, you cannot say an IQ score is twice as large as another IQ score. So while an IQ of 130 is 65 scaled points greater than an IQ of 65, it is not twice as great.

Ratio Level of Measurement

The numbers indicating the values of a variable at the **ratio level of measurement** represent fixed measuring units and an absolute zero point (zero means absolutely no amount of whatever the variable indicates). Income is measured on a ratio scale, as no income equals zero dollars and cents! Weight is also measured on a ratio scale, as the scale of ounces and pounds has a genuine zero point. Kelvin temperature is another example of a ratio scale because in classical physics, zero on the Kelvin scale means absolute zero, the case in which all motion stops. Speed in terms of time in track and field races would also be considered to be measured on a ratio scale (see **Exhibit 4.9**).

Exhibit 4.9   A Ratio Level of Measurement for Speed

Source: From "Data Collection and Analysis" *Neuroscience for Kids* by Dr. Eric H. Chudler, Department of Bioengineering, University of Washington.

For most statistical analyses in social science research, the interval and ratio levels of measurement can be treated as equivalent, but there is an important difference: On a ratio scale, 10 is 2 points higher than 8 and is also 2 times greater than 5. Ratio numbers can be added and subtracted, and because the numbers begin at an absolute zero point, they can be multiplied and divided (so ratios can be formed between the numbers). For example, people's ages can be represented by values ranging from 0 years (or some fraction of a year) to 120 or more. A person who is 30 years old is 15 years older than someone who is 15 years old ($30 - 15 = 15$) and is twice as old as that person ($30/15 = 2$). Of course, the numbers also must be mutually exclusive and exhaustive so that every case can be assigned one and only one value.

Comparison of Levels of Measurement

Table 4.1 summarizes the types of comparisons that can be made with different levels of measurement as well as the mathematical operations that are legitimate.

Table 4.1   Properties of the Four Different Levels of Measurement

Examples of Comparison Statements	Appropriate Math Operations	Nominal	Ordinal	Interval	Ratio
		Relevant Level of Measurement			
A is equal to (not equal to) B	= (≠)	XX	XX	XX	XX
A is greater than (less than) B	> (<)		XX	XX	XX
A is three more than (less than) B	+ (−)			XX	XX
A is twice (half) as large as B	X (/)				XX

Source: Schutt, R. K. (2009). *Investigating the social world: The process and practice of research* (6th ed.). Thousand Oaks, CA: Pine Forge Press.

All four levels of measurement allow researchers to assign different values to different cases. Scores obtained on ordinal, interval, or ratio scales of measurement all allow for mathematical operations and are thus often referred to as quantitative variables. By contrast, a nominal level of measurement involves classifying observations using an arbitrary number as a code for group membership (e.g., *females* = 1; *males* = 2). Thus, a nominal level of measurement does not allow for mathematical operations and is used for what are often referred to as qualitative variables. Keep in mind that researchers choose levels of measurement in the process of creating operational definitions for their variables; the level of measurement is not inherent in the variable itself. Many variables can be measured at different levels with different procedures.

Levels of measurement are especially important for statistical analyses that we will cover in depth in Chapter 10. We will learn in Chapter 10 that different types of statistical procedures require different levels of measurement of variables. For example, **nonparametric statistics** test hypotheses for variables that use either a nominal or an ordinal scale of measurement. A commonly used nonparametric statistical procedure that will be covered in Chapter 10 is the *chi-square* test. Let's imagine for a moment that you are interested in the question of whether there are more women than men majoring in psychology. To answer this question, you could perform a chi-square statistic test comparing percentages of female and male psychology majors. You would use the nonparametric chi-square test because gender is a categorical variable, meaning that it is measured on a nominal scale that can only be analyzed using nonparametric statistics.

Similarly, recall Keyes's ratings of how frequently people experience particular positive emotions, such as joy. Here research participants selected among one of five choices, which could be coded as: *all of the time* = 5, *most of the time* = 4, *some of the time* = 3, *a little of the time* = 2, and *none of the time* = 1. Remember, with an ordinal level of measurement such as this Likert scale used by Keyes, we can only say that a response of 4 is higher than a response of 3, but we cannot say how much higher, as we could if we had used an interval level of measurement. As we have learned, with an ordinal level of measurement, the distance between two points, or among each response, is not equal. In this example, then, we can conclude that people with higher-numbered responses reported experiencing positive emotions more often than did people with lowered-number responses. And with an ordinal level of measurement, we could then determine the median for our sample (see Chapter 10). The median is a statistic that indicates the middle position among responses by research participants. The advantage of the median for ordinal data is that it does not assume equal distance between points on the response scale. The median thus provides a sound quantitative description and summary of ordinal data. These ordinal data can in turn be analyzed with nonparametric statistics to evaluate whether the observed difference in medians is due to chance. Similar nonparametric statistics are often used with qualitative research covered in Chapter 11.

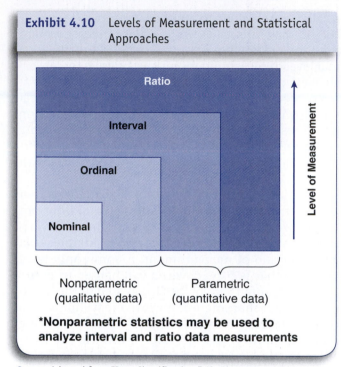

Exhibit 4.10 Levels of Measurement and Statistical Approaches

Nonparametric (qualitative data)

Parametric (quantitative data)

*Nonparametric statistics may be used to analyze interval and ratio data measurements

Source: Adapted from "Data Classification," Six Sigma Material.

On the other hand, **parametric statistics** are used with variables that are measured on either an interval or ratio scale. A commonly used parametric statistical procedure that will be covered in Chapter 10 is the *t-test statistic*. Imagine you wanted to compare SATs of female and male college applicants. A *t*-test would allow you to compare average SATs of these two groups. The SAT would be considered a variable that is measured on an interval scale and thus suitable to be analyzed with parametric statistics, such as the *t*-test. In general, parametric statistics are preferable because they provide a more powerful test than do nonparametric statistics of a research hypothesis. That is, parametric statistics provide the best chance of establishing whether there is a relationship between independent and dependent variables. **Exhibit 4.10** depicts the relationship of levels of measurement and parametric and nonparametric statistics.

PSYCHOMETRIC TESTS AND MEASUREMENT

Psychometrics is a school of psychology that studies the application of psychological tests as objective measures of the mind and mental processes. The word *psychometric* literally means "to measure the mind." For social historians and critics, psychometric testing mixed the idealism and hubris of a fledgling field of psychology of the early 20th century, which would come to touch the lives of millions of people and leave an enduring imprint on national culture (Brown, 1992; Lemann, 1999). As Lemann (1999) wrote in his book titled *The Big Test: The Secret History of the American Meritocracy,*

> It was magical: the idea that the mysterious, inaccessible human mind would now yield its content to psychologists who knew the right questions to ask. Testing touched upon the mythic themes: the ability to see the invisible (what was inside people's heads), the oracular ability to predict the future (what someone's grades would be in courses he hadn't even chosen yet). (p. 18)

Most of these psychometric tests referred to by Lemann here were not designed to measure intelligence itself but some closely related construct, such as scholastic aptitude, school achievement, or some specific cognitive abilities (Neisser et al., 1996). They would be so widely used for selection purposes that critics would come to liken them to a metric for "social ordering" of people based on their test scores (Brown, 1992; Lemann, 1999). The impact would start early, beginning with the SSAT for preparatory school, followed by the SAT or ACT for college, then the GRE for graduate school, the MCAT for medical school, the LSAT for law school, and the GMAT for business school. As Neisser and colleagues pointed out in their "Report of a Task Force Established by the American Psychological Association," published in a 1996 *American Psychologist* article, "Intelligence: Knowns and Unknowns," scores on these psychometric instruments "matter, and the stakes can be high" (p. 78).

Culture Counts

We thus begin with a warning about the psychometrics of measurement as embodied in the score derived from an intelligence test, IQ. Like any theoretical construct, intelligence is only partially captured by IQ test scores, and while certainly important, it should not be confused with virtue, wisdom, or fulfillment. In fact, while clearly linked to educational achievement, IQ may be overshadowed as a predictor of health and longevity by personality traits such as conscientiousness (e.g., Friedman et al., 1995). But the reason for our warning is not about the science of intelligence as represented by IQ tests (see Gray & Thompson, 2004; Lichtenberger & Kaufmann, 2009)—that has been well established—but from the misuse of IQ as a tool to stigmatize racial and ethnic groups of people. Recall from Chapter 2 the importance of *culture* in psychological research. There is perhaps no greater example than that of the study of psychometric intelligence to illustrate the need for understanding and appreciating the indispensable role of culture in the expression and measurement of human traits.

At the center of the controversy is the well-established 15-point gap in IQ between African American and white American groups (Neisser et al., 1996). In trying to understand this disparity, two important points are especially relevant. First is that throughout the industrial and nonindustrial world, all caste-like minorities show a similar 15-point gap in IQ between them and the nonstigmatized members of their societies. Citing the work of Ogbu (1978, 1994), Neisser and colleagues pointed out that these caste-like minorities include the Harijans of India, the Maoris of New Zealand, the Baraku of Japan, the Oriental Jews of Israel, and the West Indians of Great Britain. This gap, Neisser and company noted, occurs even for stigmatized and nonstigmatized groups of the same race, as for example Baraku and other Japanese. Second, the controversy is not about whether group IQ disparities exist but about the bases or causes of these differences and their public policy implications. The most egregious of these ideas is the notion that race-based cognitive inequalities are permanently encoded in the genes, and so too are the social inequalities that arise from them (Holt, 2009). From this **hereditarian** view of intelligence, an often vitriolic debate has ensued, virtually unabated, seemingly reignited over the years by such scholarly books as *The Bell Curve* (1994) by the late Harvard professor of psychology Richard J. Hernstein and Charles Murray, and *The g Factor* (1998) by University of California, Berkeley Professor Emeritus Arthur R. Jensen. But as Neisser and colleagues (1996) concluded, genetic interpretations for these racial and ethnic group IQ disparities have been unsupported by research.

To understand how the group-IQ disparity has been erroneously interpreted as evidence of genetic inferiority, consider the following well-known plant analogy developed by evolutionary biologist Richard Lewontin (1976). As shown in **Exhibit 4.11**, imagine having a packet of virtually identical seeds, half of which you plant in a pot containing fertile soil and the other half you plant in a pot of barren soil. The group of seeds planted in the poor soil will inevitably grow, but their growth will be stunted in comparison to the group of seeds planted in the rich soil. Keep in mind that because the two groups of seeds are genetically identical, any differences in growth *between* the two potted plants are entirely due to the *environment,* which in this case is the soil. By the same token, *within* each

Exhibit 4.11   The plant analogy used to explain why group differences in IQ are determined by the environment

Source: From "How heritability misleads about race" by Ned Block in *Cognition 56*(2), 99–128. Copyright © 1995, Elsevier. Reprinted with permission.

group of seeds, some plants will grow larger than others. In contradistinction to the group differences observed between the two pots, the differences in plant heights within each pot are entirely due to genetic variation within each group of seeds.

Now to apply this analogy to race/ethnic differences in IQ, we know that genetic variation can produce individual differences in IQ within a group (e.g., Bouchard & McGue, 1981); yet we also know that the average IQ difference between groups can still only be determined by the environment (e.g., Gray & Thompson, 2004). That is, genes along with environmental factors will influence individual differences in IQ, but only culture and environment will determine group differences in IQ. The critical lesson to take from this analogy is that any interpretation for racial/ethnic differences in IQ cannot use within-group genetic variation to account for between-group differences (Gray & Thompson, 2004).

Thus, Neisser and company argued that the black/white IQ differential reflects **outcome bias**. Imagine flipping a coin that consistently comes up heads for any reason. In probability theory, the coin would be considered to be biased, regardless of any consequences that the outcome may or may not have. By analogy, an IQ test for which the black mean falls approximately one standard deviation (about 15 points) or less below the mean of whites would also be considered *ipso facto* evidence of outcome bias (Neisser et al., 1996). Some have argued that this is yet another example of the pervasive outcome bias that blacks experience in American society, which accompanies similar disparities in income, health, longevity, occupational achievement, and dealings with the criminal justice system (see Neisser et al., 1996).

In 1995, social psychologists C. M. Steele and J. Aronson proposed that negative stereotypes (e.g. "genetic deficit") that have been traditionally used to explain racial IQ differences shape both intellectual identity and actual test performance of African Americans. According to their theory, sustained academic achievement requires identification with school and its sub-domains (e.g., standardized testing). Identification is typically defined in terms of demonstrated academic success and accomplishment, as, for example, being a student in an elite university. The nexus of the theory is that negative stereotypes about race and IQ threaten performance of African Americans who have become identified by academic achievement. This phenomenon is referred to as **stereotype threat**. It is viewed as a strictly situational threat that can be elicited by the mere recognition that a negative group stereotype could apply in a given setting. And for those African American individuals whose identities and self-images are defined by their academic accomplishment, the mere labeling of a test as an intelligence measure is sufficient to elicit stereotype threat. Yet if the individual does not identify with the domain, then no stereotype threat will be evoked.

The theory gained support through a series of laboratory experiments comparing test performance of high-achieving majority and minority students under conditions when stereotype threat is induced and when it is not. In the stereotype condition, participants were told that they were given a test of intelligence, and in the nonthreat condition, they were told that they were given a test of problem-solving developed by the researchers. For example, black and white students from Stanford University took a standardized test composed of the most difficult items of the Verbal GRE. The researchers described the same test as either an *ability-diagnostic measure of intelligence* or as *an ability-nondiagnostic, laboratory measure of problem-solving* unrelated to intelligence. Keep in mind that all participants received the same test. Steele and Aronson (1995) found a larger majority–minority difference in test performance in the threat condition than in the nonthreat condition, which supported their hypothesis that stereotype threat detracts from minority group performance on standardized tests. In a follow-up, Steele and Aronson (1995) investigated whether an even more subtle change in the testing conditions might also lead to this racial difference in test performance. Here they manipulated stereotype threat by having participants either record or not record their race on a demographic questionnaire before taking a test that was described as nondiagnostic in both conditions. Steele and Aronson (1995) replicated their findings, demonstrating that the recording of race on a demographic questionnaire alone was sufficient to reduce performance of African American students.

Since being first introduced in the literature by Steele and Aronson (1995), the theory of stereotype threat has been rapidly incorporated into mainstream psychology; for example, it is now covered in two thirds of a sample of current introductory psychology textbooks (Sackett, Hardison, & Cullen, 2004). The theory and empirical

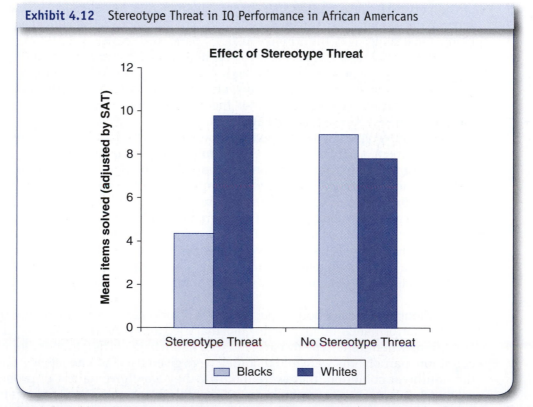

Exhibit 4.12   Stereotype Threat in IQ Performance in African Americans

Effect of Stereotype Threat

Source: Created by Kevin Murray based on data from "The Effects of Stereotype Threat on the Standardized Test Performance of College Students" by J. Aronson, C. M. Steele, M. F. Salinas, and M. J. Lustina in *Readings About the Social Animal*, 8th Edition.

data have unmistakable relevance to the raging debates about interpreting racial group differences in IQ. As Steele (1997) wrote,

> To the set of possible causes for these group differences, our (C. M. Steele & Aronson, 1995) findings add a new one: the differential impact of stereotype threat on groups in the testing situation itself. Thus, stereotype threat may be a possible source of bias in standardized tests, a bias that arises not from item content but for group differences in the threat that societal stereotypes attach to test performance. (p. 622)

Psychometric Principles

At the heart of the psychometric approach is that people have certain levels of **psychological traits**, such as those related to intelligence, personality, or attitudes and that these presumed enduring and stable dispositions can be measured by objective tests. Equally important for the psychometric approach are competencies, such as those related to scholastic aptitude or academic achievement that can also be measured by objective pencil-and-paper tests.

Psychometrics provides us with the most powerful set of tools and concepts for the measurement of human traits. Psychometrics requires the **standardization** of

Exhibit 4.13 *Psychometrics of Educational Testing*

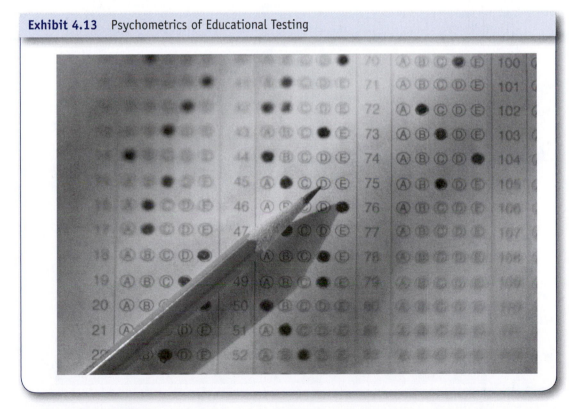

Source: © Comstock/Thinkstock.

both test administration and test scoring. Standardization simply means that testing, scoring, and interpretation procedures are uniform across all administrations of the test. In constructing a psychometric test, a researcher identifies a **standardization sample**, which is defined as a random selection of people drawn from a carefully defined population. As we will study in Chapter 5, random sampling simply means that each person of the targeted or defined population has an equal chance of being selected to be part of the standardization sample. The tests, administered uniformly to the standardization sample, are then scored according to the same specified and objective criteria for each examinee. From the standardization sample, the **norms** of the test are calculated. The norms of a test involve two measures: The first is the **mean** or average score for the standardization sample. The second measure is the **standard deviation**, which indicates the degree to which an individual score deviates from the sample mean (see Chapter 10 for details).

Let us consider a widely used standardized test of IQ known as the Wechsler Adult Intelligence Scale-Fourth Edition (WAIS-IV; Wechsler, 2008). In "norming" the WAIS-IV, the developers gave the IQ test to a standardization sample of 2,200 English-speaking people who were randomly selected from a carefully defined population. The norming of the test came from a stratified sampling of the population. A **stratified sample** is formed by randomly selecting from relatively uniform subpopulations called strata. Strata are defined along specified, objective

Exhibit 4.14 Single Score (Clouds) Compared to a Normal Sample (Solid)

features. For the WAIS-IV, the test developers used data gathered in October 2005 by the U.S. Bureau of Census to stratify their standardization sample along the following variables: age, sex, race/ethnicity, self or parent educational level, and geographic region. Thus the final standardization sample included representative proportions of whites, African Americans, and other racial/ethnic groups, consisting of 2,200 male and female examinees divided into 13 age groups from the youngest age bracket of 16 years through 17 years 11 months to the oldest age bracket of 85 years through 90 years, 11 months from four major geographic regions: Northeast, Midwest, South, and West (Wechsler, 2008).

As part of the standardization process, the test scores generated from a standardization sample are plotted or graphed. The graph shows the range of scores as well as the distribution of scores, which is simply a tally of the number of examinees who obtained a certain score. As we will cover in Chapter 10, this kind of graph provides a frequency distribution for the scores generated from a sample. For many human traits, from height to weight to intelligence and personality predispositions, scores are distributed along a **normal curve** that is presented in **Exhibit 4.13** (Kosslyn & Rosenberg, 2001). When the distribution of scores approximates a normal curve, most scores fall near the center, with gradually fewer scores as you move toward either extreme. In general, the larger the sample, the more closely will the distribution of scores resemble the normal curve, which is also known as the *bell curve,* due its bell shape—bilaterally symmetrical with a single peak in the middle.

Exhibit 4.15 shows the normal curve for WAIS-IV IQ scores. WAIS-IV raw scores are converted by a specific statistical formula to standard scores, with a mean of 100 and a standard deviation of 15. As you can see in **Exhibit 4.15**, about two thirds of scores from the standardization sample fall within one standard deviation above and below the mean of 100. In other words, two thirds of all scores fall with

Exhibit 4.15 Normal Distribution of IQ Scores

the range of 85 to 115. What this means is that a person with an IQ of 115 earns a score that falls one standard deviation unit above the mean of 100. In qualitative terms, an IQ of 115 would be classified as falling in the *High Average* range. Thus, you can see how a person's score on a standardized test can be compared and interpreted relative to others in the standardized sample.

EVALUATING MEASURES

For a test to be meaningful or useful, it must be both *reliable* and *valid*. As we learned in Chapter 2, *reliability* refers to the consistency in the measurement, as for example the degree of agreement among raters using the same instrument to code videotapes of the same behavior. Or reliability can also be assessed on the basis of test-retest, as in the case of IQ scores remaining similar for examinees tested in early adulthood and then 10 years later. *Validity* is different from reliability and refers to the meaning of what is measured. Validity can be evident by what a measure might predict, as for example, IQ scores predict school success. In the following sections, we will learn that the quality of a test depends on the extent to which it generates reliable and valid measurement.

Measurement Reliability

A reliable test yields consistent scores when the construct being measured is not changing (or the measured scores change in direct correspondence to actual changes in the construct). If a test is reliable, it is affected less by measurement error or chance variation than if it is unreliable. Reliability is a prerequisite for measurement validity: We cannot really measure a construct if the test we are using gives inconsistent results. In fact, because it usually is easier to assess test reliability than test validity, you are more likely to see an evaluation of measurement reliability in a research report than an evaluation of measurement validity.

A construct such as intelligence is presumed to remain stable over time. This means that the same measurements of the same construct separated by a period of time should be highly consistent. In other words, a measure such as the WAIS-IV IQ should have high **test-retest reliability**; scores should remain similar over time. Thus, if you take the WAIS-IV IQ and then retake it again 2 years later, the test is performing reliably if you receive a similar score both times—presuming that nothing dramatic happened during the 2 years to change your IQ. (Recall that an examinee's IQ is computed relative to the norms for his/her same-age peers; that is, built into the IQ is an adjustment for normal age-related changes.) Of course, if serious events transpire between the test and the retest, as for example an examinee sustains a severe closed head injury that could affect IQ being measured, then the scores are likely to diverge. But this would not be attributable to diminished test-retest reliability of the WAIS-IV but rather to the effects of a brain injury on IQ. In a similar vein, often research involves different raters coding the same behavior. Here consistency among raters needs to be established so that the same behavior is coded reliably. This type of reliability is referred to as **interobserver reliability**, which indexes the degree to which raters consistently code the same observed behavior.

Tests usually consist of many items, all of which are typically intended to measure the same construct, whether it be IQ, a personality trait, or reading comprehension. When researchers use multiple items to measure a single construct, they must be concerned with **interitem reliability** (or interitem or internal consistency). The idea is that if the items of a test are all measuring the same construct, the correlation among these items should be high. The goal is to have consistency across items within a test. One frequently used measure of internal consistency is the **split-half reliability** coefficient. Here you randomly divide all items that are supposed to measure the same trait or construct into two sets. Calculate the total score for each randomly divided half. The correlation between the two total scales is the split-half reliability coefficient. **Cronbach's alpha** is another **reliability measure** commonly used to assess interitem reliability. Very similar to split-half reliability, Cronbach's alpha is computed by several iterations of randomly dividing a scale of items into sets of split halves. You (or the computer program) compute the reliability coefficient, recomputing on next set, and so on until you have computed all possible split-half estimates of reliability.

One rather simple and straightforward way to increase the internal consistency of an instrument is to make it longer! In other words, by adding more related items to your test, you will increase the internal consistency of the test. Why is this so? In any response there is **random error of measurement**—variation due to multiple little factors that have nothing to do with the construct you are trying to measure. Perhaps an answer is influenced by a story in that morning's newspaper, by the noise of a truck passing by, and on and on. Any given response to a question will therefore contain a large component of random error of measurement. But as you increase the number of items in a test, the random error involved in each answer to each particular question will be cancelled out by the random error associated with responses to the other questions. The more you add questions related to the concept of interest, the more the random error will wash out in this way.

Finally, many standardized tests will have alternate forms, which come in very handy when an examinee might need to be retested over a relatively short period of time. Think of a study that is investigating the effects of a new drug on memory. Participants are tested before and after a 60-day treatment trial. A control group who receives a **placebo** is also tested on two occasions before and after receiving the inert substance. In order to control for practice effects that could influence test scores, alternate forms of the memory measurement would need to be administered. In selecting your memory measure, then, you would look at **alternate-forms reliability** of the test. Alternate-forms reliability reflects the degree of agreement between two slightly different tests comprised of different sets of questions or items of the same construct.

The Logic of Measurement Validity

Measurement validity refers to the extent to which measures indicate what they are intended to measure. The extent to which measurement validity has been achieved can be assessed with four different approaches: face validation, content validation, criterion validation, and construct validation. For example, returning to the Keyes study, we might wish to examine the validity of his mental health diagnostic procedures. Keyes in effect evaluated the validity of his classification scheme by empirically testing the idea that persons who are assessed as flourishing should differ from others on objective independent measures of physical health, job performance, and psychological functioning. Put plainly, Keyes is betting that empirical evidence will show the validity of his classification scheme by verifying that participants who have been diagnosed as mentally healthy and flourishing are living productive and happy lives, as objectively measured. Notice that Keyes validated his classification system by using outcome measures that are independent of the diagnostic schemes that he used to assess both mental illness and mental health.

This use of independent measures of theoretically linked outcomes to validate the assessment protocol effectively avoids a common pitfall in research design that is referred to as **circular reasoning**. A research design can be invalidated by circular reasoning. For example, if Keyes correlated the 13 symptoms he used to diagnose people as flourishing with each other (e.g., dimensions 1 and 2) and used such correlations as evidence of validity, he would be engaging in circular reasoning. This would be analogous to correlating individual items of an IQ test with each other, which might tell you about the internal consistency of the test, an aspect of reliability, but it would not tell you anything about the meaning or validity of the test, and for that you would need independent outcome measures.

Face Validity

The question of **face validity** asks whether a test "looks like" it measures what it is suppose to measure (Anastasi, 1988). Face validity is essentially a matter of opinion and lacks a firm scientific or empirical basis. It adds little or nothing to the validation of a test. In fact, if anything, problems can arise when what a psychological test is supposed to measure looks too obvious. Such an instrument may be subjected to **social desirability bias**, in which examinees respond defensively to test items based on how they wish to be perceived rather than openly and genuinely. Other test-taking strategies, such as examinees "faking bad" or "faking good," may also threaten the validity of an instrument whose measurement objective appears to be too transparent. Face validity is similar to the legal term *prima facie,* a Latin expression meaning *on its first appearance,* or *at first sight.* However, in law, prima facie evidence is an essential element of jurisprudence, whereas in psychology the face validity of an instrument is inconsequential.

Content Validity

A valid test needs to provide a full measure of a construct. For example, the WAIS-IV includes 10 core subtests, each of which is presumed to measure a distinct aspect of intelligence, such as verbal reasoning or constructional abilities of working with your hands. Thus, **content validity** refers to the extent to which test items have sufficient breadth to capture the full range of a construct intended to be measured. In this regard, Keyes went to great lengths to make sure that his measures provided the full range of the meaning of the construct of mental health. Recall that he used multiple measures to capture what he conceptualized to be the multidimensional nature of mental health. In so doing, his measurement of mental health as well as his DSM measure of mental illness would be considered to be valid from the standpoint of content validity.

Criterion Validity

The validity of a test can also be measured against a certain criterion or outcome. For example, a measure of blood-alcohol concentration or a urine test could serve as the criterion for validating a self-report measure of drinking, as long as the questions we ask about drinking refer to the same period of time. Thus, **criterion validity** addresses the extent to which test scores agree with an objective criterion that follows logically from the measured variable. The criterion that researchers select can be measured either at the same time as the variable to be validated or after that time. **Concurrent validity** exists when a measure yields scores that are closely related to scores on a criterion measured at the same time. A store might validate a test of sales ability by administering it to sales personnel who are already employed and then comparing their test scores to their actual sales performance. **Predictive validity** is the ability of a measure to predict scores on a criterion measured in the future. For example, SAT scores might be predictive of college grade point averages.

An attempt at criterion validation is well worth the effort because it greatly increases confidence that the measure is measuring what was intended. However, for many concepts of interest to psychological researchers, no one variable can reasonably be considered a criterion. If we are measuring feelings or beliefs or other subjective states, such as feelings of loneliness, what direct indicator could serve as a criterion? Even with variables for which a reasonable criterion exists, the researcher may not be able to gain access to the criterion—as would be the case with a tax return or employer document that we might wish we could use as a criterion for self-reported income.

Construct Validity

As we have learned, psychological constructs exist not as material entities but as ideas inferred on the basis of empirical relationships among measured variables. The question then becomes, how does one demonstrate the validity of a construct? This is perhaps the most important question of validity in psychology, as it speaks directly to the issue of how to build and evaluate theory (Cronbach & Meehl, 1955). At the nexus of construct validity sit two interrelated frameworks: theoretical and empirical. First is the theoretical framework in which a construct is embedded, as, for example, Keyes's construct of mental health fits within the theoretical framework of positive psychology (Sheldon & King, 2001). Second is the empirical framework that tells how a construct is to be measured, as for example Keyes used self-report and interviews to assess mental health.

In their classic 1955 paper titled *Construct Validity in Psychological Tests,* psychologists Lee Cronbach and Paul Meehl introduced the term of a **nomological network** as a way to think about construct validity. The word *nomological* is derived from the Greek term *nomology*, meaning lawful, which in construct validity refers to the interlocking relationships between the observable, measurable, or empirical and the inferable, interpretable, or theoretical. Thus, according to Cronbach and Meehl, a construct is more or less useful, meaning that its utility depends largely on the extent to which it can describe, explain, and predict observable phenomena; that is, the extent to which it can enter into a nomological network that unites empirical and theoretical frameworks.

In the Cronbach and Meehl article, the influential idea of nomological networks served largely as a philosophical foundation for understanding construct validity. What the article lacked was a specific prescription for how you would empirically examine construct validity. For this, another classic paper in psychology, *Convergent and Discriminant Validation by the Multitrait-Multimethod Matrix* by Donald Campbell and Donald Fiske (1959), would provide researchers with methodology to empirically evaluate construct validity. In this article, the researchers unveiled the **multitrait-multimethod** matrix as a method to assess construct validity. Today, we view the multitrait-multimethod matrix as the gold standard for testing the validity of new ideas and new measurements in psychology. It tells you both how good your idea is and whether your idea is new and different.

In understanding the logic of a multitrait-multimethod approach, it is helpful to recall the advantages of using multiple methods of measurement. Now with a multitrait-multimethod matrix, you use not only two or more methods of measurement, but you also identify two or more theoretical constructs to investigate. To simplify, let's think of two constructs, intelligence and the personality trait of extraversion, and each is measured with two different methods of measurement, behavioral observations and psychometric tests of intelligence (e.g., WAIS-IV) and extraversion (e.g., NEO Five Factor Personality Inventory; Costa & McRae, 1985). Within a single multitrait-multimethod matrix, two fundamental aspects of construct validity can be empirically evaluated.

First is **convergent validity,** which is established by examining whether the same trait measured by two different methods yields similar results. In our example, intelligence measured by the WAIS-IV and behavioral observations should be related, as should extraversion measured by the NEO and behavioral observations. If different measures of the same trait correlate, then this would be considered strong empirical evidence for convergent validity. Second, the matrix provides a format to examine **discriminant validity**, which is demonstrated when different traits using the same form of measurement are unrelated. In our example, intelligence and extraversion should be unrelated, whether measured using psychometric tests or by behavioral observations. Thus, construct validity requires both convergent and discriminant validity, which can be most effectively empirically evaluated via the multimethod-multitrait matrix.

Table 4.2 Multitrait-Multimethod Matrix of Correlations Between Intelligence and Extraversion

	Psychometric Measures		Observations of Behavior	
	Intelligence	Extraversion	Intelligence	Extraversion
Psychometric Measures				
Intelligence	(.90)	.30		
Extraversion	.30	(.90)		
Behavior Observations				
Intelligence	.70	.10	(.90)	.30
Extraversion	.10	.70	.30	(.90)

Source: Adapted from Kidder, L. H. (1981). *Research Methods in Social Relations.* New York: Holt, Reinhart and Winston.

Table 4.2 depicts a multitrait-multimethod matrix of our hypothetical example of two traits, intelligence and extraversion, and two methods of measurement, psychometric tests and behavioral observation. The psychometric methods of measurement are the WAIS-IV IQ test for the construct of intelligence and the NEO Five Factor Personality Inventory test for the construct of extraversion. There are three important points regarding the multitrait-multimethod matrix of correlational values (see Chapter 1) presented in Table 4.2. First, the correlational values presented in the diagonal (in parentheses) of the matrix are the Cronbach alpha reliability coefficients. This is a correlational statistic that indicates the degree of internal consistency for each of the four measurements; higher values reflect stronger reliability of the measure. As shown in the matrix, each of the four measurements had reliability coefficients of .90. Correlation values of this magnitude indicate highly reliable, internally consistent measures.

Second are the same-trait-different-method correlation coefficient values. Here we see a .70 correlation coefficient between scores on the WAIS-IV IQ test and behavioral observation recordings for the construct of intelligence. We also see an identical .70 value for the correlation between scores on the NEO Five Factor Inventory test of extraversion and behavioral observation recordings for the construct of extraversion. Thus the same-trait-different-method comparisons revealed high correlation values of .70 for intelligence and for personality. We therefore can conclude that our results demonstrated convergent validity for the each of these constructs of intelligence and extraversion. Third, the different-traits-same-method pairs for psychometric tests of intelligence and extraversion revealed a very low value of .30, as did the different-traits-same-method pairs for behavioral observations of intelligence and extraversion. For discriminant validity, there should be no relationship between two different constructs such as intelligence and extraversion that are tested with the same form of measurement, such as a psychometric instrument or behavioral observation.

To summarize, the multitrait-multimethod template is a matrix of correlation coefficient values. Recall from Chapter 1 that a correlation coefficient can range from 0.00 to +1.00 and 0.00 to −1.00. The absolute value of a correlation coefficient indicates the strength of the relationship between two variables, with a higher absolute value indicating a stronger relationship. Recall also from Chapter 1, the positive and negative signs of the correlation coefficient tell the direction of the relationship between the two variables. A positive correlation coefficient (a "plus" sign) means as one variable increases, so does the other variable. A negative correlation coefficient indicated by a "minus" sign means that as one variable increases, the other variable decreases. For the matrix, three sets of correlations are vital (see Table 4.3). First, in the diagonal of the matrix are reliability correlation coefficients (e.g., Cronbach alphas) for each measure, which you hope are high, as they indicate the extent to which the items of a given test cohere or coalesce. Second are the correlation coefficients of two different measures of the same construct, which you also hope are high, as they indicate convergent validity. Third are correlation coefficients of pairs of same measures of different constructs, which you hope are low, as they indicate discriminant validity. Last are the nonsense correlations of different traits and different measures.

Latent Variable Models

Constructs can be inferred, developed, and evaluated through the use of a set of specialized statistical techniques that are referred to as **latent variable models** (Heinen, 1996). Perhaps the most well-known of these models is **factor analysis,** which can be used when a researcher wants to identify distinct dimensions or "factors" of a given construct (DeCoster, 1998). For example, let us consider the well-known five-factor model of personality. In this model, the construct of personality has been shown to encompass five distinct but universal factors or traits: neuroticism, extraversion, openness, agreeableness, and conscientiousness. How, you may

Table 4.3   Correlation Coefficients in a Multitrait-Multimethod Matrix

Coefficients	Constructs/Traits	Methods/Measurements
1. Reliability correlation	Same	Same
2. Convergent validity correlation	Same	Different
3. Discriminant validity correlation	Different	Same
4. Nonsense correlation	Different	Different

Source: Adapted from Kidder (1981).

ask, did this model come to be? Essentially, the model is a product of factor analyses, which may be viewed as a "bottom up" inductive procedure that investigates patterns of correlations among responses to a very large set of measurable indicators or variables. In this example, these indicators or variables are objective responses to an extensive sample of thousands of personality test items. Factor analysis as a statistical technique uncovers what items coalesce or the extent to which participants respond similarly across various personality items. The more similar the scores, the more likely it is that this set of items taps a particular factor, such as extraversion.

Note the researcher labels a factor such as extraversion based on what the interrelated items appear to be measuring. That is, the researcher infers the factor on the basis of the content of interrelated items. Labeling and inferring factors are thus based on interpretation of the content that is measured. It is subjective even though it is based on empirical findings, and as a result, it often needs to be confirmed on a second independent sample of participants given the same test items. This is referred to as **confirmatory factor analysis**, which is used to determine whether the same set of factors can be replicated in new independent sample.

Constructs and factors are often used interchangeably. For our example, however, we used factor analysis in order to test the five factor model of personality. The five factors—neuroticism, extraversion, agreeableness, openness, and conscientiousness—may be viewed as distinct dimensions or traits of the construct of personality. In other research, as in our construct validity example, each of these personality traits can also be conceptualized as constructs in its own right.

CONCLUSIONS

In this chapter, you learned the essence of theoretical constructs and how they are tested and evaluated through a combination of experimentation and measurement. Research in psychology may be viewed as a dynamic interplay between conceptual and operational modes of thinking. On one hand are theoretical constructs that exist as abstract formulations in need of empirical validation. On the other hand are operational definitions that act as recipes for specifying how constructs will be produced and measured. In experimental studies, an operational definition such as a staged manipulation can be used to induce a mental state or to create the conditions that are thought to reflect the essence of the construct under investigation.

As an example, recall the staged manipulation Bushman and Baumeister used to create conditions for interpersonal violence by insulting research participants. A researcher always aims to create or design an experimental manipulation that captures the essence of a construct that is being investigated. As we know from Chapter 2, ecological validity comes into play when thinking about the marriage of theoretical constructs and their experimental instantiations. Here you would be wise to consider how realistic is the experimental manipulation in fostering the desired mental state or producing the relevant conditions for the construct under investigation and how realistic are the dependent variables used to measure the construct. And thus, as you learned, a construct will be intimately tied to the independent variables that produce it and the dependent variables that measure it.

The chapter also emphasized the importance of measurement. You learned that a dependent variable may use one of four scales of measurement: nominal, ordinal, interval, or ratio. These scales of measurement are especially important when considering arithmetic calculations. Recall, for example, that a nominal scale reflects simple categorization for which any arithmetic calculations beyond basic counting are impossible.

Last, measurement in the form of standardized tests, you learned, is a field of study in of itself to which an influential and at times controversial school of psychology, known as psychometrics, is dedicated. The source of the controversy centers on the inherent outcome bias in the race–IQ disparity. Recent social psychological studies have shown that stereotype threat is a key factor contributing to the 15-point IQ gap between African Americans and white Americans. However, the controversy is not about IQ as a psychological trait of individual difference. That, as we have seen, is well established through the scientific method of psychology, particularly psychometric studies of reliability and validity. In fact, psychometrics is based on the principles of standardization of test construction, test administration, and test scoring. In addition, psychometric tests can be evaluated in terms of various reliability coefficients, such as the Cronbach alpha that provides a quantitative measure of the internal consistency of a test. Similarly, test-retest reliability provides a quantitative measure of the stability of scores over time.

The principles of validity also represent a cornerstone of the psychometric approach. In fact, the multitrait-multimethod matrix is the gold standard for evaluating construct validity. Recall our example of a multitrait-multimethod matrix involving two constructs, intelligence and extraversion, and two methods of measurements, observational ratings and pencil-and-paper psychometric tests (i.e., WAIS-IV IQ, and NEO Extraversion). Here the two aspects of construct validity—convergent validity and discriminant validity—can both be evaluated. Recall that convergent validity is established when two different methods of measurement of the same construct correlate or produce similar results. And recall that discriminant validity is established when the same two methods of measurement of two different constructs are unrelated or uncorrelated.

END OF CHAPTER

Chapter Highlights

- Psychological theory provides a conceptual framework for a study by defining key terms, specifying how variables are to be measured or operationalized, and explaining the purpose and rationale for the research.

- Think of a conceptual framework as a network of interlocking relationships linking theoretical ideas to concrete variables and their measurements.

- Abstract concepts are formally referred to as constructs that are specified by a theory in order to describe, explain, and predict a wide range of related empirical findings.

- Constructs are operationalized in research by one or more indicators, or measures, which may be derived from observation, self-report, rating scales, clinical indicators, test scores, or some combination of these.

- An operational definition provides a recipe for how to measure (dependent variables) and to produce (independent variables) a construct.

- The scientific validity of a theory or a theoretical construct hinges on the extent to which it describes, predicts, and explains those empirical relationships that are uncovered between independent and dependent variables.

- Level of measurement indicates the type of information obtained about a variable and the type of statistics that can be used to describe its variation. The four levels of measurement can be ordered by complexity of the mathematical operations they permit: nominal (least complex), ordinal, interval, ratio (most complex). The measurement level of a variable is determined by how the variable is operationalized. Dichotomies, a special case, may be treated as measured at the nominal or ordinal level.

- Nonparametric statistics test hypotheses for variables that use either nominal or ordinal levels of measurement, and parametric statistics can be used for variables that use interval or ratio levels of measurement.

- Psychometrics is a school of psychology that studies the application of psychological tests as objective measures of the mind and mental processes.

- Psychometrics of ability testing should always be mindful of the insidious effects of stereotype threat on performance.

- In constructing a psychometric test, a researcher identifies a standardization sample, which is defined as a random selection of people drawn from a carefully defined population. From the standardization sample, the norms of the test are calculated.

- The norms of a test involve two measures: The first is the mean or average score for the standardization sample. The second measure is the standard deviation, which indicates the degree to which an individual score deviates from the sample mean.

- For many human traits, from height to weight to intelligence and personality features, scores are distributed along a normal curve. When the distribution of scores approximates a normal curve, most scores fall near the center, with gradually fewer scores as you move toward either extreme.

- For a test to be meaningful or useful, it must be both reliable and valid.

- A reliable test yields consistent scores when the construct being measured is not changing (or the measured scores change in direct correspondence to actual changes in the construct).

- Measurement reliability is a prerequisite for measurement validity, although reliable measures are not necessarily valid. Reliability can be assessed through a test-retest procedure, in terms of interitem consistency, through a comparison of responses to alternate forms of the test, or in terms of consistency among observers.

- The validity of measures should always be evaluated. There are four basic approaches: face validation, content validation, criterion validation (either predictive or concurrent), and construct validation.

- Construct validation provides the strongest approach to evaluating the validity of an idea or theory. A nomological network in construct validity refers to the interlocking relationships between the observable, measurable, or empirical and the inferable, interpretable, or theoretical.

- The multitrait-multimethod matrix as a method to assess construct validity represents the gold standard for testing the validity of new ideas and new measurements in psychology.

- In a multitrait-multimethod matrix, convergent validity is established if the same trait measured by two different methods yields similar results, and discriminant validity is established if two different traits measured by the same method yield dissimilar results.

- Constructs can be inferred, developed, and evaluated through the use of a set of specialized statistical techniques that are referred to as latent variable models, such as factor analysis.

Key Terms

Alternate-forms reliability   119

Circular reasoning   120

Concurrent validity   121

Confirmatory factor analysis   125

Construct   96

Construct validity   121

Content validity   120

Convergent validity   122

Criterion validity   121

Cronbach's alpha   119

Dichotomy   104

Discriminant validity   122

Exhaustive   103

Face validity   120

Factor analysis   124

Hereditarian   112

Interitem reliability   119

Interobserver reliability   119

Research in the News

In a May 10, 2010 *New York Times* piece, "Metric Mania" mathematics professor John Allen Paulos writes, "The problem isn't with statistical tests themselves but what we do before and after we run them." Let's imagine that you have been assigned to write a similar piece for the *New York Times* that you cleverly title "The Rule of Measurement." In your piece, you want to explain to the reader that all statistics depend on reliable and valid measurements. That is, you want to explain why reliable and valid measurement is the lifeline of statistics as well as a vital component of all research. In so doing, describe the four different levels of measurement and how each can be applied to investigate a research question.

Activity Questions

1. Richard E. Nisbett (2009) argues in his book, *Intelligence and How to Get It: Why Schools and Culture Count,* the disparity in average IQ between Americans of

European and of African descent is "purely environmental." Explain how the Lewontin (1976) analogy shows that the racial disparities in IQ are best understood in terms of environmental factors.

2. Role play what it would be like being a research participant assigned to either the stereotype threat or nonstereotype threat condition of the Steele and Aronson (1995) study. Perhaps hand out exam blue books and read the two different sets of instructions to give your students a feel for what it would be like to be in either the stereotype threat or nonstereotype condition.

3. The Implicit Association Test (IAT) is among the most widely researched web-based measures of covert thoughts and feelings. Go to https://implicit.harvard.edu/implicit/ and investigate the IAT and take one of the IAT measures. Evaluate the IAT in terms of reliability and validity. What are the pros and cons of this relatively new technology for assessing covert thoughts and feelings? What are the cultural implications?

4. Are important constructs in psychological research always defined clearly? Are they defined consistently? Search the literature for six research articles that focus on "mental illness," "mental health," "happiness," or some other construct suggested by your instructor. Is the construct defined clearly in each article? How similar are the definitions? Write up what you have found in a short report.

5. Two important human traits—intelligence and happiness—have attracted your curiosity. You are interested in construct validation of these two traits. You have at your disposal two methods of measurement: psychometric tests and behavioral observations. Show how you would use a multitrait-multimethod matrix to evaluate construct validity of intelligence and happiness using these two different methods of measurement. Make sure to address both convergent validity and discriminant validity.

6. Imagine you have been asked by a political consultant to devise a measure to assess whether people agree or disagree with a set of positions regarding a particular policy or political position. Describe how you would use a *nominal* level of measurement to gauge people's opinions. What statistic would you use to summarize your hypothetical data that you plan to collect using a nominal level of measurement? What statistical test would you use to analyze your nominal data? Now describe how you would use an *ordinal* level of measurement to gauge people's opinions. Again, identify the statistic you would use to summarize your ordinal data and also indicate the best statistical approach for your data analysis. Finally, compare and contrast your nominal and ordinal levels of measurement.

7. Stereotype threat creates a significant problem in psychometric testing of cognitive abilities. Imagine that you wanted to study the effect of stereotype threat on high-level mathematics performance in women. Explain the stereotype threat and how it is theorized to detract from women's performance in mathematics, especially at higher levels of complexity. What staged manipulation would you devise to create

or operationalize stereotype threat in this study? How might stereotype threat be reduced so that people are judged by their abilities rather than by stereotype?

8. The construct of intelligence extends well beyond what is measured by IQ tests. For example, psychologist Howard Gardner (1983, 1993) proposed the existence of multiple intelligences ranging from musical to logical-mathematical to interpersonal ability. What do you think intelligence means? What would your construct of intelligence entail? Would you include, as Howard Gardner does, a *bodily-kinesthetic intelligence* that is shown by gifted athletes, surgeons, or dancers?

Review Questions

1. Think of a construct that we covered in Chapter 1. How was it developed? How is it operationalized?

2. Why does a Likert scale use an ordinal level of measurement?

3. What are the advantages of using multiple methods or multiple forms of measurement such as behavioral observations and psychophysiological recordings?

4. Why is face validity inadequate? How would social desirability bias and face validity be related?

5. Why is IQ measured with an interval scale and Fahrenheit with a ratio scale?

6. Why can only the mode be used with data measured with a nominal scale? Why can't the arithmetic mean and standard deviation be used with nominal level of measurement?

7. What IQ score equals one-and-one third standard deviation below the mean of 100?

8. What percentages of cases are expected to fall within plus or minus 1 standard deviation of the mean of the normal curve?

9. How would you stratify a sample of 2,000 people ranging in ages from 16 to 90?

10. How would you demonstrate that a test provides an internally consistent measure of a construct?

11. Why is discriminant validity important for construct validation?

12. Describe the relationship between the four levels of measurements and parametric/nonparametric statistics.

13. Describe the research design used in stereotype threat studies.

14. How does research on stereotype threat help explain the IQ disparity between Americans of European and of African descent?

15. Discus the ethics of using staged manipulations in research.

16. Explain the principles of construct validity. Show how to construct a multitrait-multimethod matrix.

17. Why would alternate-forms reliability be important when comparing people's memory before and after receiving a treatment drug?

18. What is outcome bias?

19. What kind of evidence would you cite to demonstrate predictive validity of IQ?

20. What is circular reasoning and how can it be prevented?

Ethics in Action

1. What are the ethical implications of the erroneous conclusion that racial group difference in IQ are hardwired, fixed, and genetically immutable? How does such a mistaken claim lead to the ethically dubious argument that enrichment programs are of little or no benefit because of immutable group IQ differences?

2. Recall from Chapter 3 ("Research in the News") the importance of fully informed consent for research participants in regard to how data collected from them in a given study will be used. Now consider informed consent for research participants in a study of racial differences in group IQ. What are the major ethical obligations a researcher has in ensuring that participants are fully informed as to the purpose of a study examining racial differences group IQ?

3. In the stereotype threat studies by Steele and colleagues, participants are given the same test, but some participants are essentially told it is an IQ measure and other participants are told it a nondiagnostic measure of problem solving (i.e., not an IQ test). How would you justify this deception as ethically justified? How it in keeping is it with the principle elucidated in the APA Ethical Code (see Chapter 3): *Avoid deception in research, except in limited circumstances*?

CHAPTER 5

Sampling and Survey Research

SUBSTANTIVE THEME: HAPPINESS

Below are five statements with which you may agree or disagree. Using the 1–7 scale below, indicate your agreement with each item by placing the appropriate number on the line preceding that item. Please be open and honest in your responding.

The 7-point scale is: 1 = *strongly disagree*, 2 = *disagree*, 3 = *slightly disagree*, 4 = *neither agree nor disagree*, 5 = *slightly agree*, 6 = *agree*, 7 = *strongly agree*.

Rating	Statement
_____	1. In most ways, my life is close to my ideal.
_____	2. The conditions of my life are excellent.
_____	3. I am satisfied with my life.
_____	4. So far I have gotten the important things I want in life.
_____	5. If I could live my life over, I would change almost nothing.

$$\Sigma \text{ (sum) } \#1 - \#5 = \underline{\quad}. \quad \Sigma / 5 = \underline{\quad}.$$

Congratulations! You have just completed psychologist Ed Diener's (Diener, Emmons, Larson, & Griffin, 1985) Satisfaction With Life Scale, a widely used measure of happiness. Perhaps it will make you just a bit happier to know that you have also just encountered the key steps in the research process that we present in this chapter. You have participated in a *survey* about happiness. You have completed a *scale,* or multi-item *index,* to *measure* your happiness. You and your classmates comprise a **sample** of students. And when you calculated your average response to the five statements, you created a *statistic* that you can use to analyze the survey results. Keep that score at hand; we'll use it later.

In this chapter, you will learn about sampling and survey research methods: the procedures used to develop generalizable research findings about a large population. We first discuss why it is important to consider the key sampling question: Can findings from a sample be generalized to the population from which the sample was drawn? We then review different sampling methods. Next, we explain the major steps in designing questions and combining them in scales. We also describe four different types of surveys and give examples of some basic statistics that are useful in analyzing data obtained in **survey research**. We conclude with a discussion of ethical issues in survey research. By the chapter's end, you should be well on your way to becoming an informed critic of sample surveys and a knowledgeable creator of surveys—and you will also have expanded your knowledge about happiness. We hope *that* makes you happy!

SELECTING RESEARCH PARTICIPANTS

Do people differ in the behaviors, attitudes, or processes that you will study? You probably know some people who tend to be happy and others who don't. No doubt you have been happy at some times and unhappy at others. So you would realize that if we seek to learn about happiness, we have to be concerned with who we study and when we study them. If we were only to study happy people, we would get a very different impression than if we studied unhappy people. This is why researchers have to be concerned with sampling—the selection of individuals or other entities to represent a larger population of interest.

Of course, if we can study the entire population of interest—that is, conduct a **census**—we can avoid the problem. This is what the federal government tries to do every 10 years with the U.S. Census. But the census approach is not likely to be feasible with a large population. To conduct the 2000 census, the U.S. Bureau of the Census spent almost $4.5 billion and took 12 years planning its methods (Prewitt, 2000; U.S. Bureau of the Census, 2000a). Half a million temporary workers and up to six follow-ups were required to contact the third of American households who did not respond to the initial mailed census questionnaire (U.S. Bureau of the Census, 2000b, 2000c). Even after all that, the number of persons missed in the census was still estimated to be between 3.2 and 6.4 million (U.S. Bureau of the Census, 2001). For most survey purposes, it is much better to survey only a limited number from the total population so there are more resources for follow-up procedures required to locate respondents and overcome their reluctance to participate.

SAMPLE PLANNING

In order to plan a sample or to assess the quality of a sample selected by another researcher, you need to answer two questions:

- From what population will you select cases?
- What method will you use to select cases from this population?

Define the Population

Let's focus first on defining the population, since everything else in a sample survey depends on that. Behavioral researchers have administered happiness surveys to samples of many different populations. Some have surveyed students, some have surveyed other groups in the U.S., while others have surveyed samples of the entire U.S. population as well as samples in other countries. The results of these surveys demonstrate the importance of the population we study, for there are some surprising consistencies and some unexpected differences. Students, disabled persons, the elderly, and adult samples tend to report similar, although not identical, levels of happiness, as do men and women, African Americans and whites (Diener & Diener, 1996; Myers & Diener, 1995). However, when Ed Diener, Marissa Diener, and Carol Diener (1995) analyzed surveys of happiness in countries around the world, they found that the average level of happiness varied markedly. In addition, satisfaction with different life domains varies across cultures (Biswas-Diener, Vitterso, & Diener, 2005).

So we can't generalize happiness findings from the population in one country to the population in another country, or from one specific population, or group, within one country to another group. If we want to assess the **cross-population generalizability** of our findings, we need to compare results obtained from samples of different populations. And this is not just true in happiness research. As another example, psychologists Yuri Miyamoto, Richard Nisbett, and Takahiko Masuda (2006) have found differences in how people from Eastern and Western cultures perceive identical scenes (Westerners focus on distinctive objects, while people from Asian cultures tend to view scenes holistically). The key issue is that we define clearly the population that we actually have studied and not give the impression that we collected data about some larger or different aggregation that we really wish we could have studied.

Define Sample Components

Once we have determined a population to study, we need to develop procedures for drawing a sample from that population that is representative of the population. Before we introduce different methods for sampling from a population, you need to learn a few more terms (**Exhibit 5.1**).

In many studies, we sample directly from the **elements**, or elementary units, in the population of interest. For a survey about mental health among students at a large midwestern public university, Daniel Eisenberg, Sarah Gollust, Ezra Golberstein, and Jennifer Hefner (2007) obtained from the registrar's office a list of the entire population of students at the school. This list, from which the elements of the population are selected, is termed the **sampling frame**. The students who are selected and interviewed from that list are the elements.

Population. The entire set of individuals or other entities to which study findings are to be generalized.

Elements. The individual members of the population whose characteristics are to be measured.

Sampling frame. A list of all elements in a population.

Representative sample. A sample that "looks like" the population from which it was selected in all respects potentially relevant to the study. The distribution of characteristics among the elements of a representative sample is the same as the distribution of those characteristics among the total population. In an unrepresentative sample, some characteristics are overrepresented or underrepresented. Random selection of elements maximizes sample representativeness.

Sample generalizability depends on the amount of **sampling error**—the difference between the characteristics of a sample and the characteristics of the population from which it was selected. The larger the sampling error, the less representative the sample—and thus the less generalizable the findings obtained from that sample. Of

Exhibit 5.1   Representative and Unrepresentative Samples

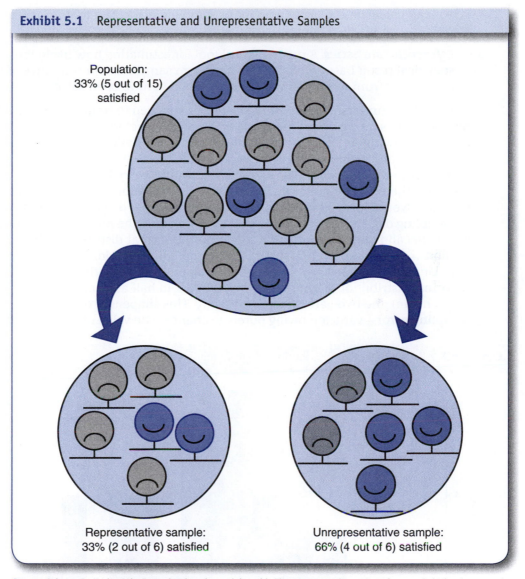

Population:
33% (5 out of 15)
satisfied

Representative sample:
33% (2 out of 6) satisfied

Unrepresentative sample:
66% (4 out of 6) satisfied

Source: Schutt, R. K. (2009). *Investigating the social world: The process and practice of research* (6th ed., p. 151). Thousand Oaks, CA: Pine Forge Press.

course, representation in a sample is never perfect, but it's important to provide information about how representative a given sample is.

Estimating Sampling Error

After we have drawn our sample and obtained our data, we can estimate the confidence we can place on the sample statistic as representative of the population—that is, we can calculate the likely amount of sampling error. The tool for calculating sampling error is called **inferential statistics**.

> *Inferential statistics.* A mathematical tool for estimating how likely it is that a statistical result based on data from a random sample is representative of the population from which the sample is assumed to have been selected.

In order to understand inferential statistics, we need to think of our sample as one possible sample out of many we could have selected from the population. Imagine drawing a great many samples from a population and calculating the average (mean) happiness level for each one. Some of the sample means would be higher and some would be lower; some would be right about at the actual mean for the entire population. If we plot the mean values for all these samples, the chart would form a **sampling distribution**, like that displayed in **Exhibit 5.2**.

Sampling distributions for many statistics, including the mean, have a "normal" shape. Recall from Chapter 4 that a graph of a normal distribution, like that in **Exhibit 5.3**, looks like a bell, with one "hump" in the middle—centered on the population mean—and the number of cases tapering off on both sides of the mean. A normal distribution is symmetric: If you fold it in half at its center (at the population mean), the two halves match perfectly. This shape is produced by **random sampling error**—variation owing purely to chance. The value of a sample statistic

Exhibit 5.2   Partial Sampling Distribution: Mean Family Income

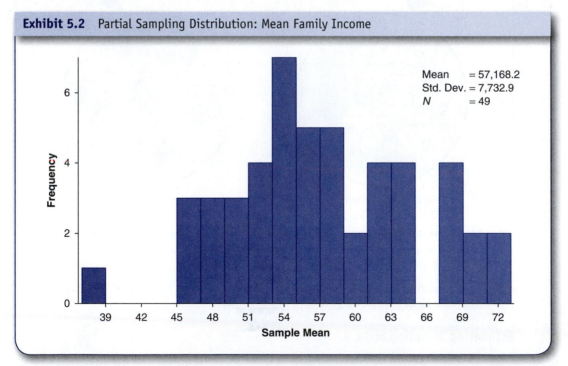

Mean = 57,168.2
Std. Dev. = 7,732.9
N = 49

Source: Schutt, R. K. (2009). *Investigating the social world: The process and practice of research* (6th ed., p. 178). Thousand Oaks, CA: Pine Forge Press.

varies from sample to sample because of chance, so higher and lower values are equally likely.

> *Random sampling error (chance sampling error).* Differences between the population and the sample that are due only to chance factors (random error), not to systematic sampling error. Random sampling error may or may not result in an unrepresentative sample. The magnitude of sampling error due to chance factors can be estimated statistically.

The properties of a sampling distribution facilitate the process of statistical inference. In the sampling distribution, the most frequent value of the **sample statistic**—the statistic (such as the mean) computed from sample data—is identical to the **population parameter**—the statistic computed for the entire population. In other words, we can have a lot of confidence that the value at the peak of the bell curve represents the norm for the entire population. A population parameter also may be termed the *true value* for the statistic in that population. A sample statistic is an estimate of a population parameter.

> *Sample statistic.* The value of a statistic, such as a mean, computed from sample data.

> *Population parameter.* The value of a statistic, such as a mean, computed using the data for the entire population; a sample statistic is an estimate of a population parameter.

In a normal distribution, a predictable proportion of cases falls within certain ranges. Inferential statistics takes advantage of this feature and allows researchers to estimate how likely it is that, given a particular sample, the true population value will be within some range of the statistics. For example, a statistician might conclude from a sample of 30 students that *we can be 95% confident that the true mean family income in the total population is between 20.1 and 25.7.* The interval from 20.1 to 25.7 would then be called the "95% confidence interval for the mean." The lower (20.1) and upper (25.7) bounds of this interval are termed the *confidence limits.* **Exhibit 5.3** marks such confidence limits, indicating the range that encompasses 95% of the area under the normal curve; 95% of all sample means would fall within this range, as does the mean of our hypothetical sample of 30 cases. The more cases in the randomly selected sample, the more confident we can be in a given sample estimate (the confidence limits will be smaller).

SAMPLING METHODS

The most important distinction that needs to be made about samples is whether they are based on a probability or a nonprobability sampling method. Sampling methods that allow us to know in advance how likely it is that any element of a

Exhibit 5.3 Normal Sampling Distribution: Mean Family Income

2.5% of total area

2.5% of total area

95% confidence interval =
95% of the total area under the curve

Lower confidence
limit = $48,459

Upper confidence
limit = $92,539

Mean Family Income = $70,499

Source: Schutt, R. K. (2009). *Investigating the social world: The process and practice of research* (6th ed., p. 179). Thousand Oaks, CA: Pine Forge Press.

population will be selected for the sample are termed **probability sampling methods**. You can only make a statistical estimate of sampling error for a probability-based sample. Sampling methods that do not let us know in advance the likelihood of selecting each element are termed **nonprobability sampling methods**.

Probability sampling methods rely on a random, or chance, selection procedure, which is, in principle, the same as flipping a coin to decide which of two people wins and which one loses. Heads and tails are equally likely to turn up in a coin toss, so both persons have an equal chance of winning. That chance, their **probability of selection**, is 1 out of 2, or .5.

Probability of selection. The likelihood that an element will be selected from the population for inclusion in the sample. In a census of all elements of a population, the probability that any particular element will be selected is 1.0. If half of the elements in the population are sampled on the basis of chance (say, by tossing a coin), the probability of selection for each element is one half, or .5. As the size of the sample decreases as a proportion of the population, so does the probability of selection.

There is a natural tendency to confuse the concept of **random sampling**, in which cases are selected only on the basis of chance, with a haphazard method of sampling. On first impression, "leaving things up to chance" seems to imply not exerting any control over the sampling method. But to ensure that nothing but chance influences the selection of cases, the researcher must proceed methodically, leaving nothing to chance except the selection of the cases themselves. The researcher must follow carefully controlled procedures if a purely random process is to be the result.

PROBABILITY SAMPLING METHODS

Probability sampling methods are those in which the probability of selection is known and is not zero (so there is some chance of selecting each element). These methods randomly select elements and therefore have no **systematic bias**; nothing but chance determines which elements are included in the sample. This feature of probability samples makes them much more desirable than nonprobability samples when the goal is to generalize to a larger population.

Don't make the mistake of thinking that a larger sample is better because it includes a greater proportion of the population. In fact, it is the number of cases that is most important; the proportion of the population that the sample represents does not affect the sample's representativeness—unless that proportion is large (Sudman, 1976). Other things being equal, a random sample of 1,000 from a population of 1 million (with a sampling fraction of 0.001, or 0.1%) is much better than a random sample of 100 from a population of 10,000 (although the sampling fraction is 0.01, or 1%, which is 10 times higher).

The four most common methods for drawing random samples are simple random sampling, systematic random sampling, stratified random sampling, and cluster sampling.

Simple Random Sampling

Simple random sampling requires some procedure that generates numbers or otherwise identifies cases strictly on the basis of chance. As you know, flipping a coin or rolling a die can be used to identify cases strictly on the basis of chance, but these procedures are not very efficient tools for drawing a sample. When a large sample must be generated, a computer program can easily generate a random sample of any size. Organizations that conduct phone surveys often draw random samples using another automated procedure, called **random-digit dialing.** A machine dials random numbers within the phone prefixes corresponding to the area in which the survey is to be conducted.

The probability of selection in a true simple random sample is equal for each element. If a sample of 500 is selected from a population of 17,000 (i.e., a sampling frame of 17,000), then the probability of selection for each element is 500/17,000, or .03. Every element has an equal chance of being selected, just like the odds in a toss of a coin (1/2) or a roll of a die (1/6).

Systematic Random Sampling

Systematic random sampling is a variant of simple random sampling. The first element is selected randomly from a list or from sequential files, and then every *n*th element is selected. This is a convenient method for drawing a random sample when the population elements are arranged sequentially, such as in folders in filing cabinets. The one problem to watch out for is **periodicity**—that is, the sequence varies in some regular, periodic pattern. For example, the houses in a new development with the same number of houses on each block (e.g., eight) may be listed by block, starting with the house in the northwest corner of each block and continuing clockwise. If the **sampling interval** is 8, the same as the periodic pattern, all the cases selected will be in the same position (see **Exhibit 5.4**). In this situation,

Exhibit 5.4   The Effect of Periodicity on Systematic Random Sampling

If the sampling interval is 8 for a study in this neighborhood, every element of the sample will be a house on the northwest corner—and thus the sample will be biased.

Source: Schutt, R. K. (2009). *Investigating the social world: The process and practice of research* (6th ed., p. 163). Thousand Oaks, CA: Pine Forge Press.

the starting point needs to be changed for each block. But in reality, periodicity and the sampling interval are rarely the same.

Stratified Random Sampling

Stratified random sampling uses information known about the total population prior to sampling to make the sampling process more efficient. First, all elements in the population (i.e., in the sampling frame) are distinguished according to their value on some relevant characteristic. That characteristic forms the sampling strata. Next, elements are sampled randomly from within these strata. For example, race may be the basis for distinguishing individuals in some population of interest. Within each racial category, individuals are then sampled randomly. Of course, using this method requires more information prior to sampling than is the case with simple random sampling. It must be possible to categorize each element in one and only one stratum, and the size of each stratum in the population must be known.

This method is more efficient than drawing a simple random sample because it ensures appropriate representation of elements across strata. It is commonly used in national surveys. Yang Yang's (2008) study of happiness over time in the U.S. used the General Social Survey, a multistage stratified probability sample of noninstitutionalized adults ages 18 and older. Recall from Chapter 4 that for the WAIS-IV, the test developers used data gathered in October 2005 by the U.S. Bureau of Census to stratify their standardization sample along the following variables: age, sex, race/ethnicity, self or parent educational level, and geographic region.

Stratified sampling can be either proportionate or disproportionate. **Proportionate stratified sampling** ensures that the sample is selected so that the distribution of characteristics in the sample matches the distribution of the corresponding characteristics in the population. So, for example, if the population ratio of undergraduates to graduates is 2 to 1, the number of students sampled in both strata can be set so as to replicate this ratio (**Exhibit 5.5**). Daniel Eisenberg and his colleagues (2007) used a slightly different sampling design, **disproportionate stratified sampling**, in a survey of student mental health at a large midwestern university. The registrar's list distinguished undergraduate and graduate students, so Eisenberg and colleagues were able to sample these two groups separately, as different strata. They knew that the mental health of graduate and professional students "has been particularly understudied," so they selected a higher fraction of graduate students than undergraduate students from the list provided by the registrar. This disproportionate sampling procedure enabled them to calculate separate statistical estimates for graduate as well as for undergraduate students.

Cluster Sampling

Cluster sampling is useful when a sampling frame of elements is not available, as often is the case for large populations spread out across a wide geographic area or

Exhibit 5.5 Stratified Random Sampling

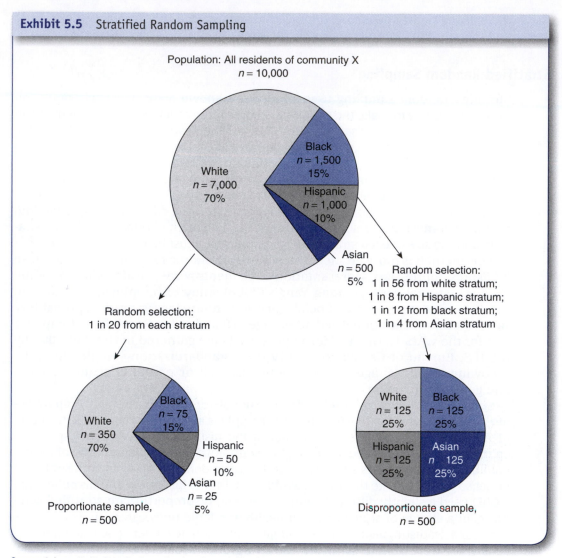

Source: Schutt, R. K. (2009). *Investigating the social world: The process and practice of research* (6th ed., p. 165). Thousand Oaks, CA: Pine Forge Press.

among many different organizations. A **cluster** is a naturally occurring, mixed aggregate of elements of the population, with each element appearing in one, and only one, cluster. Schools could serve as clusters for sampling students, blocks could serve as clusters for sampling city residents, counties could serve as clusters for sampling the general population, and businesses could serve as clusters for sampling employees.

Drawing a cluster sample is, at least, a two-stage procedure. First, the researcher draws a random sample of clusters (**Exhibit 5.6**). A list of clusters should be much easier to obtain than a list of all the individuals in each cluster in the population. Next, the researcher draws a random sample of elements within each selected

Exhibit 5.6 Multistage Cluster Sampling

Stage 1:
Randomly
select states

Stage 2:
Randomly select cities,
towns, and counties
within those states

Stage 3:
Randomly select
schools within
those cities and towns

Stage 4:
Randomly select
students within
each school

Source: Schutt, R. K. (2009). *Investigating the social world: The process and practice of research* (6th ed., p. 167). Thousand Oaks, CA: Pine Forge Press.

cluster. Because only a fraction of the total clusters are involved, obtaining the sampling frame at this stage should be much easier. For example, in a cluster sample of students, a researcher could contact the schools selected in the first stage and make arrangements with the registrar to obtain lists of students at each school. (Levy & Lemeshow, 1999). Many professionally designed surveys combine cluster and stratified probability sampling methods.

NONPROBABILITY SAMPLING METHODS

In contrast to these other sampling methods, availability sampling (also called convenience sampling) is a **nonprobability sampling method**. This method does not use a random selection procedure, so we will not know if an availability sample is a representative sample of some larger population. Nonetheless, behavioral research with samples of those students who are simply "available" for experiments or surveys have shown that availability sampling can lead to great insights about human behavior and psychological processes.

Elements are selected for **availability sampling** because they're available or easy to find. Thus, this sampling method is also known as haphazard, accidental, or convenience sampling. There are many ways to select elements for an availability sample, such as inviting interested students to come to an on-campus lab, including a survey inside a magazine (with the plea to subscribers to complete and return it), or asking questions of available students at campus hangouts. Many happiness researchers have used availability samples of students who volunteer to participate in a research project.

Quota Sampling

Quota sampling is intended to overcome the most obvious flaw of availability sampling: that the sample will just consist of whoever or whatever is available, without any concern for its similarity to the population of interest. The distinguishing feature of a quota sample is that quotas are set to ensure that the sample represents certain characteristics in proportion to their prevalence in the population.

Suppose that you wish to sample adult residents of a town in a study of support for placing a group home in the town. You know from the town's annual report what the proportions of town residents are in terms of gender, race, age, and number of children. This is where quotas come in. Let's say that 48 % of the town's adult residents are men and 52 % are women, and that 60 % are employed, 5 % are unemployed, and 35 % are out of the labor force. These percentages and the percentages corresponding to the other characteristics become the quotas for the sample. If you plan to include a total of 500 residents in your sample, 240 must be men (48 % of 500), 260 must be women, 300 must be employed, and so on. With the quota list in hand, you (or your research staff) can now go out into the community looking for the right number of people in each quota category. You may go door to door, bar to bar, or just stand on a street corner until you have surveyed 240 men, 260 women, and so on.

Exhibit 5.7 summarizes the differences between quota sampling and stratified random sampling. The key difference, of course, is quota sampling's lack of random selection.

No matter what type of sample you draw, your sample will be less representative if more potential respondents refuse to participate. Unfortunately, this is a real problem in national surveys. The rate of response to most surveys in the United States and Western Europe has been declining since the early 1950s (Groves & Couper, 1998). Growing popular cynicism and distrust of government have undermined trust in the value of social research. More recently, people have been using caller ID to screen out calls from unknown parties. Growing reliance on cell phones compounds the problem. There are no directories of cell phone numbers and calls to cell phones may go unanswered simply because the recipient must pay the cost of the call (Nagourney, 2002). As a result of these changes, it has become increasingly challenging for survey researchers to achieve the 70 % response rate that most consider necessary if their survey results are to represent the surveyed population.

Exhibit 5.7 Comparison of Stratified and Quota Sampling Methods

Feature	Stratified	Quota
Unbiased (random) selection of cases	Yes	No
Sampling frame required	Yes	No
Ensures representation of key strata	Yes	Yes

Source: Schutt, R. K. (2009). *Investigating the social world: The process and practice of research* (6th ed., p. 173). Thousand Oaks, CA: Pine Forge Press.

WRITING SURVEY QUESTIONS

Once you have chosen a population to study and a method for sampling from that population, you must decide what questions to ask in your survey. Presenting clear and interesting questions in a well-organized questionnaire is a critical task. All hope for achieving measurement validity is lost unless the questions in a survey are clear and convey the intended meaning to respondents.

Adherence to a few basic principles will go a long way toward ensuring clear and meaningful questions.

Avoid Confusing Phrasing

Try to answer the following question, one used in a 1980 "National Priorities Survey, United States Space Program" by the Planetary Society:

> The Moon may be a place for an eventual scientific base, and even for engineering resources. Setting up a base or mining experiment will cost tens of billions of dollars in the next century. Should the United States pursue further manned and unmanned scientific research projects on the surface of the Moon?
>
> Yes ☐   No ☐   No opinion ☐

Does a "yes" response mean that you favor spending tens of billions of dollars for a base or for a mining experiment? How should you answer if you favor further research projects on the Moon but oppose funding a scientific base or engineering? How do you answer if you favor unmanned scientific research projects but oppose manned projects?

In most cases, a simple direct approach to asking a question minimizes confusion. Try to use shorter rather than longer words and sentences and keep the total number of words to 20 or fewer and the number of commas to three or fewer (Peterson, 2000). Here's a good, clear question used in the General Social Survey to measure happiness:

> Taken all together, how would you say things are these days—would you say that you are very happy, pretty happy, or not too happy?

A sure way to muddy the meaning of a question is to use **double negatives**: "Do you *disagree* that rich people are *not* happy?" Respondents have a hard time figuring out which response matches their sentiments. To be safe, it's best just to avoid using negative words like "don't" and "not" in questions.

So-called **double-barreled questions** are also guaranteed to produce uninterpretable results because they actually ask two questions but allow only one answer. For example, during the Watergate scandal, Gallup poll results indicated that when the question was "Do you think President Nixon should be impeached and compelled to leave the presidency, or not?" only about a third of Americans supported impeaching President Richard M. Nixon. But when the Gallup organization changed the question to ask respondents if they "think there is enough evidence of possible wrongdoing in the case of President Nixon to bring him to trial before the Senate, or not," over half answered yes. Apparently the first "double-barreled" version of the question confused support for impeaching Nixon—putting him on trial before the Senate—with concluding that he was guilty before he had had a chance to defend himself (Kagay & Elder, 1992).

Be sure that each question is asked of only the respondents who have the information needed to answer. If you include a question about job satisfaction in a survey of the general population, first ask respondents whether they have a job. These **filter questions** create **skip patterns**. For example, respondents who answer "no" to one question are directed to skip ahead to another question, but respondents who answer "yes" go on to the **contingent question**. Skip patterns should be indicated clearly with arrows or other marks in the questionnaire as demonstrated in **Exhibit 5.8**.

Minimize the Risk of Bias

Specific words in survey questions should not trigger biases unless that is the researcher's conscious intent. Answers can be biased by subtle problems in phrasing that make certain responses more or less attractive to particular groups, so researchers have to

Exhibit 5.8 Filter Questions and Skip Patterns

Source: Schutt, R. K. (2009). *Investigating the social world: The process and practice of research* (6th ed., p. 264). Thousand Oaks, CA: Pine Forge Press.

test reactions to the phrasing of a question. When Catherine Ross (1990) was seeking to determine respondents' interests in household work rather than formal employment in her survey of stress and mental health, she took special care to phrase her questions in a balanced, unbiased way. For example, she asked, "If you could choose, would you rather do the kind of work people do on jobs or the kind of work that is done around the house?" Her response options were "Jobs," "House," "Both," "Neither," "Don't care," and "Don't know." She could easily have biased the distribution of responses to this question by referring to housework as "the kind of work that women traditionally have done around the house" or by simply referring to housework as "staying home during the day." The explicit gender-typing would probably have made men less likely to choose housework as their preference.

Avoid Making Either Disagreement or Agreement Disagreeable

People often tend to agree with a statement just to avoid seeming disagreeable. When an illegal or socially disapproved behavior or attitude is the focus, we have to be concerned that some respondents will be reluctant to agree that they have ever done or thought such a thing. In this situation, the goal is to write a question and response choices that make agreement seem more acceptable. For example, Kilpatrick and colleagues (2003) prefaced their questions about childhood sexual victimization with a statement that began as follows:

> Sometimes a person may do sexual things to a young person that the young person doesn't want. These unwanted sexual things can happen to boys as well as girls and to young men as well as young women. People who try to do unwanted sexual things to young people are not always strangers. . . . They can even be a family member.

Asking about a variety of behaviors or attitudes that range from socially acceptable to socially unacceptable will also soften the impact of agreeing with those that are socially unacceptable.

Minimize Fence-Sitting and Floating

Two related problems in question writing also stem from people's desire to choose an acceptable answer.

Fence-sitters, people who see themselves as being neutral, may skew the results if you force them to choose between opposites. In most cases, about 10% to 20% of such respondents—those who do not have strong feelings on an issue—will choose an explicit middle, neutral alternative (Schuman & Presser, 1981). Adding an explicit neutral response option is appropriate when you want to find out who is a fence-sitter.

Even more people can be termed **floaters**: respondents who choose a substantive answer when they really don't know. A third of the public will provide an opinion on a proposed law that they know nothing about if they are asked for their opinion in a closed-ended survey question that does not include "Don't know" as an explicit response choice (**Exhibit 5.9**). However, 90 % of these persons will select the "Don't know" response if they are explicitly given that option. On average, offering an explicit response option increases the "Don't know" responses by about a fifth (Schuman & Presser, 1981). It's a good idea to omit the "No opinion" or "Don't know" category when you feel that people have an opinion but are reluctant to express it.

Conducting a **survey pretest** should be the final step to check question wording. For a pretest, draw a small sample of individuals from the population you are studying, or one very similar to it, and try out the survey procedures with them. You may include in the pretest version of a written questionnaire some space for individuals to comment on each key question or, with in-person interviews, audiotape the test interviews for later review. Revise any questions that respondents do not seem to interpret as you had intended or that are not working well for other reasons.

COMBINING QUESTIONS IN INDEXES AND SCALES

Writing single questions that yield usable answers is a challenge. Even though they may seem simple, single questions are prone to error due to **idiosyncratic variation**, which occurs when individuals' responses vary because of their reactions to

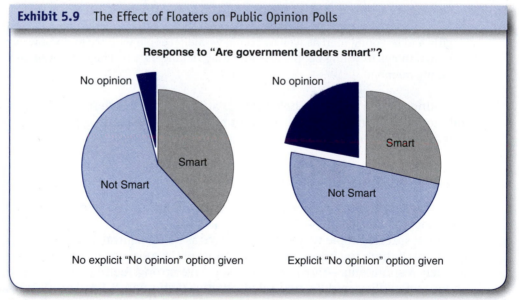

Exhibit 5.9   The Effect of Floaters on Public Opinion Polls

Source: Schutt, R. K. (2009). *Investigating the social world: The process and practice of research* (6th ed., p. 267). Thousand Oaks, CA: Pine Forge Press.

particular words or ideas in the question. Differences in respondents' backgrounds, knowledge, and beliefs almost guarantee that some will understand the same question differently.

The guidelines in this chapter for writing clear questions should help to reduce idiosyncratic variation caused by different interpretations of questions. But the best option is often to develop multiple questions about a concept and then to average the responses to those questions in a composite measure termed an **index**.

> *Index.* The sum or average of responses to a set of questions about a concept.

The idea is that idiosyncratic variation in response to particular questions will average out, so the main influence on the combined measure will be the concept that all the questions focus on. The index can be considered a more complete measure of the concept than can any one of the component questions.

Creating an index is not just a matter of writing a few questions that seem to focus on a concept. Questions that seem to you to measure a common concept might seem to respondents to concern several different issues. The only way to know that a given set of questions does, in fact, form an index is to administer the questions to people like those you plan to study. If a common concept is being measured, people's responses to the different questions should display some consistency. In other words, responses to the different questions should be correlated. Diener and company's (1985) Satisfaction With Life Scale is an example of a well-tested index. Did you find that your responses to five questions were generally consistent? Were there some idiosyncratic reasons that you answered one or more questions differently than the others? Special statistics called reliability measures help researchers decide whether responses are consistent across the questions asked of a sample.

Psychologists have developed a great many indexes that have proved to be reliable in a range of studies and are available for subsequent researchers, like the SWS scale. It usually is much better to use such an index to measure a concept than to try to devise questions to form a new index. Use of an existing index both simplifies the work involved in designing a study and facilitates comparison of findings to those obtained in other studies.

DESIGNING QUESTIONNAIRES

Survey questions are answered as part of a **questionnaire** (or **interview schedule**, as it's often called in interview-based studies). The design of the questionnaire influences how individual questions are interpreted and whether they are even answered. As a result, survey researchers must give very careful attention to the design of the questionnaire as well as to the individual questions that it includes.

> *Questionnaire.* The survey instrument containing the questions in a self-administered survey.

> *Interview schedule.* The survey instrument containing the questions asked by the interviewer in an in-person or phone survey.

The way a questionnaire should be designed varies with the specific survey method used and with other particulars of a survey project. There can be no precise formula for identifying questionnaire features that reduce error. Nonetheless, some key principles should guide the design of any questionnaire, and some systematic procedures should be considered for refining it.

Order the Questions

The order in which questions are presented will influence how respondents react to the questionnaire as a whole and how they may answer some questions. Both the major sections in the questionnaire and the questions within the sections must be organized in a logical order that would make sense in a conversation.

Question order can lead to **context effects** (also called **priming effects**) when one or more questions influence responses to subsequent questions (Schober, 1999). Fritz Strack, Leonard L. Martin, and Norbert Schwartz (1988) identified the importance of context effects in happiness surveys. They asked students two questions:

1. How happy are you with your life in general?

2. How happy are you with your dating?

The students were asked to rate their happiness in response to each question on an 11-point scale, ranging from "not so happy" to "extremely happy."

But here's the catch. Some of the questionnaires presented the questions in the order used above, on successive pages, while other questionnaires presented the questions in the reverse order, on successive pages. Can you guess the results? When students were asked the dating question first, they tended to report that they were happier with their "life in general." That is a context or priming effect. Similarly, married people tend to report that they are happier "in general" if the general happiness question is preceded by a question about their happiness with their marriage (Schuman & Presser, 1981). Focusing respondents' attention on something specific they felt happy about caused them to think more about that when they responded to the next question about their general happiness (Kahneman et al., 2006). We can also refer to context effects as a focusing illusion (see Chapter 1, *Activity Questions*).

When you design a survey, you should be aware of the potential for problems due to question order and evaluate carefully the likelihood of context effects. (Labaw, 1980).

ORGANIZING SURVEYS

Now that you have your questions prepared, you must decide what type of survey to conduct. There are five basic survey designs: mailed, group-administered, phone, in-person, and electronic. **Exhibit 5.10** summarizes the typical features of the five different survey designs. Each design differs from the others in one or more important features.

Manner of administration. The five survey designs differ in the manner in which the questionnaire is administered. Mailed, group, and electronic surveys are completed by the respondents themselves. During phone and in-person interviews, however, the researcher or a staff person asks the questions and records the respondent's answers.

Questionnaire structure. Survey designs also differ in the extent to which the content and order of questions are structured in advance by the researcher. Most mailed, group, phone, and electronic surveys are highly structured, fixing in advance the content and order of questions and most response choices. In-person interviews are often highly structured, but they may include many questions without fixed response choices. Extra questions are added as needed to clarify or explore answers to the most important questions.

Setting. Most surveys are conducted in settings where only one respondent completes the survey at a time; most mail and electronic questionnaires and phone interviews are intended for completion by only one respondent. The same is usually true of in-person interviews. On the other hand, a variant of the standard survey is a questionnaire distributed simultaneously to a group of respondents who complete the survey while the researcher (or assistant) waits. Students in classrooms are often the group involved, although this type of group distribution also occurs in surveys of employees and members of voluntary groups.

Cost. As mentioned earlier, in-person interviews are the most expensive type of survey. Phone interviews are much less expensive, but surveying by mail is

Exhibit 5.10   Typical Features of the Five Survey Designs

Design	Manner of Administration	Setting	Questionnaire Structure	Cost
Mailed survey	Self	Individual	Mostly structured	Low
Group survey	Self	Group	Mostly structured	Very low
Phone survey	Professional	Individual	Structured	Moderate
In-person interview	Professional	Individual	Structured or unstructured	High
Electronic survey	Self	Individual	Mostly structured	Very low

Source: Schutt, R. K. (2009). *Investigating the social world: The process and practice of research* (6th ed.). Thousand Oaks, CA: Pine Forge Press.

cheaper yet. Electronic surveys are now the least expensive method because there are no interviewer costs, no mailing costs, and, for many designs, almost no costs for data entry. Of course, extra staff time and expertise are required to prepare an electronic questionnaire.

Mailed, Self-Administered Surveys

A **mailed survey** is conducted by mailing a questionnaire to respondents, who then administer the survey themselves. The central concern in a mailed survey is maximizing the response rate. Even an attractive questionnaire full of clear questions will probably be returned by no more than 30% of a sample unless extra steps are taken to increase the rate of response. It's just too much bother for most potential recipients; in the language of social exchange theory, the costs of responding are perceived to be much higher than any anticipated rewards for doing so. Of course, a response rate of 30% is a disaster; even a response rate of 60% represents so much nonresponse error that it is hard to justify using the resulting data. Fortunately, the conscientious use of a systematic survey design method can be expected to lead to an acceptable 70% or higher rate of response to most mailed surveys (Dillman, 2000).

Sending follow-up mailings to **nonrespondents** is the single most important requirement for obtaining an adequate response rate to a mailed survey. The follow-up mailings explicitly encourage initial nonrespondents to return a completed questionnaire; implicitly, they convey the importance of the effort. Dillman (2000) has demonstrated the effectiveness of a standard procedure for the mailing process: Sending a brief announcement to respondents a few days before the questionnaire is mailed; sending the questionnaire itself with a well-designed, personalized cover letter (see the next section), a self-addressed stamped return envelope, and, if possible, a token monetary reward; sending a reminder postcard thanking respondents and reminding nonrespondents 2 weeks after the initial mailing; sending a replacement questionnaire with a new cover letter and self-addressed stamped return envelope only to nonrespondents 2 to 4 weeks after the initial questionnaire mailing; sending another replacement questionnaire 6 to 8 weeks after the initial survey mailing—by priority or special delivery, if possible.

The **cover letter** for a mailed questionnaire is critical to the success of a mailed survey. This statement to respondents sets the tone for the questionnaire. The cover letter or introductory statement must show that the researcher is credible, it should be personalized for the respondent (Dear Tom, not Dear Student), it should interest the respondent in the contents of the questionnaire, and it should reassure the respondent that the information will be treated confidentially.

Exhibit 5.11 is an example of a cover letter for a questionnaire.

If Dillman's procedures are followed and the guidelines for cover letters and questionnaire design also are adhered to, the response rate is almost certain to approach 70%. One review of studies using Dillman's method to survey the general population indicates that the average response to a first mailing will be about 24%; the response rate will rise to 42% after the postcard follow-up, to 50% after the first

> **Exhibit 5.11**   Sample Questionnaire Cover Letter

University of Massachusetts at Boston
Department of Sociology
May 24, 2003

Jane Doe
AIDS Coordinator
Shattuck Shelter

Dear Jane:

AIDS is an increasing concern for homeless people and for homeless shelters. The enclosed survey is about the AIDS problem and related issues confronting shelters. It is sponsored by the Life Lines AIDS Prevention Project for the Homeless—a program of the Massachusetts Department of Public Health.

As an AIDS coordinator/shelter director, you have learned about homeless persons' problems and about implementing programs in response to those problems. The Life Lines Project needs to learn from your experience. Your answers to the questions in the enclosed survey will improve substantially the base of information for improving AIDS prevention programs.

Questions in the survey focus on AIDS prevention activities and on related aspects of shelter operations. It should take about 30 minutes to answer all the questions.

Every shelter AIDS coordinator (or shelter director) in Massachusetts is being asked to complete the survey. And every response is vital to the success of the survey: The survey report must represent the full range of experiences.

You may be assured of complete confidentiality. No one outside of the university will have access to the questionnaire you return. (The ID number on the survey will permit us to check with nonrespondents to see if they need a replacement survey or other information.) All information presented in the report to Life Lines will be in aggregate form, with the exception of a list of the number, gender, and family status of each shelter's guests.

Please mail the survey back to us by Monday, June 4, and feel free to call if you have any questions.

Thank you for your assistance.

Yours sincerely,

Russell K. Schutt   *Stephanie Howard*

Russell K. Schutt, Ph.D.   Stephanie Howard
Project Director   Project Assistant

Source: Schutt, R. K. (2009). *Investigating the social world: The process and practice of research* (6th ed., p. 287). Thousand Oaks, CA: Pine Forge Press.

replacement questionnaire, and to 72% after a second replacement questionnaire is sent by certified mail (Dillman, Christenson, Carpenter, & Brooks, 1974).

Group-Administered Surveys

A **group-administered survey** is completed by individual respondents assembled in a group. The response rate is not usually a major concern in surveys that are distributed and collected in a group setting because most group members will participate. The real difficulty with this method is that it is seldom feasible, because it requires what might be called a captive audience. With the exception of students, employees, members of the armed forces, and some institutionalized populations, most populations cannot be sampled in such a setting. A standard introductory statement should be read to the group that expresses appreciation for their participation, describes the steps of the survey, and emphasizes that the survey is voluntary and that results will be treated as confidential.

Telephone Surveys

In a **phone survey,** interviewers question respondents over the phone and then record their answers. Most telephone surveys use random-digit dialing at some point in the survey process (Lavrakas, 1987). A machine calls random phone numbers within designated exchanges, whether or not the numbers are published. When the machine reaches an inappropriate household (such as a business in a survey that is directed to the general population), the phone number is simply replaced with another. However households are contacted, the interviewers must ask a series of questions at the start of the survey to ensure that they are speaking to the appropriate member of the household.

Maximizing Response to Phone Surveys

Four issues require special attention in phone surveys. First, because people often are not home, multiple callbacks will be needed for many sample members. The number of callbacks needed to reach respondents by telephone has increased greatly in the past 20 years, with increasing numbers of single-person households, dual-earner families, and out-of-home activities. Survey research organizations have increased the usual number of phone contact attempts from just 4 to 20.

Phone surveying has been the method of choice for relatively short surveys of the general population. Response rates in phone surveys traditionally have tended to be very high—often above 80%—because few individuals would hang up on a polite caller or suddenly stop answering questions in the middle of a call (at least within the first 30 minutes or so). Ross (1990) achieved a response rate of 82% over a 3-month period at the end of 1990, resulting in a final sample of 2,031 Americans. However, several social changes have made it increasingly difficult to obtain a high rate of response in a phone survey (Dillman, 2000): growing use of caller ID to screen out calls from unknown callers; the use of cell phones (which often do not have exchanges based on geographic area); and people's getting accustomed to "just saying no" to calls from telemarketers.

In addition to these problems, response rates can be much lower in harder-to-reach populations. In a recent phone survey of low-income women in a public health program (Schutt, Cruz, & Woodford, 2008), the University of Massachusetts

Center for Survey Research (CSR) achieved a 55.1% response rate from all eligible sampled clients after a protocol that included up to 30 contact attempts, although the response rate rose to 72.9% when it was calculated as a percentage of clients who CSR was able to locate (Roman, 2005).

In-Person Interviews

Face-to-face social interaction between interviewer and respondent is the unique feature of **in-person interviews**. If money is no object, in-person interviewing is often the best survey design.

In-person interviewing has several advantages: Responses rates are higher than with any other survey design; questionnaires can be much longer than with mailed or phone surveys; the questionnaire can be complex, with both open-ended and closed-ended questions and frequent branching patterns; the order in which questions are read and answered can be controlled by the interviewer; the physical and social circumstances of the interview can be monitored; and respondents' interpretations of questions can be probed and clarified.

But researchers must be alert to some special hazards due to the presence of an interviewer. Respondents should experience the interview process as a personalized interaction with an interviewer who is very interested in the respondent's experiences and opinions. At the same time, however, every respondent should have the same interview experience—asked the same questions in the same way by the same type of person, who reacts similarly to the answers. Therein lies the researcher's challenge—to plan an interview process that will be personal and engaging and yet consistent and nonreactive (and to hire interviewers who can carry out this plan). Careful training and supervision are essential, because small differences in intonation or emphasis on particular words can alter respondents' interpretations of question meaning (Groves, 1989; Peterson, 2000). Without a personalized approach, the rate of response will be lower and answers will be less thoughtful—and potentially less valid. Without a consistent approach, information obtained from different respondents will not be comparable—less reliable and less valid.

As with phone interviewing, computers can be used to increase control of the in-person interview. In a **computer-assisted personal interviewing (CAPI)** project, interviewers carry a laptop computer that is programmed to display the interview questions and to process the response that the interviewer types in, as well as to check that these responses fall within allowed ranges. Interviewers seem to like CAPI, and the data obtained are comparable in quality to data obtained in a noncomputerized interview (Shepherd, Hill, Bristor, & Montalvan, 1996). A CAPI approach also makes it easier for the researcher to develop skip patterns and experiment with different types of questions for different respondents without increasing the risk of interviewer mistakes (Couper et al., 1998).

Electronic Surveys

The widespread use of personal computers and the growth of the Internet have created new possibilities for survey research. In October 2003, more than half of American households were connected to the Internet (Cooper & Victory, 2002). As the proportion of the population that is connected increases, the Internet may become the preferred medium for survey research on many topics.

Electronic surveys can be prepared in two ways (Dillman, 2000, pp. 352–354). **E-mail surveys** can be sent as messages to respondents' e-mail addresses. Respondents then mark their answers in the message and send them back to the researcher. This approach is easy for researchers to develop and for respondents to use. However, it is cumbersome for surveys that are more than four or five pages in length. By contrast, **web surveys** are made available to Internet users on a remote server. Respondents are asked by e-mail (or regular mail) to visit the website and respond to the web questionnaire by checking answers.

Web surveys are becoming the more popular form of Internet survey because they are so flexible (see **Exhibit 5.12**). Web surveys can be quite long, with questions that are inapplicable to a given respondent hidden from them so that the survey may actually seem much shorter than it is. The questionnaire's design can feature many graphic and typographic elements. Respondents can view definitions of words or instructions for answering questions by clicking on linked terms. Lengthy sets of response choices can be presented with pull-down menus. Pictures and audio segments can be added when they are useful. Because answers are recorded directly in the researcher's database, data entry errors are almost eliminated and results can be reported quickly.

When the population to be surveyed has a high rate of Internet use, the web makes possible fast and effective surveys (Dillman, 2000). A skilled web programmer can generate a survey layout with many attractive features that make it more likely that respondents will give their answers—and have a clear understanding of the question (Smyth, Dillman, Christian, & Stern, 2004). To ensure that the appropriate people respond to a web-based survey, researchers may require that respondents enter a PIN (personal identification number) in order to gain access to the Web survey (Dillman, 2000).

Eisenberg and colleagues (2007) used a web-based survey in their survey of university students' mental health. Sample members were first mailed an introductory letter along with $2 as a token of appreciation. They then received up to four e-mail reminders with a link to the survey. They were also told they had been entered into a cash sweepstakes.

A Comparison of Survey Designs

Which survey design should be used when? Group-administered surveys are similar, in most respects, to mailed surveys, except that they require the unusual circumstance of having access to the sample in a group setting. We therefore don't

Exhibit 5.12   Survey Monkey Web Survey Example

need to consider this survey design by itself; what applies to mailed surveys applies to group-administered survey designs, with the exception of sampling issues. The features of **mixed-mode surveys** depend on the survey types that are being combined. Thus, we can focus our comparison on the four survey designs that involve the use of a questionnaire with individuals sampled from a larger population: mailed surveys, phone surveys, in-person surveys, and electronic surveys. **Exhibit 5.13** summarizes their strong and weak points.

The most important consideration in comparing the advantages and disadvantages of the four methods is the likely response rate they will generate. Because of the great weakness of mailed surveys in this respect, they must be considered the least preferred survey design from a sampling standpoint. However, researchers may still prefer a mailed survey when they have to reach a widely dispersed population and don't have enough financial resources to hire and train an interview staff or to contract with a survey organization that already has an interview staff available in many locations.

Contracting with an established survey research organization for a phone survey is often the best alternative to a mailed survey. The persistent follow-up attempts that are necessary to secure an adequate response rate are much easier over the phone than in person. A phone survey limits the length and complexity of the questionnaire but offers the possibility of very carefully monitoring interviewers (Dillman, 1978; Fowler, 1988).

In-person surveys are clearly preferable in terms of the possible length and complexity of the questionnaire itself, as well as the researcher's ability to monitor conditions while the questionnaire is being completed. Mailed surveys often are preferable for asking sensitive questions, although this problem can be lessened in an interview by giving respondents a separate sheet to fill out on their own. Although interviewers may themselves distort results, either by changing the wording of questions or by failing to record answers properly, survey research organizations can reduce this risk through careful training of the interviewers and through ongoing monitoring of interviewer performance. Some survey supervisors will have interviews tape recorded so that they can review the dialogue between interviewers and respondents and provide feedback to the interviewers to help improve their performance.

The advantages of electronic surveys are increasing as Internet usage spreads and personal computer capacity improves, but what matters is computer usage among the population to be surveyed. Some data must show a reasonably high rate of Internet usage before making a decision to conduct an Internet survey.

These various points about the different survey designs lead to two general conclusions. First, in-person interviews are the strongest design and generally preferable when sufficient resources and a trained interview staff are available; telephone surveys have many of the advantages of in-person interviews at much less cost, but response rates are an increasing problem. Second, the "best" survey design for any particular study will be determined by the study's unique features and goals rather than by any absolute standard of what the best survey design is.

Exhibit 5.13   Advantages and Disadvantages of the Four Survey Designs

Characteristics of Design	Mail Survey	Phone Survey	In-person Survey	Electronic Survey
Representative sample				
Opportunity for inclusion is known				
For completely listed populations	High	High	High	Medium
For incompletely listed populations	Medium	Medium	High	Low
Selection within sampling units is controlled (e.g., specific family members must respond)	Medium	High	High	Low
Respondents are likely to be located				
If samples are heterogeneous	Medium	Medium	High	Low
If samples are homogeneous and specialized	High	High	High	High
Questionnaire construction and question design				
Allowable length of questionnaire	Medium	Medium	High	Medium
Ability to include				
Complex questions	Medium	Low	High	High
Open questions	Low	High	High	Medium
Screening questions	Low	High	High	High
Tedious, boring questions	Low	High	High	Low
Ability to control question sequence	Low	High	High	High
Ability to ensure questionnaire completion	Medium	High	High	Low
Distortion of answers				
Odds of avoiding social desirability bias	High	Medium	Low	High
Odds of avoiding interviewer distortion	High	Medium	Low	High
Odds of avoiding contamination by others	Medium	High	Medium	Medium
Administrative goals				
Odds of meeting personnel requirements	High	High	Low	Medium
Odds of implementing quickly	Low	High	Low	High
Odds of keeping costs low	High	Medium	Low	High

Source: Adapted from *Mail and Telephone Surveys: The Total Design Method*, by Don A. Dillman. Copyright © 1978 Don A. Dillman. Published by John Wiley & Sons, Inc.

ANALYZING SURVEYS

Survey researchers, like researchers using other methods, can use a variety of statistics to test their hypotheses. One of the most common analytic approaches in survey research is contingency table analysis. A **contingency table** shows how responses to one question (the dependent variable) are distributed within the responses to another question (the independent variable). That is, we construct a contingency table to determine whether values of cases on the dependent variable are contingent on the value of those cases on the independent variable.

Exhibit 5.14 shows how responses to the happiness question varied by family income in the study reported by Daniel Kahneman and his colleagues (2006). The numbers in the table have been converted to percentages of the total number in each income category. This conversion to percentages standardizes the distributions in each column so that they each add up to 100. In order to begin to read the table, you can compare the distribution of percentages in the first column to those in the second column. You can see that the percentage of respondents in the "very happy" category is higher for the respondents making $20,000 to $49,999 (30.2%) than it is for those making less than $20,000 (22.2%). You can also see that the percentage of "very happy" respondents is even higher (41.9%) in the $50,000 to $89,999 category but then is about the same for those making $90,000 and more. Overall, you can see that as income increases, the percentage of respondents in the "not too happy" category declines and the percent in the "very happy" category increases.

Even when the association between two variables is consistent with the researcher's hypothesis, it is possible that the association was just due to the vagaries of sampling on a random basis. It is conventional in statistics to avoid concluding that an association exists in the population from which the sample was drawn unless the probability that the association was due to chance is less than 5%. In other words, a statistician normally will not conclude that an association exists

Exhibit 5.14 Distribution of Self-Reported Global Happiness by Family Income, 2004

	Percentage indicating global happiness at family income of...			
Response	*Under $20,000*	*$20,000–$49,999*	*$50,000–$89,999*	*$90,000 and over*
Not too happy	17.2	13.0	7.7	5.3
Pretty happy	60.5	56.8	50.3	51.8
Very happy	22.2	30.2	41.9	42.9

Source: From "Would You Be Happier If You Were Richer? A Focusing Illusion," by Daniel Kahneman, Alan B. Krueger, David Schkade, Norbet Schwartz, and Arthur A. Stone in *Science, 30,* June 2006: 1908–1910. Copyright © 2006, The American Association for the Advancement of Science. Reprinted with permission.

between two variables unless he or she can be at least 95% confident that the association was not due to chance. In a contingency table, estimation of the probability that an association is not due to chance can be based on the chi-square statistic (χ^2). The probability is customarily reported in a summary form such as: "$p < .05$," which can be translated as "The probability that the association was due to chance is less than 5 out of 100 (5%)."

> *Chi-square* An inferential statistic used to test hypotheses about relationships between variables in a contingency table.

When the analyst feels reasonably confident (at least 95% confident) that an association was not due to chance, it is said that the association is statistically significant. Recall from Chapter 2 that statistical significance means that an association is not likely to be due to chance, according to some criterion set by the analyst. Convention (and the desire to avoid concluding that an association exists in the population when it doesn't) dictates that the criterion be a probability less than 5%.

> *Statistical significance* The mathematical likelihood that an association is not due to chance, judged by a criterion set by the analyst (often that the probability is less than 5 out of 100 or $p < .05$).

But statistical significance is not everything. You recall from the sampling section that sampling error decreases as sample size increases. For this same reason, an association is less likely to appear on the basis of chance in a larger sample than in a smaller sample. In a table with more than 1,000 cases, the odds of a chance association are often very low indeed. For example, in the table in the Kahneman (2006) article, with a sample size of 1,173 individuals, the probability that the association between happiness and family income was due to chance was less than 1 in 1,000 ($p < .001$)! In a large sample, even a weak association may be statistically significant ($p < .05$) but still be too weak to be substantively important.

CONCLUSIONS

Sampling is a powerful tool for behavioral science research. Probability sampling methods allow a researcher to use the laws of chance, or probability, to draw samples from which population parameters can be estimated with a high degree of confidence. A sample of just 1,000 or 1,500 individuals can be used to estimate reliably the characteristics of the population of a nation comprising millions of individuals.

But researchers do not come by representative samples easily. Well-designed samples require careful planning, some advance knowledge about the population to be sampled, and adherence to systematic selection procedures—all so that the selection procedures are not biased. And even after the sample data are collected, the researcher's ability to generalize from the sample findings to the population is not completely certain. The best that he or she can do is to perform additional calculations that state the degree of confidence that can be placed in the sample statistic.

Surveying a sample of the population of interest is an exceptionally efficient and productive method for investigating a wide array of research questions. In 2 months, Eisenberg et al.'s (2007) web-based survey produced a unique, comprehensive dataset on mental health issues in a large university student body. Considerations of time and expense can make a survey the preferred data collection method for contributing to psychological science.

END OF CHAPTER

Chapter Highlights

- Sampling theory focuses on the generalizability of descriptive findings to the population from which the sample was drawn. Researchers must also consider whether statements can be generalized from one population to another.

- Sampling is unnecessary when the elements that would be sampled are identical, but the complexity of the social world makes it difficult to argue very often that different elements are identical. Conducting a complete census of a population also eliminates the need for sampling, but the resources required for a complete census of a large population are usually prohibitive.

- Nonresponse undermines sample quality: It is the obtained sample, not the desired sample, that determines sample quality.

- The likely degree of error in an estimate of a population characteristic based on a probability sample decreases when the size of the sample and the homogeneity of the population from which the sample was selected increase. Sampling error is not affected by the proportion of the population that is sampled except when that proportion is large. The degree of sampling error affecting a sample statistic can be estimated from the characteristics of the sample and knowledge of the properties of sampling distributions.

- Probability sampling methods rely on a random selection procedure to ensure no systematic bias in the selection of elements. In a probability sample, the odds of selecting elements are known, and the method of selection is carefully controlled.

- A sampling frame (a list of elements in the population) is required in most probability sampling methods. The adequacy of the sampling frame is an important determinant of sample quality.

- Simple random sampling and systematic random sampling are equivalent probability sampling methods in most situations. However, systematic random sampling is inappropriate for sampling from lists of elements that have a regular, periodic structure.

- Stratified random sampling uses prior information about a population to make sampling more efficient. Stratified sampling may be either proportionate or disproportionate. Disproportionate stratified sampling is useful when a research question focuses on a stratum or on strata that make up a small proportion of the population.

- Cluster sampling is less efficient than simple random sampling but is useful when a sampling frame is unavailable. It is also useful for large populations spread out across a wide area or among many organizations.

- Nonprobability sampling methods can be useful when random sampling is not possible, when a research question does not concern a larger population, and when a preliminary exploratory study is appropriate. However, the representativeness of nonprobability samples cannot be determined.

- Surveys are the most popular form of social research because of their versatility, efficiency, and generalizability. Many survey datasets are available for social scientists to use in teaching and research.

- Survey designs must minimize the risk of errors of observation (measurement error) and errors of nonobservation (errors due to inadequate coverage, sampling error, and nonresponse). The likelihood of both types of error varies with the survey goals. For example, political polling can produce inconsistent results because of rapid changes in popular sentiment.

- Social exchange theory asserts that behavior is motivated by the return expected to the individual for the behavior. Survey designs must maximize the social rewards, minimize the costs of participating, and establish trust that the rewards will outweigh the costs.

- A survey questionnaire or interview schedule should be designed as an integrated whole, with each question and section serving some clear purpose and complementing the others.

- Questions must be worded carefully to avoid confusing respondents, encouraging less-than-honest responses, or triggering biases. Inclusion of "Don't know" choices and neutral responses may help, but the presence of such options also affects the distribution of answers. Open-ended questions can be used to determine the meaning that respondents attach to their answers. Answers to any survey questions may be affected by the questions that precede them in a questionnaire or interview schedule.

- Questions can be tested and improved through review by experts, focus group discussions, cognitive interviews, behavior coding, and pilot testing. Every questionnaire and interview schedule should be pretested on a small sample that is like the sample to be surveyed.

- Interpretive questions should be used in questionnaires to help clarify the meaning of responses to critical questions.

- The cover letter for a mailed questionnaire should be credible, personalized, interesting, and responsible.

- Response rates in mailed surveys are typically well below 70% unless multiple mailings are made to nonrespondents and the questionnaire and cover letter are attractive, interesting, and carefully planned. Response rates for group-administered surveys are usually much higher.

- Phone interviews using random-digit dialing allow fast turnaround and efficient sampling. Multiple callbacks are often required, and the rate of nonresponse to phone interviews is rising. Phone interviews should be limited in length to about 30 to 45 minutes.

- In-person interviews have several advantages over other types of surveys: They allow longer and more complex interview schedules, monitoring of the conditions when the questions are answered, probing for respondents' understanding of the questions, and high response rates. However, the interviewer must balance the need to establish rapport with the respondent with the importance of maintaining control over the delivery of the interview questions.

- Electronic surveys may be e-mailed or posted on the web. Interactive voice response systems using the telephone are another option. At this time, use of the Internet is not sufficiently widespread to allow e-mail or web surveys of the general population, but these approaches can be fast and efficient for populations with high rates of computer use.

- Mixed-mode surveys allow the strengths of one survey design to compensate for the weaknesses of another. However, questions and procedures must be designed carefully, using "unimode design" principles, to reduce the possibility that responses to the same question will vary as a result of the mode of delivery.

- In deciding which survey design to use, researchers must take into account the unique features and goals of the study. In general, in-person interviews are the strongest, but most expensive, survey design.

- Most survey research poses few ethical problems because respondents are able to decline to participate—an option that should be stated clearly in the cover letter or introductory statement. Special care must be taken when questionnaires are administered in group settings (to "captive audiences") and when sensitive personal questions are to be asked; subject confidentiality should always be preserved.

Key Terms

📖 Research in the News

1. *The Boston Globe*'s Stan Grossfeld (2007) reported on the problem of steroid drug use by professional athletes. It is hard to determine the scope of the problem because many athletes refuse to talk about it. Do you think your classmates would respond honestly to questions in a confidential survey about recent drug use? What about professional athletes? Why might their orientation to a survey about drug use differ?

2. A recent survey found that 4 in 10 college students endure stress often (Fram & Tompson, 2008). Propose a probability sampling design to study this issue that combines stratification and clustering. What challenges would a survey research organization confront in implementing your design?

Activity Questions

1. Response rates to phone surveys are declining even as phone usage increases. Part of the problem is that lists of cell phone numbers are not available and wireless service providers do not allow outside access to their networks. Cell phone users may also have to pay for incoming calls. Do you think regulations should be passed to increase the ability of survey researchers to include cell phones in their random-digit-dialing surveys? How would you feel about receiving survey calls on your cell phone? What problems might result from "improving" phone survey capabilities in this way?

2. In-person interviews have for many years been the "gold standard" in survey research because the presence of an interviewer increases the response rate, allows better rapport with the interviewee, facilitates clarification of questions and instructions, and provides feedback about the interviewee's situation. However, researchers who design in-person interviewing projects are now making increasing use of technology to ensure consistent questioning of respondents and to provide greater privacy while answering questions. But having a respondent answer questions on a laptop while the interviewer waits is a very different social process than actually asking the questions verbally. Which approach would you favor in survey research? What tradeoffs can you suggest there might be in terms of quality of information collected, rapport building, and interviewee satisfaction?

3. Select a random sample using the table of random numbers in Appendix E. Compute a statistic based on your sample and compare it to the corresponding figure for the entire population. Here's how to proceed:
   a. First, select a very small population for which you have a reasonably complete sampling frame. One possibility would be the list of asking prices for houses advertised in your local paper. Another would be the listing of some characteristic of states in a U.S. Census Bureau publication, such as average income or population size.

b. The next step is to create your sampling frame, a numbered list of all the elements in the population. If you are using a complete listing of all elements, as from a U.S. Census Bureau publication, the sampling frame is the same as the list. Just number the elements (states). If your population is composed of housing ads in the local paper, your sampling frame will be those ads that contain a housing price. Identify these ads and then number them sequentially starting with 1.

c. Decide on a method of picking numbers out of the random number table in Appendix E, such as taking every number in each row, row by row (or you may move down or diagonally across the columns). Use only the first (or last) digit in each number if you need to select 1 to 9 cases or only the first (or last) two digits if you want fewer than 100 cases.

d. Pick a starting location in the random number table. It's important to pick a starting point in an unbiased way, perhaps by closing your eyes and then pointing to some part of the page.

e. Record the numbers you encounter as you move from the starting location in the direction you decided on in advance until you have recorded as many random numbers as the number of cases you need in the sample. If you are selecting states, 10 might be a good number. Ignore numbers that are too large (or small) for the range of numbers used to identify the elements in the population. Discard duplicate numbers.

f. Calculate the average value in your sample for some variable that was measured—for example, population size in a sample of states or housing price for the housing ads. Calculate the average by adding up the values of all the elements in the sample and dividing by the number of elements in the sample.

g. Go back to the sampling frame and calculate this same average for all elements in the list. How close is the sample average to the population average?

h. Estimate the range of sample averages that would be likely to include 90% of the possible samples.

4. Consider how you could design a split-ballot experiment to determine the effect of phrasing a question or its response choices in different ways. Check recent issues of the local newspaper for a question used in a survey of attitudes about some social policy or political position. Propose some hypothesis about how the wording of the question or its response choices might have influenced the answers people gave and devise an alternative that differs only in this respect. Distribute these different questions to two halves of a large class (after your instructor makes the necessary arrangements) to test your hypothesis.

Review Questions

1. Discuss how cross-population generalizability would be essential for cultural studies in psychology.

2. What is sampling error? How does it affect sample generalizability?

3. Compare and contrast probability sampling and nonprobability sampling.

4. What is a sampling distribution? Discuss the relationship of sampling distributions and inferential statistics, particularly in relation to statistical significance.

5. What is the difference between sample statistic and population parameter?

6. What is a contingency table? What inferential statistic is used to analyze contingency table data?

7. Describe two types of errors that can occur in survey deigns. How can they be minimized?

8. Discuss how social exchange theory can be used in survey designs.

9. What are the advantages of in-person interviews over other types of surveys?

10. What considerations are important in deciding which survey design to use?

Ethics in Action

1. How much pressure is too much pressure to participate in a probability-based sample survey? Is it OK for the U.S. government to mandate legally that all citizens participate in the decennial census? Should companies be able to require employees to participate in survey research about work-related issues? Should students be required to participate in surveys about teacher performance? Should parents be required to consent to the participation of their high school-age students in a survey about substance abuse and health issues? Is it OK to give monetary incentives for participation in a survey of homeless shelter clients? Can monetary incentives be coercive? Explain your decisions.

2. Federal regulations require special safeguards for research on persons with impaired cognitive capacity. Special safeguards are also required for research on prisoners and on children. Do you think special safeguards are necessary? Why or why not? Do you think it is possible for individuals in any of these groups to give "voluntary consent" to research participation? What procedures might help make consent to research truly voluntary in these situations? How could these procedures influence sampling plans and results?

CHAPTER 6

True Experiments I

Single-Factorial Designs

MEMORY ENHANCEMENT IN HEALTHY OLDER ADULTS USING A BRAIN PLASTICITY-BASED TRAINING PROGRAM: A RANDOMIZED, CONTROLLED STUDY

"Memory Enhancement in Healthy Older Adults Using a Brain Plasticity-Based Training Program: A Randomized, Controlled Study" is the title of a recently published study in the prestigious *Proceedings of the National Academy of Sciences*. In this study, Merzenich and colleagues (Mahncke et al., 2006) examined whether healthy participants aged 60 years or older would show improved mental abilities following brain plasticity training that involved "working out"—performing a prescribed 5-day-a-week regimen of cognitive exercises on their home computers. An interesting research question indeed, we might think, and one that resonates with popular fads touting the benefits of mental calisthenics, but the issue for us is: What is the scientific and most rigorous way to test whether brain exercises actually work? Can a causal relationship be demonstrated between brain plasticity training and improved memory?

Recall from Chapters 1 and 2 the idea of the research toolbox, our veritable playbook of methods for experimental and nonexperimental designs for rigorous hypothesis testing. For the Merzenich study, the question posed is one of cause and effect, and as such, it dictates an experimental design known simply as a **true experiment**. As you also recall from Chapter 1, an experiment is a controlled investigation in which one or more variables are manipulated. And as you know, variables differ in the degree to which they can be controlled or manipulated. In a true experiment, a researcher has complete control over the manipulation of the independent variable. Such experimental control allows for testing whether systematically varying the independent variable causes changes in the dependent variable. For the Merzenich study, this meant investigating whether varying training could lead to improved memory.

In many areas of science, such as chemistry and physics, true experiments are de rigueur, the standard approach to establishing causality. In these sciences in which all other extraneous sources can be controlled, a true experiment can provide the empirical ammunition for a causal explanation often formulated in terms of a particular theoretical model. In psychology, different circumstances and challenges prevail, yet here too true experiments are quite common. However, causal explanations are much more difficult to establish than in chemistry or physics and certainly much trickier, even when a true experiment is performed. For example, the Strack, Martin, and Stepper (1988) study discussed in Chapter 2 represented a true experiment in which changes in the independent variable of stimulating either smile or scowl facial muscles had a direct effect on how participants perceived funny cartoons. Did the induced facial expressions cause affective reactions to these particular cartoons? No, but what might be concluded is that facial expressions modulated affective reactions, meaning that particular muscle contractions either facilitated or dampened emotional responses to cartoons.

In this chapter, we learn about true experiments—their basic ingredients as well as how to design and conduct them. We examine true experiments in light of the difficulties of establishing causality in psychology. We use the Merzenich study to help illustrate the practice and principles of true experiments.

BASICS OF EXPERIMENTATION

The defining feature of an experiment is the degree of **control** a researcher exercises over all aspects of the study design. In an experiment, the researcher controls with whom, with what, and how the study is conducted. That is, the researcher directly controls the formation of groups, or, in the Merzenich study, *who* receives brain plasticity computer-based training, active computer-based training, and no training. The researcher also directly controls *what* levels of the independent variables are to be manipulated—for example, Merzenich produced three levels of values of the independent variable of treatment or cognitive training. Third, the researcher controls *how* the experiment is conducted by holding constant certain aspects, such as the time, place, and setting of the study. For example, all participants in the Merzenich study are measured on the same outcome measures of cognition, and participants in either brain plasticity or active computer training received an equal number of sessions.

Experimental Control

Such **experimental control** is thus built in to a study's design. As we will see later in this chapter, a researcher can also exercise statistical control in analyzing data. But unlike statistical control that involves rather complicated data analytic strategies, experimental control is relatively straightforward and direct. A researcher exercises experimental control in a study by holding constant as many extraneous variables as possible. If a variable is held constant, it cannot account for the results of the experiment. That is, the statistically significant results of a study establishing a relationship between changes in the independent variable and performance on a dependent variable cannot be confounded by a *third variable* (see Chapter 2) provided that this third variable has been held constant. For example, participants in all groups in the Merzenich experiment should be treated identically, with the sole exception that some participants receive the treatment and others do not. Thus, the only difference between the groups is the manipulated variable, which in this case refers to the group who received the treatment versus the groups who did not receive the treatment. Similarly, as you recall in psychometrics, variables are held constant through *standardization* of test administration and test scoring (see Chapter 4).

Randomization

Another technique to control for the unwanted effects of a variable is known as **randomization**. This might seem counterintuitive that randomization, a process that can be as simple as shuffling cards or tossing a coin, would be such an important technique in counteracting unwanted effects. But such is the case that researchers randomize unwanted effects that cannot be experimentally controlled either by holding them constant or by measurement. Think about a common memory experiment that studies how many trials are needed for participants to learn a list of words that vary in terms of visual imagery. Here our independent variable is visual imagery of words. However, we know that irrespective of imagery, words presented at the beginning and the end of a list tend to be remembered better than words in the middle of a list. The position of the word on a list, whether at the beginning, known as the *primacy effect,* or at the end, known as the *recency effect,* can confound the results of an experiment that may be examining visual imagery and recall. To control for this position effect, an experimenter could randomize the order of presentation of the words so that each list would present the same words in a different order.

As we will elaborate below, randomization is used in assigning participants to groups or to different levels of an independent variable. For example, as shown in **Exhibit 6.1**, if we have two groups or two conditions, we could simply flip a coin with heads being assigned to one group and tails to the other. A table of random numbers (found in the back of statistics books) can also be used to assign participants to groups. To generate odd and even numbers, we would select a row of numbers in the table. Simply proceed across the row, noting whether the number is odd or even. If you reach the end of one row, continue; just select a different row of numbers and proceed until all participants have been assigned to a group. Use a simple decision rule: If the random number is even, assign participant to group 1, and if the random number is odd, assign the participant to group 2. As we will learn, this process of **random assignment** ensures that any extraneous influence is just as likely to affect one group as the other group.

In many psychology studies, however, an experimenter cannot use random assignment to create experimental and control groups. In these instances, the levels of the independent variable are selected rather than directly manipulated by the experimenter; that is, participants are selected and grouped after the fact or, **ex post facto**, on the basis of a particular characteristic, such as gender, race, age, or diagnoses. Under these circumstances, the researcher conducts a **quasiexperiment**. For example, suppose Merzenich and colleagues chose to examine whether brain plasticity training improves memory in both young adult and elderly groups. They would form their groups not by random assignment but by selecting, on the basis of age, young and elderly participants. They would therefore use a quasiexperiment because they could not randomly assign participants to different levels of the independent variable of age. We will discuss quasiexperiments in more detail in Chapter 8.

Exhibit 6.1   Random Assignment to One of Two Groups

Source: Schutt, R. K. (2009). *Investigating the social world: The process and practice of research* (6th ed., p. 210). Thousand Oaks, CA: Pine Forge Press.

Independent Variables

There is perhaps no more important concept for experimental design than that of the *independent variable*. We have learned that an independent variable is something that a researcher manipulates in some way in order to determine its effects on a dependent variable. We have also learned that an independent variable must have at least two values that are referred to as levels. For example, if you wanted only to compare participants who received brain plasticity training with those who received no training, you would have an independent variable that you could label as "training" and it would have two levels—brain plasticity training and no training. In an experiment, independent variables are often referred to as **factors**. An experiment must have at least one independent variable that is manipulated by the experimenter; otherwise it would not be an experiment. An experiment with one independent variable is called a **single-factor experiment**, and as we will see in Chapter 7, experiments with more than one independent variable are often referred to as **multifactorial designs**.

Independent variables are the conditions that are directly and systematically manipulated by an experimenter. The term *condition* simply means a particular way in which participants are treated. For example, an experimenter may compare two groups of participants—those who receive treatment versus those who receive no treatment. Here condition—labeled "group"—and *treatment* can be used interchangeably to refer to the independent variable. In more complicated experiments, each participant might experience or receive all conditions. In these circumstances, you would speak of the independent variable in terms of various kinds of conditions or treatments, but not as groups, as there is only one group of participants that receives all conditions.

In the Merzenich study, treatment or cognitive training is the independent variable, with three levels. The group of participants who received the level of independent variable that is the focus of the study (i.e., computer-based brain plasticity training) is called the **experimental group** or **treatment group**. The group of participants who received the computer-based active training is called the **comparison group**. The group that received no training is called the **control group**. Do not confuse a control group with a control variable, which is defined as a variable that is held constant. The control group provides a means to determine changes that might occur naturally in the absence of treatment. The control group thus provides a **baseline** against which the treatment or experimental group can be compared.

Dependent Variables

All true experiments have as the dependent variable a **posttest**—that is, measurement of the outcome in both groups after the experimental group has received the treatment. Many randomized experiments also have **pretests** that measure the dependent variable prior to the experimental intervention. A pretest can be exactly the same as a posttest, just administered at a different time. Pretest scores permit a direct measure of how much the experimental and comparison groups changed over time, such as a change in memory among elderly persons. Oftentimes, however, using identical pre- and posttests is to be avoided, especially if performance is likely to be influenced by practice in taking the same measure twice. This creates problems because a researcher wants to ensure that any observed pre- and posttests changes are attributable to the independent variable and not to practice effects. Here the use of pretest and posttest measures that have alternate forms would be wise, and as you recall from Chapter 4, you can check to see if your pretest and posttest measures have good *alternate-forms reliability*.

Control Variables

Some researchers' control variables are others' independent variables! What this means is that a control variable is a potential independent variable that is held constant throughout the experiment because its influence is thought to be extraneous, peripheral, or unimportant to the goal of the study. Recall from Chapter 2 that the researcher uses control variables to show that these factors do not explain the results; if they do, then, the results are considered to be confounded. Ideally, holding certain control variables constant while systematically manipulating only the independent variable allows the researcher to show that the desired effect on the dependent variable could only be accounted for by the changes in the independent variable.

The great challenge is, of course, in identifying or selecting which variables are to be controlled for or held constant, as there are more control variables than a researcher could ever desire to hold constant in practice. Some variables are rather straightforward to hold constant, such as the time of the day the study is conducted, temperature of the room, and the instructions introducing the study. These can be easily incorporated in the study design so that all participants are tested at the same time of day under the same room temperature and receive the same instructions introducing the experiment. For example, in the Merzenich et al. study, both experimental and comparison groups received training on their home computers on exactly the same schedule for 60 minutes per day, 5 days a week, for 8 to 10 weeks. This study design feature helped to control for the effects of computer training such that any changes in memory scores could be attributable to the independent variable of treatment (whether the participants received either brain plasticity training or an educational DVD).

Other effects of other control variables that are not held constant in the study design may be quantified and measured. That is, a researcher might need to quantify the effects of a variable known to be strongly related to the independent variable as well as the dependent variable but thought to be extraneous. In the Merzenich et al. study, let's imagine we found out that the experimental group differed from the comparison and the control groups on an important variable that could affect both the treatment and the outcome. For the sake of illustration, let's consider what it would mean if the experimental group as a whole had lower blood pressure, which in turn, could influence both responses to the brain plasticity training as well as performance on the cognitive outcome measures. In this hypothetical example, any result pointing to a brain plasticity training effect on memory would be considered confounded, influenced by a *third variable*—in this case, blood pressure.

RESEARCH DESIGN ALTERNATIVES

A researcher is faced with a number of decisions in designing an experiment. One of the most important of these decisions pertains to the assignment of participants to the various levels of the independent variables. The two main alternatives to consider are to assign only some participants to each level of the independent variable or to assign each participant to each level of the independent variables. These two alternatives constitute two types of experimental designs: between-subjects and within-subjects. With a **between-subjects design**, independent groups of participants receive the different levels of the independent variable. By contrast, a **within-subjects design** is one in which all research participants receive all levels of the independent variable.

Between-Subjects Design

For a between-subjects design with two levels of an independent variable, some participants receive one level and others receive the other level of the independent variable; the same participants never receive all levels of the independent variable. As you can see, a different group of participants must be assigned to each level of the independent variable. For this reason, between-subjects designs require a large number of people to be enrolled in a study. Such a design is, however, often used in treatment outcome studies. In these studies, a primary concern of the researcher is to ensure that there is no chance of one treatment contaminating the other. A between-subjects design provides the best bet in making sure that one treatment does not contaminate the other. The Merzenich study used a between-subjects design. In this study, the participants assigned to the experimental group received only brain plasticity training, and those assigned to the comparison group received only the educational DVD. If somehow experimental and comparison groups became exposed to each other's training, then the experimenter would not be able to attribute the improved memory to brain plasticity training. **Exhibit 6.2** provides a simple schematic of a between-subjects design. As in the Merzenich study, **Exhibit 6.2** shows that participants are randomly assigned to one of the three

Exhibit 6.2 Schematic of a Between-Subjects Design

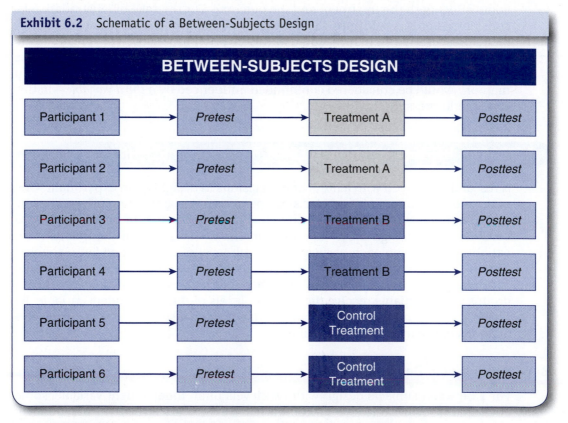

Source: From Experiment-Resources.com. Reprinted with permission.

levels of the independent variable labeled A, B, and C, with all receiving both pre-tests and posttests.

Randomization and Matching

A major concern for a between-subjects design is to ensure that there are as few differences as possible among participants in the various treatment groups. How then are experimental and treatment groups to be formed? How then are the levels of the independent variable to be manipulated or assigned? As we know, the answer to both these questions is random assignment. That is, a true experiment requires the investigator to randomly assign participants to groups, as for example to the treatment or experimental group or to the control group. Random assignment helps to ensure that groups are similar prior to the manipulation of the independent variable. The idea behind random assignment is this: People all have different psychologies, and these **individual differences** are equalized or neutralized when researchers use random assignment to form experimental and control groups. For example, Merzenich et al. used random assignment to create their experimental, comparison, and control groups. In the experimental group, participants received a treatment, brain plasticity training, which the researchers hypothesized would improve memory. In the comparison group, participants also received computer-based training, but it did not include any mental exercises targeted to improve memory.

The comparison group served to control for the potential extraneous and perhaps beneficial effects on cognition participants might have experienced from computer work. The researchers aimed to show that although both experimental and comparison groups received computer-based training, only the experimental group who received brain plasticity computer-based training would show improved performance on subsequent outcome measures of cognition.

How can you be sure that random assignment worked in creating equivalent groups prior to the introduction of the treatment variable? A **pretest** measure before treatment is often used to evaluate whether random assignment was successful (that sampling or selection biases did not lead to an initial difference between the groups). Of course, the idea behind random assignment is to wash out existing individual differences between groups on the dependent variable. But one is never completely sure of this, since the comparison groups could differ on the basis of chance. We all know that some people have better memories than others and some have worse memories. As in the Merzenich et al. study, if you want to demonstrate that treatment improves memory, you want to make sure that your groups are equivalent in memory *before* they received treatment. If they are indeed equivalent before the treatment but differ after the treatment, then your randomized experimental design provided sufficient control for you to support your hypothesis! So why not pretest research participants on their memory abilities to check the equivalence of the groups at the start of the experiment in addition to using random assignment to form the treatment and control groups?

Merzenich and colleagues used standardized tests of memory as pretest and posttest measures to assess the effectiveness of their brain-plasticity training. By identifying subjects' initial scores on the dependent variable, this pretest provides a more complete picture of the conditions in which their intervention had (or didn't have) an effect (Mohr, 1992). A randomized experimental design with a pretest and posttest is termed a **randomized comparative change design**, or a **pretest-posttest control group design**.

An experiment may have multiple posttests and perhaps even multiple pretests. Multiple posttests can identify just when the treatment has its effect and for how long. This is particularly important when treatments are delivered over a period of time (Rossi & Freeman, 1989). However, strictly speaking, an experiment does not require a pretest. Random assignment is thought to equate experimental and comparison groups before the intervention is administered to the experimental group so that in principle a pretest is unnecessary. Any subsequent difference in outcome between the experimental and comparison groups is therefore likely to be due to the intervention (or to other processes occurring during the experiment), and the likelihood of a difference just on the basis of chance can be calculated. This is fortunate, because the dependent variable in some experiments cannot be measured in a pretest: For example, if you want to test the effect of class size on student reactions to a teacher, you can't measure their reactions to the teacher until they have been exposed to the experimental treatment—the classes of different size. There can also be a disadvantage to having a pretest, even when it is possible to do so: The act of taking the pretest can itself cause participants to change.

Of course, random assignment cannot guarantee that the groups are perfectly identical at the start of the experiment. Randomization removes bias from the assignment process, but only by relying on chance, which itself can result in some intergroup differences. Fortunately, researchers can use statistical methods to determine the odds of ending up with groups that differ very much on the basis of chance, and these odds are low even for groups of moderate size. The larger the group, the less likely it is that even modest differences will occur on the basis of chance and the more possible it is to draw conclusions about the relationship between the independent and dependent variables.

Matching is another procedure sometimes used to equate groups, but by itself it is a poor substitute for randomization. Matching of individuals in a treatment group with those in a control group might involve pairing persons on the basis of similarity of gender, age, year in school, or some other objective characteristic. The basic problem is that, as a practical matter, individuals can only be matched on a few characteristics; unmatched characteristics between the experimental and control groups may still influence the results of the study. When matching is used as a substitute for random assignment, the research becomes *quasiexperimental* instead of being a true experiment (see Chapter 8).

Matching can be combined with random assignment. This is referred to a **matched-pairs design**, which for between-subjects studies provides a better bet that the groups are equivalent before the introduction of the independent variable manipulation. In a matched-pairs design, we first create pairs of participants that are matched on a variable that is strongly related to the dependent variable. We then randomly assign one of the pairs to the experimental condition and the other to the control condition. That is, each member of the pair is assigned to *different* levels of the independent variable (see **Exhibit 6.3**). In short, an effective matched pairs design provides a degree of experimental control of between-subject individual differences that is comparable to that of a within-subjects design. As such, a matched-pairs design provides greater power to detect statistical significance than simple random assignment of a between-subjects design.

Within-Subjects Design

In a within-subjects design, each research participant receives each level of the independent variable. And when the same participant can be tested repeatedly over time, the term **repeated-measures**, **within-subjects design** is commonly used. Often such a design is more efficient, because the performance of each participant is compared across all of the different experimental conditions. In this

Exhibit 6.3 Matched-Pairs Design Combines Matching and Random Assignment

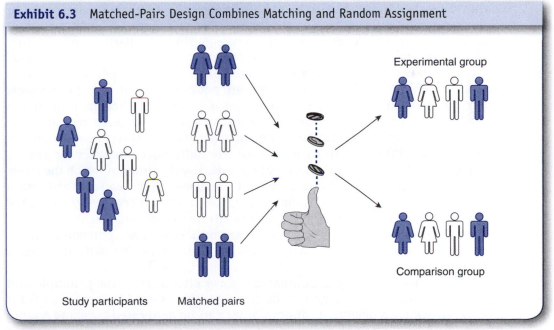

Source: Schutt, R. K. (2009). *Investigating the social world: The process and practice of research* (6th ed., p. 228). Thousand Oaks, CA: Pine Forge Press.

sense, each participant serves as his or her own control (McBurney & White, 2010). What this means is that differences in performance are more likely attributed to the different experimental conditions, that is, the manipulation of the independent variable. This provides a major advantage for a within-subjects design over a between-subjects design. Indeed, absent in a within-subjects design is the concern, always present in a between-subjects design, that somehow random assignment failed to equate treatment and control groups, confounding the results of the study.

Another important advantage of a within-subjects design is that fewer research participants are needed because all participants will receive all treatments. A within-subjects design is also desirable when an experimenter is sure that the effect of one treatment will not carry over to, or contaminate, the other condition or conditions of the experiment. Finally, a within-subjects design is essential for longitudinal studies, which will be discussed in Chapter 8. In a longitudinal study, the same research participants are followed over time, as for example when the same child is tested at age 6, then at age 10, and then again at age 13. Widely used in developmental psychology, a **longitudinal research design** can collect data for decades, as participants might be followed over their lifespans, and these data are ordered in time so that developmental trajectories or courses can be examined.

By the same token, however, an important source of experimental error for a within-subjects design is the problem of **carryover effects** from one treatment or condition to the next (Elmes et al., 2006). This of course is not a source of experimental error for a between-subjects design, since the participants are only exposed to one treatment. But a major concern for any within-subjects manipulation arises if performance in one condition affects performance in a subsequent condition. If carryover effects are not controlled in a within-subjects design, any results will be confounded by the order of presentation of the conditions. Under these circumstances, a researcher will not be able to attribute the results of a study to a particular treatment or a particular level of an independent variable. True differences in treatment, or true differences between or among levels of the independent variable, may be masked by the order in which the levels of the independent variable were presented. Carryover effects can also arise from rather routine factors, such as fatigue participants might experience by the end of an experiment, or from familiarity or practice effects participants might experience over the course of a study. Thus, these carryover effects are considered to be confounding variables that present major challenges for within-subjects manipulations.

Randomization is a way to combat carryover effects. Here the principle and objective are the same as when random assignment is used to form groups for a between-subjects design. A random order can be generated by using a table of random numbers or by as simple a task as writing the different orders of treatment on slips of paper and then drawing them out of a hat. Randomization ensures that any differences in treatment orders are due to chance only.

However, generally there are fewer treatment orders than participants, and for this reason randomization is really not an effective technique for equating order of treatments.

Counterbalancing

A commonly used technique to control for the order of treatments is known as **counterbalancing**. Counterbalancing the order of treatment tends to be more effective than randomizing the order of treatment because it ensures that each treatment or level of the independent variable occurs in each time period of the experiment. That way, every treatment has the same chance of being influenced by confounding variables related to a treatment coming before and after it. Complete counterbalancing begins by calculating all possible treatment orders. For two treatments, this will be very straightforward. For example, let's say your two treatments are computer-based neural plasticity training and computer-based educational training. You would have only two orders: computer-based neural plasticity training then computer-based educational training and computer-based educational training then computer-based neural plasticity training. Half the participants receive computer-based neural plasticity training then computer-based educational training, and half receive computer-based educational training then computer-based neural plasticity training.

As the number of treatments, conditions, or levels of the independent variable increases, so too does the number of possible orders. For five treatments, you have 120 different orders. This is calculated as follows: $5! = 5 \times 4 \times 3 \times 2 \times 1$. Four treatments have 24 different orders ($4! = 4 \times 3 \times 2 \times 1$). Three treatments have six different orders ($3! = 3 \times 2 \times 1$). As you can see, in experimental design, fewer levels of the independent variables are easier to manage and require fewer research participants. Overall, however, even with as few as four treatments, complete counterbalancing becomes unwieldy and impractical.

With complete counterbalancing often untenable, researchers will frequently use what is called a **Latin-square design** as a way to combat confounds of carryover effects in within-subjects experiments. A Latin-square design is an *incomplete* counterbalancing arrangement in which each possible order of treatments occurs equally often across research participants. For example, consider a Latin square for counterbalancing the order of three treatment conditions: memory (M), reasoning (R), and processing speed (PS). As shown in **Table 6.1**, in this arrangement, memory will be administered first, second, or third equally often, as will the treatment of reasoning and processing speed. This arrangement is presented in a Latin square with rows representing the participants in the study and columns representing the order of these treatments. That is, participant 1 receives memory first, followed by reasoning, and then processing speed; participant 2 receives reasoning first, following by processing speed, and then memory; and participant 3 receives processing speed, memory, and then reasoning. The same order of treatments is presented for participants 4 through 6.

Usually, however, a researcher will need to use more research participants than treatments. What this means is that a researcher will need to use some number in calculating sample size that is a multiple of the number of the treatments in the Latin square. So if there are three treatments, then a researcher could use sample sizes of 3, 6, 9, 12, 15, and so on, as long as the sample size can be divided by 3 (the number of treatments for this example) with no remainder. A Latin-square design thus provides a practical remedy to the problem of carryover effects. The constraint it places on sample size is not too burdensome. And keep in mind that an advantage of a within-subjects design is that it requires fewer subjects than a between-subjects design.

However, an important cautionary note is important to keep in mind: Because the same Latin-square arrangement can be used over and over (see **Table 6.1**), there is a possibility that somehow the order of the treatments becomes confounded with the effects of the treatments. In other words, just as random assignment can fail in a between-subjects design, so can a Latin square for counterbalancing order of treatments in a within-subjects design. There is a statistical test for square uniqueness that will determine whether the Latin square proved

Table 6.1 A Latin Square for Counterbalancing the Order of Three Treatments Across Six Research Participants

		Order		
		1st	2nd	3rd
	Participant Number			
	1	M	R	PS
Square 1	2	R	PS	M
	3	PS	M	R
	4	M	R	PS
Square 2	5	R	PS	M
	6	PS	M	R

M = memory

R = reasoning

PS = processing speed

effective in counterbalancing order of treatments (please refer to Kirk, 1994, as the statistical test for square uniqueness is beyond the scope of this book). In the final analysis, complete counterbalancing remains the safest technique for within-subjects designs.

Selecting a Between- or Within-Subjects Design

As you can see, there are pros and cons to weigh when considering whether to manipulate an independent variable between subjects or within subjects. For between-subject designs, there is always the threat that random assignment will fail to neutralize individual differences and that groups will not be equal prior to treatment or manipulation of the independent variable. Remember, randomization procedures deal in probability, which means that groups formed by random assignment could still differ by chance. On the other hand, if carryover effects are to be avoided at all cost, then a between-subjects design will certainly be favored over a within-subjects design. As we will learn below, a well-known use of a between-subjects design is in pharmacological investigations of the effectiveness of a drug. These studies, known as *randomized clinical trials,* use a between-subjects design, as carryover effects from another treatment would be fatal, invalidating the investigation. For many studies in psychology, individual differences are of vital interest; a researcher may be studying memory, for example, for the sole purpose of investigating how individuals differ in their recall under certain experimental conditions. Here a researcher will opt for a within-subjects design.

There is an additional interesting question that extends beyond the pros and cons of a between- and within-subjects design. Let's imagine that we take the *same* independent variable, and in one experiment, we use a within-subjects design and in the other experiment, we use a between-subjects design. How would these two experiments fare? Greene (1996) did just that when he contrasted within- and between-subjects designs using the same independent variable. In the Greene study, research participants performed an experimental task of short-term memory and forgetting known as the Petersons' Distractor Task (Peterson & Peterson, 1959). On this task, participants are asked to recall in correct order short lists of three letters (such as FVR). These nonsense syllables were presented briefly on a computer monitor, and then after delays for either 5 or 25 seconds, participants were asked to recall them. This is not as easy as it may sound, as during the delay participants must count digits rapidly. The idea behind the task is that counting during the delay would prevent rehearsal, the process of internal repetition, thereby distracting participants from remembering the three letters. The independent variable was the length of time counting, which we can label as the delay interval, with two levels, 5- or 25-second duration. Prior studies using within-subject designs have shown recall declines as the length of the delay interval increases.

Greene performed the experiment two ways: In his between-subjects design, one group recalled the three consonants after a 5-second delay of rapidly counting digits, and another group after a 25-second delay. For his within-subjects design, all participants were tested at both of the delay intervals, meaning on some trials they recalled the three consonants after counting rapidly for 5 seconds, and on other trials they recalled the three consonants after counting rapidly for 25 seconds. Greene's results for the within-subjects manipulation replicated prior studies of poorer recall for longer delays. However, his between-subjects design failed to show this effect of poorer recall for longer delays, as performance did not differ significantly for the group of participants who had the 5-second delay versus the group who had the 25-second delay.

Why these findings differed for the between- and within-subjects designs is not entirely clear. Perhaps in the between-subjects manipulation, a fixed delay of either 5 or 25 seconds for each group was less distracting. Indeed, it seems more distracting to switch between these two delays, as each participant did in the within-subjects design. These considerations fit well under the rubric of design sensitivity and internal validity, which we now discuss.

INTERNAL VALIDITY

Ideally, we want to design an experiment in which all extraneous factors are sufficiently controlled so that changes in the dependent variables result solely from changes in the independent variable. How then might independent, dependent, and control variables be optimally arranged in order for us to demonstrate causality? The concept of **internal validity** speaks to the logic of experimental design—the extent to which procedures and methods are optimally arranged so that the effects of the independent variable on the dependent variable can be "evaluated unambiguously" (Underwood, 1957, p. 86). That is, the internal validity of an experiment is defined as the extent to which the systematic manipulation of one or more independent variables produces the predicted or hypothesized effect on the dependent variable. The goal is to design experiments with high internal validity that will allow the researcher to establish causal relationships among the key variables under study.

To put it simply, the objective is to design an internally valid experiment that works! By "work," we mean whether an experiment will have sufficient sensitivity to detect the effects it purports to investigate. We use the term **design sensitivity** when thinking about the extent to which a researcher has constructed the best possible study to evaluate the topic under investigation. Some questions to consider when evaluating internal validity are as follows: Are the levels of the independent variable sufficiently distinct? Are the experimental conditions effectively designed to create the hypothesized effect? Is the manipulation strong enough to create an effect? Does the dependent variable provide enough precision of measurement to pick up the effects of the independent variable? Did the randomization procedures provide adequate control? How are participants assigned to the experimental conditions? Should all participants receive all levels of the independent variable? Or is the hypothesis of the study best addressed by random assignment to different conditions so that participants receive only one level of the independent variable?

Methods and Procedures

Every research study follows certain methods and procedures, which together act as a recipe for how the experiment will be carried out. Included in the methods and procedures are the specific instructions, stimuli, and events to be presented to all research participants. As Aronson, Brewer, and Carlsmith (1985) described, an important aspect of experimental design is in "setting the stage" as to how to introduce the study (see also Cozby, 2009). The "cover story" of Strack et al. (1988) that is detailed in Chapter 2 would be a good example of how a researcher sets the stage for an experiment. Recall that in the Strack et al. study, some participants held a pen between their lips to inhibit smiling, whereas other participants held the pen between their teeth to facilitate smiling. The researchers wanted to see whether these facial contractions alone would be sufficient to influence emotional reactions to cartoons. To accomplish this, they needed an experimental methodology in which participants would either smile or frown without being instructed to do so, that is, without them recognizing the associated emotional states accompanying these facial contractions. Thus, their cover story began with, "The study you are participating in has to do with psychomotoric coordination. . . ."

There are many structural features of a design that could affect the internal validity of an experiment. These include not only cover story (when used) but also instructions read to participants, the setting of the study, and the time of day that the study was run. Look to see whether the design effectively held constant such features as the instructions that were read to all participants. At the same time, check to see whether the design randomized other features, as for example time of day of study, that could be a source of invalidity. In short, carefully assessing what it was like to be a research participant will help you toward evaluating the internal validity of an experiment.

Next, consider the nature of an independent variable that is manipulated directly by an experimenter. Here, devising an effective manipulation of the independent variable is particularly important. Recall that an independent variable must have at least two levels. Each level of the independent variable needs to be sufficiently distinct. Let us say you reward small children with either one treat or two treats for correct answers on a task. To your surprise, however, performance of children who receive one treat did not differ from those who received two treats. This represents a **null result**, which occurs when an independent variable fails to produce any effect on the dependent variable. The most likely reason for a null result in this hypothetical scenario is that manipulation of one treat vs. two treats represented much too small a range to produce the desired effect on the dependent variable of test performance. Returning to the Merzenich study, these investigators devised an independent variable composed of three distinct and very different levels: (1) brain plasticity computer-based training; (2) active computer-based training; and (3) no training. Their independent variable was clearly of sufficient range to test for the desired effect of brain plasticity training on pencil-and-paper measures of mental abilities. The take-home lesson for internally valid experimental design is to devise levels of an independent variable that are truly distinct so that its effect on the dependent variable can be objectively assessed and clearly interpreted (Underwood, 1957).

In many instances, manipulating the independent variable can be as straightforward as assigning participants to either treatment or control groups. However, all research studies are faced with the problem of ***demand characteristics***. As we leaned in Chapter 2, demand characteristics occur when participants form expectations as to the true purpose of the study and then alter their responses in the experiment to fit with their preconceived notions of the study. An experimenter may also send signals unwittingly as to how a research participant is expected to respond, usually in ways to confirm the researcher's hypothesis, such as showing the predicted beneficial effect for treatment.

Demand characteristics are an important threat to internal validity. As a control for demand characteristics, an experiment will often include a **placebo** condition. This design feature is most often associated with drug studies in which a control group is administered a pharmacologically inert preparation or placebo drug. If the placebo group improves as much as the treatment group, this improvement would be attributable to the demand characteristics participants develop from simply being administered a druglike substance.

Placebo effects are also not just limited to drug studies. For example, Merzenich and colleagues controlled for placebolike effects by having their active control (comparison) group engaged in computer use following the same schedules (60 minutes per day, 5 days per week, for 8 to 10 weeks) as the experimental group. The researchers could thus investigate placebo effects by comparing cognitive outcome measures for the active computer-based comparison group with the no-contact control group. To rule out the possibility of placebo effects, both groups, the computer-based comparison group and the no-contact control group, should show similar responses on outcome measures. Also to combat expectancies of both participants and researchers, **double-blind** procedures are often added as a standard design feature of an experiment, particularly in a drug trial study. A double-blind feature of a study means that both experimenter and participant are deliberately kept blind to (unaware of) or kept in the dark as to whether the participant is receiving the treatment or placebo.

Psychological studies often use very straightforward independent variable manipulations, such as varying the meaningfulness of a to-be-remembered list of words or simply changing the order of presentation of two questions, as in the focusing illusion study that we will cover in Chapter 12. In other studies, however, manipulations of an independent variable can be much more complicated. For example, a researcher might rig a cyberspace game to exclude players in order to measure their experiences of social rejection (Eisenberger, Lieberman, & Williams, 2003). **Staged manipulations** like this frequently use a confederate who typically is presented as another participant in an experiment but is actually an accomplice of the researcher. The accomplice or confederate is used to help create the psychological state or social situation that is the topic of investigation.

The famous Milgram study discussed in Chapter 3 employed confederates in order to create a psychological state of obedience. As you learned in Chapter 3, these kinds of studies raise serious ethical concerns that need to be reviewed by an IRB before one ever even pilots them (Knapp & VandeCreek, 2006). If your study is approved by an IRB, then, pilot a **manipulation check** to measure directly whether the independent variable manipulation creates the intended effect on people.

Measuring Dependent Variables

The selection of the dependent variable is also important in designing a sensitive, internally valid experiment. Here you want to make sure your dependent variable is sufficiently sensitive as a measure so that it can capture a range of performance. A dependent variable can often be problematic because it has a restricted range. For example, when a dependent variable fails to discriminate various degrees of poor performance, meaning that all scores are confined to the very low end of the range, this is referred to as a **floor effect**. Think of a test in which all items are failed as an illustration of a floor effect. The opposite circumstance is called a **ceiling effect** in which the dependent variable is seriously restricted in range by very high scores. Think of getting 100% correct on a test as an illustration of a ceiling effect.

Both floor and ceiling effects are major design problems that can detract from internal validity because they prevent the influence of an independent variable from being accurately measured by a dependent variable. Merzenich and colleagues reported problems with ceiling effects for their pretest and posttest memory measures. Their sample as a whole had rather high scores. This may have limited the extent to which Merzenich and colleagues could have demonstrated the predicted treatment effect of brain plasticity training on memory. Participants all had fairly strong memories.

The lesson is: In experimental design, you want research participants to show a sufficient range of scores on a dependent variable. The greater the range in scores a dependent variable shows, the greater the likelihood that these changes result from changes in the independent variable. Why this matters is that a genuine relationship between changes in a dependent variable resulting from changes in an independent variable may be masked, undetected, or missed when an insensitive or coarse measure of the dependent variable is employed. Under these circumstances, the experiment could produce null results. This may occur even though the actual hypothesized effect may very well be at work in the sample, but the dependent variable lacked sufficient calibration to capture it.

Various measures—or different formats of measures—of dependent variables are used across psychological studies. Some researchers will use measures that they have constructed for the expressed purpose of the study. For example, they may code videotapes of behavior of children in a play situation. These devised coding protocols are referred to as behavioral measures. Formal rating scales of symptoms can also be considered under the rubric of behavioral measures of a dependent variable. These are widely used in studies of schizophrenia, a notable example of which is the Positive and Negative Symptom Syndrome Scale developed by Kay, Opler, and Fiszbein (1987). The advantage of using "off-the-shelf" behavioral measures of symptom scales is that they generally will have manuals detailing critical reliability and validity data for the instrument and they are commonly used by other researchers.

Psychometric tests of mental abilties provide another type of measurement that can be used to assess a dependent variable. These tests, such as those of memory, intelligence, or attention, undergo rigorous standardization that provides norms that allow scores to be compared to particular age groups. (Psychomertric tests are discsussed in Chapter 4.) These tests also have the added advantage of extensive reliability and validity stiudies. Last, physiological measures are also used to assess dependent variables. These include galvanic skin response as well as measures of various aspects of brain activity, such as event-related potentials or functional magentic resonance imaging. These measures will require specialized training and expertise in order to be used to assess dependent variables.

Minimizing Experimental Error

We aim to design an internally valid experiment or study that minimizes **experimental error**. Experimental error is broadly defined as any influence on the dependent variable that is not due solely to the systematic change in the independent variable. You have already learned that there are many potential sources of experimental error. Experimental error may arise from some particular sources that come with within-subjects designs. These may arise when participants have different responses to repeated testing; some may become bored; others might adopt idiosyncratic strategies in response to the order of presentation of the experiment. Other problems could arise if the conditions are always presented in the same order, and perhaps at the same time of day. For example, in an experiment that is always run early in the morning, the first condition comes when participants are still a bit tired. All of these extraneous factors can increase experimental error and detract from internal validity.

Statistical Control

As we have learned, internal validity has to do with the logic of arranging experiments. Statistics, on other hand, in the form of calculating odds, probabilities, and mathematical quantities, can also influence internal validity. That is, internal validity can also be enhanced by statistical techniques. The basic idea of **statistical control** is to quantify the effects of variables that cannot be randomized but are known to be strongly related to the dependent variable, independent variable, or both. These are control variables for which an experimenter collects data. For example, blood pressure might be collected in a study examining the effects of age on memory, because it could serve as a third variable or alternative explanation of age-related changes in memory. That is, blood pressure could confound the relationship of age and memory. However, in this example, blood pressure could be used as a control variable to statistically adjust the dependent variable of scores on tests of memory.

There are different statistical techniques available to compare groups on a dependent variable, such as memory, while controlling for group differences on a control variable, such as blood pressure. The most well known of these statistical techniques is **analysis of covariance**, which allows the researcher to test whether a difference on a dependent measure exists, even after controlling or covarying for the effects of specific control variables. Analysis of covariance is beyond the scope of this book (see e.g., Kirk, 1994, for description). However, the principle to keep in mind is that a dependent measure can be adjusted statistically, which in effect eliminates the confounding influence of a specified third variable. This statistical test allows the experimenter to conclude that observed group differences on a dependent variable could not be attributable to unwanted effects of a third variable.

Table 6.2 presents pre- and posttraining scores on a measure of auditory memory for the three groups of the Merzenich study. As you can see in **Table 6.2**, only the brain plasticity training group showed a significant improvement in memory following training. Note a potential problem in these results pertains to the pretraining memory scores: As you can see in **Table 6.2**, the brain plasticity group had the lowest pretest memory scores. This raises concerns as to whether the subsequent posttest improvement for the brain plasticity training group was confounded by their relatively low pretest scores. Here, analysis of covariance could be used to statistically equate the three groups on pretest memory scores. This would adjust the scores on the dependent variable—the posttest outcome measure—for the initial differences on the pretest measure. If the results still remain significant, then we would have more confidence in concluding that

Table 6.2   Training Improves Global Memory Score

Group	Pretest	Posttest	Difference p value
Experimental	48.9 ± 1.3	51.2 ± 1.2	$2.3 \pm 0.9 \, p = .019$
Comparison	50.2 ± 1.2	51.2 ± 1.2	$1.0 \pm 0.9 \, p = .29$
Control	51.2 ± 1.0	52.3 ± 1.1	$1.1 \pm 0.9 \, p = .22$

Source: Adapted from Mahncke et al., 2006.

neural plasticity training improved memory, even after controlling for the relatively lower pretest scores for the experimental group. Absent this statistical control, however, the beneficial effect of brain plasticity training on memory can be questioned.

Table 6.2 presents the prettest and posttest scores on memory for experimental brain plasticity training ($n = 53$), comparison with DVD educational ($n = 53$), and control ($n = 56$) groups. As you can see, in relation to their pretest scores, the experimental brain plasticity group showed a significant improvement of 2.3 points in postest memory scores. By contrast, neither the comparison nor the control group showed a significant improvement in posttest memory scores. The researchers concluded that only the participants in the experimental group showed improvements in nontrained, standardized assessments of memory (Mahncke et al., 2006).

Hypothesis Testing and Statistical Reasoning

Notice in Table 6.2 the pretraining/posttraining difference scores in memory test points were 2.3 for brain plasticity, 1.0 for comparison, and 1.1 for control groups. These absolute difference scores may be viewed as the *effect size,* which as you recall from Chapter 2 refers to the strength of the treatment—brain plasticity training—on the outcome measure of memory. The effect size for the brain plasticity training would appear to be rather modest—a mean 2.3-point improvement on the posttest from the pretest baseline measure. Yet the results did show a statistically significant difference pointing to an improvement on the memory posttest for the experimental group following treatment with the brain plasticity training.

It is not uncommon in psychological research for a finding to achieve statistical significance yet to involve a rather small effect size. Statistical significance and effect size address two distinct aspects of results. Recall that statistical significance tells us the likelihood that the observed effect revealed by data analysis could be due to chance. In other words, statistical significance answers the question: Does the treatment work? Effect size tells us the strength of the relationship between the treatment and the outcome measure; it answers the practical question: How much impact does the treatment have?

Effect size and statistical significance also play distinct roles in hypothesis testing. Statistical significance is used to test what is referred to as the **null hypothesis**. The null hypothesis is defined as the hypothesis of no difference or no relationship, which the researcher tries to reject, nullify, or disproof. An example of a null hypothesis from the Merzenich study is:

> The pretest and posttest changes scores in memory will be the same for the three groups, indicating that brain plasticity training did not improve memory scores.

The alternative hypothesis, the **research hypothesis** in this example, usually predicts a specific relationship typically on the basis of theory, which in this case is that brain plasticity training improves memory. The alternative hypothesis in this study was:

> Participants in the experimental group who receive brain plasticity training will have higher posttest than pretest memory scores in relation to those of the comparison and control groups.

Statistics do not directly test the research hypothesis. That is, a significance level of less than 5% allows for the rejection of the *null* hypothesis of no difference between the groups, but it does not allow for the acceptance of the research hypothesis of better outcome for the experimental group. As we learned, groups may differ for a number of reasons, apart from that attributable to the independent variable, and we hope that any existing differences have been washed out by randomization. However, we should keep in the mind that our statistical analytical techniques are set up to test the null hypothesis, not the alternative or research hypothesis. We therefore do not interpret significant results as support for the alternative hypothesis, that is, the research hypothesis that predicts that changes in the dependent variable result from changes in the independent variable. These peculiar and counterintuitive circumstances of statistics and hypothesis testing are yet another reminder for us of the importance of cautious skepticism in interpreting research findings.

Two types of errors must be weighed in making decisions about whether to reject or accept the null hypothesis. **Type I error** occurs when the null hypothesis is wrongly rejected. To use a legal analogy, the maxim that "all defendants are innocent until proven guilty" is akin to a null hypothesis. A jury makes a Type I error when it wrongly convicts an innocent defendant. In science, what is the likelihood of a Type I error, that is, rejecting the null hypothesis when in fact it is true? The answer is the level of statistical significance stated as a probability (i.e., *p*-value). A probability of a Type I error is the significance level. So if statistical analysis of the results showed a *p*-value of less than .03, then the chances are less than 3% that the obtained results are due to chance; there is less than 3% chance of a Type I error of wrongfully rejecting the null hypothesis (see Chapter 10).

Type II error occurs when the null hypothesis is wrongfully accepted. A jury makes a Type II error when it fails to convict a guilty defendant. When you as a researcher commit a Type II error, you have in effect shot yourself in the foot! In psychological, research Type II errors are difficult to gauge in terms of how often they may occur. This is likely because studies that are plagued by Type II errors have by definition failed to achieve statistical significance and therefore are seldom reviewed for publication. This helps to explain the problem of *publication bias* in the psychological literature that we discussed in Chapter 2.

Why might Type II errors occur? Type II errors are typically understood as a problem of *statistical power*—the extent to which a study is adequately designed to find the predicted significant effect. Among the factors related to statistical power, there are two of particular interest—sample size and effect size. Sample size refers to the number of research participants/observations/data points that are expected to be collected and analyzed. In general, larger samples provide greater statistical power. The idea is that if only a handful of research participants are tested, then a negative finding of no difference or no relationship may arise simply because not enough people were tested. Similarly, different treatments will have different effects, as, for example, brain plasticity training may have a relatively small effect on memory for healthy people. A small treatment effect means a small effect size, and a small effect size can be very difficult to detect. On the other hand, a large treatment effect translates into a large effect size, and a large effect size is easier to detect. Statistical power increases as effect size increases. When designing an experiment, a researcher calculates what effect size would be expected when an independent variable is manipulated. The calculation is simply the difference in means between experimental and control groups divided by the overall variability or spread in scores for the two groups combined. The numbers for these calculations can be taken from a previously published study or from **pilot data** collected by the experimenter to test out the procedures and measures before formally running the study. Tables available in statistical books as well as on the Internet can be used to assess and interpret the meaning of an obtained effect size. These tables provide information about how large a sample is necessary to obtain the effect size calculated from a prior study.

EXTERNAL VALIDITY

Whenever we hear of a new research finding, one of our first questions is, To whom do the results of the study apply? Doctors, for example, may fail to pursue for their patients a treatment, which has been demonstrated to be effective in experiments, if they think the results have limited applicability and relevance. Relevance and applicability depend on external validity. The concept of **external validity** addresses the extent to which results of a particular study that involves a sample of subjects will generalize to the wider population. The need for generalizable findings can be thought of as the Achilles heel of randomized experimental design. The design components that are essential for a randomized experiment and that minimize the threats to internal validity make it more difficult to achieve external validity in the form of sample generalizability (being able to apply the findings to some clearly defined larger population), cross-population generalizability (generalizing across subgroups and to other populations and settings, conditions, and outcomes) and *ecological validity* (discussed in Chapter 2) or the real-world impact of research (see **Exhibit 6.4**).

Sample Generalizability

Research participants, who can be recruited for a laboratory experiment, randomly assigned to a group, and kept under carefully controlled conditions for

Exhibit 6.4   Greater Generalizability and Applicability, Greater External Validity

Source: Reprinted with permission of Dr. David J. McKirnan, Department of Psychology, University of Illinois at Chicago.

the study's duration, are unlikely to be a representative sample of any large population of interest to social scientists. Can they be expected to react to the experimental treatment in the same way as members of the larger population? The generalizability of the treatment and of the setting for the experiment also must be considered (Cook & Campbell, 1979). The more artificial the experimental arrangements are, the greater the problem will be (Campbell & Stanley, 1966).

A researcher can take steps both before and after an experiment to increase a study's generalizability. The Merzenich team's (2006) study is likely to yield more generalizable findings than are laboratory experiments that rely on college students as research participants. In studies like the Merzenich et al. investigation as well as some field experiments, participants can even be selected randomly from the population of interest, and, thus, the researchers can achieve results that are generalizable to that population. For example, some studies of the effects of income supports on the work behavior of poor persons have *randomly sampled* persons within particular states before randomly assigning them to experimental and comparison groups. When random selection is not feasible, the researchers may be able to increase generalizability by selecting several different experimental sites that offer marked contrasts on key variables (Cook & Campbell, 1979).

Note that the random assignment of research participants to groups is not the same as random sampling of individuals from some larger population (see **Exhibit 6.5**).

Exhibit 6.5   Random Sampling and Random Assignment Increase External and Internal Validity, Respectively

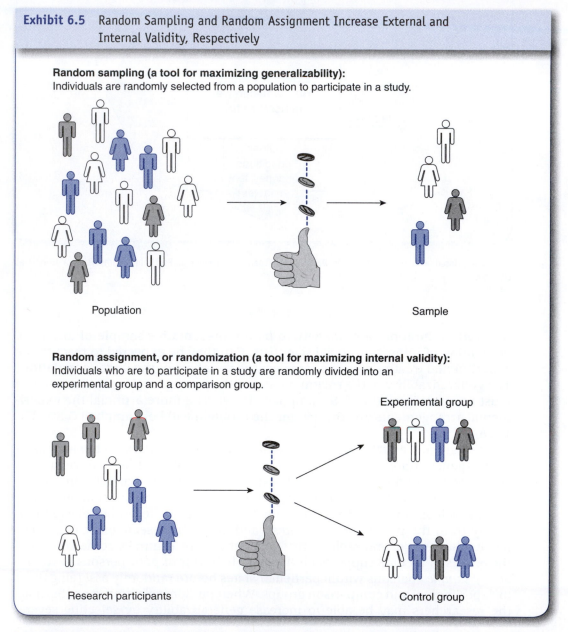

Random sampling (a tool for maximizing generalizability):
Individuals are randomly selected from a population to participate in a study.

Population

Sample

Random assignment, or randomization (a tool for maximizing internal validity):
Individuals who are to participate in a study are randomly divided into an experimental group and a comparison group.

Experimental group

Research participants

Control group

Source: Schutt, R. K. (2009). *Investigating the social world: The process and practice of research* (6th ed., p. 227). Thousand Oaks, CA: Pine Forge Press.

In fact, random assignment (randomization) does not help at all to ensure that the research participants are representative of some larger population; instead, representativeness is the goal of random sampling. What random assignment does—create two or more equivalent groups—is useful for maximizing the likelihood of internal validity, not generalizability. As sketched in **Exhibit 6.5**, random sampling and random assignment are vital in constructing sensitive and valid designs. Random sampling by maximizing generalizability increases the external validity of the results of a study. Similarly, random assignment by equating treatment and control groups prior to the manipulation of the independent variable enhances the ability of an experiment to generate internally valid results.

Ecological Validity

As we touched upon in Chapter 2, ecological validity is a form of external validity that is concerned with the real-life impact of results generated from research studies. We have already learned that ecological validity is especially important in studies that want to investigate whether some form of training or treatment can improve real-live functioning. Ecological validity rests largely on the extent to which the researchers select the proper outcome measures. In general, laboratory experiments often fall short on ecological validity. The researcher tries to balance experimental control and internal validity, on one hand, with general applicability of ecological validity on the other hand. As we have seen, for example, the Stanford Prison Experiment described in Chapter 3 is thought of as an experiment with considerable ecological validity. However, it lacked experimental control and internal validity in that many of the particular features of the environment that triggered the abusive behavior of the guards could not be specified and measured.

On the other hand, the Merzenich team's study can be criticized for its limited ecological validity in the selection of outcome measures that they used to demonstrate the effectiveness of their neural plasticity training. What their experiment showed is that brain plasticity training improved performance on standardized tests of mental ability. However, it is unclear whether the improved performance on these tests translated to real-life improvement. To do so, Merzenich and company would need as a dependent measure of outcome an assessment of everyday functioning in life, and they would then need to demonstrate that the brain plasticity training group had higher levels of everyday functioning than did the comparison and control groups.

CAN CAUSALITY BE ESTABLISHED?

As we have seen, the results of the Merzenich study indicated that the experimental computer-based training group showed a statistically significant improvement on the outcome measure of memory as assessed by standardized neuropsychological tests. The experimental group sustained its improved memory at a 3-month follow-up. By contrast, neither the active computer-based training group nor the no-contact control group showed any significant change on the outcome measure of memory at the end of the study or at the 3-month follow-up. The comparison and control groups had similar responses on the outcome measures. Merzenich and colleagues concluded that their brain plasticity-based program significantly improved memory in mature adults. Was this causal conclusion justified? How confident can we be in this conclusion? Do you think that this effect is likely to generalize to other people and settings?

We can say that brain plasticity improved cognition in the Merzenich group's study because only participants who received this training showed improved performance on the outcome measures of memory. This improvement occurred after the treatment. This is important because causality requires demonstrating that the predicted effect followed treatment. This time order criterion (or, as we learned in Chapter 2, *temporal precedence*) of causality is clearly demonstrated in the Merzenich and company study. However, two aspects of their data raise concern as to whether a causal relationship can be concluded between their demonstrated association of brain plasticity and improved memory. The first aspect concerns pre-existing differences among the three groups on the pretest memory measure, with the experimental group showing the lowest scores prior to receiving brain plasticity training. The second concern centers on the strength of the brain plasticity training on the posttest outcome measure of memory. As we have discussed, the Merzenich results pointed to a rather small effect for the brain plasticity training on memory scores for the experimental group. Both aspects of their data—pretest differences and small effect size—pose major problems for drawing a causal connection between brain plasticity training and memory improvement. Also important to remember is that our statistics test the null hypothesis, not the research hypothesis. A statistically significant finding tells us the obtained results are unlikely due to change, but this is a far cry from establishing a causal prediction formulated in the research hypothesis. We can therefore safely conclude that the Merzenich data pointed to an empirical association of treatment and better memory scores for the experimental group, but we should exercise caution (in the spirit of the scientific method) in drawing any causal conclusion that brain plasticity training by itself produced memory improvement in the experimental group.

In addition, we must be mindful of the multiple influences at work in any psychological study; only the influence of a sole independent variable is studied in a single-factor experiment. As we will learn in Chapter 7, most psychological experiments involve more than one independent variable. There are many advantages of manipulating two or more independent variables simultaneously within the same experiment. Chief among these is that so-called multifactorial experiments allow us to examine an important issue of validity, that is, whether results generalize across several independent variables. And as we will also learn in Chapter 7, *interactions* between and among independent variables can be tested in these multifactorial experiments. In this sense, then, multifactorial experiments offer a more realistic chance of arriving at a causal explanation. As a preview to the next chapter, we will learn how two independent variables interact, meaning the effects produced by one independent variable are not the same across levels of a second independent variable. For now, however, we end this chapter looking at some common errors in reasoning that can lead to invalid causal explanations.

Mistakes in Reasoning About Causality

Recall that in Chapter 1 we learned that we are naturally prone to making certain errors of reasoning, such as when confirmatory bias influences our collection and interpretation of evidence. These errors of reasoning, or *heuristic biases* (see Chapter 1), come in many different forms, including those that predispose us to infer causation on the basis of correlation. Consider the old adage, "Correlation does not prove causation." This maxim is meant to remind us that a correlation between two variables might be caused by something other than an effect of the presumed independent variable on the dependent variable—that is, it might be a spurious relationship. If we measure children's shoe sizes and their academic knowledge, for example, we will find a positive association. However, the association results from the fact that older children have larger feet as well as more academic knowledge. Shoe size does not cause knowledge, or vice versa.

Do storks bring babies? If you believe that correlation proves causation, then you might think so. The more storks that appear in certain districts in Holland, the more babies are born. But the association in Holland between number of storks and birthrate is spurious. In fact, both the number of storks and the birthrate are higher in rural districts than in urban districts. The rural or urban character of the district (the extraneous variable) causes variation in the other two variables.

If you think the point is obvious, consider a social science example. Do schools with more resources produce better student outcomes? Before you answer the question, consider the fact that parents with more education and higher income tend to live in neighborhoods that spend more on their schools. The parents are more likely to have books in the home and provide other advantages for their children. Do parents cause variation in both school resources and student performance? If so, there would be an association between school resources and student performance that was at least partially spurious.

Finally, researchers should make sure that their causal conclusions reflect the unit of analysis in their study. Experiments involve investigating group differences. As such, the group is the proper unit of analysis. What this means is that conclusions about group-level processes should be made based on experimental data collected from groups, and conclusions about individuals should be based on individual-level data. Ignoring this individual versus group-unit level of analysis distinction can give rise to two kinds of errors in casual conclusion.

First, an error of reasoning known as the ecological fallacy occurs when you make conclusions about an individual based only on analyses of group data. For example, a research participant who received the computerized cognitive training will have better memory than a person who did not participate in the study. Essentially, the mistake is taking the average for the group and blindly applying it to an individual member of the group. However, don't be too quick to reject all the conclusions about individual processes based on group-level data; just keep in mind the possibility of an ecological fallacy. If we don't have individual-level data, we can't be sure that patterns at the group level, often summarized by the arithmetic average or mean, will hold at the individual level. Second, when data about individuals are used to make inferences about group-level processes, a problem occurs that can be thought of as the mirror image of the ecological fallacy: the **reductionist fallacy**, also known as reductionism or individualist fallacy (see **Exhibit 6.6**).

Exhibit 6.6   Errors in Causal Conclusion

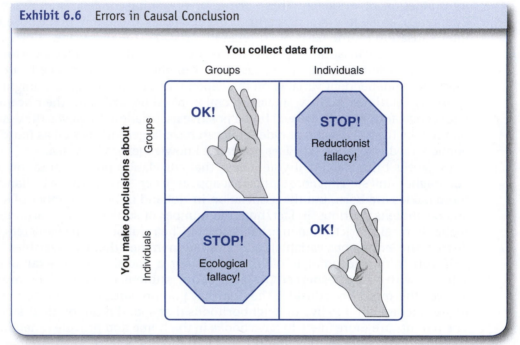

Source: Schutt, R. K. (2009). *Investigating the social world: The process and practice of research* (6th ed., p. 193). Thousand Oaks, CA: Pine Forge Press.

In summary, the fact that errors in causal reasoning can be made should not deter you from carrying out experiments nor make you unduly critical of researchers who make inferences about individuals on the basis of group data. However, just because a person is a member of a group with a certain average, such as a high memory score, does not mean you can conclude that the person will have a strong memory!

CONCLUSIONS

We have learned of a particularly well-controlled and powerful research design known simply as a true experiment. In a true experiment, a researcher has complete control over the manipulation of the independent variable. Such experimental control allows for testing whether systematically varying the independent variable causes changes in the dependent variable. That is, a researcher aims to design an internally valid experiment that will establish causal relationships among the key variables under study.

A pivotal question in designing a true experiment is how participants will be allocated to control and experimental conditions. In a between-subjects design, participants are randomly assigned to control and experimental groups. Random assignment is critical in forming equivalent control and experimental groups before the introduction of the independent variable. We use this design to ensure that participants are exposed to only one level of the independent variable, for example, a particular treatment, and not to any other types of treatment.

In a within-subjects design, all participants receive all conditions of the experiment. Each participant serves as his or her own control. As such, a within-subject design requires fewer participants than a between-subjects design. A within-subject design provides one of the most powerful techniques of experimental control of factors that could either confound or obscure the effect of the independent variable on the dependent variable. However, conditions must be presented in counterbalanced order to avoid confounding influences of carryover effects.

Other important considerations for designing and conducting experiments are to employ independent and dependent variables that are sufficiently sensitive to test the research hypothesis. Experimental error can also be minimized by statistical control in the use of pretest measures that allow for statistically equated control and experimental groups before the treatment is implemented. The more factors controlled through design and statistical tools, the more likely it is that an experiment will produce internally valid results. Unfortunately, often it is the case that the design components, which are essential for a true experiment and which minimize the threats to internal validity, make it more difficult to achieve external validity in the form of sample generalizability and real-world impact.

END OF CHAPTER

Chapter Highlights

- We want to design an experiment in which all extraneous factors are sufficiently controlled so that changes in the dependent variables result solely from changes in the independent variable.

- An experiment provides the best test of whether manipulation of an independent variable causes changes in a dependent variable. A true experiment uses random assignment to form equivalent control and experimental groups before treatment (pretest) that can be directly compared on the dependent variable following treatment (posttest).

- The concept of internal validity is synonymous with causality. The internal validity of an experiment is defined as the extent to which the systematic manipulation of one or more independent variables produces the predicted or hypothesized effect on the dependent variable. The goal is to design an internally valid experiment that will allow the researcher to establish causal relationships among the key variables under study.

- A sound experiment uses pretest and posttest measures of a dependent variable. Group differences on pretest confound interpretation of any subsequent group differences on posttest. When this happens, posttest scores can be statistically adjusted to take into account the problematic pretest differences.

- A within-subjects design in which all participants receive all conditions of the experiment in counterbalanced order provides us with one of the most powerful techniques of experimental control of factors that could either confound or obscure the effect of the independent variable on the dependent variable. However, carryover effects can be a serious concern in a within-subjects design.

- In a between-subjects design, participants receive only one level of the independent variable. We use this design to ensure that participants are exposed to only one level of the independent variable, for example, a particular treatment, and not to any other types of treatment.

- In science, random does not mean haphazard, arbitrary, unplanned, by habit, or done without awareness. In science, randomization refers to a precise technique by which we control the influences of any and all confounding variables and biases from corrupting the design of our experiment.

- An effective matched-pairs design provides a degree of experimental control of between-subject individual differences that is comparable to that of a within-subjects design. As such, a matched-pairs design provides greater power to detect statistical significance than simple random assignment of a between-subjects design.

- Ceiling and floor effects can pose problems for the measurement of a dependent variable, reducing its sensitivity to changes in the independent variable.

- More complicated manipulations of an independent variable called staged or event manipulations create a psychological state in the participants that mimics a reaction to a real-life situation. These kinds of manipulations raise serious ethical concerns that need to be reviewed by an IRB before ever even piloting them. If approved by an IRB, then pilot a manipulation check to measure directly whether the independent variable manipulation creates the intended effect on people.

- Sample generalizability and real-world impact of the results (ecological validity) increase external validity of experiments.

- We should exercise caution (in the spirit of the scientific method) in drawing any causal conclusion that an independent variable caused a change in a dependent variable.

Key Terms

Analysis of covariance   191

Baseline   176

Between-subjects design   177

Carryover effects   182

Ceiling effect   189

Comparison group   176

Condition   175

Control   173

Control group   176

Counterbalancing   183

Demand characteristics   188

Design sensitivity   186

Double-blind   188

Ecological fallacy   199

Effect size   192

Ex post facto   174

Experimental control   173

Experimental error   190

Experimental group   176

External validity   192

Factors   175

Floor effect   189

Individual differences   179

Internal validity   186

Latin-square design   183

Longitudinal research design   182

Manipulation check   189

Matching   180

Matched-pairs design   181

Multifactorial designs   175

Null hypothesis   192

Null result   187

Pilot data   194

Placebo   188

Posttest   176

Pretest   176

Pretest-posttest control group design   180

Quasiexperiment   174

Random assignment   174

Randomization   174

Randomized comparative change design   180

Reductionist fallacy   200

Repeated-measures, within-subjects design   181

Research hypothesis   192

Single-factor experiment   175

Spurious relationship   199

Staged manipulation   189

Statistical control   191

Treatment   175

Treatment group   176

True experiment   172

Type I error   193

Type II error   193

Within-subjects design   177

Research in the News

1. The April 27, 2009, issue of the *New Yorker* contains a lengthy article by Margaret Talbot titled "Brain Gain: The Underground World of 'Neuroenhancing' Drugs." Talbot addresses the use of psychiatric drugs as brain boosters or cognitive enhancers by healthy adults. She details cases of healthy college students with stellar grades seeking even better academic results by using stimulants that are prescribed for the treatment of attention-deficit hyperactivity disorder. This "off-label" use (meaning that the drug has neither its manufacturer's nor the FDA's approval) has become increasingly popular not only among students but also with many other professions, including scientists and researchers. In fact, psychologist Martha Farah of the University of Pennsylvania and her colleagues (Greely et al., 2008) reviewed the empirical evidence for the use of cognitive enhancers from 40 laboratory studies involving healthy research participants. In their review appearing in *Nature* (2008), "Towards Responsible Use of Cognitive Enhancing Drugs by the Healthy" they concluded cognitive enhancers may help people who don't meet diagnostic criteria for any kind of cognitive impairment. Discuss the scientific evidence for the use of "neuroenhancers" and the kind of study you would design to investigate their effectiveness.

Activity Questions

1. "The Problem with Prozac" headlines the column written by science journalist Martin Enserink (2008) in *ScienceNOW*, a website devoted to daily news about research. Enserink reports on a controversial new study that claims that Prozac and other so-called selective serotonin reuptake inhibitors (SSRIs), which are widely used to treat depression, are largely ineffective for the vast majority of patients who take them. Design a true experiment to examine the effectiveness of Prozac. Your design must contain each of these six features:

   1. Experimental or treatment group is the group that will receive the experimental treatment, manipulation of the variable under study.

   2. Control group is used to produce comparisons. The treatment of interest is deliberately withheld or manipulated to provide a baseline performance with which to compare the experimental or treatment group's performance.

   3. Independent variable is the variable that you as an experimenter manipulate in order to determine its influence on the dependent variable.

   4. Dependent variable is what you will measure in the study.

   5. Random assignment is how you will form your treatment and control groups. When you use random assignment, each participant has an equal probability of being selected for either the treatment or control group.

   6. Double blind means that neither the participant nor the experimenter knows whether the research participant is in the treatment or the control condition.

2. You have found a statistically significant result but one that is of a very small effect size. How would you interpret these results, and what implications might these findings have in designing future studies, especially in regard to sample size?

Review Questions

1. How would you define a true experiment? How does a true experiment compare with other study designs of the "research toolbox" presented in Chapter 1?

2. Compare and contrast between-subject designs and within-subjects designs.

3. Compare and contrast experimental control and statistical control.

4. Describe the relationship between statistical significance and Type I error and the relationship between statistical power and Type II error.

5. What is the main objective or purpose of randomly assigning research participants in a between-subjects design?

6. How does a matched-pairs design increase the likelihood that experimental and control groups will be similar before the treatment is employed?

7. How does counterbalancing reduce the likelihood of confounds related to carry-over effects?

8. What is a Latin-square design and when would you consider using it?

9. What is a null hypothesis? What is a research hypothesis?

10. Why is it important to understand that statistics allow for the rejection of the null hypothesis but do not provide a direct test of the research hypothesis?

11. Why is causality so difficult to establish even with a true experiment?

12. What are ceiling effects? What are floor effects? What kinds of problems do these pose for the researcher?

13. What are individual differences? Compare how between-subjects designs and within-subjects designs address the problem of individual differences.

14. What is a null result? How might experimental error and design sensitivity contribute to a null result?

15. What does *statistical significance* mean? What does *effect size* mean? How are statistical significance and effect size similar? How are they different?

16. What is external validity? What is internal validity? What is the relationship between external validity and internal validity?

17. Explain staged manipulation as a device to create an independent variable.

18. Describe the design of the study by Merzenich and colleagues. How did these researchers arrange the independent and dependent variables and control variables?

19. Discuss some of the alternative explanations for the findings of the Merzenich et al. study.

20. Under what circumstances would you recommend the use of double-blind procedures?

Ethics in Action

1. Randomization and double-blind procedures are key features of experimental design that are often used by studies to investigate the efficacy of new treatments for serious and often incurable, terminal diseases. What ethical issues do these techniques raise in studies of experimental treatments for incurable, terminal diseases?

2. What about the random assignment used in the Merzenich team's study? What are the ethical concerns that two-thirds of their research participants were not given the opportunity to receive the treatment? How could a similar study be designed so that all participants eventually receive the desired treatment?

3. Are cognitive enhancers described in *Research in the News* a form of cheating and will they add to inequality of opportunity and contribute to an uneven playing field?

CHAPTER 7

True Experiments II

Multifactorial Designs

SUBSTANTIVE THEME: SOCIAL AND EMOTIONAL INFLUENCES ON THINKING AND PERCEIVING

Psychologists have long been interested in how emotions influence our perceptions, thoughts, and actions. Yet the study of human emotions may at first appear experimentally intractable, meaning that it does not lend itself to controlled laboratory research. That is, how can emotions be manipulated in the laboratory? And would these laboratory manipulations provide a realistic depiction of true human emotional experience? But as you recall from Chapter 2, elegant experimental studies by Paul Ekman and other researchers (e.g., Strack et al., 1988) have indeed shown that emotions can be covertly induced (without a person even knowing) and reliably manipulated by specific facial contractions. In this chapter, we continue to focus on the human face as an exquisite and efficient organ of emotional communication. But we now ask an even more complex question, one that seeks to figure out how it is that the face acts as a social signaling system that influences our perceptions and reactions (Hess, Adams, & Kleck, 2009). As Hess and colleagues aptly put in the cogent subtitle of their recent review "The face is not an empty canvas."

Instead, the idea is that the emotional salience of the human face reflects an intricate interaction among distinct features of the face. Note the term *interaction,* which, we will learn in this chapter, has a specific statistical meaning. But before we learn about statistical interactions, an analogy might be helpful. Different drugs, for example, may interact to produce harmful or beneficial effects. Consider the effects of valium and alcohol that, when taken together, can interact to produce feelings of depression. Using each alone, however, may produce a very different emotional effect. Similarly, two drugs may work together or synergistically to enhance or magnify one or more effects. In other words, elements interact to generate effects that otherwise would not have occurred with each drug alone.

In a similar vein, psychologists often are very excited by the prospect of studying how different factors, either directly or indirectly, influence experience. From our research toolbox from Chapter 1, we introduce a study design that is ideally suited to disentangle both direct and interactive influences on measured responses. We referred to this as a complex experimental design, which is used when a researcher seeks to manipulate two or more independent variables at the same time. These complex experimental designs are more realistic, as we will see, in part because they allow a researcher to examine how independent variables interact with each other. These complex designs are also more efficient than an experimental analysis limited to a one-at-a-time variable manipulation. Instead of having to conduct a series of independent single-factor experiments, we can effectively combine these experiments into one. Up until now, we have focused on single-factor experiments in which only one independent variable is manipulated, such as the Merzenich team's memory enhancement study from Chapter 6. Now think of a true experiment from Chapter 6 with two or more independent variables.

These complex experimental designs are referred to as **factorial designs**. As we have learned, a factor is simply another name for an independent variable. We use the term **multifactorial** for experiments that vary two or more independent variables and, as we will see, provide direct tests of the main effects of each independent variable as well as the interaction effects between and among the independent variables. Factorial experiments can vary the independent variables between subjects, others can vary them within subjects, and still others can combine between-subjects and within-subjects manipulation of the independent variables. As we will learn, multifactorial experiments have provided a powerful and economical research design to begin to disentangle the intricacies of human emotional experience.

MULTIFACTORIAL DESIGNS

We begin our discussion of multifactorial designs by returning to the now familiar concept of the independent variable. As you know, so far we have examined single-factor experiments, which by definition involve just one independent variable. As you also know, all independent variables must have two or more levels. Thus, all single-factor experiments must incorporate one and *only one* independent variable with two or more levels. So in the Merzenich group study of Chapter 6, the single-factor experiment had one independent variable, which we called "treatment," with groups of participants randomly assigned to one of three treatment levels or conditions: brain plasticity training, educational DVD, and no treatment. Thus, in a single-factor experiment, a researcher can always add a new level to an existing independent variable, as for example when a baseline, no-treatment group is incorporated into the study design. By contrast, in a multifactorial experiment, an altogether new independent variable is devised and incorporated into the research design. It is therefore important to understand the difference between adding a level to an existing independent variable, as done in a single-factor experiment, versus devising an entirely new and distinct independent variable altogether, as done in a multifactorial experiment.

How then does a researcher add a second independent variable? **Exhibit 7.1**, adapted from a study by Rowe, Hirsh, and Anderson (2007) illustrates a multifactorial design with two independent variables. As shown in **Exhibit 7.1**, there are two independent variables: mood induction, with two levels, happy or sad, and cognitive exercise, also with two levels, verbal or visual. Note that the two independent variables—mood induction and cognitive exercises—are *qualitatively* different

Exhibit 7.1 Independent Variables (IV) of Mood Induction and Cognitive Tests, Each With Two Levels

	Cognitive Exercises (IV)	
Mood Induction *(IV)*	Verbal *(Level)*	Visual *(Level)*
Happy *(Level)*	Verbal word associations	Visual attention
Sad *(Level)*	Verbal word associations	Visual attention

Source: Adapted from Rowe et al., 2007.

from each other. Note also that we have not simply added a new level to an existing independent variable, but rather we have devised two distinct independent variables, one mood and the other cognition, that are each manipulated within the same multifactorial experiment.

Exhibit 7.1 illustrates a multifactorial design that could be used to study how emotions may influence thinking (e.g., Rowe et al., 2007). We have two independent variables, mood induction and cognitive exercises, each with two levels. To induce a positive mood, participants listen to a jazzed-up version of Bach's *Brandenberg Concerto No. 3* (played by Hubert Lewis), and for a sad mood, they listen to Prokofiev's *Alexander Nevsky's Russia under the Mongolian Yoke* played at half speed. For the other independent variable, participants perform a verbal exercise of generating remote word associations and a visual exercise of detecting and selecting targets presented on a computer monitor. The idea behind the study is an interesting one of how emotion (mood induction) might influence thinking (cognitive exercises) and whether a particular mood state might be better for performing a particular cognitive exercise.

As with a single-factor experiment, in a multifactorial design, each independent variable can be studied either between subjects or within subjects. For example, in a between-subjects multifactorial research design for the study illustrated in Exhibit 7.1, you would need four groups of research participants, each randomly assigned to one of the four experimental conditions: (1) happy mood/verbal; (2) happy mood/visual; (3) sad mood/verbal; and (4) sad mood/visual. That is, some participants would receive the happy mood induction followed by the verbal task; some would receive the happy mood induction followed by the visual task; others would receive the sad mood induction followed by the verbal task; and still others would receive the sad mood induction followed by the visual task. For a within-subjects multifactorial research design, all participants would be run through each of the four experimental conditions. Thus, the same participants would receive the happy mood induction followed by the verbal task and then the visual task and the sad mood induction followed by the verbal task and then the visual task. As you know from Chapter 6, it would be necessary to counterbalance the order of tasks between moods, and, in turn, between participants.

As we will learn in this chapter, there are many advantages to a multifactorial research design. More complex than a single-factor experiment, a multifactorial design provides a more realistic model of rich psychological phenomena. It offers an economical and efficient design to evaluate and to test the separate and joint influences of one or more independent variables on a dependent variable. For example, we learn through studies that use multifactorial design as illustrated in Exhibit 7.1 that mood influences performance in different ways depending on the cognitive task. That is, a happy mood improves performance for generating remote verbal associations, a test of creative problem solving, but it detracts from performance on a visual task that requires attention to detail (see Rowe et al., 2007). In this sense, then, as we will learn very shortly, these results show that mood and cognition *interact,* meaning the influence of the independent variable of mood induction differed depending upon the level of the second independent variable, that is, whether the cognitive exercise involves either verbal creativity or visual attention to fine details. Had we studied each of these two independent variables separately using two single-factor experiments, we would not have discovered this interaction of mood and cognition.

In this chapter, we discuss a within-subjects factorial experiment in which participants received all levels of the two independent variables. We follow this with a discussion of a factorial experiment that uses between-subjects manipulation of two independent variables.

Notations and Terms

The simplest multifactorial experimental design contains two independent variables, each with two levels or values. Factorial experiments are typically designated or identified by a numbering notation. For example, a **2 × 2 factorial design** has two independent variables, with two levels or values. In this notation, the *number of numbers* tells how many factors or independent variables there are, and the *number values* tell how many levels of the independent variables. A 3 × 4 (spoken as "three-by-four") factorial design indicates two independent variables, one with three levels, and the other with four levels. The order of the numbers makes no difference, so that a 3 × 4 factorial design could be just as easily identified as a 4 × 3. In a factorial design, every level of each independent variable is combined. For a 3 × 4 design, this means the three levels of one independent variable are combined with the four levels of the other independent variable for a total of 12 levels or treatments. Thus, the number of treatment groups that we have in any factorial design can be calculated by simply multiplying through the number notation. In our 2 × 2 example, we have 2 × 2 = 4 groups. In a 3 × 4 factorial design, we have 3 × 4 = 12 groups. A factorial experiment allows us to examine all these combinations.

Theory and Experimentation

How might complex experimental designs be applied to fascinating theoretical questions? As with all research designs, theory serves as the starting point for all investigations. Theory, as we have learned, provides us with the conceptual framework for how particular psychological phenomena might work in real life. We learned in Chapter 2, for example, that theories of *embodied cognition* can be used as a conceptual model for us to understand how we experience, perceive, and communicate emotional information (Niedenthal, 2007). Recall that the major thrust of this theory is that when we perceive and think about emotion, we re-enact or re-experience its perceptual, somatovisceral, and motoric features (which is collectively referred to as "embodiment"). We further learned that the embodiment of emotion, when induced in human participants in the laboratory by covert manipulation of facial expression, causally affected how emotional information is processed (Niedenthal, 2007).

For example, as discussed in Chapter 2, participants in the Strack et al. (1988) study rated cartoons as funnier than did participants who held a pen between the teeth (to induce smiling) than when holding a pen between the lips (to inhibit smiling). More recently, Havas, Glenberg, and Rinck (2007) had research participants judge sentences that described a pleasant or unpleasant occurrence while holding a pen between the teeth (i.e., smiling) or between the lips (i.e., prevents smiling). The results showed that reading times for understanding sentences that described pleasant events were faster when participants were smiling than when participants were prevented from smiling. Similarly, reading times for understanding sentences that described unpleasant events were faster when participants were prevented from smiling than when they were smiling.

We thus see that theory and experimentation are closely intertwined. To wit, theory guides how an experiment is designed, how independent variables are developed and manipulated, how dependent variables are measured, and what specific hypotheses are tested. For complex multifactorial designs, the role of theory may be even more prominent than for single-factor experiments. After all, developing and creating two or more independent variables and specifying how they may interact are certainly advanced when a researcher has a well-developed theoretical model. In the following section, we present a study of facial expression of emotion that incorporates the simplest complex design: the 2 × 2 design. You will learn how theory informed and inspired the construction of the research design, providing both the rationale and motivation for devising the two independent variables and for formulating the study hypotheses.

A COMPLEX WITHIN-SUBJECTS EXPERIMENT

What makes the human face such a vital and universal signal system of emotional perception and expression? Why are facial expressions so universally recognizable? Why is a face of anger so readily distinguishable from a face of fear? In their 2003 paper published in *Psychological Science* titled "Perceived Gaze Direction and the Processing of Facial Displays," researchers Reginald B. Adams and Robert E. Kleck wondered about these very same questions (see Appendix C). They theorized that eye-gaze direction and facial expressions represent two distinct and isolable features of the human face, which, among others, may be especially important in conveying social information. They suggested that these facial features have played critical roles in our evolutionary past for both survival and cooperation. According to their theory, eye-gaze direction and facial expressions can each be understood in terms of **approach-avoidance motivation**. That is, both can share informational value as signals of approach, propelling behavior forward, setting the stage for direct expression, confrontation or "fight;" conversely, they may fuel avoidance, triggering inhibition, culminating in "flight" from negative stimuli, of potential danger and threat. (see Adams & Kleck, 2003; Elliot, 2006).

As an example, Adams and Kleck cited evidence that has long linked anger and direct eye gaze with approach motivation. On the other hand, fear and averted gaze, they emphasized, have been shown to be associated with avoidance motivation. They further showed in a related report published in *Science* (Adams et al., 2003) that a particular part of the brain, the amygdala, known to be responsive to threat, is differentially engaged when research participants view fearful as well as angry facial displays of emotion coupled with either direct or averted eye gaze. As they wrote,

> The issue of gaze becomes pertinent because anger faces signal impending aggression on the part of the expressor, whereas fear faces indicate potential environmental threat perceived by the expressor. Thus, when coupled with direct gaze (i.e., eye contact with observer) anger faces should indicate more clearly that threat is directed at the observer, whereas when coupled with averted gaze (i.e., laterally shifted gaze) fear faces should indicate more clearly where in the environment that threat is located. (Adams et al., 2003, p. 1536)

Here we thus see an excellent example of how to thoughtfully weave a theory that leads to direct experimentation. That is, Adams and Kleck constructed a theory, which proposes that facial expressions of emotions and gaze direction operate as a **social signaling system** that governs our basic evolved behavioral tendencies for approach or avoidance (see also Hess et al., 2009). They further reasoned that our fluency in perceiving facial expressions of emotions reflects a dynamic interaction of signals associated with gaze direction and affective displays etched on our visages. Now let's learn from Adams and Kleck how a theory can be translated into a complex experiment.

Decoding Facial Expressions of Emotion

We naturally and automatically perceive facial expressions of emotion holistically as messages. (e.g., "That person is mad about something"). These facial expressions are nonetheless complex stimuli, configurations of more basic elementary features. Consider for example the eye region of the face, one of the key sources of information for decoding emotional expression (e.g., Whalen, 1998). **Exhibit 7.2**, taken from Whalen et al. (2004), compares the "eye whites" known as sclera of standardized (Ekman) fearful and happy faces (see Chapter 2). Note in **Exhibit 7.2** the larger size of fearful eye whites in comparison to that of happy eye whites. In an ingenious brain imaging study, Whalen and colleagues recorded neural activity while participants viewed a series of slides, each with either fearful white eyes or happy white eyes (**see Exhibit 7.2**). Consistent with the findings of Adams and Kleck (2003), Whalen and colleagues also found the amygdala of the human brain to be especially sensitive to fearful white eyes but not to happy white eyes. These scientific findings give credence to "wide-eyed" fear shown in horror movie actors!

Exhibit 7.2 Fearful Eye Whites Are Larger Than Happy Eye Whites

17ms   17ms

Fear   Happy

Source: From "Human Amygdala Responsivity to Masked Fearful Eye Whites" by Paul J. Whalen, Jerome Kagan, Robert G. Cook, F. Caroline Davis, Hackjin Kim, Sara Polis, Donald G. McLaren, Leah H. Somerville, Ashly A. McLean, Jeffrey S. Maxwell, Tom Johnstone in *Science, 17,* December 2004: Vol. 306. no. 5704, p. 2061. Copyright © 2004, AAAS. Reprinted with permission.

Experimentation often deconstructs complex phenomena such as facial expression of emotions into discrete components. As you recall from Chapter 2, Paul Ekman's Facial Action Coding System is an especially good example of how seemingly holistic facial displays of specific emotions can be broken down into combinations of facial muscle movements. Likewise, Whalen and colleagues showed how critical basic features like eye whites influence how we perceive facial expressions of emotion. So too with Adams and Kleck (2003), we see how they conceptualized perceptions of facial displays of affect as represented by a dynamic interplay of countenance expression and eye gaze.

Devising Independent Variables

Adams and Kleck (2003) thus investigated two aspects of the face that they thought would be particularly important for emotional expression. These were (a) facial muscle contractions that form different emotional expressions, such as anger or fear, and (b) gaze direction, such as direct or averted eyes. Their challenge was to devise a way to separate gaze direction and facial expression so that the effects of each on perception could be studied. Their literature review indicated that different emotional expressions can be perceived more readily if associated with certain directions of the eyes. They were particularly interested in studies that showed anger expression to be more quickly perceived when accompanied by a direct gaze, in contrast to fear faces being more quickly perceived when coupled with an averted gaze. Based on these studies, Adams and Kleck formulated a two-prong hypothesis: (a) Anger faces with direct gaze would be more readily perceived than anger faces with averted gaze and (b) fear faces with averted gaze would be more readily perceived than fear faces with direct gaze.

To test their hypothesis, the researchers had to first create **experimental stimuli**, that is, to construct facial stimuli that varied in expression and gaze direction. They did so by using Adobe Photoshop to doctor gaze direction of faces of anger and fear, some of which were taken from the Ekman series (see Chapter 2). They created four types of faces: (1) anger with direct gaze, (2) anger with averted gaze, (3) fear with direct gaze, and (4) fear with averted gaze.

Next, the researchers had to organize their four types of faces into an **experimental task** for participants to perform. The experimental task they constructed had participants view one at a time on a computer monitor a face that had an expression of either anger or fear and a gaze direction of either direct or averted. For each face, participants made a speedy judgment as to whether the face displayed anger or fear by responding via a right or left mouse click. The participants were instructed to label each face (fear/anger) as quickly and accurately as possible.

The final step centered on whether to use a within-subjects or a between-subjects manipulation. They opted for a within-subjects design. What this meant is that all participants received all four types of faces. This allowed for the comparison of participants' response times in emotional judgment for the four different kinds of faces—those with anger and direct gaze, those with anger and averted gaze, those with fear and direct gaze, and those with fear and averted gaze. In so doing, with a within-subjects design, individual differences that could figure very prominently in processing emotions are automatically controlled. In other words, people may vary greatly in their responses to emotional faces. Because in a within-subjects design each participant serves as his or her own control, these individual differences are effectively held constant.

The second advantage is that within-subject designs are more economical than between-subjects designs. That is, fewer participants are needed to perform the experimental task. However, fewer participants require that you collect more observations per participant. Here for point of clarification, let us suppose observations are analogous to items of a test. The reliability of a test can often be increased by simply adding more items. The same principle is good to keep in mind in light of the reduced number of participants that is commonly used in within-subjects designs. For example, Adams and Kleck had a sample size of 32 participants. Yet their experimental task had 240 slides consisting of 60 anger/direct gaze, 60 anger/averted gaze, 60 fear/direct gaze, and 60 fear/averted eye gaze. The 240 slides were presented in a random order. The large number of items or slides of their experimental task provided a sufficient number of observations to reliably measure emotional perception.

The 2 × 2 Design

The experiment manipulated two independent variables: emotional expression and gaze direction. Each independent variable had two levels, with anger or fear faces the two levels of emotional expression, and directed or averted eyes the two levels of gaze direction. In other words, each face varied in expression (anger or fear) and gaze direction (direct or averted). The 2 × 2 factorial design produced four combinations of conditions: anger/direct gaze faces; anger/averted gaze faces; fear/direct gaze faces; and fear/averted gaze faces. The dependent measure was response time in milliseconds for judging faces as expressions of either anger or fear

Now let us diagram the Adams and Kleck (2003) 2 × 2 factorial experiment with their two independent variables, gaze direction with two levels (direct/averted) and facial expression with two levels (anger/fear). Let us call *Direction of Eye Gaze* Factor A and *Type of Emotional Expression* Factor B. **Table 7.1** shows the four combinations: (1) direct gaze/anger (A1B1), (2) averted gaze/anger (A2B1), (3) direct gaze/fear (A1B2), and (4) averted gaze/fear (A2B2). The number presented in the upper left cell of **Table 7.1** is the mean response time to correctly judge faces displaying anger expressions with direct gaze (mean = 862.3) The number presented in the upper right cell of **Table 7.1** is the mean response time to correctly judge faces displaying anger expressions with averted gaze (mean = 914.1). The number presented in the bottom left cell of **Table 7.1** is the mean response time to correctly judge faces displaying fear expressions with direct gaze (mean = 944.5). The number presented in the bottom right cell of **Table 7.1** is the mean response time to correctly judge faces displaying fear expressions with averted gaze (mean = 891.2).

You can see that the numbers in the two left cells are the response times for Condition A1: direct gaze/anger and direct gaze/fear. The numbers in the two right cells are response times for Condition A2: averted gaze/anger and averted gaze/fear. We can average the numbers in the two left cells and find the average response time to faces with direct gaze to be 903.4, as shown in the bottom left column. Likewise, we can average the numbers in the two right cells and find the average response time to faces with averted gaze to be 902.7. These response times to faces with direct gaze (903.4) and averted gazes (902.7) are called the *column means* because they are calculated by averaging the columns of the table. Looking at the column means shows us that faces with direct gaze were responded to as quickly as faces with averted gaze. Less than one millisecond difference between these two conditions tells us that gaze direction by itself had no effect on response times for emotional judgments.

Table 7.1 Mean Response Times in Milliseconds to Correctly Labeled Anger and Fear Expressions, as a Function of Gaze Direction

	Direction of Eye Gaze (A) (Independent variable A)		Row Means (Main Effect of Emotional Expression)
Type of Emotional Expression (B) (Independent variable B)	Direct (A1)	Averted (A2)	
Anger (B1)	862.3 *A1B1*	914.1 *A2B1*	888.2
Fear (B2)	944.5 *A1B2*	891.2 *A2B2*	917.9
Column Means (Main Effect of Gaze Direction)	903.4	902.7	

Source: Adapted from Adams & Kleck, 2003.

The effect of type of facial expression on response time can be examined by looking at the rows of **Table 7.1**. The numbers in the two upper cells are the response times for Condition B1: anger/direct gaze and anger/averted gaze. The numbers in the two lower cells are the response times for Condition B2: fear/direct gaze and fear/averted gaze. We can average the numbers in the two upper cells and find the average response time to facial expressions of anger to be 888.2 as shown in the end of the upper right row. Likewise, we can average the numbers in the bottom right row and find the average response times to facial expressions of fear to be 917.9 as shown in the end of the bottom right row. These response times to anger expression (888.2) and fear expression (917.9) are called *row means* because they are calculated by averaging the rows of the table. Looking at the row means shows us that anger faces were responded to more quickly than were fear faces.

Main Effects

There are two factors or independent variables presented in **Table 7.1**. We are interested in the effects of each of these factors on the dependent variable. What effect does gaze direction have on mean responses times? What effect does the type of emotional expression of the face have on mean response times? In a factorial experiment, the effects of each independent variable on a dependent variable are referred to as the **main effect** of that independent variable. A main effect can be calculated for each independent variable. In the Adams and Kleck study, because there are two independent variables, two main effects can be calculated. We have already done so in **Table 7.1** when we calculated column means and row means. The column means tell us the main effect of gaze direction. These values were 903.4 for faces with direct gaze and 902.7 for faces with averted gaze (averaging over whether the faces displayed either anger or fear expressions). For the main effect of gaze direction, we compared average response times for faces with direct gaze with those with averted gaze. We can see that the column means are nearly identical—there's less than 1 millisecond difference. We therefore conclude that that the main effect of gaze direction of the faces did not significantly influence the dependent variable of response time.

For the main effect of type of facial emotional expression, we look at the row means in **Table 7.1**. These values are 888.2 milliseconds for angry faces versus 917.9 milliseconds for fearful faces. We can see that participants responded faster to angry faces than to fearful faces, regardless of whether these emotional expressions were displayed in conjunction with either direct or averted eye gaze. The difference of 29.7 milliseconds in response time between facial expressions of anger versus facial expressions of fear was statistically significant, meaning that it was unlikely due to chance. We can therefore conclude the main effect of type of facial expression of emotion did influence the dependent variable of response time. In the Adams and Kleck study, participants made faster judgments in correctly labeling angry facial expressions than fearful facial expressions.

Interactions

So far we have based our conclusion on the main effects of the two independent variables: gaze direction and emotional expression. We concluded the main effect of gaze direction did not influence response rates to the facial expressions: Regardless of their emotional expression, faces with direct gaze were labeled as quickly as faces with averted gaze. In contrast, the main effect of emotional expression did influence response rates: Regardless of their gaze direction, anger faces were correctly labeled more quickly than were fear faces. However, before interpreting the main effect of emotional expression, we must first look to see if there is a statistical **interaction** between the two independent variables. A statistical interaction occurs when the effects of one level of the independent variable depend on the particular level of the other independent variable.

In the Adams and Kleck study, we see in **Table 7.1** that direct gaze decreased response time in judging anger faces (from 914.1 milliseconds to 862.3 milliseconds) but increased response time in judging fear faces (from 891.2 milliseconds to 944.5 milliseconds). **Table 7.1** also shows that averted gaze reduced response time in judging fear faces (from 944.5 milliseconds to 891.2 milliseconds) but increased response time in judging anger faces (from 862.3 milliseconds to 914.1 milliseconds). This pattern reflects an interaction between type of emotional expression and gaze direction. The interaction means that the effect of emotional expression depended on gaze direction of the face. In simple words, we can describe the interaction as: On one hand, direct gaze led to faster judgment of anger faces but slower judgment of fear faces. On the other hand, averted gaze led to faster judgment of fear faces but slower judgment of anger faces.

Interpreting Results of Multifactorial Designs

Thus factorial designs provide two distinct sources of information: (1) main effect of each independent variable by itself and (2) any interaction effect of the independent variables. Keep in mind that main effects are statistically independent of interaction effects. That is, you can have no significant main effects but still have significant interaction effects or vice versa.

How then do we interpret results generated from a multifactorial 2 × 2 experiment that produces significant main and interaction effects? We always begin by looking to see if there is an interaction between the independent variables, and if so, we interpret the interaction first, before the main effects.

An interaction indicates that any interpretation of a main effect of an independent variable by itself will be misleading. This is because the interaction tells us that the effects of the independent variable depend upon the particular level of the other independent variable. We therefore cannot interpret a main effect of an independent variable without first taking into consideration whether that effect interacts with another independent variable.

In the Adams and Kleck study, for example, we would be wrong to conclude on the basis of the main effect of emotional type that responses times are faster for anger faces than fear faces. Why? Because the data showed that this main effect is qualified by the significant interaction of emotion type and gaze direction. The main effect of emotion type depended on gaze direction of the faces—direct gaze, faster response to anger faces; averted gaze, faster response times to fear faces.

We often graph main effects and interactions as a way to help us to understand and interpret our data. **Exhibit 7.3** depicts the absence of the main effect for the independent variable of gaze direction on the dependent variable of response time. The values plotted in this figure are the column means from **Table 7.1**. Similarly, **Exhibit 7.4** plots the row means from **Table 7.1** and shows the main effect for the other independent variable of emotional expression. **Exhibit 7.4** shows graphically what we have already noted about the effect of faster response times for anger faces than fear faces.

Exhibit 7.3   Absence of the Main Effect of the Independent Variable of Gaze Direction on the Dependent Variable of Response Time of Emotion Judgment

Exhibit 7.4   Main Effect of Faster Response Times in Emotional Judgment for Anger Faces Than Fear Faces

Exhibit 7.5   Statistical Interaction of Emotional Expression and Gaze Direction

However, in **Exhibit 7.5**, we plot the interaction of emotion type and gaze direction. To do this, we plot the values in each of the four cells of **Table 7.1**. Each cell value reflects what is referred to as a **simple main effect**. A simple main effect compares the influence of one level of an independent variable at a given level of another independent variable.

To interpret an interaction, we need to look at simple main effects. The simple effects in **Table 7.1** reveal a pattern of a classic **cross-over interaction**. In **Exhibit 7.5**, the two lines cross over, depicting the interaction of emotional expression and gaze direction. That is, **Exhibit 7.5** shows the interaction, characterized on one line by faster response times for anger faces with direct gaze than for anger faces with averted gaze and on the other line by faster response times for fear faces with averted gaze than for fear faces with direct gaze.

Finally, if, on the other hand, the lines in **Exhibit 7.5** did not cross over and in fact were parallel to each other, we would conclude that no interaction occurred between the independent variables. For example, if there were no interaction between the independent variables, the horizontal lines in **Exhibit 7.5** would appear on visual inspection to be parallel.

The 2 × 2 Logic

We now have learned that the simplest of the complex designs, the 2 × 2 design is far from simple! The logic behind the 2 × 2 is at once compelling and elusive. It is compelling because it provides a direct test of the main effect of each of the two independent variables as well a direct test of the interaction effect between them. These effects are independent of each other. That is, either of the two independent variables may or may not affect the dependent variable, and an interaction between the two independent variables may or may not be present. For example, the 2 × 2 factorial design used by Adams and Kleck revealed two important findings: a significant effect for facial expression and a significant effect for the interaction of facial interaction and gaze direction. By contrast, the independent variable of gaze direction of faces did not influence response times.

Exhibit 7.6   Artificial data illustrating no effect of Eye Gaze or Emotional Expression and no interaction of the two.

Means	Direction of Eye Gaze (A) (Independent variable A)		Row (Main Effect of Emotional Expression)
Type of Emotional Expression (B) **(Independent variable B)**	Direct (A1)	Averted (A2)	
Anger (B1)	800 A1B1	800 A2B1	**800**
Fear (B2)	800 A1B2	800 A2B2	**800**
Column Means (Main Effect of Eye Gaze)	**800**	**800**	

Let us deconstruct the logic behind the 2 x 2 design used by Adams and Kleck. In a 2 x 2 design, there are eight possible patterns of results. These eight patterns are: 1) no effect of Eye Gaze or Emotional Expression and no interaction of the two; 2) main effect only of Eye Gaze; 3) main effect only of Emotional Expression; 4) main effects of Eye Gaze and Emotional Expression, but no interaction of the two; 5) interaction effect only of Eye Gaze and Emotional Expression; 6) main effect of Eye Gaze and interaction of Eye Gaze and Emotional Expression; 7) main effect of Emotional Expression and interaction of Eye Gaze and Emotional Expression; and 8) main effects of Eye Gaze and Emotional Expression, plus interaction effect.

Exhibit 7.6 presents artificial data of the most disappointing pattern of findings of no effect for the independent variable of Eye Gaze or the independent variable of Emotion Expression, as well no effect of the interaction of the two. We set the simple main effects to a value of 800, in order to demonstrate a pattern of results of no main effects or interaction effect. This null effect is depicted in Exhibit 7.7 by the two horizontal lines that overlap each other. By contrast, Exhibit 7.8 depicts a main effect for independent variable of Emotional Expression but no effect of Eye Gaze or for the interaction. Here you see that the two lines now diverge.

Exhibit 7.7 plots artificial data from Exhibit 7.6 illustrating a 2 x 2 design that yields no effect of Eye Gaze or Emotional Expression and no interaction of the two.

Exhibit 7.8 illustrates a 2 x 2 design that yields main effect of Emotion Expression, but no effect of Eye Gaze or the interaction of the two.

Now let us consider a pattern of results from our 2 x 2 design that yields main effects of Eye Gaze and Emotional Expression, but no interaction of the two. These

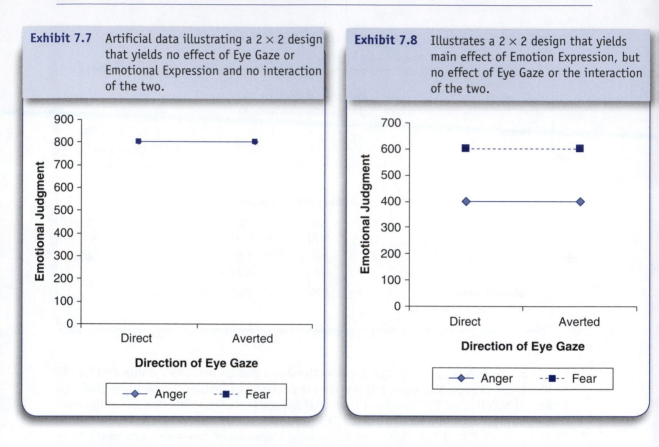

Exhibit 7.7   Artificial data illustrating a 2 × 2 design that yields no effect of Eye Gaze or Emotional Expression and no interaction of the two.

Exhibit 7.8   Illustrates a 2 × 2 design that yields main effect of Emotion Expression, but no effect of Eye Gaze or the interaction of the two.

artificial data are presented in **Exhibit 7.9**. As you can see in the row and cell means there is a main effect for Eye Gaze and for Emotional Expression, but these variables do not interact. Experimentalists often use the term additivity to indicate the absence of interaction between independent variables. In fact, we can think of *additivity* and *no interaction* as synonymous. For example, if you have two main effects but no interaction, we can say the values of one independent variable exert a similar, *additive* effect on the values of the other independent variable. This is can be seen in **Exhibit 7.10**.

Exhibit 7.10 plots artificial data from **Exhibit 7.9** illustrating a 2 × 2 design that yields main effects of Eye Gaze and Emotional Expression but no interaction of the two.

Our final pattern to illustrate is one in which there is an interaction effect between Eye Gaze and Emotional Expression, but no main effect for either of these variables. These artificial data are presented in **Exhibit 7.11**. When we plot this interaction in **Exhibit 7.12**, the lines do not look parallel. In fact, compare **Exhibit 7.9** and **Exhibit 7.11**. As you can see, when the values in **Exhibit 7.11** are graphed in **Exhibit 7.12** the lines actually cross over one another, giving credence to its name, crossover interaction. We have seen also a crossover interaction in the actual Adams and Kleck study (see **Exhibit 7.5**) as well as an effect of Emotional Expression

Exhibit 7.9 Artificial data illustrating main effects of Eye Gaze and Emotional Expression but no interaction of the two.

Direction of Eye Gaze (A)
(Independent variable A)

Means

Row
(Main Effect of
Emotional Expression)

Type of Emotional Expression (B) (Independent variable B)	Direct (A1)	Averted (A2)	
Anger (B1)	500 A1B1	530 A2B1	515
Fear (B2)	600 A1B1	630 A2B2	615
Column Means (Main Effect of Eye Gaze)	**650**	**580**	

(see **Exhibit 7.4**). **Exhibit 7.12** provides a clear depiction of how the crossover interaction can also be referred to as an antagonistic interaction. This is because as you can see in the values presented in **Exhibit 7.11**, the two independent variables of Eye Gaze and Emotional Expression show opposite effects on the dependent variable of response time. To wit, direct eye gaze led to faster responses to anger faces but slower responses to fear faces, whereas averted gaze led to faster responses to fear faces, but slower responses to angry faces.

Exhibit 7.12 plots artificial data from **Exhibit 7.11** illustrating a 2×2 design that yields interaction effect of Eye Gaze and Emotional Expression but no main effects.

Exhibit 7.10 Artificial data illustrating a 2×2 design that yields main effects of Eye Gaze and Emotional Expression, but no interaction of the two.

Exhibit 7.11   Artificial data illustrating interaction of Eye Gaze and Emotional Expression but no main effect of Eye Gaze or Emotional Expression.

	Direction of Eye Gaze (A) (Independent variable A)		Row
Means			(Main Effect of Emotional Expression)
Type of Emotional Expression (B) (Independent variable B)	Direct (A1)	Averted (A2)	
Anger (B1)	500 *A1B1*	600 *A2B1*	**650**
Fear (B2)	600 *A1B1*	500 *A2B2*	**650**
Column Means (Main Effect of Eye Gaze)	**650**	650	

Exhibit 7.12   Artificial data illustrating a 2 × 2 design that yields interaction effect of Eye Gaze and Emotional Expression, but no main effects.

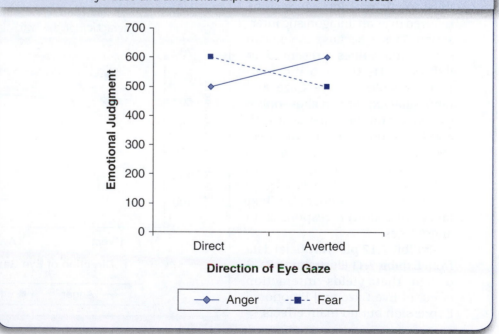

A COMPLEX BETWEEN-SUBJECTS EXPERIMENT

We know that true experiments, whether single or multifactorial, require independent variables that we can directly manipulate. Many variables of interest to psychologists, however, are not easy to manipulate. Consider for example the idea taken from evolutionary psychology of the **social brain hypothesis**. According to this theoretical perspective, intelligent thought is shaped by our "social connectivity"—the degree to which we enjoy friendships, love, companionship, and intimacy. You might think what an interesting idea it is that our advanced intellectual capacities evolved to solve social problems related to forming friendships, bonds, and alliances, to identifying foes and cheaters, and to building trust, reciprocity, and fairness. But how could you test it experimentally?

Staged Event Manipulations

Recall that in Chapter 6 we saw that an experimenter can create independent variables by staging or manipulating an event. We called this a *staged* or *event manipulation* that can be employed when the primary goal is to induce a particular psychological state in research participants. For example, the famous Milgram study used a staged event to create obedience in the research participants.

Baumeister and colleagues (Baumeister, Twenge, & Nuss, 2002) sought to induce a specific psychological state that they described as **social exclusion**, defined simply as a belief of ending up alone in life without loved ones, friends, and acquaintances. Their research challenge was to simulate a situation within their experiment so that participants would come to believe in a future foreshadowed by a solitary, isolative, and lonely life. In other words, Baumeister and colleagues needed to figure out how to implant, so to speak, in their research participants a belief of a future of social isolation. If successful in the event manipulation, social exclusion could then be directly manipulated as an independent variable that could be randomly assigned.

As part of their staged event, Baumeister and colleagues also wanted to manipulate a second independent variable, intellectual thought. In so doing so, they could examine which aspects of intellectual thought might be affected by social exclusion. Manipulating intellectual thought proved, however, to be easier, both experimentally and ethically, than inducing social exclusion.

Here the researchers took passages and test items from the reading comprehension section of the familiar Graduate Record Exam (GRE). From the GRE, they identified two aspects of intellectual thought and directly manipulated each across participants. One aspect entailed reading GRE passages, referred to as the **encoding** condition of new information. The other aspect entailed answering questions about the read passages, referred to as the **recall** condition of passages.

2 × 3 Design

The staged manipulations thus produced two independent variables. One independent variable, labeled *intellectual thought*, had two conditions: encoding and recall. The other independent variable, labeled *social connectivity*, had three conditions. In the condition labeled *future alone,* participants were told that they would end up alone in later life. In the condition labeled *future belonging,* participants were told they would have a life full of rewarding relationships. In the condition labeled *misfortune control condition,* they were told they that later in their lives, they would become increasingly accident prone.

The 2 × 3 factorial design produced six combinations of conditions. These were (1) encoding/future alone, (2) encoding/future belonging, (3) encoding/future misfortune, (4) recall/future alone, (5) recall/future belonging, and (6) recall/future misfortune. The researchers randomly assigned participants to one of these six experimental conditions. They made the obvious choice of a between-subjects design. A within-subjects design would definitely not work for this study: You can't tell the same people in one condition that their futures will be lonely and bereft of social contact and then in another condition tell them that they will have lives full of rich social relationships! Baumeister thus used a between-subjects design controlling for individual differences in GRE performance by randomly assigning participants to one of the six experimental conditions. As we know, a between-subjects design requires more participants than a within-subjects design. Baumeister had a sample size of 65 undergraduates. Compare that to the sample of 32 undergraduates used in the within-subjects experiment of Adams and Kleck discussed previously.

For the experimental task, as already described, participants read passages from the GRE verbal section. Then, following a specified time delay, they answered questions about these passages. Baumeister and colleagues considered the comparison of test scores for encoding/future alone vs. recall/future alone conditions to be a crucial comparison. They hypothesized that social exclusion would lower scores for only those participants in the recall/future alone condition but not for participants assigned to either the encoding/future alone or any of the other conditions. In other words, test scores would not be reduced even for participants in the encoding/future alone condition. These persons read the GRE passages after being told that they would end up alone later in life, but *before* answering the multiple-choice questions, they had learned from the experimenter the forecast of their lonely demise was bogus. By contrast, in the recall/future alone condition, participants read or encoded the GRE passages under normal conditions, but they were tested on recall of the passage information under the influence of the personality feedback that described their futures as those of aloneness.

Exhibit 7.13 provides a schematic outline of the experiment. Research participants could be randomly assigned to either the encoding or the recall condition. In the *encoding affected condition,* participants received the feedback about their futures first, read the GRE passages, and were then told the feedback was not true, followed by answering recall questions about the GRE passages. Thus in the encoding condition, participants read or encoded the passages after receiving "news" that that they would either end up alone in later life (future alone), become increasingly accident prone in later life (future misfortune), or would have a life full of rewarding relationships (future belonging). However, they were then told that their future horoscopes were wrong before they completed the recall test of the passages. For the *recall affected condition,* participants received the same experimental events as the

Exhibit 7.13 Schematic Outline of Sequence of Experimental Events for Baumeister et al. (2002)

Sequence of Experimental Events

Group

Recall   Read GRE Passages → Future Forecast either:

1. Future Misfortune →
2. Future Alone →   Complete GRE Passage Questions → Told forecast was bogus
3. Future Belonging →

Encoding   Future forecast either:

1. Future Misfortune →
2. Future Alone →   Read GRE Passages →Told forecast was bogus →   Complete GRE Passage Questions
3. Future Belonging →

encoding affected condition but in a different sequence. That is, participants read the GRE passages, received one of the three kinds of feedback information about their futures, and then after completing the recall questions for the GRE passages were told that the forecasts about their futures were wrong.

Manipulation Check

Baumeister and colleagues took several steps to increase the believability of the bogus feedback in forecasting a future alone life. As they wrote:

> Because this feedback was randomly assigned and would therefore be given to at least some people who presumably have rich networks of friends, several steps were taken to enhance credibility. First, each participant was given accurate feedback about his or her level of extraversion, on the basis of an accurate scoring of the trait scale. Second, the experimenter added that the participant may well have many friends and acquaintances at present, which is common in young people in university settings. The experimenter went on to say, however, that once the person is past the age at which people are constantly forming new friendships, the current friends will tend to drift apart and not be replaced, so that the individual will spend more and more time alone. (p. 819)

At this point, you might still be a bit skeptical about the staged manipulation of the Baumeister et al. study. Did it effectively create the psychological state of future loneliness, future belonging, or future misfortune in the participants randomly assigned to any one of these feedback conditions? Perhaps reading exactly what these descriptions entailed might be helpful. Participants randomly assigned to the crucial "future alone" condition heard the following personality description:

> You're the type who will end up alone later in life. You may have friends and relationships now, but by your mid-20s most of these will have drifted away. You may even marry or have several marriages, but these are likely to be short-lived and not continue into your 30s. Relationships don't last, and when you're past the age where people are constantly forming new relationships, the odds are you'll end up being alone more and more. (p. 819)

Participants randomly assigned to the "future belonging" condition heard the following personality description:

> You're the type who has rewarding relationships throughout life. You're likely to have a long and stable marriage and have friendships that will last into your later years. The odds are that you'll always have friends and people who care about you. (p. 819)

Participants randomly assigned to the "nonsocial future misfortune" condition heard the following personality description:

> You're likely to be accident prone later in life—you might break an arm or a leg a few times, or maybe be injured in car accidents. Even if you haven't been accident

prone before, these things will show up later in life and the odds are you will have a lot of accidents. (p. 819)

As a research participant, would you be convinced? Or would you dismiss them as meaning nothing more or less than you would a horoscope from a fortune teller? Fortunately, as researchers we don't need to assume the role of a movie critic in assessing the extent to which the staged manipulations actually worked. As we learned in Chapter 6, sound experimental design often includes a manipulation check. In the Baumeister et al. study, a simple questionnaire provided at the end of the study as part of the debriefing would have helped to determine the degree to which the participants actually bought the bogus feedback. Unfortunately, the study did not include any manipulation check that might have helped to determine objectively that the participants believed the fake feedback.

Main Effects and Interactions

Exhibit 7.14 presents the results for the Baumeister experiment. The 2 × 3 multifactorial design provides a test for the main and interaction effects of social connectivity. Let us begin as we always should by first examining for a statistical interaction for the independent variables of social connectivity and intelligent thought. We do so by looking at each of the six simple main effects presented in each of the six cells in **Exhibit 7.14**. What value stands out? As shown **Exhibit 7.14**, the readings scores are markedly lower for the recall/future alone condition. Otherwise, the scores are essentially the same across the other five conditions.

Exhibit 7.14 Scores for Graduate Record Examination Reading Passages Comprehension

	Intelligent Thought (Independent variable A)		**Row Means (Main Effect of B)**
	Encoding	Recall	
Social Feedback (Independent Variable B)			
Future Alone	4.78	2.75	**3.76**
Future Misfortune	4.60	4.58	**4.59**
Future Belonging	4.40	4.75	**4.57**
Column Means (Main Effect of A)	**4.59**	**3.02**	

Note: Higher scores indicate better performance; adapted from Baumeister, Twenge, & Nuss, 2002.

The researchers specifically predicted that reading scores would be significantly reduced for this condition only. In other words, they predicted a statistical interaction in which the effects of social exclusion would affect only those participants who took the reading test believing that that they would end up alone in life. The effect depended exclusively on the interaction of aloneness and having to recall information to answer questions. The effect did not occur for participants who read the passages believing that they would end up alone in life, but later took the recall testing knowing, if not relieved, that they were not doomed to a life of aloneness. By ostensibly removing the social aloneness effect, the experimenters showed that reading scores recovered to levels seen in the future belonging and future misfortune conditions.

Exhibit 7.15 depicts the interaction of social connectivity and intelligent thought. To do so, we graph the simple main effects for each of the six conditions. For ease of illustration, we use a line graph that is commonly used to depict statistical interaction. As Exhibit 7.15 shows, all but the recall/future alone condition have similar reading scores.

We run into the same pattern of findings in the Baumeister study as we did in the Adams and Kleck study. That is, in both studies, had we only looked at the main effects, we would have made erroneous interpretations and drawn false

Exhibit 7.15 The Interaction of Social Connectivity and Intelligent Thought

Source: Adapted from Baumeister, Twenge, & Nuss, 2002.

conclusions from the results. Keep in mind that multifactorial experiments provide a powerful research design to investigate interactions. Arguably, the ability to test interactions is the primary reason we pursue such a complex research design. The lesson is by now familiar: Statistical interactions should be examined by graphing simple main effects; consider any main effect in a multifactorial experiment of two or more independent variables only after examining for interactions.

Interpreting Results

The results of the Baumeister study revealed a statistical interaction between social connectivity and intellectual thought. As these researchers hypothesized, intellectual processes related to the recall but not to the encoding of passages declined in participants who were told that they would end up alone in life.

The findings pointed to a specific effect that could not be attributable to the general effects of hearing bad news. If the later were the case, we would have expected the future misfortune condition to also show reductions in intellectual thought. This of course did not materialize, as only the recall/future alone condition showed reduced scores.

As you can see, the Baumeister study was well designed, incorporating a misfortune future condition that effectively served to rule out a general effect of receiving bad news for their findings. However, as with all studies, there were limitations. As we discussed earlier, the researchers failed to include a manipulation check for their rather elaborate staged event.

Also, as we have learned, between-subjects designs are at the mercy of random assignment to control for or neutralize individual differences. The dependent measure used here, the GRE, is designed to capture individual differences in intellectual aptitude. A pretest measure (see Chapter 6) would have provided additional control for any individual differences that might have occurred by chance but still could have influenced the findings. Finally, a sample of college students is of limited generalizability.

Statistical Analysis of Complex Designs

An important inferential statistic is the **analysis of variance** (abbreviated ANOVA), which is also known as the *F*-test. The analysis of variance is a general statistical procedure that is used to evaluate the likelihood that results obtained in a study are due to chance. It is used when there are more than two levels of an independent variable, such as the Merzenich study in Chapter 6, which compared a group of research participants who received brain plasticity training with a comparison group who received an educational DVD as well as a control group who received no treatment. In studies such as the Merzenich investigation in which only one factor or independent variable is varied systematically, a researcher employs what is referred to as a *simple analysis of variance* to evaluate whether the obtained results of the study are statistically significant, meaning that they are unlikely due to chance. This simple analysis of variance is also called a *one-factor analysis of variance* or a simple ANOVA. We will learn more about simple ANOVA in Chapter 10.

Now, as we have learned in this chapter, researchers are often interested in varying or manipulating two or more independent variables. Examples of these complex experiments with two or more factors or independent variables are the Adams and Kleck as well as the Baumeister and colleagues studies covered in this chapter. Such complex or multifactor experimental designs also require results to be evaluated by a multifactorial ANOVA. In comparison to a simple ANOVA, a multifactorial ANOVA is much more computationally complex given that there are both main and interaction effects that need to be tested. We will learn more about multifactorial ANOVA in Chapter 10. For now, in this section, we would like to introduce you to the elementary logic and a basic conceptual understanding of ANOVA as a general inferential statistical procedure in evaluating the probability that the results of a study are due to chance.

The advantage of ANOVA procedures is that the effects of all independent variables can be tested simultaneously. So instead of statically comparing pairs of conditions, levels or groups, ANOVA tests all of the effects simultaneously, thereby reducing the likelihood of chance findings. By the same token, ANOVA provides a statistical significance test (*F*-test) for each of the main effects of an experiment as well as their interactions for studies with two or more independent variables. Thus, as with other statistical tests, an ANOVA/*F*-test allows us to determine whether each of these effects—main effects and interactions—are due to chance.

In nearly all sets of data, there will be variability, which is referred to statistically as variance. ANOVA (hence the name *analysis of variance*) provides statistical procedures for identifying the sources of this variability. In fact, for each main effect and interaction effect, ANOVA computes an *F* statistic, which is a ratio of two types of variance: systematic and error variance. For the simple ANOVA, **systematic variance** is computed by summing the deviation of the means for each experimental condition from the grand mean (the mean of the means of all conditions of an experiment). Ideally, a researcher hopes to design experiments that will maximize systematic variance, as the sources of systematic variation are the main effects for each independent variable and the interactions between the independent variables. A researcher also hopes to design experiments that will minimize **error variance**, which in simple ANOVA is defined as the deviation of individual scores in each group or condition from its respective mean. Systematic variance is also referred to as *between-groups variance* and error variance as *within-group variance*. The *F* statistic can then be stated as the ratio of between-group variance to within-group variance.

> *F* ratio = between-group variance/within-group variance

Recall that statistics provide a direct test of the null hypothesis. Under the null hypothesis, the *F* ratio should be 1, meaning that the between-group variance should be the same as the within-group variance. The greater the ratio of between-group variance is to the within-group variance, the more likely it is that the null hypothesis is false and therefore should be rejected. Thus, the larger the *F* ratio, the more likely it is the results of the experiment are statistically significant and not due to chance (see Chapter 10).

In summary, in this section, we wanted to present the basic logic underlying ANOVA as a general procedure used for inferential statistics. Keep in mind, however, that the computational details of ANOVA differ depending on the experimental design. This holds for the simple ANOVA used for a single-factor experiment versus the multifactorial ANOVA used for a complex experiment. But the formula for the ANOVA procedures also takes into account whether a researcher varies the independent variables between subjects or within subjects.

CONCLUSIONS

We examined in depth two examples of multifactorial experiments. We learned that the Adams and Kleck study employed a within-subjects manipulation of two independent variables, each with two levels: facial expression and gaze direction. This 2×2 factorial design tested main effects for facial expression and gaze direction as well as the interaction of these two independent variables. The results showed a very interesting interaction of facial expression and gaze direction: anger faces were more readily recognized when coupled with direct gaze, whereas fear faces were more readily recognized when coupled with averted gaze. The Baumeister study illustrated a 2×3 factorial design with between-subjects manipulations of two independent variables: intelligent thought with two levels, encoding or recall, and social connectivity with three levels: future alone, future belonging, or future misfortune. Here too, the results showed a very interesting interaction of intelligent thought and social connectivity: Passage recall but not passage encoding was negatively affected by thoughts of a future alone. Both studies reveal that multifactorial designs allow us to test both main and interaction effects, and we learned that interaction effects always take precedence over main effects. In other words, we always consider interaction effects before looking at main effects. We also learned that within-subjects designs can be limited by small sample size, but this problem can be addressed by making sure to use a sufficient number of observations per participants. For between-subjects designs, our concerns center on the degree to which random assignment can control or neutralize individual differences. Overall, multifactorial experiments provide a powerful research design to help us understand the rich and complex influences that shape psychology.

END OF CHAPTER

Chapter Highlights

- Multifactorial experiments have two or more independent variables, and these variables may have two or more levels.

- Multifactorial experiments can vary the independent variables between subjects, others can vary them within subjects, and still others can combine between-subjects and within-subjects manipulation of the independent variables.

- Fewer participants are required for a within-subjects design, but more observations are needed per participant in order to ensure reliable data measures.

- A 2 × 2 factorial design has two independent variables with two levels or values. In this notation, the *number of numbers* tells how many factors or independent variables there are, and the *number* values tells how many levels of the independent variables.

- A 3 × 4 (spoken as "three-by-four") factorial design indicates two independent variables, one with three levels and the other with four levels. The order of the numbers makes no difference, so a 3 × 4 factorial design could be just as easily identified as a 4 × 3.

- A multifactorial design allows for the testing of effects of all possible combinations of the levels of the independent variables on the dependent variable. It provides information as to the main effect of each independent variable as well as any interactions between and among independent variables.

- A statistical interaction occurs when the effects of one level of the independent variable depend on the particular level of the other independent variable.

- Statistical interactions should be examined by graphing simple main effects before considering any main effects of independent variables.

- A graph of two variables that interact will show nonparallel lines. These nonparallel lines cross over each other when a classic type of interaction, known as the crossover interaction, is present.

- A graph of two parallel lines is a clear visual indication of additivity, that is, there is no interaction between independent variables.

- In a complex design with two independent variables, the sources of systematic variation are the main effects for each of the independent variables and the interaction between the independent variables.

- The analysis of variance (abbreviated as ANOVA), also known as the *F*-test, is a general statistical procedure used when there are more than two levels of an independent variable or for complex experimental designs with two or more independent variables.

- The larger the *F* ratio, the more likely it is the results of the experiment are statistically significant and not due to chance.

Key Terms

Research in the News

The December 26, 2006, *New York Times* editorial, "Exercise for Your Aging Brain" reports on a study published in the *Journal of American Medical Association* (*JAMA*) on cognitive training in the elderly. The editorial reads in part,

> When tested five years later, these participants has less of a decline in the skill they were trained in than did a control group that received no cognitive training. The payoff from mental exercises seemed far greater than we are accustomed to getting for physical exercise—as if 10 workouts at the gym were enough to keep you fit five years later.

The *JAMA* study is titled "Long-term Effects of Cognitive Training on Everyday Functional Outcomes in Older Adults" by Willis and colleagues (2006). Imagine that you been asked to design a multifactorial experiment to compare effects of physical exercise and cognitive exercise on everyday functioning for older adults. Your two independent variables are physical exercise and cognitive exercise, and each will have two levels, high intensity and low intensity. High-intensity physical exercise involves increasingly demanding aerobics and high-intensity cognitive exercise involves increasingly demanding problem-solving tasks. Low-intensity physical exercise involves breathing exercises and low-intensity cognitive exercise involves simple puzzles. For your dependent variable, you will use the measure of functional everyday outcomes borrowed from Willis and colleagues. In developing your experiment, choose between a complex within-subject designs and a complex between-subjects design. Explain your choice. What is your research hypothesis? Present artificial data in a 2 × 2 table that you think might be consistent with your hypothesis.

Activity Questions

1. As a researcher, you are interested in pursuing the Rowe et al. (2007) study described earlier in the chapter. As you recall, the Rowe et al. study demonstrated an interaction

between mood and cognition. Based on this finding, you also hypothesize an interaction between mood and cognition. State precisely the hypothesis, that is, the specific nature of the interaction. In **Exhibit 7.16** are the mean scores (range from 0–100; higher score, better performance) for the artificial data. Do these results suggest an interaction between mood and cognition? If so, describe the nature of the interaction. Draw a figure showing these results.

2. Cognitive psychologists often theorized about a mental dictionary in which words are organized in networks of associates of varying degrees of "connectivity" (Carmazza, 1996; Nelson, Schrieber, & McEvoy, 1992; Nestor et al., 1998). **Exhibit 7.17** illustrates this model of network connectivity. As you can see in **Exhibit 7.17**, DINNER and DOG each belong to high- and low-connected networks of associates, respectively. Notice also in **Exhibit 7.17** the size of the two networks (number of associates). Nelson and colleagues (1992) have shown that pairs of words belonging to high-connected yet small-in-size networks are easiest to remember. They have developed a large normative data base consisting of four distinct types of words: (1) high connectivity-small network size (e.g., MONKEY-ZOO); (2) low connectivity-small network size (e.g., BEE-HIVE); (3) high connectivity-large network size (e.g., WHISKEY-DRUNK); and (4) low connectivity-large network size (e.g., BIRTHDAY-PARTY). In support of the Nelson et al. model, we (Nestor et al., 1998) have reported highest rates of recall for words of high connectivity-small network size, followed by words of low connectivity-small network size, then by words of high connectivity-large network size, and finally by words of low connectivity-large network size. Identify the independent variables and their levels that are used to test the network model of memory. Present, in a 2 × 2 table, artificial data that would be consistent with the pattern of recall demonstrated by Nestor et al. (1998). Describe what you would expect analysis of these artificial data to yield in terms of main effects and interaction. Draw a figure showing these results.

Review Questions

1. Compare and contrast single-factor experiments with multifactorial experiments. Discuss the implications of adding a new level to an existing and sole independent variable of a single-factor experiment versus devising an altogether new independent variable in a multifactorial experiment.

Exhibit 7.16 Expected Results Based on Rowe et al. (2007)

	Cognitive Exercises (IV)	
Mood Induction *(IV)*	Remote Association Test	Selective Attention Test
Happy *(Level)*	85	60
Sad *(Level)*	67	89

Exhibit 7.17   High Connectivity (Upper Panel) and Low Connectivity (Lower Panel) Among the Associates of Two Different Words

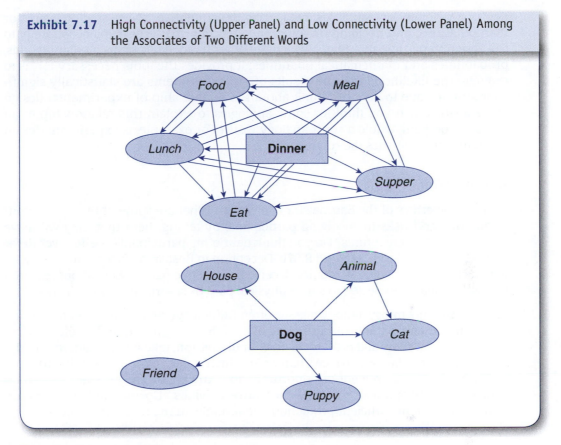

Source: From Nelson et al., 1992.

2. Among the many advantages of multifactorial experiments is testing for interactions between and among independent variables. First, discuss the meaning of interaction and why it is so important in multifactorial experiments. Second, describe the cross-over interaction covered in this chapter. Last, be sure to explain why it is crucial in interpreting results that interactions be examined before looking at any main effects.

3. When there is no interaction between independent variables present, the results are considered to be additive. What are the implications of additivity when interpreting main effects of independent variables?

4. Compare and contrast the advantages of using between-subjects complex (or factorial) designs and within-subjects complex (or factorial) designs. When would you choose one over the other?

5. As you may have surmised from this chapter as well as other chapters, experimental design and statistics are intimately connected. Experimental design deals with

devising independent variables, measuring dependent variables, staging events or manipulations, and deciding on a within-subjects or between-subjects strategy to test research participants. Statistics, on the other hand, deals with calculating odds, probabilities and mathematical quantities: It provides the tools necessary for us to evaluate the likelihood that the results of our experiments are statistically significant and not due to chance. Think about the relationship of experimental design and statistics. Can you think of some analogies to explain this relationship to an educated person? Would a sport analogy work? For example, is experiment design the game, and statistics the referee?

Ethics in Action

1. Critique the ethics of the Baumeister et al. study. What are some of the ethical considerations and risks in deceiving participants by telling them that they will have lonely and unhappy futures? Do you think debriefing participants is effective? Refer to the APA Ethics Code, Standard 8.07b, Deception in Research, covered in Chapter 3, which states, "Psychologists do not deceive prospective participants about research that is reasonably expected to cause physical pain or severe emotional distress."

2. College students in psychology classes often fulfill a course requirement by participating in a research study. Discuss some of the ethical dilemmas and challenges this poses for researchers and professors. In your discussion, take into consideration APA Ethics Code, Standard 8.04b (see Chapter 3), which states, "When research participation is a course requirement or opportunity for extra credit, the prospective participant is given the option of equitable alternative activities." Do you think this standard provides a student sufficient protection and leverage in the research process?

CHAPTER 8

Quasiexperimental and Nonexperimental Designs

We have now learned about true experiments that manipulate either one or more independent variables. We learned that single-factor experiments manipulate one independent variable and multifactorial experiments manipulate two or more independent variables. What allows us to label single and multifactorial experiments as "true"? Randomization, we shout from the highest mountain! For between-subjects design, this means randomly assigning participants to different conditions or levels of the independent variables. For within-subjects designs, this means participants receive all levels or conditions of the independent variables in a randomized or counterbalanced order.

QUASIEXPERIMENTAL DESIGN

In many instances, however, we cannot directly manipulate an independent variable. Gender, race, age, ethnicity, socio-economic status (SES), locale, diagnosis, personality traits, and personal history are just some examples of independent variables that are not possible for an experimenter to directly manipulate . Rather, for these kinds of variables, an experimenter either selects participants who have a particular characteristic or studies participants who have been exposed to specified events, such as war or trauma, or might live in certain settings or situations, such as a neighborhood or a geographic region. When particular individual characteristics are used for the bases of selecting research participants, an experimenter is often interested in studying the effects of these **subject variable**s on a dependent measure. Here a subject variable such as gender is treated as a type of independent variable. Similarly, when exposures to events, situations, or settings that emanate from the "real world" define how participants are selected, we refer to this type of independent variable as a **natural treatment**. In studies of the effects of a natural treatment on a dependent variable, exposure and nonexposure would form two levels of the independent variable.

A reasonable question to ask is, How can these subject variables and natural treatments be considered true independent variables? After all, we have repeatedly learned that independent variables of true experiments are completely controlled and directly manipulated by the experimenter. Then how is it that subject variables and natural treatments are considered independent variables? The answer is that subject variables and natural treatments belong to a distinct class of independent variables that many behavioral researchers term "quasi-independent." A **quasiexperiment** is one that investigates the effects of a quasi-independent variable on a dependent variable. The word *quasi* means "as if" or "to a degree." A quasiexperiment resembles a true experiment except for the degree to which an experimenter can directly control and manipulate one or more of the independent variables. By that, we mean whether the experimenter can randomly assign participants to experimental and control conditions.

The label *quasi* unfortunately often takes on a negative connotation. It often implies, if not telegraphs, a lower status of second-class citizenship for a quasiexperiment in relation to a true experiment. This, however, is not how we want to think about a quasiexperimental research design. Truth be told, if ethical and practical for the research question or problem, a true experiment would be our first option. But for many vital problems in psychology, a pure, true experiment is simply out of the question. A researcher who studies child abuse cannot randomly assign participants to victimized and nonvictimized groups. A researcher who studies gender differences in cognition cannot randomly assign people to male and female groups. A researcher who studies schizophrenia cannot assign persons to mentally ill and healthy groups. The list could go on and on, but the point is simple: Quasiexperiments offer a fertile research design for investigating some of the most important and creative questions in psychology. Thus, as to the often-asked question of which is the best research design, the answer depends solely on the type of question under investigation.

In this chapter, we will learn how natural treatments and subject variables can be arranged in quasiexperimental designs. We will discuss two major types of quasiexperimental designs (other types can be found in Cook & Campbell, 1979; Mohr, 1992):

- *Nonequivalent-control-group designs:* Nonequivalent-control-group designs have experimental and comparison groups that are designated before the treatment occurs and are not created by random assignment.

- *Before-and-after designs:* Before-and-after designs have a pretest and posttest but no comparison group. In other words, the participants exposed to the treatment serve, at an earlier time, as their own controls.

Exhibit 8.1 presents a schematic that provides the general outline of these two quasiexperimental designs using two studies as examples, which we will discuss below. It might be helpful to think of nonequivalent-control designs and before-and-after designs as belonging to a large and extended family of quasiexperimental research approaches. In addition, we will learn about three relatives of the before-and-after-designs: interrupted-time-series design, multiple-group before-and-after design, and repeated-measures-panel design. But before (no pun intended) we delve into these different types of designs, let us first look at how natural treatments and subject characteristics can be identified and studied as quasi-independent variables.

Natural Treatments as Quasi-Independent Variables

Suppose we wanted to study the psychological effects of September 11, 2001 (9/11). We select as our quasi-independent variable 9/11. It is a quasi-independent variable because we cannot directly control or manipulate via random assignment exposure to 9/11. It is considered a natural treatment created by events in the real world over which an experimenter has no control. Some examples of natural treatments are historical events such as war, presidential assassinations, and terrorist attacks; natural disasters such as hurricanes, earthquakes, and tsunamis; and more ordinary, system-level practices and policies such as new educational curricula, school closings, and changes in rules governing drug prescriptions of physicians. We have learned that these natural treatments fall into the class of quasi-independent variables that cannot be directly manipulated; the researcher can provide only an "after-the-fact" or **ex post facto** analysis

Exhibit 8.1   Quasiexperimental Designs

Quasiexperimental Designs

Nonequivalent control group design (Wageman, 2005)

Experimental group:		O_1	X_a	O_2
Comparison group 1:		O_2	X_b	O_2
Comparison group 2:		O_3	X_c	O_2
		Pretest	*Treatment*	*Posttest*
Team interdependence	Group	Team performance	Independent tasks	Team performance
	Hybrid	Team performance	Mixed tasks	Team performance
	Individual	Team performance	Individual tasks	Team performance

Before-and-after design:
Soap-opera suicide and actual suicide (Phillips, 1982)

Experimental group:	O_{11}	X_1	O_{21}
	O_{12}	X_2	O_{22}
	O_{13}	X_3	O_{23}
	O_{14}	X_4	O_{24}
	Pretest	*Treatment*	*Posttest*
	Suicide rate	Soap-opera suicides	Suicide rate

Key: O = Observation (pretest or posttest)
         X = Experimental treatment

Source: Lik, Michael (2008). *Solving the Problems Cell Phones Create for Survey Research. Presentation to the Harvard Program on Survey Research Spring Conference, New Technologies and Survey Research.* Cambridge, MA: Institute if Quantitative Social Science, Harvard University, May 9.

(Latin: that which is done afterward) of its effect on a particular dependent variable such as memory, suicide rates, or grades.

Subject Variables as Quasi-Independent Variables

Suppose again that we wanted to study 9/11, but this time we are interested in gender differences in response to 9/11. Now we have two quasi-independent variables, one we consider as a natural treatment, 9/11, and the other a subject variable, gender. In many instances, however, research designs incorporate both a nonmanipulated—that is, a quasi-independent—variable along with a manipulated independent variable.

For example, we recently compared social attention and nonsocial attention as measured by speeded target detection in persons with schizophrenia and in a control group of healthy volunteers (Nestor et al., 2010). Diagnosis of schizophrenia was the quasi-independent variable: We selected participants on the subject variable of diagnosis and formed our experimental group based on the presence of existing schizophrenia and our control group based on the absence of schizophrenia. We manipulated within subjects two forms of attention, social and nonsocial, and presented these two experimental tasks in a counterbalanced order.

The schizophrenia study is an example of a quasiexperiment that used a **mixed-factorial design**. We described this as mixed-factorial design because, as we know, it combines both between- and within-subjects factors. To wit, the presence or absence of a diagnosis of schizophrenia is the between-subjects factor that is used to form patient and control groups. It is a quasi-independent variable that obviously cannot be manipulated and is not under the complete control of the experimenter. By contrast, type of attention, social or nonsocial, is the within-subjects factor that is manipulated and under the complete control of the experimenter.

A more familiar example of a mixed-factorial design with one nonmanipulated, quasi-independent variable comes from the *Research in the News* section of Chapter 7. Recall the *JAMA* study of healthy 65-and-older participants who received 10 sessions of training to improve either one of three different kinds of mental skill: memory, reasoning, or attention. Following training, the participants were evaluated annually over a 5-year period. Participants were randomly assigned to one of the three cognitive treatments or training. Here in this study, cognitive training is the true independent variable that is manipulated between subjects. Each of the five posttests given annually constitutes the within-subject variable. However, technically this is not manipulated and thus would be considered a quasi-independent variable, as all participants received the same sequence of tests annually over 5 years. But how could we make this example a better illustration of a mixed-factorial design with a nonmanipulated independent variable? We could simply add gender as a quasi-independent variable, and this would allow us to examine whether males and females showed similar or different responses to cognitive training.

Nonequivalent-Control-Group Designs

Recall that in Chapter 6 we learned the importance of using random assignment in creating experimental and control groups. We learned that random assignment provides us with the best chance of ensuring that the groups would be equivalent at the beginning of the experiment before the treatment or the manipulation of the independent variable. The logic, now so familiar to us, can be simply stated: If groups formed by random assignment subsequently differed on the dependent variable, then such difference, in principle, would be attributable to treatment or the independent variable. Now with quasiexperiments, we know that our control and experimental groups are not formed by random assignment. Rather, the groups are selected on the basis of pre-existing, immutable subject characteristics or exposure to some kind of natural treatment.

As a result, the control group can never be considered to be equivalent to the experimental group. Their pre-existing differences cannot be equalized by random assignment as would be the case in a true experiment. This is the most common quasiexperiment, which is referred to as a *nonequivalent-control-group design.* Thus, nonequivalent-control-group designs have experimental and control groups that have been predetermined or predesignated by either an existing subject characteristic or an already-occurred natural treatment and are not created by random assignment.

Consider a study by Ruth Wageman (1995) that used a quasiexperimental design to investigate how the organization of work tasks and rewards affected work team functioning. Her research question was whether it was preferable to organize work and work rewards in a way that stressed either interdependence or individual autonomy. More than 800 Xerox service technicians in 152 teams participated. Wageman allowed district managers to choose which intervention they would implement in their work team. Thus, management of some teams stressed interdependence, others, autonomy, and still others, a hybrid model in which members worked part of the time as an interdependent team and part of the time as autonomous individuals (see **Exhibit 8.1**).

Notice that Wageman did not use random assignment to determine which team received which management style. And while she did compare pretest and posttest team performance, her three groups likely differed considerably regardless of whether their district managers stressed interdependence, individual autonomy, or a combination of the two. Also important to keep in mind is that her research design could not disentangle the effects of the intervention itself from the effects of the district manager, who not only implemented the strategy but also decided which one to use. In this regard, there may be important *interactions* among the characteristics of the managers and the intervention they chose to apply to their work teams. For example, the hybrid model may be effective with a certain management personality, whereas emphasizing work team interdependence might be better suited for managers with a different personality style. And this, as we know from Chapter 7, would constitute an interaction whereby the effect of one variable, in this case management intervention, differs depending on the effect of another variable, in this case, personality style of manager.

These confounds clearly limit the extent to which we can draw internally valid conclusions from this study. Wageman did, however, report a surprising finding: Team performance improved more for the hybrid model of management than with either interdependence or autonomy (see **Exhibit 8.2**). Such a finding would no doubt be of great interest to those who might study management or organizational psychology. Indeed, they may have a more sanguine take on the study as resonating with realism and practicality that would be otherwise lacking in a design with strong experimental controls, such as random assignment. In this regard, then, we can see that quasiexperimental studies with nonequivalent control or comparison groups often receive high marks for their external validity in general, and their *ecological validity* in particular. That is, they are often high in generalizability and high in realism. We now look at some research techniques that can be used in quasiexperiments to try to make the control group as comparable as possible to the experimental group.

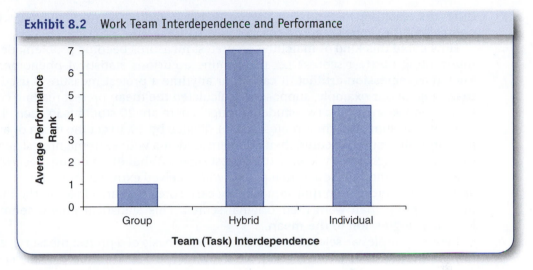

Exhibit 8.2   Work Team Interdependence and Performance

Note: 7 = high rank, 1 = low rank.

Source: Reprinted from "Interdependence and Group Effectiveness," by Ruth Wageman in *Administrative Science Quarterly, 40:* 145–180 by permission of Administrative Science Quarterly. Copyright © 1995.

Matching

Two methods of selection of a control group can be used: individual matching and aggregate matching. In **individual matching**, individual cases in the treatment group are matched with similar individuals in the control group. In some situations, this can create a control group that is very similar to the experimental group, as when Head Start participants were matched with their siblings in order to estimate the effect of participation in Head Start (Currie & Thomas, 1995). However, in many studies, it may not be possible to match on the most important variables.

In most situations when random assignment is not possible, the second method of matching makes more sense: identifying a comparison group that matches the treatment group in the aggregate rather than trying to match individual cases. This is referred to as **aggregate matching**. It means finding a comparison group that has similar distributions on key variables: the same average age, the same percentage female, and so on. For this design to be considered quasiexperimental, however, individuals must not have been able to choose whether to be in the treatment group or the control group.

Matching, however, is not without problems. A researcher matches on a variable that is highly related to the dependent variable. Oftentimes, a researcher can collect pretest measures and then match participants either individually or in the aggregate on pretest scores. For example, suppose you are studying the effects of two different teaching methods on reading comprehension. Because you could not randomly assign students to one of the two different teaching methods, you might decide to administer a pretest measure of reading competence before the study begins. You would then match participants on their pretest reading scores. This would allow you to determine the effects of the two different teaching methods on the posttest of reading comprehension while controlling for pretest reading competence.

How could this kind of matching on pretest measures become problematic for interpreting posttest scores? Let us examine a curious statistical phenomenon known as **regression artifact**. It can occur anytime a pretest measure is used for matching. In our example, suppose we calculated the mean pretest reading comprehension score for the two student groups. There are 20 students in each class, so we would sum all of their pretest scores, divided by 20, to get the mean or average for each group. We could then compare students with extreme pretest scores (that is, very high or very low) with posttest scores. What often occurs, regardless of any kind of intervention, is that people who received extreme scores on a test of ability when retested on that same ability earn sores that are closer to the mean of their group than were their original scores. This statistical phenomenon is known as **regression to the mean**.

In our example, we selected participants on the basis of a pretest measure, reading comprehension, and then matched them on the basis of their pretest scores. Any subsequent differences in posttest measures may have been related to the effect of the teaching method or may have been due to regression to the mean. In other words, regression to the mean may be a confounding factor for interpreting results of studies that match groups on pretest measures. Regression to the mean is important to consider whenever random assignment is not or cannot be used and groups are matched on a pretest measure.

Before-and-After Designs

The common feature of before-and-after designs is the absence of a comparison group. Because all cases are exposed to the experimental treatment, the basis for comparison is provided by comparing the pretreatment to the posttest measures. These designs are thus useful for studies of interventions that are experienced by virtually every case in some population, such as total coverage programs like Social Security or studies of the effect of a new management strategy in a single organization. The simplest type of before-and-after design is the fixed-sample panel design, with one pretest and one posttest (see Chapter 5).

The **interrupted-time-series design** is often used in quasiexperimental research to examine observations before and after a naturally occurring treatment. In the simplest time series design, there is a single experimental group for which we have obtained multiple observations before and after a naturally occurring treatment. Such a design might be used to examine the effects of a public policy change on a particular behavior, such as the influence of changing the age of legal drinking on car accidents in young drivers. Here you would look at accident rates over several years and you would need to know when the time series is interrupted by the natural treatment, which in this example would when the public policy or law changed. You could compare accidents before and after the new law went into effect.

Consider the study done by John Gibbons and colleagues (2007) as an example of an interrupted-time-series design to examine the effects of a naturally occurring treatment. These researchers investigated the effect of public health warnings about the safety of antidepressant drugs issued by U.S. and European regulators in 2003 and 2004. The warnings, which discouraged the use of antidepressants in children and adolescents, coincided with a sharp jump in adolescent suicide rates in children and adolescents (ages 5–19 years). The researchers wanted to know whether the policies that discouraged the use of antidepressants in treating children and adolescents had inadvertently led to untreated depression in the young that in turn contributed to their jump in suicide rates. In this quasiexperimental research, then, the naturally occurring treatment is the policy change discouraging the use of antidepressants in children and adolescents. Thus, Gibbons et al. (2007) compared suicide rates of children and adolescents before and after the regulators issued their warnings. By way of background, the researchers cited several prior studies, all of which should have told the regulators that their warnings to discourage antidepressant use lacked empirical support and that it could indeed be harmful to the mental health and well-being of depressed children and adolescents. For example, an earlier study by Gibbons, Hur, Bhaumik, and Mann (2005) found an inverse or negative association between lower rates of antidepressant prescriptions and higher rates of adult suicide both within countries over time and between countries. Ludwig and Marcotte (2005) found a similar inverse association between lower antidepressant prescription rates and higher adult suicide rates from 1980 to 1999 in 26 European countries, and this inverse association held for the United States (Grunebaum et al., 2004) and Norway (Bramness, Walby, & Tverdal, 2007). Isacsson (2001), in a study heralding antidepressants as a "medical breakthrough" in preventing suicides, demonstrated that a 3.5-fold increase in antidepressant prescriptions in Sweden corresponded to a 19% decrease in suicides.

In their most recent investigation, Gibbons et al. (2007) found a similar inverse association between lower antidepressant prescription rates and heightened suicide risk for children and adolescents. These researchers correlated annual rates of antidepressant prescriptions and suicide for children and teens. For example, as you can see in **Exhibit 8.3**, they plotted suicide rates before and after the warnings from 1998 to 2005 in the Netherlands. Over a 3-year period between 2003 and 2005 after the regulators issued the warnings, antidepressant prescription rates showed a 22% decline, and the suicide rate showed a 49% increase for children and teens. The United States showed a similar pattern of lower antidepressant prescription rates and higher suicide rates for children and adolescents. For example, following the warnings, the prescription rates for children and teens showed a small decline, which Gibbons et al. speculated meant that the most vulnerable children were likely left untreated. Suicide rates for children and teens showed a 14% increase from 2003 to 2004. Compare this to adults 60 years or older. Here antidepressant prescription rates continued to increase, and suicide rates continued to decrease for adults age 60 and over.

Exhibit 8.3 Suicide Rate in Children and Adolescents (Up to Age 19) in the Netherlands, 1998 to 2005 (Gibbons et al., 2007)

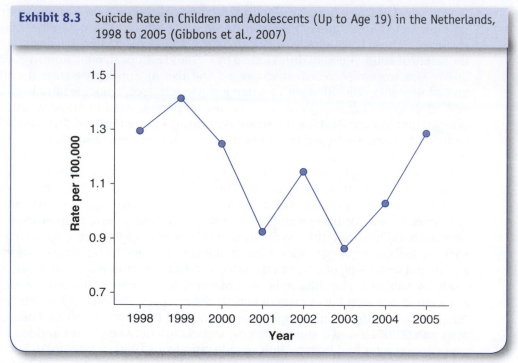

Gibbons and colleagues interpreted these findings as showing that regulatory policies discouraging the use of antidepressants in children and adolescents may have inadvertently increased suicide rates for these groups. The results have remarkable ecological validity as they suggested antidepressants may help reduce suicide rates of children, adolescent, and adults across counties and states. The studies may be viewed as quasiexperiments of the effects of a natural treatment (public health warnings) on a dependent variable or outcome measure (suicide rates).

David P. Phillips's (1982) study of the effect of TV soap-opera suicides on the number of actual suicides in the United States illustrates a powerful **multiple group before-and-after design.** In this type of quasiexperimental design, several before-and-after comparisons are made involving the same independent and dependent variables but with different groups. Phillips identified 13 soap-opera suicides in 1977 and then recorded the U.S. suicide rate in the weeks prior to and following each TV story. In effect, the researcher had 13 different before-and-after studies, one for each suicide story. In 12 of these 13 comparisons, deaths due to suicide increased from the week before each soap-opera suicide to the week after (see Exhibit 8.4).

Another type of before-and-after design involves multiple pretest and posttest observations of the same group. These may be **repeated-measures panel designs,**

Exhibit 8.4 Real Suicides and Soap-Opera Suicides

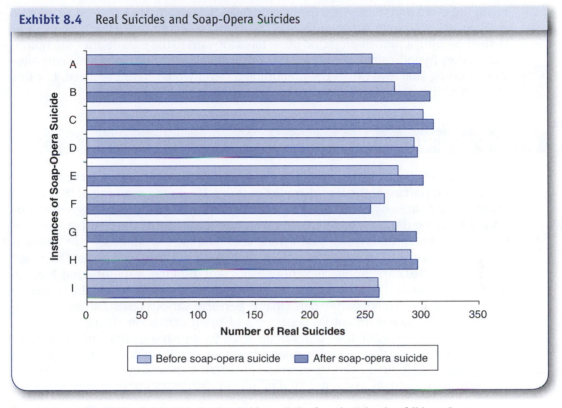

Source: Adapted from Philips (1982:1347). Reprinted with permission from the University of Chicago Press.

which include several pretest and posttest observations, and **time series designs**, such as the interrupted-time-series study of Gibbons and colleagues, which include many (preferably 30 or more) such observations in both pretest and post-test periods. Repeated-measures panel designs are stronger than simple before-and-after panel designs because they allow the researcher to study the process by which an intervention or treatment has an impact over time.

In a time series design, you compare the trend in the dependent variable up to the date of the intervention or event whose effect is being studied and the trend in the dependent variable after the intervention. A substantial disparity between the preintervention trend and the postintervention trend is evidence that the intervention or event had an impact (Rossi & Freeman, 1989).

Time series designs are particularly useful for studies of the impact of new laws or social programs that affect everyone and that are readily assessed by some ongoing measurement. For example, Paul A. Nakonezny, Rebecca Reddick, and Joseph Lee Rodgers (2004) used a time series design to identify the impact of the Oklahoma City terrorist bombing in April 1995 on the divorce rate in Oklahoma. They hypothesized that people would be more likely to feel a need for support in the aftermath of such a terrifying event and thus be less likely to divorce. Nakonezny et al. first calculated the average rate of change in divorce rates in Oklahoma's 77 counties in the 10 years prior to the bombing and then projected these rates forward to the 5 years after the bombing. As they hypothesized, they found that the actual divorce rate in the first years after the bombing was lower than the prebombing trend would have predicted, but this effect diminished to nothing by the year 2000 (**see Exhibit 8.5**).

A QUASIEXPERIMENT OF MEMORIES OF 9/11

Sharot, Martorella, Delgado, and Phelps recruited participants who had been in the vicinity (Manhattan) of the World Trade Center (WTC) on the morning of 9/11 when the terrorist attacks occurred. The researchers employed **functional magnetic resonance imaging (fMRI)**, a widely used technique that records the brain at work, in real time, while an individual performs a task. The fMRI technology can be combined with various behavioral exercises, and these performance tasks can entail highly controlled experiments of various aspects of thinking, remembering, feeling, and concentration. The fMRI uses a blood oxygen dependent level (BOLD) signal to measure brain activation while participants perform various tasks. Different cognitive tasks will elicit different fMRI patterns of brain activation. Thus, some brain areas will be more active than other brain areas while participants perform certain tasks. By examining these patterns, researchers can identify various neural networks that underlie different kinds of performance, whether involving memory, attention, perception, or virtually any other kind of information processing.

Exhibit 8.5 Divorce Rates in Oklahoma Before and After the Oklahoma City Bombing

Source: From "Did Divorce Rates Decline after the Oklahoma City Bombing?" by Paul A. Nakonezny, Rebecca Reddick and Joseph Lee Rodgers in *Journal of Marriage and Family, 66*(1), July 2004: 90. Copyright © 2004 National Council on Family Relations. Reprinted with permission of Wiley Blackwell Publishing.

Experimental Stimuli and Task

How does the brain remember emotional events such as 9/11? What networks of brain areas are activated by memories of 9/11? Brain imaging techniques, such as fMRI, go a long way in addressing these questions. Also of critical importance is the behavioral activation task that is coupled or combined with fMRI. In the Sharot study, for the experimental task, participants viewed words that numerous prior studies have shown to be effective cues for memory. As you can see in **Exhibit 8.6**,

Exhibit 8.6	Word Cues Used as Experimental Stimuli in Sharot et al. (2007)	
hands	reading	sleep
circle	reporter	weather
classes	evening news	breakfast
drink	lunch	New York City
evening	radio	teacher
street corner	homework	writing
building	greed	work
e-mail	exam	food
quiet	morning	noise
walking	transportation	mail
boredom	red	dream
thought	afternoon	clothes
cool	phone	photograph
mom	office	weekday
airplane	sibling	music
hearing	weekend	paper
coffee	moral	sidewalk
shopping	dad	significant other
stair	money	university
hot	family	friend

Source: From "How personal experience modulates the neural circuitry of memories of September 11" by T. Sharot, E. A. Martorella, M. R. Delgado, and E. A. Phelps in *Proceedings of the National Academy of Science, 104,* 389–39, 2007. Reprinted with permission.

some examples of the experimental stimuli were word cues, such as *morning, New York City, lunch, evening,* and *weather*. The researchers wanted to see if these words would cue different memories depending on the experimental condition in which they were presented. There were two experimental conditions: September 2001 and summer 2001. The same list of word cues was presented in both conditions. For example, a trial in the September 2001 condition, a participant saw on a screen: September 2001 morning. In a trial in the summer 2001 condition, a participant saw on a screen: summer 2001 morning. The same word cues were used across both conditions. That way, the researchers could compare word-cued 9/11 memories with word-cued summer 2001 memories.

The fMRI recorded brain responses to these memories in response to the word cues listed in **Exhibit 8.6**. Later, outside the fMRI scanner, participants again saw the same word cues paired either with September 2001 or summer 2001. But this time, participants rated each word-cued memory on six characteristics: (1) arousal, (2) vividness, (3) reliving, (4) remember/know, (5) confidence, and (6) valence. These six characteristics have been demonstrated in previous research to be distinctive attributes of memories.

To summarize, Sharot and colleagues used memory as a within-subjects variable with two levels: summer 2001 and September of 2001. All participants received the same word cues, presented one at a time for both conditions—summer 2001 and September 2001. As one of the dependent measures, the researchers recorded brain activity while participants viewed cue words in both summer 2001 and September 2001 conditions. In addition, the other dependent measure was ratings of the word cues on the six characteristics that the participants completed outside the fMRI.

Ex Post Facto Variables and Comparison Groups

Sharot and colleagues found that not only did 9/11 memories have higher ratings than did summer 2001 memories on each of these attributes, but individuals differed considerably in their ratings. Wondering what might account for these differences, the researcher examined surveys that all participants had completed. Among the information surveyed included distance or proximity to the WTC on the day that terrorists attacked. Put simply, Sharot and colleagues wanted to know whether being closer to the WTC on that day influenced memory and brain responses for 9/11. They subsequently divided their participants into two groups, those who were closer to the WTC, defined as a mean 2.08 miles, labeled as the *Downtown* group, and those farther away from the WTC, defined as a mean distance of 4.53 miles, labeled as the *Midtown* group.

Here we have an example of researchers creating comparison groups ex post facto, or after the fact, meaning, in this instance, after the fMRI and word-rating data had been collected. In addition, they created a new subject variable based on their participants' ratings of their memories on the six characteristics listed above. From these six characteristics, the researchers computed a new subject variable—a single score that they labeled "recollective experience enhancement." We can see this quasiexperimental approach is very different from a factorial experiment in which groups are formed by random assignment and variables are defined conceptually and operationally a priori.

Correlational Relationships

As we know, quasiexperiments lack design features that improve internal validity, thus lessening confidence in causal conclusions. On the other hand, researchers are often interested in examining the relationship between variables, as, for example, Sharot and colleagues wanted to examine whether being closer to the WTC would be associated with more intense recollections of the 9/11 attacks. As you know, the degree and direction of a relationship between two variables can be tested with a single statistic known as the **correlation coefficient** (the symbol for correlation is r). Correlation coefficients vary from –1.00 through 0.00 to +1.00. The number value of the correlation indicates the strength of the relationship between the two variables—a larger number indicates a stronger relationship. The sign, whether positive or negative, indicates the direction of the relationship. A *positive* correlation indicates that as one variable increases, so too does the other. A *negative* correlation indicates that as one variable increases, the other decreases.

Sharot et al. found a statistically significant, negative correlation between WTC distance and 9/11 memories ($r = -0.67$). Remember that *statistically significant* means unlikely due to chance and *negative* refers to the direction of the relationship between the two variables. The negative direction means that participants who were closer to WTC (in this case, shorter distance, lower score on the distance variable) had higher ratings (in this case, higher scores on the recollective experience enhancement variable).

Researchers often use **scatter diagrams** to graph correlations. A scatter diagram is a graph of a correlation. A correlation always involves two variables. Let's call one variable x and the other y. Let us say a participant had a score of 5 on one variable, labeled x, and a score of 10 on another variable, labeled y. Make a two-dimensional graph with a horizontal x-axis and a vertical y-axis. Now plot the participant's scores of 5, 10 (5 to the right, and 10 up). Each participant can be represented by a point on the graph, in this example, 5, 10, which represents scores on x and y variables. So if there are 12 participants, there should be 12 points. The direction of the points on the graph will signify whether the correlation between the two variables across all participants is either positive or negative. For a positive correlation, the graph will depict points that fall on an imaginary line that tilts upward to the right. For a negative correlation, the graph will depict points that fall on an imaginary line that tilts downward to the right.

A real-life example of a negative correlation taken from Sharot et al. can be seen in **Exhibit 8.7**. On the horizontal x-axis is the distance-from-WTC variable. On the vertical y-axis is the recollective experience enhancement variable. Each of the 24 participant scores on distance and memory variables are plotted. Each point on

Exhibit 8.7 Correlation scatter plot across all groups for enhancement in recollective experience, defined as the average differential scores on all subjective scales for 9/11 memories vs. summer memories, with participants' distance from the WTC defined by ranking participants from the individual closest to the WTC to the individual farthest from the WTC

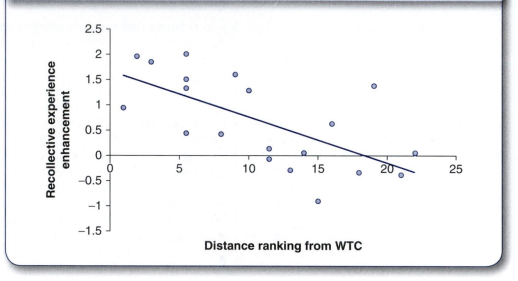

Source: From Sharot et al., 2007.

the graph depicts a participant's score on these two variables. As you can see, the direction of the points on the graph tilts downward to the right. The imaginary line provided by all computer graphic programs clearly illustrated the right downward tilt. This, then, is an example of a statistically significant negative correlation between WTC distance and memory rating scores. This scatter plot shows that the shorter the WTC distance, meaning closer to the site of the terrorist attacks, the more intense personal recollection of 9/11.

Now consider the influence of distance from the WTC on fMRI patterns of brain activation associated with 9/11 memories. Participants who were downtown and closest to the WTC on that day showed a different pattern of brain activation from participants who were further way from the WTC. The Downtown group consisting of participants who were closest to the WTC showed the greatest activation of the **amygdala**, an almond-shaped structure found deep in the brain that plays a key role in fusing memories with emotion. The amygdala, which is adjacent to the **hippocampus** that is known to be crucial in remembering, thus played an important role in providing the emotional tone and intensity for memories in those participants who were the closest to the WTC on that day. The fMRI data showed the intense activation of the amygdala during retrieval of 9/11 memories relative to summer memories in research participants.

The two groups, Midtown and Downtown, showed different brain responses for the two types of memory, 9/11 and summer 2001 memories. The Downtown group showed greater amygdala activation for 9/11 memories than for 2001 memories. The Midtown group did not (in fact, they showed signs of the opposite pattern, greater amygdala activation for 2001 summer memories than for 9/11). As we learned in Chapter 7, this outcome is referred to as an *interaction*. An interaction occurs when the effects of one independent variable depends on the level of another independent variable. In the Sharot study, the effect of the group variable (e.g., Midtown vs. Downtown) depended upon whether the cue words came in the September 2001 condition or in the summer 2001 condition. In this example, there are two independent variables, group and memory condition. Each has two levels: group (Downtown/Midtown) and memory condition (September 2001/Summer 2001). Group interacted with memory as seen in the effect it had on the dependent variable: fMRI activation of the amygdala. The interaction showed that only the Downtown group when presented with cue words in the September 11 condition had selective activation of the amygdala. **Exhibit 8.8** provides a graphical representation of how the different effects the two independent variables of memory (9/11, summer) and group (Midtown, Downtown) had on the dependent variable of fMRI response. This, as you recall from Chapter 7, is referred to as a crossover two-way interaction because there are two independent variables (memory condition, group) that exert different effects on the dependent variable, which when plotted in a graph reveal lines that cross over each other.

Control and Natural Treatments

Let's pause for a moment and examine the research design used by Sharot and colleagues. First, we can see that they used a complex within-subjects design because all their research participants received both levels of the independent variable of memory. That is, all the research participants in the study viewed the cue words in both the September 2001 and summer 2001 memory conditions. Second, Sharot and colleagues used a control condition. Most experiments have either a control group, as in the case of a between-subjects design, or a **control condition**, as in the case of a within-subjects design. With a within-subjects design, Sharot used the summer 2001 memory condition as the control condition. Why? Because it provided a **baseline** measure to compare memories—9/11 memories versus 2001 summer memories. That is, a key characteristic of a control condition is that it provides a baseline against which an important variable of an experiment can be compared. By using a baseline control measure, Sharot and colleagues could compare, within the same research participants, patterns of brain activation associated with 9/11 memories with those associated

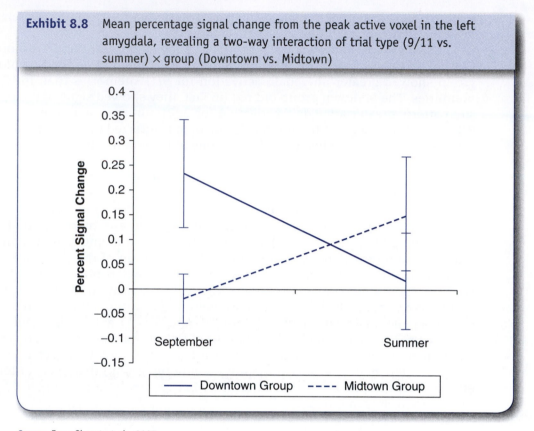

Exhibit 8.8 Mean percentage signal change from the peak active voxel in the left amygdala, revealing a two-way interaction of trial type (9/11 vs. summer) × group (Downtown vs. Midtown)

Source: From Sharot et al., 2007.

with the summer of 2001. Third, the design included two independent variables, memory condition and group, each with two levels. Thus, it would meet the criteria of a complex multifactorial design described in Chapter 7. However, because of the nature of the independent variables, it is further distinguished as a quasiexperimental design.

Such a sound and rigorous quasiexperimental design appeared eminently capable of answering the research question as to how 9/11 memories differ from regular memories. When evaluating research, ask yourself two simple questions: Can the experimental design provide an answer to the research question? Or is the experimental design doomed by uncontrolled or confounding variables such that any results would be suspect and leave the research question unanswered? Because we can answer yes to the first question and no to the second question, we can now look at the exciting findings of Sharot and colleagues with confidence that they conducted a well-designed quasiexperimental study that indeed did reveal some very interesting and distinctive aspects of memories of 9/11.

Why is the Sharot study a good example of a quasiexperiment? First, it examined a natural treatment, in this case the influence of 9/11, on personal recollections. Second, as is the case of any study that examines the effects of natural treatments on any given dependent variable, memories of 9/11 could not be directly manipulated. Third, the researchers could not use random assignment to create comparison groups. Instead, they performed an ex post facto analysis on how distance from the WTC would affect 9/11 memories and then used this variable to create two comparison groups: Downtown and Midtown groups. This proved to be an excellent variable; it could be easily measured and did vary across their research participants. Not to mention it proved to be a key factor influencing personal recollections of 9/11 as well as patterns of brain activation associated with those memories. Fourth, while the groups were not formed by random assignment, participants did not decide whether they would enter either of the two groups. If they did decide group membership, the study would not have been considered a quasiexperiment. Rather, as we will see later, it would have been considered a nonexperiment.

QUASIEXPERIMENTAL RESEARCH OF CULTURE AND COGNITION

In Chapter 1, we introduced you to the importance of culture for studying and understanding human behavior. And again in Chapter 4, we learned that culture figures prominently in our understanding of measurement of psychological constructs, especially in the psychometrics of assessing human intelligence. Culture is traditionally studied using nonexperimental research designs. As you recall from our toolbox of research methods (see Chapter 1), nonexperimental approaches can involve a variety of research techniques and designs, such as ethnographic studies, correlational analyses, and qualitative investigations. Together, this body of research illuminates how culture shapes our thinking and how our thinking shapes culture (e.g., Nisbett, Peng, Choi, & Norenzayan, 2001). Now in this section, we learn how researchers study culture experimentally and how these studies using simple but ingenious techniques have produced some rather interesting and powerful results.

You might ask why researchers would use an experimental approach to study culture. After all, culture is an important characteristic of individuals that would hardly seem suited to experimental studies. A very good point, we would reply, and you are indeed correct that culture cannot be directly manipulated; it cannot be randomly assigned. However, in defense of an experimental approach to culture, consider the following scenario: Many scholars and researchers have long been fascinated by differences in value orientations between Western (e.g., Europe and North America) and Eastern (e.g., East Asia and China) cultures. And in fact, converging lines of evidence reliably characterize Western culture as individualistic versus the collectivistic value orientation of the East (e.g., Nisbett et al., 2001).

For example, psychologist L.-H. Chiu (1972; cited in Nisbett et al., 2001, p. 295) is quoted as follows:

> Chinese are situation-centered. They are obliged to be sensitive to their environment. Americans are individual-centered. They expect their environment to be sensitive to them. Thus, Chinese tend to assume a passive attitude while Americans tend to possess an active and conquering attitude in dealing with their environment. (p. 236)

An experimentally minded researcher takes these findings and asks the following questions: What are the processes and mechanisms underlying these robust cultural differences in value orientation? What effect do such cultural differences have on thinking, perception, and reasoning? Can these differences be manipulated? In other words, how can we uncover how these differences emerge, under what conditions they might be activated, and how they may affect individual psychology? We would argue for an experimental approach in studying these questions.

Constructivist Theories of Culture

How then can we study these fascinating cultural differences experimentally? Enter researchers Ying-yi Hong, Michael W. Morris, Chi-yue Chiu, and Veronica Benet-Martinez, who published a paper in 2000 in the *American Psychologist,* titled "Multicultural Minds: A Dynamic Constructivist Approach to Culture and Cognition." We use this paper as a model to illustrate how quasiexperimental research can be effectively applied to the study of culture and cognition. As we have emphasized throughout this book, sound research begins with theory. Accordingly, we note that Hong et al. (2000) framed their work in what is known as **constructivist theory**. In constructivist theory, culture is conceptualized as the rich blend of images, metaphors, practices, and discourses about human life that prevail in a given group or society (Shweder & Sullivan, 1993). This blend, likened to a "cultural menu," provides the raw materials from which people construct their own individual life stories or narratives. As McAdams and Pal (2006) write, "Culture then, provides each person with an extensive menu of stories about how to live, and each person chooses from the menu" (p. 212).

Two important implications follow from such a constructivist model of culture. First is that within the same person, there may exist two very different cultural menus. In fact, studies cited by Hong et al. have shown that many bicultural individuals often describe experiencing two internalized cultures that take turns in guiding their thoughts and perceptions. Second is that within any person, there is a dynamic ebb and flow to one's internalized culture; it is not relied on continuously for interpretation and meaning, but instead only a small subset of cultural knowledge may come to the fore at any given time. Of particular interest is that each of these implications can be tested experimentally. The first is rather straightforward: recruit bicultural individuals as research participants. The second is much more difficult. Hong et al.'s constructivist theory defines the process through which bicultural individuals alternate between two internalized cultural mental sets as **frame switching**. According to their model, the bicultural individuals, when triggered by cues in the social environment, can switch between two interpretive frames rooted in their two different cultures. To test this model experimentally, then, requires techniques, tasks, and stimuli capable of eliciting certain cultural states of mind. In addition, these experimental procedures need to be nontransparent so that the induced cultural mental set is not apparent to the research participant.

Experimental Tasks and Stimuli

We can thus see that constructivist theory requires methods that are not traditionally used in cultural studies. By the same token, however, it is important to incorporate interpretive tasks that have been well studied in traditional nonexperimental cultural psychology. Such tasks are important because they have an established track record of being sensitive to and influenced by cultural knowledge in a well-understood manner. In addition, constructivist theory would likely be best tested with an experimental task that would require participants to interpret some sort of ambiguous stimuli that could be viewed differently depending upon one's cultural frame. In light of these considerations, Hong et al. decided upon films of animated fish in which it was ambiguous as to whether an individual fish was leading or being chased by the other fish (see **Exhibit 8.9**). In a prior study using these films, Morris and Peng (1994) showed that Chinese participants and American participants provided different explanations for the individual fish's behavior. The Chinese participants were more likely than the American participants to attribute the behavior of the individual fish to external forces related to the group of fish as a whole. By contrast, the American participants explained the behavior in terms of the internal dispositions of the single fish. The researchers argued that how Americans and Chinese naturally explain ambiguous behaviors may be directly related to their culture. They reasoned that the weight accorded to internal dispositions resonates with the American culture of individualism, as does the weight accorded to external group factor to collectivism of Chinese culture (Su et al., 1999).

Hong et al. sought to extend these findings by investigating whether they could experimentally induce frame switching in bicultural individuals. To do so, they adopted a well-known experimental technique from cognitive psychology called **priming.** Priming occurs when exposure to a stimulus facilitates responses to a subsequent event. That is, initial exposure primes subsequent processing. Hong et al. hoped priming would allow them to test a key element of their theory. They theorized *accessibility* of cultural knowledge would determine the extent to which such knowledge guides thinking, perceiving, and interpreting. They saw priming as a way to manipulate levels of accessibility of knowledge. For bicultural participants

Exhibit 8.9   Points A and C are the average ratings for American and Chinese research participants, respectively, on the internal and external attribution scales.

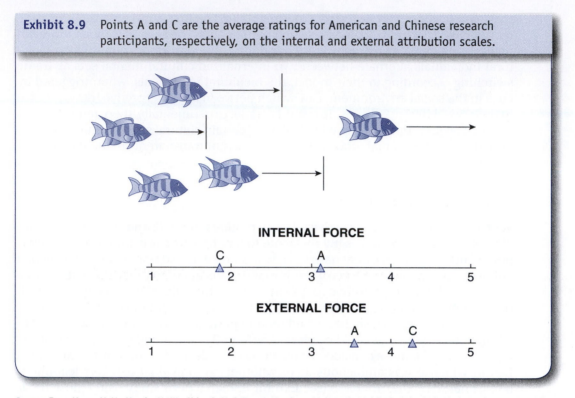

Source: From Hong, Y.-Y., Morris, M. W., Chiu, C.-Y, & Benet-Martinez, V. (2000). Multicultural minds: A dynamic constructivist approach to culture and cognition. *American Psychologist, 55,* 709–720. Copyright © 2000 American Psychological Association.

(e.g., Hong Kong Chinese undergraduate students), visual icons should prime switching between their American and Chinese cultural frames (see **Exhibit 8.10**). Thus, in their studies, Hong et al. had bicultural participants, randomly assigned to either the American cultural priming condition or the Chinese cultural priming condition, watch the film clips of the animated fish. The results followed the same pattern as did the findings of the cross-national studies of Morris and Peng (2004). As predicted, participants were less likely to attribute the behavior of the single fish to external group factors related to social pressure after American priming than after Chinese priming.

We thus see how quasiexperimental research can be applied to cultural studies that have long been the province of nonexperimental and correlational approaches. In thinking about the experimental design used by Hong and colleagues, several points are worth keeping in mind. First, participants were selected on the basis of their biculturalism. As such, we can best classify these studies as quasiexperimental in nature. However, Hong and colleagues did also randomly assign participants to the cultural priming conditions. In this regard, then, cultural priming

Exhibit 8.10   Examples of Iconic Images Used as Cultural Primes

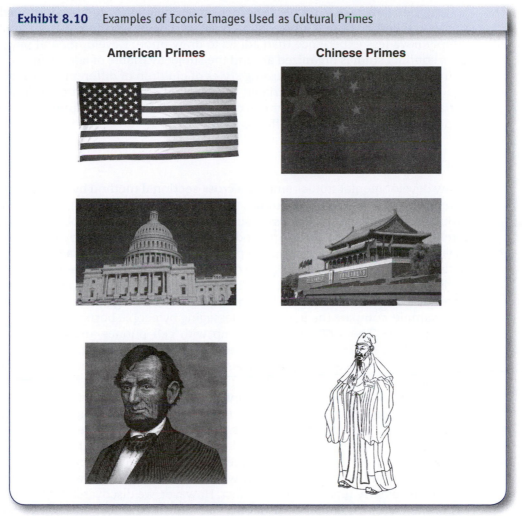

Source: From Hong et al. (2000). Lincoln: © JupiterImages/Liquidlibrary/Thinkstock; Tiananmen Square: © Can Stock Photo, Inc./devon; Flag of People's Republic of China: © Stockbyte/Thinkstock.

represented a true independent variable. Given nonrandom selection of participants but random assignment to priming conditions, the Hong study may be best characterized as a mixed-factorial design.

DEVELOPMENTAL STUDIES

Developmental psychology is defined as the scientific study of progressive psychological changes that unfold across the entire life span as human beings age. Key topics include the development of intelligence, personality, morality, problem solving, and language. Key questions focus on principles that govern human development, whether, for example, children are *qualitatively* different from adults or simply have less experience than adults to draw upon. Developmental psychologists conduct studies organized around the subject variable of age, as for example in investigations comparing learning styles of children of different ages. However, age as a quasi-independent variable is typically correlated with countless other variables, and these associations can complicate and confound our understanding of developmental changes or effects.

Cross-Sectional Design

Many developmental studies employ a **cross-sectional method** by taking groups of people of different ages (for example, 6, 10, and 13) and then comparing these age groups on psychological processes such as moral reasoning, problem solving, or intelligence. A cross-sectional method is, however, confounded by **cohort effects** that result from comparing groups of persons who are at different ages at one point in time. A **cohort** is defined as a group of individuals sharing a certain characteristic, such as age, year of high school graduation, or locale. Different age groups have different cohort effects that are the consequences of being born at different times. For example, compare the use of text messaging by people born in 1990 with those born in 1950. The 1990 cohort grew up with cell phones and text messaging, whereas the 1950 cohort was likely well into their 40s before these technologies even existed. This would likely translate into a large cohort effect influencing any cross-sectional study of text messaging between these different age groups.

A cross-sectional method is also confounded by **period effects** that are defined as historical influences that may affect responses to the dependent variable (see Schaie, 1977). As a hypothetical, let us say we conducted studies in the 1960s on alcohol consumption and aging. We compared cohorts born in 1900 and 1940, and we found the 1900 cohort consumed much less alcohol than the 1940 cohort. Based on our cross-sectional studies, we concluded that lower alcohol consumption by the elderly reflected an age effect. However, we discovered that other studies in the historical annals have shown that individuals born in 1900 consumed less alcohol even when compared to older cohorts born in the 1880s. We then recall from our American history classes that the 1900 cohort came of age during Prohibition. We now change our conclusion, realizing that these period effects in the form of historical differences between the 1900 and 1940 cohorts may have confounded our interpretation of reduced alcohol consumption in aging.

Longitudinal Design

We can see that cohort effects and period effects are important limitations to keep in mind when using a cross-sectional method. To avoid cohort and period effects, developmental psychologists often use a **longitudinal method** in which the same research participants are followed over time, as for example when the same child is tested at age 6, then at age 10, and then again at age 13. A longitudinal study can go on for decades, as participants might be followed over their life span. A well-known longitudinal study conducted by psychiatrist George Vaillant followed 268 graduates from Harvard College classses of 1942, 1943, and 1944. A June 2009 *Atlantic Monthly* piece by Joshua Wolf Shenk captures the richnes of a longitudinal method when he writes in describing Vaillant's work:

> Is there a formula—some mix of love, work, and psychological adaptation—for a good life? For 72 years, researchers at Harvard have been examining this question, following 268 men who entered college in the late 1930s through war, career, marriage and divorce, parenthood and grandparenthood, and old age. Here, for the first time, a journalist gains access to the archive of one of the most comprehensive longitudinal studies in history. Its contents, as much literature as science, offer profound insight into the human condition—and into the brilliant, complex mind of the study's longtime director, George Vaillant.

In a longitudinal study, samples all share the same age and thus there are no cohort effects. However, a longitudinal method is not without problems. In practical terms, following people over time is obviously very hard, and participant **attrition** or dropout can threaten sample size. A longitudinal study also may take decades to complete as the cohort ages. In addition, what are known as **secular trends** pose a main confound for longitudinal studies. Secular trends occur when a researcher cannot attribute longitudinal results to hypothesized age-related developmental processes, as for example to the age-related transition to adulthood. Rather, secular trends related to general changes that have taken place in society may have influenced or confounded the longitudinal study.

As a result, developmental researchers now often design studies that are able to distinguish longitudinal or age-related effects from secular trends. For example, Nelson and colleagues (2006) conducted a 5-year longitudinal study on weight-related health behavior in a sample of more than 2,500 adolescents. They collected observations of *longitudinal* changes in two age cohorts—early adolescence to midadolescence and midadolescence to late adolescence—as well as *secular* changes in physical activity, television video viewing, and leisure-time computer use. Thus, as we can see, Nelson and colleagues were able to tease apart longitudinal trends from secular trends and to determine the extent to which changes in heath-related behavior could be attributable to age versus time. They found substantial longitudinal changes in physical activity, reflected by decreases of about 1 hour per week for the early-to-midadolescent cohort and nearly 2 hours per week for the mid-to-late-adolescent cohort. Their findings also showed dramatic secular trends in midadolescent computer use reflected by increases of more than 2 hours per week for girls and nearly 5 hours per week for boys.

Cross-Sequential Design

Researchers (e.g., Baltes, 1968; Schaie, 1965, 1977) have developed some ingenious designs to manage confounds that occur in developmental research. One of these designs is referred to as a **cross-sequential design**. A cross-sequential design requires two or more age groups tested at two or more time intervals. The advantage of a cross-sequential design is that it allows for three important effects to be studied simultaneously. These effects are: cross-sectional, longitudinal, and time lag. **Exhibit 8.11** depicts a **cross-sequential design**, indicated by the central box.

Now let us imagine that we have four groups of adolescents and we want to examine what percentage of each group uses the highly popular social technology—Facebook. Let's suppose that we interview our research participants about their Facebook use in years 2007, 2008, 2009 and 2010, and we obtained data presented in **Exhibit 8.11**. In the central box of **Exhibit 8.11**, we have five age groups, with participants of 18, 17, 16, 15, or 14 years of age, and with two testing or interview times, 2008 and 2009. For the cross-sectional method, you can look down column 2008 or column 2009. By looking at either one of these columns, you can investigate cross-sectional effects by comparing participants of different ages tested in the same year. For the longitudinal method, look at any one of the four rows of the central box. This will allow you to investigate the same participant interviewed in successive years, 2008 and 2009. For the time-lag method, look along the diagonal of the box, and you see that you can examine participants of the same age interviewed at different times either in year 2008 or 2009. Thus, with a **time-lag design**, the effects of time of testing can be investigated while holding age constant. As shown in **Exhibit 8.11**, the time lag method for our imagined data indicated that 75% of 17-year olds used Facebook in 2008 compare to 100% Facebook use in 17-years olds in 2009.

Exhibit 8.11 Percentage of adolescents who use Facebook

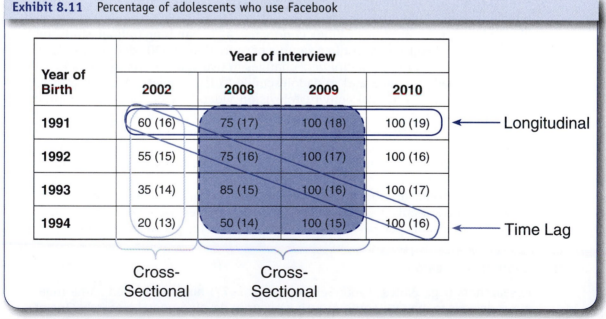

Note: Numbers in parentheses indicate age at time of interview.

To illustrate how the cross-sequential design may be used to address some of the important confounds in developmental research, consider the following example taken from **Exhibit 8.11** of 16-year old participants born in 1991 who were first interviewed in 2007. Cross-sectional effects can be investigated by comparing these 16 year olds to different age groups who were also interviewed in 2007. Longitudinal effects can be assessed by re-interviewing the same participants in 2008 now 17 years of age. If both these cross-sectional and longitudinal comparisons show similar age effects, then we can be reasonable confident that our results are not confounded by cohort effects and time of interview effects. In addition, if time-lag comparisons of 16-year old participants interviewed in 2007 with those interviewed 2008 yield similar results to both cross-sectional and longitudinal analyses, then there would appear to be no evidence of secular trends confounding our results.

A Developmental Study of Brain Maturation

Attention deficit hyperactivity disorder (ADHD) is the most common psychiatric diagnosis given to children, occurring in approximately 3% to 5% of school-age children. Is ADHD due to a brain deficit or to a delay in brain development? In the Shaw et al. (2007) study, titled "Attention-Deficit/Hyperactivity Disorder Is Characterized by a Delay in Cortical Maturation," two groups of children, those with and without ADHD—223 in each group—had repeated structural **magnetic resonance imaging** (MRI) exams of the brain from ages 6 to 16. By tracking these children over the course of 10 years and collecting multiple MRI scans on each child, the researchers were able to examine developmental trajectories of brain regions and structures and their size, density, and thickness for both ADHD and control participants.

In a normally developing brain, the **cerebral cortex** (the brain's outer layer or "bark," which is thought to be the seat of higher thinking) thickens during early childhood, but then reverses course and thins out, losing brain cells or neurons, as the brain matures through adolescence. Children differ considerably in the timing of these developmental or growth trajectories in brain maturation. We can think of these as maturational or developmental differences that children show in their schedules of peaks and troughs of thickening and thinning of the cerebral cortex.

Shaw measured these differences in children with ADHD and healthy controls, who had been scanned (MRI) between two and five times within intervals of 2 or 3 years. The researchers examined cortical thickness using both cross-sectional and longitudinal analyses. For the cross-sectional analysis, they compared for each age (ages 5 to 16) the brain scans of children with ADHD and healthy controls. For the longitudinal analysis, the researchers examined changes in brain thickness measured over time in the repeated MRI scans for each child. Shaw et al. (2007) found a substantial delay of about 3 years in the age of reaching peak cortical thickness for the ADHD children. While ADHD children showed the same sequence of brain development as the healthy control children, brain maturation occurred more slowly on a delayed schedule.

Developmental studies require tremendous resources. Seldom does a study combine cross-sectional and longitudinal methods, as the Shaw study did. Shaw and colleagues also employed, as their dependent measure, MRI of brain anatomy. As a biological measure of the structure of the brain, MRI might arguably be free of confounds of time and cohort that plague cross-sectional and longitudinal studies of psychological changes. As such, a cross-sequential design might have been unnecessary for the Shaw study. However, as we have seen in **Exhibit 8.11**, a cross-sequential design is rather straightforward under those rare circumstances a researcher has the resources to combine both longitudinal and cross-sectional methods. A cross-sequential design increases the internal validity of developmental research.

NONEXPERIMENTAL RESEARCH

Numerous topics of vital importance are studied systematically and empirically using nonexperiments. That is to say, many topics of interest in psychology can be studied by using neither true randomized experiments nor quasiexperiments. Think back to the 9/11 study. Recall that this study used a quasiexperimental design. What made this quasiexperimental instead of nonexperimental? In a word, the WTC distance variable, because this variable allowed the researchers to create two groups: Midtown Manhattan and Downtown Manhattan. They then could test whether memories and concomitant brain activation differed as a function of WTC distance. Had they simply used as a control group subjects who lived on the West Coast and compared their 9/11 memories with those from Manhattan, then this design would be considered nonexperimental. The distinction between quasiexperiments and nonexperiments is not cut and dried. In both cases, the researcher selects independent variables that cannot be directly controlled and manipulated. In neither instance can causality be established.

However, quasiexperiments test the effects of natural treatments as quasi-independent variables. Different levels of quasi-independent variables can be established and even quantified as in the case of the WTC distance. By contrast, for nonexperiments, the researcher has even less control over the independent variable, and seldom can specific levels of the independent variable be precisely established or quantified, as in the WTC distance variable. The bottom line is that both approaches have major limitations in terms of internal validity needed for establishing causality, but quasiexperiments as a rule will allow us more confidence and greater precision in interpreting results.

Ex Post Facto Control Group Designs

The **ex post facto control group design** is similar to the **nonequivalent control group design** and is often confused with it, but it does not meet as well the criteria for quasiexperimental designs. This design has experimental and comparison groups that are not created by random assignment, but unlike nonequivalent control group designs, individuals may decide themselves whether to enter the treatment or control group. As a result, in *ex post facto* (after-the-fact) designs, the people who join the treatment group may differ because of what attracted them to the group initially, not because of their experience in the group.

Susan Cohen and Gerald Ledford (1994) studied the effectiveness of self-managing teams in a telecommunications company with an ex post facto design (**Exhibit 8.12**). They compared work teams that they rated as self-managing with those they found to be traditionally managed (meaning that a manager was responsible for the team's decisions). They found that the self-reported quality of work life was higher in the self-managed groups than in the traditionally managed groups.

What distinguishes this nonexperimental design from a quasiexperimental design is the fact that the teams themselves and their managers had some influence on how they were managed. As the researchers noted, "If the groups which were already high performers were the ones selected to be self-managing teams, then the findings could be due to a selection bias rather than any effects of self-management" (Cohen & Ledford, 1994, p. 34). Keep in mind that **selection bias** is a source of internal invalidity that occurs when existing characteristics of participants may influence the formation of treatment and comparison groups. Thus, existing characteristics of employees and managers or their team composition might have influenced which "treatment" they received, as well as the outcomes achieved. This leaves us less certain about the effect of the treatment itself.

Exhibit 8.12 Ex Post Facto Control Group Design

	Self-Managing Work Teams		
Treatment Group	O_1	X	O_2
Comparison Group	O_1		O_2
Treatment group	Pretest: Measures of satisfaction and productivity	Self-managing work team	Posttest: Measures of satisfaction
Comparison group	Pretest: Measures of satisfaction and productivity		Posttest: Measures of satisfaction

Source: Based on Cohen & Ledford, 1994.

Key: O = Observation (present or posttest)

X = Experimental treatment

CONCLUSIONS

The critical advantage of quasiexperiments and nonexperiments is that they allow us to study topics of vital interest and also variables that would otherwise be unethical to manipulate directly. In this chapter, we have learned that carefully controlled and well-designed quasiexperiments and nonexperiments provide a powerful and valid research design to investigate topics that cannot be studied by randomized experiments.

There is always an implicit trade-off in experimental design between maximizing internal validity and external validity. Quasiexperimental and nonexperimental approaches cannot establish causality, as both approaches use quasi-independent variables that cannot be manipulated via random assignment. Associations between pairs of variables can be investigated and tested for statistical significance by computing a correlation coefficient. However, temporal order of what came first cannot always be established. Likewise, questions regarding nonspuriousness of a demonstrated relationship come into play because of potentially extraneous influences that could not be controlled.

On the other hand, the more that assignment to treatments is randomized and all experimental conditions are controlled, the less likely it is that the research participants and setting will be representative of the large population. In this sense, then, quasiexperiments and nonexperiments may be viewed as earning higher grades on external validity than true experiments. That is to say, quasiexperiments and nonexperiments are used to study how a particular phenomenon may naturally occur over time and, in some instances for developmental studies, over the life span. The researcher cannot directly control or manipulate these so-called natural treatments, and this will generally add to the external validity of the results while limiting confidence in their internal validity.

END OF CHAPTER

Chapter Highlights

- Subject variables and natural treatment belong to a distinct class of independent variables that many researchers call quasi-independent variables. A quasiexperiment is one that investigates the effects of one or more quasi-independent variables: subject variables, naturally occurring variables, or both.

- The most common quasiexperiment is a nonequivalent-control-group design in which experimental and control groups that have been predetermined or predesignated by either an existing subject characteristic or an already-occurred natural treatment and are not created by random assignment.

- Nonequivalent control group designs have experimental and control groups that have been predetermined or predesignated by either an existing subject characteristic or an already-occurred natural treatment and are not created by random assignment. The goal, of course, is to try to make the control group as comparable as possible to the experimental group.

- Matching individuals or groups on a variable that is highly related to the dependent variable is commonly used to equate participants before the study. However, matching on a pretest measure can present confounds related to regression to the mean for interpreting posttest results. Regression to the mean is important to consider whenever random assignment is not or cannot be used and groups are matched on a pretest measure.

- A quasiexperimental design is needed to study the psychological effect of September 11, 2001 (9/11) because we cannot directly control or manipulate via random assignment exposure to 9/11. Sharot et al. created a new variable, ex post facto, called distance from the World Trade Center (WTC) and found a significant correlation between being closer to WTC and experiencing greater intensity of 9/11 memories.

- Quasiexperimental research can be effectively applied to the study of culture and cognition. For example, Hong et al.'s constructivist theory defines the process through which bicultural individuals when triggered by cues in the social environment can switch between two interpretive frames rooted in their two different cultures. Experimental techniques involving cultural priming have been effective in studying this frame switching.

- Age used as a subject variable is confounded with numerous other factors that pose serious threats to internal validity. In developmental studies, a cross-sequential design allows for examination of three important age-related effects—cross-sectional, longitudinal, and time-lag—while providing some measure of control of secular and cohort confounds. A cross-sequential design increases the internal validity of developmental research.

- The ex post facto control group design is similar to the nonequivalent control group design and is often confused with it, but it does not meet as well the criteria for quasiexperimental designs. This design has experimental and comparison groups that are not created by random assignment, but unlike nonequivalent control group designs, individuals may decide themselves whether to enter the treatment or control group.

Key Terms

Research in the News

Science writer Jonah Lehrer featured the work of developmental and personality psychologist Walter Mischel in a May 18, 2009, piece in the *New Yorker*. In the article, Lehrer describes the "marshmallow test" that Mischel invented to study the development of self-control in preschool children. Mischel's longitudinal studies showed that preschool children who could delay eating a second marshmallow experieneced better outcomes in school, work, and health than did preschool children who failed to refrain from eating a second marshmallow. What confounds does the Mischel research present? How would a researcher use a cross-sequential design to study the development of self-control? Would the marshmallow test still predict outcome for preschool children today?

Activity Questions

1. Each of our 5 reseach participants has a pair of scores, which we call x and y:

   x y

   2 4

   6 8

   10 12

   14 16

   18 20

   a. Plot these scores in a scatter diagram. What do the points on the graph represent? What is the direction of the points on your graph? What does it signify? What is the direction of the relationship between the pairs of scores? Now reverse the scores:

   x y

   4 2

   8 6

   12 10

   16 14

   20 18

   b. Plot these scores in a scatter diagram. What is the direction of points on the graph? How would you describe the relationship between the pairs of scores? Describe the difference betweens scatter diagram a and scatter diagram b.

2. As we learned in this chapter, John Gibbons and colleagues examined the effect of public health warnings about the safety of antidepressant drugs issued by U.S. and European regulators in 2003 and 2004. The researchers wanted to know whether the policies that discouraged the use of antidepressants in treating children and adolescents had inadvertently led to untreated depression in the young that in turn contributed to their jump in suicide rates. To answer this question, Gibbons et al. (2007) compared suicide rates of children and adolescents before and after the regulators issued in 2003 and 2004 the warning discouraging antidepressants in young persons. Carefully review this study published in the *American Journal of Psychiatry.* How would you evaluate the research design? Would you consider this an example of a quasiexperiment that used an interrupted-time-series design? Why? What confounds should we consider? Explain your answers.

3. The work by Gibbons and others also illustrates the important role quasiexperimental research can play in social policy. Think of some other examples of high-impact quasiexperimental research. Discuss the pros and cons of quasiexperimental research in influencing public policy and social discourse. The discussion about intelligence from Chapter 4 might be a good starting point for a debate on quasi-experimental research in the world today.

Review Questions

1. Explain why natural treatments and subject variables are considered quasi-independent variables. What are the experimental design implications when studying quasi-independent varaibles? What are the sources of invalidity in quasiexperimental research, and how might they be mitigated?

2. The three broad approaches to research design covered in this chapter and in Chaper 7 may be described as experimental, quasiexperimental, and nonexperimental. How would you rate these approaches (i.e., "+"/strength "−"/weakness) on the following five criteria: (a) external validity, (b) internal validity, (c) random assignment, (d) use of control/comparison groups, and (e) ecological validity?

3. Compare and contrast before-and-after and nonequivalent control group designs. What kinds of research questions would be better studied with a before-and-after design than with a nonequivalent control group design? Explain your reasoning with examples taken from the scientific literature.

4. Describe individual matching and aggregate matching. What is the rationale for using these techniques and what are their limitations?

5. Discuss the use of age as a subject variable in quasiexperimental research, particularly in developmental psychology. Compare the use of age as a quasi-independent variable in developmental psychology research with elderly versus child research participants. Why does age in geriatric research pose more problems in terms of potential confounds than it does in child developmental studies?

6. Compare and contrast longitudinal and cross-sectional designs. Describe confounds related to a cross-sectional design and how they are addressed in a longitudinal design. Describe confounds related to a longitudinal design.

7. What is a cross-sequential design? How does a cross-sequential design incorporate features of longitudinal, cross-sectional, and time-lag designs? What are the advantages and disadvantages of a cross-sequential design?

8. What is an ex post facto control group design? What kind of research questions might be investigated with an ex post facto control group design? What are its limitations? What is a major source of invalidity with this design?

9. Describe how a quasiexperimental research approach can be used to study culture and cognition. What are some of the experimental techniques used to examine cultural effects on cognition? How would you describe the theoretical rationale underlying these techniques? How would you assess their external validity and ecological validity?

10. Describe a quasiexperimental research approach that uses a mixed-factorial design. What kinds of research questions might be studied using this approach? What are its advantages and disadvantages?

Ethics in Action

1. Imagine you are a developmental psychologist interested in studying age-related changes in moral reasoning in children (ages 8–12) and early adolescents (ages 13–17). As you likely know, to participate in research, minors (generally below the age of 18) require either parental consent or permission from a legally authorized person. Consult the APA Ethics Code (Standard 3.10b Informed Consent, Standard 8.02a Informed Consent to Research). Explain the difference between informed consent and assent. Explain what ethical safeguards are necessary for research with minors as well as for other vulnerable populations.

2. In their book *Practical Ethics for Psychologists: A Positive Approach,* Knapp and VandeCreek cite Fisher (2000), who proposed that researchers adopt a "duty-based" perspective toward their participants and "treat them as moral agents with intrinsic worth and helpful perspectives, instead of simply the means by which investigators can reach their research goals" (Knapp & VandeCreek, 2005, p. 13). What is your positon on a duty-based perspective toward research participants? How might reseachers move toward achieving such a perspective? Are there some research approaches that are more suited for a duty-based perspective than others? Weigh the pros and cons of such a perspective in designing and conducting research.

C H A P T E R   9

Small-N and
Single-Subject Designs

"**S**am" had not been an easy patient on the psychiatric hospital's inpatient ward. Although he was outgoing, friendly, and energetic, he also frequently chased, pushed, punched, and kicked peers and repeatedly hit himself on his forehead—to the point of causing abrasions. Those who knew his background were not terribly surprised by Sam's behavior: Sam had been diagnosed with schizoaffective disorder, bipolar type, mild mental retardation (his full scale IQ was 58), and a seizure disorder, and he took a range of medications for these disorders. Yet the psychologists and others on Sam's treatment team focused on his behavior during their assessment, not on his psychiatric symptoms per se, for it was his aggressive and threatening behavior that endangered Sam and other patients on their ward and prevented him from living in the community.

The plan developed to modify Sam's behavior focused on reinforcers that Sam had identified himself. In their article about this case, Dr. Sarah W. Bisconer and her colleagues (2006) mentioned reinforcers ranging from having a diet soda or hot chocolate to receiving stickers, listening to a Walkman, helping staff with meals, walking with staff, or even going to a restaurant. But would these reinforcers have the desired effect? In order to ensure delivery of the treatment program, the team psychologist trained the others in use of the reinforcers. In order to ensure maintenance of an objective behavioral record, the team psychologist developed a behavior checklist for the nurses to complete (see Exhibit 9.1; Bisconer et al., 2006). The combination of a treatment plan and a systematic scheme for observing target behaviors provides the basis for a single-subject design.

As clinicians, we must often give our attention to the progress of a single case and consider the progress of that case. Too often, we think we "know" when a client is improving and are too quick to attribute that improvement to our own treatment efforts. Single-subject designs provide an alternative, more systematic procedure for testing for changes in a subject's behavior. They were also recommended by B. F. Skinner for the behavioral analysis required in operant conditioning experiments (Saville, 2003). In this chapter, you will learn how single-subject designs can be used to systematically test the effectiveness of a particular intervention as well as to monitor client progress.

Single-subject designs (sometimes referred to as single-case designs) offer an alternative to group designs. The very name suggests that the focus is on an $N = 1$, a single subject, although many researchers instead refer to this type of design as a "small-N design" and apply it to between one and nine subjects. The structure of these designs makes them useful for research on interventions in behavior analysis and clinical practice, in which the focus is on a single individual (Saville, 2003; Yarnold, 1992). In particular, the clinical processes of assessment, establishing intervention goals and specific outcomes, providing the intervention, and evaluating progress have direct parallels to the structure of single-subject design, which depends on identifying target problems, taking preintervention measures, providing the intervention, taking additional measures, and making decisions about the efficacy of the intervention.

Contrast this design with group designs. In Chapters 6 through 8, we noted that group designs do not naturally conform to practice, particularly when the practice involves interventions with individuals. The analysis of group designs typically refers to the "group's average change score" or "the number of subjects altering their status." By describing the group, we miss each individual's experience with the intervention (Callahan & Barisa, 2005).

In this chapter, we first take you through the components of single-subject designs, including their basic features, measurement of the target problem, and

Exhibit 9.1 Behavior Plan: Target Behavior Data Form

Day	Shift	Aggression toward others	Aggression toward self	PRN	R
Monday	Day				
	Evening				
	Night				
Tuesday	Day				
	Evening				
	Night				
Wednesday	Day				
	Evening				
	Night				
Thursday	Day				
	Evening				
	Night				
Friday	Day				
	Evening				
	Night				
Saturday	Day				
	Evening				
	Night				
Sunday	Day				
	Evening				
	Night				

Source: From Bisconer, Green, Mallon-Czajka, & Johnson, 2006.

PRN, *pro re nata* medication, R, restraints.

Place a vertical mark (I) in appropriate cell for each incident of target behaviour or use of PRN medication or restraints.

interpretation of the findings. We then describe different designs and illustrate their roles in behavioral research, practice evaluation, and client monitoring. Finally, we discuss the generalizability of findings from single-subject designs and the ethical issues associated with single-subject designs.

FOUNDATIONS OF SMALL-N DESIGNS

The underlying principle of small-N and single-subject designs as a behavioral research tool is simple: If an intervention with a client, agency, or community is effective, there will be an improvement from the period prior to intervention to the period during and after the intervention. Formally, a small-N design is "an in-depth study of a single or relatively few subjects under tightly controlled experimental conditions in which the independent variable(s) is repeatedly manipulated over successive trials or conditions and in which the dependent variable(s) is repeatedly measured" (Saville & Buskist, 2003).

Small-N and single-subject designs typically have four components:

1. Repeated measurement of the dependent variable;

2. Baseline phase;

3. Treatment phase(s), with all subjects exposed to each phase;

4. Graphic display, perhaps supplemented by statistical analysis.

Repeated Measurement

These designs require the repeated measurement of a dependent variable or, in other words, the target problem. So, both prior to starting an intervention and during the intervention itself, you must be able to measure the subject's status on the target problem at regular time intervals, whether the intervals are hours, days, weeks, months, or the like. In the ideal research situation, measures of the target problem are taken with the client prior to actually implementing the intervention, for example, during the assessment process, and then continued during the course of the intervention. To gather information may mean withholding the intervention until the repeated measures can be taken. In the case of Sam, nursing staff assessed behavior three times daily for 3 months before the intervention began and then for 39 months afterwards. Alternatively, repeated measures of the dependent variable can begin when the client is receiving an intervention for other problems. For example, a child may be seen for behavioral problems, but eventually, communication issues will be a concern. The repeated measurement of the communication issues could begin prior to that specific intervention focus.

There are times when it is not possible to delay the intervention, either because there is a crisis or because to delay intervention would not be ethically appropriate. Yet, you may still be able to construct a set of preintervention measures by using data already collected or asking about past experiences. Client records may have information from which a baseline can be produced. Some client records, such as report cards, may have very complete information, but other client records, such as case files, may or may not. When using client records, you are limited to the information that is available, and even that information may be missing. Another option is to ask clients about past behavior, such as how many drinks they had each week in the last several weeks. Similarly, if permission is granted, significant members of the client's network could be asked questions about the client's behaviors. Trying to construct measures by asking clients or family members depends on the client's or family member's memories or opinions and assumes that the information is both remembered and reported accurately. Generally, behaviors and events are easier to recall than moods or feelings. Even the recall of behaviors or events becomes more difficult with the passage of time and probably should be limited to the last month. Although recognizing the limits of these retrospective data collection methods is important, the limitations should not preclude using the information if that is all that is available, particularly for evaluating practice.

There are other times when using retrospective data is quite feasible and realistic. Agencies often collect quite a bit of data about their operations, and these data can be used to obtain repeated measurements. For example, if an agency director was trying to find an outreach method that would increase the number of referrals, previous monthly referral information could be used and the intervention begun immediately.

Baseline Phase

The baseline phase, typically abbreviated by using the letter A, represents the period in which the intervention to be evaluated is not offered to the subject. During the baseline phase, repeated measurements of the dependent variable are taken or reconstructed. These measures reflect the status of the client on the dependent variable prior to the implementation of the intervention. The baseline phase measurements provide two aspects of control analogous to a control group in a group design. First, in a group design, we expect the treatment group to have different scores than the control group after the intervention. In a single-subject design, the subject serves as the control as the repeated baseline measurements establish the pattern of scores that we expect the intervention to change. Without the intervention, researchers assume that the baseline pattern of scores would continue its course. Second, in a control group design, random assignment controls for threats to internal validity. In a single-subject design, the repeated baseline measurements allow the researcher to discount some of the threats to the internal validity of the design.

Patterns

In the baseline phase, measurements are taken until a pattern emerges. Different types of patterns are summarized in Exhibit 9.2. One type of pattern is a stable line. A stable line, as displayed in Exhibit 9.2a, is a line that is relatively flat, with little variability in the scores so that the scores fall in a narrow band. This kind of line is desirable because changes can easily be detected (unlike the variable pattern in Exhibit 9.2b), and it is likely that there are few problems of testing, instrumentation, statistical regression, and maturation in the data.

Exhibit 9.2 Different Baseline Patterns

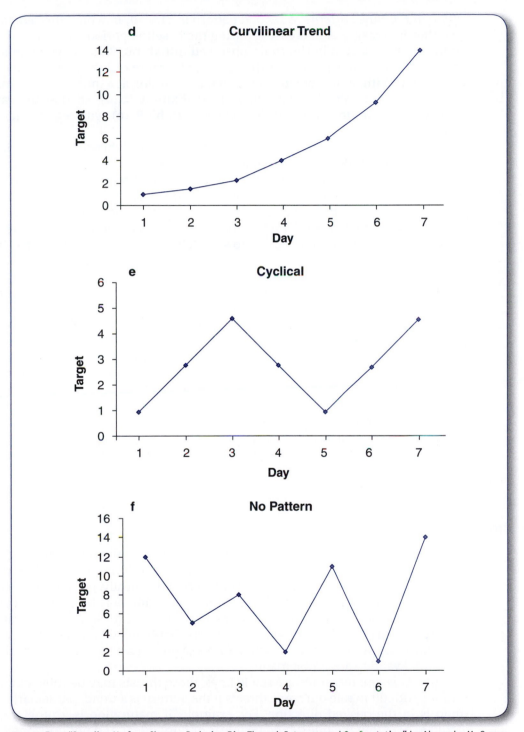

Source: From "Standing Up for a Change: Reducing Bias Through Interpersonal Confrontation" by Alexander M. Czopp, Margo J. Monteith, and Aimee Y. Mark in *Journal of Personality and Social Psychology, 90:* 784–803. Copyright © 2006 American Psychological Association.

Different Baseline Patterns. A second pattern is a **trend,** in which the scores may be either increasing or decreasing during the baseline period. Some trends may be linear, as reflected in the trend observed in **Exhibit 9.2c**. As you can see in this trend, the scores seem to be increasing at a more or less constant rate over time. You can imagine instead a trend that is declining at a more or less constant rate. Trends may also be even curvilinear (**Exhibit 9.2d**), so that the rate of change is accelerating over time, or **cyclical**, (**Exhibit 9.2e**), with regular increases and decreases.

Finally, there are situations, such as the display in **Exhibit 9.2f**, in which no pattern is evident. With such baseline patterns, it is important to consider the reasons for the variability in scores. Is it due to the lack of reliability of the measurement process? If so, then an alternative measure might be sought. On the other hand, the client may be using a good measure but not reporting information consistently, for example, completing a depression scale at different times of day. Also, the variability in scores may be due to some changing circumstance in the life of the client.

You know you have a pattern when you can predict with some certainty what might be the next score. To be able to predict the next score requires a minimum of three observations in the baseline stage. When there are only two measures, as in **Exhibit 9.3a**, can you predict the next score with any certainty? The next data point could be higher, lower, or the same as the previous data points (see **Exhibit 9.3b**). With three measures, your certainty increases about the nature of the pattern. But even three measures might not be enough, depending on the pattern that is emerging. In **Exhibit 9.3c**, is the pattern predictable? You probably should take at least two more baseline measures, but three or four additional measures may be necessary to see a pattern emerge. As a general rule, the more data points, the more certain you will be about the pattern; it takes at least three consecutive measures that fall in some pattern for you to have confidence in the shape of the baseline pattern.

Internal Validity

Findings of causality depend on the internal validity of the research design (see Chapter 6). When repeated measurements are taken during the baseline phase, several threats to internal validity are controlled. Specifically, problems of maturation, instrumentation, statistical regression, and testing may be controlled by the repeated measurement because patterns illustrative of these threats to internal validity should appear in the baseline. On the other hand, when the measurement in the baseline phase is reconstructed from existing data or memory, these threats to internal validity are problematic.

When baseline measures are stable lines, these threats may be ruled out, but it is more difficult to rule out some threats if the pattern is a trend, particularly if the trend is in the desired direction. For example, if maturation is a problem, you would expect that the line would be linear or curvilinear and not horizontal. Perhaps you have a client who has suffered a loss and you are measuring sadness. If there is a maturation effect, the level of sadness should decline from time point to

Exhibit 9.3   Predicting a Pattern

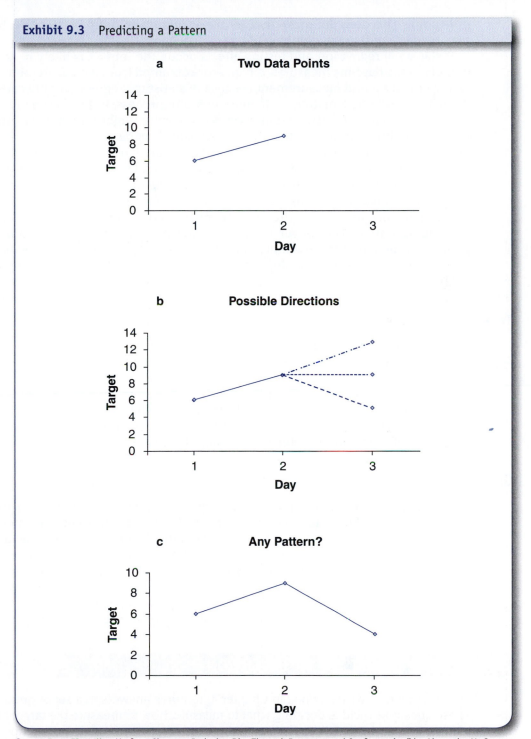

Source: From "Standing Up for a Change: Reducing Bias Through Interpersonal Confrontation" by Alexander M. Czopp, Margo J. Monteith, and Aimee Y. Mark in *Journal of Personality and Social Psychology, 90:* 784–803. Copyright © 2006 American Psychological Association.

time point. This does not mean that an intervention would not be effective, but it may be more difficult to demonstrate its effectiveness.

If statistical regression and testing effects occur, the impact is likely to appear initially in the baseline measures. A high score obtained from a measurement may be lower in a second measurement because of statistical regression or because of the respondent's acclimation to the measurement process. If there were only one baseline measure, then the first intervention measure might reflect these effects. But with multiple measures, the effect of statistical regression, if present, should occur in the beginning of measurement, and continued measurement should produce a stable baseline pattern. The testing effect should be observable early in the baseline measurement process as the subject adjusts to the testing requirements.

Repeated measurement in a baseline will not control for an extraneous event (history) that occurs between the last baseline measurement and the first intervention measurement. The longer the time period between the two measurement points, the greater the possibility that an event might influence the subject's scores. Later, we will describe single-subject designs that will control for the potential threat of history.

Treatment Phase

The **treatment phase**, signified by a **B**, represents the time period during which the intervention is implemented. As during the baseline phase, repeated measurements of the same dependent variable using the same measures are obtained. Ultimately, the patterns and magnitude of the data points will be compared to the data points in the baseline phase to determine whether a change has occurred. Tony Tripodi (1994) and David Barlow and Michel Hersen (1984) recommend that the length of the treatment phase be as long as the baseline phase.

Graphing

The phases of a single-subject design are virtually always summarized on a graph. Graphing the data facilitates monitoring and evaluating the impact of the intervention. The *y*-axis is used to represent the scores of the dependent variable, while the *x*-axis represents a unit of time, such as an hour, a day, a week, or a month. Although you may make your graph by hand, both statistical software and spreadsheet software offer the tools to present data in graphs. For example, James Carr and Eric Burkholder (1998) provide simple, step-by-step instructions for using Microsoft Excel to create graphs for different types of single-subject designs.

MEASURING TARGETS OF INTERVENTION

Measurement, as we described in Chapter 4, requires answers to a set of questions. These questions include deciding what to measure, how to measure the target of the intervention, and who will do the measuring. With each decision, there are important issues to consider. For behavioral research, there should be some certainty based on theoretical literature, empirical support, or practice experience to suggest that the chosen intervention is an appropriate method to address the target problem.

The dependent variable in a single-subject design is the concern or issue that is the focus of the intervention. This target for change may be one specific problem or different aspects of that problem. For example, Dr. Bisconer and her colleagues (2006) focused on both the frequency of Sam's aggressive behavior toward others and self and the frequency of his positive behaviors, such as voicing needs, using appropriate verbal greetings, and not touching others without permission. The target problems can be measured simultaneously or sequentially. In the study of Sam, they were measured simultaneously—at least three times daily.

Once the target of the intervention has been identified, you must determine how you will operationalize the outcome. Generally, in a research study, operationalization occurs prior to the beginning of the study. The "target behavior data form" developed by Dr. Bisconer and her colleagues required nursing staff to tally the frequency of aggressive behaviors three times each day.

Measures of behaviors, status, or functioning are often characterized in four ways: frequency, duration, interval, and magnitude.

- **Frequency** refers to counting the number of times a behavior occurs or the number of times people experience different feelings within a particular time period. This is the approached used for the study of Sam. Frequency counts are useful for measuring targets that happen regularly, but counting can be burdensome if the behavior occurs too often. On the other hand, if the behavior happens only periodically, the counts will not be meaningful.

- **Duration** refers to the length of time an event or some symptom lasts and usually is measured for each occurrence of the event or symptom. Rather than counting the number of aggressive behaviors three times per day, the nurses could have been asked to time the length of each aggressive outburst. The nurses would have needed a clear operational definition that specified what constitutes the beginning of an aggressive behavior and what constitutes the end of such a behavior. A measure of duration requires fewer episodes than do frequency counts of the target problem.

- Rather than look at the length of an event, we can examine the **interval,** or the length of time between events. Using a measure of interval, the nurses would calculate the length of time between aggressive behaviors. Just as a clear operational definition was necessary for the duration measure, they would need a clear definition when measuring the interval between aggressive behaviors. This kind of measure may not be appropriate for events or symptoms that happen frequently unless the intent of the intervention is to delay their onset.

- Finally, the **magnitude** or intensity of a particular behavior or psychological state can be measured. A scale might be developed by which the nurses rate or score the intensity of the aggressive behavior—how loud the screaming is, whether there is hitting that caused noticeable injury, and the like. Often, magnitude or intensity measures are applied to psychological symptoms or attitudes such as measures of depressive symptoms, quality of peer interactions, or self-esteem.

It is important to consider who will gather the data and to understand the potential consequence of each choice. Participants or clients can be asked to keep logs and to record information in the logs. Participants can complete instruments at specified time points, either through self-administration or by an interview. Or the behavioral researcher may choose to observe the participant's behavior. In addition, the reliability and validity of the instruments should have been tested on subjects of the same age, gender, and ethnicity as the client who is the focus of the single-subject design (Nelson, 1994).

A particular problem in gathering the data is the issue of reactivity. In Chapter 4, we suggested that it is important to have measures that are nonreactive; that is, you want measures that do not influence the responses that people provide. The very process of measurement might change a subject's behavior. If you ask a subject to keep a log and to record each time a behavior occurred, the act of keeping the log may reduce the behavior. Staff, knowing that supervisors are looking for certain activities, may increase the number of those activities. Tony Tripodi (1994) suggests that changes due to reactivity may be short in duration and observable in the baseline, so repeated measurements in the baseline might mitigate this problem. Nonetheless, it is important to recognize that there might be reactivity and to choose methods that limit reactivity.

An additional concern about measurement is the feasibility of the measurement process. Repeatedly taking measures can be cumbersome, inconvenient, and difficult. Is it going to be possible to use the method time and time again? Is the method too time-consuming for the subject and/or the researcher or practitioner? Will continuous measurements reduce the incentive of the subject to participate in the research or treatment?

Finally, the choice of measurement must be sensitive enough to detect changes. If the measuring device is too global, it may be impossible to detect incremental or small changes, particularly in such target problems as psychological status, feelings, emotions, and attitudes. In addition, whatever is measured must occur frequently enough or on a regular basis so that repeated measurements can be taken. If an event is a fairly rare occurrence, unless the research is designed to last a long time, it will be impractical to take repeated measures.

ANALYZING SMALL-N AND SINGLE-SUBJECT DESIGNS

When you are engaged with a client, you typically are most concerned about the client's status and whether the intervention is making a difference for that client. If the intervention seems to be making a difference, then you continue with the intervention as it is needed; if the intervention is not leading to meaningful change, then you will likely abandon the intervention and try another intervention or vary the intensity of the intervention you are already providing. Because the methods described in this chapter help you to *systematically* describe the changes that have or have not occurred with your clients, how then can we use single-subject designs to decide whether the intervention has been effective? One way is to visually examine the graphed data. Visual inspection is the most common method of evaluating the data, and in the following sections, we describe the presentation and possible interpretations of the data. A second option is to use a statistical technique such as the two-standard deviation-band, chi-square analysis, or time series to analyze the data (see Barlow & Hersen, 1984; Bloom, Fischer, & Orme, 2003; Franklin, Allison, & Gorman, 1997).

Regardless of whether you use visual inspection or one of these statistical approaches, the overriding issue is the practical (or clinical) significance of the findings. Has the intervention made a meaningful difference in the well-being of the subject? Although practical significance at times is subjective, there are several principles you might apply to reduce the uncertainty. These include:

- *Setting criteria.* One simple method is to establish with the client or community the criteria for success. If the intervention reaches that point, then the change is meaningful.

- *Cut-off scores.* A second method, particularly useful for psychological symptoms, is whether the intervention has reduced the problem to a level below a clinical cut-off score. For example, if you are using the Center for Epidemiologic Studies Depression Index, you would determine whether the depressive symptom scores fall below the cut-off score for depression for that particular scale. Visual inspection or a statistical test may lead you to conclude that the intervention did reduce the number of reported symptoms of depression, but the number did not fall below a cut-off score for depression. Is it a clinically meaningful change if the client is still depressed?

- *Costs and benefits.* A third way to view practical significance is to weigh the costs and benefits to produce the change (see Chapter 10). Do efforts to increase depression in a company's workforce result in sufficient change to be worth the cost and effort to produce the improvement in mental health?

Visual Analysis

Visual analysis is the process of looking at a graph of the data points to determine whether the intervention has altered the subject's preintervention pattern of scores. Three concepts that help guide visual inspection are level, trend, and variability.

Level

One option is to examine the **level** or the amount or magnitude of the target variable. A question that you might ask is whether the amount of the target variable has changed from the baseline to the intervention period. One option to describe the level is simply to inspect the actual data points, as illustrated in **Exhibit 9.4a**. It appears that the actual amount of the target variable—anxiety—has decreased.

Alternatively, the level of the phase scores may be summarized by drawing a line at the typical score for each phase separately. For example, the level may be summarized into a single observation using the mean (the average of the observations in the phase) or the median (the value at which 50% of the scores in the phase are higher and 50% are lower). The median is typically used in place of the mean when there are outliers or one or two extreme scores that greatly alter the mean. The mean of the baseline scores is calculated, and a horizontal line is drawn across the baseline phase at the mean. Then the mean of the intervention scores is calculated, and a horizontal line is drawn at the mean score across the intervention phase. How these lines appear is displayed in **Exhibit 9.4b**. The summary line for the baseline phase can then be compared to the summary line for the intervention phase. You can see how this method simplifies the interpretation of the level.

Changes in level are typically used when the observations fall along relatively stable lines. Imagine the case, displayed in **Exhibit 9.4c**, where there is an ascending trend in the baseline phase and a descending trend in the intervention phase. As you can see, the direction has changed but the mean for each phase may not have changed or changed only insignificantly.

Trend

Another way to view the data is to compare trends in the baseline and intervention stages. As we have suggested earlier, a trend refers to the direction in the pattern of the data points and can be increasing, decreasing, cyclical, or curvilinear. When there is a trend in the baseline, you might ask whether the intervention altered the direction of the trend. When the direction does not change, you may be interested in whether the **rate** of increase or decrease in the trend has changed. Does it alter the slope of the line? Because the published data from the study of Sam included only one data point to summarize behavior over the 3-month baseline period, we cannot use this method of comparing trend lines for the further analysis of these data. However, you can examine the reported trend after the baseline period to see if it seems that the behavior plan used by hospital staff to lessen Sam's aggressive behavior had any impact (see **Exhibit 9.5**). What would you conclude?

Variability

The interpretation of visually inspecting scores may depend on the stability or variability of the data points. By **variability** we mean how different or divergent the scores are within a baseline or intervention phase. Widely divergent scores in

Exhibit 9.4 Level

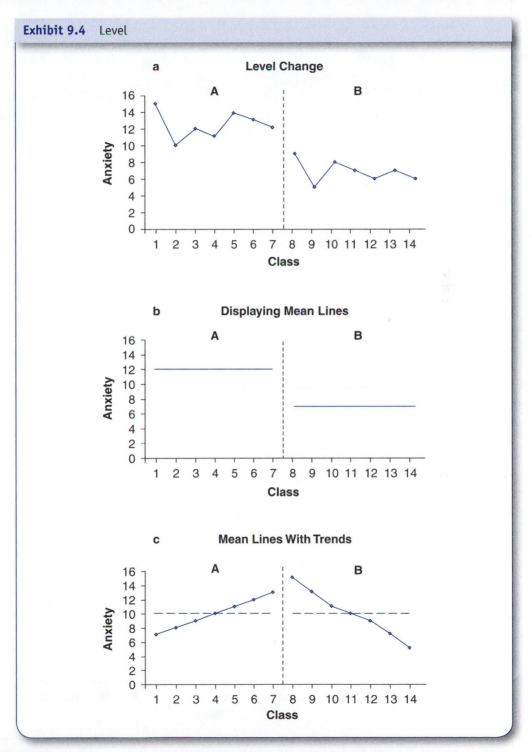

Source: Engel, R. J. and Schutt, R. K. (2009). *The practice of research in social work* (2nd ed., p. 219). Thousand Oaks, CA: SAGE.

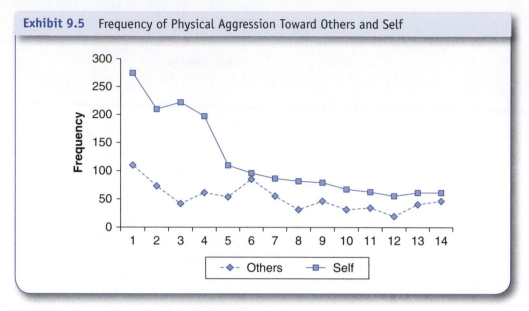

Exhibit 9.5   Frequency of Physical Aggression Toward Others and Self

Source: From Bisconer, Green, Mallon-Czajka, & Johnson, 2006.

the baseline make the assessment of the intervention more difficult, as do widely different scores in the intervention phase. One way to summarize variability with a visual analysis is to draw range lines, as was done in Exhibit 9.6. Whether the intervention had an effect depends on what goal was established with the client.

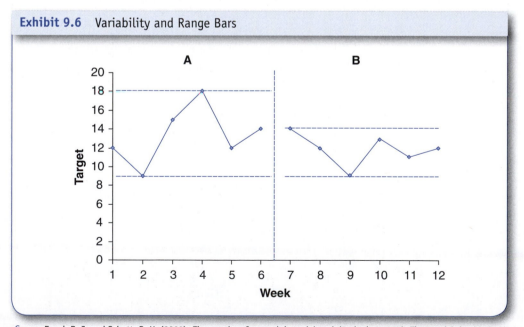

Exhibit 9.6   Variability and Range Bars

Source: Engel, R. J. and Schutt, R. K. (2009). *The practice of research in social work* (2nd ed., p. 222). Thousand Oaks, CA: SAGE.

As you can see in this graph, the only change has been a reduction in the spread of the points. But this does not mean that the intervention has not been effective, as it depends on the goal of the intervention. There are some conditions and concerns for which the lack of stability is the problem, and so creating stability may represent a positive change.

Interpreting Visual Patterns

We next turn to patterns of level and trend that you are likely to encounter, although the patterns we present are a bit neater or more ideal than what actual data might look like. Exhibit 9.7a displays a situation in which there is a stable line (or a close approximation of a stable line), and so the level of the target problem is of interest. The target in this exhibit is the amount of anxiety, with lower scores being desired. For Outcome A, the intervention has only made the problem worse, for Outcome B the intervention has had no effect, and Outcome C suggests that there has been an improvement.

In addition to the level–level comparisons, two other common patterns are displayed in Exhibit 9.7b, labeled Outcomes D and E. In both cases, there have been trend changes from no trend to a deteriorating trend, Outcome D, and an improving trend, Outcome E.

Exhibit 9.7c displays common patterns when there is a trend in the baseline. As you can see, the baseline phase is marked by an increase in anxiety from week to week. In the case of Outcome F, the intervention had no effect on the level of anxiety. For Outcome G, there was no change in the direction of the trend, but the rate of deterioration has slowed, suggesting that the intervention has been effective at least in slowing the increase of the problem but has not alleviated the problem. Outcome H represents the situation in which the intervention has improved the situation only to the extent that it is not getting worse. Finally, for Outcome I, the intervention has resulted in an improvement in the subject's status.

TYPES OF SMALL-N AND SINGLE-SUBJECT DESIGNS

You now have the different tools and components necessary to use a single-subject design. We will now describe the different types of these designs.

Basic Design (A-B)

The *A-B design* is the basic single-subject design. It includes a baseline phase with repeated measurements and an intervention phase continuing the same measures (see Exhibit 9.8).

This is the type of design that Dr. Bisconer and colleagues (2006) used in their study of Sam: They assessed Sam's behavior for 3 months (the "A phase"), then they implemented their planned treatment and continued to assess his behavior (the "B phase").

Exhibit 9.7 Typical Baseline-Intervention Patterns

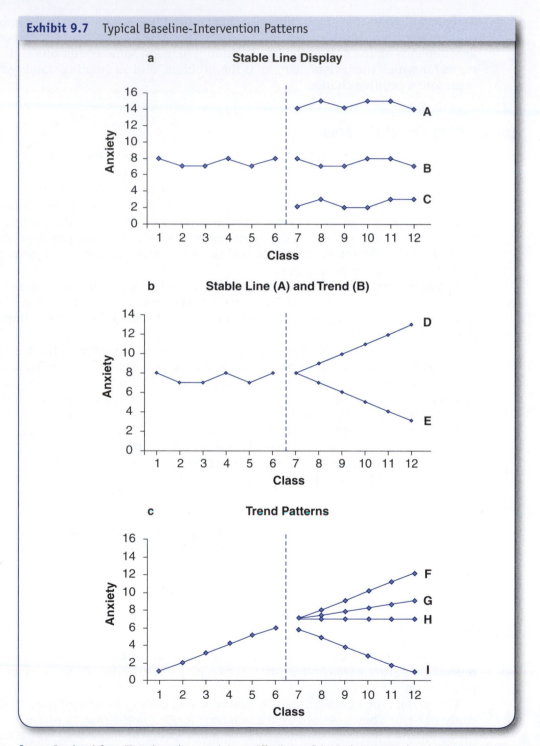

Exhibit 9.8   A-B Design of Behavior

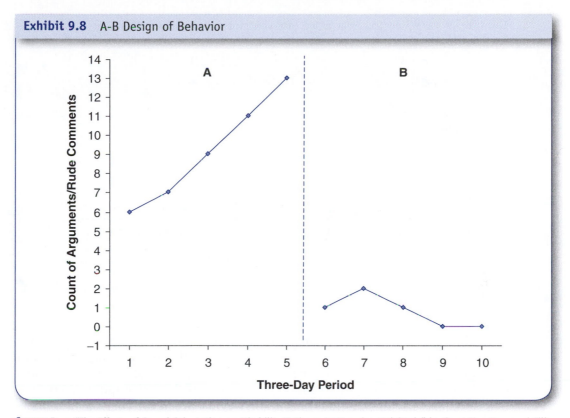

You have already seen in **Exhibit 9.5** that there was considerable improvement in Sam's behavior after the intervention began. However, you can also see in that figure that the frequency in Sam's aggressive behavior toward himself did not decline as much as the frequency of his aggression toward others, and there were increases in that behavior in intervals 4, 6, and 9. This same complexity in the B phase is also apparent in **Exhibit 9.9**, in which you can see some increases in staff injury in periods 4, 6, and 9. It is hard to know what to make of these fluctuations, since there was only one intervention and it is maintained throughout the B period. (And can you see how helpful it would have been to see what the trend was over a period of time during the baseline, "A," phase.)

The example points to the limits of the A-B design as a tool for research. The design cannot rule out other extraneous events, so it is impossible to conclude that the treatment *caused* the change. Perhaps the use of more psychotropic medication in periods 4, 6, and 9 (see **Exhibit 9.9**), not the treatment plan, was responsible for some of the reduction in aggressive behavior. More complicated single-subject designs can provide firmer answers to such questions.

Withdrawal Designs

There are two withdrawal designs: the *A-B-A design* and the *A-B-A-B design*. By withdrawal, we mean that the intervention is concluded (A-B-A design) or is

Exhibit 9.9   Frequency of Restrictive Interventions and Nursing Staff Injury

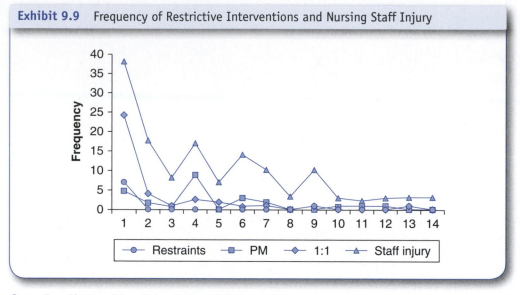

Source: From Bisconer, Green, Mallon-Czajka, & Johnson, 2006.

stopped for some period of time before the intervention is begun again (A-B-A-B design). The premise is that if the intervention is effective, the target problem should be improved only during the course of intervention, and the target scores should worsen when the intervention is removed. If this assumption is correct, then the impact of an extraneous event (history) between the baseline and intervention phase would not explain the change.

This premise, however, poses a problem. Ideally, the point of intervention is to reduce or eliminate the target problem without the need for ongoing intervention. We would like the impact of the intervention to be felt long after the client has stopped the intervention itself. Practice theories, such as behavioral or cognitive behavioral treatment, are based on the idea that the therapeutic effects will persist. This concern, referred to as the **carryover effect**, may inhibit the use of these designs for research.

A-B-A Designs

The A-B-A design builds on the A-B design by integrating a posttreatment follow-up that would typically include repeated measures. This design answers the question left unanswered by the A-B design: Does the effect of the intervention persist beyond the period in which treatment is provided? Depending on the length of the follow-up period, it may also be possible to learn how long the effect of the intervention persists.

The follow-up period should include multiple measures until a follow-up pattern emerges. The practicality of this depends on whether the relationship with the client extends beyond the period of the actual intervention. For example, the effect of an intervention designed to reduce problem behaviors in school might be amenable to repeated measurement after the end of the intervention, given that the client is likely still to be in school. On the other hand, a voluntary client who has come to a family service agency for treatment of depression might be more difficult to locate or might be unwilling to go through repeated follow-up measurements. In cases like this, consider simplifying and adapting the methods of collecting data to further reduce the burden on ex-clients, such as using phone interviews rather than face-to-face interviews.

Through replication and the aggregation of findings, the A-B-A design provides additional support for the effectiveness of an intervention. For example, Kirsten Ferguson and Margaret Rodway (1994) explored the effectiveness of cognitive-behavioral treatment on perfectionism by applying an *A-B-A design* to nine clients. They used two standardized scales to measure perfectionist thoughts and a non-standardized client rating of perfectionist behaviors. In the baseline stage, clients completed the measurement twice a week (once a week at the beginning of an assessment with the practitioner and once a week at home 3 days after the session). Data were collected over 4 weeks. The intervention stage lasted 8 weeks, with assessment prior to each counseling session, although only one follow-up measure was obtained, 3 weeks after the last counseling session.

A-B-A-B Designs

The A-B-A-B design builds in a second intervention phase. The intervention in this phase is identical to the intervention used in the first B phase. The second intervention phase makes this design useful for behavioral research. The design replicates the intervention. For example, if during the follow-up phase the effects of the intervention began to reverse (see Exhibit 9.10a), then the effects of the intervention can be established by doing it again. If there is a second improvement, the replication reduces the possibility that an event or history explains the change.

Just as with the A-B-A design, there is no guarantee that the effects will be reversed by withdrawing the intervention. If the practice theory holds, then it is unlikely that the effects will actually reverse themselves. So it may be that this first intervention period has to be short and ended just as evidence of improvement appears. Even if the effect is not reversed during the follow-up, reintroducing the intervention may demonstrate a second period of additional improvement, as displayed in Exhibit 9.10b. This pattern suggests that the changes between the no-treatment and treatment phases are due to the intervention and not the result of history.

Kam-fong Monit Cheung (1999) used an A-B-A-B design to evaluate the effectiveness of a combination of massage therapy and social work treatment on six residents in three nursing homes. Measurements included an assessment of activities of daily living and the amount of assistance received. In the first 7 weeks (the A phase), residents received their usual social work services, and in the second 7 weeks (the B phase), residents received massage therapy and social work services. In the third 7-week period (the second A phase), residents received just social work services, and in the fourth 7-week period (the second B phase), massage therapy resumed. The measurements at the baseline were retrospectively constructed from client, nursing aide, and social work assessments. Subsequent measurements were taken from logs and reported behavior by the clients.

Exhibit 9.10 Graphic Display of the Burns Perfectionism Scale

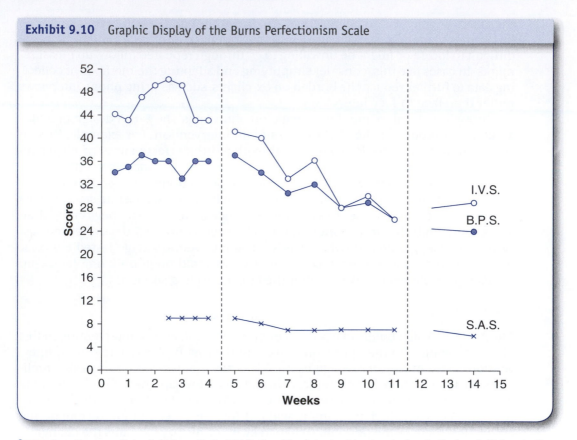

Source: From Ferguson, K. L., & Rodway, M. R. (1994). Cognitive behavioral treatment of perfectionism: Initial evaluation studies. *Research on Social Work Practice, 4,* 283–308.

Multiple-Baseline Designs

In the withdrawal designs, the individual serves as the control for the impact of the intervention. Yet the withdrawal designs suffer from the problem that often the target behavior does not reverse itself, and it may not be ethical to withdraw treatment early. A solution to these problems is to add additional subjects, target problems, or settings to the study. This method provides behavioral researchers with a feasible method of controlling for the effects of history.

The basic format is a **concurrent multiple baseline design** in which a series of A-B designs (although A-B-A or A-B-A-B designs could also be used) are implemented at the same time for at least three cases (clients, target problems, or settings). Therefore, the data will be collected at the same time. The unique feature of this design is that the length of the baseline phase is staggered (see **Exhibit 9.11**) to control for external events (i.e., history) across the three cases. The baseline phase for the second case extends until the intervention data points for the first

Exhibit 9.11   A-B-A-B Designs

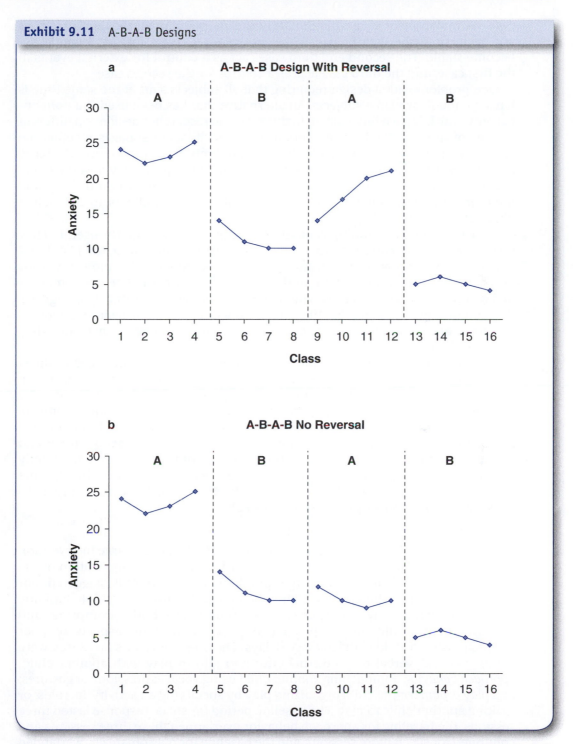

Source: Engel, R. J. and Schutt, R. K. (2009). *The practice of research in social work* (2nd ed., p. 232). Thousand Oaks, CA: SAGE.

case become more or less stable. Similarly, the intervention for the third case does not begin until the data points in the intervention phase for the second case become stable. The second and third cases act as a control for external events in the first case, and the third case acts as a control for the second case.

One problem with a design requiring that all subjects start at the same time is having enough available subjects. An alternative that has been used is a **nonconcurrent multiple baseline design**. In this case, the researcher decides on different lengths of time for the baseline period. Then as clients or subjects meeting the selection criteria become available, they are randomly assigned to one of the baseline phases. For example, Carla Jensen (1994) used this approach to test the effectiveness of an integrated short-term model of cognitive-behavioral therapy and interpersonal psychotherapy. Jensen randomly assigned clients to a baseline phase of 3, 4, or 5 weeks.

As a research tool, multiple baseline designs are particularly useful. They introduce two replications so that if consistent results are found, the likelihood that some external event is causing the change is reduced. If some extraneous event might have an impact on all three cases, the effect of the event may be picked up by the control cases. The pattern of change in **Exhibit 9.12** suggests that something occurred that affected not only Client A but also simultaneously Clients B and C, as they report changes and improvement even before they received the intervention.

Across subjects. When a multiple baseline is used across subjects, each subject receives the same intervention sequentially to address the same target problem. For example, David Besa (1994) used a multiple-baseline design to assess the effectiveness of narrative family therapy to reduce parent–child conflict with six families. Besa used a nonconcurrent approach because he could not find six family pairs to start at the same time. Families were started sequentially and essentially paired together based on the similarity of the problem. Each family identified a child's behavior that produced conflict. The length of the baseline varied: Family 1, 7 weeks; Family 2, 10 weeks; Family 3, 10 days; Family 4, 15 days; Family 5, 3 weeks; and Family 6, 4 weeks.

Across target problems. In this case, there is one client, and the same intervention is applied to different but related problems or behaviors. The application of the intervention as it relates to the target problems or behaviors is staggered. For example, Christina Johnson and Jeannie Golden (1997) used a multiple-baseline design to examine whether an intervention using both prompting and reinforcement would have a positive impact on different aspects of peer interactions for a child with language delays. The three behaviors measured were *social response,* verbal or nonverbal efforts to join in play with another child; *approach behavior,* approaching another child using vocal expressions or gestures; and *play organizer,* the child organizing play by specifying an activity, its rules, or inviting another child to play. The baseline period for social response lasted three sessions, the baseline for approach behavior overlapped these three sessions and continued for seven more sessions, and the baseline for play organizer overlapped the above two baselines and continued for four more sessions, lasting a total of

Exhibit 9.12   Multiple Baseline Design

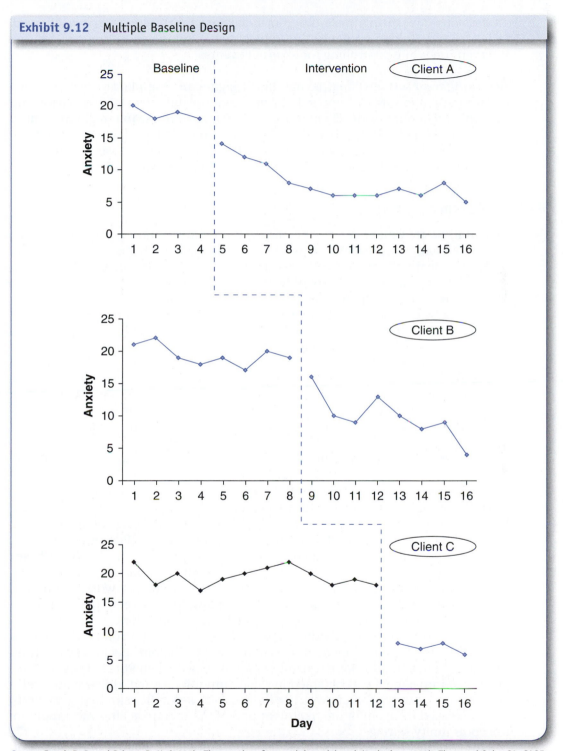

Source: Engel, R. J. and Schutt, R. K. (2009). *The practice of research in social work* (2nd ed., p. 233). Thousand Oaks, CA: SAGE.

14 sessions. Measuring these different behaviors for different periods allowed Johnson and Golden to determine which behaviors were influenced by the intervention while controlling for external events.

Across different settings. Multiple-baseline designs can be applied to test the effect of an intervention as it is applied to one client, dealing with one behavior but sequentially applied as the client moves to different settings. You might imagine a client with behavioral problems in school, at home, and at play with friends. A behavioral intervention might be used, with the application of rewards introduced sequentially across the three settings, starting with home, then school, then play.

Multiple-Treatment Designs

In a multiple-treatment design, the nature of the intervention changes over time and each change represents a new phase of the design. This is the design used by Paul L. Beare, Susan Severson, and Patricia Brandt (2004) in a single-subject study of a long-term adult hospital resident they called "Ed." Ed was profoundly mentally retarded, with an IQ of 16, never initiated conversation, and made no eye contact with others. Ed had moved 4 years earlier into a group home and was working in a sheltered workshop where he folded precreased corner pads used for packing furniture. Three challenging behaviors interfered with Ed's function-ing: self-injurious thigh slapping—so prolonged that it had led to a thick callous; vigorously tugging at his clothes—so vigorous that he destroyed some clothes each day; and restraining his own arms by crossing them under his legs. The treatment team developed a differential reinforcement plan in an attempt to reduce the self-injurious behavior. Preferred food was the chosen reinforcer. Ed's behavior was measured every 13 minutes throughout each 6-hour workday by a trained job coach. The specific measures are described in **Exhibit 9.13** (Beare et al., 2004).

Paul Beare and his colleagues (2004) developed what they termed an A-B-BC-BCD-BCD design for the single-study study of Ed. For the first intervention, Phase B, Ed received a food reward when he folded a pad. Ed's task engagement increased, but the slapping did not stop (**Exhibit 9.14**). Then, in Phase BC, Ed was given a food reward only when he folded a pad without slapping himself. In the BCD phase, reinforcement occurred only when both clothes manipulation and slapping were avoided. In the final BCD stage, Ed was moved to a community worksite and his behavior was observed there. **Exhibit 9.14** displays the apparent effects of these various treatment phases on the different challenging behaviors.

Take a minute to inspect **Exhibit 9.14**. You can see that time on task increased as soon as the food reinforcement started in Phase B. Slapping declined sharply at the start of Phase C and clothes manipulation dropped when Phase D began. This positive improvement was obtained in the community setting. However, the self-restraining behaviors, which were not the focus of a specific reinforcement strat-egy, decreased throughout the treatment period but then rose after movement to the community setting.

This complex research design yields a more convincing picture of the effect of the treatment program on Ed's behavior than would be possible with a simple A-B

Exhibit 9.13   Multiple Baseline Designs With History?

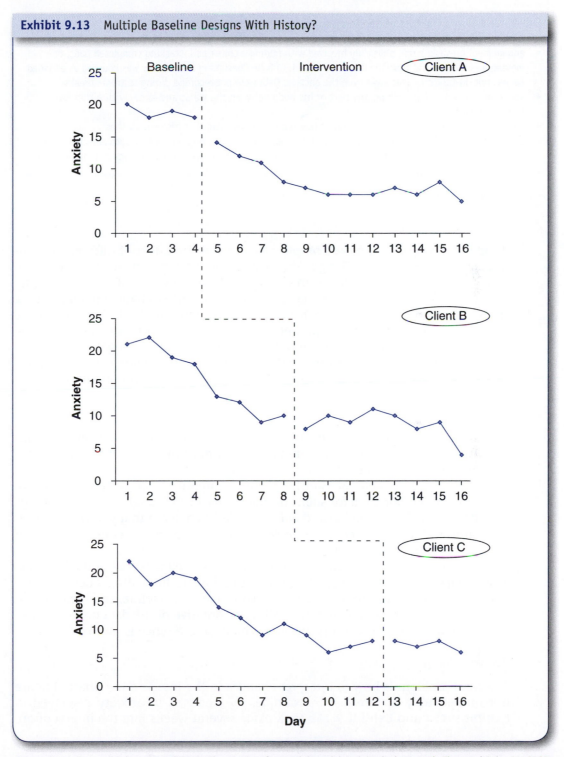

Source: Engel, R. J. and Schutt, R. K. (2009). *The practice of research in social work* (2nd ed., p. 235). Thousand Oaks, CA: SAGE.

> **Exhibit 9.14** Partial List of Challenging Behaviors
>
> - engagement on-task: being physically involved with folding a comer pad, stacking completed pads, or moving an unfolded pad from the floor to the work surface. Consuming a reinforcer was counted as engaged. Ed was not on-task if he was away from the enclave. Data were not recorded during restroom breaks.
> - self-injurious slapping: striking any part of his body between the waist and knee, with either hand, irrespective of force.
> - clothes manipulation: pulling, tugging, or holding on to any article of his own clothes.
> - self-restraint: clasping one or both hands under the opposite arm pit, trapping one or both arms between legs, placing one or both hands down front of pants, clasping hands together behind back or in front of self.

Source: From Beare, Severson, & Brandt, 2004, p. 34.

design. It also allows a more complete analysis of the effect of differential reinforcement: Ed's most challenging behaviors only changed when they were the focus of specific reinforcement; in general, reducing the rate of one challenging behavior did not also result in changing the rate of other challenging behaviors. However, it also appears that the frequency of self-restraining behavior might have varied in part in relation to the propensity to engage in the other behaviors. Thus, these rich findings also suggest the value of other lines of investigation.

Other types of multiple-treatment designs can change the *intensity* of the intervention, the number of treatments, or the nature of the intervention itself.

Problems of Interpretation

Dr. Bisconer's (2006) analysis of the case of Sam and the hypothetical examples presented earlier were quite neat, but the use of multiple treatments can complicate the analysis considerably—as can the complexity of the real world that you are studying. The results of Paul Beare and company's (2004) study of Ed give some idea of the potential for such complications, even though the basic findings of that study were straightforward. It is possible, even likely, that you will encounter patterns that are much more ambiguous and that make conclusions from visual inspection less certain.

One problem occurs when there are widely discrepant scores in the baseline, as was the case in **Exhibit 9.2f**. When scores in the baseline differ, it becomes difficult to determine whether there is any pattern at the baseline, and measures of level or a typical score may not be at all representative of the data points. Therefore, judging whether the intervention has made a difference is more difficult.

Delayed Change

A second problem is how to interpret changes in the intervention phase that are not immediately apparent. For example, the changes in anxiety displayed in **Exhibit 9.15a** and **Exhibit 9.15b** took place several weeks into the intervention.

Exhibit 9.15   Percentage scores for engagement on-task, self-slapping, clothes manipulation, and self-restraint exhibited by a 46-year-old worker with severe disabilities

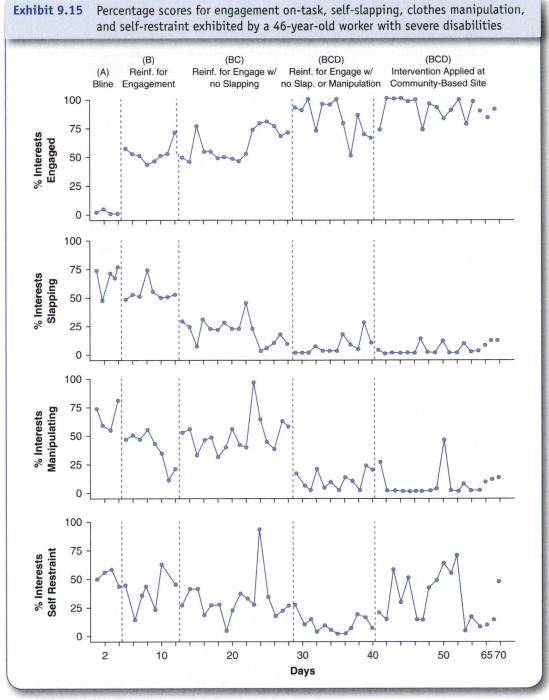

Source: From Beare, Severson, & Brandt, 2004, p. 38.

Is the change due to the intervention or is it due to some extraneous event or factor unrelated to the intervention? There is no easy answer to this question. It may depend on the nature of the intervention and when it is hypothesized that change will occur. Not all treatment modalities will produce instantaneous improvement. On the other hand, the alternative interpretation—"something else happened" (i.e., history)—is equally plausible.

Another problem occurs when there is improvement in the target problem scores during the baseline phase, even prior to the onset of the intervention. This improvement may occur for a variety of reasons, including the impact of an event or the passage of time (i.e., maturation). The effectiveness of the intervention may then depend on whether there is a shift in level or in the rate of the improvement. In **Exhibit 9.16a**, you see a pattern in which the intervention had no impact, as the improvement continues unchanged after the intervention has begun. Based on the pattern of scores in **Exhibits 9.16b** and **9.16c**, there may have been an intervention effect on the target problem. In **Exhibit 9.16b**, there was a shift in level, while in **Exhibit 9.16c**, the rate of improvement has accelerated. Of course, these changes may still be due to an event occurring between the last baseline measure and the first intervention measure.

Distorted Pictures

The act of graphing can create visual distortions that can lead to different conclusions As you can see in **Exhibit 9.17**, three different pictures of the baseline data appear, with the lines becoming increasingly flat, depending on the scale that is used on the vertical axis. Furthermore, the nature of the graph may prevent small but meaningful changes from being visually evident. So a small change in the unemployment rate may not be visible, yet the change includes the employment of many individuals. Therefore, when making a graph, it is important to make the axes as proportionate as possible to minimize distortions.

Statistical Analysis

Because of these problems of visual interpretation, some single-subject researchers have begun to analyze their data statistically. At first impression, it may seem peculiar to use statistics to analyze data from just one subject—or a very few subjects. But when there are many observations, it can be very helpful to use statistics to test for changes in levels or trends of the value of the dependent variable. Statistical tests may indicate that a trend that looks somewhat important when displayed in a graph is no different than what would be expected on the basis of chance. But in spite of the logical appeal of statistical tests, most single-subject (and small-N) data are still analyzed through visual inspection. The requirements that appropriate statistical tests impose on research design—such as having a prolonged baseline period or withdrawing the treatment at random intervals—can be difficult, if not possible, to impose in clinical settings. Moreover, the particular statistics most appropriate for these designs, such as time-series analysis and randomization tests, can be difficult to learn (Kazdin, 1982). So for now we just recommend that you should plan to review discussions of appropriate statistical tests if you plan to use a single-subject design (see Franklin, Allison, & Gorman, 1997).

Exhibit 9.16   Delayed Change

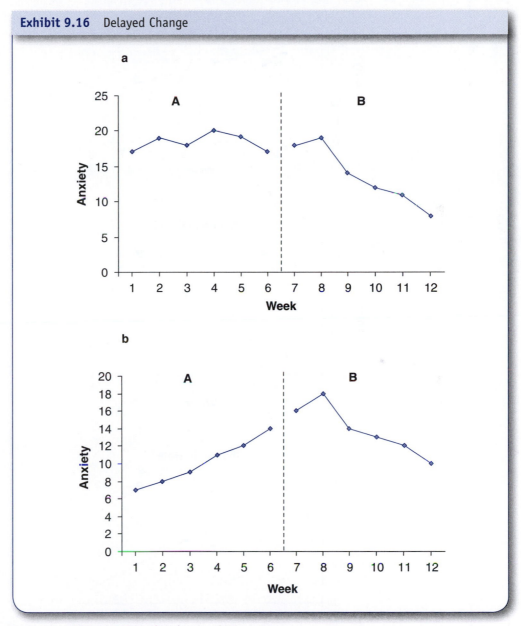

Adapted from Philips (1982:1347). University of Chicago Press.

Exhibit 9.17 Improvement in the Baseline

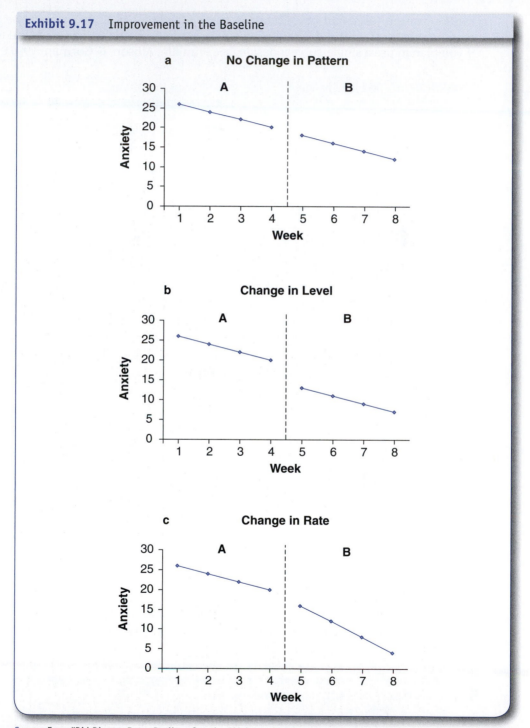

Source: From "Did Divorce Rates Decline after the Oklahoma City Bombing?" by Paul A. Nakonezny, Rebecca Reddick, and Joseph Lee Rodgers in *Journal of Marriage and Family*, Vol. 66, Issue 1, July 2004:90. Copyright © 2004 National Council on Family Relations. Reprinted with permission of Wiley Blackwell Publishing.

Exhibit 9.18   Distorted Pictures

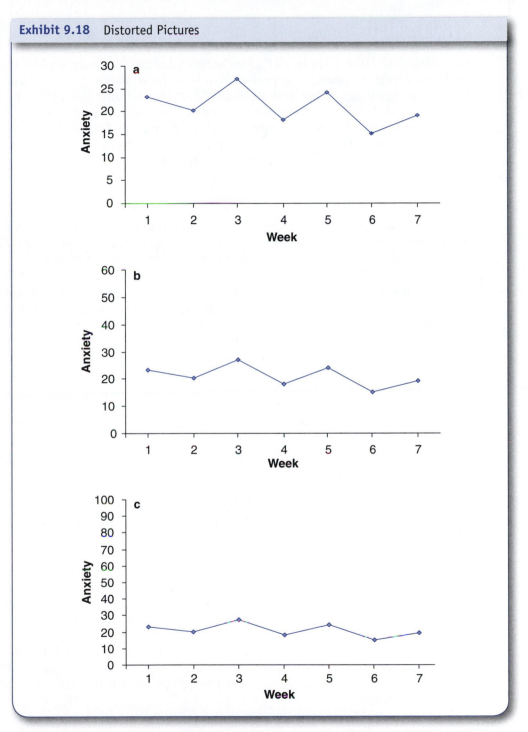

Source: Based on Cohen, Susan G., and Gerald E. Ledford, Jr. 1994. "The Effectiveness of Self-Managing Teams: A Quasi-Experiment." *Human Relations, 47*: 13–43.

GENERALIZABILITY

Generalizability in the context of single-subject design—or group design, for that matter—is not an issue of representativeness or drawing generalizations to broader populations; rather, it is an issue of external validity. Therefore, the ideal is to take what has been tested in one research context and apply the findings to different settings, clients, or communities, to other providers, and even to other problems related to the target concern of the research. To do so when the sample consists of a single subject engaged in a particular intervention provided by a particular individual is challenging. To demonstrate the external validity of single-subject design requires replication both of the research conditions and beyond the research conditions.

David Barlow and Michel Hersen (1984) suggest that three sequential replication strategies be used to enhance the external validity of single-subject design. These are direct replication, systematic replication, and clinical replication.

Direct replication. **Direct replication** involves repeating the same procedures, by the same researchers, including the same providers of the treatment, in the same setting, and in the same situation, with different clients. Barlow and Hersen (1984) would add that even the clients should have similar characteristics. The strength of the findings is enhanced by having successful outcomes with these other clients. When the results are inconsistent, differences in the clients can be examined to identify characteristics that may be related to success or failure.

Systematic replication. From direct replication, the next step is **systematic replication**, which involves repeating the experiment in different settings using different providers and other related behaviors (Barlow & Hersen, 1984). Systematic replication also increases the number and type of clients exposed to the intervention. Through systematic replication, the applicability of the intervention to different conditions is evaluated. Like direct replication, systematic replication helps to clarify conditions in which the intervention may be successful and conditions in which the intervention may not be successful.

Clinical replication. The last stage is **clinical replication**, which Barlow and Hersen (1984) define as combining different interventions into a clinical package to treat multiple problems. The actual replication takes place in the same setting and with clients who have the same types of problems. In many ways, findings from practice evaluation can enhance clinical replications.

For any replication effort to be successful, the treatment procedures must be clearly articulated, identified, and followed. Failing to adhere to the treatment procedures changes the intervention, and therefore, there is not a true replication of the experiment.

CONCLUSIONS

Single-subject designs are useful for doing research, evaluating practice, and monitoring client progress. Single-subject designs have been underutilized as a research tool by behavioral researchers. Yet researchers using these designs can make a unique contribution to clinical practice knowledge because so much of practice is with individuals. Done systematically, the success or failure of different interventions can be evaluated with distinct clients and under differing conditions. Single-subject researchers can also use statistical analyses to achieve more explicit tests for effects than have been possible with graphic techniques (Callahan & Barisa, 2005; Huitema, 2002; Yarnold, 1992). Furthermore, single-subject designs may be useful in understanding the process of change and how it varies with particular clients.

END OF CHAPTER

Chapter Highlights

- Single-subject designs are tools for behavioral researchers to evaluate the impact of an intervention on an individual.

- Single-subject designs have four essential components: the taking of repeated measurements, a baseline phase (A), a treatment phase (B), and data analysis (often based on graphing).

- Single-subject A-B designs can be improved by adding a treatment withdrawal phase (A-B-A), by using multiple subjects at different baselines, or by trying multiple treatments.

- Repeated measurement controls for many of the potential threats to internal validity. The period between the last baseline measure and the first treatment measure is susceptible to the effect of history.

- The baseline phase typically continues, if practical, until there is a predictable pattern. To establish a pattern requires at least three measurements. The pattern may include a stable line, an increasing or decreasing trend line, or a cycle of ups and downs dependent on time of measurement.

- Researchers often measure behaviors, status, or level of functioning. These measures are typically characterized by frequency (counts), duration (length of time), interval (time between events), or magnitude (intensity).

- Reactivity to the process of measurement may impact the outcomes, and efforts to limit reactivity are important.

- Data analysis typically involves visually inspecting graphs of the measurements. A researcher may look for changes in level (magnitude) or rate or in directional changes in the trend line or reductions in variability. The most important criterion is whether the treatment has made a practical (or clinical) difference in the subject's well-being.

- Results of single-subject designs can be difficult to interpret due to discrepancies in baseline measures, delayed changes, improvements in the baseline period, and distortions due to graphing. Some researchers use statistical tests to lessen these problems.

- Generalizability from single-subject designs direct replication, systematic replication, and clinical replication.

Key Terms

Baseline phase (A)   279

Carryover effect   294

Clinical replication   308

Concurrent multiple baseline design   296

Cyclical   282

Direct replication   308

Duration   285

Frequency   285

Interval   285

Level   288

Magnitude   285

Noncurrent multiple baseline design   298

Practical (or clinical) significance   287

Rate   288

Stable line   279

Systematic replication   308

Treatment phase (B)   284

Trend   282

Variability   288

Visual analysis   287

Research in the News

1. In "Exercise Your Brain, or Else You'll . . . Uh . . .," *The New York Times'* Katie Hafner reported on the many exercises that baby boomers are taking up to keep their brains active, reduce forgetfulness, and, hopefully, lessen the risk of Alzheimer's disease. Design a single-subject experiment to test the impact of one of these brain exercise games on a friend. What indicators could you use to track the impact of the game?

2. "Exercise, the studies increasingly suggest, may be as good for your brain as it is for your body," according to research reviewed in a *Boston Globe* article by Carey Goldberg on April 21, 2008. Consider your friends and their exercise patterns.

How could you design a single-subject study using an A-B-A-B design to investigate the effect of exercise on the mood of one of them? What challenges would you face in carrying out the study? What would be the advantages and disadvantages of carrying out this study if you were a therapist and your friend was a patient?

Activity Questions

1. Behavioral research seeks to confirm an intervention's effectiveness by observing scores when clients no longer receive the intervention. Yet the carryover effect may necessitate using a withdrawal design—ending a treatment prematurely—to do this successfully. Debate the merits of the withdrawal design in social work research. What are the advantages and disadvantages? Do the benefits outweigh the risks or vice versa?

2. Stress is a common occurrence in many students' lives. Measure the frequency, duration, interval, and magnitude of school-related stress in your life in a 1-week period of time. Take care to provide a clear operational definition of stress and construct a meaningful scale to rate magnitude. Did you notice any issues of reactivity? Which of the measurement processes did you find most feasible? Finally, do you believe that your operational definition was sufficient to capture your target problem and to detect changes?

Review Questions

1. Visual analysis is used to communicate the impact of an intervention in visual form. What are the three primary ways that the pattern of scores established during a baseline or intervention stage may be viewed? When is each of them best used? What information is conveyed and what information may be omitted by choosing each one of them over the others?

2. Single-subject designs lack the inclusion of additional subjects serving as controls to demonstrate internal validity. How do the measurements during the baseline phase provide another form of control?

3. Behavioral research seeks to confirm an intervention's effectiveness by observing scores when clients no longer receive the intervention. Yet the carryover effect may necessitate using a withdrawal design—ending a treatment prematurely—to do this successfully. Debate the merits of the withdrawal design in social work research. What are the advantages and disadvantages? Do the benefits outweigh the risks or vice versa?

4. Use of single-subject methodology requires frequent measurement of symptoms or other outcomes. In their *American Psychologist* article introducing single subject designs to the broader practitioner community, Jeffrey J. Borckardt and his colleagues (2008, p. 88) urge practitioners to discuss with patients before treatment begins the plan to use de-identified data in reports to the research community.

Patients who do not consent still receive treatment—and data may still be recorded on their symptoms in order to evaluate treatment effects. Should the prospect of recording and publishing de-identified data on single subjects become a routine part of clinical practice? What would be the advantages and disadvantages of such a routine?

5. What are the weaknesses of single-subject designs compared true experimental designs? In what circumstances are single-subject designs useful? Which features add to single-subject designs more of the strengths of true experimental designs? Explain your reasoning.

Ethics in Action

1. The relationship between the patient and therapist is the single most important factor in the therapeutic process. Do you think a therapist's use of a single-subject design to study the treatment process harms her relationship with the patient, presuming she told the patient? Should she share her findings with the patient after the therapy is concluded? While it is in process? What if the patient abruptly announces that he is terminating? Should therapists in private practice have to have their single-subject study plans reviewed by some type of ethics board?

2. As you learned in this chapter, single-subject designs have been used to study behavior modification with patients who were not considered intellectually capable of providing informed consent. Do you think that it is ever permissible to include such patients in single-subject research? Who, if anyone, should be authorized to give consent in these cases? What special protections should be required? Now compare your answers to those you can find in the FAQ list at the website of the Office for Human Research Protections, U.S. Department of Health & Human Services: http://www.hhs.gov/ohrp/informconsfaq.html.

C H A P T E R   1 0

Quantitative Data Analysis

DOES SPENDING MONEY ON OTHERS PROMOTE HAPPINESS?

Can money buy happiness? Yes, but not in ways you might imagine. According to a March 2008 article in *Science* (Dunn, 2008), social psychologist Elizabeth Dunn and colleagues found an interesting association between increased happiness and spending money on others. How did they show this? Dunn and colleagues performed three different types of research: a cross-sectional national representative survey, a longitudinal field study, and an experimental laboratory investigation. In each study, the researchers reported statistics that supported their hypothesis that spending money on other people has a more positive impact on happiness than spending money on oneself.

The Dunn experimental study provides a platform for us to introduce several common statistics used in psychological research. Following Dunn, we will imagine that we have 60 research participants rate their happiness in the morning and then we give each participant an envelope that contains either $5 or $20, which they are to spend by 5:00 P.M. that day. We randomly assign participants to either the *personal spending* condition in which they are instructed to spend the money on a bill, an expense, or a gift for themselves, or to the *prosocial spending* condition in which they are instructed to spend the money on a gift for someone else or for a charity. We thus have constructed two independent variables, each with two levels: amount of money given ($5 vs. $20) and spending (personal vs. prosocial). Now, we randomly assign 15 research participants to each of the resulting four conditions: (1) personal spending $5; (2) personal spending $20; (3) prosocial spending $5; and (4) prosocial spending $20. We call participants after 5:00 P.M. on that same day and ask them to rate their happiness from 1 to 10, with 1 = *very unhappy* and 10 = *very happy*. Thus, we have a 2 × 2 between-subjects factorial design. Our dependent measure is happiness rating.

In this chapter, we use the Dunn experimental design to learn how statistics can be used to test the hypothesis that spending money on others can promote happiness. We also use the 13-item maximization/satisficer questionnaire from Chapter 1 to learn how to employ statistics to analyze percentages and correlational data. Here we will imagine whether the percentages of maximizers and satisficers differ in young and older age groups. We will also examine the correlation of age and maximizer/satisficer score.

Think of this chapter as a review of fundamental psychological statistics if you completed a statistics course before you picked up *Research Methods in Psychology: Investigating Human Behavior* or as an introductory overview if your first exposure to statistics has been the statistics sections in our earlier chapters. Even though you can take a whole course on statistics for psychology (for good reason—there's a *lot* to learn), we don't want you to think of this chapter as something different from research methods. Rather, think of statistical analysis as flowing naturally from the design of a study and the method of observation or data collection.

STATISTICAL APPROACH

As we learned in Chapter 2, there are two major types of statistics. **Descriptive statistics** are used to describe the variables in a study, both one at a time and in terms of their relations to each other. In our example, we would report the composition of our sample with descriptive statistics about age, gender, socioeconomic status, and other such variables. We would also examine descriptive statistics for our dependent measure, happiness, and we would describe the relationship between variables in our study using other descriptive statistics. Much important research is purely descriptive, ranging from reports on self-esteem among college students to the prevalence of mental illness in the general population.

As you learned in Chapter 5, inferential statistics are used to estimate characteristics of a population from those we found in a random sample of that population. But inferential statistics can also be used for another purpose: to test hypotheses about the relationship between variables. How likely is it that the relationship we found between the independent and dependent variables in our experiment was due to chance? To put this inferential question another way: How confident can we be that the effect we observed was not simply due to chance? There are many different inferential statistical tests that help to answer this question in particular circumstances; we will present the most commonly used in this chapter.

Level of Measurement Matters

Before we calculate statistics involving a variable, we must identify that variable's level of measurement. You may recall from Chapter 4 that there are four levels of measurement: nominal, ordinal, interval, and ratio. Each level has different arithmetic properties and so different statistics are appropriate for variables measured at these different levels.

In the Dunn et al. example, the independent variable of spending (personal vs. prosocial) reflects a nominal scale of measurement. This represents a categorical variable in which participants are assigned either to spend on themselves or to spend on others. On the other hand, the dependent variable of happiness asks participants to rate their happiness on a 1-to-10 scale with 1 = *very unhappy* and 10 = *very happy*. This happiness variable uses an ordinal scale of measurement. An ordinal scale involves minimal arithmetic distinctions. It allows us to rank responses from lowest to highest, but it does not identify the numerical difference between responses of, say, 1 and 2 or 6 and 10. So even though we know that 1 is for *very unhappy* and 10 is for *very happy,* it does not really mean that a response of 10 is 9 units more happiness than a response of 1.

It is at the interval and ratio levels of measurement that the values of the variable reflect actual numbers on a scale with fixed intervals. In our study, we operationalized the independent variable, amount of money to spend, by providing participants with either $5 or $20. We know that $20 is $15 dollars more than $5 because we are using a scale with fixed intervals: dollars. In addition, that scale begins at an absolute zero point ($0), so the level of measurement is ratio. We can therefore calculate the ratio between the two values and conclude that $20 is four times greater than $5.

Although conceptually different, ratio and interval measures can be analyzed with the same statistical procedures. These procedures are more powerful than those that are allowable with an ordinal (or nominal) level of measurement. The levels of measurement of both independent and dependent variables are thus important factors to consider when designing experiments and other types of research and when planning statistical analyses of the resulting data. Now would be a good time to review our more complete discussion of levels of measurement in Chapter 4.

UNIVARIATE DISTRIBUTIONS

Both frequency distributions and graphs are used to describe the distribution of variables one at a time. As we will see, a univariate distribution is a probability or frequency distribution of only one variable.

Frequency Distributions

Often the first step in statistical analysis is to construct a frequency distribution for key variables. A **frequency distribution** shows the number of cases and/or the percentage of cases who receive each possible score on a variable. For many descriptive purposes, the analysis may go no further than a frequency distribution.

Constructing and reading frequency distributions for variables with few values is not difficult. For example, consider data from the 2006 General Social Survey on voting. The frequency distribution of voting in **Exhibit 10.1**, for example, shows that 69.2% of the respondents eligible to vote said they voted, and 30.8% reported they did not vote. The total number of respondents to this question was 4,126, although 4,510 actually were interviewed. The rest were ineligible to vote, just refused to answer the question, said they did not know whether they had voted, or gave no answer.

Political ideology was measured with a question having seven response choices, resulting in a longer but still relatively simple frequency distribution (see **Exhibit 10.2**). The most common response was moderate, with 38.9% of the

Exhibit 10.1   Frequency Distribution of Voting in the 2004 Presidential Election

Value	Frequency	Valid Percentage
Voted	3,037	69.2
Did not vote	1,089	30.8
Not eligible	335	
Don't know	34	
No answer	15	
Total	4,510	100.0
N		(4,126)

Source: National Opinion Research Center.

Exhibit 10.2   Frequency Distribution of Political Views

Value	Frequency	Valid Percentage
Extremely liberal	139	3.2%
Liberal	524	12.1
Slightly liberal	517	11.9
Moderate	1,683	38.9
Slightly conservative	618	14.2
Conservative	685	15.8
Extremely conservative	167	3.9
Total	4,333	100.0%

Source: National Opinion Research Center.

sample that responded choosing this label to represent their political ideology. The distribution has a symmetric shape, with somewhat more respondents identifying themselves as conservative rather than liberal. About 4% of the respondents identified themselves as extremely conservative and about 3% as extremely liberal.

Many frequency distributions (and graphs) require grouping of some values after the data are collected. There are two reasons for grouping:

- There are more than 15 to 20 values to begin with, a number too large to be displayed in an easily readable table.

- The distribution of the variable will be clearer or more meaningful if some of the values are combined.

Inspection of **Exhibit 10.3** should clarify these reasons. In the first distribution, which is only a portion of the entire ungrouped GSS age distribution, it is very difficult to discern any shape, much less the central tendency. In the second distribution, age is grouped in the familiar 10-year intervals (except for the first, abbreviated category), and the distribution's shape is immediately clear.

Once we decide to group values, or categories, we have to be sure that we do not distort the distribution. Adhering to the following guidelines for combining values in a frequency distribution will prevent many problems:

- Categories should be logically defensible and preserve the distribution's shape.

- Categories should be mutually exclusive and exhaustive so that every case should be classifiable in one and only one category.

Exhibit 10.3 Grouped Versus Ungrouped Frequency Distributions

Ungrouped		Grouped	
Age	Percentage	Age	Percentage
18	0.4%	18–19	1.5%
19	1.0	20–29	15.6
20	1.1	30–39	19.8
21	1.2	40–49	21.5
22	1.6	50–59	17.9
23	1.4	60–69	11.8
24	1.4	70–79	7.7
25	1.6	80–89	4.3
26	1.8		100.0%
27	1.9		(4,492)
28	1.8		
29	1.8		
30	1.9		
31	1.5		
32	2.2		
33	2.0		
34	2.0		
35	1.8		
36	2.3		
37	2.0		
38	2.1		
39	2.1		
40	2.1		
41	2.1		
42	2.2		
43	2.1		
44	2.2		
45	1.8		
46	2.0		
. . .	. . .		

Source: National Opinion Research Center.

Graphing

Several different types of graph are commonly used to depict frequency distributions. The most common and most useful are bar charts and histograms. For bar charts and histograms, each figure has two axes, the horizontal axis (the *x*-axis) and the vertical axis (the *y*-axis), and labels to identify the variables and the values, with tick marks showing where each indicated value falls along the axis.

A **bar chart** contains solid bars separated by spaces. It is a good tool for displaying the distribution of variables measured at the nominal level because there is, in effect, a gap between each of the categories. The bar chart of our 13-item maximizer/satisficer questionnaire that we introduced in Chapter 1 is presented in **Exhibit 10.4**. This bar chart graphs how many students were classified as either maximizers or satisficers on the 13-item maximizer/satisficer questionnaire. Seven students were classified as maximizers (scores > 61.75), and the remaining 22 students as satisficers (scores < 61.75).

A **histogram** displays a frequency distribution of a quantitative variable. **Exhibit 10.5** shows a histogram of scores on the maximization-satisficer question for a sample of 29 college students. The figure shows that the most common score was 53.00.

Both graphs and frequency distributions allow the researcher to display the distribution of cases across the categories or scores of a variable. Graphs have the

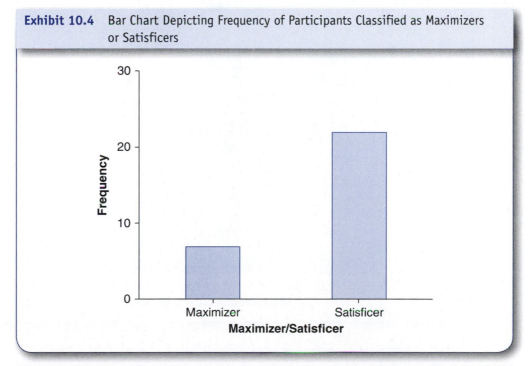

Exhibit 10.4   Bar Chart Depicting Frequency of Participants Classified as Maximizers or Satisficers

Source: From "Shocking numbers and graphic accounts: Quantified images of drug problems in the print media" by J. D. Orcutt and J.B. *Turner in Social Problems, 49,* 190–206, 1993.

advantage of providing a picture that is easier to comprehend, although frequency distributions are preferable when exact numbers of cases having particular values must be reported and when many distributions must be displayed in a compact form.

Beware of Deceptive Graphs

If graphs are misused, they can distort, rather than display, the shape of a distribution. Compare, for example, the two graphs in **Exhibit 10.6**. The first graph shows that high school seniors reported relatively stable rates of lifetime use of cocaine between 1980 and 1985. The second graph, using exactly the same numbers,

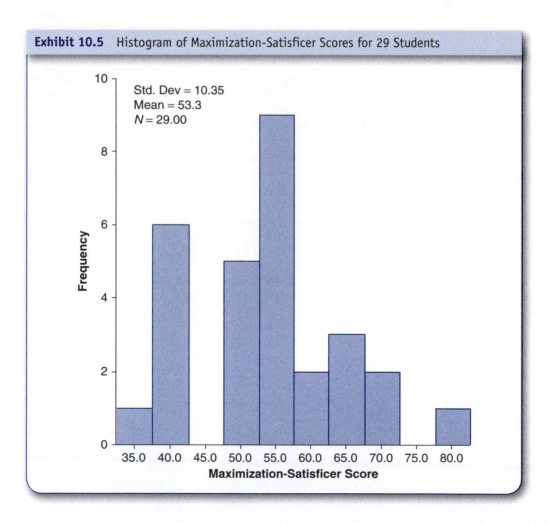

Exhibit 10.5 Histogram of Maximization-Satisficer Scores for 29 Students

Std. Dev = 10.35
Mean = 53.3
N = 29.00

appeared in a 1986 *Newsweek* article on the "coke plague" (Orcutt & Turner, 1993). To look at this graph, you would think that the rate of cocaine usage among high school seniors had increased dramatically during this period. But in fact, the

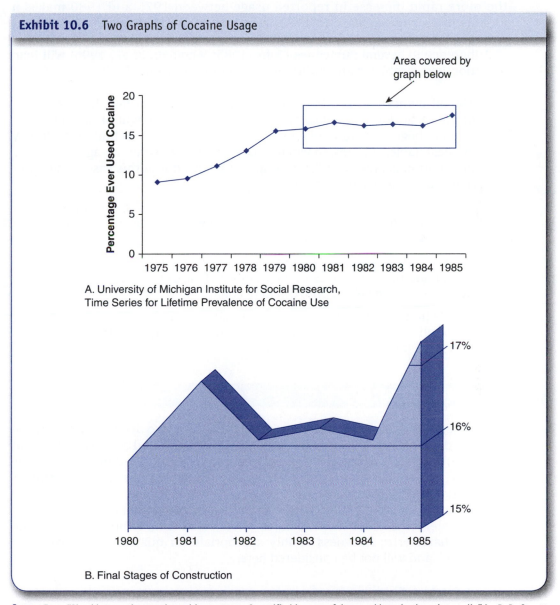

Exhibit 10.6 Two Graphs of Cocaine Usage

A. University of Michigan Institute for Social Research, Time Series for Lifetime Prevalence of Cocaine Use

B. Final Stages of Construction

Source: From "Shocking numbers and graphic accounts: Quantified images of drug problems in the print media" by J. D. Orcutt and J. B. Turner in *Social Problems, 49,* 190–206, 1993.

difference between the two graphs is due simply to changes in how the graphs are drawn. In the plague graph, the percentage scale on the vertical axis begins at 15 rather than at 0, making what was about a 1-percentage-point increase look very big indeed. In addition, omission from the plague graph of the more rapid increase in reported usage between 1975 and 1980 makes it look as if the tiny increase in 1985 were a new, and thus more newsworthy, crisis.

Adherence to several guidelines (Tufte, 1983; Walgreen et al., 1996) will help you spot these problems and avoid them in your own work:

- The difference between bars can be exaggerated by cutting off the bottom of the vertical axis and displaying less than the full height of the bars. Instead, begin the graph of a quantitative variable at 0 on both axes. It may be reasonable, at times, to violate this guideline, as when an age distribution is presented for a sample of adults, but in this case be sure to mark the break clearly on the axis.

- Bars of unequal width, including pictures instead of bars, can make particular values look as if they carry more weight than their frequency warrants. Always use bars of equal width.

- Either shortening or lengthening the vertical axis will obscure or accentuate the differences in the number of cases between values. The two axes should be of approximately equal length.

- Avoid chart junk that can confuse the reader and obscure the distribution's shape (a lot of verbiage or umpteen marks, lines, lots of cross-hatching, etc.).

DESCRIPTIVE STATISTICS

Whichever type of display is used, the primary concern is to display accurately the distribution's shape, that is, to show how cases are distributed across the values of the variable. Three features of shape are important: central tendency, variability, and skewness (lack of symmetry). All three features are represented in a graph or in a frequency distribution.

Descriptive statistics involve mathematical calculations that allow us to make precise statements about these features of collected data, although the statistic used to characterize skewness is only appropriate for quantitative variables, is rarely used, and will not be considered here.

Measures of Central Tendency

Central tendency is usually summarized with one of three statistics: the mode, the median, or the mean. For any particular application, one of these statistics may be preferable, but each has a role to play in data analysis. To choose an appropriate measure of central tendency, the researcher must consider level of measurement, the skewness of the distribution of the variable (if it is a quantitative variable), and the purpose for which the statistic is used.

Mode

The **mode** is the most frequent value in a distribution. It is also termed the **probability average** because, being the most frequent value, it is the most probable. For a nominal scale of measurement, the mode, defined as the most frequent score, is the only measure of central tendency. The mode indicates the most frequently occurring value. It is a simple count. It does not use the actual values of a scale, as we have seen in the gender example. The most frequent score or mode for our maximization/satisficer questionnaire was 53 (**see Exhibit 10.5**).

The mode is used much less often than the other two measures of central tendency because it can so easily give a misleading impression of a distribution's central tendency. One problem with the mode occurs when a distribution is **bimodal**, in contrast to being **unimodal**. A bimodal (or trimodal, etc.) distribution has two or more categories with an equal number of cases and with more cases than any of the other categories. There is no single mode. Imagine that a particular distribution has two categories that both have just about the same number of cases. Strictly speaking, the mode would be the category with more cases, even though the other frequent category had only slightly fewer cases. Another potential problem with the mode is that it might happen to fall far from the main clustering of cases in a distribution. With such a distribution, it would be misleading to say simply that the variable's central tendency was whatever the modal value was. However, when the issue is what the most probable value is, the mode is the appropriate statistic. Which ethnic group is most common in a given school? The mode provides the answer.

Median

The **median** is the position average or the point that divides the distribution in half (the 50th percentile). The median is inappropriate for variables measured at the nominal level because their values cannot be put in order, and so there is no meaningful middle position. To determine the median, we simply array the distribution of values in numerical order and find the value of the case that has an equal number of cases above and below it. If the median point falls between two cases (which happens if the distribution has an even number of cases), the median is defined as the average of the two middle values and is computed by adding the values of the two middle cases and dividing by 2. The median in a frequency distribution is determined by identifying the value corresponding to a cumulative percentage of 50. In our example, the median, abbreviated as *Mdn*, was 53 for our maximization/satisficer questionnaire, which as you can see is identical to the mode.

Mean

The **mean**, or arithmetic average, takes into account the value of each case in a distribution; it is a weighted average. The mean is computed by adding up the values of all the cases and dividing by the total number of cases, thereby taking into account the value of each case in the distribution:

Mean = Sum of value of cases/Number of cases

In algebraic notation, the equation is $\bar{Y} = \Sigma Y_i/N$. For example, to calculate the mean of eight cases, we add the values of all the cases (ΣY_i) and divide by the number of cases (N):

$$(28 + 117 + 42 + 10 + 77 + 51 + 64 + 55)/8 = 444/8 = 55.5$$

Because computing the mean requires adding up the values of the cases, it makes sense to compute a mean only if the values of the cases can be treated as actual quantities—that is, if they reflect an interval or ratio level of measurement, or if they are ordinal and we assume that ordinal measures can be treated as interval. It would make no sense to calculate the mean of a variable measured at the nominal level, such as religion. For example, imagine a group of four people in which there were two Protestants, one Catholic, and one Jew. To calculate the mean, you would need to solve the equation (Protestant + Protestant + Catholic + Jew) + 4 = ? Even if you decide that Protestant = 1, Catholic = 2, and Jew = 3 for data entry purposes, it still doesn't make sense to add these numbers because they don't represent quantities of religion.

By contrast, it makes perfect sense to compute the mean score for the maximization/satisficer questionnaire from Chapter 1 that we gave to our class of 29 students. We found a mean score of 53.28 for the maximization/satisficer questionnaire, with scores ranging from a low of 36 to a high of 78. We can see that our three measures of central tendency are nearly identical. Three measure of central tendency all falling together characterizes a symmetric distribution of values for the maximization/satisficer questionnaire. This can be seen in the histogram plotting the maximizer/satisficer scores in **Exhibit 10.5**.

Median vs. Mean

Both the median and the mean are used to summarize the central tendency of quantitative variables, but their suitability for a particular application must be carefully assessed. The key issues to be considered in this assessment are the variable's level of measurement, the shape of its distribution, and the purpose of the statistical summary. Consideration of these issues will sometimes result in a decision to use both the median and the mean and will sometimes result in neither measure being seen as preferable. But in many other situations, the choice between the mean and median will be clear-cut as soon as the researcher takes the time to consider these three issues.

Level of measurement is a key concern because to calculate the mean, we must add up the values of all the cases—a procedure that assumes the variable is measured at the interval or ratio level. So even though we know that coding *Agree* as 2 and *Disagree* as 3 does not really mean that *Disagree* is 1 unit more of disagreement than *Agree,* the mean assumes this evaluation to be true. Because calculation of the median requires only that we order the values of cases, we do not have to make this assumption. Technically speaking, then, the mean is simply an inappropriate statistic for variables measured at the ordinal level (and you already know that it is completely meaningless for variables measured at the nominal level). In practice, however, many social researchers use the mean to describe the central tendency of variables measured at the ordinal level.

The shape of the distribution of a variable should also be taken into account when deciding whether to use the median or mean. When a distribution is perfectly symmetric, so that the distribution of values below the median is a mirror image of the distribution of values above the median, the mean and median will be the same. But the values of the mean and median are affected differently by skewness, or the presence of cases with extreme values on one side of the distribution but not the other side. Because the median takes into account only the number of cases above and below the median point, not the value of these cases, it is not affected in any way by extreme values. Because the mean is based on adding the values of all the cases, it will be pulled in the direction of exceptionally high (or low) values. When the value of the mean is larger than the value of the median, we know that the distribution is skewed in a positive direction, with proportionately more cases with higher than lower values. When the mean is smaller than the median, the distribution is skewed in a negative direction.

This differential impact of skewness on the median and mean is illustrated in **Exhibit 10.7**. On the first balance beam, the cases (bags) are spread out equally, and the median and mean are in the same location. On the second and third balance beams, the median corresponds to the value of the middle case, but the mean is pulled toward the value of the one case with an extremely high value. For this reason, the mean age (47.1) for the 4,492 cases represented partially in the detailed age distribution in **Exhibit 10.3** is higher than the median age (46). Although in the distribution represented in **Exhibit 10.3** the difference is small, in some distributions the two measures will have markedly different values, and in such instances the median may be preferred.

The single most important influence on the choice of the median or the mean for summarizing the central tendency of quantitative variables should be the purpose of the statistical summary. If the purpose is to report the middle position in one or more distributions, then the median is the proper statistic, whether or not the distribution is skewed. For example, data from the 2006 General Social Survey indicate a median age of 46 years for the U.S. population. This means half the U.S. population is younger than 46 years old, and half the population is older than that. However, if

Exhibit 10.7 The Mean as a Balance Point

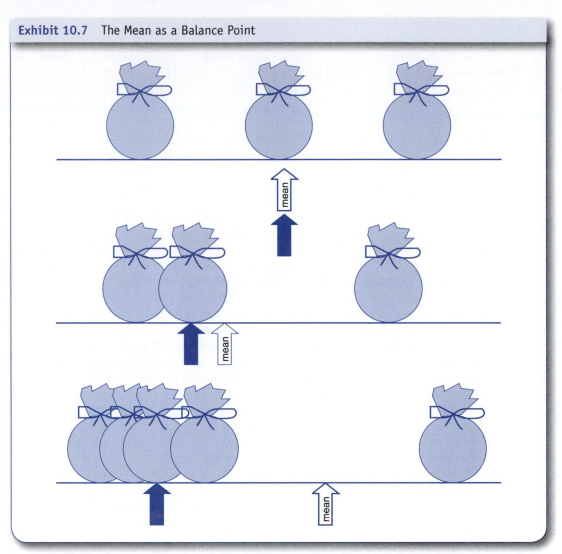

Source: Schutt, R. K. (2009). *Investigating the social world: The process and practice of research* (6th ed., p. 507). Thousand Oaks, CA: Pine Forge Press.

the purpose of the research is to show how likely different groups are to have age-related health problems, the measure of central tendency for these groups should take into account people's ages, not just the number of people who are older and younger than a particular age. For this purpose, the median would be inappropriate, because it would not distinguish between two distributions like those presented in Exhibit 10.8. In the top distribution, everyone is between the ages of 35 and 45, with a median of 41. In the bottom distribution, the median is still 41, but almost half of the cases (4/9, 44%) have ages above 60. Here in the second distribution, despite a median of 41 identical to the first distribution, the higher mean captures the important fact that it has a greater number of older people.

Exhibit 10.8   Insensitivity of Median to Variation at End of Distribution

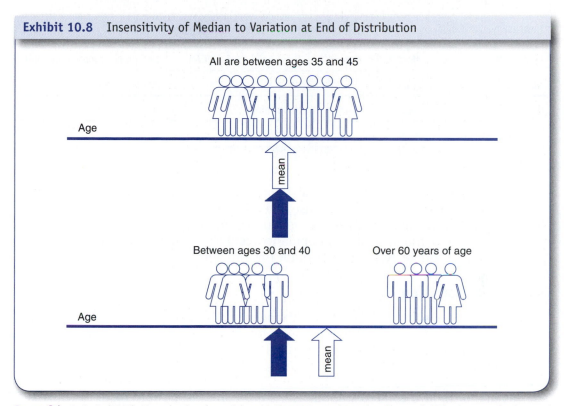

Source: Schutt, R. K. (2009). *Investigating the social world: The process and practice of research* (6th ed., p. 508). Thousand Oaks, CA: Pine Forge Press.

Keep in mind that it is not appropriate to use either the median or the mean as a measure of central tendency for variables measured at the nominal level, because at this level of measurement, the different attributes of a variable cannot be ordered as higher or lower (see **Exhibit 10.9**). Technically speaking, the mode should be used to assess the central tendency of variables measured at the nominal level (and it can be used with variables measured at the ordinal, interval, and ratio levels). The median is most suited to assess the central tendency of variables measured at the ordinal level (and it can also be used to measure the central tendency of variables at the interval and ratio levels). Finally, the mean is only suited to measuring the central tendency of variables measured at the interval and ratio levels.

It is not entirely legitimate to represent the central tendency of a variable measured at the ordinal level with the mean: Calculation of the mean requires summing the values of all the cases, and at the ordinal level, these values indicate only order, not actual quantities. Nonetheless, many social scientists use the mean with ordinal-level variables and find that this is potentially useful for comparisons among variables and as a first step in more complex statistical analyses. As shown in **Exhibit 10.9**, the median and mode can also be useful as measures of central tendency for variables measured at interval and ratio levels when the goal is indicate middle position (median) or the most frequent value.

Exhibit 10.9 Measures of Central Tendency (MCT) and Scales of Measurement

Level of Measurement	Most Appropriate MCT	Potentially Useful MCT	Definitely Inappropriate MCT
Nominal	Mode	None	Median, mean
Ordinal	Median	Mean, mode	None
Interval, ratio	Mean	Median, mode	None

Note: MCT = measure of central tendency.

In general, the mean is the most common measure of central tendency for quantitative variables, both because it takes into account the value of all cases in the distribution and because it is the foundation for many other advanced statistics. However, the mean's very popularity results in its use in situations for which it is inappropriate. Keep an eye out for this problem.

Measures of Variation

You already have learned that central tendency is only one aspect of the shape of a distribution—the most important aspect for many purposes but still just a piece of the total picture. A summary of distributions based only on their central tendency can be very incomplete, even misleading. For example, three towns might have the same median income but still be very different in their social character due to the shape of their income distributions. As illustrated in **Exhibit 10.10**, Town A is a homogeneous middle-class community; Town B is very heterogeneous; and Town C has a polarized, bimodal income distribution, with mostly very poor and very rich people and few in between. However, all three towns have the same median income.

The way to capture these differences is with statistical measures of variation or variability. Three popular measures of variability in a set of data are the range, the variance, and the standard deviation (which is the most popular measure of variability). To calculate each of these measures, the variable must be at the interval or ratio level (but many would argue that, like the mean, they can be used with ordinal-level measures, too). Statistical measures of variation are used infrequently with variables measured at the nominal level, so these other measures will not be presented here. It's important to realize that measures of variability are descriptive statistics that capture only part of what we need to be concerned with about the distribution of a variable. In particular, they do not tell us about the extent to which a distribution is skewed, which we've seen is very important for interpreting measures of central tendency. Researchers usually evaluate the skewness of distributions just by eyeballing them.

Range

The **range** is a simple measure of variation, calculated as the highest value in a distribution minus the lowest value, plus 1:

$$\text{Range} = \text{Highest value} - \text{Lowest value} + 1$$

Exhibit 10.10   Frequency Polygon of Years of Education

Source: National Opinion Research Center.

It often is important to report the range of a distribution to identify the whole range of possible values that might be encountered. However, because the range can be drastically altered by just one exceptionally high or low value (termed an **outlier**), it does not do an adequate job of summarizing the extent of variability in a distribution.

Variance

The **variance** is the average squared deviation of each case from the mean, so it takes into account the amount by which each case differs from the mean. An example of how to calculate the variance, using the following formula:

$$\sigma^2 = \frac{\Sigma(y_i - \bar{y}_i)^2}{N}$$

Symbol key: $\bar{Y}$ = mean; N = number of cases; Σ = sum of all cases; Y_i = value of case i on variable Y; σ^2 = variance. **Exhibit 10.11** shows an example of calculating the variance. The variance is used in many other statistics, although it is more conventional to measure variability with the closely related standard deviation than with the variance.

Standard Deviation

The **standard deviation** is simply the square root of the variance. It is the square root of the average squared deviation of each case from the mean:

$$\sigma = \sqrt{\frac{\Sigma(Y_i - \bar{Y}_i)^2}{N}}$$

Symbol key: $\bar{Y}$ = mean; N = number of cases; $\sum$ = sum of all cases; Y_i = value of case i variable Y; $\sqrt{}$ = square root; σ = standard deviation.

Standard deviation is thus the square root of the average squared deviation of each case from the mean. When the standard deviation is calculated from sample data, the denominator is supposed to be $N - 1$, rather than N, an adjustment that has no discernible effect when the number of cases is reasonably large. You also should note that the use of *squared* deviations in the formula accentuates the

Exhibit 10.11   Calculation of the Variance Y = 24.27, Variance = 434.15, *SD* = 20.81

Case #	Score (Y_i)	Y_i - $\bar{Y}$ (mean)	$(Y_i - \bar{Y})^2$
1	21	−3.27	10.69
2	30	5.73	32.83
3	15	−9.27	85.93
4	18	−6.27	39.31
5	25	0.73	0.53
6	32	7.73	59.75
7	19	−5.27	27.77
8	21	−3.27	10.69
9	23	−1.27	1.61
10	37	12.73	162.05
11	26	1.73	2.99
Total			434.15

impact of relatively large deviations, because squaring a large number makes that number count much more.

The standard deviation can be used to answer two simple questions: (1) How much variation, dispersion, or spread is there in a set of scores, numbers, or data points? and (2) How far from the average is a particular score? In our example using the maximizer/satisficer questionnaire, our group had a standard deviation of 10.35 on this test. As we will learn, this standard deviation value tells us that most of the students (approximately 68%) in our sample had scores on the questionnaire 10.35 points above or below the mean. That is, for the maximizer/satisficer questionnaire, our group had a mean of 53.28, with most scores falling between 42.93, that is (53.28 − 10.35), and 63.30, that is (53.28 + 10.35). We can also say that a student with a score of 63.30 falls "one standard deviation unit above the mean." In the next section, you will learn the importance of a statement like this.

SAMPLING DISTRIBUTIONS

You learned about sampling distributions in Chapter 5. The basic idea was that the value of the mean or any other statistic we obtain for a random sample is not likely to equal exactly the population mean or, more generally, the population **parameter**. By chance alone, any sample statistic, such as the mean, is very likely to be a little bit lower or a little bit higher than a hypothetical population parameter; sometimes the sample statistic will be quite a bit higher or lower than the population parameter. You can think of the mean for this sample as being one of the mean values we would obtain if we repeatedly drew new random samples from the population—in fact, we can imagine that we draw an infinite number of random samples from this population and calculate the mean of each. The distribution of the means of all these samples would be a **sampling distribution** (distribution of sample statistics).

The mean of the distribution of sample means is the actual population mean. We can calculate a statistic called the **standard error of the mean** to indicate the degree to which the means of the samples vary from the population mean. You can think of the standard error as an estimate of the standard deviation of the sampling distribution.

INFERENTIAL STATISTICS

You might wonder how we can calculate the mean and standard deviation of the sampling distribution when we can't possibly draw an infinite number of random samples from a population and calculate the means of all those samples. Well, the fact is that we can't. However, what we can do is determine how confident we can be that the mean (or some other statistic) of a random sample from a population is within a certain range of the population mean. This is the logic behind calculating confidence limits around the mean, as we did in Chapter 5. And as you recall, confidence limits assume a normal distribution of values. A normal distribution is a distribution that results from chance variation around a mean. It is symmetric and tapers off in a characteristic shape from its mean. If a variable is normally distributed (see **Exhibit 10.12**), 68% of the cases will be between plus and minus 1 standard deviation from the distribution's mean, and 95% of the cases will lie between plus and minus 1.96 standard deviations from the mean. And as we will learn, this correspondence of the standard deviation to the normal distribution enables us to infer how confident we can be that the mean (or some other statistic) of a population sampled randomly is within a certain range of the hypothetical population mean. Now that you know how to compute the standard deviation, it is just a short additional step to computation of the confidence limits around a mean. There are just four more steps:

1. Calculate the standard error (*SE*). This is the estimated value of the standard deviation of the sampling distribution (σ) from which your sample was selected. It equals the standard deviation divided by the square root of the sample size minus 1: $SE = \sigma\sqrt{(n-1)}$.

2. Decide on the degree of confidence that you wish to have that the population parameter falls within the confidence interval you compute. It is conventional to calculate the 95%, 99%, or even the 99.9% confidence limits around the mean. Most often, the 95% confidence limits are used, so we will just show the calculation for this estimate.

3. Multiply the value of the *SE* × 1.96. This is because 95% of the area under the normal curve falls within ±1.96 standard deviation units of the mean.

4. Add and subtract the number in step 3 from the sample mean. The resulting numbers are the upper and lower confidence limits.

Recall that the standard deviation for the maximization/satisficer questionnaire is 10.35 for our sample of 29 students. The standard error of the mean is the standard deviation of 10.35 divided by the square root of the sample size of 29, minus 1. This equals a standard error of the mean of 1.96 for the maximization/satisficer questionnaire. Multiply *SE* of 1.96 by 1.96 because 95% of the area under the normal curve falls within ±1.96 standard deviation units of the mean (step 3). Thus we can say with 95% certainty that the population mean is within 3.84 +/– of the obtained sample mean of 53.28 for the satisficer/maximizer questionnaire: The 95% confidence interval of the mean is 49.44 to 57.12.

This represents one use of inferential statistics: to estimate a population parameter from a sample statistic. We just inferred that the mean of the population is likely to be between 49.44 and 57.12.

Hypothesis Testing

Inferential statistics are also used to test hypotheses. As we learned in Chapter 6, the logic of hypothesis testing centers on two hypotheses: the null hypothesis and the research (or alternative) hypothesis. In a test of the difference between two means, the **null hypothesis** states that the population means are equal; any differences observed in the study sample merely reflect random error. The null hypothesis predicts that the independent variable will have no effect on the dependent variable—the intervention will not work. The null hypothesis runs counter to the theory of the study—it's the reverse of what a researcher expects to demonstrate by conducting an investigation.

On the other hand, the **research hypothesis** states that the population means are not equal, that differences demonstrated between control and experimental groups reflect the manipulation of the independent variable, as well as some random error. In other words, the research hypothesis states the investigator's prediction that there will be an association between the independent and dependent variables.

In our study about prosocial spending and happiness, the null and research hypotheses would be:

Ho (null hypothesis): the population mean for happiness in the *prosocial spending* group is **equal** to the population mean for happiness in the *personal spending* group.

H1 (research hypothesis): the population mean for happiness in the *prosocial spending* group is **not equal** to the population mean for happiness in the *personal spending* group.

The notion of the null hypothesis may strike you as counterintuitive. Why, in essence, would you predict that your study would not work, that there would be no meaningful difference between the control and experimental groups, or that the independent variable will have no systematic effect on the dependent variable? There are two reasons why the null hypothesis is vital: First, it provides a precise statement—the population means are equal, and any observed differences are merely due to chance or normal variation. Second, it can be directly tested.

Note that the null hypothesis states that there is no difference between the means beyond what would be expected by normal variation—chance. The key term here is *normal variation*. How do we know what differences are simply due to normal variation? We do so by using inferential statistics to test the significance of observed differences in sample data. The extent to which an observed finding is merely due to normal variation can be determined by looking at the sampling distribution of a statistic.

As we have learned, when a result (such as a difference in means) is not likely due to chance, it is said to be statistically significant. **Statistical significance** is a function of where the obtained value or study result falls on the normal sampling distribution. This is measured in standard deviation units that are referred to as Z values and are provided in the Z-table that can be found in Appendix D as well as on line (key search words: *normal distribution z-table*). In the normal sampling distribution, $Z = 1$ standard deviation unit.

As shown in **Exhibit 10.12**, about 68 % of the normal curve falls within +/– 1 standard deviation units ($z = 1$). About 95 % of the normal curve falls within +/– 1.96 standard deviation units ($z = 1.96$), and about 99 % of the normal curve falls within +/– 2.58 standard deviation units ($z = 2.58$). In testing for statistical significance, an obtained value that falls beyond +/– 1.96 standard deviation units is in an area of less than 5 % of the normal curve (2.5 % for each tail of the curve); this is considered unlikely due to chance. In statistical terms, the finding is statistically significant at a 0.05 level. This means that there is a 5 % probability that the finding is due to chance (you are wrong!), and a 95 % probability that the finding is reliable or statistically significant (you are right!).

t-Test

Two of the most popular inferential statistics are used to test whether group means from a sample are statistically significant: the *t*-test for two groups and the *F*-test for more than two groups. The formulas for each require that you have the following information about the sample: sample size, means, and variance. Each formula is a ratio: The numerator is simply the differences in group means over the denominator, which is the total variance for the entire sample. Essentially, these numbers are plugged into a particular formula that generates a statistical value. The greater the obtained *t*-value or *F*-value, the less likely that the obtained *t*- or *F*-value is due to random variation and the more likely it is due to the effect of the independent variable.

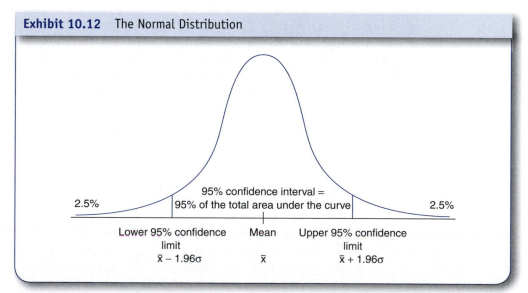

Exhibit 10.12   The Normal Distribution

95% confidence interval =
95% of the total area under the curve

2.5%   2.5%

Lower 95% confidence   Mean   Upper 95% confidence
limit   limit
$\bar{x} - 1.96\sigma$ $\bar{x}$ $\bar{x} + 1.96\sigma$

Source: National Opinion Research Center.

The two-sample *t*-test is commonly used to compare the means of two groups on a dependent variable measured using either an interval or ratio scale. It provides a *t*-statistic that has a known sampling distribution. The *t*-test formula for equal-sized groups is:

$$t = \frac{\bar{X}_1 - \bar{X}_2}{\sqrt{\frac{S_1^2}{N_1} + \frac{S_2^2}{N_2}}}$$

Symbol key: $\bar{X}_1$ = mean of sample 1; $\bar{X}_2$ = mean of sample 2; S_1^2 = variance of sample 1; S_2^2 = variance of sample 2; N = total number of cases

Thus, to calculate the value of the two-sample *t*-test, divide the observed difference between the two group means by the total variation within each group (which is assumed to reflect error). This calculation provides a *t*-statistic with an exact value. The value of *t* increases as the difference between the two group means increases. The sampling distribution of this *t*-statistic assumes that there is no difference in the population means, or, stated in another way, the expected value of the *t*-statistic under the null hypothesis is zero. Using this sampling distribution, we can determine the likelihood that the computed value of the *t*-statistic is due to chance or normal variation.

The *t*-value we calculate with our data is compared with a **critical *t*-value** provided in the **Student's *t*-table**. The table—found in Appendix E—provides exact critical *t*-values for different levels of significance and different **degrees of freedom** that is taken from Lowry (2010). (The full table of critical *t* values can be found in Appendix E.)

Degrees of freedom (abbreviated as *df*) are determined on the basis of sample size. Degrees of freedom equal the total number of participants minus the number of groups. Consider two groups of 10 participants, for a total sample size of 20. The degrees of freedom equal 18. As the sample size increases, so do the degrees of freedom. So a critical *t*-value at .05 level is greater for 18 degrees of freedom ($t = 2.10$) than for 60 degrees of freedom ($t = 2.00$). Larger sample sizes provide greater degrees of freedom, and this adds to the statistical power of the study. This is based on the idea discussed earlier that larger sample sizes provide better estimates (lower standard error of estimate) of population parameters than do smaller samples. With a smaller sample, you will need a large *t*-value in order to achieve statistical significance.

One final piece of information needed to read a statistical table pertains to the issue of a **one-tailed test** versus a **two-tailed test**. A one-tailed test is used when a research hypothesis specifies a direction of difference (e.g., treatment group will perform better than control group); otherwise, a two-tailed test is used. In practical terms, two-tailed tests are the convention for scientific publications in psychology. **Exhibit 10.13** is an abbreviated *t*-table of critical values for 5, 10, 18, and 20 degrees of freedom (Lowry, 2010; Lowry's full table of critical *t* values can be found in Appendix E. On each row, the numbers after the *df* (degrees of freedom) indicate the critical value that +*t* or −*t* must equal or be greater than in order for the

Exhibit 10.13 An Abbreviated *t*-Table of Critical Values for 5, 10, 18, and 20 Degrees of Freedom (*df*)

	Level of Significance					
	.05	.025	.01	.005	.0005	one-tailed test
df	—	.05	.02	.01	.001	two-tailed test
5	2.02	2.57	3.36	4.03	6.87	
10	1.81	2.23	2.76	3.17	4.59	
18	1.73	2.10	2.55	2.88	3.92	
20	1.72	2.09	2.53	2.85	3.85	

Source: Lowry, 2010. Reprinted with permission of Richard Lowry.

obtained result to be considered statistically significant. Each critical value is presented in the table columns for both one-tailed and two-tailed tests. Now returning to our example from Lowry (2010), you can see that for 18 degrees of freedom the critical *t*-values for the .05 level of significance using a one-tailed and a two-tailed test, respectively, are 1.73 and 2.10. By convention, when a *t*-test for a directional hypothesis meets or exceeds the critical *t*-value for a one-tailed test, the results are considered statistically significant and the null hypothesis of no difference between the sample means can be rejected. For a nondirectional hypothesis, the two-tailed test is used.

Exhibit 10.14 presents another example of a sampling distribution of *t*-values with 18 degrees of freedom for one-tailed and two-tailed tests of significance

Exhibit 10.14 Sampling Distribution of *t*-Values With 18 Degrees of Freedom

$t = -1.73$ (.05) $t = +1.73$ (.05)
$t = -2.10$ (.025) $t = +2.10$ (.025)

Source: Lowry, 2010. Reprinted with permission of Richard Lowry.

(Lowry, 2010). Using a two-tailed test, the *t*-value would have to equal or exceed +2.10 or –2.10 in order to be statistically significant at or beyond the .05 level. What this means is that when you obtain an absolute (unsigned) value of *t* equal to or greater than 2.10, the result is statistically significant. And as you can also see in **Exhibit 10.14**, for a one-tailed test of significance, the obtained *t*-statistic must be equal to or greater than +1.73 or –1.73 in order to be judged statistically significant at the .05 level.

Now to return to our imagined study and fictitious data, and the pivotal question: Are happiness ratings for prosocial spending statistically or significantly different from those for personal spending? One way to address this question is to calculate a *paired t-test* that compares pretest happiness and posttest happiness ratings for prosocial and personal spending groups. Prosocial spending had a mean happiness rating at pretest of 5.76 (standard deviation = .91) and at posttest of 7.10 (standard deviation = 0.87). A paired *t*-test indicated that the pretest and posttest difference of 1.34 after prosocial spending achieved a very high level of statistical significance. This is reflected by a *t*-value of –6.69, $df = 29$, $p < .001$. A paired *t*-test indicated that the pretest and posttest difference in happiness ratings for participants instructed to spend on themselves did not reach statistical significance, $t = .837$, $df = 29$, $p = .41$.

The Analysis of Variance

Whereas the *t*-test is used to evaluate results of an experiment with two groups, the analysis of variance (abbreviated ANOVA), also referred to as the *F* test, is used to evaluate the results of an experiment with multiple groups. As we learned in Chapter 6, researchers often have more than two groups in an experiment. For example, Merzenich and colleagues (Mahncke et al., 2006) compared three groups of research participants, some who received brain plasticity training, other participants who received an educational DVD, and still other participants received no treatment (see Chapter 6). In this experimental design, Merzenich and colleagues had one factor or independent variable, which we can call treatment, with three levels or groups. To evaluate the results of an experiment such as the Merzenich study with more than two groups requires the analysis of variance.

Following Elmes Kantowitz, & Roediger (2006), we describe the analysis of variance as a set of *general* statistical procedures that can be applied to evaluate the results of findings generated from a much wider variety of experimental designs than the *t*-test. The analysis of variance comes in different flavors, so to speak, depending on the experimental design. A **simple ANOVA** is used when one and only one factor is varied across more than two levels, such as in the Merzenich study of cognitive training. A simple ANOVA is also referred to as a one-factor analysis of variance, or **one-factor ANOVA**. However, as we learned in Chapters 7 and 8, experimenters often manipulate more than one factor or independent variable simultaneously. For these complex or multifactorial designs, the analysis of variance is also appropriate, and this type of ANOVA is often referred to as a **multifactor ANOVA**. In comparison to the simple ANOVA, the multifactor ANOVA is much more computationally complex given that there are both main and interaction effects that need to be tested. The ANOVA formulas will also differ depending on whether a between-subjects or within-subjects design is used.

Simple ANOVA. The ANOVA procedure is essentially a comparison of variance estimates. As we learned earlier in this chapter, the variance of the population can be estimated from a particular sample of observations. That is, the formula for estimating variance presented earlier is

$$\sigma^2 = \frac{\Sigma(y_i - \bar{y}_i)^2}{N}$$

The simple ANOVA calculates two independent estimates of variance. One measures the variability between the different groups—the greater the differences in the means of the different groups, the larger the estimate of variability between groups. This is referred to as the **between-groups variance.** It is based on how much the individual group means differ from the overall mean for all scores in the experiment; this overall mean is referred to as the *grand mean.* As the differences between each group mean and the grand mean increases, so too will the between-group variance. As you also recall from Chapter 7, for the simple ANOVA, the between-groups variance represents *systematic variance* due to the manipulation of the independent variable. Good experimental design seeks to maximize systematic variance by using powerful and effective independent variables that will distinguish the groups.

The other estimate of variance is the **within-groups variance**. The within-groups variance provides an estimate of how much the participants in each of the groups differ from one another. It reflects the deviation of the individual scores in each group from their respective group means. As you recall from Chapter 7, for the simple ANOVA, the within-groups variance is thought to represent in part *error variance,* which the researcher hopes to minimize through statistical control and experimental design features, such as random assignment.

At the heart of calculating ANOVA is the basic quantity known as **sums of squares**, which is shorthand for the *sum of squared deviations from the mean.* To understand sums of squares, we return to the equation for estimating sample variance, σ^2. The sum of squares is the numerator in the equation used to calculate the sample variance, σ^2. For the simple ANOVA, three sums of squares are important: First, the total sums of squares (SS Total) is the sum of squared deviations of each and every individual score from the grand mean, which is the mean of all scores in all groups in the study. Second is the sum of squares between groups (SS Between), which is the sum of squared deviations of the group means from the grand mean. Third is the sum of squares within groups (SS Within), which is the mean of the sum of squared deviations of the individual scores within groups, conditions, or level from their respective mean.

The formula for finding the total sums of squares is:

$$SS\ Total = \Sigma\Sigma X^2 - T^2/N$$

To calculate $\Sigma\Sigma X^2$ square each observation within each group, so X^2 and then sum together all these squared values, so ΣX^2 For the two summation signs, $\Sigma\Sigma$, one Σ is for adding together the squared values within each group, and the other Σ is for then adding together the ΣX^2 across the different groups. T is the total for all observations and N is for the total number of observations in the study.

The formula for finding the between-groups sums of squares is:

$$SS\ Between = \Sigma(\Sigma X)^2/n - T^2/N$$

First take the sum of the values for each group, so (ΣX), next square the sum, so $(\Sigma X)^2$, and then divide by the number of observations on which it is based. For the second part of the formula, the T^2/N term, T is the total for all observations and N is for the total number of observations in the study. Finally, the sums of squares within groups is calculated by subtracting the value for SS Between from the value for SS Total, so

$$SS\ Within = SS\ Total - SS\ Between$$

Once you have calculated SS Between, SS Within, and SS Total, your next step is to compute the *mean squares* for between and within sums of squares. The mean square for the between sums of squares is calculated by dividing the value for the between sums of square by its corresponding degrees of freedom, which is simply the number of groups minus one. The mean square for the within sums of squares is calculated by dividing the value for the within sums of squares by its corresponding degrees of freedom, which is the number of groups multiplied by the number of observations per group – 1. Each mean square provides an estimate of the population variance. The F statistic is found by dividing the mean squares between by the mean squares within.

$$F = mean\ squares\ between/mean\ squares\ within$$

As with the t statistic, this value is then compared to a critical F value for particular degrees of freedom and level of statistical significance, usually set at a .05 level of probability. If the simple ANOVA yields an F that exceeds the critical value that is provided in the *Critical values of the F distribution* table (see Appendix F), then the null hypothesis can be rejected. The ANOVA thus indicated that the groups differed significantly.

Multifactor ANOVA. We use the **multifactor ANOVA** when we have two or more independent variables within the same experiment. The simplest multifactor ANOVA is the 2×2 ANOVA, which is used for an experiment that simultaneously varies two factors each with two levels. As we know from Chapter 7, the advantage of the multifactor ANOVA is that the effects of all independent variables can be tested simultaneously. So instead of statically comparing each pair of conditions, levels, or groups, the multifactor ANOVA tests all of the effects simultaneously, thereby reducing the likelihood of chance findings. And as with the simple ANOVA, the multifactor ANOVA provides a statistical significance test (*F* test) for each of the main effects of an experiment as well as their interactions. Thus, as we have just seen, like other statistical tests, the ANOVA/*F* test allows us to determine whether each of these effects—main effects and interactions—are due to chance (see Appendix F).

For our purposes, returning to our imagined study fictitious data on spending and happiness, we have a 2×2 research design that allows us to test each of the two independent effects, spending and amount, as well as the interaction of the two. In other words, we want to know whether the spending effect differs as a function of the amount of money spent. Our dependent variable is the posthappiness rating score.

Our 2×2 ANOVA revealed a highly statistically significant main effect for type of spending (prosocial or personal). This is notated as follows: $F(1, 55) = 38.04$, $p < .001$. The (1, 55) is the degrees of freedom and the 38.04 is the *F*-value. Like the *t*-value, the *F*-value increases as the difference between the means increases. The $p < .001$ indicates the probability is less than one out of 1,000 that the effect of type of spending is due to chance. By contrast, the 2×2 ANOVA did not indicate a significant effect for amount of spending, since $F(1, 55) = .080$, $p = .779$. The telling value here is the *p*-value of .779, which means that there is about 78% probability that there is no true difference as a function of amount of money spent across personal and prosocial conditions. In addition, the interaction of spending and amount (signified as spending $\times$ amount) was not statistically significant: $F(1, 55) = .035$, $p = .852$.

In general, as we learned in Chapter 7, ANOVA results are examined by first evaluating the interaction of the independent variables and then looking at main effects of each independent variable. In our example, the two-way interaction of spending $\times$ amount was far from statistically significant. This indicated that happiness ratings did not vary as a function of whether the participants received either $5 or $20 for either prosocial or personal spending conditions. Likewise, the main effect of amount of money had no significant effect on happiness across both prosocial and personal spending conditions. However, the main effect of spending had a significant effect on happiness ratings across both money amounts. Regardless of whether participants received

$5 or $20, they reported higher happiness ratings for prosocial spending than for personal spending.

Type I and Type II Errors

Note that the researcher is faced with a decision: reject/accept the null hypothesis. In principle, inferential statistics allow *only* for the rejection/acceptance of a null hypothesis. However, recall from Chapter 6 that there is nothing in inferential statistics that directly tests the research hypothesis. That the null hypothesis is rejected does not necessarily lead to the automatic acceptance of the research hypothesis. The reason, simply stated, is that the null hypothesis could be rejected on the basis of a number of factors that might have nothing to do with the research hypothesis.

What, then, is a researcher to do? Recall from Chapter 2 the importance of design studies that allow for ruling out alternative explanations. This can be done by controlling for confounding factors. These are factors that might also influence the independent and dependent variable relationship, but through some extraneous, spurious process that is incidental to the theory being tested and evaluated. Also, state the research hypothesis as precisely as possible, such as the direction of the predicted group difference and the nature of the predicted relationship. As we have learned in factorial research designs, main and interaction effects can be statistically tested. A research hypothesis that is supported by a specifically predicted interaction effect is more difficult to attribute to extraneous, spurious factors.

In our imagined study using fictitious data, both the *t*-test and ANOVA provided highly statistically significant evidence in favor of rejecting the null hypothesis concerning the effect of type of spending. However, as we know from Chapter 6, because we are dealing with statistical probabilities rather than certainties, we can make one of two possible errors when testing the null hypothesis. A *Type I error* occurs when we reject the null hypothesis, but the null hypothesis is actually true. Here we decided that based on our sample statistics, the population means are not equal, but in fact they are. The statistical significance level indicates the chances of making a Type I error. A significance level of .05 means there is less than a 5% chance of making a Type I error, and a significance level of .01 means there is less than a 1% chance of making a Type I error. In our study, we obtained a very high *F*-value of 38.04, which would be highly improbable if the population means are equal. In fact, this value reached a level of significance of $p < 0.001$, meaning there is less than one chance in 1,000 we would obtain this *F*-value if the null hypothesis were true. Thus, the significance level, also known as the alpha (signified by the Greek letter α) level indicates the probability of a Type I error.

As we learned in Chapter 6, *Type II error* occurs when we accept the null hypothesis as true when in fact it is false. You have mistakenly decided that the population means are equal when in fact they are not! Your failure to find statistically significant results means that you will conclude that your research hypothesis is wrong. The probability of a Type II error, which is referred to as β, is a function of three factors. First is the level of significance (Type I error) itself: Setting a very stringent significance level for making a Type I error increases the likelihood for making a Type II error. That is, if we make it very difficult to commit a Type I error of rejecting the null hypothesis of no difference, the likelihood of a Type II error of incorrectly accepting the null hypothesis must increase. Second, the probability of committing a Type II error decreases with increasing sample size. Recall that another way to say this is that **statistical power** increases with larger sample size (see Chapter 6). A statistically underpowered study is one in which the probability of committing a Type II error is high. Third, **effect size** also influences the likelihood of committing a Type II error. Effect size is a measure of the magnitude of the effect of an independent variable on a dependent variable. Effect size differs from statistical significance, which indicates only the statistical probability that an observed finding is due to chance. An effect size indicates the magnitude of an observed finding, as for example how much improvement is associated with a significant treatment effect. In general, Type II error increases if the effect size is small. A small effect size is difficult to detect and therefore might result in mistakenly accepting the null hypothesis (see also Chapter 6).

Chi-Square

The *t*-test and *F*-test are two of the inferential statistics that are most commonly used to test hypotheses in behavioral research, but they are by no means the only ones. Now that we have reviewed the basics of hypothesis testing, we will introduce two other popular statistics: chi-square (χ^2) and Pearson's correlation coefficient (*r*). We will again present the formulas for each of these statistics.

Chi-square is most commonly used to test hypotheses involving two categorical variables whose relationship is displayed in a *contingency table* (also called a "crosstab" or a percentage table), which we introduced in Chapter 5. Recall the 13-item maximizer/satisficer questionnaire that we used in Chapter 1 to classify people as either maximizers or satisficers. Now let's imagine we want to test the hypothesis that the percentage of maximizers and satisficers differs between the young (18–35 years of age) and older (36–53 years of age) research participants.

The frequency data are presented in a 2×2 **contingency table**, with young and older groups in the two rows and maximizer and satisficer along the two columns. (See **Exhibit 10.15**.) A contingency table presents frequencies or percentages for the dependent variable for all levels of an independent variable. For example, a 2×4 contingency table has two rows and four columns. The convention for notation is to present the number of rows and then the number of columns. It is called a contingency table because the idea is to test whether the numbers in the table are "contingent" or dependent upon each other.

As can be seen in **Exhibit 10.15**, for the young group, six of the 20 were classified as maximizers (30%) and 14 of the 20 as satisficers (70%); for the older group, three of the 20 were classified as maximizers (15%) and 17 of the 20 as satisficers

Exhibit 10.15   A Contingency Table Showing Frequency and Relative Frequency in Percentages of Maximizers and Satisficers for Young and Older Groups

	Maximizer	Satisficer
Age Group		
Young	6	14
%	30%	70
Older	3	17
%	15%	85%

(85%). While twice as many participants were classified as maximizers in the young group as in the older group, that alone does not indicate whether this group difference could have occurred by chance alone. Calculating the chi-square statistic allows us to determine the likelihood that we would have seen such a group difference when in the population we were sampling from there was actually no difference. According to the null hypothesis, there would be no difference in maximization between the age groups, meaning that these two variables are independent of each other. In this example, we would use the **two-variable chi-square (χ^2)**, also known as the **chi-square (χ^2) test of independence**. Our two variables are age and maximizer-satisficer score, and our null hypothesis states that there is no relationship between age and percentages of maximizers/satisficers. The formula for calculating chi-square test of independence is:

$$\chi^2 = \sum \frac{(O - E)^2}{E}$$

O is the observed frequency, and

E is the expected frequency.

The degrees of freedom for the two-dimensional chi-square statistic are:

$$df = (C - 1)(R - 1)$$

C is the number of columns or levels of the first variable and R is the number of rows or levels of the second variable.

The greater the differences in frequencies between what is observed and what would be expected on the basis of chance, the larger the chi-square value and the less likely it is that the differences are due to chance. For our 2 × 2 table, the null hypothesis states that the **expected frequencies** for maximizers and satisficers should be equal (i.e., 50%) for the young and the older groups. Statistical tables (see Appendix G) are available that provide the significance level of a chi-square value, taking into account the number of rows and columns in the table (the table's so-called "degrees of freedom"). Our present example (*using artificial data*) yielded a chi-square value of 12.01 that is significant at the 0.001 level. This statistically significant level allows us to reject the null hypothesis that age and maximizers are independent with 99.9% confidence. We can conclude that it is very likely that maximization and age are highly related.

Correlation

The most commonly used statistic to measure the relationship between two quantitative variables is **Pearson's correlation coefficient, or r.** The formula for computing the Pearson correlation coefficient is:

$$r = \frac{N\sum XY - (\sum X)(\sum Y)}{\sqrt{\left[N\sum X^2 - (\sum X)^2\right]\left[N\sum Y^2 - (\sum Y)^2\right]}}$$

Symbol key: N = number of paired scores; X = the score on one variable; Y = the score on the other variable; $\sum X$ = sum of the X scores; $\sum Y$ = sum of the Y scores, $\sum XY$ = sum of the product of the paired X and Y scores; $\sum X^2$ = sum of the squared X scores; $\sum Y^2$ = sum of the squared Y scores; $(\sum X)^2$ = square of the sum of the X scores; $(\sum Y)^2$ = square of the sum of the Y scores

We introduced the correlation coefficient in Chapter 8, and you may recall that it can vary from −1.00 through 0.00 to +1.00. The numerical value of the correlation indicates the strength of the relationship between the two variables—a larger number indicates a stronger relationship. The sign, whether positive or negative, indicates the direction of the relationship. A *positive* correlation indicates that as one variable increases, so too does the other. A *negative* correlation indicates that as one variable increases, the other decreases. Now continuing with our artificial data set of 40 research participants divided into young (ages 18–35) and older (ages 36–53)groups, let us compute the correlation between age and maximization/satisficer scores. For our hypothetical sample of 40 research participants, the correlation formula yielded a coefficient value of −.80, which an inferential test tells us was highly statistically significant ($p < .001$), thus indicating that the r of −.80 was highly unlikely due to chance (see Appendix H). We can conclude (the beauty of artificial data!) that there is a highly statistically significant relationship between age and maximizer/satisficer score in our make-believe sample of 40 research participants.

We know that our significant findings mean that we can reject the null hypothesis. And we can't emphasize enough the importance of rejecting the null hypothesis for only those findings that achieve statistical significance. The stringent level of significance required in order to reject the null hypothesis (at least .05) reminds us of the importance of not committing a Type I error. By the same token, however, when we must accept the null hypothesis because of statistically nonsignificant findings, we must consider the possibility of a Type II error. The problem, of course, is that our nonsignificant findings could be due to the limitations of the study design. For example, with a real data set, we might not have drawn a larger sample of students, so a significant correlation could not be achieved. The take-home message is that when we fail to reject the null hypothesis due to a nonsignificant finding, we have to recognize that this outcome could be due to limitations in our study design (of course, the same could be said when we obtain a statistically significant result).

THE ETHICS OF STATISTICS

We end this chapter by discussing some of the ethical issues that arise in reporting and analyzing data. As you recall from Chapter 3, the ethical principle most relevant to statistical analysis and reporting data is *integrity,* which is embodied in the APA Ethics Code, Standard 8.10b, *Reporting Research Results.*

How Not to Lie With Statistics

Using statistics ethically means, first and foremost, being honest and open. Findings should be reported honestly, and researchers should be open about their thinking that guided their decisions to use particular statistics. Although we use a humorous subtitle for this section (after Darrell Huff's [1954] little classic, *How to Lie With Statistics),* make no mistake about the intent: It is possible distort social reality with statistics, and it is unethical to do so knowingly, even when the error is due more to carelessness than to deceptive intent.

Summary or descriptive statistics can easily be used unethically, knowingly or not. When we summarize a distribution in a single number, even in two numbers, we are losing much information. Neither central tendency nor variation describes a distribution's overall shape. And taken separately, neither measure tells us about the other characteristic of the distribution (central tendency or variation). So reports using measures of central tendency should normally also include measures of variation. And we should also inspect the shape of any distribution for which we report descriptive statistics to ensure that the summary statistic does not mislead us (or anyone else) because of an unusual degree of skewness.

It is possible to mislead those who read statistical reports by choosing descriptive or summary statistics that accentuate a particular feature of a distribution. For example, imagine an unscrupulous realtor trying to convince a prospective home buyer in Community B that it is a community with very high property values when it actually has a positively skewed distribution of property values (see **Exhibit 10.16**). The realtor compares the mean price of homes in Community B to that for Community A (one with a homogenous mid-priced set of homes) and therefore makes Community B look pricier. In truth, the higher mean in Community B reflects a very skewed, lopsided distribution of property values—most residents own small, less pricey houses. A median would provide a better basis for comparison.

Exhibit 10.16   Using the Mean to Create a More Favorable Impression

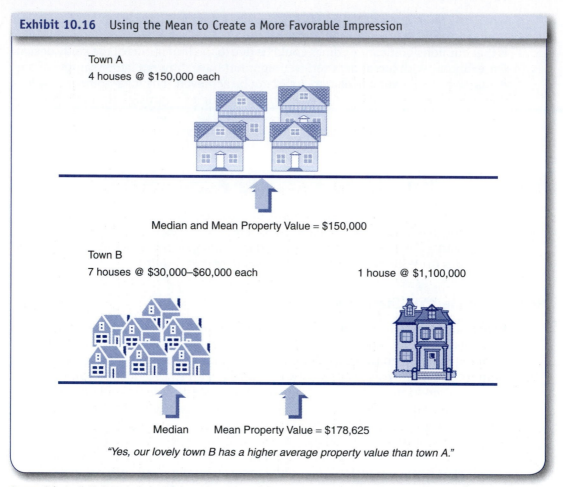

Town A
4 houses @ $150,000 each

Median and Mean Property Value = $150,000

Town B
7 houses @ $30,000–$60,000 each   1 house @ $1,100,000

Median   Mean Property Value = $178,625

"Yes, our lovely town B has a higher average property value than town A."

Source: Schutt, R. K. (2009). *Investigating the social world: The process and practice of research* (6th ed., p. 515). Thousand Oaks, CA: Pine Forge Press.

You can also easily see that an improperly constructed graph can distort the shape of a distribution. Recall how grouping data matters mightily. Whenever you need to group data in a frequency distribution or graph, you can reduce the potential for distortion by first looking at the entire data set, that is, the ungrouped distribution of raw numbers. You should then select a grouping procedure that does not distort the shape of the distribution of the original ungrouped set of raw numbers. When you create graphs, be sure to consider how the axes and their "tick" marks for grouping or scaling you choose may change the distribution's apparent shape.

Finally, when the data analyst begins to examine relationships among variables in some real data, psychological research becomes most exciting. The moment of truth, it would seem, has arrived. Either the hypotheses are supported or they are not. But, in fact, this is also a time to proceed with caution and to evaluate the analyses of others with even more caution. This is especially true for large data sets, which often provide us with many opportunities to check out a great many relationships. Indeed, when relationships are examined among three or more variables at a time, the possibilities become almost endless.

However, this range of possibilities presents a great hazard for data analysis and for the accurate, truthful presentation of results. It becomes tempting to search around in the data until something emerges. Rejected hypotheses are forgotten in favor of highlighting what's going on in the data. It's not wrong to examine data for unanticipated relationships; the problem is that inevitably some relationships among variables will appear just on the basis of chance association alone. If you search hard and long enough, it will be possible to come up with something that really means nothing.

A reasonable balance, then, must be struck between deductive data analysis—inferential statistics to test hypotheses—and inductive analysis to explore patterns in a data set. A priori hypotheses, meaning those formulated well in advance of data collection, must be tested as they were originally stated; any subsequently revised hypotheses are labeled *post hoc* (in Latin, "after this") and must be analyzed statistically using a more stringent level of significance. This adjustment in statistical significance is necessary in order to compensate for the increased probability of a Type I error that comes when exploring data and testing **post hoc hypotheses**. Unanticipated findings, often referred to as serendipitous results, need not be ignored, and in fact can be very important discoveries, but they must be reported as a product of exploring post hoc hypotheses. Future researchers can try to test deductively, in the form of a priori hypotheses, serendipitous findings borne of data exploration and post hoc statistical analyses.

CONCLUSIONS

Statistics serve two important functions in research. First is to describe the distribution of scores on all variables of interest and the relations between some of those variables. Second, statistics are used to determine the likelihood that an observed finding is due to chance. Inferential statistics allow researchers to determine how confident they can be that a statistical description based on a random sample holds true in the population from which the sample was drawn. Inferential statistics also allow researchers to test the likelihood that a relationship between two (or more) variables occurred on the basis of chance.

END OF CHAPTER

Chapter Highlights

- Sample statistics are used to estimate population parameters.
- Mode, median, and mean are measures of central tendency.

- Range, variance, and standard deviation are measures of variability.

- Measures of central tendency and variability are used as descriptive statistics to characterize a sample.

- The standard error indicates the variability in a distribution of sample statistics. It is used in inferential statistics to determine the degree of confidence that an estimate of a population parameter falls within a specified range.

- A relative frequency distribution (a percentage distribution) indicates the probability associated with each of the possible values for a variable.

- Two popular types of graphic displays for frequency distributions are bar charts and histograms.

- The sampling distribution of many statistics reflects a normal bell curve with a mean of 0 and standard deviation of 1.

- Inferential statistics are used to make inferences about the true difference in the population on the basis of sample data.

- The chi-square test for independence is used to assess the statistical significance of frequency data for two variables measured at the nominal level.

- The most commonly used statistic to measure the relationship between two quantitative variables is the Pearson correlation coefficient, which is generally referred simply as the correlation (r). An inferential test is used to estimate the likelihood that the value of r is due to chance.

- The t-test, an inferential statistic, can be used to test the difference in means between two groups or the difference of means for one group measured at two points in time.

- The F-test, an inferential statistic, can be used to test the differences in means for more than two groups or for two or more independent variables.

- Inferential statistics provide a direct test of the null hypothesis of no difference in population means.

- To select a critical value for a statistic, such as a t- or F-test, the researcher must specify the degrees of freedom, significance level, and directionality of the test (i.e., one-tailed or two-tailed).

- The significance level indicates the probability of a Type I error of mistakenly rejecting the null hypothesis of no difference in population means.

- A small sample size and a small effect size increase the probability of a Type II error of mistakenly accepting the null hypothesis.

- Nonsignificant results are best described as a failure to reject the null hypothesis. This failure may be due to limitations in experimental design.

Key Terms

Bar chart   319

Between-groups variance   338

Bimodal   323

Central tendency   322

Chi-square (χ^2)
test of independence   343

Contingency table   342

Correlation   000

Critical t-value   335

Degrees of freedom   335

Descriptive statistics   314

Effect size   342

F-test   334

Frequency distribution   316

Histogram   320

Inferential statistics   315

Mean   323

Median   323

Mode   338

Multifactor ANOVA   338

Normal distribution   332

Null hypothesis   333

One-factor ANOVA   337

One-tailed test   335

Outlier   329

Parameter   331

Pearson's correlation
coefficient, or *r*   344

Post hoc hypotheses   347

Probability average   323

Range   328

Research hypothesis   333

Sampling distribution   331

Simple ANOVA   337

Skewness   322

Standard deviation   330

Standard error of the mean   331

Statistical power   342

Statistical significance   333

Student's *t*-table   335

Sums of squares   338

t-test   334

Two-tailed test   335

Two-variable chi-square (χ^2)   343

Unimodal   323

Variability   322

Variance   329

Within-groups variance   338

Research in the News

1. The controversy around a major study of National Football League (NFL) retirees has prompted Congressional hearings. At issue is the design of the study that examines concussions sustained while playing professional football and dementia in later life.

In a piece in the *New York Times* (December 20, 2009), which nicely amplifies the meaning of statistical power, reporter Alan Schwartz quoted Amy Borenstein, an epidemiologist testifying before the Congressional hearing, as saying, "The design suffers from a total lack of statistical power to detect an effect if one truly exists." Imagine that you have been hired to design a better study of NFL retirees, one that has sufficient statistical power to detect an effect, if one truly exists, between football concussions and later diagnosis of dementia. Explain statistical power and how you might design a better study. What would be an appropriate comparison group for NFL retirees?

2. In a piece appearing in the *Wall Street Journal*, April 24, 2007, "Shattering the Bell Curve," David A. Shaywitz reviews two books by author Nassim Taleb titled *Fooled by Randomness* and *The Black Swan*. In both these books, Taleb, Shaywitz writes, provides a provocative critique of the normal distribution, arguing in effect that most important things in life are not normally distributed. This, of course, runs counter to the central idea presented in this chapter that places the normal distribution front and center in any statistical testing of a hypothesis. Taleb, as Shaywitz describes, contends that

> Height follows the bell curve in its distribution. Wealth does not: It follows an asymmetric, L-shaped pattern known as a 'power law,' where most values are below average and a few far above. In the realm of the power law, rare and extreme events dominate the action.

Debate the pros and cons of the normal distribution versus the power law. How does the power law present a countervailing force to the normal distribution? Does the power law pose a threat to statistical reasoning in psychological research? What advantages/disadvantages do you see in normal distribution versus power law?

Activity Questions

1. You have two groups of research participants. One group ($n = 35$) receives SAT coaching and the other group ($n = 35$) does not. You want to compare actual SAT scores between coached and noncoached groups.
   a. What is the scale of measurement of your dependent variable?
   b. What statistical test would you use to compare the two groups on SAT scores?
   c. What level of statistical significance would you use? What are the degrees of freedom and what is the critical value?
   d. What is the null hypothesis and what is the research hypothesis?
   e. What is the Type I error and what is the Type II error?
   f. What is the probability of making a Type I error?
   g. What are some of the study confounds? What control variables would you recommend?

2. You want to examine the effects of age and on scores on the maximizer/satisficer questionnaire. You have three age groups: 20 young (ages 18–35), 20 middle-aged (50–65), and 20 old (66–80). You calculate the percentages of maximizers and

satisficers for each age group. You want to know whether the percentage of maximizers and satisficers differs for the three age groups.

a. What is the scale of measurement of your dependent variable?

b. What statistical test would you use to compare the three age groups?

c. What level of statistical significance would you use? What are the degrees of freedom and what is the critical value?

d. What is the null hypothesis and what is the research hypothesis?

e. What is the Type I error and what is the Type II error?

f. What is the probability of making a Type I error?

g. What is the best tabular format for presenting your data?

h. What are some of the study confounds? What control variables would you recommend?

3. You want to examine the effects of age on scores on the maximizer/satisficer questionnaire. You collected a sample of 600 research participants that is composed of equal proportions of young (ages 18–35), middle-aged (50–65), and old (66–80) people. You want to know whether there is an association between age and score on the maximizer/satisficer questionnaire.

a. What is the scale of measurement for age? What is the scale of measurement for the maximizer/satisficer questionnaire?

b. What statistical test would you use to examine the association of age and maximizer/satisficer score?

c. What level of statistical significance would you use? What are the degrees of freedom and what is the critical value?

d. What is the null hypothesis and what is the research hypothesis?

e. What is the Type I error and what is the Type II error?

f. What is the probability of making a Type II error?

g. What are some of the study confounds? What control variables would you recommend?

4. Recall from Chapter 7 the Adams and Kleck (2003) study that examined the processing of facial displays of emotions. In this study, research participants judged faces that varied in expression (anger/sad) and eye gaze (direct/averted). The study aimed to separate the influences of expression and eye gaze on reaction time for labeling faces as either sad or angry.

a. What is the scale of measurement for the dependent variable?

b. What are the independent variables and how many levels are there for each independent variable?

c. What statistical test would you use? What are the main effects and the interaction effects?

d. What is the null hypothesis and what is the research hypothesis?

   e. What is the Type I error and what is the Type II error?

   f. What is the probability of making a Type I error?

   g. What are some of the study confounds? What control variables would you recommend?

Review Questions

1. Explain why "levels of measurement matter" in statistics.

2. Discuss the considerations that come into play in choosing mean versus median.

3. Discuss the relationship of statistical power to sample size and effect size.

4. What descriptive statistic is used for summarizing data measured using a nominal scale? Why?

5. What is the best descriptive statistic of central tendency for data measured using an ordinal scale? Why?

6. What are two popular types of graphic displays for frequency distributions? Describe them in relation to the level of measurement of the variables to be graphed.

7. What is the difference between a sample statistic and a population parameter? Why is this difference so important in statistical reasoning?

8. Discuss the difference between descriptive and inferential statistics.

9. What is the standard error? What does it measure and why it used?

10. How do you select a critical value for a statistic, such as a t- or F-test? What does a critical value for a statistic mean? Why it important?

Ethics in Action

1. *How to Lie With Statistics* is small but classic book by Darrell Huff (1954) with a timeless and vital message for all researchers, which is echoed in the APA Ethics Code for reporting data accurately. How would you guard against distorting data in both graphic presentation and statistical description and analyses?

2. Actual falsification of data is fraudulent and always unethical. Unfortunately, when it does occur, it is always incalculably harmful to the research enterprise and abjectly deceitful to participants and to the public at large. It can involve completely fabricating data or omitting participant responses in order to skew the data. Why do you think cheating occurs in research and how might teachers, courses, and textbooks (like this one) better address this ethical challenge?

3. Honest mistakes in reporting data can also occur. When these occur, the APA Ethics Code (Standard 8.10b, Reporting Research Results) states that researchers should take steps to correct the errors. Describe some honest mistakes that can occur in recording data and in using and reporting statistics. How might you safeguard against them?

CHAPTER 11

Qualitative Methods

You know, my husband is a very nice person. He's a very easygoing person you know. But, I mean he's wrapped up in his job, and it's just that I—I know I don't understand it enough you know. Like I just sort of feel like "hey, I've been giving, giving, giving to kids and the husband for 30 odd years, when is it going to be my turn?" (Brinegar, Salvi, Stiles, & Greenberg, 2006, p. 170)

The woman who made these comments in a therapy session was 58 years old, white, moderately depressed, and concerned with a difficult marriage and letting go of her grown children. In many respects, there was nothing unusual about "Margaret's" comments or about the successful brief client-centered therapy provided by her therapist, a clinical psychology doctoral student. But Margaret had given her consent to participate in the York University Depression Project, and so her therapy sessions were recorded, analyzed by a research team, and then excerpted in a journal article (after identifying information was removed; Brinegar, Salvi, Stiles, & Greenberg, 2006). In this way, Margaret's therapy provided a basis for investigating therapeutic process and for improving therapeutic practice.

For us, Margaret's statement introduces qualitative methods, in which psychologists learn about human behavior by listening to people or observing their behavior in a natural setting. Her statement also reminds us that some aspects of human orientations and behaviors are ill suited to investigation with experiments or surveys. In this chapter, you will learn how Meredith Glick Brinegar, Lima M. Salvi, William B. Stiles, and Leslie S. Greenberg (2006) and others have used qualitative methods to illuminate the process of psychotherapy. You will also learn, from a variety of examples, that some of our greatest insights into human behavior can result from what appear to be very ordinary activities: listening, talking, participating, observing.

But you will also learn that qualitative research is much more than just doing what comes naturally. Qualitative researchers must question respondents strategically, observe keenly, take notes systematically, and prepare to spend more time and invest more of their whole selves than often occurs with experiments or surveys. Moreover, if we are to have any confidence in the validity of conclusions based on qualitative methods, each element of the research design must be reviewed as carefully as we would review the elements of an experiment or survey.

The chapter begins with an overview of the major features of qualitative research as reflected in research on psychotherapy. The next section discusses the different ways of collecting qualitative data, ranging from intensive interviewing to observations and group discussions. We also discuss ways of combining methods and techniques for analyzing qualitative data. We conclude with a discussion of ethical issues in qualitative research. By the chapter's end, you should appreciate the hard work required to translate "doing what comes naturally" into systematic research, be able to recognize strong and weak points in qualitative studies, and be ready to do some of it yourself.

FUNDAMENTALS OF QUALITATIVE RESEARCH

You have seen in the excerpt from Meredith Glick Brinegar et al. (2006) that the "data" used in qualitative research can be ordinary speech. You will see in this chapter other examples of qualitative research in which the data are observations of human behavior as it occurs in a natural setting. More generally, qualitative methods involve "an interpretive, naturalistic approach to the world" in which things are studied "in their natural settings, attempting to make sense of, or interpret, phenomena in terms of the meanings people bring to them" (Denzin & Lincoln, 2005, p. 3). Attitudes are assessed by listening to people talk, not by requesting answers to a series of questions with fixed response choices. Behavior is observed as it happens, not based on responses to planned treatments delivered to randomly assigned groups.

There are many different types of qualitative methods, but we will begin by pointing out several common features that distinguish these methods from experimental and survey research designs (Denzin & Lincoln, 2000; Maxwell, 1996; Wolcott, 1995):

Collection primarily of qualitative rather than quantitative data. Any research design may collect both qualitative and quantitative data, but qualitative methods emphasize observations about natural behavior, attitudes, and artifacts that capture life as it is experienced by the participants rather than in categories predetermined by the researcher.

Exploratory research questions, with a commitment to inductive reasoning. Qualitative researchers typically begin their projects seeking not to test preformulated hypotheses but to discover what people think, how they act, and why, in some setting. Only after many observations do qualitative researchers try to develop general principles to account for their observations. (Levitt, Butler, & Hill, 2006).

A focus on previously unstudied processes and unanticipated phenomena. Previously unstudied attitudes and actions can't adequately be understood with a structured set of questions or within a highly controlled experiment. So qualitative methods have their greatest appeal when we need to explore new issues, investigate hard-to-study groups, or determine the meaning people give to their lives and actions.

Of course, this does not mean that qualitative research must begin with a completely blank slate. For example, Meredith Glick Brinegar and her colleagues (2006) used the Assimilation of Problematic Experiences Sequence (APES) to guide their analysis of Margaret's psychotherapy experience. However, as qualitative researchers, they explained,

> The theory is not considered a rigid treatise to be voted up or down in light of supporting or disconfirming evidence. Rather, theory is a flexible (permeable) account that was constructed as a way of understanding previous observations and now must be elaborated, extended, qualified, and modified to encompass the observations at hand. (p. 165)

A focus on human subjectivity, on the meanings that participants attach to events and that people give to their lives. Unlike quantitative methods, in which the researcher attempts to measure attitudes and behavior "objectively" with standardized instruments, the qualitative researcher tries to learn how people make sense of what is happening to them. In their qualitative investigation of male survivors of childhood sexual abuse, Frances K. Grossman, Lynn Sorsoli, and Maryam Kia-Keating (2006) describe their focus as "one crucial dimension of

Exhibit 11.1 Assimilation of Problematic Experiences Scale (APES)

0. **Warded off/dissociated.** Client is unaware of the problem; the problematic voice is silent or dissociated. Affect may be minimal, reflecting successful avoidance.

1. **Unwanted thoughts/active avoidance.** Client prefers not to think about the experience. Problematic voices emerge in response to therapist interventions or external circumstances and are suppressed or avoided. Affect is intensely negative but episodic and unfocused; the connection with the content may be unclear.

2. **Vague awareness/emergence.** Client is aware of a problematic experience but cannot formulate the problem clearly. Problematic voice emerges into sustained awareness. Affect includes acute psychological pain or panic associated with the problematic material.

3. **Problem statement/clarification.** Content includes a clear statement of a problem—something that can be worked on. Opposing voices are differentiated and can talk about each other. Affect is negative but manageable, not panicky.

4. **Understanding/insight.** The problematic experience is formulated and understood in some way. Voices reach an understanding with each other (a meaning bridge). Affect may be mixed, with some unpleasant recognition but also some pleasant surprise.

5. **Application/working through.** The understanding is used to work on a problem. Voices work together to address problems of living. Affective tone is positive, optimistic.

6. **Resourcefulness/problem solution.** The formerly problematic experience has become a resource, used for solving problems. Voices can be used flexibly. Affect is positive, satisfied.

7. **Integration/mastery.** Client automatically generalizes solutions; voices are fully integrated, serving as resources in new situations. Affect is positive or neutral (i.e., this is no longer something to get excited about).

Note: Assimilation is considered as a continuum, and intermediate levels are allowed, for example, 2.5 represents a level of assimilation halfway between vague awareness/emergence (2.0) and problem statement/clarification (3.0).

Source: From "Assimilation of problematic experiences" by W. B. Stiles in J. C. Norcross (Ed.), *Psychotherapy relationships that work: Therapist contributions and responsiveness to patients*. Copyright © 2002. Reprinted by permission of Oxford University Press, Inc.

survivors' recovery . . . finding a way to 'make sense' of what happened to them in the past, and to make some kind of meaning of the place the abuse has in their current lives" (p. 434).

Reflexive research design, in which the design develops as the research progresses. Qualitative research is sensitive to how "the activity of studying something will always change it, will affect it" (Banister, Burman, Parker, Taylor, & Tindall, 1994, p. 14). Each component of the design may need to be reconsidered or modified in response to new developments or to changes in some other component. . . . (Maxwell, 1996).

Sensitivity to the researcher's subjectivity. Many qualitative researchers question the possibility of achieving an objective perspective on human behavior—coming to conclusions about the data that any psychologist would see as valid—and instead focus attention on how their own backgrounds might influence their observations. Sarah Knox, Alan W. Burkard, Adanna J. Johnson, Lisa A. Suzuki, and Joseph G. Ponterotto (2003) explain how they "explored their potential biases and expectations" prior to interviewing African American and European American therapists about their experiences of addressing race in their psychotherapy:

> Two researchers indicated that they had been supervised by someone of a different race than their own. . . . In terms of personal experiences, three authors stated that the time they spent living in a culturally diverse area had affected them. . . . When discussing their approach to or experience of addressing race in therapy, 1 researcher indicated having had only positive experiences with addressing race; . . . One researcher was struggling with whether she should address race with clients of her same racial background. (p. 468)

What do these fundamental features of qualitative methods add up to? As you will soon see, when these features are specified and combined in different ways, they provide a rich array of useful techniques for investigating human behavior. These qualitative techniques can be used as supplements or as alternatives to experimental or survey designs when investigations focus on previously unstudied issues, how people interpret their experiences, or on the broader social context of behavior. Qualitative methods may be the only reasonable choice for some people or settings where controlled designs and systematic measures are not feasible.

METHODS FOR COLLECTING QUALITATIVE DATA

There are several distinctive approaches to collecting qualitative data. We will focus on three of them: **qualitative interviewing**, **participant observation**, and **focus groups**. Participant observation and intensive interviewing are often used in the same project; focus groups are a unique data-collection strategy that combines some elements of these two approaches.

Qualitative interviewing A qualitative method that involves open-ended, relatively unstructured questioning in which the interviewer seeks in-depth information on the interviewee's feelings, experiences, and perceptions (Lofland & Lofland, 1984).

Participant observation A qualitative method for gathering data that involves developing a sustained relationship with people while they go about their normal activities.

Focus groups A qualitative method that involves unstructured group interviews in which the focus group leader actively encourages discussion among participants on the topics of interest.

QUALITATIVE INTERVIEWING

Qualitative interviewing is used to find out about people's experiences, thoughts, and feelings, often with a goal of understanding how they make sense of their experiences. Qualitative interviewing can be used by itself or combined with the participant observation approach that you will learn about next (Wolcott, 1995).

Unlike the more structured interviewing that may be used in survey research (discussed in Chapter 9), qualitative interviewing relies on open-ended questions. Rather than asking standard questions in a fixed order, qualitative interviewers may allow the specific content and order of questions to vary from one interviewee to another. Rather than presenting fixed responses, qualitative interviewers expect respondents to answer questions in their own words (Banister et al., 1994).

What distinguishes qualitative interviewing from less planned forms of questioning is consistency and thoroughness. For example, Heidi Levitt, Mike Butler, and Travis Hill (2006) used qualitative interviews "as one path through which [psychotherapy] researchers can develop understandings of this ['moment-to-moment'] interpersonal process of change" (p. 314). The researchers' description of their 1.5-hour interviews captures the logic of intensive interviewing:

> The main questions asked clients to describe whatever was significant or important to them about their general psychotherapy, specific psychotherapy moments, and therapeutic relationship. Additional probes were used to further clarify the meanings in their responses. . . . Interview questions were designed to promote discussion in a nonleading manner. (Levitt et al., 2006, p. 315)

So qualitative interviewing engages researchers more actively with subjects than standard survey research does. The researchers must listen to lengthy explanations, ask follow-up questions tailored to the preceding answers, and seek to learn about interrelated belief systems or personal approaches to things rather than measure a limited set of variables. As a result, qualitative interviews are often much longer than standardized interviews, sometimes as long as 15 hours, conducted in several different sessions. The qualitative interview becomes more like a conversation between partners than an interview between a researcher and a subject (Kaufman, 1986). Some call it "a conversation with a purpose" (Rossman & Rallis, 1998).

The qualitative interview follows a preplanned outline of topics. It may begin with a few simple questions that gather background information while building rapport. These are often followed by a few general "grand tour" questions that are meant to elicit lengthy narratives (Miller & Crabtree, 1999). Some projects may use semi-structured interviews with a standard set of questions asked in a predefined order, particularly when the focus is on developing knowledge about prior events, standard processes, or some narrowly defined topic. But more exploratory projects, particularly those aiming to learn about interviewees' interpretations of the world, may let each interview flow in a unique direction in response to the interviewee's experiences and interests (Kvale, 1996; Rubin & Rubin, 1995; Wolcott, 1995). In either case, qualitative interviewers must adapt nimbly throughout the interview, paying attention to nonverbal cues, expressions with symbolic value, and the ebb and flow of the interviewee's feelings and interests. "You have to be free to follow your data where they lead" (Rubin & Rubin, 1995, p. 64).

Selecting Interviewees

Random selection is rarely used to select respondents for intensive interviews, but the selection method still must be considered carefully. Researchers should try to select interviewees who are knowledgeable about the subject of the interview, who are open to talking, and who represent the range of perspectives (Rubin & Rubin, 1995). As Frances Grossman and her colleagues explain, subjects must be screened carefully for eligibility.

> Participants were recruited through letters written to clinicians in the community and by posted flyers seeking resilient men with histories of childhood sexual abuse. . . . Brief telephone screenings were conducted to ascertain whether participants had a history of childhood sexual abuse that met the criteria of being perpetrated by a member of the immediate or extended family. . . . Participants were also screened for resiliency; specifically . . . if they had never been sexually abusive to anyone and were functioning well. . . . (Grossman et al., 2006, p. 435)

Selection of new interviewees should continue, if possible, at least until the **saturation point** is reached, the point when new interviews seem to yield little additional information (see **Exhibit 11.1**). As new issues are uncovered, additional interviewees may be selected to represent different opinions about these issues.

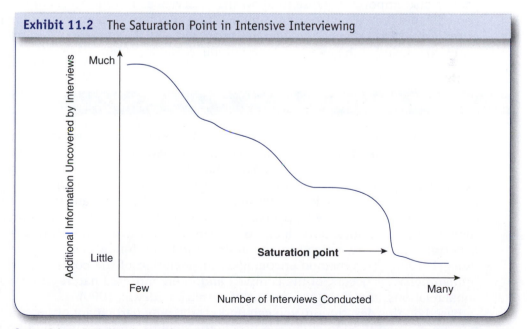

Exhibit 11.2 The Saturation Point in Intensive Interviewing

Source: Schutt, R. K. (2009). *Investigating the social world: The process and practice of research* (6th ed., p. 342). Thousand Oaks, CA: Pine Forge Press.

Asking Questions and Recording Answers

Qualitative interviewers must plan their main questions around an outline of the interview topic. The questions should generally be short and to the point. More details can then be elicited through nondirective probes (e.g., "Can you tell me more about that?" or "uh-huh," echoing the respondent's comment, or just maintaining a moment of silence). Follow-up questions can then be tailored to answers to the main questions.

Tape recorders commonly are used to record intensive and focus-group interviews. Most researchers who have tape recorded interviews feel that they do not inhibit most interviewees and, in fact, are routinely ignored. The occasional respondent is very concerned with his or her public image and may therefore speak "for the tape recorder," but such individuals are unlikely to speak frankly in any research interview. In any case, constant note taking during an interview prevents adequate displays of interest and appreciation by the interviewer and hinders the degree of concentration that results in the best interviews.

Developing Rapport

In the first few minutes of the interview, the goal is to show interest in the interviewee and to explain clearly what the purpose of the interview is (Kvale, 1996). During the interview, the interviewer should maintain an appropriate distance from the interviewee, one that doesn't violate cultural norms; the interviewer should maintain eye contact and not engage in districting behavior. An appropriate pace is also important; pause to allow the interviewee to reflect, elaborate, and generally not feel rushed (Gordon, 1992). When an interview covers emotional or otherwise stressful topics, the interviewer should give the interviewee an opportunity to unwind at the interview's end (Rubin & Rubin, 1995).

PARTICIPANT OBSERVATION

Participant observation is a qualitative method in which natural social processes are studied as they happen (in "the field" rather than in the laboratory) and left relatively undisturbed. It is the seminal qualitative research method—a means for observing human behavior as the research subjects experience it, in its totality, and for understanding subjects' interpretations of their behavior and that of others (Wolcott, 1995). By observing people and interacting with them in the course of their normal activities, **participant observers** seek to avoid the artificiality of experimental designs and the unnatural structured questioning of survey research (Koegel, 1987). This method encourages consideration of the context in which human behavior occurs, of the complex and interconnected nature of interpersonal relations, and of the sequencing of events (Bogdewic, 1999).

Based on this description, you can understand why participant observation is *not* the method used to study the psychotherapeutic process: It would be too intrusive to have an observer sitting in sessions, and of course the observer couldn't interrupt to ask questions—not to mention the impact that a third party could have on the process itself. You can also understand why participant observation was the method used to study the process of change in group homes in the Boston McKinney Project (Schutt, 2011). This project was funded by the National Institute of Mental Health in 1990 to test the value for homeless mentally ill persons of living in group homes or independent apartments. The research design included random assignment to group or independent living (after an initial screen for eligibility and safety) and standard measures that were administered to subjects. But the group homes that principal investigator Stephen M. Goldfinger, MD, one of your co-authors (RKS) and several other co-investigators developed for this study were different from the traditional group homes used by most mental health agencies. The McKinney group homes were termed "evolving consumer households," and they were supposed to shift from staff management to resident control over the 1.5-year study period. But how would this occur?

> We knew that the development of consumer-managed collective households was a sufficiently novel and unprecedented approach that we could not guarantee that all Evolving Consumer Households would move systematically and uniformly toward the goal of independence and tenant control. Studying the process of housing evolution of each of these "micro-cultures" became the responsibility of a team of three anthropologists. Each ethnographer spent several days per week speaking with and observing tenants and staff in at least two group households. (Goldfinger et al., 1997, pp. 34–35)

The first concern of every participant observer is to decide what balance to strike between observing and participating. This decision must take into account the specifics of the situation being studied, the researcher's own background and personality, the larger sociopolitical context, and ethical concerns. Consider the "mix" of participating and observing in the Boston McKinney Project:

> Data collection consisted principally of participant observation, the hallmark of the anthropological method. Participant observation involves spending time with people in their own settings, talking with them about their lives, and following events as they develop over time. In this instance, it involved both attending formal events and joining in more informal activities, such as grocery shopping, sports, walks, card games, watching TV, cooking, or just "hanging out." Informal interviews with residents and staff were also part of the data collection process. (Ware, 1999, p. 5)

Which balance of participating and observing is most appropriate also changes, often many times, during most projects. In public settings involving other people, in which observing while standing or sitting does not attract attention, your activities as an observer may be no different than those of others who are simply observing others to pass the time. However, when you take notes, when you systematically check out the different areas of a public space or different people in a crowd, when you arrive and leave at particular times, you are acting differently in important respects from others in the setting. If you observe in this way in a public place, you should always remember to evaluate how your actions in the setting and your purposes for being there may affect the actions of others and your own interpretations.

This is the problem of **reactive effects**. It is not "natural" in most social situations for someone to be present who will record her or his observations for research and publication purposes, and so individuals may alter their behavior. The observer is even more likely to have an impact when the social setting involves few people or if observing is unlike the usual activities in the setting. Observable differences between the observer and those being observed also increase the likelihood of reactive effects. A McKinney ethnographer (unpublished notes) described how she tried to overcome her "unusual" status in a group home:

> I finally try to explain who I am and what I'm doing there. I allude to the fact that everyone has been "very polite," and not asked, but that they must have been wondering. I say that I am an anthropologist. [a resident asks] "What's that?" [I say] That's someone who studies social processes, and my job here is to study this experiment that we're all involved in together and try to explain what works and doesn't work and why . . . by being with people and talking to people.

Observers in the Boston McKinney Project (unpublished notes) visited each group home for several hours each week and so did not simply "blend" into the setting as if they were residents.

> [a resident] tried to explain further who I was to [another]. "She's not staff, she just comes and visits us there—she's with the housing project."

Most **field researchers** adopt a role that involves some active participation in the setting. Usually they participate in enough group activities to develop rapport with members and to gain a direct sense of what group members experience. Notes from the medical anthropology team in the Boston McKinney Project (Schutt, 2011) provide a good example of the rapport-building function of participation. On different occasions, over the 18 months that they observed in a particular house, a team member might play cards with house residents, help out in the yard, walk or even drive to a store, or meet for lunch or a local show. Such active participation in resident activities often led to more feelings of trust and to lengthy conservations about a range of issues. As a McKinney ethnographer noted, after being introduced by a resident to a staff member:

> There have been a lot of indications recently from various tenants of my acceptance on the "inside," but this one definitely felt the nicest.

But being a participant as well as an observer inevitably creates some boundary issues: Participants in the setting can simply forget about the researcher's role and the researcher can start to function simply as a participant. McKinney observers were at times asked by residents for cash, offered food, solicited for advice, and considered as possible romantic partners.

Experienced participant observers try to lessen some of the resulting problems by evaluating both their effect on others in the setting and the effect of others on their observations. Participant observers write about these effects throughout the time they are in the field and while they analyze their data. They also try to preserve some physical space and regular time when they can concentrate on their research, and they schedule occasional meetings with other researchers to review the field-work. The McKinney observers often commented on these issues in their notes:

> I think I overreacted, because I was so pleased with the way that things had worked out at the meeting and I could not have left [the resident this ethnographer was talking to] thinking that it was otherwise. . . . I showed him the minutes. . . . I felt like I had gone too far.

Entering the Field

Entering the field, the setting under investigation, is a critical stage in a participant observation project because it can shape many subsequent experiences. Researchers must learn in advance how participants dress and what their typical activities are so as to avoid being caught completely unprepared. Finding a participant who can make introductions is often critical (Rossman & Rallis, 1998), and formal permission may be needed in an organizational setting (Bogdewic, 1999). It can take weeks or even months until entry is possible.

In the following field notes, one McKinney ethnographer describes how two of them introduced themselves to staff at meeting:

> I started in with a brief description of our responsibilities: . . . We were going to hang out and take notes and help out and sometimes do formal interviews in order to get an overall sense of how this group home was another stage in the unfolding of treatment programs for the mentally ill and the homeless in MA. . . . Except for situations of danger or self-destruction, we weren't there to judge anyone's performance but simply to record how everyone worked together to make the program a success. We also mentioned that if anyone felt uncomfortable with anything we were doing to please discuss it. . . . There were quite a few questions on the nature of anthropology and our role and "what, specifically, we are looking for." [We] talked about how looking for specifics would be biasing . . . about us trying to treat the house as a different culture, to try to make sense of what we all normally take for granted as normal and ordinary. . . . We left, with many assurances of how glad they were to meet with us and how they were looking forward to seeing us again. I remember warm smiles and enthusiastic goodbyes.

Managing Relationships

Researchers must be careful to manage their relationships in the research setting so they can continue to observe and interview diverse members of the social setting throughout the long period typical of participant observation (Maxwell, 1996). Every action the researcher takes can develop or undermine this relationship. Interaction early in the research process is particularly sensitive, because participants don't know the researcher and the researcher doesn't know the routines. You can sense the tension in a McKinney ethnographer's note about comments directed to her by a staff member who had just criticized some other staff who had just left:

> [Referring to the ethnographer] . . . don't put that down! On second thought, maybe you should!! No, really, go ahead. They gotta find out somehow!

As the observers established rapport with house residents, interaction became more natural, although never completely so.

> We played a game [of Yahtzee] and I won (!) The game was fun. It was one of those circumstances where I find myself really overplaying the "fun" aspect of things. . . . After playing two games interest waned and we stopped.

Experienced participant observers have developed some sound advice for others seeking to maintain relationships in the field (Bogdewic, 1999; Rossman & Rallis, 1998; Whyte, 1955; Wolcott, 1995):

- Develop a plausible (and honest) explanation for yourself and your study.

- Maintain the support of key individuals in groups or organizations under study.

- Be unobtrusive and unassuming. Don't "show off" your expertise.

- Don't be too aggressive in questioning others (e.g., don't violate implicit norms that preclude discussion of illegal activity with outsiders). Being a researcher requires that you not simultaneously try to be the guardian of law and order. Instead, be a reflective listener.

- Ask very sensitive questions only of informants with whom your relationship is good.

- Be self-revealing, but only up to a point. Let participants learn about you as a person, but without making too much of yourself.

- Don't fake your social similarity with your subjects. Taking a friendly interest in them should be an adequate basis for developing trust.

- Avoid giving or receiving monetary or other tangible gifts but without violating norms of reciprocity. You can't be a participant observer without occasionally helping others, but you will lose your ability to function as a researcher if you come to be seen as someone who gives away money or other favors.

- Be prepared for special difficulties and tensions if multiple groups are involved. It is hard to avoid taking sides or being used in situations of intergroup conflict.

Taking Notes

Notes are the primary means of recording participant observation data (Emerson, Fretz, & Shaw, 1995). It is almost always a mistake to try to take comprehensive notes while engaged in the field—the process of writing extensively is just too disruptive. The usual procedure is to jot down brief notes about highlights of the observation period. These brief notes (called **jottings**) can then serve as memory joggers when writing the actual **field notes** at a later session. It will also help to maintain a daily log and to record in it each day's activities (Bogdewic, 1999). With the aid of the jottings and some practice, researchers usually remember a great deal of what happened—as long as the comprehensive field notes are written immediately afterward, or at least within the next 24 hours, and before they have been discussed with anyone else.

Although there is no fixed formula to guide note taking, observers try to identify the who, what, when, where, why, and how of activities in the setting. Their observations will usually become more focused over time as the observer develops a sense of the important categories of people and activities and gradually develops a theory that accounts for what is observed (Bogdewic, 1999). Banister et al. (1994) suggest writing notes to address each of the following issues:

1. *Describe the context,* including the physical setting.

2. *Describe the participants,* including potentially important variables such as age, gender, and clothing.

3. *Describe who the observer is,* including links to the context being observed.

4. *Describe the actions of participants,* including both verbal and nonverbal behavior and action sequences.

5. *Consider alternative interpretations of the situation,* including giving some rationale for them.

6. *Explore your feelings in being an observer,* including your experience of the observation.

Usually, writing up notes takes much longer—at least 3 times longer—than the observing did. Field notes must be as complete, detailed, and true as possible to what was observed and heard. Direct quotes should be distinguished clearly from paraphrased quotes, and both should be set off from the researcher's observations and reflections. Pauses and interruptions should be indicated. The surrounding context should receive as much attention as possible, and a map of the setting always should be included, with indications of where individuals were at different times.

Careful note taking yields a big payoff. On page after page, field notes will suggest new concepts, causal connections, and theoretical propositions. Social processes and settings can be described in rich detail, with ample illustrations. Exhibit 11.2 contains field notes recorded by Norma Ware, the lead anthropologist studying group homes in the Boston McKinney Project (Schutt, 2011). The notes contain observations of the setting, the questions the anthropologist asked, the answers she received, and her analytic thoughts about one of the residents. What can be learned from just this one page of field notes? The mood of the house at this time is evident, with joking, casual conversation, and close friendships. "Dick" remarks on problems with household financial management, and, at the same time, we learn a bit about his own activities and personality (a regular worker who appears to like systematic plans). We see how a few questions and a private conversation elicit information about the transition from the shelter to the house, as well as about household operations. The field notes also provide the foundation for a more complete picture of one resident, describing "Jim's" relationships with others, his personal history, his interests and personality, and his orientation to the future. We can see analytic concepts emerge in the notes, such as the concept of "pulling himself together" and of some house members working as a "team." You can imagine how researchers can go on to develop a theoretical framework for understanding the setting and a set of concepts and questions to inform subsequent observations.

Complete field notes must provide even more than a record of what was observed or heard. Notes also should include descriptions of the methodology: where researchers were standing or sitting while they observed, how they chose people for conversation or observation, what counts of people or events they made and why. Sprinkled throughout the notes also should be a record of the researchers' feelings and thoughts while observing: when they were disgusted by some statement or act, when they felt threatened or intimidated, why their attention shifted from one group to another, and what ethical concerns arose. Notes like these provide a foundation for later review of the likelihood of bias or of inattention to some salient features of the situation.

Notes may, in some situations, be supplemented by still pictures, videotapes, and printed material circulated or posted in the research setting. Such visual material can bring an entirely differently qualitative dimension into the analysis and call attention to some features of the social situation and actors within it that were missed in the notes (Grady, 1996). Commentary on this material can be integrated with the written notes (Bogdewic, 1999).

Exhibit 11.3   Field Notes From an Evolving Consumer Household (ECH)

I arrive around 4:30 p.m. and walk into a conversation between Jim and somebody else as to what color jeans he should buy. There is quite a lot of joking going on between Jim and Susan. I go out to the kitchen and find Dick about to take his dinner out to the picnic table to eat (his idea?) so I go ask if I can join him. He says yes. In the course of the conversation, I find out that he works 3 days a week in the "prevoc" program at the local day program, Food Services branch, for which he gets $10 per week. Does he think the living situation will work out? Yes. All they need is a plan for things like when somebody buys something and then everybody else uses it. Like he bought a gallon of milk and it was gone in two days, because everyone was using it for their coffee. I ask if he's gone back to the shelter to visit and he says, "No. I was glad to get out of there." He came to [the ECH] from [a shelter] through homeless outreach [a Department of Mental Health program]. Had been at [the shelter] since January. Affirms that [the ECH] is a better place to live than the shelter. Why? Because you have your own room and privacy and stuff. How have people been getting along with each other? He says, "Fine."

I return to the living room and sit down on the couch with Jim and Susan. Susan teases Jim and he jokes back. Susan is eating a T.V. dinner with M & M's for dessert. There is joking about working off the calories from the M & M's by doing sit-ups, which she proceeds to demonstrate. This leads to a conversation about exercise during which Jim declares his intention to get back into exercise by doing sports, like basketball.

Jim seems to have his mind on pulling himself together, which he characterizes as "getting my old self back." When I ask him what he's been doing since I saw him last, he says, "Working on my appearance." And in fact, he has had a haircut, a shave, and washed his clothes. When I ask him what his old self was like, he says, "You mean before I lost everything?" I learn that he used to work two jobs, had "a family" and was into "religion." This seems to have been when he was quite young, around eighteen. He tells me he was on the street for 7–8 years, from 1978–1985, drinking the whole time. I ask him whether he thinks living at [the ECH] will help him to get his "old self back" and he says that it will "help motivate me." I observe that he seems pretty motivated already. He says yes, "but this will motivate me more."

Jim has a warm personality, likes to joke and laugh. He also speaks up—in meetings he is among the first to say what he thinks and he talks among the most. His "team" relationship with Bill is also important to him—"me and Bill, we work together."

Source: Martin, Lawrence L. and Peter M. Kettner (1996). *Measuring the performance of Human Service Programs*. Thousand Oaks, CA: SAGE.

Managing the Personal Dimensions

Our overview of participant observation would not be complete without considering its personal dimensions. Because field researchers become a part of the social situation they are studying, they cannot help but be affected on a personal, emotional level. At the same time, those being studied react to researchers not just as researchers but as personal acquaintances—often as friends, sometimes as personal rivals. Managing and learning from this personal side of field research is an important part of any project.

The impact of personal issues varies with the depth of researchers' involvement in the setting. The more involved researchers are in multiple aspects of the ongoing social situation, the more important personal issues become and the greater the risk of "going native." In a moment of intense interaction, a McKinney ethnographer reported giving some advice to a staff member:

> [She] asked [a resident] and I what she should do. I told her that it probably should be up to [another resident] to make sure he takes his meds sometime in the evening.

There is no formula for successfully managing the personal dimension of field research. It is much more art than science and flows more from the researcher's own personality and natural approach to other people than from formal training.

If you plan a field research project, follow these guidelines (Whyte, 1955):

- Take the time to consider how you want to relate to your potential subjects as people.

- Speculate about what personal problems might arise and how you will respond to them.

- Keep in touch with other researchers and personal friends outside the research setting.

- Maintain standards of conduct that make you comfortable as a person and that respect the integrity of your subjects.

When you evaluate participant observers' reports, pay attention to how they defined their role in the setting and dealt with personal problems. Don't place too much confidence in such research unless the report provides this information. The primary strengths of participant observation—learning about the social world from the participants' perspectives, as they experience it, and minimizing the distortion of these perspectives by the methods used to measure them—should not blind us to its primary weaknesses—the lack of consistency in the data collected, particularly when different observers are used, and the many opportunities for direct influence of the researchers perspective on what is observed. Whenever we consider using the method of participant observation, we also must realize that the need to focus so much attention on each setting studied will severely restrict the possible number of settings or people we can study.

SYSTEMATIC OBSERVATION

Observations can be made in a more systematic, quantitative design that allows systematic comparisons and more confident generalizations. A researcher using systematic observation develops a standard form on which to record variation within the observed setting in terms of variables of interest. Such variables might include the frequency of some behavior(s), the particular people observed, the weather or other environmental conditions, and the number and state of repair of physical structures. In some systematic observation studies, records will be obtained from a random sample of places or times.

Antonio Pascual-Leone and Leslie S. Greenberg (2007) used a systematic observation strategy to investigate emotional processing in experiential therapy. Therapy clients gave their informed consent and their therapy sessions were videotaped. The researchers reviewed a total of 102 sessions, rated each one with their Classification of Affective-Meaning States (CAM) form, and identified 34 sessions in which clients exhibited global distress. These sessions were then coded systematically.

> Ratings began with a confirmation of the preselected global distress marker, which served as the rater's first code. Using the CAMS, the rater then coded emotion event continuously for the presence of any one of the given possible emotion codes. Raters were instructed to make codes as they saw them unfold sequentially and indicated the time at which they initiated a change in code. . . . Raters using the Experiencing Scale were operationally independent from raters using the CAMS. High experiencing in the last 15% of each event was used as an indicator of good within-session outcome. (Pascual-Leone & Greenberg, 2007, p. 881)

The systematic observations give us greater confidence in the measurement of emotional processing than we would have based on unstructured descriptive reports by observers or self-reports by patients to survey questions. However, for some purposes, it might be more important to know how emotional the patient felt during the therapy session, so interviews or perhaps just general observational reports on the videotaped sessions might be preferred.

FOCUS GROUPS

Focus groups are groups of unrelated people, usually about 7 to 10, that are formed by a researcher and then led in group discussion of a topic for 1 to 2 hours. The researcher asks specific questions and guides the discussion to ensure that group members address these questions, but the resulting information is qualitative and relatively unstructured. Focus groups do not involve representative samples; instead, individuals are recruited who have the time to participate, have some knowledge pertinent to the focus group topic, and share key characteristics with the target population.

Awareness of the value of focus groups for exploring new topics prompted Vetta L. Sanders Thompson, Anita Bazile, and Maysa Akbar (2004) to use this methodology to study African Americans' perceptions of psychotherapists:

> The current study represents a preliminary effort to understand what values and concerns may affect African American mental health attitudes and service use, as well as what efforts by the psychological community may prove beneficial in promoting an image of multicultural sensitivity and competence. (p. 19)

A focused discussion mimics the natural process of forming and expressing opinions, but the leader must create the expectation that all group members will participate and that no particular perspective or participant is favored. The researcher, or group moderator, uses an interview guide, but the dynamics of group discussion often require changes in the order and manner in which different topics are addressed (Brown, 1999). Focus group methods thus share with other field research techniques an emphasis on discovering unanticipated findings and exploring hidden meanings. For example, Thompson, Bazile, and Akbar (2004) discovered that "There was surprising consensus on the barriers to seeking mental health services . . . need[ing] to seek psychotherapy was associated with weakness and diminished price" (p. 22). They further observe:

> Well I think that also goes with an African American dream to be considered a strong family. Mental illness is considered a weakness and we wouldn't even recognize it in the first place, because strong families just don't do that. (p. 22)

No formal procedure exists for determining the generalizability of focus group answers, but the careful researcher should conduct at least several focus groups on the same topic and check for consistency in the findings. Some focus group experts advise conducting enough focus groups to reach the point of "saturation," when an additional focus group adds little new information to that which already has been generated (Brown, 1999). In any case, it is always important to consider how recruitment procedures have shaped the generalizability of focus group findings.

Vetta Sanders Thompson and her colleagues (2004) used newspaper advertisements and posted announcements to recruit 134 African American women and 66 African American men from a Midwestern city—an unusually large sample for a focus group study that ultimately consisted of 24 mixed-sex groups ranging in size from 3 to 12 members. In spite of the large number of participants, the researchers duly cautioned the readers of *Professional Psychology* about the limitations of their sample:

> Although we made an effort to obtain a diverse sample . . . , it is likely that there were regional differences in service use attitudes and preferences, as well as in knowledge about mental health. This sample was composed of volunteers, and it is impossible to know how individuals who chose to participate differ from those who did not. It is plausible that individuals who had concerns about mental health issues in the African American community were more likely to agree to participate in a study of this nature. In addition, the provision of a monetary incentive may have resulted in a larger proportion of low-income participants. (Thompson et al., 2004, p. 21)

MIXED METHODS

In simplest terms, mixed methods combine the strengths of different approaches to improve a research investigation. There are different ways of combining methods (Creswell et al., 2008). Often, some qualitative methods are combined with some quantitative methods, but particular types of qualitative or quantitative methods can also be "mixed" (Tashakkori & Teddlie, 2003). For example, a qualitative focus group may identify issues to be included in a quantitative survey. Alternatively, a quantitative experimental study may be followed by qualitative interviews that explore the process by which a treatment had an effect. Some mixed-methods designs may have a dominant method, with supplementary methods used to focus attention on some specific questions. For example, Stanley Milgram supplemented his experiment on obedience to authority with qualitative observations about participants' subjective reactions to the experimental treatment (see Chapter 3). Other mixed-methods designs may give equal attention to different methods. No matter how mixed methods are used, successful implementation of a mixed-methods design requires careful planning.

Deborah Gioia and John S. Brekke (2009) used mixed methods to investigate the impact of neurocognition on daily living in the community for individuals with schizophrenia. It is an important question for behavioral scientists, since there is a very large gap between the sophistication of neurocognitive tests and the limited knowledge about how, or whether, performance on cognitive tests is related to community functioning.

The mixed-method study began with the selection of 10 individuals with schizophrenia who had been scored as high or low in neuropsychological functioning based on tests administered to a large sample. Deborah Gioia then spent 3 to 5 hours on each of 3 days with each of these 10 individuals. She observed them as they engaged in such community activities as shopping, managing money, or ordering a meal in a restaurant. Gioia wrote detailed field notes after each observational session and then categorized the behavioral strategies of each person as "rote," "instrumental," "facilitative social" or "independent social." **Exhibit 11.4** includes the definition of one category—"rote tasks"—and some of the information provided about a participant who exemplified this behavioral strategy.

Exhibit 11.4   Definition of Rote Behavioral Strategy

Task	Definition	Participant Example
Rote tasks	Tasks that are generally purposeful and productive, but are done repeatedly in a repetitive or scripted fashion—folding clothes, putting away groceries, cleaning, sweeping—and are often directed by others.	RL is a single white male is [sic] his 50s living in supported housing. He does not work or attend school and is most comfortable doing assigned chores. He sweeps the courtyard daily, helps with lifting and unloading supplies. He is seen by the staff as dependable and helpful. He does not venture beyond these daily tasks and sometimes needs reminders. RL keeps a box with every receipt and check-stub from his social security checks dating back at least a decade. . . .

Source: Gioia & Brekke, 2009, p. 100, Figure 1.

Among their 10 participants, Gioia and Brekke (2009) found that differences in observed functioning paralleled neuropsychological scores: "The low NP group showed a restricted range of rote and instrumental behavior, with rote behavior predominant in the ratings" (p. 102). Although their conclusions can only be tentative due to the limited size of their sample, Gioia and Brekke's research helps to give us more confidence in the generalizability of neuropsychological tests to community functioning. A behavioral researcher should always consider whether data of another type should be collected in research designed with a single method in mind and whether additional research using different methods is needed before a research question can be answered with sufficient confidence. The ability to apply diverse techniques to address different aspects of a complex research question is one mark of a sophisticated behavioral researcher.

QUALITATIVE DATA ANALYSIS

The focus on text—on qualitative data rather than on numbers—is the most important feature of qualitative analysis. The "text" that qualitative researchers analyze is most often transcripts of interviews or notes from participant observation sessions, but text can also refer to pictures or other images that the researcher examines. Qualitative data analysts often seek to describe their textual data in ways that capture the setting or people who produced this text on their own terms rather than in terms of predefined measures and hypotheses. In this way, qualitative data analysis tends to be inductive: The analyst identifies important categories in the data, as well as patterns and relationships, through a process of discovery. There are often no predefined measures or hypotheses.

Good qualitative data analyses also are distinguished by their focus on the interrelated aspects of the setting, group, or person under investigation—the case—rather than breaking the whole into separate parts. The whole is always understood to be greater than the sum of its parts, and so the social context of events, thoughts, and actions becomes essential for interpretation. Within this framework, it doesn't really make sense to focus on two variables out of an interacting set of influences and test the relationship between just those two.

Qualitative data analysis is an iterative and reflexive process that begins as data are being collected rather than after data collection has ceased (Stake, 1995). Next to her field notes or interview transcripts, the qualitative analyst jots down ideas about the meaning of the text and how it might relate to other issues. This process of reading through the data and interpreting them continues throughout the project. The analyst adjusts the data collection process itself when it begins to appear that additional concepts need to be investigated or new relationships explored.

Documentation

The data for a qualitative study most often are notes jotted down in the field or during an interview—from which the original comments, observations, and feelings are reconstructed—or text transcribed from audiotapes. What to do with all this material?

Many field research projects have slowed to a halt because a novice researcher becomes overwhelmed by the quantity of information that has been collected. A 1-hour interview can generate 20 to 25 pages of single-spaced text (Kvale, 1996).

The first formal analytical step is documentation. The various contacts, interviews, written documents, and whatever it is that preserves a record of what happened all need to be saved and listed. Documentation is critical to qualitative research for several reasons: It is essential for keeping track of what will be a rapidly growing volume of notes, tapes, and documents; it provides a way of developing an outline for the analytic process; and it encourages ongoing conceptualizing and strategizing about the text. You can see in **Exhibit 11.5** how Grossman et al. (2006) documented their interviews.

Exhibit 11.5	Reported Perpetrators and Approximate Age Range Over Which Sexual Abuse Occurred	
Participant	*Approximate age range*	*Perpetrators*
Earl	7–13	uncle, male friend of father's
Brad	4–12	older sister, female babysitter, male stranger
Ron	4–10	grandfather, older brother
Morgan	2–11	mother, older brother
Will	2–13	stepfather, older sister, other men and women in group
Paul	4–6	grandfather
Martín	7–8	school principal and wife
Uhan	5–7	female babysitter, male neighbor
Malcolm	7	sister
Burt	2–13	father, mother, male church camp director, other men
Web	2–14	father, mother
Bill	2–17	mother, older sister, older foster sister, male border, female babysitter
Amhad	11–12	Big brother
Christos	3–15	uncle, male and female cousins, older neighborhood boy, older male and female children of friends of mother
Tomas	7–10	adult male cousin
Alejandro	4–15	two uncles

Source: Grossman, F. K., Sorsoli, L., & Kia-Keating, M. (2006). A gale force wind: Meaning making by male survivors of childhood sexual abuse. *American Journal of Orthopsychiatry, 76*(4), 434–443.

Conceptualizing, Coding, and Categorizing

Identifying and refining important concepts is a key part of the iterative process of qualitative research. Sometimes, conceptualizing begins with a simple observation that is interpreted directly, "pulled apart," and then put back together more meaningfully. Frances Grossman and her colleagues (2006) provide an example (Exhibit 11.6):

Exhibit 11.6 Categories of Meaning Making

Categories of Meaning Making	
Type of Meaning Making	*Narrative Example*
Meaning making through actions	
Altruistic behaviors	"Certain kids when I was in school, I'd defend them if I could. Like, if they were kind of outcast, I was like 'I know how that feels.' So I would try to help them out."
Creative expressions	"Create characters. Fantasize. That was the safe space."
Meaning making by developing cognitive frameworks	
Finding ways to understand the abuser's psychology	"He was gang-raped when he was about 6 years old. When he would abuse me, it was a replication of what had happened to him."
Finding ways to understand the role of the self	"I blamed my neediness for what got me into the situation."
Using a socio-cultural framework	"Many women of that generation had none of their needs met. . . . There she is in the suburbs; she's supposed to be a housewife. The women were forced to be like that at that time. It was a horrible mess."
Developing a philosophical view	"When I was 4 or 5, I was convinced that there was another world below where we were [where] things would be much better for me."
Meaning making through spirituality	"I've been forgiven for a lot of things that I've done in my life. And because of that, there is really nothing that anyone does to me that I shouldn't be able to forgive. So whatever my sister has done, whatever anyone has done to me, it all pales in comparison to what I've done to God, from a religious viewpoint."

Source: Grossman, F. K., Sorsoli, L., & Kia-Keating, M. (2006). A gale force wind: Meaning making by male survivors of childhood sexual abuse. *American Journal of Orthopsychiatry, 76*(4), 434–443.

Researchers should check their coding with others in order to establish reliability. Analytic insights are tested against new observations, the initial statement of problems and concepts is refined, the researcher then collects more data, interacts with the data again, and the process continues. Grossman et al. (2006) describe this process in their study of childhood sexual abuse survivors:

> To establish reliability, all members of the research team first coded the same interview transcript, which was then reviewed in detail to identify and resolve

discrepancies. Following this initial meticulous phase of establishing reliability, all other interview transcripts were coded by two members of the research team, who separately coded each transcript and then reviewed and reconciled any differences. The contents coded as meaning making and therapy were then carefully reread and categorized thematically. (p. 436)

Examining Relationships and Displaying Data

Examining relationships is the centerpiece of the analytic process, because it allows the researcher to move from simple description of the people and settings to explanations of why things happened as they did it with those people in that setting. The process of examining relationships can be captured in a **matrix** that shows how different concepts are connected or perhaps what causes are linked with what effects.

Exhibit 11.7 displays a matrix used to capture the relationship between therapists' race and the way that they discussed race in a cross-racial dyad.

Exhibit 11.7 Domains, Categories, and Frequencies of Therapists' Discussion of a Specific Cross-Racial Dyad: Discussing Race Had Positive Effect

Domain	Category	Frequency: AA	Frequency: EA
1. When therapists addressed race	Early in therapy	Variant	Typical
	Middle of therapy	Variant	Variant
2. Why therapists addressed race	Perceived discomfort in client	Typical	Variant
	Because client raised race	Variant	Variant
	Because client struggled with personal vs. community expectations	—	Variant
3. Therapists' comfort addressing race	Felt comfortable	Typical	Variant
	Felt discomfort	—	Typical
4. How therapists addressed race	Directly (e.g., questions, confrontations)	Typical	Typical
	Followed client's lead	Variant	Variant
5. Perceived effect of addressing race	Positive	General	General
	Increased trust/security m relationship	Typical	Typical

Note: AA = African American: EA = European American: dashes indicate that the category did not emerge for these participants.

Source: Knox, S., Burkard, A. W., Johnson, A. J., Suzuki, L. A., & Ponterotto, J.G. (2003). African American and European American therapists' experiences of addressing race in cross-racial psychotherapy dyads. *Journal of Counseling Psychology, 50*(4), 466-481.

Permission granted by American Psychological Association, as per their guidelines at: http://www.apa.org/about/contact/copyright/index.aspx.

Authenticating Conclusions

No set standards exist for evaluating the validity or "authenticity" of conclusions in a qualitative study, but the need to consider carefully the evidence and methods on which conclusions are based is just as great as with other types of research. Individual items of information can be assessed in terms of at least three criteria (Becker, 1958):

- *How credible was the informant?* Were statements made by someone with whom the researcher had a relationship of trust or by someone the researcher had just met? Did the informant have reason to lie? If the statements do not seem to be trustworthy as indicators of actual events, can they at least be used to help understand the informant's perspective?

- *Were statements made in response to the researcher's questions, or were they spontaneous?* Spontaneous statements are more likely to indicate what would have been said had the researcher not been present.

- *How does the presence or absence of the researcher or the researcher's informant influence the actions and statements of other group members?* Reactivity to being observed can never be ruled out as a possible explanation for some directly observed social phenomenon. However, if the researcher carefully compares what the informant says goes on when the researcher is not present, what the researcher observes directly, and what other group members say about their normal practices, the extent of reactivity can be assessed to some extent. Confidence in the conclusions from a field research study is also strengthened by an honest and informative account about how the researcher interacted with subjects in the field, what problems he or she encountered, and how these problems were or were not resolved.

Heidi Levitt and her colleagues (2006) were very careful to authenticate critical conclusions in their psychotherapy study.

It was noticeable that clients rarely discussed symptomatic change per se as an important outcome of their psychotherapy. To check this interpretation, after the hierarchy was formed, the researchers reread all the interviews to identify any discussion of specific symptoms (e.g., sleeping, eating, anxiety changes, sexual functioning changes). Although clients did mention symptoms in connection with the medication that they took, they did not describe symptom reduction as a reason why an experience in therapy was important to them. (p. 322)

ETHICAL ISSUES IN QUALITATIVE RESEARCH

No matter how hard the qualitative researcher strives to study the social world naturally, leaving no traces, the very act of research itself imposes something "unnatural" on the situation, so the qualitative researcher may have an impact that has ethical implications. Four ethical issues should be given particular attention:

Voluntary participation. Ensuring that subjects are participating in a study voluntarily is not often a problem with intensive interviewing and focus group research, but it often is a point of contention in participant observation studies. Practically, much field research would be impossible if the participant observer were required to request permission of everyone having some contact, no matter how minimal, with a group or setting being observed. And should the requirement of voluntary participation apply equally to every member of an organization being observed? What if the manager consents, the workers are ambivalent, and the union says no? Requiring everyone's consent would limit participant observation research to settings without serious conflicts of interest.

Subject well-being. Every field researcher should consider carefully before beginning a project how to avoid harm to subjects. It is not possible to avoid every theoretical possibility of harm nor to be sure that any project will cause no adverse consequences whatsoever to any individual. Direct harm to the reputations or feelings of particular individuals is what researchers must carefully avoid. They can do so, in part, by maintaining the confidentiality of research subjects. They also must avoid adversely affecting the course of events while engaged in a setting. The ethical problem becomes more difficult when subjects appear to be in harm's way, and the researcher must decide whether to take some action to lessen the likelihood of harm. A McKinney ethnographer's notes included an instructive example:

> I took his statements about cutting himself quite seriously, though I did not consider it a direct suicide threat since he was smiling when he said it. I told him that I thought he should talk to someone besides me about it because it sounded very serious and that he needed professional help.

These problems are rare in qualitative interviewing and focus groups, but researchers using these methods should try to identify negative feelings and help distressed subjects cope with their feelings through debriefing or referrals for professional help.

Identity disclosure. Current ethical standards require informed consent of research subjects, and most would argue that this standard cannot be met in any meaningful way if researchers do not disclose fully their identity. But how much disclosure about the study is necessary, and how hard should researchers try to make sure that their research purposes are understood? In field research on Codependents Anonymous, Leslie Irvine (1998) found that the emphasis on anonymity and expectations for group discussion made it difficult to disclose her identity. Less-educated subjects may not readily comprehend what research is or be able to weigh the possible consequences of the research for themselves. Should researchers inform subjects if the study's interests and foci change while it is in progress? What balance do you think should be struck between the disclosure of critical facts and a coherent research strategy?

Confidentiality. Field researchers normally use fictitious names for the characters in their reports, but doing so does not always guarantee confidentiality to their research subjects. Individuals in the setting studied may be able to identify those whose actions are described and thus may become privy to some knowledge about their colleagues or neighbors that had formerly been kept from them. Therefore, researchers should make every effort to expunge possible identifying material from published information and to alter unimportant aspects of a description when necessary to prevent identity disclosure. In any case, no field research project should begin if some participants clearly will suffer serious harm by being identified in project publications. Procedures for protecting privacy and maintaining confidentiality should be negotiated with participants early in the study if at all possible.

These ethical issues cannot be evaluated independently. The final decision to proceed must be made after weighing the relative benefits and risks to participants. Few qualitative research projects will be barred by consideration of these ethical issues. The more important concern for researchers is to identify the ethically troublesome aspects of their proposed research and resolve them before the project begins and to act on new ethical issues as they come up during the project.

CONCLUSIONS

Qualitative research allows the careful investigator to obtain a richer and more intimate view of human behavior than is possible with more structured methods. And the emphases in qualitative research on inductive reasoning and incremental understanding help to stimulate and inform other research approaches. Exploratory research to chart the dimensions of previously unstudied behaviors and intensive investigations of the subjective meanings that motivate individual action are particularly well served by the techniques of participant observation, intensive interviewing, and focus groups.

The very characteristics that make qualitative research techniques so appealing restrict their use to a limited set of research problems. It is not possible to draw representative samples for study using participant observation, and, for this reason, the generalizability of any particular field study's results cannot really be known. Only the accumulation of findings from numerous qualitative studies permits confident generalization, but here again, the time and effort required to collect and analyze the data make it unlikely that many field research studies will be replicated.

In the final analysis, qualitative research involves a mode of thinking and investigating different from that used in experimental and survey research. As a research methodologist, you must be ready to mix and match the methods as required by the research problem to be investigated and the setting in which it is to be studied.

END OF CHAPTER

Chapter Highlights

- Qualitative methods are most useful in exploring new issues, investigating hard-to-study groups, and determining the meaning people give to their lives and actions. In addition, many behavioral research projects can be improved, in some respects, by taking advantage of qualitative techniques.

- Qualitative researchers tend to develop ideas inductively, try to understand the social context and sequential nature of attitudes and actions, and explore the subjective meanings that participants attach to events. They rely primarily on participant observation, intensive interviewing, and, in recent years, focus groups.

- Intensive interviews involve open-ended questions and follow-up probes, with specific question content and order varying from one interview to another. Intensive interviews can supplement participant observation data.

- Field researchers must develop strategies for entering the field; developing and maintaining relations in the field; and sampling, recording, and analyzing data. Selection of sites or other units to study may reflect an emphasis on typical cases, deviant cases, and/or critical cases that can provide more information than others. Sampling techniques commonly used within sites or in selecting interviewees in field research include theoretical sampling, purposive sampling, snowball sampling, quota sampling, and in special circumstances, random selection with the experience sampling method.

- Recording and analyzing notes is a crucial step in field research. Jottings are used as brief reminders about events in the field, while daily logs are useful for chronicling the researcher's activities. Detailed field notes should be recorded and analyzed daily. Analysis of the notes can guide refinement of methods used in the field and of the concepts, indicators, and models developed to explain what has been observed.

- Systematic observation techniques quantify the observational process to allow more systematic comparison between cases and greater generalizability.

- Focus groups combine elements of participant observation and intensive interviewing. They can increase the validity of attitude measurement by revealing what people say when they present their opinions in a group context instead of in the artificial one-on-one interview setting.

- Four ethical issues that should be given particular attention in field research concern voluntary participation, subject well-being, identity disclosure, and confidentiality.

Key Terms

Research in the News

1. Williams syndrome results from a genetic error that leads to social gregariousness combined with poor comprehension of social dynamics. In a *New York Times* story about the syndrome, reporter David Dobbs (2007) described the experience of two teenage twins with Williams who spoke to a motorcycle club about their problems, leaving club members in tears. How would you have planned a participant observation study to learn about the sociability of "bikers" in a situation like this? What behaviors would you have looked for?

2. What a *New York Times* article termed "the grim neurology of teenage drinking" (Butler, 2006) often begins with a very social process. What questions would you ask a focus group of teens about social occasions at which some engage in binge drinking? What follow-up questions could encourage discussion about social pressure to drink?

Activity Questions

1. Conduct a brief observational study in a public location on campus where students congregate. A cafeteria, a building lobby, or a lounge would be ideal. You can sit and observe, taking occasional notes unobtrusively, without violating any expectations

of privacy. Observe for 30 minutes. Write up field notes, being sure to include a description of the setting and a commentary on your own behavior and your reactions to what you observed.

2. Devise a plan for using a focus group to explore and explain student perspectives on some current event. How would you recruit students for the group? What types of students would you try to include? How would you introduce the topic and the method to the group? What questions would you ask? What problems would you anticipate, such as discord between focus group members or digressions from the chosen topic? How would you respond to these problems?

3. Conduct a three-question qualitative interview with a classmate about her first date, car, college course, or something else that you and your classmates agree on. Then collect all the responses and analyze them in a "committee of the whole." Follow the procedures discussed in the section on qualitative analysis.

4. Using any of the major search engines, search the Web for the topic "Freud" and "psychoanalysis," keeping field notes on what you find. Categorize each site and write a brief report based on the data you have collected. What are the different views of Freudian psychoanalysis and who holds these views?

Review Questions

1. The variable extent to which a researcher participants in a situation being observed allows qualitative researchers to adapt to very different social situations but also creates some difficult challenges. Identify a social situations in which different levels of participation would be appropriate and identify the unique challenges they would create.

2. You read in this chapter a quote from an ethnographer in the McKinney housing study who learned that a house resident was talking seriously about cutting himself. If you were the ethnographer, would you have immediately informed house staff about this? Would you have told anyone? What if the resident asked you not to tell anyone? In what circumstances would you feel it is ethical to take action to prevent the likelihood of a subject harming him or herself or others?

3. Compare the method of qualitative interviewing to the design of structured surveys described in Chapter 5. What are the comparative advantages and disadvantages of qualitative interviewing?

4. Devise a plan for using a focus group to explore and explain student perspectives on some current event. How would you recruit students for the group? What types of students would you try to include? How would you introduce the topic and the method to the group? What questions would you ask? What problems would you anticipate, such as discord between focus group members or digressions from the chosen topic? How would you respond to these problems?

Ethics in Action

1. The McKinney ethnographers observed a variety of problems in the group homes, ranging from arguments between tenants, conflicts with staff over chores, and incoherent speech to drug use. Do you think the ethnographers should ever have intervened in these problems? Notified staff about them? Called police? What ethical standards do your answers suggest you would favor in ethnographic research?

2. Would it ever be ethical for participant observers to conduct their observations covertly, without revealing their identity as a researcher to the group or individuals they are observing? Do you believe that social scientists should simply avoid conducting research on groups or individuals who refuse to admit researchers into their lives? Would there be any advantages to a strategy of covert observation? Might there be practical problems with this approach?

3. Should any requirements be imposed on researchers who seek to study other cultures, to ensure that procedures are appropriate and interpretations are culturally sensitive? What practices would you suggest for cross-cultural researchers to ensure that ethical guidelines are followed? (Consider the wording of consent forms and the procedures for gaining voluntary cooperation.)

C H A P T E R   1 2

Essentials of APA Report Writing

Throughout the book, we have selected reports published in scientific journals of specific psychological investigations to serve as our "case studies." Each chapter highlighted a particular study, beginning in Chapter 1 with the introduction of the maximization-satisficer scale (Iyengar, Wells, & Schwartz, 2006) through the qualitative research on psychotherapy process (Brinegar, Salvi, Stiles, & Greenberg, 2006) covered in Chapter 11. We went behind the scenes, so to speak, of each of these studies to learn how theory, method, measurements, design, statistics, and data interpretation all come together to create a scientific paper. Now in this final chapter comes perhaps the most crucial stage in the practice of research—written communication of the findings. Written or print communication is the primary medium by which research is disseminated. Without a written report, the most ground-breaking findings will go undocumented, the perfect experiment will remain unknown, and new theoretical perspectives will be unrealized. How then should we go about composing a written report of research findings? What format are we to follow? Are there habits and practices that lead to effective report writing?

To answer these questions, we will break down report writing into smaller steps that will, we hope, make what is often a daunting task more manageable and perhaps even enjoyable. We will focus on the basics that you need to know to begin report writing. Two distinct types of reports are covered: *empirical studies* are reports of original research and *literature reviews* are critical evaluations of works that have already been published (see Chapter 2). We will also look at two different media of expression for communicating research. One, of course, is the traditional written article that is published in a scientific journal. The other is the poster presentation, a very popular option for communicating research at psychological conventions. An article and poster share the same basics of style and organization of report writing.

Let's begin with an illustrative case of writing a report of an empirical study. As a class exercise, students in our research methods course answered two questions, each of which we presented and handed out on separate sheets of paper. One question asked students to rate their current happiness on a 1 to 10 scale with 1 = *very unhappy* and 10 = *very happy*. The other question asked students how many dates they had in the past 30 days. We manipulated the order in which we presented the two questions. Half the class received the happiness question first, followed by the dating question, and the other half of the class received the dating question followed by the happiness question. Our research question asked: Would the order of the presentation of questions influence answers? For the purpose of this illustration, we use artificial data. On the basis of these artificial data, we calculate the correlation of the two questions for each of the orders of presentation. Our results indicate no statistically significant correlation between answers when students responded to the happiness question first, followed by the dating question. However, answers did correlate significantly when students responded to the dating question first, followed by the happiness question. Our task is now to write up these results. Below we will learn how to compose a written report of this empirical study.

APA FORMAT

The American Psychological Association (APA) format provides us with a blueprint for report writing. The format is presented in clear and precise detail in the *Publication Manual of the American Psychological Association* (APA, 2009). We will present the general guidelines for using the *Publication Manual,* outlining both style and organization of report writing. For additional information, there are several other sources that you may helpful in learning about report writing using APA format. These include: *APA: The Easy Way!* by Houghton and Houghton (2007), *The APA Pocket Handbook* by Jill Rossiter (2007), *The Psychologist's Companion* by R. J. Sternberg (2003), *Concise Rules of APA Style* (APA, 2005), and a computer program called *APA-Style Helper,* which can be used with most word processors to make sure that your paper is formatted in APA style. The *Publication Manual,*

Concise Rules of APA Style, and *APA-Style Helper* can be purchased directly from the APA websites at http://www.apa.org and http://www. apastyle.org.

As we will learn, the APA format for organization of a written report of an empirical study is rather straightforward: title, abstract, introduction, method, results, discussion, references, author notes, footnotes, tables, figure captions, and figures. Becoming familiar with APA writing style, on the other hand, is much more difficult. *Concise, clear,* and *interesting* are adjectives that frequently describe APA writing style. These terms, however, are not intended to intimidate. For beginners as well as for seasoned veterans of APA writing style, clarity, brevity, and felicitous phrasing are aspirational. In other words, live with imperfection, remember there is no good writing, there is only good rewriting, and it is better to write and to rewrite than to have never written at all!

APA style emphasizes written language that is sensitive to racial and ethnic identity, gender, age, sexual orientation, and disabilities. The goal is to eliminate sexism and ethnic bias in writing. For example, *gender* is the correct term to describe males and females as social groups, as in the phrase "gender differences evidently in average income." The term *sex* is the correct term to describe biological features of men and women, as in "sex chromosomes" or "sex-determining gene." However, gender pronouns can often be sexist. Other biased terms are *he, his, man, men, mankind,* and so forth, in representing both men and women. In describing people, a general rule is to refer to people in terms as they prefer. Often the best policy is not to assume but rather to inquire politely and respectfully so that you will be sensitive to any terms or labels that might be offensive. In research reports of studies of persons with disabilities, be very mindful of the stigmatizing effects of diagnostic labels. For example, do not use the term "schizophrenic" as a noun, but rather use the phrase "a person with the diagnosis of schizophrenia." Similarly, when comparing a group of people with a disability, such as a diagnosis of schizophrenia, with a control group, do not describe the control group as the "normal group." Instead, write "We compared people with the disorder and without the disorder." Also, people in a research study are referred to as *participants*. This term is used to distinguish human and animal subjects.

APA style also emphasizes the importance of proper documentation and citation. Consider the following statement: "The prevalence of schizophrenia in the general population is 1 %" (Gottesman, 1991). Notice that the statement is substantiated by the Gottesman (1991) study that empirically demonstrated the 1 % prevalence rate of schizophrenia in the general population. In report writing, any written statement or claim such as the example citing the prevalence of schizophrenia needs to be documented. Documentation in the form of citing a reference allows the reader to know that the statement is supported and substantiated by evidence. In addition, it allows the reader to check the reference to determine the accuracy of the statement and learn the details of the cited study.

You should only cite references or sources that you have read first hand. For references that you have not read yourself, use a secondary citation for the work. For example, imagine that you read in your textbook the following: "Aristotle emphasized the importance of distinguishing in moral reasoning actions that are bad and criminal versus those that are mad and insane." You would write, "Aristotle as cited by Nestor and Schutt (2011) emphasized the importance of distinguishing bad and criminal acts from mad and insane acts in moral reasoning." Here our textbook, Nestor and Schutt (2011), is a secondary source for the reference citing Aristotle. In general, however, use secondary sources sparingly, as mistakes in describing and understanding ideas can be perpetuated in secondary sources when authors fail to read the original or primary work. The mechanics of APA style of documentation are covered below in the reference section in the organization of report writing.

Proper documentation is essential, an ethical imperative. Your ideas, thoughts, sentences, phrases, and words must be clearly separated from those from other sources. Always err on the side of crediting others. Even for what you may believe to be your truly original ideas and insights, there are almost always others who have had similar thoughts published in the literature. Citing these helps also to place ideas and thoughts in context as well as to show how ideas of others may have influenced your work. Never present another person's published work or parts of published work as your own. In other words, do not plagiarize. **Plagiarism** is a serious ethical as well as legal problem that can result in expulsion, grade failure, job loss, and litigation for violating copyright laws (Hard, Conway, & Moran, 2006). Directly quoting another author with the proper reference is a must. However, filling a paper with many direct quotes or with very lengthy quotes is self-defeating and counterproductive—why bother reading a paper filled with quotes? As a result, good writing requires paraphrasing with proper citation of the author(s). When paraphrasing, you put into your own words another cited or referenced author's own ideas. It is not easy finding different words for the same idea. In general, do not use three or more consecutive words in a sentence that are the same as those written in the original source. Use quotes with citation if you do, or better still, revise your sentence. In the following sections, we will examine six essential parts of an APA written report of an empirical study: abstract, introduction, method, results, discussion, and references.

REPORT ORGANIZATION IN APA FORMAT

APA style requires that all reports be typed, entirely double-spaced, in 12-point serif font with at least 1-inch margins for right and left, and top and bottom. The alignment of the text is set to the left margin; do not right justify. All pages are numbered consecutively, beginning with the title page. Page numbers are placed in the top margin 1 inch from the right side of the paper. The number appears by itself with no punctuation.

Title

Appearing as the first page of your report is the title page. It contains the title of the report, author's name and school affiliation, a running head, page header, and page number. A running head is a short title of the paper that should be no more than 50 characters in length. A good title conveys specific information as to the major thrust of the study. Typically, the title of the paper describes the relationships between independent and dependent variables of the study. Consider the title of a 2004 published paper in the APA journal *Neuropsychology* by the first author of your current text (PGN) and his colleagues, "Neuropsychological Correlates of Diffusion Tensor Imaging in Schizophrenia." The title indicates that the study examined the relationship of neuropsychological performance and diffusion tensor imaging (structural brain imaging of white matter) in schizophrenia. In general, when choosing a title, look to your research question and hypothesis. The title we chose for our in-class exercise described above is "Focusing Illusion in College Students." Here the theoretical construct of the paper, focusing illusion, is placed front and center in the title. This informs the reader of the topic and rationale for the study in a way that the study variables for our in-class exercise—order of questions and their answers—could not.

Abstract

The abstract is presented on the second page, following the title page. It comes at the beginning of the paper, but the abstract is the last section that the author writes. The abstract is a brief paragraph, no more than 120 words, that states what was done to whom and the major results or findings. The abstract parallels the structure and organization of the paper: Begin with a sentence or two that summarizes the introduction, followed by a sentence or two for the method, then the results, and finally the discussion. Expect your earlier drafts of the abstract to be too long, and then you can start to whittle it down to size. This is the best approach, as editing works best for shortening rather than lengthening.

Introduction

In the introduction, we describe what our plan is and the reason our study needs to be done. We begin by providing a theoretical description of our research question or principal problem. So for our in class-exercise, the concept of focusing illusion is pivotal. Our first order of business, then, is to whet the appetite of the reader. Borrowing from Kahneman et al. (2006), consider the following as our opening sentence:

> *When people are led to think about the impact of any single thing on their happiness, such as money, they tend to overstate its importance.*

Our initial statement, both general and nontechnical, leads to a more specific description of the key phenomenon under study, focusing illusion (Kahneman et al., 2006):

> *Exaggerating the impact of any one factor can lead to a particular form of cognitive bias, known as a focusing illusion.*

We then present a simple example used in previous research studying focusing illusion.

For example, consider two simple questions: (1) How happy are you? (2) How many dates did you have last month?

We now draw connections with previous research.

Previous studies (Kahneman et al., 2006; Strack, Martin, & Schwartz 1988), have shown a strong correlation in responses to these two questions when participants are presented with the dating question first, followed by the happiness question. However, the correlation disappeared when participants answered the happiness question first followed by the dating question (Strack et al., 1988).

In your own words, elaborate on the meaning of these studies.

The dating question (coming first) may have drawn attention to that part of life, leading people to exaggerate its importance in their responses to the more general question regarding their happiness.

Now tell the reader how you plan to study the focusing illusion.

The purpose of this study is to examine whether the order of presentation of these two simple questions to be answered by college students in a research methods class would induce a focusing illusion.

Notice that this simple sentence reports two important facts about our study. First is that focusing illusion will be studied by manipulating the order of presentation of two simple questions, and, second, our sample consists of college students who will answer the two questions.

Our next and often final step in the introduction is to present our main hypothesis. Setting the stage for the method, the hypothesis, as outlined in Kahneman et al. (2006), reported here is intended to focus the reader on the primary reason for the study.

It is hypothesized that when college students are asked first about the number of dates they had in the past 30 days, that aspect of life will influence their responses to the second question about their overall level of happiness. By contrast, for students who are presented the happiness question first, followed by the dating question, their answers to these two questions will be unrelated.

This text tells the reader our principal prediction, essentially why we are doing the study. The focusing illusion is expected to be induced by the order of presentation of our two questions. When respondents first answer the question as to how many dates they have had in the past 30 days, this factor becomes exaggerated, creating, we predict, a focusing illusion that unduly influences participants' answers to the second general question regarding their overall level of happiness. By contrast, when we present the dating question second, after the general question of happiness, no focusing illusion will be induced, and there will be no relationship between answers to these two questions.

These sentences are meant to engage you in the process of writing an introduction. Each sentence helps the reader to understand why the study is needed and how it is conducted. An introduction must thus provide background and context for the study. This is done by reporting a brief history of the topic followed by a balanced summary of previous research that is relevant to the topic. In researching a topic, searching a database such as PsychInfo or Google Scholar is an important first step (see Chapter 2).

For example, when we entered "focusing illusion, cognitive bias," Google Scholar revealed more than 27,000 links. Of course the sheer number of these links is overwhelming. Accordingly, we pursued another tactic, one with which your professor can surely help you. We knew from our studies that focusing illusion belongs to an area of research in cognitive psychology referred to as heuristic or cognitive biases based on the pioneering works of psychologist Daniel Kahneman and his collaborator Amos Tversky. In 2006, Kahneman and colleagues published a study in the international journal *Science* titled "Would You Be Happier If You Were Richer? A Focusing Illusion." In their review of the literature, Kahneman and colleagues provided a concise background for the topic of focusing illusion that included several references that you can find easily and then read thoroughly. Once read, you can then describe in your own words these studies in your introduction and how they are related to your topic. (How to cite studies that appear in the body of text in APA style will be covered in a separate section later in this chapter.)

You want to look for papers that are most relevant to your topic, such as a study that you might wish to replicate. For example, in their paper, Kahneman and colleagues carefully described an experimental study by Strack and colleagues (1988) published in the *European Journal of Social Psychology* that used the dating question followed by the happiness question to induce a focusing illusion in their college student sample. You want to read the Strack et al. article as your primary source, and then in your own words describe and explain in the introduction how and why you want to replicate this study. In essence, in writing an introduction, think of yourself as a detective. In our study, the Kahneman et al. literature review served as a major clue and the Strack experimental study as the smoking gun!

In the end of the introduction, present your hypotheses. This should flow from your summary of previous research. For example, perhaps you have identified areas in which existing research is lacking or questions that have yet to be addressed. Present your hypothesis as a possible means to address a question left unanswered by previous studies and offer what you expect to find in your study.

Method

The method section is the most straightforward section of the report. It is often written first and in fact while the study is being conducted so as to serve as an official record to document procedures, measures, and actions of participants. It is written in the past tense. The method section must be presented clearly so that another researcher should be able to repeat or reproduce the study exactly. Also of critical importance to keep in mind is that the validity of a study's findings will be judged largely on the extent to which its method provided variables that adequately captured the phenomena under study. For example, does presenting the dating question first constitute a valid means to induce a focusing illusion? Similarly, recall from Chapter 6 that an experimenter can create independent variables by staging or manipulating an event. We called this a *staged* or *event manipulation* that can be employed when the primary goal is to induce a particular psychological state in research participants. For example, the famous Milgram study used a staged event to create obedience in the research participants. In Chapter 7, Baumeister and colleagues sought to induce a specific psychological state of social exclusion, creating bogus feedback to participants about ending up alone in life without loved ones, friends, and acquaintances. These manipulations should be described in detail in the method. When you do so, readers will be able to evaluate whether a staged event truly represents the phenomenon that it is intended to induce. The take-home message is that evaluating and critiquing any research begins by carefully examining the study method. Unlike the introduction, results, and discussion, the method section is divided into the following subsections: participants, materials, design, and procedure.

Participants. Report how many participants were in the study and how they were recruited. Parenthetically, recall that we have learned that the number of participants or the size of a study sample represents an important piece of information that you should consider in evaluating and critiquing a study. Likewise, how participants were recruited, with random sampling as the gold standard for research, is yet another piece of information included in all method sections that is essential for evaluating and critiquing a study. In addition, present in your method age, gender, education, student status, and any other important characteristics, such as whether participants were compensated, received course credit, or volunteered for no material benefit. Again, describe your participants so that a reader can evaluate the *generalizability* of your sample. Also include in the participant subsection of the method that your study was approved by the Institutional Review Board (IRB) and was in accordance with APA ethical guidelines (see Chapter 3).

Materials. Describe measures, variables, and type of apparatus or stimuli used in the study. If your study only used a survey, then in the material subsection you would describe the survey, such as the number of items and the nature of the questions. For example, in our focusing illusion study, you could present the two-item questionnaire:

- On a scale of 1 to 10, with 1 = *very unhappy* and 10 = *very happy*, rate how happy you are with your life in general.

- How many dates did you have last month?

Design. Report the type of design used in the study. Specify the independent and dependent variables. Indicate whether your study employs within-groups or between-groups design. For example, the focusing illusion study used a between-groups comparison of participants' responses as a function of the order of presentation of a two-item questionnaire. The order of presentation is the independent variable and the dependent variable is the answers to the two questions.

Procedure. Here, specify the sequence of steps of the study, essentially what you had the participants do and how you collected their data. For example, in our focusing illusion study, we would write the following:

> *We manipulated the order of presentation of a two-item questionnaire. Participants were randomly assigned to either one of two orders of presentation. Thirty participants answered the happiness item first followed by the dating item and 30 participants answered the dating item first followed by the happiness item.*

Results

In the results section, summarize your findings and the statistical tests you performed. Report your findings in sufficient detail, but do not overwhelm the reader with such detail that the most relevant findings in regard to the study hypotheses are lost in a sea of numbers. Report all relevant findings, including those that run counter to your hypotheses and expectations, such as findings that are statistically nonsignificant or much smaller in magnitude (effect size) than predicted by your theory. Individual scores or raw data are not reported, with the exception of single-subject designs that by definition focus on one or a small number of participants. Do not hide unexpected, disappointing, or uncomfortable results by omission.

You typically begin the results section by providing descriptive statistics of your study sample. Often descriptive statistics are presented in a table with means and standard deviations. **Exhibit 12.1** is taken from a recent publication by us (Nestor et al., 2010) in the APA journal *Neuropsychology.* This is a typical table that provides descriptive data in the form of means and standard deviations for both patient and control groups. Note that uppercase and italicized *N* refers to the total number of cases, whereas lowercase and italicized *n* refers to the number of cases of a group or subsample, as for instance when you may want to report scores separately for males and females, or, as in **Exhibit 12.1**, patients and controls.

In our illustrative study, let us present in text (as opposed to in a table) means (*M*) and standard deviations (*SD*) for responses to each of the two questions for our entire sample of 60 (*N* = 60) participants:

> *The entire sample of 60 participants had a mean happiness rating of 6.75 with a standard deviation of 1.34 and a mean number of dates for the past 30 days of 6.63 with a standard deviation of 2.35.*

Exhibit 12.1 Neuropsychological scores for patients with schizophrenia for WAIS-III. ($n = 22$) and IGT ($n = 23$) and for control participants for WAIS-III ($n = 23$) and IGT ($n = 24$)

Demographic Information	Patients	Controls
Age	38.78 ± 9.90	41.5 ± 7.35
Education	12.83 ± 1.99	15.00 ± 1.98
SES	3.75 ± 1.22	2.42 ± 1.06
Parental SES	2.83 ± 1.11	2.71 ± 1.27
WAIS-III IQ		
Full scale	91.83 ± 13.74	105.22 ± 16.24
Verbal	95.35 ± 14.78	104.22 ± 14.16
Performance	88.87 ± 12.20	105.30 ± 18.07
WAIS-III Index		
Verbal comprehension	99.96 ± 15.88	103.13 ± 14.47
Perceptual organization	94.74 ± 16.05	107.48 ± 17.56
Working memory	91.91 ± 13.54	105.75 ± 15.68
Processing speed	81.04 ± 10.1	101.87 ± 14.48
Iowa Gambling Task		
Block 1	−2.17 ± 12.02	−1.17 ± 10.87
Block 2	−1.25 ± 10.01	4.33 ± 9.08
Block 3	1.25 ± 9.97	6.91 ± 9.65
Block 4	−1.58 ± 9.55	3.83 ± 10.30
Block 5	−0.08 ± 9.16	4.67 ± 11.31

Note: Values are means plus or minus standard deviations. SES = socioeconomic status; WAIS-III = Wechsler Adult Intelligence Scale–Third Edition; IGT = Iowa Gambling Test (IGT).

Source: From "Neuropsychological correlates of diffusion tensor imaging in schizophrenia" by P. G. Nestor, M. Kubicki, R. J. Gurrera, M. Niznikiewicz, M. Frumin, R. W. McCarley, and M. E. Shenton in *Neuropsychology*, *18*, 629–637. Copyright © 2004 American Psychological Association.

In writing the results, we assume that the reader has a professional knowledge of statistics. We therefore would not need to indicate in our report that one standard deviation unit means that about two-thirds of the entire sample responses fall between +/− one standard deviation unit of the mean. The reader will likely know this, just as the reader will likely know the arithmetic mean. (Of course, for class exercises and assignments, you may very well need to show that you understand these concepts!)

There are numerous approaches to the analysis of data, including both quantitative (Chapter 10) and qualitative (Chapter 11). In the results section, we want to clearly present our data analytic approach. For our illustrative study on focusing illusion, this means that we specify the statistics used to test our hypothesis. This will allow the reader to judge whether we used the most direct and powerful statistical test of the theory and hypothesis of the study. First, let us make clear our statistic test used to test the hypothesis. For example:

> *The focusing illusion predicted that answers to the two questions should be correlated only when the dating question came first, followed by the happiness question. To test this hypothesis, we computed the Pearson correlation (symbol for Pearson correlation is r) between the responses of the two questions for each of the two orders of presentation. The results indicated a significant correlation for answers when the dating question came first, followed by the happiness question (r = .493, p = .006). By contrast, when the happiness question came first, followed by the dating question, the results indicated no significant correlation (r = .031, ns). Thus, as predicted, and in support for the theory of focusing illusion, answers to these two questions correlated significantly only when participants responded to the dating question first followed by the happiness question.*

Several points of both substance and style are important to keep in mind. First, notice that the text specifically links the statistical test, Pearson correlation, to the main theory and hypothesis of the study, that being under what conditions does a focusing illusion occur. Second, without being repetitious or redundant, we remind the reader that we manipulated the order of presentation of the two questions, which served as the independent variable of our study. Third, we report the quantitative results of our statistical analyses, and we present the Pearson correlation as a three-decimal number. Because a correlation statistic cannot be greater than 1, we do not use a zero before the decimal fraction. The same principle for recording holds for significance level. Note we present the exact *p*-value for a statistically significant result. For a nonstatistically significant result, we do not present the exact *p*-value, which we know by definition is greater than .05; instead, use the symbol *ns* to indicate a nonsignificant value. Fourth, we make a simple declarative statement as to whether the obtained results either supported or failed to support the hypothesis and theory of focusing illusion of the study. Any additional interpretive statements and conclusions are not appropriate for the results section and are addressed more fully in the discussion section that follows the results section.

Discussion

Now, having reported the results, you are ready to evaluate and interpret their implications, particularly in relation to your original hypothesis. Keep in mind that the culture of scientific report writing favors a modest, conservative, careful, and cautious style. Even when significant results are obtained in favor of the original hypothesis, you as a writer of the research report should always avoid sweeping generalizations and inflated pronouncements. Keep in mind that your findings still represent the results only of one study. Emphasize the importance of independent replication of any obtained significant finding. Present clearly and forthrightly aspects of the findings that may not fit with the results and that may raise questions and problems of interpretation and meaning. Qualify results to the specific conditions of the study.

Content of the discussion section begins with a clear statement as to whether the obtained results either supported or did not support the original hypothesis. If the results failed to support the hypothesis, offer explanations; these are typically referred to as *post hoc,* meaning they occur "after the fact." Here, consider similarities and differences between your study and the work of others. Oftentimes you might return to the method section and look to see how your study conditions and participants aligned with the work of others. For example, imagine a study that used a staged event or manipulation to create a certain condition. Perhaps the manipulation lacked credibility and thus failed to induce the desired state of mind. This is why it is important to collect data as part of debriefing, when you can ask participants their thoughts and feelings about a staged event. This provides both a methodological check on the validity of the study design and evidence to substantiate with numbers a post hoc explanation as to whether a staged event actually produced the desired effect. Thus, a discussion must include previous relevant studies. These serve to place your current study in a scientific context. Emphasize both theoretical and practical implications of you results.

The *Publication Manual* (APA, 2009) emphasizes critical factors that need to be accounted for when interpreting results in the discussion section. First, consider sources of potential bias and other threats to both internal validity of the study design and external validity of the study sample of participants. Consideration of internal validity is relatively straightforward and transparent and can be largely done by carefully reviewing the method and results sections. External validity is trickier. Here, be mindful of cultural and ethical sensitivities: Research studies that produce empirical results about groups of people can be misused prejudicially. Second, in interpreting results, always make sure to account for the imprecision of measurements: There are no perfect measurements in psychology. Third, take into account the number of tests used and the extent to which they overlap or are redundant. For example, a correlation can be artificially inflated between two tests that use the same form of measurement, such as pencil and paper. That is why researchers often use a multimethod approach with different forms of measurements (e.g., behavior observation, pencil and paper) of the same trait (see Chapter 4).

Also, when interpreting results, be mindful of the inherent nature of statistical analysis of data collected across several measures. The number of statistical tests, such as the number of correlations computed, can lead to chance findings. For example, imagine you have a set of 10 test scores that you correlated with a set of

10 brain volume measures. A 10×10 correlation matrix will have a total of 100 values, each test score correlated with each brain volume measure. By chance alone, five of these correlations are expected to be significant. Let's say these significant correlations coincided with those that you had predicted beforehand. How, then, would you know for certain whether the obtained correlations represented genuine statistical support for the hypothesis or, conversely, were simply due to chance that comes with computing a large number of statistical tests or correlations? This is a rather complicated problem. The important point to remember is that any written discussion about data interpretation needs to be mindful of the inherent limitations of statistical testing. Finally, in the discussion section you want to address any other weaknesses or limitations of your study.

The discussion section concludes with a commentary on the meaning and importance of your findings. Here, make sure your interpretations are well reasoned and based on the empirical evidence from your results section. Again, a common mistake is to overstate the impact of your study and to overinterpret the significance and meaning of your results. Whether brief or extensive, your closing commentary must be tightly reasoned and crystal clear. It revisits why the research problem is important (as presented in the introduction) and carefully addresses implications beyond the particulars of your study. It comments on the theoretical, clinical, or practical significance of your results. As stated in the *Publication Manual* (APA, 2009), in this concluding section, you might also touch upon the extent to which any real-life applications are warranted on the basis of your research and what problems remain unresolved or newly emerged because of your findings.

For our illustrative case, we begin our discussion by restating our major findings. For example, we begin the discussion:

> *The study examined whether a focusing illusion could be induced simply by manipulating the order of presentation of two simple questions. In support of the hypothesis, the results indicated that responses to the two test items correlated significantly but only when participants answered the dating question first, followed by the happiness question. These results suggested that presenting the dating question first created a focusing illusion whereby participants exaggerated the specific impact of their current level of dating when considering the second, more global question of how happy they are with their lives in general. In stark contrast, and also consistent with the hypothesis, participants showed no evidence of a focusing illusion when presented with the happiness question first, followed by the dating question. That is, the responses to the two questions did not correlate when participants answered the happiness question first, followed by the dating question.*

Next, we need to place our findings in context. How do our results relate to previous research? Revisit the literature review of your introduction. In a real full-length paper, you would have a fairly extensive literature review. For our illustration, our introduction does include two important sources, the Kahneman et al. review and Strack et al. experiment, and we would therefore make sure we address our findings in relation to these two key works. In addition, in a real, full-length paper, in the introduction section you would have cast the phenomenon of focusing illusion within a wider theoretical framework. For example,

> Research on focusing illusion emanates from a school of cognitive psychology that studies how our thinking can be deceived or distorted by heuristic biases or mistakes of reasoning. These errors of thinking have been likened to curious blind spots or mental tunnels in our minds (Piattelli-Palmarini, 1995). Focusing illusion is just one type of heuristic bias but one that may be a source of error in significant decisions that people make.

But most important for our exercise in report writing is to emphasize the limitations of our study. Indeed, even though our artificial results supported the hypothesis and conformed to previous research, our study (i.e., class exercise) on focusing illusion had several major limitations and flaws. How do you report these? First, be straightforward and open: Do not hide them or hope that they will be overlooked. Second, carefully explain the limitations, and comment as to the degree of importance in relation to your study. How much of a threat to internal validity do they pose? How much of a threat to external validity? In other words, simply listing limitations and flaws will not be well received but rather will come across as rote and dull. Instead, explain clearly and thoroughly; make sure the reader knows not only the limitations but also the relative importance of these for the current study.

In our example, two important limitations come immediately to mind. One might be classified as a threat to external validity and the other to internal validity. The external validity of our findings is clearly threatened by the simple fact that all participants were enrolled in a research methods class and answered the two-item questionnaire as part of an in-class exercise. The limited generalizability of this sample is clearly a major point to emphasize in your discussion. Likewise, for internal validity, we failed to control for any number of variables, such as age, education, relationship/marital status, depression, or other mental status conditions, all of which could have influenced our results.

References

Two important "must knows" regarding references: First, for references cited in the body of the text, whether in the introduction, method, results, or discussion, you list the last names of the authors of the work followed by the date of publication. For example,

Strack, Martin, and Schwartz (1988) reported that. . . .

Or you could write:

Previous work (Strack, Martin, & Schwartz, 1988) demonstrated that . . .

Note that when the authors' last names appear outside the parentheses, use the word *and,* but use an ampersand (&) when they appear inside the parentheses.

For two authors, always list in your text both names in the order that they appear on the referenced publication. For referenced works by three or more authors, list all names the first time you cite the work as in the above example. Thereafter, list only the first author, followed by *et al.* and the year of publication:

Strack et al. (1988) suggested that. . . .

Second, following the discussion and beginning on a separate page under the label *References* that is centered at the top of the page is the reference section of your report. Here you list the reference for each work cited in your paper. Only references contained in the body of your text are included in the reference section. There should be no entries on your list of references that have not been cited in the body of your text. Likewise, there should be no reference cited in the body of your text that is not also included in your reference list.

A reference to a journal article contains the following: author(s), date, title, journal (italicized), volume (italicized), and page range:

Nestor, P. G., Kubicki, M., Gurrera, R. J., Niznikiewicz, M., Frumin, M., McCarley, R. W., & Shenton, M. E. (2004). Neuropsychological correlates of diffusion tensor imaging in schizophrenia. *Neuropsychology, 18,* 629–637.

For a reference to a book cited in the text and listed in the reference, you need the following information: author(s) date, title (italicized), city in which book was published, and publisher. From an example taken from Houghton and Houghton (2007):

Shotton, M. A. (1989). *Computer addiction? A study of computer dependency.* London, England: Taylor & Francis.

For a reference to a journal article read on the Internet that was originally in print, list the author(s), publication date, article title [Electronic version], journal title, volume, issue, and pages. From an example taken from Houghton & Houghton (2007):

Ostroff, C. (1998). The relationship between satisfaction, attitudes, and performance: An organizational level analysis [Electronic version]. *Journal of Applied Psychology, 12*(2), 963–974.

LITERATURE REVIEW

Now let's imagine that you have been assigned to write a literature review. What is a literature review and how would you go about completing such a task? Literature reviews are critical examinations of empirical studies that have already been published. In a literature review, you evaluate published studies in terms of their methods as well as their conceptual foundation. Consider for example the methods employed in terms of samples studied, measurements, and operational definitions of critical independent and dependent variables. Also consider the ideas and concepts that have inspired the various studies. But perhaps what makes a literature review so challenging is that you, as the author, need to abstract common themes and weave together theories and results from a number of studies to describe the "big picture" of your topic of research. The emphasis is on analyses, critique, and evaluation of both theories and empirical work conducted to test these theories. Do not simply summarize studies but rather draw connections, abstract common themes, and identify gaps, inconsistencies, and contradictions in the literature. Develop a case for the steps that are needed to advance research and to solve these problems.

Selecting a topic is the first and most important step in writing a good literature review. Choose a topic that comes from a well-defined and well-studied area of research. For inspiration and ideas, browse through some recent APA journals, particularly those that specialize in literature reviews, such as *Psychological Bulletin* or *Psychological Review*. Make sure you choose an area that you find personally interesting. Within that area, narrow your topic so that you will have a manageable number of studies to review. A broad topic such as memory, schizophrenia, or culture generates countless articles that would be impossible to cover in a literature review. Instead, think of a specific topic that targets a particular area of research that you plan to review. For example, you might want to review a specific aspect of memory, such as false memory. You could then review neuropsychological and psychological evidence for and against the concept of false memory. And then you could address wider implications of false memory, particularly for courtroom proceedings. In short, keep in mind literature reviews will be easier to write and more pleasurable for the reader to understand and appreciate if you choose a current, well-studied, and specific topic.

Here are some helpful tips for browsing for a topic or for actually collecting studies that will be the basis of your literature review. In Chapter 2, we described both *popular science literature* and *science journalism* as excellent sources for generating research ideas. So too for selecting a topic for a literature review, these works often are both highly engaging and scientifically sound. For traditional scientific literature, along with the aforementioned *Psychological Bulletin* and *Psychological Review, Current Directions in Psychological Science* features well-written articles by authors who are often leaders in a specific topic of research. You can get leads from these articles by looking at listed citations. You can then use these citations to find works that will help you to develop a specific topic and a particular line of research that you would like to review.

Before finalizing your topic, try to find at least one published article from the traditional scientific literature that could serve as a foundation for your paper. A pivotal article could be one that is especially well-written, references valuable citations, addresses an interesting question or theme, or integrates different but related lines of research. Oftentimes, an older review of the literature published 5 to 10 years ago will help you to provide a historical background for your topic. More recent articles can be accessed in periodicals published within the past few years through your library using search engines such as Google Scholar or PsycInfo (see Chapter 2).

In our earlier example of writing a report on an empirical study, the review paper by Kahneman and colleagues served as a pivotal article for us. We found the article to be especially well written, with clear, concise, and engaging prose, containing a number of valuable citations, including the Strack et al. (1988) study that served as the foundation for our in-class exercise. We found fascinating the overall theme cultivated by Kahneman and colleagues of how our minds can deceive us and can lead to erroneous decisions. The eye-catching title alone, "Would You Be Happier If You Were Richer? A Focusing Illusion," resonated with intrigue and fun and, published in the prestigious international journal *Science,* underscored the relevance and impact of the topic. Also adding to the luster of the article is the fact that the lead author, psychologist Daniel Kahneman, won the 2002 Nobel Prize in Economic Sciences for his pioneering studies on decision-making under uncertainty!

Once you have finalized your topic, you will read and review a number of articles. How many studies should you review? For published reviews, 100 or more studies may be cited. Luckily, most professors will require you to review between 5 and 15 articles. Fewer articles mean that your literature review will not be exhaustive. You will have to be especially discriminating in selecting the most useful and representative articles. Often helpful are index cards, a summary sheet, or even a table that lists the following key features of each article: What is the research question or problem (introduction); how was it studied (method); what were the findings (results); and how were they understood and interpreted (discussion)? Answers to each of these key questions can be found in the body of the text in particular sections of the paper (presented in parentheses), and all will be contained in the abstract, which will give you a helpful overview of the study.

Read for content and depth. Examine the articles to see how previous works are described and how much emphasis is given to any particular study. For example, key works are given more attention with respect to both methodological detail and theoretical contribution. Less important studies may be cited but not described in any detail. In reading an article, think about the principles of construct validity that we covered in Chapter 4. As you recall, constructs are synonymous with ideas or theories. For example, let's imagine that you are writing a review paper on the topic of false memory. In reviewing the literature, you would want to identify the methods used to study false memory. You would look to see whether different methods to assess false memory, such as psychological studies and brain imaging, converge to reveal a consistent pattern of evidence. Studies using different methods of the same construct should agree, so this would be a critical point for you to develop in your literature review.

A literature review does not follow the same organization and structure as an article reporting an empirical study. You will have an abstract that appears on the first page that summarizes your review. But you will not have prescribed method and results sections for a literature review. Nevertheless, you will identify headings for major sections that well help you to organize the structure of the paper. Try to make headings as specific as possible. For clues, look at published literature reviews to see how authors typically use headers to delineate major sections of their articles. Outline your paper with sections, some of which will correspond to the headers that you will use in the final written product. Here are a set of steps that might be helpful to keep in mind when writing a literature review (APA, 2009; University of Washington Psychology Writing Center, 1997–2005):

- Introduce and define research question or problem, and explain its importance and meaning.

- Focus research question to the studies reviewed.

- Describe studies, explain their methods and results.

- Identify relationships, gaps, inconsistencies across studies.

- Discuss how the research area may be advanced and improved.

Consider a literature review published by one of us, "Mental Disorder and Violence: Personality Dimensions and Clinical Features" (Nestor, 2002). First, I introduced the research question, identifying what it is and why it is worth examining: For example, my research question asked, How do some mental disorders increase the risk of violence? I then explained why this research question is worth examining. To wit, understanding of these factors may lead to prevention of violence for at-risk individuals. Next, I narrowed the research topic to the studies reviewed. I distinguished between two approaches, actuarial and clinical, each of which has been used to study mental disorders and violence. I then described how these two approaches had until recently revealed divergent and inconsistent findings, with age and past history serving as strong actuarial predictors of violence in contrast to the failure of clinical variables, such as symptoms and diagnoses, to predict violence. Last, I presented a model generated from my review of these studies for understanding violence and mental disorders:

> The risk of violence may be understood in terms of four fundamental personality dimensions: 1) impulse control; 2) affect regulation; 3) narcissism; and 4) paranoid cognitive personality style. . . . This review supports the hypothesis that these four fundamental personality dimensions operate jointly, and in varying degrees, as clinical risk factors for violence among groups with these classes of mental disorders. p. 1973

POSTER PRESENTATION

A poster is a very effective and economical way to communicate results of your research. In fact, many research studies that will be eventually published in peer-reviewed scientific journals are first presented in what are referred to as poster sessions at national or regional conferences. Most if not all psychological conventions include poster sessions in which the bulk of new research is presented. These sessions are typically held in a large room in a convention hall that contains large poster boards for presenters. A session usually holds a fairly large number of researchers simultaneously presenting their individual posters. During the session, convention members may stop by and read the poster and may ask questions of the presenters about the study. Oftentimes, conventiongoers like to "window-shop" at poster sessions, quickly looking at posters and asking questions only if especially interested in the study. Do not be offended, and keep in mind that brevity and clarity of communication are hallmarks of good posters.

A poster includes the same major sections that are found in a published article: title, abstract, introduction, method, results, discussion, and references. However, a poster contains much less detail than an article, and information is often presented in bulleted lists of major points. The amount space a conference provides for each poster varies, but dimensions of 3 to 4 feet high and 5 to 6 feet wide are common. Exhibit 12.2 provides an example of a common poster layout adapted from Cozby (2010) and the 2010 website of Psi Chi The International Honor Society in Psychology: http://www.psichi.org/.

Posters can be constructed using large-format printing technology that is often made available through your psychology department. Or, if a poster printer is not available, a series of separate pages can be laid out following the example presented in Exhibit 12.2. Each page corresponds to particular section, such as abstract or introduction, and each section is printed on letter-sized paper, numbered, and tacked to the poster board in the proper sequence. In general, you want to construct your poster so that one or two important points can be easily gleaned.

Exhibit 12.2   Example Poster Layout

Source: Adapted from "Sample Poster Arrangements" on the 2010 website of *Psi Chi The International Honor Society in Psychology.*

A simple figure and an easy-to-read table are generally included in a poster. Try to make your poster as visually friendly as possible. Text should be presented in a large font along with simple figures and tables. The idea is to keep it concise and visually pleasing. Finally, make sure to have available for viewers printed handouts summarizing your poster. The handouts must include presenters' (authors') names, the title of the poster, name of the organization or conference where the poster was presented, and date (year, month). This information is necessary in order to cite a poster in APA format:

Presenters, A. A. (Year, Month). Title of poster. Poster session presented at the meeting of the Organization Name, Location.

You can see how easily our report on the focusing illusion exercise with artificial data could be presented in a poster. Look back at the text (italics) for the introduction, method, results, and discussion sections of our report. Note that text for each of these sections is sufficiently concise and brief for a poster presentation. As you can also see in **Exhibit 12.3**, we present a table and figure that would be well suited for a poster presentation of our artificial data. You can see that the table and figure visually depict the two major points of the study. That is, **Exhibit 12.4a** depicts a scatter diagram (see Chapter 8) plotting the significant correlation between responses to the dating and happiness questions when the dating question came first followed by the happiness question. By contrast, **Exhibit 12.4b** depicts a scatter diagram (see Chapter 8) plotting the nonsignificant correlation between responses to the happiness and dating questions when the happiness question came first followed by the dating question. Thus, a viewer of the poster can see that your data showed clear evidence of a focusing illusion: When college students were asked first about the number of dates they had in the past 30 days, that aspect of their life became exaggerated, influencing their responses when they encountered the more general second question about their overall level of happiness (**Exhibit 12.4a**). By contrast, presenting the happiness question first had no influence on responses to the subsequent dating question (**Exhibit 12.4b**).

Exhibit 12.3	Happiness ratings and number of dates for participants who answered the dating question followed by happiness question ($n = 30$) versus participants who answered the happiness question followed by the dating question ($n = 30$)	
	Happiness	*Number of Dates*
Date question followed by happiness question	6.57 ± 1.17	6.93 ± 1.48
Happiness question followed by date question	6.93 ± 1.48	6.13 ± 2.47

Note: Values are means plus or minus standard deviations (based on artificial data; see text).

Exhibit 12.4a   Scatter diagram plotting the significant correlation between responses to the dating and happiness questions when the dating question came first followed by the happiness question

Date Question Followed by Happiness Question

$r = .493, p < .05$

Exhibit 12.4b   Scatter diagram plotting the nonsignificant correlation between responses to the dating and happiness questions when the happiness question came first followed by the dating question

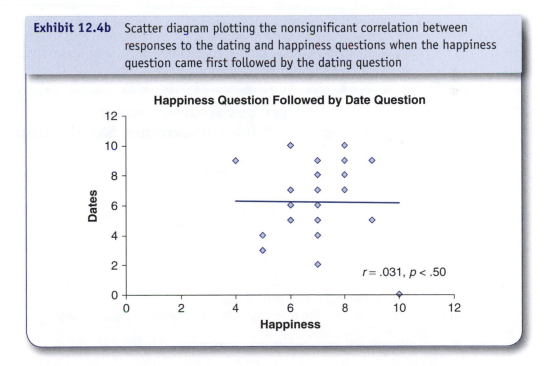

Happiness Question Followed by Date Question

$r = .031, p < .50$

SAMPLE PAPER

In the following pages, we present a sample manuscript by Iyengar et al. (2006) titled "Doing Better but Feeling Worse: Looking for the 'Best' Job Undermines Satisfaction." We present this paper as an example of a prepublication manuscript that was submitted to the journal *Psychological Science,* where it was eventually published. We covered this study in Chapter 1, so we have come full circle! Now we use this prepublication manuscript as a model to guide you in writing your own papers in APA style. In reading through the sample manuscript, pay close attention to its organization, that is, the order of presentation of the section headings of the report—title, abstract, introduction, method, results, references, author notes, footnotes, tables, and figures. Also pay close attention to the APA style requirements for page numbering, reference citations, and the format of figures and tables.

Writing is not easy, and writing in APA style can be overwhelming. It is important therefore to think of APA format as providing a general organization for your papers. It is meant to be helpful to you in structuring and ordering your ideas, providing a format to follow in reporting results of your psychological studies. You want to master the general APA format for organization as well as the general rules for citations and references. For more specific questions, such as citations for different kinds of sources, whether newspaper articles or online documents, consult the *Publication Manual.* Remember, even the most seasoned authors or researchers will make errors in APA style. Fortunately, editorial offices of journal articles are equipped with experts who can correct these errors. So the take-home message is do not be discouraged and afraid to make mistakes. For your papers, just make sure to follow the general APA format for organization and referencing. This, we hope, will help rather than hinder you in presenting your research results.

Doing Better but Feeling Worse:
Looking for the "Best" Job Undermines Satisfaction

Sheena S. Iyengar
Columbia University

Rachael E. Wells
Columbia University

Barry Schwartz
Swarthmore College

KEYWORDS: Maximizing, job search, satisfaction
Word Count: 3,917, excluding title page, abstract, references, and tables

Abstract

Expanding upon Simon's (1955) seminal theory, this investigation compares the choice making strategies of maximizers to those of satisficers and finds that maximizing tendencies, while positively correlated with objectively better decision outcomes, are also associated with more negative subjective evaluations of these decision outcomes. Specifically, graduating university students were administered a scale that measured maximizing tendencies, and then followed over the course of the year as they searched for jobs. Students with high maximizing tendencies secured jobs with 20% higher starting salaries. However, maximizers were less satisfied than satisficers with the jobs they obtained, and experienced more negative affect throughout the job search process. These effects were mediated by maximizers' greater reliance on external sources of information, and their fixation on realized and unrealized options during the choice search and selection process.

Doing Better but Feeling Worse: Looking for the "Best" Job Undermines Satisfaction

"Success is getting what you want. Happiness is wanting what you get."

—Attributed to Dale Carnegie circa 1944

Half a century ago, Simon (1955, 1956, 1957) introduced an important distinction between "maximizing" and "satisficing" as choice making strategies. To maximize is to seek the best, requiring an exhaustive search of all possibilities. To satisfice is to seek "good enough," searching until an option is encountered that crosses the threshold of acceptability. For example, compare the strategies of a maximizer versus a satisficer selecting a TV show from one of 400 cable channels. The maximizer would channel-surf, exploring *all* the channels, spending so much time deciding on a show that little time would be left for viewing. The satisficer would most likely channel surf until he/she encounters the first acceptable show, put down the remote, and actually watch the show. Simon based his distinction on the idea that the limited information processing capacities of organisms made maximizing impossible. In the modern world of almost unimaginable choice, this distinction is even more pertinent (see Iyengar & Lepper, 2000; Schwartz, 2004a; Schwartz, 2004b).

Expanding upon Simon's classic theory, recent studies by Schwartz, Ward, Monterosso, Lyubomirsky, White, and Lehman (2002) comparing the decision making processes of maximizers and satisficers revealed that those exhibiting maximizing tendencies, like the channel surfer described above, were less satisfied with their decision outcomes than their satisficing counterparts. Researchers asked participants about recent purchasing decisions and used a "maximization scale" to measure individual differences in maximizing tendencies. Their findings suggested that the experiences of maximizers differed from those of satisficers both during the decision making process and when evaluating their final decision outcome. Specifically, while they were involved in the decision making process, maximizers were more likely to engage in an exhaustive search of all available options and compare their decisions to those of others (Schwartz et al., 2002). Even though maximizers invested more time and effort during the decision process and explored more options than satisficers—presumably in order to achieve greater satisfaction—they nonetheless felt worse about the outcome that they achieved. Results showed that maximizing tendencies were positively correlated with regret, depression, and decision difficulty, and negatively correlated with happiness, life satisfaction, optimism, and satisfaction with decision outcomes (Schwartz et al., 2002).

Such differences in the subjective choice making experiences between maximizers and satisficers are attributed to the fact that maximizers create a more onerous choice making process for themselves. Initially, maximizers focus on increasing their choice sets by exploring multiple options, presumably because expanded choice sets allow for greater possibilities to seek out and find the elusive "best." Yet, as the number of options proliferates, cognitive limitations prevent decision makers from evaluating and comparing all options (Iyengar & Jiang, 2004; Iyengar & Lepper, 2000; Miller, 1956). Identifying the "best" becomes increasingly difficult, compelling maximizers to rely on external (often social) rather than internal standards to evaluate and select outcomes (Lyubomirsky & Ross, 1997). In addition, the inevitability of tradeoffs among attractive options intensifies the sting of passing up one attractive alternative when choosing a more attractive one, and increases expectations about the quality and utility of the chosen alternative.

But, do the very strategies that render maximizers less happy with their decision outcomes also enable them to achieve better objective decision outcomes? Perhaps there is utility associated with the strategic pursuit of real and imagined options, and the careful observation of others' choice making experiences—utility that may be reflected in the form of more effective deliberations and objectively better outcomes. Unlike prior investigations of the relationship between maximizing tendencies and decision outcomes, the current investigation examines the effects of maximizing tendencies on both the objective outcome associated with the decision as well as the subjective experience of the decision maker throughout the process.

Thus, expanding upon this nascent literature, the present study allows us to test the hypotheses that during the choice search and selection process, maximizers will invest more heavily in gathering information from external sources (thereby incurring search costs and perhaps prioritizing externally valued criteria) and will fixate more on realized and unrealized options (thereby incurring opportunity costs), both of which together will contribute to more successful decision outcomes, yet also result in greater negative affect and reduced subjective well being. We chose to test these predictions within the consequential domain of graduating college students' job search processes, which allowed us to examine the influence of maximizing tendencies on both actual and perceived decision outcomes, and afforded us the opportunity to examine reactions to the decision process as decisions were being made. Regardless of the finite number of offers made to job seekers, during the search process itself maximizers face both the search costs and the raised expectations associated with contemplating an almost limitless set of employment possibilities. To determine how a maximizing orientation affects both the *affective* experiences and the *objective* outcomes of the job search process, we measured the maximizing tendencies of participants from multiple institutions during the fall of their final year and subsequently followed them throughout their job search. Specifically, the longitudinal questionnaire study measured both how well applicants actually did and how well they thought they did. This methodology allowed us to test the following predictions: that compared to satisficers, maximizers would desire more options, plan to apply for more jobs, rely more on social comparison and other external sources of information, obtain jobs with higher expected returns (i.e., salary), but also experience greater negative affect than satisficers throughout the process and at the conclusion of their job search.

METHOD

Participants

Graduating students (predominantly undergraduate seniors) were recruited from 11 colleges and universities that varied in geographical region, university rank, and school size. Females comprised 69.7% of the sample. The median age of participants was 21 (range: 20 to 57), and 64% of participants were Caucasian, 26% Asian, and 10% Other. Participants majored in the social sciences (36%), arts/humanities (25%), engineering (16%), natural sciences and math (11%), and business (15%). At T1, 548 participants responded, followed by response rates of 69.5% and 56% at T2 and T3 respectively. Five $200 prizes were raffled off amongst participants who completed all three surveys.

Procedures

Career services from 11 participating institutions directed students who were just beginning their job searches in November, 2001 (T1) to our survey website. T1 participants were notified via email of our follow up online surveys in February, 2002, as they were completing applications, interviewing, and getting offers (T2), and in May 2002, as they were accepting offers (T3). While it is difficult to calculate the percentage of students who, upon encountering the online advertisement, chose to participate in the survey, consultations with career services staff provided us with numerical estimates of the total number of students who utilized career services in their job search within the given academic year. Since the advertisement was available only to those students who were affiliated with career services between the months of September and November (approximately 25%), we calculated that response rates ranged from 17.4% to 53.2% across a sampling of participating institutions.

Measures

Maximizing tendencies. At T1, participants completed 11 maximization items drawn from Schwartz et al. (2002), each of which were rated on a scale from 1 (*Strongly Disagree*) to 9 (*Strongly Agree*) ($\alpha = 0.6$). Two sample items are: "When I am in the car listening to the radio, I often check other stations to see if something better is playing, even if I am relatively satisfied with what I'm listening to" and "When shopping, I have a hard time finding clothes that I really love." Individual item scores were averaged to create a composite maximizing score. Overall, men ($N = 166$, $M = 5.48$) and women ($N = 382$, $M = 5.10$) from our sample population showed significantly higher maximizing tendencies than those in a recent national adult sample (Kliger & Schwartz, 2005; men: $N = 3261$, $M = 4.9$, $t(165) = 7.03$, $p < 0.0001$; women: $N = 4692$, $M = 4.77$ $t(381) = 6.28$, $p < .0001$), a difference which may be at least partly attributable to the age difference between the two samples, as maximization tendencies have found to be negatively correlated with age (Kliger & Schwartz, 2005).

Option fixation. We used three measures to examine option fixation. At T1, we measured the number of options that participants pursued: "For approximately how many jobs do you anticipate applying?" Participants provided responses in numerical form. Note that the number of anticipated applications ranged from 1 to 1000, exhibiting extreme right skewness (skew = 7.5) and kurtosis (69.0), and was therefore log-transformed. At T2, we measured participants' fixation on unrealized options on a scale from 1 (Strongly disagree) to 9 (Strongly agree): "I often fantasize about jobs that are quite different from the actual job(s) that I am pursuing." At T3, we measured participants' regret with their choice set size on a scale from 1 (Not at all) to 9 (To a large extent): "I wish I had pursued more options in my job search process."

Reliance on external influences. We created a single composite measure of five items ($\alpha = 0.70$) to test reliance on external influences. At T1 participants were asked: "How much have you been using the services offered by the career services office at your school during the job search?," "To what extent have you consulted experts' ranking such as 'top companies,' 'fastest growing fields,' etc.?," "How much do you seek advice from your family regarding the job search (i.e., input, suggestions, etc.)?," and "To what extent do you compare your own job search process and results to those of your peers?" The question regarding peer comparison was repeated at T2. Participants responded on a scale from 1 (*Very little*) to 9 (*Very much*).

Job market performance. Participants were asked how many interviews they had received at T2 and T3, how many job offers they had received at T3, and their annual salary (in dollars per year/hour) when they accepted a full-time job offer at T3. In the case of jobs with hourly wages, we determined how many hours per week participants were required to work and converted this information into an estimated annual salary.

Negative affect. Participants' negative affect with the job search process was measured at all three time periods. At T1 and T2, participants were asked, "To what extent does each of the following describe how you are generally feeling about the job search process?," rating each of seven emotions from 1 (*Not at all*) to 9 (*Extremely*) (T1 α = .86; T2 α = .89): "pessimistic," "stressed," "tired," "anxious," "worried," "overwhelmed," and "depressed." At T3, the same question was repeated; however, for those who had accepted job offers, it was modified to read: "To what extent does each of the following describe how you are feeling about the offer you accepted and your upcoming new job?" and three emotions were added (T3 α = .92): "regretful," "disappointed," and "frustrated." Composite measures for T1, T2 and T3 were constructed.

Outcome satisfaction. We measured participants' satisfaction with their accepted job offers by averaging their responses [on a scale from 1 (*Not at all*) to 9 (*Very satisfied*) / (*Very confident*)] on two items: (a) "How satisfied are you with the offer you have accepted?" and (b) "How confident are you that you made the right choice about where to work next year?" (α = .88).

Demographics and Other Control Variables

We gathered information on age, sex, ethnicity, family income-level, university-affiliation, and rank (as measured by *U.S. News and World Report*, "Best National Universities," 2001), geographic location, and information on academic standing, including major, overall GPA, and job-related activities (i.e., current stage in the job search process).

RESULTS

Preliminary Analysis

Table 1 reports the means and standard deviations for all hypothesized variables, with maximizers and satisficers separated by a median split. Attrition analyses demonstrate that our initial sample differed from T2 and T3 samples in terms of demographics: East Asians, children of foreign-born parents, and older students comprised less of the later samples, while those who did not identify themselves with one specific ethnicity comprised a greater portion of the sample at T3. However, T1, T2, and T3 samples did not differ as a function of our hypothesized variables (including maximizing score, number of logged anticipated applications, fixation on unrealized options, and reliance on external influences). Further analyses reveal that the subsample of participants who reported having completed the job search at T3 was comprised of significantly more business majors and fewer arts/humanities majors, younger job seekers, and those with higher GPAs, socioeconomic backgrounds, and a heavier reliance on external influences. All regression analyses reported below controlled for gender, university rank, age, academic major, cumulative GPA (collected at T2), and whether a job offer had been accepted. See Table 2 for full regression models including control variables. Note that, following Killeen (2005), as we report our regression results, we provide the probabilities of replicating our effects (denoted by p_{rep}) in addition to reporting standard p values.

Main Effects for Maximizing Tendencies

As illustrated in Table 2, maximizing tendencies were observed to be positively correlated with increased option fixation, greater reliance on external influences, improved job market performance, and more negative affective experiences. At T1, those with greater maximizing tendencies anticipated applying for more jobs ($\beta = .13$, $t(537) = 2.35$, $p < .05$, $p_{rep} = .93$); however, this effect was attenuated amongst those attending high ranked universities ($\beta = -.50$, $t(537) = -2.33$, $p < .05$, $p_{rep} = .93$). Among students in top-15 ranked universities, the median for both maximizers and satisficers was 30, while in lower ranked universities, the median

Table 1 Mean Differences Between Maximizers and Satisficers*

	Maximizers' Mean	Satisficers' Mean
Anticipated applications	20[+]	10
Fixation on unrealized options	5.17 (2.55)	4.02 (2.47)
Regret with choice set size	5.09 (2.39)	4.52 (2.20)
Reliance on external influences	5.02 (1.65)	4.65 (1.62)
Salary (in $10K)	4.45 (1.34)	3.71 (1.35)
Negative Affect (T1)	5.54 (1.56)	4.81 (1.59)
Negative Affect (T2)	5.40 (1.67)	4.81 (1.83)
Negative Affect (T3)	4.50 (1.82)	3.91 (1.78)
Outcome Satisfaction	7.02 (1.78)	7.58 (1.55)

*Standard deviations are provided in parentheses.

[+]*Note.* The scores reported for anticipated applications are medians, rather than means, and are only for students from universities not ranked within the top 15 as university rank significantly interacted with maximizing tendencies university rank.

Table 2 Regression Analyses Betas

	1 Logged Anticipated Applications	2 Fixation on Unrealized Options	3 Regret with Choice Set Size	4 Reliance on External Influences	5 Salary - Initial Model	6 Salary - Mediator Model	7 Negative Affect (T1) - Initial Model	8 Negative Affect (T1) - Mediator Model
1. Control Variables								
Female sex (0-M; 1-F)	.03	.00	.04	−.07	−.16*	−.11	.04	.04
Top 15-ranked university	.73**	.01	.02	.05	.29**	.27**	.11*	.03
Age	.11*	−.00	.13*	−.17**	.06	.10	−.05	−.08+
Business major	.25**	−.06	.05	.33**	.11	.03	.08	.01
Social sciences major	.24**	−.08	.02	.18	−.00	.02	.08	.01
Science/math major	.03	−.16*	−.05	−.01	.08	.06	−.01	−.02
Engineering major	.21**	−.12	−.06	.11	.32+	.36*	.06	.00
Education major	−.01	−.04	.00	−.04	—	−.20	−.03	−.03
Arts/humanities major	.12	−.08	.08	−.04	−.28+	.20**	.08	.04
Cumulative GPA		−.09	−.18**	.02	.19*	.15*	—	—
S had already accepted an offer by point of DV measurement	−0.09*	−.01	−.18**	.21**			−.19**	−.16**
Salary (in $10K)								

(Continued)

Table 2 (Continued)

	Logged Anticipated Applications	Fixation on Unrealized Options	Regret with Choice Set Size	Reliance on External Influences	Salary- Initial Model	Salary- Mediator Model	Negative Affect (T1) - Initial Model	Negative Affect (T1)- Mediator Model
2. Maximizing Variables								
Maximizing score	.13*	.23**	.18**	.17**	.20**	.15*	.26**	.25**
Maximizing score*Top-15 ranked university	−.50*							
3. Proposed Mediators								
Logged anticipated applications						—		.29**
Fixation on unrealized options						—		
Regret with choice set size						—		
Reliance on external influence						.27**		
Full Model R²	.14	.08	.14	.28	.49	.54	.13	.20
Δ R² vs. Control Model	.01	.05	.03	.03	.04	.09	.07	.14
Δ R² vs. Previous Model of Same DV						.05		.07
Model F-Ratio	7.06	2.60	3.34	11.28	10.22	11.29	6.98	10.97
Degrees of freedom	537	372	263	366	115	115	535	535
p_{rep}	.99	.98	.99	.99	.99	.99	.99	.99

Table 3 Regression Analyses Betas

	9 Negative Affect T2- Initial Model	10 Negative Affect T2- Mediator Model	11 Negative Affect T2- Ctrl for Neg. Affect T1	12 Negative Affect T3 - Initial Model	13 Negative Affect T3 - Mediator Model	14 Negative Affect T3 - Ctrl for Neg. Affect T1	13 Outcome Satisfaction - Initial Model	14 Outcome Satisfaction- Ctrl for Neg. Affect T1	15 Outcome Satisfaction- Ctrl for Neg. Affect T1
1. Control Variables:									
Female sex (0-M; 1-F)	-.01	-.01	-.02	-.04	-.04	-.07	.05	.08	.10
Top 15-ranked university	.09+	.01	.01	-.03	-.05	-.08	-.05	-.04	-.02
Age	-.10*	-.13**	-.06	.00	-.00	.01	-.08	-.10	-.10
Business major	-.00	-.02	-.02	.05	-.02	.02	-.08	-.20	-.21
Social sciences major	.02	.00	-.01	.12	.09	.08	-.04	-.17	-.16
Science/math major	.01	.06	.06	-.08	-.04	-.02	.09	.02	.03
Engineering major	.05	.05	.05	.07	.09	.09	.04	-.14	-.14
Education major	.05	.05	.03	.09	.10+	.06	–		
Arts/humanities major	.04	.04	.01	.06	.07	.06	-.02	-.02	-.02
Cumulative GPA	-.03	.01	.01	-.08	-.02	-.00	.20*	.02	.01
S had already accepted an offer by point of DV measurement	-.31**	-.30**	-.24**	-.53**	-.53**	-.52**	–		
Salary (in $10K)							.12	.22+	.19

(Continued)

413

Table 3 (Continued)

	Negative Affect T2- Initial Model	Negative Affect T2- Mediator Model	Negative Affect T2- Ctrl for Neg. Affect T1	Negative Affect T3 - Initial Model	Negative Affect T3 - Mediator Model	Negative Affect T3 - Ctrl for Neg. Affect T1	Outcome Satisfaction - Initial Model	Outcome Satisfaction- Ctrl for Neg. Affect T1	Outcome Satisfaction- Ctrl for Neg. Affect T1
2. Maximizing Variables									
Maximizing score	.18**	.11*	.01	.16**	.06	.03	−.28**	−.14	−.10
Maximizing score* Top-15 ranked university									
3. Proposed Mediators									
Logged anticipated applications		.21**	.04						
Fixation on unrealized options		.25**	.15**		.10+	.04		−.27**	−.21*
Regret with choice set size					.21**	.16**		−.34**	−.31**
Reliance on external influence					.18**	.11*			
Negative Affect T1			.59**			.31**			−.23*
Full Model R²	.14	.24	.52	.35	.42	.50	.16	.34	.38
Δ R² vs. Control Model	.03	.13	.41	.02	.09	.17	.07	.25	.29
Δ R² vs. Previous Model of Same DV		.10	.28		.07	.08		.18	.03
Model F-Ratio	4.70	8.07	25.75	11.18	11.85	15.16	1.75	4.05	4.46
Degrees of freedom	365	365	365	257	257	257	115	115	115
p_{rep}	.99	.99	.99	.99	.99	.99	.85	.99	.99

was 20 for maximizers and 10 for satisficers. At T2, those with greater maximizing tendencies fantasized more about jobs that they were not pursuing ($\beta = .23$, $t(372) = 4.48$, $p < .001$, $p_{rep} = .99$), such that every one-unit increase in maximizing was associated with a .59 increase in this measure. At T3 those with greater maximizing tendencies reported that they "wished that they had pursued still more options" ($\beta = .18$, $t(263) = 2.96$, $p < .01$, $p_{rep} = .97$), such that every one-unit increase in maximizing was associated with a .40 increase in this measure. Additionally, those with greater maximizing tendencies were more reliant on external influences during T1 and T2 of the job search process ($\beta = .17$, $t(366) = 3.63$, $p < .001$, $p_{rep} = .99$). Every one-unit increase in maximizing was associated with a 0.27 increase in this measure.

Indeed, job seekers with greater maximizing tendencies were offered an average of $7,430 more in salary than their satisficing counterparts ($\beta = .20$, $t(115) = 2.83$, $p < .01$, $p_{rep} = .96$), such that every one-unit increase in the maximizing composite score was associated with a $2,630 increase in the annual salary obtained. Based on a median split of the maximizing scale, the mean salary of maximizing job seekers was $44,515 while that of satisficing job seekers was $37,085. This difference in salary between maximizing and satisficing job seekers was unaccounted for by the number of interviews or job offers received, as maximizing tendencies did not prove to be a significant predictor of either number of interviews (T2 poisson regression $\beta = .09$, $X^2 = 1.43$, ns; T3 poisson $\beta = .05$, $X^2 = .55$, ns) or offers attained (T3 poisson regression $\beta = .09$, $X^2 = 1.80$, ns).

Greater maximizing tendencies were also associated with experiences of greater negative affect at all three times of the job search process (T1: $\beta = .26$, $t(535) = 6.32$, $p < .001$, $p_{rep} = .99$; T2: $\beta = .18$, $t(365) = 3.56$, $p < .001$, $p_{rep} = .99$; T3: $\beta = .16$, $t(257) = 2.98$, $p < .01$, $p_{rep} = .97$). Every one-unit increase in maximizing was associated with .40, .31, and .28 increases in negative affect at T1, T2, and T3, respectively. Those with greater maximizing tendencies also reported less satisfaction with their accepted job offers even when controlling for annual salary achieved ($\beta = -.28$, $t(115) = -2.92$, $p < .01$, $p_{rep} = .97$), such that every one-unit increase in maximizing was associated with a .43 decrease in reported satisfaction.

Mediators of Maximizing Tendencies

As illustrated in Table 2, results suggest that the relationship of maximizing tendencies with job market performance and negative affective experience was mediated by a combination of reliance on external influences and option fixation. Reliance on external influences ($\beta = .27$, $t(115) = 3.41$, $p < .01$, $p_{rep} = .98$) acted as a partial mediator of the effect of maximizing on job market performance. The positive correlational relationship between maximizing and negative affect was observed to be partially mediated at T2 by logged anticipated applications ($\beta = .21$, $t(365) = 4.14$ $p < .001$, $p_{rep} = .99$) and fixation on unrealized options

($\beta = .25$, $t(365) = 5.15$, $p < .001$, $p_{rep} = .99$), and fully mediated at T3 by fixation on unrealized options ($\beta = .10$, $t(257) = 1.81$, $p < .10$, $p_{rep} = .85$), regret with choice set size ($\beta = .21$, $t(257) = 3.82$, $p < .001$, $p_{rep} = .99$), and reliance on external influence ($\beta = .18$, $t(257) = 3.01$, $p < .01$, $p_{rep} = .97$). In fact, the relationship between maximizing tendencies and outcome satisfaction was also fully mediated by fixation on unrealized options ($\beta = -.27$, $t(115) = -2.81$, $p < .01$, $p_{rep} = .96$) and regret with choice set size ($\beta = -.34$, $t(257) = -3.80$, $p < .001$, $p_{rep} = .99$). Even when T1 negative affective experience is included as a control in the regression models, similar results emerge.

DISCUSSION

Maximizers do better financially in their job search but feel worse. In their quest for placement after graduation, those with greater maximizing tendencies not only pursue and fixate on realized and unrealized options to a greater degree, but they also rely on more external sources of information than do more satisficing job seekers. These efforts result in higher payoffs; maximizers earn starting salaries that are 20% higher than those of satisficers. Yet, despite their relative success, they are less satisfied with the outcomes of their job search, and more "pessimistic," "stressed," "tired," "anxious," "worried," "overwhelmed," and "depressed" throughout the process. Why?

Perhaps maximizers are merely high achievers with more past successes and superior credentials who have rightly learned to expect more of themselves. No matter how well they do, maximizers feel worse because they fail to match these high expectations. Certainly there is evidence to suggest that maximizers have histories of past success; we find significantly more maximizers within top-ranked universities. However, there is also evidence to suggest that equating maximizing tendencies with capability oversimplifies the story. After all, we do not find a significant relationship between maximizing and another marker of academic success, GPA. Furthermore, if one assumed maximizers' success on the job market to simply be about better credentials, one would expect proxies for high qualifications such as university rank and GPA to mediate the effects of maximizing on job market performance. Yet we find that even when controlling for these two indices, maximizing tendencies are still predictive of salary. Thus, whatever the relationship between maximizing and high achievement, past achievement in and of itself seems inadequate to explain high expectations as the putative source of maximizers' negative affect. Why, then, do maximizers feel worse when they do better?

Perhaps the fact that maximizers start the job search process at T1 feeling worse suggests that they are simply dispositionally less happy than satisficers, and therefore less satisfied with the outcome of *any* decision. Contrary to this "dispositional unhappiness" prediction, even after accounting for initial negative affect at T1, we observe that option fixation and regret with choice set size mediate the effect of maximizing on outcome satisfaction at T2 and T3. Our findings support earlier research by Schwartz et al. (2002) that suggest that even when controlling for dispositional happiness, maximizing tendencies make an independent contribution to subjective evaluations.

Instead, we suggest that maximizers may be less satisfied and experience greater negative affect with their resulting jobs because their pursuit of the elusive "best" induces them to consider a large number of possibilities, thereby increasing their potential for regret and/or anticipated regret, engendering unrealistically high expectations, and creating mounting opportunity costs. Such effects may be integral to identifying maximizing as a goal, and may detract from the satisfaction that maximizers ultimately derive from their decisions.

Although we treat maximizing tendencies as a global individual difference measure, it may well be that maximizing strategies to find the "best" are simply a set of learned behaviors or search strategies designed specifically for decision making tasks, and not necessarily even *all* decision making tasks. In fact, mediation analyses demonstrate that individual differences in maximizing tendencies are explained by differences in option fixation and reliance on external sources of information. Nonetheless, whether global or specific, maximizing tendencies seem to cast a long shadow on people's evaluations of their decision and search outcomes.

Of course, the findings from this investigation are limited in that salary is merely one measure of objective success in the job search process. Our present investigation does not allow us to assess whether maximizers' lesser job satisfaction stems from other measures of job search success, such as working conditions, colleagues, organizational commitment, and opportunities for advancement. Additionally, our affective measures allow us to assess decision makers' experiences with the process and their *expected* satisfaction with their impending employment, but are limited in that they do not assess job seekers' affective experience with their resulting employment.

Psychologists and economists alike have assumed the provision of choice to be beneficial, as it allows decision makers more opportunities for preference matching, and more generally enables utility maximization. However, the present investigation is part of a growing body of literature that posits that decision makers' appraisals of their decision outcomes may have less to do with their ability to preference match or increase the expected value of their decision outcomes than it does with the decision makers' social values (Iyengar & Lepper, 1999), mispredicted expectations during the decision process (Frederick & Loewenstein, 1999; Kahnmen, 1999; Loewenstein & Schkade, 1999; Wilson, 2002; Wilson & Gilbert, 2003), and the affect experienced during the decision process itself (Botti & Iyengar, 2004). Maximizers, then, epitomize the type of decision maker who may overestimate the affective benefits that result from pursuing the best objective outcome, and underestimate the affective costs of a process that involves evaluating as many options as possible and fixating on choices that may be non-existent. Even when they get what they want, maximizers may not always want what they get. Individual decision makers as well as policy makers are thus confronted by a dilemma: if the subjective well being of the decision maker and the objective value of the decision outcome are at odds, which should be prioritized? What should people do when "doing better" makes them feel worse?

REFERENCES

Best National Universities. (2001, September 17). *U.S. News & World Report, 131,* 106.

Botti, S., & Iyengar, S. S. (2004). The psychological pleasure and pain of choosing: When people prefer choosing at the cost of subsequent outcome satisfaction. *Journal of Personality and Social Psychology, 87,* 312–326.

Frederick, S., & Loewenstein, G. (1999). Hedonic adaptation. In D. Kahneman, E. Diener, & N. Schwarz (Eds.), *Well-being: The foundations of hedonic psychology* (pp. 302–329). New York: Russell Sage.

Iyengar, S. S., & Jiang, W. (2004). *Choosing not to choose: The effect of more choices on retirement savings decisions.* Manuscript submitted for publication, Columbia University.

Iyengar, S. S., & Lepper, M. R. (1999). Rethinking the value of choice: A cultural perspective on intrinsic motivation. *Journal of Personality and Social Psychology, 76,* 349–366.

Iyengar, S. S., & Lepper, M. R. (2000). When choice is demotivating: Can one desire too much of a good thing? *Journal of Personality and Social Psychology, 79,* 995–1006.

Kahneman, D. (1999). Objective happiness. In D. Kahneman, E. Diener, & N. Schwarz (Eds.), *Well-being: The foundations of hedonic psychology* (pp. 3–25). New York: Russell Sage.

Killeen, P. R. (2005). An alternative to null-hypothesis significance tests. *Psychological Science, 16,* 345–353.

Kliger, M. & Schwartz, B. (2005). *Maximizing tendencies: Evidence from a national sample.* Unpublished raw data, Simmons Company.

Loewenstein, G., & Schkade, D. (1999). Wouldn't it be nice? Predicting future feelings. In D. Kahneman, E. Diener, & N. Schwarz (Eds.), *Well-being: The foundations of hedonic psychology* (pp. 85–108). New York: Russell Sage.

Lyubomirsky, S., & Ross, L. (1997). Hedonic consequences of social comparison: A contrast of happy and unhappy people. *Journal of Personality and Social Psychology, 73,* 1141–1157.

Miller, G. A. (1956). The magic number seven plus or minus two: Some limits in our capacity for processing information. *Psychological Review, 63,* 81–97.

Schwartz, B. (2004a). *The paradox of choice: Why more is less.* New York: Ecco.

Schwartz, B. (2004b). The tyranny of choice. *Scientific American, April,* 71–75.

Schwartz, B., Ward, A., Monterosso, J., Lyubomirsky, S., White, K., & Lehman, D. R. (2002). Maximizing versus satisficing: Happiness is a matter of choice. *Journal of Personality and Social Psychology, 83,* 1178–1197.

Simon, H. A. (1955). A behavioral model of rational choice. *Quarterly Journal of Economics, 59,* 99–118.

Simon, H. A. (1956). Rational choice and the structure of the environment. *Psychological Review, 63,* 129–138.

Simon, H. A. (1957). *Models of man, social and rational: Mathematical essays on rational human behavior.* New York: Wiley.

Wilson, T. D. (2002). *Strangers to ourselves: Discovering the adaptive unconscious.* Cambridge: Harvard University Press.

Wilson, T. D., & Gilbert, D. T. (2003). Affective forecasting. In M. P. Zanna (Ed.), *Advances in experimental social psychology* (Vol. 35, pp. 345–411). San Diego: Academic Press.

Authors' Note

Sheena S. Iyengar, Management Division, Graduate School of Business, Columbia University; Rachael E. Wells, Management Division, Graduate School of Business, Columbia University; Barry Schwartz, Psychology Department, Swarthmore College.

This research was supported by a National Science Foundation Young Investigator Career Award.

Correspondence can be addressed to: Sheena S. Iyengar, Management Division, Columbia University Business School, by email, ss957@columbia.edu, or telephone, (212) 854–8308. Detailed statistical information yielded by analyses of differences in sub-sample characteristics is also available upon request.

CONCLUSIONS

The APA format provides us with a blueprint for report writing. We learned that written language must be sensitive to racial and ethnic identity, gender, age, sexual orientation, and disabilities. The goal is to eliminate sexism and ethnic bias in writing. We also learned the importance of proper documentation and citation. In report writing, any written statement or claim such as the example citing the prevalence of schizophrenia must be documented. Documentation in the form of citing a reference allows the reader to know that the statement is supported and substantiated by evidence. In addition, it allows the reader to check the reference to determine the accuracy of the statement and learn the details of the cited study. Proper documentation is essential, an ethical imperative. Your ideas, thoughts, sentences, phrases, and words must be clearly separated from those from other sources. Always err on the side of crediting others. Even for what you may believe to be your truly original ideas and insights, there are almost always others who have had similar thoughts published in the literature. Citing these helps also to place ideas and thoughts in context as well as to show how ideas of others may have influenced your work. Never present another person's published work or parts of published work as your own. In other words, do not plagiarize.

Two of the most common types of reports are empirical studies and literature reviews. APA format for organization of a written report of an empirical study is rather straightforward: title, abstract, method, results, discussion, references, author notes, footnotes, tables, and figures with captions. Literature reviews are critical examinations of empirical studies that have already been published. In a literature review, you evaluate published studies in terms of their methods as well as their conceptual foundation. A literature review does not follow the same organization and structure as an article reporting an empirical study. You will have an abstract that appears on the first page that summarizes your review. But you will not have the prescribed method and results sections for a report on an empirical study. Instead, you will identify headings for major sections that well help you to organize the structure of the paper. Try to make headings as specific as possible. For clues, look at published literature reviews to see how authors typically use headers to delineate major sections of their articles.

In summary, writing in psychology is both a communal and a learning process. We read the works of others. We can learn how to structure a report, organize ideas, and develop a line of argument by outlining and diagramming a work that we find to be especially well written. We can ask peers and teachers to provide feedback on our own written work. We might also ask our instructor to identify key ingredients of a text that make a particular article well written. And as we stated at the outset, stay positive and open, and remember it's better to have rewritten than to have never written!

END OF CHAPTER

Chapter Highlights

- Our psychological knowledge advances through written research.

- The American Psychological Association (APA) format provides us with a blueprint for report writing.

- APA style emphasizes written language that is sensitive to racial and ethnic identity, gender, age, sexual orientation, and disabilities.

- APA style also emphasizes the importance of proper documentation and citation.

- Plagiarism is a serious ethical as well as legal problem that can result in expulsion, grade failure, job loss, and litigation for violating copyright laws.

- Two common types of research articles are empirical studies and literature reviews.

- Empirical studies are reports of original research and literature reviews are critical evaluations of works that have already been published.

- The parts of a written report are: (1) title, (2) title and affiliations of authors, (3) abstract, (4) introduction, (5) method, (6) results, (7) discussion, (8) references, (9) author notes, (10) footnotes, (11) tables, (12) figure captions, and (13) figures.

- We examined in detail how to write six essential sections of an empirical study: abstract, introduction, method, results, discussion, and references.

- Four steps that might be helpful to keep in mind when writing a literature review are: (1) introduce and define research question or problem; (2) narrow research question to the studies reviewed; (3) describe studies in detail and identify relationships, gaps, inconsistencies in the literature; and (4) discuss how the research problem may be ameliorated or rectified.

Key Terms

Abstract   387

APA format   384

Discussion   393

Introduction   387

Method   389

Plagiarism   386

References   396

Research in the News

In Chapter 2, we learned about meta-analyses as a type of literature review that has become widely used by researchers over the past 15 years. In meta-analyses, researchers use quantitative procedures to statistically combine the results of numerous studies. As a form of a literature review, meta-analyses are, however, not without controversy. Consider a January 12, 2010, op-ed piece appearing in the *New York Times* by Richard A. Friedman, M.D., titled "Before You Quit Antidepressants . . ."

In his commentary, Friedman takes issue with a recent meta-analysis appearing in *The Journal of the American Medical Association (JAMA)* authored by Fournier and colleagues that questioned the effectiveness of antidepressant drugs. The *JAMA* article, based on a meta-analysis of six studies of 718 patients, indicated that antidepressant medication is no more effective than a placebo pill for the treatment of mild to moderate forms of depression. Disputing these findings, Friedman wrote,

> The study is a so-called meta-analysis—not a fresh clinical trial, but a combined analysis of previous studies. A common reason for doing this kind of analysis is to discover potential drug effects that might have been missed in smaller studies. By aggregating the data from many studies, researchers gain the statistical power to detect broad patterns that may have not been evident before. . . . But meta-analyses can be tricky. First, they are only as good as the smaller studies they analyze. And then there are hundred of studies out there, how to decide which ones to include. (Friedman, 2010)

Debate the issue of meta-analysis as a valid form of literature review. How would you compare and contrast meta-analysis with the traditional form of literature review we covered here in this chapter? How would you evaluate the selection of studies included in the Fournier article? How would you respond to criticism leveled by Friedman? Would you have reported the results differently? How might you have reported the results to avoid this ensuing controversy?

Activity Questions

1. Plagiarism is no joke. What are the regulations on plagiarism in class papers at your school? What do you think the ideal policy would be? Should this policy take into account cultural differences in teaching practices and learning styles? Do you think this ideal policy is likely to be implemented? Why or why not? Based on your experiences, do you believe that most student plagiarism is the result of misunderstanding

about proper citation practices, or is it the result of dishonesty? Do you think that students who plagiarize while in school are less likely to be honest as researchers?

2. The National Academy of Sciences wrote a lengthy report on ethics issues in scientific research. Visit the site and read the free executive summary you can obtain at http://www.nap.edu/catalog.php?record_id=10430. Summarize the information and guidelines in the report.

3. Write an abstract of no more than 120 words describing our in-class exercise that investigated focusing illusion in college students.

4. Read the Kahneman et al. (2006) article. Outline the paper so that you can understand the structure and organization of ideas presented. Identify the major thesis of the paper, its background, and evidence in favor of and against the research question.

Review Questions

1. Describe how you would, according to APA style, organize a report of an empirical study. Describe the content you must include for each of the major sections of your report.

2. Describe how you would, according to APA style, organize a written literature review. What is the rationale for your literature review and how would go about accomplishing your objective or aim?

3. What are the pros and cons of a scientific poster? How does a scientific poster differ from a written manuscript or article? How would you describe the relationship between a poster and a written manuscript?

Ethics in Action

1. The APA Ethics Code (Standard 8.10b, Reporting Research Results) indicates that when mistakes in reporting data occur and are published, the researchers should take steps to correct the errors. How would a researcher go about making corrections to data already published? How might errors be avoided?

2. In a July 2010 *Scientific American* piece, "When Scientists Lie," essayist Michael Shermer comments on the recent book by vice provost of California Institute of Technology David Goodstein titled *On Fact and Fraud: Cautionary Tales from the Front Lines of Science* (2010). Both the Shermer essay and the Goodstein book resonate with the thrust of this chapter devoted to the topic of reporting research results. In his book, Goodstein writes, as reported by Shermer, "Injecting falsehoods into the body of science is rarely, if ever, the purpose of those who perpetuate fraud. They almost always believe that they are injecting a truth into the scientific record." In other words, in many instances of scientific fraud and deceit, the perpetrators fool themselves into believing that their finding or discovery will turn out to be true when subsequent investigators perform the proper studies. What do you make of this? Comment on these apparent acts of conscious and unconscious self-deception, that is, how scientists might fool themselves into believing and defending "research lies." What are the ethical and practical implications of these costly misrepresentations?

Appendix A

Summaries of Frequently Cited Research Articles

Actual research studies are used throughout the text to illustrate particular research approaches and issues. You can use the following summaries at any point to review the design of these studies. The chapter number in brackets indicates the text chapter in which the study is introduced.

Aronson, E., & Mills, J. (1959). The effect of severity of initiation on liking for a group. *Journal of Abnormal and Social Psychology, 59*, 177–181. [Chapter 3]. Classic experimental study of students at an all-women's college in the 1950s. Students were assigned randomly to either read embarrassing words or listen to a boring, taped discussion prior to being allowed to join a group in order to determine the effect of severity of initiation on liking for the group.

Beare, P. L., Severson S., & Brandt P. (2004). The use of a positive procedure to increase engagement on-task and decrease challenging behavior. *Behavior Modification, 28*, 28–44. [Chapter 9]. Single-subject study of a profoundly mentally retarded long-term adult hospital resident to determine whether a differential reinforcement plan could reduce his self-injurious behavior.

Bisconer, S. W., Green, M., Mallon-Czajka, J., & Johnson, J. S. (2006). Managing aggression in a psychiatric hospital using a behaviour plan: A case study. *Journal of Psychiatric and Mental Health Nursing, 13*, 515–521. [Chapter 9]. Single-subject study of a psychiatric hospital inpatient to determine whether a treatment program based on reinforcers could reduce his aggressive and threatening behavior.

Brinegar, M. G., Salvi, L. M., Stiles, W. B., & Greenberg, L. S. (2006). Building a meaning bridge: Therapeutic progress from problem formulation to understanding. *Journal of Counseling Psychology, 53*, 165–180. [Chapter 11]. Qualitative study of brief client-centered therapy in York University Depression Project, using recordings of actual therapy sessions.

Cohen, S. G., & Ledford, Jr., G. E. (1994). The effectiveness of self-managing teams: A quasi-experiment. *Human Relations, 47*, 13–43. [Chapter 8]. A study of the effectiveness of self-managing teams in a telecommunications company, using an *ex post facto* design. Each work group identified as self-managing was matched with a traditionally managed work group that produced the same product or service.

Dunn, E. W., Aknin, L. B., & Norton, M. I. (2008). Spending money on others promotes happiness. *Science, 319*, 1687–1688. [Chapter 10]. Multimethod research using cross-sectional and longitudinal surveys and a laboratory experiment to test the hypothesis that spending money on other people has a more positive impact on happiness than does spending money on oneself.

Haney, C., Banks, C., & Zimbardo, P. G. (1973). Interpersonal dynamics in a simulated prison. *International Journal for Criminology and Penology, 1*, 69–97. [Chapter 3]. Classic study of the impact of social position—being a prisoner or a prison guard—on behavior. Male volunteers signed a contact to participate for 2 weeks in a simulated prison. Prisoners became passive and disorganized, whereas guards became verbally and physically aggressive and the experiment was terminated after 6 days.

Hard, S. F., Conway, J. M., & Moran, A. C. (2006). [Chapter 12] Faculty and college student beliefs about the frequency of student academic misconduct. *Journal of Higher Education, 77*, 1058–1080. Group-based survey about plagiarism and other misconduct in classes within one university.

Humphreys, L. (1970). *Tearoom trade: Impersonal sex in public places.* Chicago: Aldine de Gruyter. [Chapter 3]. Two-part study of men who participate in anonymous homosexual encounters. First, Humphreys worked as a covert participant by serving as a lookout (a "watch queen") in a public bathroom (and copying down license plate numbers of participants); second, he surveyed the men in their homes, without revealing how he had obtained their names.

Iyengar, S. S., Wells, R. E., & Schwartz, B. (2006). Doing better but feeling worse. Looking for the "best" job undermines satisfaction. *Current Directions in Psychological Science, 17*, 143–150. [Chapter 1, Chapter 12]. Survey of graduating students early and late in their initial job search. Contrasts starting salaries and feelings of satisfaction between students classified as maximizers and satisficers.

Keyes, C. L. M. (2007). Promoting and protecting mental health as flourishing: A complementary strategy for improving national mental health. *American Psychologist, 62*, 95–108. [Chapter 4]. Conceptualization of mental health and mental illness as on a continuum, with measures used in survey research to identify prevalence.

Levitt, H., Butler, M., & Hill, T. (2006). What clients find helpful in psychotherapy: Developing principles for facilitating moment-to-moment change. *Journal of Counseling Psychology, 53*, 314–324. [Chapter 11]. Study of process of change in psychotherapy based on 1.5-hour intensive qualitative interviews.

Levitt, H. M., Swanger, R. T., & Butler, J. B. (2008). Male perpetrators' perspectives on intimate partner violence, religion, and masculinity. *Sex Roles, 58*, 435–448. [Chapter 11]. Exploration of perspectives of intimate partner violence perpetrators in the southern U.S. Semistructured interviews analyzed using grounded theory method.

Mahncke, H. W., Connor, B. B., Appelman, J., Ahsanuddin, O. N., Hardy, J. L., Wood, R. A., Joyce, N. M., Boniske, T., Atkins, S. M., & Merzenich, M. M. (2006). Memory enhancement in healthy older adults using a brain plasticity-based training program: A randomized controlled study. *Proceedings of the National Academy of Sciences, 103*, 12523–12528. [Chapter 6]. Randomized experiment to determine whether healthy participants 60 years or older would show improved mental abilities following brain plasticity training that involved "working out"—performing a prescribed 5-day-a-week regimen of cognitive exercises on their home computers.

Meyers, D. G., & Diener, E. (1996). Most people are happy. *Psychological Science 7*, 181–185. [Chapter 5]. Comparison of findings about happiness ("subjective well-being") from surveys in 43 nations in which nationally representative samples were selected.

Milgram, S. (1965). Some conditions of obedience and disobedience to authority. *Human Relations, 18*, 57–75. [Chapter 3]. Attempt to identify through laboratory experiments the conditions under which ordinary citizens would resist instructions from authority figures to inflict pain on others. Men were recruited through local newspaper ads, told they were to participate in a study of learning, and instructed to help a "student" memorize words by administering an electric shock (with a phony machine).

Nakonezny, P. A., Reddick, R., & Rodgers, J. L. (2004). Did divorces decline after the Oklahoma City bombing? *Journal of Marriage and Family, 66*, 90–100. [Chapter 8]. Time series design to identify the impact of the Oklahoma City terrorist bombing in April 1995 on the divorce rate in Oklahoma.

Average rate of change in divorce rates in Oklahoma's 77 counties in the 10 years prior to the bombing compared with those 5 years after the bombing.

Nestor, P. G., Klein, K., Pomplun, M., Niznikiewicz, M., & McCarley, R. W. (2010). Gaze cueing of attention in schizophrenia: Individual differences in neuropsychological functioning and symptoms. *Journal of Clinical and Experimental Neuropsychology, 32*, 281–288. [Chapter 8]. Quasiexperimental study comparing experimentally manipulated effect of social and nonsocial attention as measured by speeded target detection in persons with schizophrenia and in a control group of healthy volunteers.

Phillips, D. P. (1982). The impact of fictional television stories on U.S. adult fatalities: New evidence on the effect of the mass media on violence. *American Journal of Sociology, 87*, 1340–1359. [Chapter 7]. Quasiexperimental study of the effect of TV soap opera suicides on the number of actual suicides in the United States, using a multiple-group before-and-after design. Soap opera suicides in 1977 were identified, and then the suicide rates in the week prior to and during the week of each suicide story were compared. Deaths due to suicide increased from the control period to the experimental period in 12 of the 13 comparisons.

Phoenix, A. (2003). Neoliberalism and masculinity: Racialization and the contradictions of schooling for 11- to 14-year-olds. *Youth & Society, 36*, 227–246. [Chapter 8]. Interview study of 78 11- to 14-year-old boys in 12 London schools in 1998 and 1999. Both group and individual interviews were conducted to explore how boys manage their everyday school interactions and how this influences their focus in school.

Rowe, G., Hirsh, J. B., & Anderson, A. K. (2007). Positive affect increases the breadth of attentional selection. *Proceedings of the National Academy of Sciences, 104*, 383–388. [Chapter 7]. A multifactorial experimental study of how emotions may broaden attentional allocation to both external visual and internal conceptual space.

Schutt, R. K. (2011). *Homelessness, housing and mental illness*. With Stephen M. Goldfinger. Cambridge: Harvard University Press. [Chapter 11]. Comprehensive analysis of group and independent living alternatives for homeless persons with severe mental illness. Multimethod study using experimental design, surveys, and participant-observation (ethnography).

Strack, F., Martin, L. L., & Stepper, S. (1988). Inhibiting and facilitating conditions of the human smile: A nonobtrusive test of the facial feedback hypothesis. *Journal of Personality and Social Psychology, 54*, 766–777. [Chapters 2, 5]. Experimental study of students to test hypothesis that induced involuntary smiling would increase happiness.

Wageman, R. (1995). Interdependence and group effectiveness. *Administrative Science Quarterly, 40*, 145–180. [Chapter 8]. Quasiexperimental study of effect of task design and reward allocation on work team functioning, with 800 Xerox service technicians in 152 teams. Team performance was influenced positively by management that stressed either interdependence or autonomy, but hybrid management models were associated with poorer team performance.

Appendix B

Questions to Ask About a Research Article

1. What is the basic research question or problem? Try to state it in just one sentence. (Chapter 1)

2. How would you classify the methods and design of the study? (Chapter 1)

3. Describe the theoretical framework of the study. How did the theoretical framework influence the design and methods of the study? How did the theoretical framework provide a rationale for the study? (Chapters 2, 6, 7)

4. Did the theoretical framework seem appropriate for the research question addressed? Can you think of a different theoretical perspective that might have been used? (Chapter 1, 7)

5. What prior literature was reviewed? Was it relevant to the research problem? To the theoretical framework? Does the literature review appear to be adequate? Are you aware of (or can you locate) any important studies that have been omitted? (Chapter 2)

6. What is the research hypothesis of the study? How is it linked to the theoretical framework of the study? How does the research hypothesis translate theoretical constructs into operational procedures? (Chapters 2, 4)

7. Identify independent variable(s). How many independent variables and how many levels for each independent variable? Describe whether the researchers used random assignment in allocating participants to the different levels of the independent variable(s). Discuss the implications of independent variables created by random assignment versus selected on the basis of pre-existing characteristics. (Chapters 2, 6, 7, 8)

8. Identify the dependent variable. What level of measurement does the dependent variable incorporate? How does the level of measurement of the dependent variable impact the kinds of statistical tests employed? What are the advantages/disadvantages of using parametric versus nonparametric statistics? (Chapters 4, 10)

9. How was the study sample recruited? How would you define the sampling methods? How representative is the study sample of the targeted population?

How do these considerations affect generalizability of the results? How do these considerations affect external validity of the study? (Chapter 5)

10. Comment on the sample size of the study. How did the sample size affect the statistical power of the study? Do you think the study had adequate statistical power? What about the effect sizes? (Chapters 2, 6, 10)

11. Did the researchers vary the independent variable(s) between subjects or within subjects? Do you think the design was optimal? What threats to internal validity need to be considered in relation to how participants were assigned to the conditions of the experiment? (Chapters 6, 7)

12. State the research hypothesis and null hypothesis for the study. State the Type I error for this study. State the Type II error. What level of statistical significance was used? What does this mean for this study? (Chapters 2, 6, 10)

13. Would you describe the study as a single-factor or multifactor experiment? Why? What are the statistical implications? (Chapters 6, 7, 10)

14. What were the main results? What statistical tests were used to analyze the data? Were they appropriate, especially in regard to the level of measurement of the dependent variable? What statistical effects did the research design allow to be tested? Did the design allow for testing of statistical interactions? If so, what interactions were tested? If not, explain why the design did not allow for testing of statistical interactions. (Chapters 6, 7, 10)

15. Can you think of a different research approach for studying this topic? How might a qualitative research approach investigate the theory and hypothesis? Would a small-N design be worth considering? (Chapters 9, 11)

16. Did the discussion carefully weigh the evidence and pay sufficient attention to the limitations of the study in reference to external and internal validity? (Chapter 12)

17. Did the study seem consistent with current ethical standards? Were any trade-offs made between different ethical guidelines? Was an appropriate balance struck between adherence to ethical standards and use of the most rigorous scientific practices? (Chapter 3)

18. Did the author(s) adequately represent the findings in the discussion and/or conclusion sections? Were conclusions well grounded in the findings? Are any other interpretations possible? (Chapters 2, 6, 7, 8, 12)

19. Compare the study to others addressing the same research question. Did the study yield additional insights? In what ways was the study design more or less adequate than the design of previous research? (Chapters 2, 6, 7, 8, 12)

20. What additional research questions and hypotheses are suggested by the study's results? What light did the study shed on the theoretical framework used? (Chapters 2, 6, 7, 8, 12)

Appendix C

How to Read a Research Article

The discussions of research articles throughout the text may provide all the guidance you need to read and critique research on your own. But reading about an article in bits and pieces in order to learn about particular methodologies is not quite the same as reading an article in its entirety in order to learn what the researcher found out. The goal of this appendix is to walk you through an entire research article, answering the review questions introduced in Appendix B. Of course, this is only one article and our "walk" will take different turns than would a review of other articles, but after this review you should feel more confident when reading other research articles on your own.

We will use for this example the study by Adams and Kleck (2003) published in *Psychological Science* titled "Perceived Gaze Direction and the Processing of Facial Displays" reprinted on pages 435–442 of this appendix. As you recall, Adams and Kleck used a complex experimental design to study how facial expression of emotions and eye gaze direction influence how we perceive others. We have reproduced below each of the article review questions from Appendix B, followed by our answers to them. After each question, we indicate the chapter where the question was discussed. You can also follow our review by reading through the article itself and noting my comments (also refer to Chapter 7).

1. *What is the basic research question or problem? Try to state it in just one sentence.* (Chapter 1)

How do facial expressions of emotions and gaze direction operate as social signals telling us whether to approach or to avoid a person? This is essentially the question that inspired Adams and Kleck (2003) to experimentally investigate how we naturally and automatically perceive facial expressions of emotion holistically as messages. (e.g., "that person is mad about something").

2. *How would you classify the methods and design of the study?* (Chapter 1)

According to our research toolbox, we would classify the Adams and Kleck study as using an experimental design. As we will see below, Adams and Kleck created photos of faces in which they varied two independent variables—eye gaze direction (direct/averted) and expression (anger/fear).

3. *Describe the theoretical framework of the study. How did the theoretical framework influence the design and methods of the study? How did the theoretical framework provide a rationale for the study?* (Chapters 2, 6, 7)

Theories of *embodied cognition* provide the conceptual framework for the Adams and Kleck study. These researchers theorized that when a research participant views a photo display of a facial emotion, he or she automatically reenacts or re-experiences its perceptual, somatovisceral, and motoric features (which is collectively referred to as "embodiment"). This reenactment influences to a large degree how emotions are perceived and communicated. Thus, emotions as embodied experiences provided Adams and Kleck a rationale for understanding how facial feature serve as key signals in emotion perception and communication.

4. *Did the theoretical framework seem appropriate for the research question addressed? Can you think of a different theoretical perspective that might have been used?* (Chapters 1, 7)

Yes, the theoretical framework provided a strong basis for investigating the research question and for designing the experiment. First the theory specified a mechanism through which perceived emotions may influence our behavior, that is, whether we approach or avoid a stimulus. The mechanism is one of embodiment—when we view an emotional stimulus, such as facial expression of anger, we reenact its perceptual, somatovisceral, and motoric features, and these experiences influence our subsequent perceptions and actions.

5. *What prior literature was reviewed? Was it relevant to the research problem? Does the literature review appear to be adequate? Are you aware of (or can you locate) any important studies that have been omitted?* (Chapters 2, 7)

As is often the case for empirical articles appearing in *Psychological Science*, literature reviews are brief and to the point. However, it is clear from the literature review that the article is well grounded in theory and builds upon prior studies of social communication. Indeed, as Adams and Kleck stated, "Surprisingly, the interaction between gaze direction and facial expression of emotion in human perception has remained a virtually uncharted inquiry in the analysis of social communication" (p. 644).

6. *What is the research hypothesis of the study? How is it linked to the theoretical framework of the study? How does the research hypothesis translate theoretical constructs into operational procedures?* (Chapters 2, 4, 7)

Their literature review indicated that different emotional expressions can be perceived more readily if associated with certain directions of the eyes. Adams and

Kleck were particularly interested in studies that showed anger expression to be more quickly perceived when accompanied by a direct gaze, in contrast to fear faces being more quickly perceived when coupled with an averted gaze. Based on these studies, Adams and Kleck formulated a two-pronged hypothesis: (1) anger faces with direct gaze would be more readily perceived than anger faces with averted gaze and (2) fear faces with averted gaze would be more readily perceived than fear faces with direct gaze.

7. *Identify independent variable(s). How many independent variables and how many levels for each independent variable? Describe whether the researchers used random assignment in allocating participants to the different levels of the independent variable(s). Discuss the implications of independent variables created by random assignment versus selected on the basis of pre-existing characteristics.* (Chapters 2, 6, 7, 8)

The experiment manipulated two independent variables: emotional expression and gaze direction. Each independent variable had two levels, with anger or fear faces the two levels of emotional expression, and direct or averted the two levels of gaze direction. In other words, each face varied in expression (anger or fear) and gaze direction (direct or averted). The 2 × 2 factorial design produced four combinations of conditions: anger/direct gaze faces; anger/averted gaze faces; fear/direct gaze faces; and fear/averted gaze faces. They used a within-subjects design. What this meant is that all participants received all four types of faces. This allowed for the comparison of participants' response times in emotional judgment for the four different kinds of faces—those with anger and direct gaze, those with anger and averted gaze, those with fear and direct gaze, and those with fear and averted gaze.

8. *Identify the dependent variable. What level of measurement does the dependent variable incorporate? How does the level of measurement of the dependent variable impact the kinds of statistical tests employed? What are the advantages/disadvantages of using parametric versus nonparametric statistics?* (Chapters 4, 7, 10)

The dependent measure was response time in milliseconds for judging faces as expressions of either anger or fear. Response time reflects a ratio level of measurement that allows for the most powerful data analytic techniques—parametric statistics.

9. *How was the study sample recruited? How would you define the sampling methods? How representative is the study sample of the targeted population? How do these considerations affect generalizability of the results? How do these considerations affect external validity of the study?* (Chapter 5)

The researchers recruited 13 male and 19 female undergraduate students. As in many psychological studies using undergraduates as research participants, the sampling method here would be defined as one of convenience. As such, it is unclear as to the representativeness of the study sample. The sample of convenience detracts from both the generalizability of the results and the overall external validity of the study.

10. *Comment on the sample size of the study. How did the sample size affect the statistical power of the study? Do you think the study had adequate statistical power? What about the effect sizes?* (Chapters 2, 6, 7, 10)

The sample size of 32 college students is small. However, because the researchers used a within-subjects design, fewer research participants were needed. Their significant findings (see below and also Chapter 7) indicated sufficient statistical power. However, the effect sizes were in milliseconds, but this is consistent with prior studies of emotional influences on human perception.

11. *Did the researchers vary the independent variable(s) between subjects or within subjects? Do you think the design was optimal? What threats to internal validity need to be considered in relation to how participants were assigned to the conditions of the experiment?* (Chapters 6, 7)

The researchers vary the independent variables within subjects. The within-subjects design was optimal. What this meant is that all participants received all four types of faces. This allowed for the comparison of participants' response times in emotional judgment for the four different kinds of faces—those with anger and direct gaze, those with anger and averted gaze, those with fear and direct gaze, and those with fear and averted gaze. In so doing, with a within-subjects design, individual differences that could figure very prominently in processing emotions are automatically controlled. In other words, people may vary greatly in their responses to emotional faces. Because in a within-subjects design each participant serves as his or her own control, these individual differences are effectively held constant.

The second advantage is that within-subject designs are more economical than between-subjects designs. That is, fewer participants are needed to perform the experimental task. However, fewer participants require that you collect more observations per participant. Here for a point of clarification, let us suppose observations are analogous to items of a test. The reliability of a test can often be increased by simply adding more items. The same principle is good to keep in mind in light of the reduced number of participants that are commonly used in within-subjects designs. For example, Adams and Kleck had a sample size of 32 participants. Yet their experimental task had 240 slides consisting of 60 anger/direct gaze slides; 60 anger/averted gaze; 60 fear/direct gaze; and 60 fear/averted gaze. The 240 slides were presented in a random order. The large number of items or slides of their experimental task provided a sufficient number of observations to measure reliably emotional perception.

12. *State the research hypothesis and null hypothesis for the study. State the Type I error for this study. State the Type II error. What level of statistical significance was used? What does this mean for this study?* (Chapters 2, 6, 7, 10)

The research hypothesis predicted that anger faces with direct gaze would be more readily perceived than anger faces with averted gaze, whereas fear faces with averted gaze would be more readily perceived than fear faces with direct gaze. The null hypothesis stated that there would be no difference in responses to faces as a function of expression (anger/fear) and eye gaze (direct/averted). The Type I error would occur if we wrongly rejected the null hypothesis of no difference in responses to faces as a function of expression (anger/fear) and eye gaze (direct/averted) as false when in fact it was true. The Type II error would occur if we wrongly accepted the null hypothesis of no difference in responses to faces as a function of expression (anger/fear) and eye gaze (direct/averted) as true when in fact it was false. Per convention, the researchers set a .05 level of statistical significance. This means that there is a 5% chance that their findings could be attributed to chance. Or there is a 95% chance that the null hypothesis is false and therefore should be rejected in favor of the research hypothesis.

13. *Would you describe the study as a single-factor or multifactor experiment? Why? What are the statistical implications?* (Chapters 6, 7, 10)

A multifactor experiment by definition must have two or more independent variables. The current study design manipulated two independent variables and therefore would be properly described as a multifactor experiment. The principal statistical implication and advantage are that a multifactor experimental design is required in order to test interactions of two or more independent variables. Recall the research hypothesis, which essentially states faster responses to both anger faces with direct gaze and fear faces with indirect gaze. Thus, the research hypothesis here predicts an interaction of facial expression and eye gaze. That is, the effect of facial expression on response times differs depending on eye-gaze direction. Or the effect of eye-gaze direction on responses times differs depending on the type of facial expression. We know that these two statements are identical, and each illustrates the meaning of statistical interaction: The influence of an independent variable differs depending upon the level of a second independent variable.

14. *What were the main results? What statistical tests were used to analyze the data? Were they appropriate, especially in regard to the level of measurement of the dependent variable? What statistical effects did the research design allow to be tested? Did the design allow for testing of statistical interactions? If so, what interactions were tested? If not, explain why the design did not allow for testing of statistical interactions.* (Chapters 6, 7, 10)

The main results pointed to an interaction whereby direct gaze led to faster judgment of anger faces but slower judgment of fear faces. On the other hand, averted gaze led to faster judgment of fear faces but slower judgment of anger faces. The proper statistical test was the 2×2 ANOVA (see Chapter 10), as the dependent variable of response times to judge faces represented a ratio level of measurement.

15. *Can you think of a different research approach for studying this topic? How might a qualitative research approach investigate the theory and hypothesis? Would a small-N design be worth considering?* (Chapters 9, 11)

The Adams and Kleck study presented an example of a classic 2×2 factorial design, which was ideally suited for testing the research hypothesis. Given the theoretical framework of emotional embodiment along with their hypothesis, neither a qualitative research approach nor a small-N design would be worth considering.

16. *Did the discussion carefully weigh the evidence and pay sufficient attention to the limitations of the study in reference to external and internal validity?* (Chapter 12)

Yes, the discussion carefully weighed the evidence of both experiments and placed their current findings within the context of prior studies. As is the case in most published scientific articles, issues of external validity and internal validity are not directly and explicitly addressed (except in instances when these are very much related to the central topic under investigation). As a research consumer and as a student in this course, it is essential to keep issues of internal validity and external validity in the forefront when evaluating a published study.

17. *Did the study seem consistent with current ethical standards? Were any trade-offs made between different ethical guidelines? Was an appropriate balance struck between adherence to ethical standards and use of the most rigorous scientific practices?* (Chapter 3)

The study was consistent with ethical standards. All studies must be approved by the host IRB, as was the case for the current investigation. Participants were either paid for their time or received course credit.

18. *Did the author(s) adequately represent the findings in the discussion and/or conclusion sections? Were conclusions well grounded in the findings? Are any other interpretations possible?* (Chapters 2, 6, 7, 8, 12)

Yes, the authors adequately represented their findings in the discussion section. The data clearly favored their interpretation, which was well grounded in their theoretical framework.

19. *Compare the study to others addressing the same research question. Did the study yield additional insights? In what ways was the study design more or less adequate than the design of previous research?* (Chapters 2, 6, 7, 8, 12)

Yes, as the authors wrote,

> Although many aspects of facial information appear to be independently processed (e.g., lip reading, emotional expression, gender, and age: Bruce & Young, 1986; Young, 1988), the current findings suggest that gaze direction and facial expressions of emotions are not. By merging the study of facial expressions with the perception of gaze direction, the current research confirms that these cues interact meaningfully in the perceptual processing of emotionally relevant facial information. (p. 646)

20. *What additional research questions and hypotheses are suggested by the study's results? What light did the study shed on the theoretical framework used?* (Chapters 2, 6, 7, 8, 12)

One important question raised by the current findings is: How do gaze direction and facial expression influence perceptual judgments for other kinds of facial expressions, such as surprise, sadness, or joy? With respect to the importance of the current finding of the interactive effects of gaze direction and facial expressions on perceptual judgment, Adams and Kleck wrote,

> This finding is important for a number of reasons. It suggests that gaze direction is an important cue in perceptual processing of facial displays of emotion, which has not been previously demonstrated in the research literature. It also suggests that the effects of gaze direction on the processing of emotion depend on the specific type of emotion displayed by the face. An understanding of the precise nature of this interaction and the brain mechanisms that support it await further research developments. (p. 646)

RESEARCH REPORT

Perceived Gaze Direction And The Processing Of Facial Displays Of Emotion

Reginald B. Adams, Jr., and Robert E. Kleck
Dartmouth College

Abstract—*There is good reason to believe that gaze direction and facial displays of emotion share an information value as signals of approach or avoidance. The combination of these cues in the analysis of social communication, however, has been a virtually neglected area of inquiry. Two studies were conducted to test the prediction that*

Source: Research Report from "Perceived Gaze Direction and the Processing of Facial Displays of Emotion," by Reginald B. Adams, Jr., and Robert E. Kleck in Psychological Science, Vol. 14, No. 6, November 2003, pp. 644–647.

direct gaze would facilitate the processing of facially communicated approach-oriented emotions (e.g., anger and joy), whereas averted gaze would facilitate the processing of facially communicated avoidance-oriented emotions (e.g., fear and sadness). The results of both studies confirmed the central hypothesis and suggest that gaze direction and facial expression are combined in the processing of emotionally relevant facial information.

An attraction to the eye region of the face may be innately prepared (e.g., Baron-Cohen, 1997; Driver et al., 1999; Hess & Petrovich, 1987). Compelling cross-species evidence for this contention is apparent in the eyespot configurations that appear on lower-order animals such as birds, reptiles, fish, and insects (Argyle & Cook, 1976). These spots are thought to mimic the eyes of larger animals, thereby warding off potential predators. In humans, both adults and infants prefer to look at the eyes compared with other facial features (Janik, Wellens, Goldberg, & Dell'Osso, 1978; Morton & Johnson, 1991), and are particularly sensitive to the gaze direction displayed by others (Baron-Cohen, 1997, Driver et al., 1999; Macrae, Hood, Milne, Rowe, & Mason, 2002).

The ability to detect the direction of gaze displayed by another is believed to play a pivotal role in the development of person and affective construal processes (Baron-Cohen, 1997; Macrae et al., 2002; Perrett & Emery, 1994). A particular direction of gaze, however, can convey multiple social meanings. Direct gaze in both humans and nonhuman primates, for example, can communicate threat (Argyle & Cook, 1976; Redican, 1982) or friendliness (Kleinke, 1986; Van Hoof, 1972). Thus, other contextual cues must be utilized when reading social meaning into the behavior of the eyes. Argyle and Cook (1976) have noted that "if the suitable experimental situations could be devised . . . [subjects] who are exposed to the same gaze, but with different context cues, would react differently, and evaluate the looker and the looker's intentions quite differently" (p. 96).

Facial expressions can offer critical contextual information that is either consistent or inconsistent with the behavioral intentions communicated by a specific gaze behavior. Fundamentally, the behavioral intentions to approach and avoid drive biological behavior (e.g., Baron-Cohen, 1997; Brothers & Ring, 1992; Davidson & Hugdahl, 1995). Both gaze behavior and emotion have been found to be associated with the behavioral motivations to approach or avoid (see Argyle & Cook, 1976; Davidson & Hugdahl, 1995; Harmon-Jones & Segilman, 2001). Positive emotions, anger, and direct gaze, for example, are associated with approach motivation. Negative emotions (other than anger) and averted gaze are associated with avoidance motivation. Thus, as a signaling system, facial expressions of emotion and gaze behavior may combine to signal these basic behavioral tendencies. Given the importance of perception of gaze direction in the affective construal process, the perceptual primacy of the eyes over other facial cues, and the shared signal value of gaze direction and facial expressions of emotion (approach-avoidance), there is good reason to believe that gaze direction might influence how efficiently facial expressions of emotion are processed by perceivers.

Address correspondence to Reginald B. Adams, Jr., Department of Psychological and Brain Sciences, Dartmouth College, 6207 Moore Hall, Hanover, NH 03755; e-mail: rba@alum.dartmouth.org.

Surprisingly, the interaction between gaze direction and facial expressions of emotion in human perception has remained a virtually uncharted area of inquiry in the analysis of social communication. Ample evidence supports the contention that certain patterns of gaze behavior and facial expressions of emotion co-occur in both humans (e.g., Argyle & Cook, 1976; Fehr & Exline, 1987) and nonhuman primates (e.g., Hinde & Rowell, 1962; Redican, 1982) in a manner consistent with a shared underlying approach-avoidance signal value. Showing that behaviors generally co-occur, however, does not establish their mutual effect on perceptual processing. In the current research, we aimed to clarify the role of gaze direction in emotion perception by investigating its influence on how efficiently emotion information is recognized in the face. Direct gaze was predicted to facilitate the processing of facially communicated approach-oriented emotions (e.g., anger and joy), whereas averted gaze was predicted to facilitate the processing of facially communicated avoidance-oriented emotions (e.g., fear and sadness).

STUDY 1

Method

Participants

Thirteen male and 19 female undergraduate students were recruited. Participants received $10 and came to the laboratory in small groups of no more than 6 people.

Materials

Pure expressions. Facial photographs of 15 male and 15 female stimulus persons showing highly recognizable expressions of anger and fear (referred to here as "pure" expressions) were presented. For each stimulus person, we included one photograph showing a pure expression of anger and one photograph showing a pure expression of fear. These photographs were selected from the Pictures of Facial Affect (Ekman & Friesen, 1978), a set developed by Kirouac and Doré (1984), the Montreal Set of Facial Displays of Emotion (Beaupré, Cheung, & Hess, 2000), and a set developed by us (Adams & Kleck, 2001). All stimulus persons were of European descent. Because each face was presented twice in the averted-gaze condition (left and right), each was also presented twice in the direct-gaze condition to balance out the design. Thus, a total of 240 pure expressions of anger and fear were included in this study. Gaze direction was manipulated using Adobe Photoshop™.

Blended expressions. Eight male and 8 female "blended" target faces were also used in this study. Each face displayed anger and fear, which were blended using a morphing algorithm included in the Morph 2.5™ software for the Macintosh. Exemplar faces were selected from the Pictures of Facial Affect (Ekman & Friesen, 1978) and the Montreal Set of Facial Displays of Emotion (Beaupré et al., 2000). The anger and fear expressions for each stimulus person were blended at approximately equal levels. The resulting images were inspected by an expert in the Facial Action Coding System (FACS; see Ekman & Friesen, 1978) and were verified to be physically viable, ecologically valid expressions. Each blended expression was presented in three gaze conditions (left, right, and direct), and the direct-gaze face for each stimulus person appeared twice to balance out the design. Thus, 64 presentations of blended expressions were randomly intermingled among the presentations of the 240 pure emotional expressions.

All pure and blended expressions were digitized, cropped in order to display only the head and neck of each individual, and presented in black and white on a computer screen at an approximate size of 4×3 in.

Procedure

Each participant was seated approximately 24 in. in front of a 15-in. monitor with a serial mouse for data acquisition with millisecond precision. Stimulus trials were presented using Superlab Pro™ (see Haxby, Parasuraman, Lalonde, & Abboud, 1993). Participants were instructed to indicate via a right or left mouse click whether each face displayed anger or fear. Each face was presented in the center of the computer screen. Each trial began with a 500-ms fixation point, which was immediately replaced by a blank screen for 50 ms before the onset of the stimulus face. The face remained on the screen until a response was made. Participants were asked to label each face as quickly and as accurately as possible.

Results

Pure expressions

Prior to analyses, the data were trimmed and log-transformed. Responses more than 3 standard deviations above or below the mean were excluded from analysis (0.76%), as were trials resulting in incorrect responses (10.1%). For ease of interpretation, we converted data back into milliseconds for reporting the means and standard errors.

The central hypothesis was tested with a 2 (anger vs. fear expression) × 2 (direct vs. averted gaze) repeated measures analysis of variance. A significant main effect of emotion emerged, $F(1, 31) = 8.05$, $p = .01$, $r = .45$; anger faces were correctly labeled more quickly ($M = 888.2$ ms, $SE = 23.9$ ms) than were fear faces ($M = 917.9$ ms, $SE = 25.5$ ms). This main effect was qualified by the predicted interaction between emotion and gaze direction, $F(1, 31) = 40.37$, $p < .0001$, $r = .75$ (see Table 1). As expected, anger expressions were more quickly decoded when displayed in

Table 1 Mean response latencies (in milliseconds) to correctly label anger and fear expressions, as a function of gaze direction

Type of emotional expression	Response latency		Standard error	
	Direct gaze	Averted gaze	Direct gaze	Averted gaze
Anger	862.3	914.1	23.5	25.6
Fear	944.5	891.2	27.5	24.4

conjunction with direct than with averted gaze, $t(31) = 4.88$, $p < .0001$, $r = .66$. Fear expressions, in contrast, were more quickly decoded when displayed in conjunction with averted than with direct gaze, $t(31) = -5.27$, $p < .0001$, $r = .69$.

Blended expressions

The use of emotion-blended expressions allowed us to test whether gaze direction could shift the relative perceptual dominance of one emotion over the other. Using the proportion of fear versus anger labels as the dependent variable of interest, we computed a direct t-test comparison. Blended expressions were given approximately equal numbers of fear labels and anger labels when displaying direct gaze ($M = .51$, $SE = .025$), whereas they were given more fear labels than anger labels when displaying averted gaze ($M = .68$, $SE = .028$), $t(31) = 5.86$, $p < .0001$, $r = .72$.

Discussion

Study 1 offers preliminary evidence for the role of gaze direction in facilitating the processing of facial displays of emotion. The reaction time data for labeling pure anger and fear expressions showed that gaze directly influences the time it takes to make correct emotion judgments. The categorical index for the blended expressions showed that gaze direction can shift the relative perceptual dominance of one emotion over another. These findings suggest that gaze direction influences the processing of facial anger and fear displays, in terms of both processing speed and perceptual interpretation. To replicate these findings and firmly establish that these processing differences are not restricted to threat-related emotional expressions (perhaps as part of an early-warning mechanism), we conducted Study 2 using different approach- and avoidance-oriented emotional expressions, joy and sadness.

STUDY 2

Method

Participants

Seventeen male and 11 female undergraduate students were recruited. Participants received either partial course credit or $7. They came to the laboratory in small groups of no more than 6 people.

Materials

As in Study 1, facial stimuli displaying pure facial expressions (in this case, joy or sadness) were used. All stimuli were selected from the same facial sets and prepared according to same parameters as described for Study 1. Blended expressions combining joy and sadness expressions, however, did not yield suitable stimuli, and therefore were not included in this study. Notably, researchers have historically had difficulty blending expressions of positive and negative emotions (Nummenmaa, 1990).

Procedure

The task was identical to the task in Study 1, except that joy and sadness emotion judgments were made and participants saw a total of 240 rather than 304 stimuli.

Results

The dependent measure of interest was the mean latency of response for correctly labeling faces as displaying either joy or sadness. Prior to analyses, the data were trimmed and log-transformed. Outliers (1.2%) and incorrect responses (5.1%) were dropped from the analyses. As for Study 1, the means and standard errors reported here were transformed back to milliseconds.

To test the hypothesis that gaze would influence the speed with which facial expressions were labeled, we computed a 2 (joy vs. sadness expression) × 2 (direct vs. averted gaze) repeated measures analysis of variance. A main effect for emotion emerged, $F(1, 27) = 15.26, p < .0001, r = .6$; joyous faces ($M = 609.5$ ms, $SE = 16.0$ ms) were correctly labeled more quickly than sad faces ($M = 633.9$ ms, $SE = 15.2$ ms). The predicted interaction between emotion and gaze direction was found, $F(1, 27) = 20.97, p < .0001, r = .66$ (see Table 2). As expected, joy expressions were more quickly decoded when displayed with direct than averted gaze, $t(27) = 3.51$, $p < .01, r = .56$. Sadness expressions were more quickly decoded when displayed with averted than direct gaze, $t(27) = -2.63, p < .02, r = .45$.

Discussion

The results for joy and sadness expressions are consistent with those for anger and fear expressions, reported in Study 1. The latencies to correctly label the emotional expressions varied as a joint function of gaze direction and whether the facial display in question represented an approach- or avoidance-oriented emotion.

GENERAL DISCUSSION

In the current studies, anger and joy expressions (which are approach oriented) were more quickly labeled when presented with direct than with averted gaze, whereas fear and sadness expressions (which are avoidance oriented) were more

Table 2 Mean response latencies (in milliseconds) to correctly label joy and sadness expressions, as a function of gaze direction

Type of emotional expression	Response latency		Standard error	
	Direct gaze	Averted gaze	Direct gaze	Averted gaze
Joy	600.8	618.3	15.5	17.0
Sadness	641.4	626.4	15.2	15.8

quickly labeled when presented with averted than with direct gaze. The finding that gaze and facial expression are combined in the perceptual processing and interpretation of emotion suggests a process that is potentially highly evolved. As noted, a fundamental dimension of behavioral intention is approach and avoidance. The ability to detect another's intention to either approach or avoid is seen by many researchers as a principal mediating factor governing social interaction. Given that both emotion expression and gaze behavior reflect these underlying approach-avoidance motivational intentions, the integration of these cues in social perception likely subserves an adaptive function.

The present findings might seem counterintuitive given recent research on gaze direction. For instance, Macrae et al. (2002) used a gender detection task to test the effects of gaze direction on the processing efficiency of person construal. They found that participants were faster to correctly label the gender of faces displaying direct gaze than faces displaying averted or closed eyes. In addition, Driver et al. (1999) used a letter discrimination task to test the effects of gaze direction as an attentional cuing device. They found that the gaze direction of a stimulus face triggers a reflexive shift of attention in the same direction in the observer. From these studies, one might conclude that direct gaze ought to facilitate the processing of all facial displays of emotion as a function of where the observer's attentional resources are allocated; direct gaze seems to shift attentional resources toward the face, whereas averted gaze appears to shift attentional resources away. The current studies, however, demonstrate that the influence of gaze direction on the perception of facial displays of emotion varies depending on the motivational orientation associated with the emotion being expressed.

Although many aspects of facial information appear to be independently processed (e.g., lip reading, emotional expression, gender, and age; Bruce & Young, 1986; Young, 1998), the current findings suggest that gaze direction and facial expressions of emotion are not. By merging the study of facial expressions with the study of perception of gaze direction, the current research confirms that these cues interact meaningfully in the perceptual processing of emotionally relevant facial information. This finding is important for a number of reasons. It suggests that gaze direction is an important cue in the perceptual processing of facial displays of emotion, which has not been previously demonstrated in the research literature. It also suggests that the effects of gaze direction on the processing of emotion depend on the specific type of emotion displayed by the face. An understanding of the precise nature of this interaction and the brain mechanisms that support it awaits further research developments.

Acknowledgments—The authors would like to thank Katharine D. Adams and Abigail A. Marsh for helpful comments on an earlier draft; Brent F. Jones for help creating the stimuli and implementing the studies; and Punam A. Keller, C. Neil Macrae, Jennifer A. Richeson, and George L. Wolford for suggestions regarding experimental design and data analysis. This research was supported in part by a Doctoral Dissertation Improvement Grant from the National Science Foundation (Award No. 0121947) to Reginald B. Adams, Jr., and by a Rockefeller Reiss Family Senior Faculty grant to Robert E. Kleck.

REFERENCES

Adams, R.B., Jr., & Kleck, R.E. (2001). [Young adult facial displays]. Unpublished set of photographs.

Argyle, M., & Cook, M. (1976). *Gaze and mutual gaze.* New York: Cambridge University Press.

Baron-Cohen, S. (1997). *Mindblindness: An essay on autism and theory of mind.* Cambridge, MA: MIT Press.

Beaupré, M., Cheung, N., & Hess, U. (2000, October). *La reconnaissance des expressions émotionnelles faciales par des décodeurs africains, asiatiques et caucasiens.* Poster presented at the annual meeting of the Société Québécoise pour la Recherche en Psychologie, Hull, Quebec, Canada.

Brothers, L., & Ring, B. (1992). A neuroethological framework for the representation of minds. *Journal of Cognitive Neuroscience, 4,* 107–118.

Bruce, V., & Young, A. (1986). Understanding face recognition. *British Journal of Psychology, 77,* 305–327.

Davidson, R.J., & Hugdahl, K. (Eds.). (1995). *Brain asymmetry.* Cambridge, MA: MIT Press.

Driver, J., Davis, G., Ricciardelli, P., Kidd, P., Maxwell, E., & Baron-Cohen, S. (1999). Gaze perception triggers reflexive visuospatial orienting. *Visual Cognition, 6,* 509–540.

Ekman, P.F., & Friesen, W.V. (1978). *The Facial Action Coding System: A technique for the measurement of facial movement.* Palo Alto, CA: Consulting Psychologists Press.

Fehr, B.J., & Exline, R.V. (1987). Social visual interaction: A conceptual and literature review. In A.W. Siegman & S. Feldstein (Eds.), *Nonverbal behavior and communication* (pp. 225–325). Hillsdale, NJ: Erlbaum.

Harmon-Jones, E., & Segilman, J. (2001). State anger and prefrontal brain activity: Evidence that insult-related relative left-prefrontal activation is associated with experienced anger and aggression. *Journal of Personality and Social Psychology, 80,* 797– 803.

Haxby, J.V., Parasuraman, R., Lalonde, F., & Abboud, H. (1993). SuperLab: General-purpose Macintosh software for human experimental psychology and psychological testing. *Behavior Research Methods, Instruments, & Computers, 25,* 400–405.

Hess, E.H., & Petrovich, S.B. (1987). *Pupillary behavior in communication.* Hillsdale, NJ: Erlbaum.

Hinde, R.A., & Rowell, T.E. (1962). Communication by posture and facial expression in the rhesus monkey. *Proceedings of the Zoological Society of London, 138,* 1–21.

Janik, S.W., Wellens, A.R., Goldberg, M.L., & Dell'Osso, L.F. (1978). Eyes as the center of focus in the visual examination of human faces. *Perceptual & Motor Skills, 47,* 857–858.

Kirouac, G., & Doré, F.Y. (1984). Judgment of facial expressions of emotion as a function of exposure time. *Perceptual & Motor Skills, 59,* 147–150.

Kleinke, C.L. (1986). Gaze and eye contact: A research review. *Psychological Bulletin, 100,* 78–100.

Macrae, C.N., Hood, B.M., Milne, A.B., Rowe, A.C., & Mason, M.F. (2002). Are you looking at me? Gaze and person perception. *Psychological Science, 13,* 460–464.

Morton, J., & Johnson, M. (1991). CONSPEC and CONLEARN: A two-process theory of infant face recognition. *Psychological Review, 98,* 164–181.

Nummenmaa, T. (1990). Sender repertoires of pure and blended facial expressions of emotion. *Scandinavian Journal of Psychology, 31,* 161–180.

Perrett, D.I., & Emery, N.J. (1994). Understanding the intentions of others from visual signals: Neurophysiological evidence. *Cognitive/Current Psychology of Cognition, 13,* 683–694.

Redican, W.K. (1982). An evolutionary perspective on human facial displays. In P. Ekman (Ed.), *Emotion in the human face* (pp. 212–280). New York: Cambridge University Press.

van Hoof, J.A.R.A.M. (1972). A comparative approach to the phylogeny of laughter and smiling. In R.A. Hinde (Ed.), *Non-verbal communication* (pp. 209–241). New York: Cambridge University Press.

Young, A.W. (1998). *Face and mind.* Oxford, England: Oxford University Press.

Appendix D

Proportions of Area Under Standard Normal Curve

A — Z	B	C	A — Z	B	C	A — Z	B	C
0.00	.0000	.5000	0.30	.1179	.3821	0.60	.2257	.2743
0.01	.0040	.4960	0.31	.1271	.3783	0.61	.2291	.2709
0.02	.0080	.4920	0.32	.1255	.3745	0.62	.2324	.2676
0.03	.0120	.4880	0.33	.1293	.3707	0.63	.2357	.2643
0.04	.0160	.4840	0.34	.1331	.3669	0.64	.2389	.2611
0.05	.0199	.4801	0.35	.1368	.3632	0.65	.2422	.2578
0.06	.0239	.4761	0.36	.1406	.3594	0.66	.2454	.2546
0.07	.0279	.4721	0.37	.1443	.3557	0.67	.2486	.2514
0.08	.0319	.4681	0.38	.1480	.3520	0.68	.2517	.2483
0.09	.0359	.4641	0.39	.1517	.3483	0.69	.2549	.2451
0.10	.0398	.4602	0.40	.1554	.3446	0.70	.2580	.2420
0.11	.0438	.4562	0.41	.1591	.3409	0.71	.2611	.2389
0.12	.0478	.4522	0.42	.1628	.3372	0.72	.2642	.2358
0.13	.0517	.4483	0.43	.1664	.3336	0.73	.2673	.2327
0.14	.0557	.4443	0.44	.1700	.3300	0.74	.2704	.2296
0.15	.0596	.4404	0.45	.1736	.3264	0.75	.2734	.2266
0.16	.0636	.4364	0.46	.1772	.3228	0.76	.2764	.2236
0.17	.0675	.4325	0.47	.1808	.3192	0.77	.2794	.2206
0.18	.0714	.4286	0.48	.1844	.3156	0.78	.2823	.2177
0.19	.0753	.4247	0.49	.1879	.3121	0.79	.2852	.2148
A — −Z	B	C	A — −Z	B	C	A — −Z	B	C

(Continued)

(Continued)

A (Z)	B	C	A (Z)	B	C	A (Z)	B	C
0.20	.0793	.4207	0.50	.1915	.3085	0.80	.2881	.2119
0.21	.0832	.4168	0.51	.1950	.3050	0.81	.2910	.2090
0.22	.0871	.4129	0.52	.1985	.3015	0.82	.2939	.2061
0.23	.0910	.4090	0.53	.2019	.2981	0.83	.2967	.2033
0.24	.0948	.4052	0.54	.2054	.2946	0.84	.2995	.2005
0.25	.0987	.4013	0.55	.2088	.2912	0.85	.3023	.1977
0.26	.1026	.3974	0.56	.2123	.2877	0.86	.3051	.1949
0.27	.1064	.3936	0.57	.2157	.2843	0.87	.3078	.1922
0.28	.1103	.3897	0.58	.2190	.2810	0.88	.3106	.1894
0.29	.1141	.3859	0.59	.2224	.2776	0.89	.3133	.1867
0.90	.3159	.1841	1.21	.3869	.1131	1.52	.4357	.0643
0.91	.3186	.1814	1.22	.3888	.1112	1.53	.4370	.0630
0.92	.3212	.1788	1.23	.3907	.1093	1.54	.4382	.0618
0.93	.3238	.1772	1.24	.3925	.1075	1.55	.4394	.0606
0.94	.3264	.1736	1.25	.3944	.1056	1.56	.4406	.0594
0.95	.3289	.1711	1.26	.3962	.1038	1.57	.4418	.0582
0.96	.3315	.1685	1.27	.3980	.1020	1.58	.4429	.0571
0.97	.3340	.1660	1.28	.3997	.1003	1.59	.4441	.0559
0.98	.3365	.1635	1.29	.4015	.0985	1.60	.4452	.0548
0.99	.3389	.1611	1.30	.4032	.0968	1.61	.4463	.0537
1.00	.3413	.1587	1.31	.4049	.0951	1.62	.4474	.0526
1.01	.3438	.1562	1.32	.4066	.0934	1.63	.4484	.0516
1.02	.3461	.1539	1.33	.4082	.0918	1.64	.4495	.0505
1.03	.3485	.1515	1.34	.4099	.0901	1.65	.4505	.0495
1.04	.3508	.1492	1.35	.4115	.0885	1.66	.4515	.0485
1.05	.3531	.1469	1.36	.4131	.0869	1.67	.4525	.0475
1.06	.3554	.1446	1.37	.4147	.0853	1.68	.4535	.0465
1.07	.3577	.1423	1.38	.4162	.0838	1.69	.4545	.0455
1.08	.3599	.1401	1.39	.4177	.0823	1.70	.4554	.0446
1.09	.3621	.1379	1.40	.4192	.0808	1.71	.4564	.0436
1.10	.3643	.1357	1.41	.4207	.0793	1.72	.4573	.0427
1.11	.3665	.1335	1.42	.4222	.0778	1.73	.4582	.0418
1.12	.3686	.1314	1.43	.4236	.0764	1.74	.4591	.0409
1.13	.3708	.1292	1.44	.4251	.0749	1.75	.4599	.0401
1.14	.3729	.1271	1.45	.4265	.0735	1.76	.4608	.0392
A (−Z)	B	C	A (−Z)	B	C	A (−Z)	B	C

A Z	B	C	A Z	B	C	A Z	B	C
1.15	.3749	.1251	1.46	.4279	.0721	1.77	.4616	.0384
1.16	.3770	.1230	1.47	.4292	.0708	1.78	.4625	.0375
1.17	.3790	.1210	1.48	.4306	.0694	1.79	.4633	.0367
1.18	.3810	.1190	1.49	.4319	.0681	1.80	.4641	.0359
1.19	.3830	.1170	1.50	.4332	.0668	1.81	.4649	.0351
1.20	.3849	.1151	1.51	.4345	.0655	1.82	.4656	.0344
1.83	.4664	.0336	2.13	.4834	.0166	2.43	.4925	.0075
1.84	.4671	.0329	2.14	.4838	.0162	2.44	.4927	.0073
1.85	.4678	.0322	2.15	.4842	.0158	2.45	.4929	.0071
1.86	.4686	.0314	2.16	.4846	.0154	2.46	.4931	.0069
1.87	.4693	.0307	2.17	.4850	.0150	2.47	.4932	.0068
1.88	.4699	.0301	2.18	.4854	.0146	2.48	.4934	.0066
1.89	.4706	.0294	2.19	.4857	.0143	2.49	.4936	.0064
1.90	.4713	.0287	2.20	.4861	.0139	2.50	.4938	.0062
1.91	.4719	.0281	2.21	.4864	.0136	2.51	.4940	.0060
1.92	.4726	.0274	2.22	.4868	.0132	2.52	.4941	.0059
1.93	.4732	.0268	2.23	.4871	.0129	2.53	.4943	.0057
1.94	.4738	.0262	2.24	.4875	.0125	2.54	.4945	.0055
1.95	.4744	.0256	2.25	.4878	.0122	2.55	.4946	.0054
1.96	.4750	.0250	2.26	.4881	.0119	2.56	.4948	.0052
1.97	.4756	.0244	2.27	.4884	.0116	2.57	.4949	.0051
1.98	.4761	.0239	2.28	.4887	.0113	2.58	.4951	.0049
1.99	.4767	.0233	2.29	.4890	.0110	2.59	.4952	.0048
2.00	.4772	.0228	2.30	.4893	.0107	2.60	.4953	.0047
2.01	.4778	.0222	2.31	.4896	.0104	2.61	.4955	.0045
2.02	.4783	.0217	2.32	.4898	.0102	2.62	.4956	.0044
2.03	.4788	.0212	2.33	.4901	.0099	2.63	.4957	.0043
2.04	.4793	.0207	2.34	.4904	.0096	2.64	.4959	.0041
2.05	.4798	.0202	2.35	.4906	.0094	2.65	.4960	.0040
2.06	.4803	.0197	2.36	.4909	.0091	2.66	.4961	.0039
2.07	.4808	.0192	2.37	.4911	.0089	2.67	.4962	.0038
2.08	.4812	.0188	2.38	.4913	.0087	2.68	.4963	.0037
2.09	.4817	.0183	2.39	.4916	.0084	2.69	.4964	.0036
2.10	.4821	.0179	2.40	.4918	.0082	2.70	.4965	.0035
2.11	.4826	.0174	2.41	.4920	.0080	2.71	.4966	.0034
2.12	.4830	.0170	2.42	.4922	.0078	2.72	.4967	.0033
A −Z	B	C	A −Z	B	C	A −Z	B	C

(Continued)

(Continued)

A	B	C	A	B	C	A	B	C
Z			Z			Z		
2.73	.4968	.0032	2.94	.4984	.0016	3.15	.4992	.0008
2.74	.4969	.0031	2.95	.4984	.0016	3.16	.4992	.0008
2.75	.4970	.0030	2.96	.4985	.0015	3.17	.4992	.0008
2.76	.4971	.0029	2.97	.4985	.0015	3.18	.4993	.0007
2.77	.4972	.0028	2.98	.4986	.0014	3.19	.4993	.0007
2.78	.4973	.0027	2.99	.4986	.0014	3.20	.4993	.0007
2.79	.4974	.0026	3.00	.4987	.0013	3.21	.4993	.0007
2.80	.4974	.0026	3.01	.4987	.0013	3.22	.4994	.0006
2.81	.4975	.0025	3.02	.4987	.0013	3.23	.4994	.0006
2.82	.4976	.0024	3.03	.4988	.0012	3.24	.4994	.0006
2.83	.4977	.0023	3.04	.4988	.0012	3.25	.4994	.0006
2.84	.4977	.0023	3.05	.4989	.0011	3.30	.4995	.0005
2.85	.4978	.0022	3.06	.4989	.0011	3.35	.4996	.0004
2.86	.4979	.0021	3.07	.4989	.0011	3.40	.4997	.0003
2.87	.4979	.0021	3.08	.4990	.0010	3.45	.4997	.0003
2.88	.4980	.0020	3.09	.4990	.0010	3.50	.4998	.0002
2.89	.4981	.0019	3.10	.4990	.0010	3.60	.4998	.0002
2.90	.4981	.0019	3.11	.4991	.0009	3.70	.4999	.0001
2.91	.4982	.0018	3.12	.4991	.0009	3.80	.4999	.0001
2.92	.4982	.0018	3.13	.4991	.0009	3.90	.4999	.0000
2.93	.4983	.0017	3.14	.4992	.0008	4.00	.4999	.0000
A	B	C	A	B	C	A	B	C
−Z			−Z			−Z		

Source: Abridged from Fisher and Yates (1974).

Appendix E

Critical Values for t Distribution

	Confidence Intervals (%)					
	80	90	95	98	99	99.9
	Level of Significance for One-Tailed Test					
	.10	.05	.025	.01	.005	.0005
	Level of Significance for Two-Tailed Test					
df	.20	.10	.05	.02	.01	.001
1	3.078	6.314	12.706	31.821	63.657	636.619
2	1.886	2.920	4.303	6.965	9.925	31.598
3	1.638	2.353	3.182	4.541	5.841	12.941
4	1.533	2.132	2.776	3.747	4.604	8.610
5	1.476	2.015	2.571	3.365	4.032	6.859
6	1.440	1.943	2.447	3.143	3.707	5.959
7	1.415	1.895	2.365	2.998	3.499	5.405
8	1.397	1.860	2.306	2.896	3.355	5.041
9	1.383	1.833	2.262	2.821	3.250	4.781
10	1.372	1.812	2.228	2.764	3.169	4.587
11	1.363	1.796	2.201	2.718	3.106	4.437
12	1.356	1.782	2.179	2.681	3.055	4.318
13	1.350	1.771	2.160	2.650	3.012	4.221
14	1.345	1.761	2.145	2.624	2.977	4.140
15	1.341	1.753	2.131	2.602	2.947	4.073

(Continued)

(Continued)

df	.20	.10	.05	.02	.01	.001
16	1.337	1.746	2.120	2.583	2.921	4.015
17	1.333	1.740	2.110	2.567	2.898	3.965
18	1.330	1.734	2.101	2.552	2.878	3.922
19	1.328	1.729	2.093	2.539	2.861	3.883
20	1.325	1.725	2.086	2.528	2.845	3.850
21	1.323	1.721	2.080	2.518	2.831	3.819
22	1.321	1.717	2.074	2.508	2.819	3.792
23	1.319	1.714	2.069	2.500	2.807	3.767
24	1.318	1.711	2.064	2.492	2.797	3.745
25	1.316	1.708	2.060	2.485	2.787	3.725
26	1.315	1.706	2.056	2.479	2.779	3.707
27	1.314	1.703	2.052	2.473	2.771	3.690
28	1.313	1.701	2.048	2.467	2.763	3.674
29	1.311	1.699	2.045	2.462	2.756	3.659
30	1.310	1.697	2.042	2.457	2.750	3.646
40	1.303	1.684	2.021	2.423	2.704	3.551
60	1.296	1.671	2.000	2.390	2.660	3.460
120	1.289	1.658	1.980	2.358	2.617	3.373
¥	1.282	1.645	1.960	2.326	2.576	3.291

Source: Abridged from Fisher and Yates (1974, Table V).

Appendix F

Critical Values of F

Critical Values of F for a = .05

$df_{denominator}$	\multicolumn{10}{c}{$df_{numerator}$}
	1	2	3	4	5	6	8	12	24	¥
1	161.40	199.50	215.70	224.60	230.20	234.00	238.90	243.90	249.00	254.30
2	18.51	19.00	19.16	19.25	19.30	19.33	19.37	19.41	19.45	19.50
3	10.13	9.55	9.28	9.12	9.01	8.94	8.84	8.74	8.64	8.53
4	7.71	6.94	6.59	6.39	6.26	6.16	6.04	5.91	5.77	5.63
5	6.61	5.79	5.41	5.19	5.05	4.95	4.82	4.68	4.53	4.36
6	5.99	5.14	4.76	4.53	4.39	4.28	4.15	4.00	3.84	3.67
7	5.59	4.74	4.35	4.12	3.97	3.87	3.73	3.57	3.41	3.23
8	5.32	4.46	4.07	3.84	3.69	3.58	3.44	3.28	3.12	2.93
9	5.12	4.26	3.86	3.63	3.48	3.37	3.23	3.07	2.90	2.71
10	4.96	4.10	3.71	3.48	3.33	3.22	3.07	2.91	2.74	2.54
11	4.84	3.98	3.59	3.36	3.20	3.09	2.95	2.79	2.61	2.40
12	4.75	3.88	3.49	3.26	3.11	3.00	2.85	2.69	2.50	2.30
13	4.67	3.80	3.41	3.18	3.02	2.92	2.77	2.60	2.42	2.21
14	4.60	3.74	3.34	3.11	2.96	2.85	2.70	2.53	2.35	2.13
15	4.54	3.68	3.29	3.06	2.90	2.79	2.64	2.48	2.29	2.07
16	4.49	3.63	3.24	3.01	2.85	2.74	2.59	2.42	2.24	2.01
17	4.45	3.59	3.20	2.96	2.81	2.70	2.55	2.38	2.19	1.96
18	4.41	3.55	3.16	2.93	2.77	2.66	2.51	2.34	2.15	1.92

(Continued)

(Continued)

$df_{denominator}$	$df_{numerator}$									
	1	2	3	4	5	6	8	12	24	¥
19	4.38	3.52	3.13	2.90	2.74	2.63	2.48	2.31	2.11	1.88
20	4.35	3.49	3.10	2.87	2.71	2.60	2.45	2.28	2.08	1.84
21	4.32	3.47	3.07	2.84	2.68	2.57	2.42	2.25	2.05	1.81
22	4.30	3.44	3.05	2.82	2.66	2.55	2.40	2.23	2.03	1.78
23	4.28	3.42	3.03	2.80	2.64	2.53	2.38	2.20	2.00	1.76
24	4.26	3.40	3.01	2.78	2.62	2.51	2.36	2.18	1.98	1.73
25	4.24	3.38	2.99	2.76	2.60	2.49	2.34	2.16	1.96	1.71
26	4.22	3.37	2.98	2.74	2.59	2.47	2.32	2.15	1.95	1.69
27	4.21	3.35	2.96	2.73	2.57	2.46	2.30	2.13	1.93	1.67
28	4.20	3.34	2.95	2.71	2.56	2.44	2.29	2.12	1.91	1.65
29	4.18	3.33	2.93	2.70	2.54	2.43	2.28	2.10	1.90	1.64
30	4.17	3.32	2.92	2.69	2.53	2.42	2.27	2.09	1.89	1.62
40	4.08	3.23	2.84	2.61	2.45	2.34	2.18	2.00	1.79	1.51
60	4.00	3.15	2.76	2.52	2.37	2.25	2.10	1.92	1.70	1.39
120	3.92	3.07	2.68	2.45	2.29	2.17	2.02	1.83	1.61	1.25
¥	3.84	2.99	2.60	2.37	2.21	2.09	1.94	1.75	1.52	1.00

Source: Abridged from Fisher and Yates (1974, Table V).

Note: In ANOVA, $df_{numerator} = df_{between}$; $df_{denominator} = df_{within}$. In regression, $df_{numerator} = df_{regression}$; $df_{denominator} = df_{residual}$.

Critical Values of F for a = .01

$df_{denominator}$	$df_{numerator}$									
	1	2	3	4	5	6	8	12	24	¥
1	4052	4999	5403	5625	5764	5859	5981	6106	6234	366
2	98.49	99.01	99.17	99.2	99.3	99.3	99.3	99.4	99.4	9.50
3	34.12	30.81	29.46	28.71	28.24	27.91	27.49	27.05	26.60	26.12
4	21.20	18.00	16.69	15.98	15.52	15.21	14.80	14.37	13.93	13.46
5	16.26	13.27	12.06	11.39	10.97	10.67	10.27	9.89	9.47	9.02

$df_{denominator}$	$df_{numerator}$									
	1	2	3	4	5	6	8	12	24	¥
6	13.74	10.92	9.78	9.15	8.75	8.47	8.10	7.72	7.31	6.88
7	12.25	9.55	8.45	7.85	7.46	7.19	6.84	6.47	6.07	5.65
8	11.26	8.65	7.59	7.0	6.63	6.37	6.03	5.67	5.28	4.86
9	10.56	8.02	6.99	6.42	6.06	5.80	5.47	5.11	4.73	4.31
10	10.04	7.56	6.55	5.99	5.64	5.39	5.06	4.71	4.33	3.91
11	9.65	7.20	6.22	5.67	5.32	5.07	4.74	4.40	4.02	3.60
12	9.33	6.93	5.95	5.41	5.06	4.82	4.50	4.16	3.78	3.36
13	9.07	6.70	5.74	5.20	4.86	4.62	4.30	3.96	3.59	3.16
14	8.86	6.51	5.56	5.03	4.69	4.46	4.14	3.80	3.43	3.00
15	8.68	6.36	5.42	4.89	4.56	4.32	4.00	3.67	3.29	2.87
16	8.53	6.23	5.29	4.77	4.44	4.20	3.89	3.55	3.18	2.75
17	8.40	6.11	5.18	4.67	4.34	4.10	3.79	3.45	3.08	2.65
18	8.28	6.01	5.09	4.58	4.25	4.01	3.71	3.37	3.00	2.57
19	8.18	5.93	5.01	4.50	4.17	3.94	3.63	3.30	2.92	2.49
20	8.10	5.85	4.94	4.43	4.10	3.87	3.56	3.23	2.86	2.42
21	8.02	5.78	4.87	4.37	4.04	3.81	3.51	3.17	2.80	2.36
22	7.94	5.72	4.82	4.31	3.99	3.76	3.45	3.12	2.75	2.31
23	7.88	5.66	4.76	4.26	3.94	3.71	3.41	3.07	2.70	2.26
24	7.82	5.61	4.72	4.22	3.90	3.67	3.36	3.03	2.66	2.21
25	7.77	5.57	4.68	4.18	3.86	3.63	3.32	2.99	2.62	2.17
26	7.72	5.53	4.64	4.14	3.82	3.59	3.29	2.96	2.58	2.13
27	7.68	5.49	4.60	4.11	3.78	3.56	3.26	2.93	2.55	2.10
28	7.64	5.45	4.57	4.07	3.75	3.53	3.23	2.90	2.52	2.06
29	7.60	5.42	4.54	4.04	3.73	3.50	3.20	2.87	2.49	2.03
30	7.56	5.39	4.51	4.02	3.70	3.47	3.17	2.84	2.47	2.01
40	7.31	5.18	4.31	3.83	3.51	3.29	2.99	2.66	2.29	1.80
60	7.08	4.98	4.13	3.65	3.34	3.12	2.82	2.50	2.12	1.60
120	6.85	4.79	3.95	3.48	3.17	2.96	2.66	2.34	1.95	1.38
¥	6.64	4.60	3.78	3.32	3.02	2.80	2.51	2.18	1.79	1.00

Source: Abridged from Fisher and Yates (1974, Table V).

Note: In ANOVA, $df_{numerator} = df_{between}$; $df_{denominator} = df_{within}$. In regression, $df_{numerator} = df_{regression}$; $df_{denominator} = df_{residual}$.

Critical Values of F for a = .001

$df_{denominator}$	$df_{numerator}$									
	1	2	3	4	5	6	8	12	24	¥
1	405284	500000	540379	562500	576405	585937	598144	610667	623497	636619
2	998.5	999.0	999.2	999.2	999.3	999.3	999.4	999.4	999.5	999.5
3	167.5	148.5	141.1	137.1	134.6	132.8	130.6	128.3	125.9	123.5
4	74.14	61.25	56.18	53.44	51.71	50.53	49.00	47.41	45.77	44.05
5	47.04	36.61	33.20	31.09	29.75	28.84	27.64	26.42	25.14	23.78
6	35.51	27.00	23.70	21.90	20.81	20.03	19.03	17.99	16.89	15.75
7	29.22	21.69	18.77	17.19	16.21	15.52	14.63	13.71	12.73	11.69
8	25.42	18.49	15.83	14.39	13.49	12.86	12.04	11.19	10.30	9.34
9	22.86	16.39	13.90	12.56	11.71	11.13	10.37	9.57	8.72	7.81
10	21.04	14.91	12.55	11.28	10.48	9.92	9.20	8.45	7.64	6.76
11	19.69	13.81	11.56	10.35	9.58	9.05	8.35	7.63	6.85	6.00
12	18.64	12.97	10.80	9.63	8.89	8.38	7.71	7.00	6.25	5.42
13	17.81	12.31	10.21	9.07	8.35	7.86	7.21	6.52	5.78	4.97
14	17.14	11.78	9.73	8.62	7.92	7.43	6.80	6.13	5.41	4.60
15	16.59	11.34	9.34	8.25	7.57	7.09	6.47	5.81	5.10	4.31
16	16.12	10.97	9.00	7.94	7.27	6.81	6.19	5.55	4.85	4.06
17	15.72	10.66	8.73	7.68	7.02	6.56	5.96	5.32	4.63	3.85
18	15.38	10.39	8.49	7.46	6.81	6.35	5.76	5.13	4.45	3.67
19	15.08	10.16	8.28	7.26	6.61	6.18	5.59	4.97	4.29	3.52
20	14.82	9.95	8.10	7.10	6.46	6.02	5.44	4.82	4.15	3.38
21	14.59	9.77	7.94	6.95	6.32	5.88	5.31	4.70	4.03	3.26
22	14.38	9.61	7.80	6.81	6.19	5.76	5.19	4.58	3.92	3.15
23	14.19	9.47	7.67	6.69	6.08	5.65	5.09	4.48	3.82	3.05
24	14.03	9.34	7.55	6.59	5.98	5.55	4.99	4.39	3.74	2.97
25	13.88	9.22	7.45	6.49	5.88	5.46	4.91	4.31	3.66	2.89
26	13.74	9.12	7.36	6.41	5.80	5.38	4.83	4.24	3.59	2.82
27	13.61	9.02	7.27	6.33	5.73	5.31	4.76	4.17	3.52	2.75
28	13.50	8.93	7.19	6.25	5.66	5.24	4.69	4.11	3.46	2.70
29	13.39	8.85	7.12	6.19	5.59	5.18	4.64	4.05	3.41	2.64
30	13.29	8.77	7.05	6.12	5.53	5.12	4.58	4.00	3.36	2.59
40	12.61	8.25	6.60	5.70	5.13	4.73	4.21	3.64	3.01	2.23
60	11.97	7.76	6.17	5.31	4.76	4.37	3.87	3.31	2.69	1.90
120	11.38	7.31	5.79	4.95	4.42	4.04	3.55	3.02	2.40	1.56
¥	10.83	6.91	5.42	4.62	4.10	3.74	3.27	2.74	2.13	1.00

Source: Abridged from Fisher and Yates (1974, Table V).

Note: In ANOVA, $df_{numerator} = df_{between}$; $df_{denominator} = df_{within}$. In regression, $df_{numerator} = df_{regression}$; $df_{denominator} = df_{residual}$.

Appendix G

Critical Values of Chi-Square

df	.10	.05	.01	.001
1	2.71	3.84	6.64	10.83
2	4.60	5.99	9.21	13.82
3	6.25	7.81	11.34	16.27
4	7.78	9.49	13.28	18.47
5	9.24	11.07	15.09	20.52
6	10.64	12.59	16.81	22.46
7	12.02	14.07	18.48	24.32
8	13.36	15.51	20.09	26.12
9	14.68	16.92	21.67	27.88
10	15.99	18.31	23.21	29.59
11	17.28	19.68	24.72	31.26
12	18.55	21.03	26.22	32.91
13	19.81	22.36	27.69	34.53
14	21.06	23.68	29.14	36.12
15	22.31	25.00	30.58	37.70
16	23.54	26.30	32.00	39.25
17	24.77	27.59	33.41	40.79
18	25.99	28.87	34.80	42.31
19	27.20	30.14	36.19	43.82
20	28.41	31.41	37.57	45.32
21	29.62	32.67	38.93	46.80
22	30.81	33.92	40.29	48.27
23	32.01	35.17	41.64	49.73

(Continued)

(Continued)

df	.10	.05	.01	.001
24	33.20	36.42	42.98	51.18
25	34.38	37.65	44.31	52.62
26	35.56	38.88	45.64	54.05
27	36.74	40.11	46.96	55.48
28	37.92	41.34	48.28	56.89
29	39.09	42.56	49.59	58.30
30	40.26	43.77	50.89	59.70
40	51.80	55.76	63.69	73.40
50	63.17	67.50	76.15	86.66
60	74.40	79.08	88.38	99.61
70	85.53	90.53	100.42	112.32

Source: Abridged from Fisher and Yates (1974).

Appendix H

Critical Values of the Correlation Coefficient

	Level of Significance for One-Tailed Test			
	.05	*.025*	*.01*	*.005*
	Level of Significance for Two-Tailed Test			
df	*.10*	*.05*	*.02*	*.01*
1	.988	.997	.9995	.9999
2	.900	.950	.980	.990
3	.805	.878	.934	.959
4	.729	.811	.882	.917
5	.669	.754	.833	.874
6	.622	.707	.789	.834
7	.582	.666	.750	.798
8	.549	.632	.716	.765
9	.521	.602	.685	.735
10	.497	.576	.658	.708
11	.476	.553	.634	.684
12	.458	.532	.612	.661
13	.441	.514	.592	.641
14	.426	.497	.574	.623
15	.412	.482	.558	.606
16	.400	.468	.542	.590

(Continued)

(Continued)

df	.10	.05	.02	.01
17	.389	.456	.528	.575
18	.378	.444	.516	.561
19	.369	.433	.503	.549
20	.360	.423	.492	.537
21	.352	.413	.482	.526
22	.344	.404	.472	.515
23	.337	.396	.462	.505
24	.330	.388	.453	.496
25	.323	.381	.445	.487
26	.317	.374	.437	.479
27	.311	.367	.430	.471
28	.306	.361	.423	.463
29	.301	.355	.416	.456
30	.296	.349	.409	.449
35	.275	.325	.381	.418
40	.257	.304	.358	.393
45	.243	.288	.338	.372
50	.231	.273	.322	.354
60	.211	.250	.295	.325
70	.195	.232	.274	.303
80	.183	.217	.256	.283
90	.173	.205	.242	.267
100	.164	.195	.230	.254

Source: Abridged from Fisher and Yates (1974, Table VII).

Glossary

2 × 2 factorial design An experimental design that has two independent variables, each with two levels, resulting in four conditions.

A priori A term that means "to come before," as in, a testable hypothesis should be formulated before experimentation or observation.

Abstract A section of a written report that summarizes the major points of the study.

Additivity In a factorial design, additivity is the term used when there is no interaction between independent variables.

Aggregate matching A comparison group is selected that has similar distributions on key variables as the treatment group such as the same average age, the same percentage female, and so on.

Alternate-forms reliability A procedure for testing the reliability of responses to questions in which participants' answers are compared after the test takers have been asked slightly different versions of the questions or when randomly selected halves of the sample have been administered slightly different versions of the questions.

Alternative explanation In order to establish causality, other plausible explanations for the observed relationship must be eliminated.

Amygdala An almond-shaped structure found deep in the brain that plays a key role in fusing memories with emotion.

Analysis of covariance A statistical technique to test whether a difference on a dependent measure exists, even after controlling or covarying for the effects of specific control variables.

Analysis of variance The analysis of variance (abbreviated as ANOVA), also known as the *F*-test, is a general statistical procedure used when there are more than two levels of an independent variable or for complex experimental designs with two or more independent variables.

Anonymity Provided by research in which no identifying information is recorded that could be used to link respondents to their responses.

Antagonistic interaction See *crossover interaction*.

APA format Organization and style of writing specified by the APA.

APA American Psychological Association.

Applied research Research focus is on important questions of immediate relevance in solving practical problems.

Approach-avoidance motivation A psychological theory that states behavioral cues share informational value as signals of approach, propelling behavior forward, or conversely, they may fuel avoidance, triggering inhibition.

Attrition When research participants drop out; often a major problem in longitudinal studies.

Autonomic nervous system Part of the peripheral nervous system, the autonomic nervous system regulates bodily reactions to stress.

Availability sampling Sampling in which elements are selected on the basis of convenience.

Bar chart A graphic for qualitative variables in which the variable's distribution is displayed with solid bars separated by spaces.

Baseline Used as a comparison condition for assessing the effect of a treatment.

Baseline phase (A) The period in a single-subject design during which the intervention to be evaluated is not offered to the subject and repeated measurements of the dependent variable are taken or reconstructed.

Basic research Studies that focus on understanding the nature of abstract psychological processes and ideas rather than on the immediate solution to a problem.

Before-and-after design A quasiexperimental design consisting of several before–after comparisons involving the same variables but different groups.

Behavior coding Observation in which the research categorizes, according to strict rules, the number of times certain behaviours occurs.

Belmont Report Developed in 1979 by a national commission to specify ethical standards for the protection of human subjects.

Beneficence The Belmont Report principle that requires minimizing possible harms and maximizing benefits.

Between-groups variance Calculated by comparing the difference of each of the means of the individual groups with the overall or grand mean for all scores in the experiment; the between-groups variance represents systematic variance due to the manipulation of the independent variable.

Between-subjects design In an experiment, independent groups of participants receive the different levels of the independent variable.

Bias An often subtle process that comes in many different forms, all of which can be fatal to a research study and for which the scientific method serves as a countervailing force.

Bimodal A distribution that has two nonadjacent categories with about the same number of cases, and these categories have more cases than any others.

Cannon–Bard theory of emotion In the 1920s, in direct opposition to the James–Lange theory, Walter Cannon and Philip Bard proposed that emotional experiences come first, followed by bodily changes.

Carryover effects An important source of experimental error for a within-subjects design, this problem occurs when the effects from one treatment condition are carried over to the next.

Case studies Investigations that involve systematic investigation of a single case or a small set of very similar cases.

Ceiling effect A problem that detracts from the sensitivity of a research design can occur when a dependent variable is seriously restricted in range by very high scores.

Census Research in which information is obtained through the responses that all available members of an entire population give to questions.

Central tendency The most common value (for variables measured at the nominal level) or the value around which cases tend to center (for a quantitative variable).

Cerebral cortex The brain's outer layer or "bark," which is thought to be the seat of higher thinking.

Certificate of Confidentiality Can be issued by the National Institutes of Health to protect a researcher studying high-risk populations or behaviors from being legally required to disclose confidential information.

Chi-square (χ^2) test of independence An inferential statistic used to test hypotheses about relationships between two or more categorical variables in a contingency table.

Circular reasoning This represents a problem in conceptualization and design that can be minimized by using distinct and different measures of the same variables.

Clinical replication of single-subject designs Used to enhance generalizability of single-subject designs, clinical replication involves combining different interventions into a clinical package to treat multiple problems.

Cluster A naturally occurring, mixed aggregate of elements of the population.

Cluster sampling Sampling in which elements are selected in two or more stages, with the first stage being the random selection of naturally occurring clusters and the last stage being the random selection of elements within clusters.

Code of Conduct, American Psychological Association Eighty-three standards adopted (updated) in 2002 to guide psychologists' clinical and research practice.

Cognitive illusions Mistakes of reasoning that occur when our thinking deceives us; often referred to as curious blind spots or mental tunnels.

Cognitive interview A technique for evaluating questions in which researchers ask people test questions and then probe with follow-up questions to learn how they understood the question and what their answers mean.

Cohort effects A confound that occurs in a cross-sectional method when comparing groups of persons who are at different ages at one point in time.

Cohort A group of individuals sharing a certain characteristic, such as age, year of high school graduation, or locale.

Comparison group In an experiment, a group that has been exposed to a different treatment (or value of the independent variable) than the experimental group.

Computer-assisted personal interview (CAPI) A personal interview in which the laptop computer is used to display interview questions and to process responses that the interviewer types in, as well as to check that these responses fall within allowed ranges.

Computer-assisted telephone interview (CATI) A telephone interview in which a questionnaire is programmed into a computer, along with relevant skip patterns, and only legal entries are allowed; incorporates the tasks of interviewing, data entry, and some data cleaning.

Conceptual definition It provides the meaning, often rather broad in scope, of an abstract term, such as *intelligence*, *anxiety*, or *emotion*. Like a dictionary definition, it demarcates a semantic or linguistic meaning of a psychological term, that is, its usage in words, texts, and language.

Concurrent multiple baseline design A type of small-N design in which a series of A-B designs (or A-B-A or A-B-A-B designs) are implemented at the same time for at least three cases (clients, target problems, or settings).

Concurrent multiple baseline single-subject design A series of A-B designs (although A-B-A or A-B-A-B designs could also be used) are implemented at the same time for at least three cases (clients, target problems, or settings).

Concurrent validity The type of validity that exists when scores on a measure are closely related to scores on a criterion measured at the same time.

Condition A particular way in which participants are treated; a group or treatment in an experiment.

Confidentiality Provided by research in which identifying information that could be used to link respondents to their responses is available only to designated research personnel for specific research needs.

Confirmatory bias A natural tendency of the human mind to actively seek out and assign more weight to any kind of evidence that favors existing beliefs, expectations, or a hypothesis in hand.

Confirmatory factor analysis A statistical technique that is used to determine whether the same set of factors underlying a construct in one study sample can be replicated in a new independent sample.

Confounding variables Variables that represent unwanted sources of influences that can create problems for data interpretation.

Confounds The researcher fails to control for unwanted sources of influences. These factors subsequently cannot be ruled out as viable alternative explanations.

Construct validity Established by showing that same traits measured by different methods are related (convergent validity), whereas different traits measured by same methods are unrelated (discriminant validity).

Construct An abstraction or concept that is specified in a theory in order to describe, explain, and predict a wide range of related empirical findings. Constructs that are studied in psychology, such as intelligence, personality, memory, anxiety, or attention, are not directly observable material entities.

Constructivist theory Psychological theory that emphasizes general cognitive processes such as categorizing, storytelling, and persuasion as tools by which the mind creates cultural meaning.

Content validity The extent to which test items have sufficient breadth to capture the full range of a construct intended to be measured.

Context effects (priming effects) Occur in a survey when one or more questions influence how subsequent questions are interpreted.

Contingency table A bivariate (two-variable) or higher-order distribution showing the distribution of one variable for each category of another variable. Also called a *cross-tabulation*. Often used with chi-square (χ^2) test of independence to tabulate and analyze relationship between two or more categorical variables.

Contingent question A question that is asked of only a subset of survey respondents.

Control condition Serves as a comparison condition in a within-subjects design.

Control group A comparison group that receives no treatment.

Control variable A variable that is either held constant in an experiment or its effects are statistically controlled.

Control A scientific investigation must exercise control of study variables either by research design or statistical techniques.

Convergent validity An important aspect of construct validity, convergent validity measures the extent to which the same trait measured by two different methods yields similar results.

Correlation coefficient A number varying from -1.00 through 0.00 to $+1.00$ that indicates the strength of relationship between the two variables.

Correlation A statistic that measures the extent to which two variables are associated but not necessarily causally related.

Correlational research Studies that focus on the association of pairs of variables, but causation cannot be established.

Counterbalancing For a within-subjects design, a commonly used technique to control for the potentially confounding effects of order of treatments.

Covariation of the cause and effect In establishing causality, evidence that shows that when the cause is present, the effect occurs, and when the cause is absent, the effect does not occur.

Cover letter The letter sent with a mailed questionnaire. It explains the survey's purpose and auspices and encourages the respondent to participate.

Criterion validity The extent to which test scores agree with an objective criterion that follows logically from the measured variable.

Critical *t*-value The value that the *t*-statistic must exceed in order to reject the null hypothesis at a certain level of probability.

Cronbach's alpha A statistic commonly used to measure interitem reliability of an objective test.

Cross-cultural psychology This field of study investigates the universality of psychological processes across different cultures.

Cross-population generalizability Exists when findings about one group, population, or setting hold true for other groups, populations, or settings. Also called *external validity*.

Cross-sectional method Taking a large group of participants of various ages at one time and testing them.

Cross-sequential design A quasiexperimental design used in developmental psychology in which several different ages are sampled at several different time periods.

Crossover interaction In a 2 × 2 design, a type of interaction in which the effects of one independent variable on a dependent variable are reversed at different levels of the other independent variable.

Cultural psychology An area in psychology that studies how culture shapes our thinking and how our thinking shapes culture.

Culture The rich and intricate melding of shared meanings, communal practices and rituals, and collective discourses and beliefs about human life that prevails in a given group or society.

Cycle A baseline phase pattern in a single-subject design reflecting ups and downs depending on the time of measurement.

Data Information that is gained objectively from observation or experimentation that can be measured and evaluated statistically.

Debriefing A researcher's informing subjects after an experiment about the experiment's purposes and methods and evaluating subjects' personal reactions to the experiment.

Deductive research The type of research in which a specific expectation is deduced from a general premise and is then tested.

Degrees of freedom In tests of statistical significance, the number of observations that are free to vary in estimating a population parameter.

Demand characteristics Cues available that tip off participants to the scientific hypothesis of the researcher and influence how participants respond to study stimuli.

Dependent variable The observed effect, result, or outcome that is measured in response to a systematic change in the independent variable.

Descriptive statistics Statistics used to describe the distribution of and relationship among variables, usually in the form of averages and standard deviations (a statistical measure of variability).

Design sensitivity The extent to which a researcher has constructed the best possible study to evaluate the topic under investigation.

Dichotomy Variable having only two values.

Direct replication of single-subject designs Used to enhance the generalizability of a single-subject design, it involves repeating the single-subject design using the same procedures, by the same researchers, including the same providers of the treatment, in the same setting, and in the same situation, with different clients.

Direction of association A pattern in a relationship between two variables—the values of variables tend to change consistently in relation to change in the other variable. The direction of association can be either positive or negative.

Discriminant validity An approach to construct validation; established by showing evidence that different traits measured by the same methods are unrelated.

Discussion A section of a written report in which the author provides theoretical interpretation for the findings of the study.

Disproportionate stratified sampling Sampling in which elements are selected from strata in different proportions from those that appear in the population.

Doctrine of falsification Scientists should aim to falsify their theories rather than confirm them.

Double negative A question or statement that contains two negatives, which can muddy the meaning of the question.

Double-barrelled question A single survey question that actually asks two questions but allows only one answer.

Double-blind When both experimenter and participant are deliberately kept blind to (unaware of) or kept in the dark as to whether the participant is receiving the treatment or placebo; used to control for expectations of the both experimenter and participant regarding the treatment.

Dualism A school of philosophy that holds that the mind is a nonphysical substance that is fundamentally different from the physical brain.

Duration The length of time an event or some symptom lasts; usually is measured for each occurrence of the event or symptom in a single-subject design.

E-mail survey A survey that is sent and answered through e-mail.

Ecological fallacy An error in reasoning in which incorrect conclusions about individual-level processes are drawn from group-level data.

Ecological validity The extent to which a study or experiment approximates the actual real-life phenomenon under investigation.

Effect size A standardized measure of association; often the difference between the mean of the experimental group and the mean of the control group on the dependent variable, adjusted for the average variability in the two groups. The effect size measures the strength of the predicted or hypothesized relationship between the independent variable and dependent variable.

Electronic survey A survey that is sent and answered by computer, either through e-mail or on the Web.

Elements The individual members of the population whose characteristics are to be measured.

Embodiment theory of emotion Perceiving and thinking about emotions involves re-experiencing in oneself those subtle physical and mental changes of the relevant emotions.

Empirical articles Reports on a particular study written in a certain format that is divided into sections with an Abstract, Introduction, Method, Results, and Discussion.

Empirical generalization A statement that describes patterns found in data.

Empiricism A school of philosophy that holds that knowledge is gained through experience, observation, and experiment.

Encoding In cognitive experiments, the condition in which information is presented and studied.

Epistemology A branch of philosophy that studies how knowledge is gained or acquired.

Error variance Defined as the deviation of individual scores in each group or condition from its respective mean.

Ethnography A naturalistic observation method that studies people in their natural settings so that their behaviors and words can be put into proper context.

Ex post facto control group design A nonexperimental design in which comparison groups are selected after the treatment, program, or other variation in the independent variable has occurred.

Ex post facto Means literally "after the fact" and refers to investigations in which conditions of a study are determined *after* rather than *before* (a priori) some variation or event has naturally occurred.

Exhaustive Every case can be classified as having at least one attribute (or value) for the variable.

Experiment A controlled investigation in which one or more variables are manipulated.

Experimental A researcher is able to exercise control over the variable or variables that are assumed to be the causal agent(s) producing the predicted effect.

Experimental control Holding constant as many extraneous variables as possible so that any effect on the dependent variable can be attributed to changes in the independent variable.

Experimental design Random assignment of participants to groups. The effects on the dependent variable of manipulating one or more independent variables are investigated.

Experimental error Any influence on the dependent variable that is not due solely to the systematic change in the independent variable.

Experimental group In an experiment, the group of research participants that receives the treatment or experimental manipulation.

Experimental stimuli Materials that are used in constructing an independent variable.

Experimental task A task that participants performed that is used as an independent variable.

External validity The extent to which the results of a study generalize to other situations or populations.

F-test ANOVA computes an F statistic, which is the ratio of two types of variance: systematic and error variance.

Face validity The type of validity that exists when an inspection of items used to measure a concept suggests that they are appropriate "on their face."

Facial feedback hypothesis Originates from the James–Lange theory of emotion; the facial feedback hypothesis now falls under the embodiment theory of emotion. The idea is that facial movements by themselves can re-enact particular emotional feelings and that these emotional feelings can be created by simply "tricking" a person into making specific facial contractions.

Factor analysis A set of data analytic techniques used to reduce correlational data to a smaller number of dimensions.

Factorial design An experimental design in which all conditions of the independent variable are combined with all conditions of the other independent variable. The main effects of each independent variable as well as the interaction effects between and among the independent variables can be statistically tested.

Factors Another term for the independent variable in an experiment.

Federal Policy for the Protection of Human Subjects Specific regulations based on the Belmont Report principles that were adopted in 1991 by the Department of Health and Human Services and the Food and Drug Administration.

Fence-sitters Survey respondents who see themselves as being neutral on an issue and choose a middle (neutral) response that is offered.

Field notes Notes that describe what has been observed, heard, or otherwise experienced in a participant observation study. These notes usually are written after the observational session.

Field researcher A researcher who uses qualitative methods to conduct research in the field developing and maintaining relationships.

Filter question A survey question used to identify a subset of respondents who then are asked other questions.

Floaters Survey respondents who provide an opinion on a topic in response to a closed-ended question that does not include a "Don't know" option but who will choose "Don't know" if it is available.

Floor effect A problem that detracts from the sensitivity of a research design can occur when a dependent variable fails to discriminate various degrees of poor performance, meaning that all scores are confined to the very low end of the range.

Focus groups A qualitative method that involves unstructured group interviews in which the focus group leader actively encourages discussion among participants on the topics of interest.

Frame switching In constructivist theory, when a person alternates between two internalized mental sets, as when a bicultural individual moves back and forth between two internalized cultural mental sets.

Frequency In a single-subject design, counting the number of times a behavior occurs or the number of times people experience different feelings within a particular time period.

Frequency distribution Numerical display showing the number of cases, and usually the percentage of cases (the relative frequencies), corresponding to each value or group of values of a variable.

Functional magnetic resonance imaging (fMRI) A widely used technique that records the brain at work, in real time, while an individual performs a task.

Gatekeeper A person in a field setting who can grant researchers access to the setting.

Generalizability The extent to which findings derived from a sample can be applied to a wider population.

Generalization A broad statement that cannot be directly tested but rather needs to be translated into one or more hypotheses.

"Grand tour" question A broad question at the start of an interview that seeks to engage the respondent in the topic of interest; used in intensive (depth) interviewing.

Group-administered survey A survey that is completed by individual respondents who are assembled in a group.

Health Insurance Portability and Accountability Act (HIPAA) Rule adopted by the U.S. Congress in 1996 requiring researchers to have valid authorization for any use or disclosure of "protected health information" (PHI) from a health care provider.

Hereditarian Emphasizes the role of genetics in the development of human traits.

Heuristic biases Mistakes in reasoning due to our natural propensity to favor subjective impressions and personal anecdotes over cold, hard statistics.

Hippocampus Key memory center of the brain.

Histogram A graphic for quantitative variables in which the variable's distribution is displayed with adjacent bars.

Hypothesis A statement that is derived from a theory that usually specifies a relationship between two or more variables.

Idiosyncratic variation Variation in responses to questions that is caused by individuals' reactions to particular words or ideas in the question instead of by variation in the concept that the question is intended to measure.

In-person interview A survey in which an interviewer questions respondents face to face and records their answers.

Independent variable An element of the study that is systematically manipulated, changed, or selected.

Index The sum or average of responses to a set of questions about a concept.

Individual differences In a between-subjects design, people's differences can confound results, and thus random assignment in forming experimental and control groups can be used to help neutralize these differences.

Individual matching Individual cases in the treatment and control groups are matched on some variables.

Inductive research The type of research in which general conclusions are drawn from specific data.

Inferential statistics A mathematical tool for estimating how likely it is that a statistical result based on data from a random sample is representative of the population from which the sample is assumed to have been selected.

Informed consent Legal and ethical obligation to provide potential research participants sufficient information about a study so that they can make an informed decision as to whether they wish to participate.

Institutional Review Board (IRB) A group of organizational and community representatives required by federal law to review the ethical issues in all proposed research that is federally funded, involves human subjects, or has any potential for harm to subjects.

Interaction An interaction occurs when the effects of one level of the independent variable depend on the particular level of the other independent variable.

Interitem reliability An approach that calculates reliability based on the correlation among multiple items used to measure a single concept; also known as internal consistency.

Internal validity Speaks to the logic of experimental design—the extent to which procedures and methods are optimally arranged so that the effects of the independent variable on the dependent variable can be evaluated unambiguously.

Interobserver reliability When similar measurements are obtained by different observers rating the same persons, events, or places.

Interpretive questions Questions included in a questionnaire or interview schedule to help explain answers to other important questions.

Interrupted-time-series design In quasiexperiments, examines the effects of a naturally occurring treatment on the behavior of a large group of people.

Interval In a single-subject design, measuring the length of time between events, behaviors, or symptoms.

Interval level of measurement A measurement of a variable in which the numbers indicating a variable's values represent fixed measurement units but have no absolute, or fixed, zero point.

Intervening variable A hypothetical internal state that is used to explain relationships between independent and dependent variables.

Interview schedule The survey instrument containing the questions asked by the interviewer in an in-person or phone survey.

Introduction The section of a written report that identifies the problem to be investigated and why it is important.

Is-ought A philosophical distinction used to emphasize questions of science ("is") versus questions of values ("ought").

James–Lange theory The 19th-century psychologist William James (1884) and Danish physiologist Carl Lange (1887) proposed that emotions are feelings that come about as a *result* of physiological changes, such as perspiration, rapid heartbeat, muscular tension, and dryness of mouth, created by the autonomic nervous system that regulates bodily reactions to stress.

Jottings Brief notes written in the field about highlights of an observation period.

Journals Peer-reviewed scientific periodicals, such as *Psychological Science*.

Justice The Belmont Report principle that requires distributing benefits and risks of research fairly.

Latent variable models Specialized statistical techniques that are used to evaluate constructs and to develop models of possible relationships among a set of variables.

Latin-square design To combat confounds of carryover effect in within-subjects experiments, a Latin-square design is an *incomplete* counterbalancing arrangement in which each possible order of treatments occurs equally often across research participants.

Level of measurement The mathematical precision with which the values of a variable can be expressed. The nominal level of measurement, which is qualitative, has no mathematical interpretation; the quantitative levels of measurement—ordinal, interval, and ratio—are progressively more precise mathematically.

Level of target variable, single-subject design Flat lines reflecting the amount or magnitude of the target variable in a single-subject design.

Levels Can also be referred to as *conditions*; levels are the different values of an independent variable.

Likert scale An ordinal level of measurement that often involves a question about attitude or opinions that asks for a numerical rating of the extent of agreement or disagreement.

Longitudinal method Same research participants are followed over time; avoids cohort and period effects that confound cross-sectional method.

Longitudinal research design A study in which data are collected that can be ordered in time; also defined as research in which data are collected at two or more points in time.

Magnetic resonance imaging (MRI) Provides a measure of the structural anatomy of the brain.

Magnitude In a single-subject design, the intensity of a particular behavior or psychological state may be measured.

Mailed survey A survey involving a mailed questionnaire to be completed by the respondent.

Main effect In a factorial experiment, the effects of one independent variable on a dependent variable are averaged over all levels of another independent variable.

Manipulation check A pilot or "dry run" to assess whether the independent variable manipulation creates the intended effect. IRB approval is required before conducting a manipulation check.

Matched-pairs design Pairs of participants are matched on a variable that is strongly related to the dependent variable, and then one of the pairs is randomly assigned to the experimental condition and the other to the control condition. That is, each member of the pair is assigned to *different* levels of the independent variable. An effective matched-pairs design provides a degree of experimental control of between-subjects individual differences that is comparable to that of a within-subjects design.

Matching A procedure for equating the characteristics of individuals in different comparison groups in an experiment. Matching can be done on either an individual or an aggregate basis. For individual matching, individuals who are similar in terms of key characteristics are paired prior to assignment, and then the two members of each pair are assigned to the two groups. For aggregate matching, groups are chosen for comparisons that are similar in terms of the distribution of key characteristics.

Matrix A form on which can be recorded systematically particular features of multiple cases or instances that a qualitative data analyst needs to examine.

Mean The arithmetic, or weighted, average, computed by adding up the value of all the cases and dividing by the total number of cases.

Measurement The assignment of numerals to objects or events according to some objective rule.

Median The position average, or the point that divides a distribution in half (the 50th percentile).

Meta-analysis A method that provides a more unbiased evaluation of the literature than a conventional review article by using objective statistics to weigh the strength of results from individual studies.

Method The section of a written report that details the operations and procedures used in the study.

Milgram's obedience experiments Experimental laboratory-based study of obedience to authority in which subjects recruited at Yale University in the 1960s were told that they were to administer shocks when supposed "learners" failed to answer questions correctly.

Mixed-factorial design An experimental design in which one independent variable is varied between subjects and the other independent variable is varied within subjects.

Mixed-mode survey A survey that is conducted by more than one method, allowing the strengths of one survey design to compensate for the weaknesses of another and maximizing the likelihood of securing data from different types of respondents; for example, nonrespondents in a mailed survey may be interviewed in person or over the phone.

Mode The most frequent value in a distribution; also termed the *probability average*.

Multifactor ANOVA Used for experimental designs with more than one factor or independent variable varied simultaneously. In comparison to the simple ANOVA, the multifactor ANOVA is much more computationally complex given that there are both main and interaction effects that need to be tested.

Multifactorial design A multifactorial design allows for the testing of effects of all possible combinations of the levels of the independent variables on the dependent variable. It provides information as to the main effect of each independent variable as well as any interactions between and among independent variables.

Multiple-group before-and-after design A type of quasiexperimental design in which several before-and-after comparisons are made involving the same independent and dependent variables but different groups.

Multitrait-multimethod matrix In evaluating construct validity, a correlation matrix composed of at least two methods of measurement of two different constructs.

Mutually exclusive A variable's attributes (or values) are mutually exclusive when every case can be classified as having only one attribute (or value).

Natural treatment A naturally occurring event is treated as a quasi-independent variable, which can be measured but cannot be manipulated.

Naturalistic observation A type of research method used to collect behavioral data in natural environments as opposed to laboratory or other controlled settings.

Nominal level of measurement Variables whose values have no mathematical interpretation; they vary in kind or quality, but not in amount (also called the *categorical or qualitative level*).

Nomological network Derived from the Greek term *nomology*, meaning lawful; *nomological network* in construct validity refers to the interlocking relationships between the observable, measurable, or empirical and the inferable, interpretable, or theoretical.

Nonconcurrent multiple baseline design A multiple baseline design in which subjects are randomly assigned into A-B designs with different baseline phase lengths.

Nonequivalent control group design A quasiexperimental design in which experimental and comparison groups are designated before the treatment occurs but are not created by random assignment.

Nonexperimental Actions and events are carefully measured and catalogued, but independent variables cannot be directly manipulated.

Nonparametric statistics Mathematical procedures used for variables that are measured on a nominal or ordinal scale.

Nonprobability sampling method Sampling method in which the probability of selection of population elements is unknown.

Nonrespondents People or other entities who do not participate in a study although they are selected for the sample.

Normal curve When the distribution of scores approximates a normal curve, most scores fall near the center, with gradually fewer scores as you move toward either extreme.

Normal distribution See *normal curve*.

Norms The mean and standard deviation used to characterize the distribution of test scores for a standardization sample.

Null hypothesis The hypothesis of no difference or no relationship, which the researcher tries to reject, nullify, or disprove.

Null result When an independent variable fails to produce any effect on the dependent variable.

Nuremberg War Crime Trials In 1946, exposed horrific medical experiments conducted by Nazi doctors and others in the name of "science."

Office for Protection from Research Risks, National Institutes of Health Monitors IRBs, with the exception of research involving drugs (which is the responsibility of the Federal Food and Drug Administration).

One-factor ANOVA See simple ANOVA.

One-tailed test In order to reject the null hypothesis, the value of the test statistic must fall in either the upper or lower end of its sampling distribution. The the null hypothesis can only be rejected by a higher value of the test statistic falling in the upper end of the sampling distribution or by a lower value of the test statistic falling in the lower end of the sampling distribution, but not by a value falling in both ends of the distribution.

Operational definition Indicates how a concept is coded, measured, or quantified. An operational definition is among several possible objective and measurable indicators of a concept.

Ordinal level of measurement A measurement of a variable in which the numbers indicating a variable's values specify only the order of the cases, permitting "greater than" and "less than" distinctions.

Outcome bias When a test consistently produces lower scores for an identifiable class of people defined by race, gender, or ethnicity, such results reflect outcome bias.

Outlier An exceptionally high or low value in a distribution.

Parameter A numerical characteristic of a population that is estimated on the basis of a sample statistic, such as the sample mean or sample standard deviation.

Parametric statistics Mathematical procedures that require variables to be measured on either an interval or ratio scale.

Part-whole question effects These occur when responses to a general or summary question about a topic are influenced by responses to an earlier, more specific question about that topic.

Participant observation A qualitative method for gathering data that involves developing a sustained relationship with people while they go about their normal activities.

Participant observer A researcher who gathers data through participating and observing in a setting where he or she develops a sustained relationship with people while they go about their normal activities. The term *participant observer* is often used to refer to a continuum of possible roles, from complete observation, in which the researcher does not participate along with others in group activities, to complete participation, in which the researcher participates without publicly acknowledging being an observer.

Pearson's correlation coefficient, or *r* The most commonly used statistic to measure the relationship between two quantitative variables.

Peer review The process by which other independent reviewers (meaning no relationship with the researchers whose work is under review) evaluate the scientific merit of the work.

Performance-based measures Studies of data collected from standardized tests, such as intelligence tests.

Period effects An inherent confound for a cross-sectional method when historical influences may affect responses to the dependent variable.

Periodicity A sequence of elements (in a list to be sampled) that varies in some regular, periodic pattern.

Phone survey A survey in which interviewers question respondents over the phone and then record their answers.

Phrenology A now defunct field of study, once considered a science in the 19th century, that held that bumps and fissures of the skull determined the character and personality of a person.

Pilot data The experimenter collects pilot data to test out the procedures and measures before formally running the study.

Placebo Often used in treatment outcome research; an inert substance or sham procedure employed to assess the psychological effects of expecting and receiving a treatment.

Plagiarism Presenting another person's published work or parts of published work as your own. A serious ethical as well as legal problem that can result in expulsion, grade failure, job loss and litigation for violating copyright laws.

Popular science Literature often written by eminent scientists who aim to explain science for a general audience.

Population Any entire collection of people, animals, plants, or things, all of which can be referred to as units, from which information is collected.

Population parameter The value of a statistic, such as a mean, computed using the data for the entire population; a sample statistic is an estimate of a population parameter.

Positive psychology A relatively new school of psychology that seeks to learn about human thriving, flourishing, optimism, resilience, joy, and capabilities.

Post hoc In Latin, "after this;" refers to hypotheses that are formulated after data are collected and analyzed.

Post hoc hypotheses Hypotheses that are formulated after data have been collected and analyzed.

Posttest In experimental research, the measurement of an outcome (dependent) variable after an experimental intervention or after a presumed independent variable has changed for some other reason.

Practical (or clinical) significance When evaluating the impact of an intervention in a single-subject design, whether the intervention made a meaningful difference in the well-being of the subject.

Predictive validity The ability of a measure to predict scores on a criterion measured in the future.

Pretest-posttest control group design See *randomized comparative change design*.

Pretest In experimental research, the measurement of an outcome (dependent) variable prior to an experimental intervention or change in a presumed independent variable for some other reason. The pretest is exactly the same "test" as the posttest, but it is administered at a different time.

Primary source First-hand empirical report published in a peer-reviewed journal.

Priming Exposure to a stimulus facilitates responses to a subsequent event.

Probability The likelihood that a given event will occur.

Probability average See *mode*.

Probability of selection The likelihood that an element will be selected from the population for inclusion in the sample. In a census of all the elements of a population, the probability that any particular element will be selected is 1.0. If half the elements in the population are sampled on the basis of chance (say, by tossing a coin), the probability of selection for each element is one-half, or .5. As the size of the sample as a proportion of the population decreases, so does the probability of selection.

Probability sampling method A sampling method that relies on a random, or chance, selection method so that the probability of selection of population elements is known.

Program evaluation This research studies the effects on behavior of large-scale policy changes as well as social reforms and innovations occurring in government, schools, courts, prisons, businesses, health care, housing, and so forth.

Proportionate stratified sampling Sampling method in which elements are selected from strata in exact proportion to their representation in the population.

Proprietary A privately owned entity that is open only to subscribers, usually for a fee.

Pseudoscience Dubious but fascinating claims that are touted as "scientifically proven" and bolstered by fervent, public testimonials of believers who have experienced first hand or who have claimed to have witnessed the phenomenon; however, such evidence is not based on the principles of the scientific method.

Psychological traits Presumed enduring and stable dispositions such as intelligence, personality characteristics, or attitudes that can be measured by objective tests.

Psychology Broadly defined as the scientific study of people, the mind and behavior that focuses attention on virtually endless questions about how we feel, think, behave, believe, and interact.

Psychometrics A school of psychology that studies the application of psychological tests as objective measures of the mind and mental processes.

PsycINFO Specialized, noncommercial search engine sponsored by the American Psychological Association (APA) to serve as a database for citations and abstracts of the world's literature in psychology and related fields.

PsycLIT See *PsycINFO*.

Publication bias A bias that can occur due to the fact that most literature reviews include only studies that have been published. Studies that are often unpublished because of negative findings are not considered, creating a bias toward published studies that typically report positive findings.

Purposive sampling A nonprobability sampling method in which elements are selected for a purpose, usually because of their unique position.

Qualitative interviewing A method that involves open-ended, relatively unstructured questioning in which the interviewer seeks in-depth information on the interviewee's feelings, experiences, and perceptions. Also called *intensive interviewing*.

Qualitative methods A set of research techniques that is intended to *go beyond numbers* in order to study and understand phenomena in terms of the meanings people attach to them, thereby preserving and capturing the complexities and diversities of human behavior. Methods such as participant observation, intensive interviewing, and focus groups that are designed to capture social life as participants experience it with spoken words or observations rather than in categories predetermined by the researcher.

Qualitative research Emphasis is placed on understanding context—the what, how, when, and where of an event or an action. It yields data regarding meanings, concepts, definitions, characteristics, metaphors, symbols, and descriptions of events or actions.

Quasi-independent variable Considered by many researchers to be a distinct type of independent variable that can be measured and varied but cannot be directly controlled by the experiment and therefore cannot be manipulated. Subject variables and natural treatments are examples of quasi-independent variables.

Quasiexperiment A research design in which there is a comparison group that is comparable with the experimental group in critical ways, but participants are not randomly assigned to the experimental and comparison groups.

Questionnaire The survey instrument containing the questions in a self-administered survey.

Quota sampling A nonprobability sampling method in which elements are selected to ensure that the sample represents certain characteristics in proportion to their prevalence in the population.

Random assignment A procedure that is used to control for bias that ensures that each participant has an equal likelihood of being placed in either control or experimental groups. That is, the assignment of cases is done by a chance procedure, as by tossing a coin.

Random error of measurement Variation due to multiple little factors that have nothing to do with the construct you are trying to measure.

Random number table A table containing lists of numbers that are ordered solely on the basis of chance; it is used for drawing a random sample.

Random sampling A method of sampling that relies on a random, or chance, selection method so that every element of the sampling frame has a known probability of being selected.

Random sampling error Differences between the population and the sample that are due only to chance factors (random error), not to systematic sampling error. Random sampling error may or may not result in an unrepresentative sample. The magnitude of sampling error due to chance factors can be estimated statistically. Also known as *chance sampling error*.

Random-digit dialing The random dialing by a machine of numbers within designated phone prefixes, which creates a random sample for phone surveys.

Randomization Procedures that are used to counteract bias; whether randomizing order of presentation of test stimuli or randomly assigning participants to different study conditions.

Randomized comparative change design The classic true experimental design in which research participants are assigned randomly to two groups; both these groups receive a pretest, one group then receives the experimental intervention, and then both groups receive a posttest. Also called the *pretest-posttest control group design*.

Range The true upper limit in a distribution minus the true lower limit (or the highest rounded value minus the lowest rounded value, plus one).

Rate In a single-subject design, refers to the increase or decrease in the trend line of the behavior or other outcome over time.

Ratio level of measurement A measurement of a variable in which the numbers indicating a variable's values represent fixed measuring units and an absolute zero point.

Reactive effects The changes in an individual or group behavior that are due to being observed or otherwise studied.

Recall In cognitive experiments, the condition in which information is tested for recall.

Reductionist fallacy (reductionism) An error in reasoning that occurs when incorrect conclusions about group-level processes are based on individual-level data.

References The last section of an APA report, which follows the discussion section and begins on a separate page under the label *References*; lists the reference for each work cited in the body of the text.

Regression artifact A threat to internal validity that occurs when subjects who are chosen for a study because of their extreme scores on the dependent variable become less extreme on the posttest due to natural cyclical or episodic change in the variable.

Regression to the mean Trend for extreme scores on a measure to move closer to the group average when retested due to inherent unreliability of measurement.

Reliability A measurement procedure that yields consistent scores when the phenomenon being measured is not changing; the degree to which a measure or a set of data is consistent.

Reliability measure Statistics that summarize the consistency among a set of measures. Cronbach alpha is the most common measure of the reliability of a set of items included in an index.

Repeated-measures panel design A quasiexperimental design consisting of several pretest and posttest observations of the same group.

Repeated-measures, within-subjects design The term often used to describe the design when the same participant can be tested repeatedly over time.

Replication Repeating a previous research study to determine whether its findings can be duplicated.

Representative sample A sample that "looks like" the population from which it was selected in all respects that are potentially relevant to the study. The distribution of characteristics among the elements of a representative sample is the same as the distribution of those characteristics among the total population. In an unrepresentative sample, some characteristics are overrepresented or underrepresented.

Research circle A diagram of the elements of the research process, including theories, hypotheses, data collection, and data analysis.

Research hypothesis A statement derived from theory that predicts that the variables under investigation are statistically related in the population; in other words, the obtained results in the study sample are true for the general population.

Respect for persons The Belmont Report principle that requires treating persons as autonomous agents and protecting those with diminished autonomy.

Results Section of a written report that presents the major statistical findings of the study.

Review articles Critical examinations of empirical studies that have already been published.

Robust The extent to which findings of a study are reproducible or replicable given different conditions, settings, and samples.

Sample bias A particular form of bias in which some members of the population are less likely to be included than others in the study.

Sample A group of units selected from a larger group that is known as the *population*.

Sample statistic The value of a statistic, such as a mean, computed from sample data.

Sampling distribution The hypothetical distribution of a statistic across all the random samples that could be drawn from a population.

Sampling error Any difference between the characteristics of a sample and the characteristics of a population. The larger the sampling error, the less representative the sample.

Sampling frame A list of all elements or other units containing the elements in a population.

Sampling interval The number of cases from one sampled case to another in a systematic random sample.

Saturation point The point at which subject selection is ended in intensive interviewing, when new interviews seem to yield little additional information.

Scale Refers to the level of measurement of a variable, as in nominal, ordinal, interval, or ratio.

Scatter diagram A graph that is used to depict the degree of correlation between pairs of variables. It is made by plotting the scores of individuals on the two variables.

Science journalism Reports appearing in media outlets that focus on recent developments in science that are judged newsworthy.

Scientific method A formal way of knowing that is exclusively reliant upon objective, empirical investigation.

Secondary sources Second-hand accounts of scientific work that can appear in various outlets, such as review articles, textbooks, and newspapers.

Secular trends A potential confound for longitudinal studies occurs when results cannot be attributed to hypothesized age-related developmental processes but rather to general changes that have taken place in society.

Selection bias A source of internal invalidity that occurs when research participants are not randomly selected.

Self-correcting A key defining feature of science that relies on empirical evidence for evaluating whether theories and beliefs should be discarded.

Serendipity An unplanned, accidental, yet fortunate discovery that can occur in the course of a study on an unrelated topic.

Simple ANOVA Analysis of variance used for experimental designs in which one and only one factor is varied across more than two levels; also referred to as a one-factor analysis of variance or one-factor ANOVA.

Simple main effect A simple main effect compares the influence of one level of an independent variable at a given level of another independent variable.

Simple random sampling A method of sampling in which every sample element is selected only on the basis of chance, through a random process.

Single-factor experiment An experiment with one independent variable.

Skepticism An important characteristic of scientific thinking for the critical analysis of theories and findings.

Skewness The extent to which cases are clustered more at one or the other end of the distribution of a quantitative variable rather than in a symmetric pattern around its center. Skew can be positive (a right skew), with the number of cases tapering off in the positive direction, or negative (a left skew), with the number of cases tapering off in the negative direction.

Skip pattern The unique combination of questions created in a survey by filter questions and contingent questions.

Snowball sampling A method of sampling in which sample elements are selected as they are identified by successive informants or interviewees.

Social brain hypothesis According to this theoretical perspective, intelligent thought is shaped by our "social connectivity"—the degree to which we enjoy friendships, love, companionship, and intimacy.

Social desirability bias A validity threat in testing in which examinees respond defensively to test items based on how they wish to be perceived rather than openly and genuinely.

Social exclusion A psychological belief that can be manipulated experimentally in which participants are led to believe that they will end up alone in life without loved ones, friends, and acquaintances.

Social Sciences Citation Index (SSCI) A citation database that consists of world-leading social science journals across more than 50 fields of sudy.

Social signaling system According to Adams and Kleck (2003), facial expressions of emotion and gaze direction operate as a social signaling system that governs our basic evolved behavioral tendencies for approach or avoidance.

Split-half reliability Reliability achieved when responses to the same questions by two randomly selected halves of a sample or two halves of a test are about the same.

Spurious relationship A relationship between two variables that is due to variation in a third variable.

Stable line A line in the baseline phase of a single-subject design that is relatively flat, with little variability in the scores so that the scores fall in a narrow band.

Staged manipulation When a confederate who typically is presented as another participant but is actually an accomplice of the researcher; the accomplice or confederate is used to help create the psychological state or social situation that is the topic of investigation.

Standard deviation A statistic used to measure variability in a sample calculated by taking the square root of the average squared deviation of each case from the mean.

Standard error of the mean Indicates the degree to which the means of the samples vary from the population mean.

Standardization sample A random selection of people drawn from a carefully defined population.

Standardization Procedures to ensure that testing, scoring, and interpretation are uniform across all administrations of a test.

Statistical control To increase internal validity, mathematical procedures can be employed to quantify the effects of variables that cannot be randomized but are known to be strongly related to the dependent variable, independent variable, or both.

Statistical power The probability that a statistical test will correctly reject the null hypothesis, that is, when the null hypothesis is in fact false.

Statistical significance The mathematical likelihood that an association is not due to chance, judged by a criterion set by the analyst (often that the probability is less than 5 out of 100 or $p < .05$).

Stereotype threat Performance on a test is lowered when the fear that one's behavior will confirm an existing stereotype is present.

Stratified random sampling A method of sampling in which sample elements are selected separately from population strata that are identified in advance by the researcher.

Stratified sample In this method of sampling, sample elements are selected separately from population strata that are identified in advance by the researcher.

Student's t-table Provides the critical value a t statistic needs to exceed in order to reject to null hypothesis at a certain level of probability.

Subject variable In a quasiexperimental design, selection of participants on the basis of some characteristic that can be measured or described but can not be directly manipulated, such as intelligence, gender, height, or weight.

Sums of squares Shorthand for the *sum of squared deviations from the mean*. Each score is subtracted from the mean and squared, and then all these values are summed.

Survey Study in which participants answer specific questions.

Survey pretest A method of evaluating survey questions and procedures by testing them out on a small sample of individuals like those to be included in the actual survey and then reviewing responses to the questions and reactions to the survey procedures.

Survey research Research in which information is obtained from a sample of individuals through their responses to questions about themselves or others.

Systematic bias Overrepresentation or underrepresentation of some population characteristics in a sample due to the method used to select the sample. A sample shaped by systematic sampling error is a biased sample.

Systematic observation A strategy that increases the reliability of observational data by using explicit rules that standardize coding practices across observers.

Systematic random sampling A method of sampling in which sample elements are selected from a list or from sequential files, with every nth element being selected after the first element is selected randomly within the first interval.

Systematic replication of single-subject designs Repeating a single-subject design in different settings using different providers and other related behaviors to increase generalizability.

Systematic variance The sum of the deviation of the means for each experimental condition from the grand mean (the mean of the means of all conditions of an experiment). The goal is to design experiments that will maximize systematic variance.

t-test An inferential statistic to test whether a pair of group means from a sample are statistically significant.

Tearoom Trade Book by sociologist Laud Humphreys that raised ethical questions about his covert observation and subsequent interviewing of men engaging in homosexual acts in public bathrooms.

Temporal precedence In establishing causality, evidence that demonstrates that the cause comes before the effect.

Test-retest reliability The extent to which scores remain consistent on the same test administered on two different occasions to the same group of examinees.

Testable hypothesis A statement often in the form of a prediction that is made prior to the actual collection of data.

Theory A coherent set of propositions that are used as principles to describe, understand, and explain psychological or behavioral phenomena.

Third variables A problem in describing the relationship between two variables, when a third variable that is extraneous to the two variables may account for the observed relationship.

Time series designs A quasiexperiemental design consisting of many pretest and posttest observations of the same group.

Time-lag design Used to determine the effects of time of testing while holding age constant by comparing only those participants who were of the same age but tested in different years, e.g., comparing 20-year-olds tested in 1990 with 20-years-olds tested in 1995.

Transparent An important feature of the scientific method that requires procedures, methods, and data analyses of any study to be presented clearly for the purposes of replication.

Treatment Another term for condition of an experiment.

Treatment group The group that receives the variable under investigation.

Treatment phase (B) The intervention phase of a single-subject design.

Trend Repeated measurement scores that are either ascending or descending in magnitude in a single-subject design.

True experiment In a true experiment, a researcher has complete control over the manipulation of the independent variable. Such experimental control allows for testing whether systematically varying the independent variable causes changes in the dependent variable.

Tuskegee syphilis study Researchers funded by the U.S. Public Health Service followed 399 low-income African American men with syphilis in the 1930s, collecting data to study the "natural" course of the illness, without informing all participants of their illness or of the discovery of a cure (penicillin) developed in the 1950s.

Two-tailed test The null hypothesis can be rejected by high or low values of a test statistic falling in both ends of its sampling distribution.

Two-variable chi-square (χ^2) A nonparametric statistical test that is used to investigate the association between two categorical variables.

Type I error The probability that the null hypothesis is rejected when it is in fact true; equals the significance level. In other words, a researcher makes an incorrect decision to reject the null hypothesis when it is in fact true.

Type II error This incorrect decision indicates the failure to reject the null hypothesis when it is in fact false. In other words, a researcher makes an incorrect decision to accept the null hypothesis when it is in fact false.

Unimodal A distribution of a variable in which there is only one value that is the most frequent.

Validity The extent to which a study provides a true measure of what it is *meant* to investigate.

Variability In a single-subject design, the extent to which cases are spread out through the distribution or clustered in just one location.

Variable Any characteristic that can take on different values or can vary across research participants.

Variance The average squared deviation of each case from the mean, so it takes into account the amount by which each case differs from the mean.

Visual analysis The process of looking at a graph of the data points in a single-subject design to determine whether the intervention has altered the subject's preintervention pattern of scores.

Web survey A survey that is accessed and responded to on the World Wide Web.

Within-groups variance An estimate of the degree to which the participants in each of the groups differ from one another. Reflects the deviation of the individual scores in each group from their respective group means. It is also referred to as *error variance*.

Within-subjects design In an experiment, all research participants receive all levels of the independent variable.

Zimbardo's prison simulation study A simulated prison was created and volunteers were assigned the role of guards or prisoners. Reactions to playing these roles were so extreme that the experiment was terminated after 6 days.

References

Abel, E. L., & Kruger, M. (2010). Smile intensity in photographs predicts longevity. *Current Directions in Psychological Science, 21*(4), 541–542.

Adair, G., Dushenko, T. W., & Lindsay, R. C. L. (1985). Ethical regulations and their impact on research practice. *American Psychologist, 40*, 59–72.

Adams, R. B., & Kleck, R. E. (2003). Perceived gaze direction and processing of facial displays of emotion. *Psychological Science, 14*, 644–647.

Adler, P. A., & Adler, P. (1994). Observational techniques. In N. K. Denzin & Y. S. Lincoln (Eds.), *Handbook of qualitative research* (pp. 377–392). Thousand Oaks, CA: Sage.

Alam, M., Barrett, K. C., Hodapp, R. M., & Arndt, K. A. (2008). Botulinum toxin and the facial feedback hypothesis: Can looking better make you feel happier? *Journal of the American Academy of Dermatology, 58*, 1061–1072.

Altman, L. K. (1987, March 31). U.S. and France end rift on AIDS. *New York Times.* Retrieved November 15, 2010, from http://www.nytimes.com

American Psychological Association. (2005). *Concise rules of APA style.* Washington, DC: Author.

American Psychological Association. (2009). *Publication manual of the American Psychological Association* (6th ed.). Washington, DC: Author.

American Psychological Association. (2010). *APA-style helper* [Computer software]. Washington, DC: Author.

American Psychological Association. (2010). Ethical principles of psychologists and code of Conduct. Retrieved November 11, 2010, from http://www.apa.org/ethics/code/index.aspx

American Psychological Association. (n.d.). *Psychological Bulletin* description. Retrieved August 9, 2010, from http://www.apa.org/pubs/journals/bul/

Anastasi, A. (1988). *Psychological testing.* New York: Macmillan.

Aronson, E., & Mills, J. (1959). The effect of severity of initiation on liking for a group. *Journal of Abnormal and Social Psychology, 59*, 177–181.

Aronson, E., Brewer, M., & Carlsmith, J. M. (1985). Experimentation in social psychology. In G. Lindzey & E. Aronson (Eds.), *Handbook of social psychology* (3rd ed., pp. 441–486). New York: Random House.

Arwood, T., & Panicker, S. (2007). Assessing risk in social and behavioral sciences. Collaborative Institutional Training Initiative. Retrieved November 13, 2010, from https://www.citiprogram.org/rcrpage.asp?language=english&affiliation=100

Baltes, P. B. (1968). Longitudinal and cross-sectional sequences in the study of age and generation effects. *Human Development, 11,* 145–171.

Banister, P., Burman, E., Parker, I., Taylor, M., & Tindall, C. (1994). *Qualitative methods in psychology: A research guide.* Philadelphia: Open University Press.

Barkow, J. H., Cosmides, L., & Tooby, J. (Eds.). (1992). *The adapted mind: Evolutionary psychology and the generation of culture.* New York: Oxford University Press.

Barlow, D., & Hersen, M. (1984). *Single-case experimental designs: Strategies for studying behavior change* (2nd ed.). New York: Pergamon.

Baumeister R. F., Smart, L., & Boden, T. (1996). Relation of threatened egotism to violence and aggression: The dark side of high self-esteem. *Psychological Review, 103,* 5–33.

Baumeister, R. F., Twenge, J. M., & Nuss, C. K. (2002). Effects of social exclusion on cognitive processes: Anticipated aloneness reduces intelligent thought. *Journal of Personality and Social Psychology, 83,* 817–827.

Baumrind, D. (1964). Some thoughts on ethics of research: After reading Milgram's "Behavioral study of obedience." *American Psychologist, 19*, 421–423.

Baumrind, D. (1985). Research using intentional deception: Ethical issues revisited. *American Psychologist, 40*, 165–174.

Beare, P. L., Severson, S., & Brandt, P. (2004). The use of a positive procedure to increase engagement on-task and decrease challenging behavior. *Behavior Modification, 28*, 28–44.

Belluck, P. (2009, January 18). Test subjects who call the scientist Mom or Dad. *New York Times,* pp. 1, 14.

Berg, B. (2004). *Qualitative research methods for the social sciences* (5th ed.). Boston: Pearson.

Besa, D. (1994). Evaluating narrative family therapy using single-system research designs. *Research on Social Work Practice, 4*, 309–325.

Binder, A., & Meeker, J. W. (1993). Implications of the failure to replicate the Minneapolis experimental findings. *American Sociological Review, 58*, 886–888.

Bisconer, S. W., Green, M., Mallon-Czajka, J., & Johnson, J. S. (2006). Managing aggression in a psychiatric hospital using a behaviour plan: A case study. *Journal of Psychiatric and Mental Health Nursing, 13*, 515–521.

Biswas-Diener, R., Vitterso, J., & Diener, E. (2005). Most people are pretty happy, but there is cultural variation: The Inughuit, the Amish, and the Maasai. *Journal of Happiness Studies, 6*, 205–226.

Block, N. (1995). How heritability misleads about race. *Cognition, 56*, 99–128.

Bloom, M., Fischer, J., & Orme, J. (2003). *Evaluating practice: Guidelines for the accountable professional* (4th ed.). Boston: Allyn and Bacon.

Bloom, P., & Wesiberg, D. S. (2007). Childhood origins of adult resistance to science. *Science, 316*, 996–997.

Bogdewic, S. P. (1999). Participant observation. In B. F. Crabtree & W. L. Miller (Eds.), *Doing qualitative research* (pp. 33–45). Thousand Oaks, CA: Sage.

Borckardt, J. J., Nash, M. R., Murphy, M. D., Moore, M., Shaw, D., & O'Neil, P. (2008). Clinical practice as natural laboratory for psychotherapy research: A guide to case-based time-series analysis. *American Psychologist, 63*, 77–95.

Bouchard, T. J. Jr., & McGue, M. (1981). Familial studies of intelligence: A review. *Science, 212*, 1055–1059.

Bramness, J. G., Walby, F. A., & Tverdal, A. (2007). The sales of antidepressants and suicide rates in Norway and its counties, 1980–2004. *Journal of Affective Disorders, 102*, 1–9.

Brinegar, M. G., Salvi, L. M., Stiles, W. B., & Greenberg, L. S. (2006). Building a meaning bridge: Therapeutic progress from problem formulation to understanding. *Journal of Counseling Psychology, 53*(2), 165–180.

Brown, J. (1992). *The definition of a profession. The authority of metaphor in the history of intelligence testing, 1890–1930*. Princeton, NJ: Princeton University Press.

Brown, J. B. (1999). The use of focus groups in clinical research. In B. F. Crabtree & W. L. Miller (Eds.), *Doing qualitative research* (2nd ed., pp. 109–124). Thousand Oaks, CA: Sage.

Bushman, B. J., & Baumeister, R. F. (1998). Threatened egotism, narcissism, self-esteem, and direct and displaced aggression. *Journal of Personality and Social Psychology, 75*, 219–229.

Butler, K. (2006, July 4). The grim neurology of teenage drinking. *New York Times,* pp. D1, D6.

Byrne, R. (2006). *The secret*. New York: Atria Books.

Callahan, C. C., & Barisa, M. T. (2005). Statistical process control and rehabilitation outcome: The single-subject design reconsidered. *Rehabilitation Psychology, 50*, 24–33.

Campbell, D. T., & Fiske, D. W. (1959). Convergent and discriminant validation by the multitrait-multimethod matrix. *Psychological Bulletin, 56*, 81–105.

Campbell, D. T., & Stanley, J. C. (1966). *Experimental and quasi-experimental designs for research*. Chicago: Rand McNally.

Cannon, W. B. (1927). The James-Lange theory of emotion: A critical examination and an alternative theory. *American Journal of Psychology, 39*, 10–124.

Carey, S. (2000). Science education as conceptual change. *Journal of Applied Developmental Psychology, 21*(1), 13–19.

Carmazza. A. (1996). The brain's dictionary. *Nature, 380*, 485–486.

Carr, J. E., & Burkholder, E. O. (1998). Creating single-subject design graphs with Microsoft

Excel™. *Journal of Applied Behavior Analysis, 31*, 245–251.

Cava, A., Cushman, R., & Goodman, K. (2007). HIPAA and human subjects research. Collaborative Institutional Training Initiative. Retrieved June 5, 2008, from https://www.citiprogram.org/members/learners

Cave, E., & Holm, S. (2003). Milgram and Tuskegee—Paradigm research projects in bioethics. *Health Care Analysis, 11*, 27–40.

Cheung, K. M. (1999). Effectiveness of social work treatment and massage therapy for nursing home clients. *Research on Social Work Practice, 9*, 229–247.

Cloud, J. (2009, January 16). How to lift your mood? Try smiling. *Time Magazine*. Retrieved May 19, 2009, from http://www.time.com/time/health/article/0,8599,1871687,00.

Cohen, S. G., & Leford, G. E. Jr. (1994). The effectiveness of self-managing teams: A quasi-experiment. *Human Relations, 47*, 13–43.

Committee on Revising Science and Creationism. (2008). A view from the National Academy of Sciences, National Academy of Sciences and Institute of Medicine of the National Academies. *Science, Evolution, and Creationism*. Retrieved from http://www.nap.edu/catalog/11876.html

Cook, T. D., & Campbell, D. T. (1979). *Quasi-experiments: Design and analysis for field settings*. Chicago: Rand McNally.

Cooper, K. B., & Victory, N. J. (2002). *A nation online: How Americans are expanding their use of the Internet*. Washington, DC: National Telecommunications and Information Administration, Economics and Statistics Administration, U.S. Department of Commerce. Retrieved November 22, 2010, from http://www.ntia.doc.gov/ntiahome/dn/nationonline_020502.htm

Costa, P. T. Jr., & McCrae, R. R. (1985). *The NEO Personality Inventory manual*. Odessa, FL: Psychological Assessment Resources.

Couper, M. P., Baker, R. P., Bethlehem, J., Clark, C. Z. F., Martin, J., Nicholls II, W. L., & O'Reilly, J. M. (Eds.). (1998). *Computer-assisted survey information collection*. New York: Wiley.

Cozby, P. C. (2009). *Methods in behavioral research* (10th ed.). New York: McGraw-Hill.

Creswell, J. W., Plano Clark, V. L., Gutmann, M. L., & Hanson, W. E. (2008). Advanced mixed methods research designs. In V. L. Plano Clark & J. W. Creswell (Eds.), *The mixed methods reader* (pp. 161–198). Thousand Oaks, CA: Sage.

Cronbach, L., & Meehl, P. (1955). Construct validity in psychological tests. *Psychological Bulletin, 52*(4), 281–302.

Currie, J., & Thomas, D. (1995). Does Head Start make a difference? *American Economic Review, 85*, 341–365.

Darwin, C. (1988). *The expression of emotion in man and animals*. New York: Oxford University Press (Original work published in 1872).

Dawkins, R. (1976/1989). *The selfish gene*. New York: Oxford University Press.

DeCoster, J. (1998). *Overview of factor analysis*. Retrieved April 20, 2010, from http://www.stat-help.com/notes.html

Denzin, N. K., & Lincoln, Y. S. (2000). Introduction: The discipline and practice of qualitative research. In N. K. Denzin & Y. S. Lincoln (Eds.), *The handbook of qualitative research* (2nd ed.). Thousand Oaks, CA: Sage.

Denzin, N. K., & Lincoln, Y. S. (2005). Introduction: The discipline and practice of qualitative research. In N. K. Denzin & Y. S. Lincoln (Eds.), *The SAGE handbook of qualitative research* (3rd ed., pp. 1–32). Thousand Oaks, CA: Sage.

Diener, E., & Diener, C. (1996). Most people are happy. *Psychological Science, 7*, 181–185.

Diener, E., Diener, M., & Diener, C. (1995). Factors predicting the subjective well-being of nations. *Journal of Personality and Social Psychology, 69*, 851–864.

Diener, E., Emmons, R. A., Larson, R. J., & Griffin, S. (1985). The Satisfaction With Life Scale. *Journal of Personality Assessment, 49*, 71–75.

Dillman, D. A. (1978). *Mail and telephone surveys: The total design method*. New York: Wiley.

Dillman, D. A. (2000). *Mail and Internet surveys: The tailored design method* (2nd ed.). New York: Wiley.

Dillman, D. A., Christenson, J. A., Carpenter, E. H., & Brooks, R. M. (1974). Increasing mail questionnaire response: A four-state comparison. *American Sociological Review, 39*, 744–756.

Dobbs, D. (2007, July 8). The gregarious brain. *New York Times*. Retrieved on November 21, 2010, from http://www.nytimes.com/2007/07/08/magazine/08sociability-t.html?_r=1&scp=1&sq=the%20gregarious%20brain&st=cse

Duenwald, M. (2005). Is she hiding something? *Discover, 26*, 16–17.

Dunn, E. W., Aknin, L. B., & Norton, M. I. (2008). Spending money on others promotes happiness. *Science, 319*, 1687–1688.

Eisenberg, D., Gollust, S. E., Golberstein, E., & Hefner, J. L. (2007). Prevalence and correlates of depression, anxiety, and suicidality among university students. *American Journal of Orthopsychiatry, 77*, 534–542.

Eisenberger, N. I., Lieberman, M. D., & Williams, K. D. (2003). Does rejection hurt? An fMRI study of social exclusion. *Science, 302*, 290–292.

Ekman, P. (1992). Facial expressions of emotion. *Current Directions in Psychological Science, 3*, 34–38.

Ekman, P. (2003). *Emotions revealed.* New York: Owl.

Elliot, A. J. (2006). The hierarchical model of approach-avoidance motivation. *Motivation and Emotion, 30*, 111–116.

Ellsworth, P. C. (1994). William James and emotion: Is a century of fame worth a century of misunderstanding? *Psychological Review, 101*, 222–229.

Elmes, D. G., Kantowitz, B. H., & Roedinger, H. L. III. (2006). *Research methods in psychology* (8th ed.). Belmont, CA: Wadsworth.

Emerson, R. M., Fretz, R. I., & Shaw, L. L. (1995). *Writing ethnographic fieldnotes.* Chicago: University of Chicago Press.

Enserink, M. (2008, February 27). The problem with Prozac. *ScienceNOW.* Retrieved March 7, 2009, from http://news.sciencemag.org/sciencenow/2008/02/27-02.html?ref=hp

Evans, J. A. (2008). Electronic publishing and narrowing of science and scholarship. *Science, 321*, 395–399.

Ewbank, M. P., Jennings, C., & Calder, A. J. (2009). Why are you angry with me? Facial expressions of threat influence perception of gaze direction. *Journal of Vision, 9*, 1–7.

Exercise for your aging brain. (2006, December 26). *New York Times.* Retrieved April 6, 2007, from http://www.nytimes.com/2006/12/26/opinion/26tue4.html

Ferguson, K., & Rodway, M. (1994). Cognitive behavioral treatment of perfectionism: Initial evaluation studies. *Research on Social Work Practice, 4*, 283–308.

Fisher, C. (2000). Relational ethics in psychological research: One feminist's journey. In M. Brabek (Ed.), *Praticing feminist ethics in psychology* (pp. 125–142). Washington, DC: American Psychological Association.

Fisher, C. B. (2003). *Decoding the ethics code: A practical guide for psychologists.* Thousand Oaks, CA: Sage.

Fournier, J. C., DeRubeis, R. J., Hollon, S. D., Dimidjian, S., Amsterdam, J. D., Shelton, R. C., & Fawcett, J. (2010). Antidepressant drug effects and depression severity. A patient-level meta-analysis. *Journal of the American Medical Association, 303*(1), 47–53.

Fowler, F. J. (1988). *Survey research methods* (rev. ed.). Newbury Park, CA: Sage.

Fram, A., & Tompson, T. (2008, March 19). Many college students stressed out, poll finds. *Boston Globe.* Retrieved May 3, 2008, from http://www.boston.com/bostonglobe/

Franklin, R. D., Allison, D. B., & Gorman, B. S. (Eds.). (1997). *Design and analysis of single-case research.* Mahway, NJ: Erlbaum.

Friedman, H. S., Tucker, J. S., Schwartz, J. B., Tomlinson-Keasey, C., Martin, L. R., Wingard, D. R., & Criqui, M. H. (1995). Psychosocial and behavioral predictors of longevity. The ageing and death of the "Termites." *American Psychologist, 50*, 69–78.

Friedman, R. A. (2010, January 11). Before you quit antidepressants . . . *New York Times,* Retrieved March 17, 2010, from http://www.nytimes.com/2010/01/12/health/12mind.html

Gardner, H. (1983). Frames of mind: *The theory of multiple intelligences.* New York: Basic Books.

Gardner, H. (1993). *Multiple intelligences: The theory in practice.* New York: Basic Books.

Gernsbacher, M. A. (2006). How to spot bias in research. *APS Observer, 19*, 30.

Gibbons, R. D., Hur, K., Bhaumik, D. K., & Mann, J. J. (2005). The relationship between antidepressant medication use and rate of suicide. *Archives of General Psychiatry, 62*, 165–172.

Gibbons, R. G., Brown Hendricks, C., Hur, K., Marcus, S., Bhaumik, D., Erkens, J. A., Herings, R. M. C., &

Mann, J. J. (2007). Early evidence on the effects of regulator's suicidality warning on SSRI prescriptions and suicide in children and adolescents *American Journal of Psychiatry, 164*(9), 1356–1363.

Gioia, D., & Brekke, J. S. (2009). Neurocognition, ecological validity, and daily living in the community for individuals with schizophrenia: A mixed methods study. *Psychiatry: Interpersonal and Biological Processes, 72*(1), 94–107.

Gladwell, M. (2002, August 5). The naked face. *The New Yorker, 78*(2), 38–49.

Goldberg, C. (2008, April 21). Mood lifting. *Boston Globe*, pp. C1, C3.

Goldfinger, S. M., Schutt, R. K., Tolomiczenko, G. S., Turner, W., Ware, N., Penk, W. E., et al. (1997). Housing persons who are homeless and mentally ill: Independent living or evolving consumer households? In W. R. Breakey & J. W. Thompson (Eds.), *Mentally ill and homeless: Special programs for special needs* (pp. 29–49). Amsterdam: Harwood.

Goodstein, D. (2010). *On fact and fraud: Cautionary tales from the front lines of science*. Princeton, NJ: Princeton University Press.

Gordon, R. (1992). *Basic interviewing skills*. Itasca, IL: Peacock.

Grady, J. (1996). The scope of visual sociology. *Visual Sociology, 11*, 10–24.

Gray, J. R., & Thompson, P. M. (2004). Neurobiology of intelligence: Science and ethics. *Nature Reviews Neuroscience, 5*, 471–482.

Greely, H., Sahakian, B., Harris, J., Kessler, R. C., Gazzaniga, M., Campbell, P., & Farah, M. J. (2008). Towards responsible use of cognitive enhancing drugs by the healthy. *Nature, 456*, 702–705.

Greene, R. L. (1996). The influence of experimental design: The example of the Brown-Peterson paradigm. *Canadian Journal of Experimental Psychology, 50*, 240–242.

Grossfeld, S. M. (2007, December 15). There are very, very many others. *Boston Globe*, Retrieved May 3, 2008, from http://www.boston.com/bostonglobe/.

Grossman, F. K., Sorsoli, L., & Kia-Keating, M. (2006). A gale force wind: Meaning making by male survivors of childhood sexual abuse. *American Journal of Orthopsychiatry, 76*(4), 434–443.

Groves, R. M. (1989). *Survey errors and survey costs*. New York: Wiley.

Groves, R. M., & Couper, M. P. (1998). *Nonresponse in household interview surveys*. New York: Wiley.

Grunebaum, M. F., Ellis, S. P., Li, S., Oquendo, M. A., & Mann, J. J. (2004). Antidepressants and suicide risk in the United States, 1985–1999. *Journal of Clinical Psychiatry, 65*, 1456–1462.

Hafner, K. (2008, May 3). Exercise your brain, or else you'll . . . uh . . . *New York Times*. Retrieved November 20, 2010, from www.nytimes.com.

Haney, C., Banks, C., & Zimbardo, P. G. (1973). Interpersonal dynamics in a simulated prison. *International Journal of Criminology and Penology, 1*, 69–97.

Harker, L., & Keltner, D. (2001). Expressions of positive emotion in women's college yearbook pictures and their relationship to personality and life outcomes across adulthood. *Journal of Personality and Social Psychology, 80*, 112–124.

Harmon, A. (2010, April 21). Tribe wins fight to limit research on its DNA. *New York Times*. Retrieved November 15, 2010, from http://www.nytimes.com

Havas, D. A., Glenberg, A. M., & Rinck, M. (2007). Emotion simulation during language comprehension. *Psychonomic Bulletin & Review, 14*, 436–441.

Heinen, T. (1996). *Latent class and discrete latent trait models: Similarities and differences*. Thousand Oaks, CA: Sage.

Hernstein, R. J., & Murray, C. (1994). *The bell curve: Intelligence and class structure in American life*. New York: Free Press.

Hertenstein, M. J., Hansel, C. A., Butts, A. M., & Hile, S. N. (2009). Smile intensity in photographs predicts divorce later in life. *Motivation and Emotion, 33*, 99–105.

Hess, U., Adams, R., & Kleck, R. E. (2009). The face is not an empty canvas: How facial expressions interact with facial appearance. *Philosophical Transactions of the Royal Society B Biological Sciences, 364*, 3497–3504.

Hines, T. (2003). *Pseudoscience and the paranormal: A critical examination of the evidence*. Buffalo, NY: Prometheus.

Holt, J. (2009, March 29). Get smart. *New York Times Book Review*, p. BR9.

Hong, Y.-Y., Morris, M. W., Chiu, C.-Y, & Benet-Martinez, V. (2000). Multicultural minds: A dynamic constructivist approach to culture and cognition. *American Psychologist, 55*, 709–720.

Houghton, P. M., & Houghton, T. J. (2007). *APA: The easy way!* Flint, MI: Baker College.

Huff, D. (1954). *How to lie with statistics.* New York: Norton.

Huitema, B. E. (2002). Statistical analysis and single-subject designs: Some misunderstandings. In J. S. Bailey & M. R. Burch (Eds.), *Research methods in applied behavior analysis* (pp. 209–232). Thousand Oaks, CA: Sage.

Humphreys, L. (1970). *Tearoom trade: Impersonal sex in public places.* Chicago: Aldine de Gruyter.

Iacoboni, M., Freedman, J., Kaplan, J., Jamieson, K. H., Freedman, T., Knapp, B., & Fitzgerald, K. (2007, November 11). This is your brain on politics. *New York Times.* Retrieved October 3, 2007, from http://www.nytimes.com

Irvine, L. (1998). Organizational ethics and fieldwork realities: Negotiating ethical boundaries in codependents anonymous. In S. Grills (Ed.), *Doing ethnographic research: Fieldwork settings* (pp. 167–183). Thousand Oaks, CA: Sage.

Isacsson, G. (2001). Suicide prevention—A medical breakthrough. *Acta Psychiatrica Scandinavica, 102*, 113–117.

Iyengar, S. S., Wells, R. E., & Schwartz, B. (2006). Doing better but feeling worse. Looking for the "best" job undermines satisfaction. *Current Directions in Psychological Science, 17*, 143–150.

Jarrett, C. (2006, March 3). Are you a grumpy maximizer or a happy satisficer? *British Psychological Society Research Digest.* Retrieved June 10, 2008, from http://bps-research-digest.blogspot .com/2006/03/are-you-grumpy-maximiser-or-happy.html

Jensen, A. R. (1998). *The g factor: The science of mental ability.* Westport, CT: Praeger.

Jensen, C. (1994). Psychosocial treatment of depression in women: Nine single-subject evaluations. *Research on Social Work Practice, 4*, 267–282.

Johnson, C., & Golden, J. (1997). Generalization of social skills to peer interactions in a child with language delays. *Behavioral Interventions, 12*, 133–147.

Kagay, M. R., with Elder, J. (1992, October 9). Numbers are no problem for pollsters. Words are. *New York Times*, p. E5.

Kahneman, D., Krueger, A. B., Schkade, D., Schwarz, N., & Stone, A. A. (2006). Would you be happier if you were richer? A focusing illusion. *Science, 30*, 1908–1910.

Kandel, E. (2006). *In search of memory. The emergence of a new science of mind.* New York: Norton.

Kaufman, S. R. (1986). *The ageless self: Sources of meaning in late life.* Madison: University of Wisconsin Press.

Kay, S. R., Fiszbein, A., & Opler, L. A. (1987). The positive and negative syndrome scale (PANSS) for schizophrenia. *Schizophrenia Bulletin, 13*, 261–276.

Kazdin, A. E. (1982). *Single-case research designs: Methods for clinical and applied settings.* New York: Oxford.

Keyes, C. L. M. (2007). Promoting and protecting mental health as flourishing: A complementary strategy for improving national mental health. *American Psychologist, 62*, 95–108.

Kidder, L. H. (1981). *Research methods in social relations.* New York: Holt, Reinhart and Winston.

Kilpatrick, D. G., Ruggiero, K. J., Acierno, R., Saunders, B. E., Resnick, H. S., & Best, C. L. (2003). Violence and risk of PTSD, major depression, substance abuse/dependence, and comorbidity: Results from the National Survey of Adolescents. *Journal of Consulting and Clinical Psychology, 1*, 692–700.

Kirk, E. E. (2002). Evaluating information on the Internet. Cited on Johns Hopkins University Library web page: www.library.jhu.edu/research help/general/evaluating

Kirk, R. E. (1994). *Experimental design: Procedures for behavioral sciences* (3rd ed.). Pacific Grove, CA: Wadsworth.

Knapp, S. J., & VandeCreek, L. D. (2006). *Practical ethics for psychologists: A positive approach.* Washington, DC: American Psychological Association.

Kniffin, K. M., & Wilson, D. S. (2004). The effect of nonphysical traits on the perception of physical attractiveness: Three naturalistic studies. *Evolution and Human Behavior, 25*, 88–101.

Knox, S., Burkard, A. W., Johnson, A. J., Suzuki, L. A., & Ponterotto, J. G. (2003). African American and European American therapists' experiences of addressing race in cross-racial psychotherapy dyads. *Journal of Counseling Psychology, 50*(4), 466–481.

Koegel, P. (1987). *Ethnographic perspectives on homeless and homeless mentally ill women.* Washington, DC: Alcohol, Drug Abuse, and Mental Health Administration, Public Health Service, U.S. Department of Health and Human Services.

Korn, J. H. (1997). *Illusions of reality: A history of deception in social psychology.* Albany: State University of New York Press.

Koslowski, B. (1996). *Theory and evidence: The development of scienftic reasoning.* Cambridge: MIT Press.

Kosslyn, S. M., & Rosenberg, R. S. (2001). *Psychology: The brain, the person, the world.* Needham Heights, MA: Allyn and Bacon.

Kuhn, T. S. (1962). *The structure of scientific revolutions.* Chicago: University of Chicago Press.

Kvale, S. (1996). *Interviews: An introduction to qualitative research interviewing.* Thousand Oaks, CA: Sage.

Labaw, P. J. (1980). *Advanced questionnaire design.* Cambridge, MA: ABT Books.

Lang, P. J. (1994). The varieties of emotional experience: A meditation on James–Lange theory. *Psychological Review, 101,* 211–221.

Larson, C. J. (1993). *Pure and applied sociological theory: Problems and issues.* New York: Harcourt Brace Jovanovich.

Lavrakas, P. J. (1987). *Telephone survey methods: Sampling, selection, and supervision.* Newbury Park, CA: Sage.

Lehrer, J. (2009, April 26). Inside the baby mind. *Boston Sunday Globe.* Retrieved November 4, 2010, http://www.boston.com/bostonglobe/ideas/articles/2009/04/26/inside_the_baby_mind/?page=4

Lehrer, J. (2009, May 18). Don't. The secret of self-control. *The New Yorker,* 26–32.

Lemann, N. (1999). *The big test. The secret history of American meritocracy* New York: Farrar, Straus and Giroux.

Leppanen, J. M., & Nelson, C. A. (2009). Tuning the developing brain to social signals of emotions. *Nature Review Neuroscience, 1,* 37–47.

Levitt, H., Butler, M., & Hill, T. (2006). What clients find helpful in psychotherapy: Developing principles for facilitating moment-to-moment change. *Journal of Counseling Psychology, 53*(3), 314–324.

Levy, P. S., & Lemeshow, S. (1999). *Sampling of populations: Methods and applications* (3rd ed.). New York: Wiley.

Lewontin, R. (1976). Race and intelligence. In J. Block & G. Dworkin (Eds.), *The IQ controversy: Critical readings.* New York: Pantheon.

Likert, R. (1932). A technique for the measurement of attitudes. *Archives of Psychology, 140,* 1–55.

Lilienfeld, S. O. (2005). The 10 commandments of helping students distinguish science from pseudoscience in psychology. *Observer, 18,* 9. Retrieved from http://www.psychologicalscience.org/observer/getArticle.cfm?id=1843

Linehan, M. M., Heard, H. L., & Armstrong, H. E. (1993). Naturalistic follow-up of a behavioural treatment of chronically parasuicidal borderline patients. *Archives of General Psychiatry, 50,* 971–974.

Litchtenbeger, E. O., & Kaufman, A. S. (2009). *Essentials of WAIS-IV assessment.* New York: Wiley.

Locke, L. F., Silverman, S. J., & Spirduso, W. W. (1998). *Reading and understanding research.* Thousands Oaks, CA: Sage.

Lofland, J., & Lofland, L. H. (1984). *Analyzing social settings: A guide to qualitative observation and analysis* (2nd ed.). Belmont, CA: Wadsworth.

Lowry, R. (1999–2010). Concepts & applications of inferential statistics. Retrieved June 13, 2010, from http://faculty.vassar.edu/lowry/VassarStats.html

Ludwig, J., & Marcotte, D. E. (2005). Anti-depressants, suicide, and drug regulation. *Journal of Policy, Analysis and Management, 24,* 249–272.

Mahncke, H. W., Connor, B. B., Appelman, J., Ahsanuddin, O. N., Hardy, J. L., Wood, R. A., Joyce, N. M., Boniske, T., Atkins, S. M., & Merzenich, M. M. (2006). Memory enhancement in healthy older adults using a brain plasticity-based training program: A randomized controlled study. *Proceedings of the National Academy of Sciences, 103,* 12523–12528.

Mandal, M. K., & Ambady, N. (2004). Laterality of facial expression of emotion: Universal and culture-specific influences. *Behavioral Neuroscience, 15,* 23–34.

Marshall, G. D., & Zimbardo, P. G. (1979). Affective consequences of inadequately explained physiological arousal. *Journal of Personality and Social Psychology, 37,* 970–988.

Matsumoto, D., & Willingham, B. (2009). Spontaneous facial expression of emotion of congenitally and noncongenitally blind individuals. *Journal of Personality and Social Psychology, 96,* 2–10.

Maxwell, J. A. (1996). *Qualitative research design: An interactive approach*. Thousand Oaks, CA: Sage.

McAdams, D. P., & Pals, J. L. (2006). A new big five: Fundamental principles for an integrative science of personality. *American Psychologist, 61*, 204–217.

McBurney, D. H., & White, T. (2010). *Research methods* (8th ed.). Belmont, CA: Wadsworth.

McLean v. Arkansas Board of Education, 529 F Supp. 1255, 1258–1264 (E.D. Ark. 1982).

Milgram, S. (1963). Behavioral study of obedience. *Journal of Abnormal and Social Psychology, 67*, 371–478.

Milgram, S. (1964). Issues in the study of obedience: A reply to Baumrind. *American Psychologist, 19*, 848–852.

Milgram, S. (1965). Some conditions of obedience and disobedience to authority. *Human Relations, 18*, 57–76.

Milgram, S. (1974). *Obedience to authority: An experimental view*. New York: Harper & Row.

Milgram, S. (1977, October). Subject reaction: The neglected factor in the ethics of experimentation. *Hastings Law Review*, 19–23.

Milgram, S. (1992). *The individual in a social world: Essays and experiments* (2nd ed.). New York: McGraw-Hill.

Miller, A. G. (1986). *The obedience experiments: A case study of controversy in social science*. New York: Praeger.

Miller, W. L., & Crabtree, B. F. (1999). Depth interviewing. In B. F. Crabtree & W. L. Miller (Eds.), *Doing qualitative research* (pp. 89–107). Thousand Oaks, CA: Sage.

Miyamoto, Y., Nisbett, R. E., & Masuda, T. (2006). Culture and the physical environment: Holistic versus analytic perceptual affordances. *Psychological Science, 17*, 113–119.

Mohr, L. B. (1992). *Impact analysis for program evaluation*. Newbury Park, CA: Sage.

Morris, M. W., & Peng, K. (1994). Culture and cause: American and Chinese attributions for social physical events. *Journal of Personality and Social Psychology, 67*, 949–971.

Myers, D., & Diener, E. (1995). Who is happy? *Psychological Science, 6*, 10–19.

Nagourney, A. (2002, November 5). Cellphones and caller ID are making it harder for pollsters to pick a winner. *New York Times*, p. A20.

Nakonezny, P. A., Reddick, R., & Rodgers, J. L. (2004). Did divorces decline after the Oklahoma City bombing? *Journal of Marriage and Family, 66*, 90–100.

Neisser, U., Boodoo, G., Bouchard, T. J., Boykin, A. W., Brody, N., Ceci, S. J., Halpern, D. F., Loehlin, J. C., Perloff, R., Sternberg, R. J., & Urbina, S. (1996). Intelligence: Knowns and unknowns. *American Psychologist, 51*, 77–101.

Nelson, D. L., Schrieber, T. A., & McEvoy, C. L. (1992). Processing implicit and explicit representations. *Psychological Review, 99*, 322–348.

Nelson, J. C. (1994). Ethics, gender, and ethnicity in single-case research and evaluation. *Journal of Social Service Research, 18*, 139–152.

Nelson, M., Neumark Stzainer, D., Hannan, P. J., Sirard, J. R., & Story, M. (2006). Longitudinal and secular trends in physical activity and sedentary behavior during adolescence. *Pediatrics, 118*, e1627–e16343.

Nestor, P. G. (2002). Mental disorder and violence: Personality dimensions and clinical features. *American Journal of Psychiatry, 159*(12), 1973–1978.

Nestor, P. G., Akdag, S. J., O'Donnell, B. F., Niznikiewicz, M. A., Law, S., Shenton, M. E., & McCarley, R. W. (1998). Word recall in schizophrenia: A connectionist model. *American Journal of Psychiatry, 155*, 1685–1690.

Nestor, P. G., Klein, K., Pomplun, M., Niznikiewicz, M., & McCarley, R. W. (2010). Gaze cueing of attention in schizophrenia: Individual differences in neuropsychological functioning and symptoms. *Journal of Clinical and Experimental Neuropsychology, 32*, 281–288.

Nestor, P. G., Kubicki, M., Gurrera, R. J., Niznikiewicz, M., Frumin, M., McCarley, R. W., & Shenton, M. E. (2004). Neuropsychological correlates of diffusion tensor imaging in schizophrenia. *Neuropsychology, 18*, 629–637.

Nestor, P. G., Kubicki, M., Nakamura, M., Niznikiewicz, M., McCarley, R. W., & Shenton, M. E. (2010). Comparing prefrontal gray and white matter contributions to intelligence and decision making in schizophrenia and healthy controls. *Neuropsychology, 1*, 121–129.

Nicholson, S. (2008). *2nd: The face of defeat*. Toronto: Magenta Publishing for the Arts.

Nickerson, R. S. (1988). Confirmatory bias: A ubiquitous phenomenon in many guises. *Review of General Psychology*, 2, 175–220.

Niedenthal, P. M. (2007). Embodying emotion. *Science, 316*, 1002–1005.

Nisbett, R. E. (2009). *Intelligence and how to get it: Why schools and culture count*. New York: Norton.

Nisbett, R. E., Peng, K., Choi, I., & Norenzayan, A. (2001). Culture and systems of thought: Holistic vs. analytic cognition. *Psychological Review, 108*, 291–310.

Ogbu, J. U. (1978). *Minority education and caste. The American system in cross-cultural perspective*. New York: Academic Press.

Ogbu, J. U. (1994). From cultural differences to differences in cultural frames of reference. In P. M. Greenfield & R. R. Cocking (Eds.), *Cross-cultural roots of minority child development* (pp. 365–391). Hillsdale, NJ: Erlbaum.

Orcutt, J. D., & Turner, J. B. (1993). Shocking numbers and graphic accounts: Quantified images of drug problems in the print media. *Social Problems, 49*, 190–206.

Pascual-Leone, A., & Greeenberg, L. S. (2007). Emotional processing in experiential therapy: Why "the only out is through." *Journal of Consulting and Clinical Psychology, 75*(6), 875–887.

Pashler, H., McDaniel, M., Rohrer, D., & Bjork, R. (2009). Learning styles: Concepts and evidence. *Psychological Science in the Public Interest, 9*, 105–119.

Paulos, J. A. (2010, May 16). Metric mania. *New York Times Magazine*, pp. 11–12.

Peterson, L. R., & Peterson, M. J. (1959). Short-term retention of individual items. *Journal of Experimental Psychology, 58*, 193–198.

Peterson, R. A. (2000). *Constructing effective questionnaires*. Thousand Oaks, CA: Sage.

Phillips, D. P. (1982). The impact of fictional television stories on U.S. adult fatalities: New evidence on the effect of mass media on violence. *American Journal of Sociology*, 87, 1340–1359.

Piatelli-Palmarini, M. (1994). *Inevitable illusions: How mistakes of reasons rule our minds*. New York: John Wiley and Sons.

Piliavin, J. A., & Piliavin, I. M. (1972). Effect of blood on reactions to a victim. *Journal of Personality and Social Psychology, 23*, 353–361.

Pinker, S. (1997). *How the mind works*. New York: Norton.

Pinker, S. (2009, November 7). Malcolm Gladwell, eclectic detective. Retrieved December 22, 2009, from http://www.nytimes.com/2009/11/15/books/review/Pinker-t.html?pagewanted=all

Popper, K. R. (1959). *The logic of scientific discovery*. New York: Basic Books.

Prewitt, K. (2000, September 27). *Letter to the Honorable Dan Miller*. Washington, DC: U.S. Department of Commerce, Bureau of the Census. Retrieved January 19, 2003, from http://www.census.gov/newsroom/releases/archives/census_2000/cb00cn58.html

Reynolds, P. D. (1979). *Ethical dilemmas and social science research*. San Francisco: Jossey-Bass.

Roman, A. (2005). *Women's Health Network client survey: Field report*. Unpublished report. Boston: Center for Survey Research, University of Massachusetts.

Ross, C. E. (1990). *Work, family, and the sense of control: Implications for the psychological well-being of women and men*. Proposal submitted to the National Science Foundation. Urbana: University of Illinois.

Rossi, P. H., & Freeman, H. E. (1989). *Evaluation: A systematic approach* (4th ed.). Newbury Park, CA: Sage.

Rossiter, J. (2007). *The APA pocket handbook*. Grand Blanc, MI: DW Publishing.

Rossman, G. B., & Rallis, S. F. (1998). *Learning in the field: An introduction to qualitative research*. Thousand Oaks, CA: Sage.

Rowe, G., Hirsh, J. B., & Anderson, A. K. (2007). Positive affect increases the breadth of attentional selection. *Proceedings of the National Academy of Sciences of the United States of America, 104*, 383–388.

Rubin, H. J., & Rubin, I. S. (1995). *Qualitative interviewing: The art of hearing data*. Thousand Oaks, CA: Sage.

Sackett, P. R., Hardison, C. M., & Cullen, M. J. (2004). On interpreting stereotype threat as accounting for African American–White differences on cognitive tests. *American Psychologist, 59,* 7–13.

Sanders Thompson, V. L., Bazile, A., & Akbar, M. (2004). African Americans' perceptions of psychotherapy and psychotherapists. *Professional Psychology: Research and Practice, 35*(1), 19–26.

Saville, B. K. (2003). Single-subject designs. In S. F. Davis (Ed.), *Handbook of research methods in experimental psychology, Vol. 1* (pp. 80–92). Malden, MA: Blackwell.

Saville, B. K., & Buskist, W. (2003). Traditional idiographic approaches: Small-N research designs. In S. F. Davis (Ed.), *Handbook of research methods in experimental psychology, Vol. 1* (pp. 66–82). Malden, MA: Blackwell.

Schaie, K. W. (1965). A general model for the study of developmental problems. *Psychological Bulletin, 64,* 92–107.

Schaie, K. W. (1977). Quasi-experimental designs in the psychology of aging. In J. E. Birren & K. W. Schaie (Eds.), *Handbook of the psychology of aging* (pp. 39–58). New York: Van Nostrand.

Schober, M. F. (1999). Making sense of survey questions. In M. G. Sirken, D. J. Herrmann, S. Schechter, N. Schwartz, J. M. Tanur, & R. Tourangeau (Eds.), *Cognition and survey research* (pp. 77–94). New York: Wiley.

Schuman, H., & Presser, S. (1981). *Questions and answers in attitude surveys: Experiments on question form, wording, and context.* New York: Academic Press.

Schutt, R. K. (with Stephen M. Goldfinger). (2011). *Homelessness, housing and mental illness.* Cambridge: Harvard University Press.

Schutt, R. K., Cruz, E. R., & Woodford, M. L. (2008). Client satisfaction in a breast and cervical cancer early detection program: The influence of ethnicity and language, health, resources and barriers. *Women & Health, 48,* 283–302.

Schwartz, A. (2009, December 20). NFL acknowledges long term concussion effects. *New York Times.* Retrieved April 10, 2010, from http://www.nytimes.com/2009/12/21/sports/football/21concussions.html

Schwartz, B. (2004, April). The tyranny of choice. *Scientific American,* 70–75.

Seligman, M. E. P. (1991). *Learned optimism: How to change your mind and your life.* New York: Knopf.

Sharot, T., Martorella, E. A., Delgado, M. R., & Phelps, E. A. (2007). How personal experience modulates the neural circuitry of memories of September 11. *Proceedings of the National Academy of Science, 104,* 389–439.

Shaw, P., Eckstrand., K., Sharp, W., Blumental, J., Lerch, J. P., Greenstein, D., Clasen, L., Evans, A., Giedd, J., & Rapoport, J. L. (2007). Attention deficit/hyperactivity disorder is characterized by a delay in cortical maturation. *Proceedings of the National Academy of Sciences of the United States of America, 104,* 19649–19654.

Shaywitz, D. A. (2007, April 24). Shattering the bell curve. *Wall Street Journal.* Retrieved May 14, 2010, from http://online.wsj.com/article/SB117736979316179649-search.html

Sheldon, K. M., & King, L. (2001). Why positive psychology is necessary. *American Psychologist, 56,* 216–217.

Shenk, J. W. (2009, June). What makes us happy? *Atlantic Monthly.* Retrieved February 22, 2010, from http://www.theatlantic.com/magazine/archive/2009/06/what-makes-us-happy/7439/

Shepherd, J., Hill, D., Bristor, J., & Montalvan, P. (1996). Converting an ongoing health study to CAPI: Findings from the National Health and Nutrition Study. In R. B. Warnecke (Ed.), *Health survey research methods conference proceedings* (pp. 159–164). Hyattsville, MD: U.S. Department of Health and Human Services.

Sherman, L. W. (1992). *Policing domestic violence: Experiments and dilemmas.* New York: Free Press.

Sherman, L. W. (1993). Implications of a failure to read the literature. *American Sociological Review, 58,* 888–889.

Sherman, L. W., & Berk, R. A. (1984). The specific deterrent effects of arrest for domestic assault. *American Sociological Review, 49,* 261–272.

Shermer, M. (2008, May 13). A new phrenology? *Scientific American, 298*(5), 46–48.

Shermer, M. (2008). Wheatgrass juice and folk medicine. *Scientific American, 299,* 48.

Shermer, M. (2010, July). When scientists lie: Fraud, deception, and lies in research reveal how science is (mostly) self-correcting. *Scientific American, 303*(1), 34.

Shweder, R., & Sullivan, M. A. (1993). Cultural psychology: Who needs it? *Annual Review of Psychology, 44,* 497–523.

Sieber, J. E. (1992). *Planning ethically responsible research: A guide for students and institutional review boards.* Thousand Oaks, CA: Sage.

Singham, M. (2010, May 9). The new war between science and religion. *Chronicle of Higher Education*. Retrieved June 20, 2010, from http://chronicle.com/article/The-New-War-Between-Science/65400/

Sjoberg, G. (Ed.). (1967). *Ethics, politics, and social research*. Cambridge, MA: Schenkman.

Smyth, J. D., Dillman, D. A., Christian, L. M., & Stern, M. J. (2004). *How visual grouping influences answers to Internet surveys*. Extended version of paper presented at the Annual Meeting of the American Association for Public Opinion Research, Phoenix, AZ, May 13. Retrieved July 5, 2005, from http://survey.sesrc.wsu.edu/dillman/papers.htm

Stake, R. E. (1995). *The art of case study research*. Thousand Oaks, CA: Sage.

Stanovich, K. (1997). *How to think straight about psychology* (4th ed.). New York: HarperCollins.

Steele, C. M. (1997). A threat in the air. How stereotypes shape intellectual identity and performance. *American Psychologist, 52*, 613–629.

Steele, C. M., & Aronson, J. (1995). Stereotype threat and the intellectual test performance of African Americans. *Journal of Personality and Social Psychology, 69,* 797–811.

Sternberg, R. J. (2003). *The psychologist's companion: A guide to scientific writing for students and researchers* (4th ed.). New York: Cambridge University Press.

Sternberg, R. J. (2007). Critical thinking in psychology: It really is critical. In R. J. Sternberg, H. L. Roediger, & D. F. Halpern (Eds.), *Critical thinking in psychology* (p. 292). New York: Cambridge University Press.

Strack, F., Martin, L. L., & Schwartz, N. (1988). Priming and communication: Social determinants of information use in judgments of life satisfaction. *European Journal of Social Psychology, 18*, 429–442.

Strack, F., Martin, L. L., & Stepper, S. (1988). Inhibiting and facilitating conditions of the human smile: A nonobtrusive test of the facial feedback hypothesis. *Journal of Personality and Social Psychology, 54,* 768–777.

Su, S. K., Chiu, C.-Y., Hong, Y.-Y., Leung, K., Peng., K., & Morris, M. W. (1999). Self-organization and social organization: American and Chinese constructions. In T. R. Tyler, R. Kramer, & O. John (Eds.), *The psychology of social self* (pp. 193–222). Mahwah, NJ: Earlbaum.

Sudman, S. (1976). *Applied sampling*. New York: Academic Press.

Talbot, M. (2009, April 27). Brain gain: The underground world of "neuroenhancing" drugs. *New Yorker*. Retrieved May 3, 2010, from http://www.newyorker.com/reporting/2009/04/27/090427fa_fact_talbot

Taleb, N. N. (2001). Fooled by randomness: *The hidden role of chance in the markets and in life*. New York: Texere LLC.

Taleb, N. N. (2007). *The Black Swan: The impact of the highly improbable*. New York: Random House.

Tashakkori, A., & Teddlie, C. (2003). *Handbook of mixed methods in social and behavioral research*. Thousand Oaks, CA: Sage.

Todorov, A., Mandisodza, A. N., Goren, A., & Hall, C. C. (2005). Inferences of competence from faces predict election outcomes. *Science, 308,* 1623–1626.

Tolman, D. L., & Brydon-Miller, M. (2001). Interpretive and participatory research methods: Moving toward subjectivities. In D. L. Tolman & M. Brydon-Miller (Eds.), *From subjects to subjectivities: A handbook of interpretive and participatory methods* (pp. 3–11). New York: New York University Press.

Tripodi, T. (1994). *A primer on single-subject design for clinical social workers*. Washington, DC: National Association of Social Workers.

Trochim, W. M. (2006). *The research methods knowledge base* (2nd ed.). Retrieved December 11, 2008, from http://www.socialresearchmethods.net/kb/

Tufte, E. (1983). *The visual display of quantitative information*. Cheshire, CT: Graphics Press.

Tuhus-Dubrow, R. (2008, November 29). Group think. *Boston Sunday Globe*. Retrieved August 7, 2009, from http://www.boston.com/bostonglobe/ideas/articles/2008/11/23/group_think/

U.S. Bureau of the Census. (2000a, September 27). Census 2000 efficiencies result in $305 million savings. Washington, DC: U.S. Department of Commerce, Bureau of the Census. Retrieved November 22, 1010, from http://www.census.gov/newsroom/releases/archives/census_2000/cb00cn58.html

U.S. Bureau of the Census. (2000b, May 31). Census bureau director says 92 percent of U.S. households accounted for; thanks president and vice president for message to census workers.

United States Department of Commerce News. Retrieved November 22, 2010, from http://www.census.gov/newsroom/releases/archives/census_2000/cb00-cn41.html

U.S. Bureau of the Census. (2000c, April 19). Response rate for Census 2000 matches 1990 rate. *United States Department of Commerce News*. Retrieved November 22, 2010, from http://www.chrispy.net/pipermail/ctpp-news/2000-April/000040.html

U.S. Department of Commerce. (2001, October 17). *Statement of acting Census Bureau director William Barron Regarding the adjustment decision*. CB01-CS.08.

U.S. Department of Health, Education, and Welfare. (1979). *The Belmont report: Ethical principles and guidelines for the protection of human subjects of research*. Washington, DC: National Commission for the Protection of Human Subjects of Biomedical and Behavioral Research, Office of the Secretary, Department of Health, Education, and Welfare. Retrieved June 20, 2005, from http://ohsr.od.nih.gov/guidelines/belmont.html

U.S. Public Health Service. (1999). *Mental health: A report of the Surgeon General*. Rockville, MD: Author.

Underwood, B. (1957). *Psychological research*. New York: Appleton.

University of Washington Psychology Writing Center. (1997). *Writing a psychology literature review*. Retrieved January 27, 2010, from http://depts.washington.edu/psywc/handouts.shtml.

Wageman, R. (1995). Interdependence and group effectiveness. *Administrative Science Quarterly*, *40*, 145–180.

Walgren, A., Walgren, B., Peterson, R., Jorner, U., & Haaland, J. (1996). *Graphing statistics and data: Creating better charts*. Thousand Oaks, CA: Sage.

Ware, N. C. (1999). Evolving consumer households: An experiment in community living for people with severe psychiatric disorders. *Psychiatric Rehabilitation Journal*, *23*(1), 3–10.

Wechsler, D. (1997). *WAIS-III administration and scoring manual*. San Antonio, TX: The Psychological Corporation.

Wechsler, D. (2008). *WAIS-IV administration and scoring manual*. San Antonio, TX: Psychological Corporation.

Wechsler, D. (2008). *Wechsler Adult Intelligence Scale–Fourth edition (WAIS-IV)*. San Antonio, TX: Pearson.

Whalen, P. J. (1998). Fear, vigilance, and ambiguity: Initial neuroimaging studies of the amygdala. *Current Directions in Psychological Science*, *7*, 177–188.

Whalen, P. J., Kagan, J., Cook, R. G., Davis, F. C., Kim, H., Polis, S., McLaren, D. G., Somerville, L. H., McLean, A. A., Maxwell, J. S., & Johnstone, T. (2004). Human amygdala responsivity to masked fearful eye whites. *Science*, *306*, 2061.

Whyte, W. F. (1955). *Street corner society*. Chicago: University of Chicago Press.

Willis, S. L., Tennstedt, S. L., Marsiske, M., Ball, K., Elias, J., Koepke, K. M., Morris, J. N., Rebok, G. W., Unverzagt, F. W., Stoddard, A. M., & Wright, E. (2006). Long-term effects of cognitive training on everyday functional outcomes in older adults. *JAMA*, *296*, 2805–2814.

Wilson, D. S. (2007). *Evolution for everyone: How Darwin's theory can change the way we think about our lives*. New York: Delacorte.

Wilson, D. S., Van Vugt, M., & O'Gorman, R. (2008). Multilevel selection theory and major evolutionary transitions: Implications for psychological science. *Current Directions in Psychological Science*, *17*, 6–9.

Wolcott, H. F. (1995). *The art of fieldwork*. Walnut Creek, CA: AltaMira Press.

Yang, Y. (2008). Social inequalities in happiness in the United States, 1972 to 2004: An age-period-cohort analysis. *American Sociological Review*, *703*, 204–226.

Yarnold, P. R. (1992). Statistical analysis for single-case designs. In F. B. Bryant, J. Edwards, R. S. Tindale, E. J. Posavac, L. Hath, E. Henderson, & Y. Suarez-Bakazar (Eds.), *Methodological issues in applied social psychology* (pp. 177–197). New York: Plenum.

Zarracina, J. (2010, April 4). A life lesson from the majors. Smile, you live longer. *Boston Sunday Globe*, p. C10.

Index

About the Authors

Paul G. Nestor, PhD, is a Professor of Psychology at the University of Massachusetts Boston, and Assistant Professor in Psychology in the Department of Psychiatry at the Harvard Medical School. A summa cum laude and Phi Beta Kappa graduate of Boston University, he earned his MA and PhD in clinical psychology from The Catholic University of America, and was a post-doctoral fellow in the National Institute of Mental Health (NIMH) Clinical Research Training Program at Harvard Medical School. His peer-reviewed publications cover a variety of areas of behavioral science, including neuropsychology, structural and functional neuroimaging, attention, memory, personality, forensic psychology, and schizophrenia. He has authored or co-authored over 95 peer-reviewed articles in such journals as *Journal of Abnormal Psychology, Neuropsychology, American Journal of Psychiatry, Archives of General Psychiatry, Biological Psychiatry, NeuroImage, Neuropsychologia, Cortex, Schizophrenia Research, Journal of Nervous and Mental Disease, Journal of Neuroscience, Proceedings of the National Academy of Science,* and *Law and Human Behavior.* His research has been federally support by competitive grants from both the National Institute of Mental Health and the Department of Veterans Affairs, and is a past recipient of a Veterans Administration Merit Review Award, "Cognitive Neuroscience Studies of Schizophrenia." He is also the past recipient of The University of Massachusetts-Boston Chancellor's Award for Distinguished Scholarship (2003) for his research in psychology. His article, "Neuropsychological Correlates of Diffusion Tensor Imaging in Schizophrenia" was one of the top 50 downloaded from the APA website during 2005, with an annualized adjusted rate of 2,238 downloads. His teaching has been recognized by the College of Arts and Sciences Outstanding Faculty Achievement Award, University of Massachusetts-Boston (1999). He also has experience in media presentation for both television and radio, including having his research featured on the Discovery Channel series, "Most Evil" (August 2006) and WUMB "Commonwealth Journal" (January 2003). He is a licensed psychologist in Massachusetts, specializing in clinical psychology, neuropsychology, and forensic psychology.

Russell K. Schutt, PhD, is Professor and Chair of Sociology at the University of Massachusetts, Boston, and Lecturer on Sociology in the Department of Psychiatry (Beth Israel-Deaconess Medical Center) at the Harvard Medical School. He completed his BA, MA, and PhD degrees at the University of Illinois at Chicago and was a postdoctoral fellow in the National Institute of Mental Health-Funded Sociology of Social Control Training Program at Yale University (1977–1979). In addition to *Investigating Human Behavior,* he is the author or co-author of other SAGE research methods texts for sociology, social work, and criminology/criminal justice

501

and author of *Homelessness, Housing, and Mental Illness* (Harvard University Press, 2011), as well as other books and more than 60 peer reviewed articles, book chapters and other publications appearing in such journals as *Psychiatric Services, Schizophrenia Bulletin, Schizophrenia Research, Journal of Nervous and Mental Disease, Journal of Health and Social Behavior, Evaluation and Program Planning,* and *American Journal of Sociology* on topics including homelessness, service preferences and satisfaction, mental health, cognitive functioning, service systems and organizations, law, and teaching research methods. His funded research experience includes a National Cancer Institute–funded study of community health workers and recruitment for cancer clinical trials, a large translational research project for the Massachusetts Department of Public Health's Women's Health Network, a National Institute of Mental Health–funded study of housing alternatives for homeless persons diagnosed with severe mental illness, and evaluations of service programs in the Massachusetts Department of Public Health, the Massachusetts Department of Mental Health, and the Veterans Administration. He has received the Chancellor's Award for Distinguished Service and the College of Arts and Sciences Outstanding Achievement Award at the University of Massachusetts Boston.